Interactions with Search Systems

Information seeking is a fundamental human activity. In the modern world it is frequently conducted through interactions with search systems. The retrieval and comprehension of information returned by these systems is a key part of decision making and action in a broad range of settings. Advances in data availability, coupled with new interaction paradigms and mobile and cloud computing capabilities, have created a diverse set of new opportunities for information access and use.

In this comprehensive book for professionals, researchers, and students involved in search system design and evaluation, search expert Ryen White discusses how search systems can capitalize on these new capabilities, and how next-generation search systems must support higher-order search activities such as task completion, learning, and decision making. He outlines the implications of these changes for the evolution of search evaluation, as well as related challenges that extend beyond search systems in areas such as privacy and societal benefit.

RYEN W. WHITE is a Principal Researcher at Microsoft Research. His research is focused on understanding search interaction and on developing tools to help people search more effectively. White's doctoral research received the British Computer Society's Distinguished Dissertation Award. He recently received the Karen Spärck Jones Award, for contributions to information retrieval. White's research is featured in many Microsoft products.

Interactions with Search Systems

Ryen W. White
Microsoft Research

CAMBRIDGE
UNIVERSITY PRESS

32 Avenue of the Americas, New York, NY 10013-2473, USA

Cambridge University Press is part of the University of Cambridge.

It furthers the University's mission by disseminating knowledge in the pursuit of education, learning, and research at the highest international levels of excellence.

www.cambridge.org
Information on this title: www.cambridge.org/9781107034228

© Ryen W. White 2016

This publication is in copyright. Subject to statutory exception
and to the provisions of relevant collective licensing agreements,
no reproduction of any part may take place without the written
permission of Cambridge University Press.

First published 2016

A catalog record for this publication is available from the British Library.

Library of Congress Cataloging in Publication Data
White, Ryen W., author.
Interactions with search systems / Ryen W. White, Microsoft Research.
   pages cm
Includes bibliographical references and index.
ISBN 978-1-107-03422-8 (hardback)
1. Search engines – Technological innovations.   I. Title.
TK5105.884.W53   2016
025.04252–dc23   2015026053

ISBN 978-1-107-03422-8 Hardback

Cambridge University Press has no responsibility for the persistence or accuracy of URLs for external or third-party Internet Web sites referred to in this publication and does not guarantee that any content on such Web sites is, or will remain, accurate or appropriate.

To Henry, Hannah, and Resa.
Your love and patience made this possible.

Contents

Preface		*page* xi
1	**Introduction**	**1**
1.1	Historical Approaches	2
1.2	Next-Generation Search Interaction	5
1.3	Outline	10
	Part I Background	**13**
2	**Collecting and Representing Search Interaction**	**15**
2.1	Interaction Types	17
2.2	Primary Actions	21
2.3	Secondary Actions	28
2.4	Beyond Queries and Clicks	37
2.5	Collection Strategies	53
2.6	Summary	57
3	**Modeling Interests and Intentions**	**59**
3.1	Modeling Next-Generation Search Interaction	59
3.2	Models of Searcher Behavior	64
3.3	Components for Model Building	82
3.4	Summary	96
4	**Models and Frameworks for Information Seeking**	**97**
4.1	Exploring	100
4.2	Seeking	102
4.3	Gathering and Organizing	114
4.4	Using	125
4.5	Summary	137

Part II System Support — 139

5 Helping People Search — 141
- 5.1 Understanding Current Search Practices — 142
- 5.2 Current Search Support — 144
- 5.3 Search Interface Design — 158
- 5.4 Additional Search Support — 163
- 5.5 New Methods and Modalities — 171
- 5.6 Logging Richer Search Behavior — 198
- 5.7 Summary — 199

6 Exploration, Complexity, and Discovery — 201
- 6.1 Identifying Exploration — 203
- 6.2 Supporting Exploration — 205
- 6.3 Intelligent Assistants — 222
- 6.4 Discovering Insights — 224
- 6.5 Summary — 229

7 Learning and Use — 231
- 7.1 Learning — 233
- 7.2 Modeling Searcher Knowledge Level — 236
- 7.3 Learning from Oneself and Others — 241
- 7.4 Intelligent Tutors — 246
- 7.5 Applying Knowledge — 246
- 7.6 Summary — 247

8 Interaction beyond the Individual — 249
- 8.1 Collaborative Searching — 251
- 8.2 Seeking Help from Others — 253
- 8.3 Recipients — 260
- 8.4 Archiving Answers and Supporting Future Searching — 264
- 8.5 Summary — 265

9 Personalization and Contextualization — 267
- 9.1 Personalization — 269
- 9.2 Contextualization — 280
- 9.3 Explanations and Searcher Control — 301
- 9.4 Summary — 303

Part III Evaluation — 305

10 Evaluation Measures — 307
- 10.1 Process-Oriented Measures — 309
- 10.2 Outcome-Oriented Measures — 320
- 10.3 Application of Measures — 334
- 10.4 Summary — 335

11 Evaluation Methodologies — 337
- 11.1 Research Questions — 338

11.2 Methods	339
11.3 Comparing Methods	355
11.4 Summary	359

12 Data, Tools, and Privacy — 361

12.1 Logging	362
12.2 Cloud Storage	366
12.3 Release of Data	367
12.4 Privacy and Ethics	377
12.5 Obtaining Ground Truth	382
12.6 Summary	383

Part IV Opportunities and Challenges — 385

13 New Directions and Domains — 387

13.1 Mobile and Cloud Computing	387
13.2 Natural User Interaction	388
13.3 Richer Sensing	389
13.4 Augmented Reality	389
13.5 Machine Understanding and Intelligence	390
13.6 Knowledge Assistants and Proactive Search	391
13.7 New Search Scenarios	392
13.8 Applying Big Data	396
13.9 Evaluation	402
13.10 Summary	403

14 Call to Action — 405

14.1 Opportunities and Challenges	405
14.2 Summary	408

Notes	411
References	415
Index	499

Color plate section can be found between pages 304 and 305.

Preface

Information seeking is a fundamental human activity, often conducted through interactions with automated search systems. The retrieval and comprehension of information returned by these systems is a key part of decision making and action in a broad range of settings; searching skills are now even taught in schools. The processes by which people retrieve and use information has been examined in detail by the information science, information retrieval, and human-computer interaction research communities for decades.

Information scientists have targeted the cognitive and behavioral mechanisms involved in the formulation of information needs and the processes by which people search for information and update their beliefs. The goal of searching is often regarded to be to reduce uncertainty in light of the information encountered, but there may also be the intention to increase that uncertainty, for example during exploratory or leisure search scenarios. Information retrieval researchers have targeted the development of new search technologies, including more advanced methods for ranking, indexing, and crawling, that facilitates the collection and selection of potentially relevant content from large document collections such as the World Wide Web or within large enterprises (where the goal may be to locate people with specific expertise rather than find information items). Human-computer interaction researchers have investigated how people interact with technology, and they have developed interfaces to allow searchers to explore and make sense of information resources as well as generate hypotheses to guide future exploration activities and decision making. In this book I discuss how new interaction capabilities such as touch and gesture, the emergence of cloud and mobile computing, machine learning, and big (and small) data mining will change the search landscape over the next decade and beyond. By building on these and other pillars, next-generation search systems will empower people and support the activities that they value.

This is the first book devoted to discussing how the range of emerging technologies can be employed to improve the search experience. To enable this transformation, many research communities – including information retrieval, human factors, data mining, and machine learning – must cooperate on the development of systems that empower searchers and leverage the broad array of tools at their disposal to make search a productive and pleasurable experience.

There have been three documented "revolutions" in information retrieval research: (1) *cognitive* (focusing on the intellectual processes involved in the search for information), (2) *relevance* (understanding the different types of relevance and the criteria associated with each type), and (3) *interactive* (the provision of search support and the capture and use of preferences from searchers, e.g., as relevance feedback). The interactive revolution continues to the present day. Together, we will cover many of the latest technological advances in this area as we progress through this book. Importantly, we are also in the early stages of a fourth revolution: the *data revolution*, driven by the increased size of corpora such as the Web and enhanced capabilities to record, analyze, and learn from aggregated usage data at scale across a broad range of searchers, tasks, and activities. Open data movements promote the availability of data, often non-textual material such as maps and genomes, for use, reuse, and redistribution. Governmental initiatives such as Data.gov (in the United States) and Data.gov.uk (in the United Kingdom) are making a broad range of datasets, tools, and applications in topics such as agriculture, health, and education freely available for download.

The data revolution also includes the collection and analysis of "small data" describing individuals in increasing detail across a range of platforms. Data in this context includes that stored in repositories collected by search providers (comprising information such as queries and resources accessed), the signals that are available to search systems through new interaction modalities such as touch and gesture, as well as the output of a range of signals available on modern devices, including those from physiological and motion sensors. These new sources of data enable search systems to better interpret the searcher and the search situation, helping them to better adapt to received requests and operate proactively on the searcher's behalf to identify and act on available information.

Popular commercial search engines such as Google and Bing have millions of users and serve search results for billions of search queries daily. Like never before, search providers have access to significant data about the search and browsing behavior of the general population and, through the sensor network created by logging these queries, to data about world at large. Richer sensing capabilities and the Internet of Things (Höller et al., 2014) also herald the availability of a range of signals from large quantities of noisy sensors. Combining data from all of these sources at massive scale has incredible potential for understanding the human condition and tracking populations, to benefit humankind through important applications in domains such as health care. Although logs lack annotations about aspects including search intent, success, experience, and attention,[1] in the aggregate they are useful for population-scale monitoring and predicting the future. With access to such data, scientists can study how people search and consume information resources, and make discoveries to improve people's lives and make the world safer. For example, log data has recently been applied to predict influenza (Ginsberg et al., 2009), detect evidence of adverse drug reactions / interactions between medications (White et al., 2013b), and predict disease outbreaks (Radinsky and Horvitz, 2013). As part of the contribution of this book, I discuss efforts to make these data and its derivatives more widely available in the interests of science, while still respecting the privacy of individuals whose data are gathered and mined (which should be of paramount concern).

The ongoing "big data" revolution in computer science (and social science and related disciplines) has been facilitated by advances in distributed computing algorithms and technologies. By employing sophisticated data mining methods, search engines can quickly identify relevance signals in logged search behavior and use these to improve the search experience by better ranking search results, suggesting related searches or query completions, or recommending content seemingly useful to others engaged in the same or similar search tasks. For example, the rate with which particular results are clicked can be used to determine dominant search intents for ambiguous queries, and for a given search query received many times by a search engine, the popularity of particular results can be used as a way to rank order them by estimated likelihood of meeting searchers' information requirements (Joachims, 2002). Behavioral data captured in this way can also be used to refine accepted models of interaction behavior and support the creation of user models and metrics to assess system performance in offline settings.

In addition to focusing on the queries and result selections on the search engine result page (SERP), the *trails* that people follow in document corpora such as the Web (which is becoming increasing pervasive) or other hypertext collections could be used in social navigation to help guide future searchers. These trails capture traces of human behavior in a way similar to that in the physical world (e.g., read and edit wear on documents, footprints in sand, and paths through landscapes). Leveraging these trails to support future searchers realizes the vision of Vannevar Bush in his seminal 1945 paper "As We May Think": the capture of our trails through online resources allows us all to be digital trailblazers (Bush, 1945). Applying templates to sequences of logged data enables search providers to harness the procedural search knowledge of the masses, allowing them to provide strategic search support spanning the full search task, rather than simply directing searchers to potentially useful resources.

Of course, considering that humans are affected by a range of cognitive biases, and search log data are mined from their online behavior, the data can be affected by biases in how people perceive the information that they encounter. These biases can skew the behavioral signals used to direct the individual (filter bubble effects) and future searchers via aggregated behavior (e.g., search behavior fueled by cognitive biases, behavioral biases, common misconceptions, and misinformation and rumor) that need to be handled. As a result, care must be taken in interpreting behavioral signals, and steps should be taken to de-bias them – for example, by uniformly sampling clicks to remove position effects, considering the role of caption content in driving click decisions, or employing mechanisms to remove known biases during the collection of data or the analysis of experiments (e.g., controlling for the impact of neighbor effects in controlled experiments on social networks [Eckles et al., 2015]).

Beyond storing, analyzing, and using interactions with existing technologies, new sources of data are also emerging as increasingly important. Cloud computing means that people's data are no longer segregated on different machines. Search providers often have multiple product offerings, with search being only one of these. Access to data from the other services that are typically offered (electronic mail, file sharing, productivity applications, etc.) can help improve search system effectiveness. This information could be available, with user consent, in personalized search applications, whereby search providers can model preferences based on contextual clues such as the documents they have reviewed or edited, as well as those from which searches are initiated. For example, a search for "VAR" from inside an Excel spreadsheet provides additional clues that the query relates to the Excel function for variance, and not about other interpretations of the acronym (e.g., value at risk, etc.). Contextual information is also available in Web search, with the queries and Web page visits that precede a search providing valuable additional relevance signals to better rank search results and generate content recommendations. Other signals such as location, time, and even the document collection itself (e.g., hyperlinks pointing to the document currently being read) also offer useful information about the current search situation. Recent advances in modeling spatial context could be useful in modeling interests and intentions within and between locations, or other applications such as supporting more effective human motion in the world (e.g., within-building travel directions).

Although I largely focus on Web search in this book, many of the lessons also apply in other domains that might be mediated through the Web but where the information is not part of the general Web. A significant amount of electronic searching is domain specific, including legal, medical, and intellectual property. These may use technology such as Web browsers as the platform, but the accessed material may not be in the form of Web pages. Even within the context of Web search itself, there are different verticals – images, video, news, and so forth – each of which has its own presentation formats and methods of interaction. For example, in image search, infinite scrolling through pages of image thumbnails is a common practice not observed in the examination of traditional search results comprising lists of Web pages. These specialized search scenarios may deserve their own search systems, but the boundaries are also blurred and content from search verticals bleeds into the presentation of traditional SERPs, affecting signals such as click-through rates on other SERP elements (e.g., advertisements [Metrikov et al., 2014]).

Social networking websites have emerged over the past decade and have grown rapidly. Data from these networks can be used to model people's interests and address issues of data sparseness for personalization, but also provide real-time support to searchers by connecting them with friends, acquaintances, or domain experts willing to assist them in a conversation in real time. Rather than conversing directly with others, the searchers could also leverage crowdworkers to help them with their information-seeking activities or other tasks. These workers can help find search results or compose instant answers that have immediate utility (Bernstein et al., 2012), but can also be stored in repositories for future searchers with similar interests.

There is also a growing interest in the development of anticipatory services in the form of intelligent agents such as Microsoft Cortana, Apple Siri, and Google Now – all of which look deeply into the searcher's context and can leverage the power of backend search systems to answer searcher questions. Cortana and Google Now can also proactively locate relevant and timely information based on people's preferences and other signals from implicitly and explicitly provided data. Over time, by anticipating searchers' needs, these systems will reduce the volume of queries that searchers must formulate and issue on their own accord.

Advances in data availability coupled with new interaction paradigms (touch, gaze, large displays, gesture, spoken dialog) and mobile computing capabilities (more powerful tablets, smartphones, and phablets [combining features of both device forms]) have created a broad range of new opportunities for information access and use. People can now interact with search systems in more lightweight and natural ways using modalities such as touch (swipes and pinches on phone and tablets), gesture (on devices such as the Kinect or the Leap), augmented reality, and more accurate speech recognition. All of these developments make interaction easier in situ, when people may be engaged in some other in-world task where more standard interaction methods such as keyboards and mice are not available. By being able to handle coarse-grained interactions such as swipes, scrolls, pinches, and other manipulations with a single or multiple fingers, devices can offer intuitive search interfaces that are robust to noise. Gestural interaction – coupled with the incorporation of large-screen displays – enables a compelling range of possible interactive scenarios in the immersive search arena. Recent advances in machine learning have enabled significant improvements in speech recognition technology to make it usable for unconstrained scenarios such as processing voice queries on mobile devices and real-time conversations with intelligent assistants. Background noise that can degrade speech recognition also provides useful contextual signals about the ambient environment that can be useful for ranking and recommendation applications.

Mobile devices such as smartphones and slates have become powerful and versatile. The integration of sensors such as accelerometers, gyroscopes, and proximity sensors provides rich context for applications. Indeed, evidence from self-reports and log analyses suggests that people can, and will, use search technology anytime, anywhere. The availability of these devices allows search systems to help people solve tasks in situations where previously there was no help available. Almost any question (or argument!) can now be resolved with a Web search on one's mobile device. Cross-device activities, where people transition between different devices (e.g., home computer to smartphone), occur frequently, and tasks can span multiple devices are now commonplace (Montañez et al., 2014). This creates new opportunities for systems to perform so-called *slow searches* to utilize the downtime between tasks or proactively support task resumption when the searcher does restart the search. For example, if a searcher terminates a task that they were attempting on their desktop computer, and the system can predict that they will resume it sometime later on their smartphone, it could use inter-task downtime to proactively retrieve content of possible interest, automatically or via third-party human involvement.

Moving beyond handheld devices such as smartphones, wearable and augmented reality applications allow relevant information to be incorporated into people's view of the world. Although this has been proposed in a range of scenarios, including triage in emergency medical situations and printer repair, recent advances in mobile computing, recommendation, and speech recognition offer further opportunities to enhance search interaction. One example are smart glasses (e.g., head-mounted displays such as *Google Glass*), which provide additional alerts on incoming communications, directions to destinations of interest, and location-dependent information, all in the searcher's field of view and using speech input. With such "always on" technology, systems no longer need to rely on their users to request information explicitly; relevant information can be pushed toward searchers proactively, capitalizing on signals such as their current location and historic preferences. Despite the attractiveness of such a seamless interaction method, there are privacy concerns around its use in public settings and the collection and capture of data (videos, still images, audio) about other individuals without their consent that need to be considered as part of broader discussions on the societal implications of wearable technology (Hong, 2013; Hoyle et al., 2014). Microsoft *HoloLens* is another example of augmented-reality technology housed inside a head-mounted display that supports multiple modes of interaction (including gaze and speech), and also adds three-dimensional holographic representations to the user's field of view, which can be manipulated using physical gestures.

Behind many of these technological advances lie conceptual models of human-information behavior, especially around how people seek and consume information. Although a number of influential models have been proposed over the past few decades, primarily by researchers in the information science community, these models must keep pace with technological advances and searcher demands. It is clear from the advances described so far that we are in the midst of a revolution in information seeking, in terms of both interaction capabilities and data availability. A plethora of new technologies and dedicated applications are emerging to supersede generic search systems in some information settings, and searcher demands for ubiquitous access to information continues to grow. In this book I discuss how these new capabilities will affect search system design, and how the range of evaluation methods and metrics that are applied to determine the performance of search systems needs to be extended.

In this book I focus on online searching. However, many of the concepts and ideas could also be applied in other domains, such as digital libraries or specialized domains. Regardless of the information environment, given its importance and technological advances, there is still significant opportunity for substantial impact through work on search interaction. Next-generation search systems will support a range of tasks, from finding basic facts to helping people explore, learn, and use encountered information. We are only beginning a journey to a more enlightened society facilitated by next-generation search technology.

The book is divided into four parts designed to introduce core concepts, describe models and methods, cover evaluation, and cast an eye to the future. The target audience for this book spans many readers, but it is primarily aimed at scholars at all career stages, including graduate students seeking to learn more about interactions with systems, especially how evidence is collected, modeled, and applied to improve the search experience for the current searcher and for future searchers. I also discuss the future of search interaction and highlight emerging trends that I believe will be of increasing importance in the design of search systems over the next decade and beyond.

CHAPTER 1

Introduction

Information seeking is a core life activity. People seek information for a number of reasons, including to find facts (Marchionini and Shneiderman, 1988) and to learn and facilitate effective decision making (Marchionini, 2006). Searchers may also have other motivations, such as pleasure and enjoyment (Wilson and Elsweiler, 2010). Historically, people have sought information through interactions with others, either synchronously through in-person or telephone dialog or asynchronously through written communication. Increasingly, information seeking is being conducted via *automated* search systems such as Web search engines. Meeting searcher requirements across the full spectrum of search goals that individuals may have is challenging with such generic search systems. Nonetheless, search engines are offering an increasing range of reactive and proactive search services to meet and anticipate searcher needs. Helping searchers with specific search tasks requires targeted search support, as well as different methods and criteria under which to evaluate the performance of search systems in different circumstances. For example, fact-finding tasks may require only a single resource or direct answer, and strong system performance may be evidenced by low searcher engagement and short task completion times. In contrast, when the goals involve exploration, learning, or enjoyment, richer search and exploration support may be needed (e.g., diverse results or query suggestions, dynamic information visualizations), and increased engagement over a much longer timespan may be a positive indication of system performance. Understanding the nature of the search task(s) being attempted is important in both designing and evaluating the support offered by search systems.

Effective interactions with automated search systems are a critical aspect of successful searching. These interactions can range in complexity from basic text query entry and result selection to rich gestural and spoken dialog interactions. Search tasks can also continue longitudinally and increasingly, these tasks transcend devices, domains, and applications. The range of search interactions, and the support that systems offer for performing them, is expanding given technological advances. Search systems are becoming more intelligent and more aware of their users' interests and intentions, as well as of their surroundings when performing searches. This enables these systems to anticipate people's needs more accurately and to work symbiotically with searchers to support task completion directly. Developing systems capable of serving as cognitive prosthetics to amplify human intelligence was proposed by visionaries some decades ago (Bush, 1945; Licklider, 1960; Engelbart, 1962). Advances in user modeling, semantic understanding of queries and documents, machine learning, and artificial intelligence mean that this vision is closer than ever to being realized. That said, there is scant literature on the new wave of technology and its relationship with the design of next-generation search systems. I address this shortcoming in this book, where I aim to summarize past and present research and development in the important area of search interaction, but also to spend significant time discussing a future enabled by a number of recent technological advances, as well as changes in the attitudes and expectations of searchers, which is affecting how searcher data is collected and used, and the types of search support offered. I use the phrase "next-generation search systems" since I believe that we are on the cusp of a revolution of how people engage with search technology and how search systems will empower searchers. Given the importance of these recent developments, I adopt a perspective that is more systems oriented than conceptual. I also focus primarily on the Web because of the wealth of recent research in this area and the opportunity for advances at scale to enhance quality of life for individuals worldwide. In principle, much of the work covered herein could be applied to any document collection or search domain, including digital libraries and organizational intranets.

1.1 Historical Approaches

Searches are often motivated by an incompleteness (Ingwersen, 1992; Mackay, 1960; Taylor, 1968) or a "problematic situation" (Belkin, 1982a, 1982b) in the mind of the searcher that develops into a desire for information. The recognition and acceptance of an information problem typically resides at the beginning of the information-seeking process (e.g., Ellis, 1989; Marchionini, 1995; Wilson, 1997). The problem can be internally motivated (e.g., curiosity) or externally motivated (e.g., an assignment). It may be characterized by a gap (Dervin, 1977), a visceral need (Taylor, 1968), an anomaly in a searcher's knowledge state (Belkin, 1982a, 1982b), as a defect in a mental model, or as an unstable collection of noumena (Marchionini, 1995). Once the problem has been accepted, it must then be understood and defined. To do so, it must be limited and labeled, and a framework for the answer must be constructed. This is defined as the "conscious need" (Taylor, 1968). During this process, attributes of candidate solutions emerge that will ultimately guide search interactions. This process leads to the development of Taylor's "formalized need" and the possible articulation of an information-seeking task. The searcher defines the problem internally as a task with properties that allow progress to be judged and a particular search strategy to be selected.

Although much of the search interaction that I consider in this book involves richer modeling and support for search interaction behavior, I begin by focusing on the traditional lookup model that has been fundamental in the design of support for searching. This model focuses on query-document matching and is used to represent search activity in a range of applications, including generic Web search. The "10 blue links" method (Broder et al., 2010) is the dominant interaction model currently used in the

Figure 1.1. Lookup-based information retrieval model (adapted from Bates, 1989).

development of database management systems and in major commercial Web search engines offered by search providers such as Google, Yahoo!, and Microsoft. Figure 1.1 depicts this retrieval model. The development of methods and tools to support the retrieval of relevant content per this model drove many of the early advances in Information Retrieval (IR) research (e.g., Van Rijsbergen, 1979; Salton and McGill, 1983), and continues to this day in settings such as the annual Text Retrieval Conference (TREC) (Voorhees and Harman, 2005) and other evaluation fora. The components of the lookup model are the collection being searched (*Documents* in Figure 1.1), a representation of the documents that are stored the collection (*Document Surrogates*, usually as an inverted index for rapid document lookup), the underlying information need of the searcher (*Information Need*), and a query statement (*Query*, traditionally in textual form provided by the searcher at query time). To use search systems employing this model, searchers provide a query statement representing their information needs, and the system returns a ranked list of document surrogates comprising titles (the "blue links" referred to by Broder et al., 2010), result captions, uniform resource locators (URLs), and other relevant information (e.g., Web page size, topical category, most recent page modification timestamp) for examination and selection by the searcher. Beyond ranked lists of search results, other methods such as result clusters and alternative visualizations of results are also available and will be discussed in more detail later in the book (Chapter 6).

The lookup-based model has promoted our understanding of IR in many ways (e.g., as the basis by which systems are evaluated at the Text Retrieval Conference; Harman, 1993; Voorhees and Harman, 2005). Lookup tasks are usually suited to analytical search strategies that begin with carefully specified queries and yield precise results with minimal need for result set examination and item comparison, such as fact-finding or question-answering scenarios (Marchionini, 2006a). A common assumption behind this model is that the information exists in the collection and searchers need only to retrieve it by formulating an appropriate query, with or without assistance from the search system. Under this paradigm, the query is treated as a one-time conception of the searcher's information need. However, many real searches contain multiple query iterations, post-query browsing, detailed result examination, and ill-defined/exploratory needs, none of which are adequately captured in this model. Hypothesis generation, decision making (an aspect of information use), and the impact of search interaction on searcher knowledge in the short and long term are also important and require support from search systems – yet have only been given limited attention in prior research on the search process, especially in Web search settings where the focus is on outcomes that are easier to measure, e.g., relevance and satisfaction.

As Kuhn (1970) noted, major models that are central to a field eventually begin to show inadequacies as testing leads to improved understanding of the processes being studied. This applies to the lookup-based interaction model as a basis for information-seeking research. The model has come under increased scrutiny for quite some time (e.g., Bates, 1986a,b; Belkin et al., 1982a,b; Ellis, 1984; Ingwersen, 1992; Kuhlthau, 1993; Marchionini, 1995). The model inadequately represents how humans interact with search systems and the potential dynamism of information needs during a search session, and also ignores important factors such as task context and information use (Bates, 1989; Ingwersen and Järvelin, 2005). Information seeking tasks are also tackled over time across many search episodes (Kotov et al., 2011; Agichtein et al., 2012) using disparate resources, and is often interwoven with other activities, meaning that searchers may be engaged in multiple information-seeking tasks simultaneously (Spink et al., 2006).

Interactive information retrieval (IIR) focuses on how people use search systems to retrieve information from the indexed corpus (i.e., the focus is largely on information *finding*) (Ruthven, 2008). Human-computer information retrieval (HCIR; Marchionini, 2006) has emerged as an important subdiscipline focused on the role of searcher and their context on the search process. Information seeking depends on the cognitive representation of a system's features, which is largely determined by the conceptual model that system designers provide through the search interfaces that they develop. Other determinants of successful searching include searchers' knowledge of the task domain (i.e., their domain or subject-matter expertise), the information-seeking experience, and the physical setting (Marchionini and Shneiderman, 1988). To support more effective search interactions, research in HCIR leverages advancements in search user interface technology and an improved understanding of people's search strategies developed by information scientists and others, via studies of library patrons and reference librarians, but more recently via large-scale surveys, panels, and log analyses.

To help searchers, interactive search systems offer support such as relevance feedback (RF), information visualizations, and query suggestions. RF (cf. Salton and Buckley, 1990) allows searchers to provide implicit or explicit feedback about relevant information and uses these judgments to enhance subsequent searches. Information visualizations (e.g., Card et al., 1999) use graphical techniques to visually represent large-scale collections of nonnumerical information, and help searchers attain new insights in support of decision making or other related complex mental activities. Visualization techniques such as highlighting salient content in documents can also capitalize on human abilities to recognize important cues and content when presented with them, rather than needing to examine information items in detail (Ahn and Brusilovsky, 2013; Lehmann et al., 2010). Query suggestions (also known as "related searches") (e.g., Efthimiadis, 1996; Koenemann and Belkin, 1996; Jones et al., 2006) provide recommendations about query terms to add to an existing query, or specific queries to issue, that assist searchers with the challenging process of query formulation.

Oddy (1977) and Belkin et al. (1982), among others, questioned the requirement for searchers to represent their information needs in a query understandable by the system. Indeed, systems such as I^3R (Croft and Thompson, 1987), *Bead* (Chalmers and Chitson, 1992), and the *Ostensive Browser* (Campbell and Van Rijsbergen, 1996) offer "query-less" interfaces, where searcher needs are conveyed by means of examples from their browse behavior rather than textual descriptions. Research on implicit feedback (Joachims et al., 2005; Kelly and Belkin, 2004; Kelly and Teevan, 2003; White et al., 2005b) has shown that interaction behavior (mainly document retention activities such as saving, bookmarking, and printing, as well as SERP click-through) can be used to build enhanced representations of information needs for use in query refinement or future retrieval operations. The notion of implicit feedback has been extended to Web search interaction, where clicks on search results can be used as signals of user interest that have utility as features of machine-learned models for general result ranking (Joachims, 2002; Agichtein et al., 2006) or personalized result ranking (Dou et al., 2007; Teevan et al., 2011b).

1.2 Next-Generation Search Interaction

The lookup model assumes that searchers are engaged in simple tasks with known information objectives. For many tasks, information needs are dynamic and only emerge as a result of learning through reflection regarding the information acquired during the search process (Bates, 1998; Marchionini, 2006). Studies of information behavior also focus primarily on user studies as a way of learning about information behavior. Over the past two decades we have witnessed an emergence of studies of human search behavior at Web scale. Studied search behaviors range from individual query statements (Silverstein et al., 1999; Jansen et al., 2000) to fine-grained interactions such as eye gaze and mouse cursor movements (Huang et al., 2011; Buscher et al., 2012). The focus has shifted to search tasks (Jones and Klinkner, 2008) and to trails that extend beyond just search engine interactions (White and Drucker, 2007). Log analyses of this nature have largely been restricted to researchers in industrial settings given restrictions on the sharing of large quantities of anonymized usage data that is required to make this type of research on naturalistic search behavior feasible. To pursue studies of this nature, academic researchers have needed to be creative in obtaining access to data, either using data collected from university websites (e.g., Joachims [2002] used data from arXiv.org, a service run by Cornell University), creating their own rich logging infrastructure (Lagun et al., 2011; Guo et al., 2013), or even devising games to help collect data from human participants (Ageev et al., 2011; West et al., 2012). In Chapter 12, I will discuss the many issues surrounding access to large-scale behavioral data, and its impact on the scope and the nature of the research that is possible in academia and industry.

New directions in search interaction are being pursued in parallel with the development of specialized search systems. Some interaction methods may be appropriate for particular scenarios more than others. Examples of this include search engine verticals such as image search, in which "infinite scrolling" (Farago et al., 2010) has replaced pagination as the predominant mechanism to explore deep into sets of retrieved items. Activities involving exploratory data analysis may benefit from views of the data such as *TreeMaps* (Shneiderman, 1992) or a closer (dynamic) coupling between queries and retrieved results (Ahlberg and Shneiderman, 1992). Next-generation search systems will recommend appropriate tools for the current search task, as well as allow searchers to control and customize search support to make the human-machine roles during searching more cooperative (Marchionini, 2006b). In offering any new functionality, appropriate consideration must be given to searchers' desire to focus on task completion rather than learning new systems (Carroll and Rosson, 1987); in other words, additional functionality must be intuitive to use and not detract from the task completion process.

As searcher expectations for the availability of search support evolve, next-generation search systems will need to handle more complex tasks and the sophisticated search scenarios (Wilson et al., 2010). These systems will require capabilities to detect and model search tasks from search activity (Lucchese et al., 2013) and to track these tasks over time (Kotov et al., 2011). The following is an example of a typical search situation that highlights how the capabilities in next-generation search systems will help people learn and take action in the world.

Example search scenario: Elizabeth is undergoing treatment for breast cancer. Evidence of Elizabeth's health concern was apparent in her online behavior months before the first oncologist visit. Queries were seen for [small lump in breast] and other symptoms. Elizabeth's intelligent personal assistant associated her long-term activity (e.g., queries, Web page visits, social media posts, physiological signals from her wearable device), with an above average risk of breast cancer. It did this using a diagnostic model trained from the long-term activities of populations of consenting individuals. Model reliability was verified in stringent testing by medical professionals and extensive trials with breast cancer patients. The model was run against a log comprising Elizabeth's long-term activity and a personalized alert was generated about her risk level and the importance of swift medical attention in her case. Thankfully, she followed the agent's advice. A diagnosis was professionally rendered, Elizabeth updated her secure, cloud-based profile – linked by choice to her electronic health records – and used applications on her mobile device to track and monitor her course of treatment over time, as well as to connect with other breast cancer patients. This additional information is used by the search system to tailor the results that Elizabeth encounters when searching about breast cancer, as well as to find additional information proactively, such as the outcomes of recent clinical trials. In addition, the system helps her understand the nature of complex content, guides her through the stages of treatment, and aid decision making, for example selecting between treatment alternatives based on combining professional medical advice and content mined and aggregated from sources on the Web.

The preceding example depicts a situation in which search systems can play a more central role in rendering assistance proactively as well as reacting to searcher demands. Many of the technologies described in this example are available in some form in present-day computer systems. However, in current search systems, much of the responsibility for the searching, tracking, and sensing is placed on the searcher; I envisage that much of this burden will be shifted to the system over time. Access to this data allows systems to custom tailor the search experience, monitor people's task progress, and identify noteworthy patterns, trends, and anomalies. As is clear from the example, search systems need to be able to support not only information finding but also topic learning (Marchionini, 2006a). To do this effectively, the system also needs to be able to understand a searcher's level of domain knowledge – perhaps through explicit solicitation of this information, or studying their online search behavior

(White et al., 2009). There are many such complex scenarios where search systems could offer quite significant help.

Long-running search tasks such as that highlighted in the preceding example are common (Kotov et al., 2011; Agichtein et al., 2012). Agichtein et al. (2012) demonstrated that over 50% of search tasks observed in Web search engine log data transcend multiple search sessions (although decoupling active tasks from persistent interests remains a challenge). Support can be provided to help people store and rehydrate search tasks across long-running search episodes (Morris and Horvitz, 2007; Donato et al., 2010; Morris et al., 2011), as well as providing direct support for task resumption by considering "standing queries" that represent persistent interests. Standing queries are useful for information filtering (Allan, 1996) or cases where people continue the same tasks over time (Morris and Horvitz, 2007). Task states, stored on the client or (preferably for accessibility) in the cloud, allow search services to use this information to cluster search histories, support the selective application of these histories for applications such as personalization, and to suggest future actions based on what the searcher has accomplished thus far.

Next-generation search systems will also become more personal and more ubiquitous. They will learn about people's activity beyond information seeking, enabling richer models and personalized search experiences tailored to individuals' preferences. Intelligent assistants – such as Siri, Microsoft Cortana, and Google Now – can communicate directly with searchers and adapt their offerings to their users via access to personal content such as calendars, e-mails, and contact information.

Slow search (Teevan et al., 2013) describes a situation where information retrieval is unconstrained by time. Searchers may have an expectation that search systems respond quickly to their requests. However, in many search scenarios (such as long-term tasks, missions – e.g., chronic medical conditions for the searcher or a family member such as that highlighted in the earlier example) the search task may span a significant amount of time and the search system may have longer to reply to the original request and alert searchers if new information is found (e.g., notify those affected by chronic medical conditions that there is a new treatment option or study finding). If there is this additional time, the system could use that to survey available information (Lieberman, 1995; Joachims et al., 1997) or find humans to help (Horowitz and Kamvar, 2010; White et al., 2011). Search is not performed in isolation, and the social context is important in analyzing the value of the answers found, but can also have direct utility in helping people reach their goals, for example by broadcasting questions to members of the searcher's social network (Morris et al., 2010).

Wearable devices allow richer sensing of the searcher (e.g., their physiological functions; Healy and Picard, 1998; Feild et al., 2010) and contextual factors, including their intentions and even the physical environment within which they are searching. Better modeling of search situations helps search systems determine task-appropriate information so as to offer tailored support to searchers. More expressive interaction methods involving gesture, touch, and speech are becoming commonplace in computer systems generally,[1] and it is likely that there will be widespread adoption of such methods in search systems over the next decade and beyond. Richer interfaces to support exploration and learning will allow searchers to discover relationships between items and make more informed decisions about both search strategies and information use. Coupling information visualization techniques with natural interaction methods will create compelling and engaging immersive search experiences to promote effective discovery and learning.

An important theme in this book is the development and application of methods to model and support searchers *at scale*. Historically, the focus in search interaction has been on sophisticated and dynamic direct manipulation interfaces applied *client-side* within a restricted domain such as movies (e.g., Williamson and Shneiderman, 1992; Card et al., 1999) or a searcher's personal data, or simple methods such as ranked lists of surrogates applicable *server-side* on the Web but with only crude interaction support for text queries and hyperlink selections. High data volumes and bandwidth concerns have meant that only limited information can be shared with remote systems, and massive processing capabilities are needed to handle the exabytes of data collected by online services. Improvements in network bandwidth and availability, reductions in the price of hardware (especially data storage), and algorithmic and technological advances in distributed computing are finally allowing providers of next-generation search systems to offer rich and engaging search experiences to billions of searchers.

Mining the behavior of large numbers of searchers has utility for both improving the system performance and yielding insights that benefit society (e.g., via initiatives in public health; White et al., 2013b, 2014a). The ability to monitor search interactions at scale enables the study of information-seeking behavior in naturalistic settings across a broad range of information needs. Query and click-through statistics can be used to identify relevant results based on dominant search intents mined from many searchers (Joachims, 2002; Agichtein et al., 2006; Anick, 2003), and also at the individual level for applications such as the personalization of search results or the generation of query suggestions (Teevan et al., 2011b, Shokouhi, 2013). Log analyses may facilitate more complete modeling of information behavior, but it often lacks data about the rationales behind the observed search activity (i.e., what actions were taken, but not why the search is necessary). Mixed-methods approaches are necessary to develop a more complete picture of people's intentions and situations when searching. There are also drawbacks and challenges associated with collecting and using these data (including the important issue of searcher privacy), and care needs to be taken in the design of logging schemes, but also in detecting and mitigating potential biases in the data collected (including demand characteristics associated with participant awareness of the experimental setting; Orne, 1962). As an alternative to tracking attention within existing search interfaces, others have deliberately designed search interfaces to facilitate the capture of fine-grained implicit feedback (White et al., 2005a). This can be advantageous since signals can be accurately interpreted as evidence for particular aspects of documents, but such interfaces may also be unfamiliar to searchers.

Beyond the search process, there are other important issues to consider. Search engines are often part of commercial enterprises that receive revenue from online advertising, primarily via advertisements juxtaposed with search results. This has implications for how search data are employed and shared. The data that they collect is valuable for improving search engine services and attracting searchers, and more searchers means more revenue. Privacy considerations and the high business value of the data mean that it is not distributed broadly. Limited access to large-scale behavioral data for the research community is also necessary given appropriate consideration of important issues such as privacy and consent to share data for research purposes.

Proposals are emerging to release samples of the queries and clicks collected by commercial search engines in a manner that rigorously guarantees searcher privacy (Korolova et al., 2009).

As people own a broader range of devices (e.g., desktop computers, smartphones, laptops, gaming consoles, etc.), support for searching across those devices is becoming more important. Research in cross-device search is in its infancy, and there is significant opportunity to help multi-device searchers be more productive by supporting information-seeking tasks that span devices. (e.g., using searcher behavior observed on one search engine vertical to personalize the experience for the same searcher on another vertical) and cross-application (e.g., applying models learned from a person's usage of one application to tailor their search experience on another) scenarios will also grow in importance (Elkahky et al., 2015). Interest profiles developed from people's interactions within one or more domains or applications can help those same searchers when searching in other domains or using other applications. A core component of this support will involve cloud-based user profiles, accessible at any time from any device or application. These profiles can contain search histories but also useful information from other sources, such as authored documents and social media activity (with searcher consent as necessary). This would directly support cross-device/domain/application search scenarios, including supporting task resumption by rehydrating prior context (Wang et al., 2013). People's tasks are not limited to device boundaries, and increasingly search engines will consider the device-appropriateness of the information that they surface. They will support search activities across devices, including predicting whether the searcher will resume a task on another device (Wang et al., 2013; Montañez et al., 2014). If a service could predict the next device that a person will use (e.g., it can be confident that they are going to transition from a laptop to a smartphone), how long it has until that transition occurs, and the topic of the next search, it can employ a range of services, including crowdsourcing, to leverage the downtime between devices and find the best information in advance of the searcher resuming their task on the destination device.

As the capabilities of search systems improve to support richer search tasks in a broader array of search settings, there is also a need to evaluate search systems from a range of different perspectives. Evaluation metrics and methodologies need to consider search *process* in addition to the outcomes such as relevance and search satisfaction. Process-based evaluation considers factors such as searcher learning (Jansen et al., 2009; Wilson and Wilson, 2013) and cognitive load (Gwizdka, 2010) as part of system evaluation. Monitoring these signals is important in measuring the performance of next-generation search systems and creating benchmarks such as TREC that can facilitate the comparison of search systems across experimental sites. To spur progress in the design of interactive search systems, other experimental methods such as searcher simulations (especially those derived directly from behavioral data; White et al., 2005b; White, 2010) and facility for large-scale flighting of new interface developments could well be made available to researchers in *both* industry and academia through partnerships with commercial search engines and related efforts.

Interactions with search systems play an important role in the daily activities of many people. From the brief overview offered in the book thus far, it is clear that there are many opportunities for next-generation search interaction. I will discuss many of these in more detail as we move together through the book.

1.3 Outline

The remainder of the book is divided into the following four parts:

1. **Part I (Background):** I set the scene for the topics covered in this book. In Chapter 2 I discuss how search interaction is represented and modeled presently in search systems and how that support could be expanded in the future with the advent of a broad range of new technologies such as gaze tracking, touch interaction, and affective feedback. Chapter 3 describes how searcher interests and intentions are modeled, including models of interaction with next-generation search systems and the components necessary to build and deploy such models in practice. Toward better understanding searcher needs, Chapter 4 describes a range of models and frameworks that have been proposed to characterize different aspects of information seeking (i.e., information exploration, seeking information, gathering and organizing information, and applying information in practice).

2. **Part II (System Support):** I describe various types of system support for search systems, including the design of interfaces to help people locate information items, but also help people explore, learn, and apply gained knowledge. Chapter 5 describes both existing and emerging technologies to help people search more effectively. Of particular interest, as mainstream search support expands beyond its existing boundaries, is support for exploration and discovery, including recommendations (Chapter 6) and learning and information use (Chapter 7). I describe how exploration and discovery can be modeled and supported by systems. As part of this, proactive search and recommendations by anticipatory services such as Google Now and Microsoft Cortana are useful to push relevant content to searchers at opportune moments. I would expect that such anticipatory services become more central, especially as they are integrated into the operating systems of desktop and mobile devices. Chapter 8 considers the role of others both in supporting an individual searcher and in searching collaboratively as a team. Other people are frequently stakeholders in search tasks, and system designers need to consider how to integrate the viewpoints and preferences into the search process, as well as how to support coordination of information seeking across individuals and teams, so as to reduce redundancy and improve overall search effectiveness. In addition, search tasks do not occur in isolation from searchers' experiences and the surrounding context. Personalization and contextualization are important in improving the quality of search engine responses to the current situation, but methods are also needed should personal content be unavailable (e.g., using data from searchers with similar interests). I expect to see significant advances given richer sensing through wearable devices and more complete context-modeling methods. Chapter 9 discusses research in these critical areas and how it can be applied to improve future search systems.

3. **Part III (Evaluation):** An important aspect of the search process is the evaluation of the search systems. Chapters 10 and 11 discuss the evaluation of these systems, in particular the formative and summative methods that can be employed to inform system design. Given the richness of next-generation search interactions, I pay particular attention to better evaluating the search *process*, and also highlight

the need for methods that facilitate comparability across sites and systems. As an important aspect of the cross-site comparability of search systems and the reproducibility experimental findings, Chapter 12 discusses data availability and analysis, as well as the important topic of searcher privacy which must inform all decisions regarding the collection and use of data.

4. **Part IV (Opportunities and Challenges):** In light of technological advances and shifting searcher expectations regarding the role of search technology, there are significant opportunities and challenges in the design of search systems. In this part of the book I highlight emerging directions and domains in the area of search interaction (Chapter 13), and conclude by presenting a call to action for the research community and beyond (Chapter 14). There is significant opportunity for search systems to help people, and this will only grow with time as these systems assume a more central role in our lives. For example, it is quite clear that we are witnessing a pivot away from reactive search systems (only capable of responding to searcher queries) toward hybrid search systems that can answer when asked but also understand the searcher and sense their environment, so as to recommend relevant content to searchers (e.g., a searcher may issue standing queries to which the search system can apply a function of location, time, proximity to others, etc. to identify and recommend relevant content). The opportunities in this area become even more empowering when search technology is coupled with new delivery mechanisms such as intelligent agents, which can engage in direct dialog with people to understand their needs and intentions, and new presentation mechanisms such as augmented reality, which can seamlessly combine search results with searchers' views of the world.

Let us begin this journey together by examining ways in which search interaction is currently collected and represented in search systems, as well as discussing some emerging interaction methods that I expect to become more prevalent in search settings in the not-too-distant future.

PART I
Background

In this part of the book, I provide background information about the collection and application of behavioral signals beyond what is already offered in the previous chapter. I discuss the ways in which evidence of search interaction can be collected and applied in search systems. Much of the previous research in this area has focused on the science behind information seeking behaviors or the effectiveness of novel interfaces to support those behaviors. In light of the data revolution, there has been a growth in interest in the collection, modeling, and application of search interaction behaviors at scale (across many thousands and millions of individuals) in settings such as web search and web browsing. In addition, there have been a number of recent technological advances in interaction methods (e.g. touch, gesture, and speech recognition), sensing, mobile and cloud computing, and machine learning that enable a range of new opportunities for search system design.

CHAPTER 2
Collecting and Representing Search Interaction

In mainstream search systems, search interactions typically assume the form of search queries and result selections. This information can be useful as implicit feedback to improve search performance when aggregated across many searchers (Joachims, 2002; Agichtein et al., 2006). Implicit feedback can also be collected at a personal level and used to update the search experience directly in real time (e.g., rearranging available information [White et al., 2005a; White et al., 2005b]), or to tailor the results for the current query using personalization or contextualization (Dou et al., 2007; Teevan et al., 2011b; Bennett et al., 2012). Trails that people follow through document collections (Bush, 1945; Bilenko and White, 2008) and trail destinations (White et al., 2007) can also be employed to help searchers understand the corpus and the domain (White and Huang, 2010), and ultimately to attain their search goals. In addition to being used to refine search results or other features (such as related searches or query auto-completions [shown dynamically as searchers compose queries]), recorded traces of search interaction can also be used as a diagnostic tool to understand when searchers are satisfied or frustrated with their search experience (Hassan et al., 2010; Aula et al., 2010; Feild et al., 2010), and consequently, where the search system could improve its performance or provide missing search support. Sections 2.1–2.3 discuss components of the search interaction process, including SERP interactions and sequences of actions extending beyond the search engine and into the corpus being searched.

There is a growing set of opportunities for search engines to learn from aggregated search activity as a new range of interface features emerge to integrate new capabilities, such as touch and gesture. Section 2.4 discusses mechanisms for collecting and representing interests and intentions beyond queries and clicks. Other advances, such as eye-gaze tracking and spoken dialog, will change both the manner and the settings in which people interact with search systems. Because interactions depend on both software and hardware, device-dependent models of relevance may be needed to accurately associate interaction events on each device with searchers' common interests and intentions. Some progress has been made on modeling relevance on mobile devices using touch interactions (Guo et al., 2013), but more research in this area is anticipated.

Mouse cursor tracking provides insight into aspects of search behavior, beyond search result clicks (e.g., the results searchers have considered, irrespective of whether they click on them) and including non-hyperlink clicks intended to restore focus on the page or to select text (White and Buscher, 2012a). Cursor movements can be captured at scale with little impact on page load time or interface responsiveness (Huang et al. 2011), especially if that functionality is loaded after the content. Recent research has demonstrated potential applications of mouse cursor movement monitoring in areas such as relevance estimation (Huang et al., 2012; Lagun et al., 2014) and understanding SERP abandonment (Huang et al., 2011; Diriye et al., 2012).

Although there is significant scientific and practical value in mining large-scale behavioral data, there are also some shortcomings. For example, because the data are collected anonymously and the analysis is performed retrospectively, there is little or no opportunity to engage directly with searchers to understand their rationales and/or the circumstances affecting their search behavior. That is, one only gets to learn about *what* searchers were interested in and *how* they reached that goal, but not *why* they were interested in that content. Knowledge of the search situation can yield important clues about how to interpret the observed behavior. Mined search behavior is also limited to that related to the interface shown to the searcher at the time the activity was logged; it therefore cannot be used to study behavior with new results or interface variants.[1] In addition, only a subset of information-seeking behaviors is visible in interactions with search engines (Kumpulainen and Järvelin, 2010). Activity may also be missing owing to avoidance behaviors related to concerns about privacy. Understanding the rationales behind observed and unobserved activity is important in understanding the search process. Although some progress has been made in mining qualitative data collected from searchers for actionable insights (Dan et al., 2012), a complete understanding of system efficacy is only attainable by working directly with searchers to capture these rationales in-situ (Fox et al., 2005; Guo et al., 2011; Diriye et al., 2012) or retrospectively soon after the activity has been observed (Kelly, 2004; Kellar et al., 2007). The latter approach uses a method known as *stimulated recall* to elicit explanations from searchers for their observed search activity (see Kelly, 2009). Section 2.5 discusses various data collection strategies that can be applied in laboratory and natural settings to collect data on how people behave during search episodes.

Research projects in this area require careful design of methods to support interaction and monitor searcher activity. Where possible, rich data should be collected about how searchers use experimental systems and baseline comparators, and these data should be represented in a way that can be used both as implicit feedback and also during comparative evaluations (i.e., meaningful information can be extracted from the data during retrospective analysis). Studies employing retrospective log analysis are attractive because they typically use data that has already been collected. In such analyses, the challenges of designing and deploying search systems with logging capabilities, and the recruitment of large cohorts of participants – two of the most difficult aspects of search system design and evaluation – have already been addressed. That said, this sort of retrospective analysis affords experimenters little control over the system used in the study or other aspects such as the participant cohort or search tasks.[2]

The foci in log analysis include devising interesting research questions, conceptualizing and modeling search behavior, efficiently mining the data, analyzing the results obtained from the analysis, summarizing the conclusions, and deriving actionable learnings. Because so much research has already been completed in the domain of search log analysis, devising novel and creative research questions is a difficult part of research in this area. Fortunately, as technology advances, there are emerging opportunities to explore new search scenarios such as cross-device search (Wang et al., 2013; Montañez et al., 2014) or engagement with intelligent personal assistants (Jiang et al., 2015), given access to log data with new information. There are also other important applications of large-scale behavioral data, such as population monitoring (Deville et al., 2014), public health (Paul et al., 2014; Fourney et al., 2015), and politics (Weber et al., 2012). The range of significant applications that can be found for big data of this nature will continue to expand over time.

Search behavior may also be affected by biases in behavior related to a variety of different factors, ranging from the presentation order of results and caption content (Joachims et al., 2005; Yue et al., 2010), searcher issues such as domain preferences (Ieong et al., 2012), cognitive biases (Tversky and Kahneman, 1974; White, 2013), potential anxieties (White and Horvitz, 2009; White and Horvitz, 2013), and sampling bias in the distribution of searchers who use a particular system or express interest in a particular query topic. As both aggregated and personal information-seeking behavior are strong signals in search engine ranking (Joachims, 2002a; Joachims, 2002b; Bennett et al., 2012), any individual biases – such as an apparent preference for information that supports a particular viewpoint (White, 2013) or searchers who share a particular perspective (Yom-Tov et al., 2013) – has a large impact on the future performance of the engine. One area in which this may be especially apparent is in the veracity of results returned (White and Hassan, 2014). Common misconceptions about controversial topics may skew result lists, especially if personalization is performed; systems may limit retrieved information to that supportive of the searcher's current position or interests (Pariser, 2011).

2.1 Interaction Types

One of the most important decisions that must be made when modeling search behavior is the unit of analysis at which those models will be constructed. The unit of analysis impacts the type of analytics that can be performed and the ways in which search behavior can be utilized for applications such as result ranking. I focus on two types: (1) *atomic interaction events*, and (2) *sequences of these events* over time.

2.1.1 Atomic Interaction Events (Individual Actions)

In many search settings, actions are primarily composed of queries and navigation events that allow people to express their information needs and access information resources.[3] Selection of recommendations provided by the system, including query and document suggestions, can also be regarded as atomic actions. Another action type is pagination, whereby searchers request the next page of results if a limited number of results are presented on each SERP.

Some events may be excluded from analysis as they are only symptomatic of the particular search experience rather than the information need of the searcher. This highlights a more important point: in analyzing data collected from a search system, care should be taken to distinguish between events that symbolize search intentions (e.g., selecting results) and those that are only associated with the particular interface design and available affordances (e.g., paginating through search results via the "Next" button). In the case of pagination, it has been shown that searchers are more likely to re-query than examine the list of search results surfaced by the search engine in detail (e.g., Rieh and Xie, 2006). The first request for the next page of search results may both reveal important information about the quality of the *first page* of search results that search systems could leverage to measure their performance holistically and identify particular queries in which their performance may be lacking. The presence of subsequent query reformulations provides insight into searchers' perceptions of the results or the SERP more generally (Hassan, 2012).

2.1.2 Sequences of Interaction Events

Moving beyond individual actions, temporally ordered sequences of actions can be analyzed given the presence of chronological information. This allows for the development of more complex models of search interaction than is possible at the individual action level. There are various ways in which actions can be combined, both in the short term and the long term. In the short term, sequences of actions usually form *sessions* (He et al., 2002), *query chains* connecting sequences of related query reformulations (Radlinski and Joachims, 2005), or *trails* of search queries and for their associated post-query navigation behavior (as well as browsing trails generally; see White and Drucker, 2007).

2.1.2.1 Search Sessions

Search sessions have received the most attention in the research community. They comprise a connected series of search-related actions, primarily queries and result selections (clicks),[4] most often in pursuit of a single information need (Jansen et al., 2007; Silverstein et al., 1999). Session identification is usually performed using inactivity timeouts (usually thirty minutes; see Downey et al., 2007; He et al., 2002; Ozmutlu, 2006; Arlitt, 2000; Murray et al., 2006; White and Drucker, 2007), or by using the absence of overlap between search queries (Radlinski and Joachims, 2005), suggesting that the active search task has terminated.

In addition to considering the overlap between consecutive search events or inactivity thresholds, there are more sophisticated – and potentially more reliable – ways to tackle this identification task. Query reformulation strategies (Huang and Efthimiadis, 2009) and automatic segmentation based on search topics (Jones and Klinkner, 2008) have also been used. Other approaches leverage combination-of-evidence methods (He et al., 2002) or hierarchical topical classification (Jones and Klinkner, 2008) to perform accurate segmentation of behavioral data into coherent sessions. Downey et al. (2007) proposed an expressive language to model people's searching and browsing behavior and constructed predictive models for behavior based on such a language. The temporal relationship between query events was exploited in the work of Piwoworksi et al. (2009), who segmented query sequences into goal-related subsequences. Boldi et al. (2008) investigated the temporal order of queries and proposed a model of query-flow graph. Focusing on clicks rather than queries, Guo et al. (2009) developed models to efficiently model search click-through behavior and predict future clicks. I discuss click prediction in more detail in Chapter 3 (Section 3.2).

2.1.2.2 Missions and Tasks

Moving beyond atomic events such as queries and clicks, events can move into higher levels of abstraction (e.g., tactics [Han et al., 2013]). *Missions* and *goals* capture higher-level concepts at the sub-session level (Jones and Klinkner, 2008). Within a single session, missions are defined as a related set of information needs, resulting in one or more goals. Search goals reflect an atomic information need, resulting in one or more queries. The definition of a goal aligns with work on tasks, which have been modeled in various ways in recent years. For example, Liao et al. (2012) attempted to model search tasks or subtasks as an alternative to sessions and trails, allowing for more focused analysis and use of behavioral data in applications such as search result ranking. The observed shift in focus toward tasks is also indicative of a desire to consider different levels of abstraction when modeling search behavior. The concept of a task has been applied in a range of different ways, including the modeling of search satisfaction (Hassan et al., 2010) or personalization (White et al., 2013a). Because searchers can perform multiple tasks simultaneously (Spink et al., 2006), and these tasks could be interwoven in search behavior, thereby creating a noisy behavioral signal, attempts have been made to identify search tasks within sessions (Liao et al., 2012; Lucchese et al., 2013b); these have been met with reasonable success.

2.1.2.3 Moves, Tactics, and Strategies

Much of the research on modeling actions and action sequences in the search and data mining community relates strongly to research in the information science community on the size, or "chunking," of activities. Bates (1989) defines various levels of search activity, ranging from low-level moves to high-level strategies in the context of understanding the extent and the nature of searcher interactions with a search system. Table 2.1 shows the various search activities proposed by Bates and how they relate to the concepts described in this chapter.

Because they are latent, some of these activities are fairly abstract (e.g., thoughts) and challenging to model directly as part of behavioral analysis. However, there may be discernable clues in people's search behaviors that could provide indications about the nature of their thought processes or affective states at the time that the information searches are conducted. MacKay (1969) proposed that searchers' brains can be considered as a black-boxes. That is, we cannot understand the exact working mechanisms involved in cognition, we can still hypothesize about the effects of its operation indirectly through the inputs provided to it, and through the outputs resulting from it. In Chapter 5 (Section 5.5.6), I discuss how searchers' cognitive processes and even their emotional/affective states can be better understood using their observable interactions with search systems and other applications.

Table 2.1. *Levels of search activities (adapted from Bates, 1989)*

Level	Name	Definition	Search Log Analysis Equivalent
1	Move	An identifiable thought or action that is part of information searching.	Atomic search event – for example, a query or click
2	Tactic	One or several moves made to further a search.	Goal or task, including query or click chain
3	Stratagem	A larger, more complex set of thoughts and/or actions than the tactic; a stratagem consists of multiple tactics and/or moves, all of which are designed to exploit a particular search domain that is thought to contain the desired information.	Mission or session
4	Strategy	A plan, which may contain moves, tactics, and/or stratagems, for an entire information search.	Session or cross-session search task

2.1.2.4 Cross-Session Search Tasks

The behaviors covered in the top three rows Table 2.1 are observable within a single search episode (maximally defined as a search session). However, for complex search tasks, such as planning a wedding or arranging a family vacation, relevant information behavior can span many sessions and a significant timeframe (weeks or months or longer). These search tasks also involve interactions with a number of other people, which an intelligent personal assistant could help manage. Queries often repeat over time, which is evidence of long-range dependence between queries in search logs (on re-finding, see, e.g., Teevan et al., 2007). However, persistent search interests – which may be reflected in repeats of identical search queries – are not necessarily long-running tasks. Rather, such queries may reflect searchers' persistent interests (e.g., for news or social media), which can continue indefinitely.

People may also work through different phases of the task at different times (Kotov et al., 2011; Agichtein et al., 2012), rather than repeating the same behavior periodically. Even if the individual actions are numerous and dispersed, it may make sense to consider them as long-term search tasks. Agichtein et al. (2012) showed that long-term tasks are usually associated with activities such as information maintenance, undirected browsing, and transactions. Not only can these tasks span prolonged periods of time, they can also span different devices – that is, searchers can start their search on a desktop at home or in the office and resume on a smartphone while on the move (Wang et al., 2013). The latter has implications for the types of search support that can be offered to searchers, and also creates opportunity for search engines to help, especially during the "downtime" between search sessions. For example, while a searcher is engaged in another activity, the search engine could be searching on their behalf. Tasks may also span domains and applications, and data from one or more sources may have utility in another (Elkahky et al., 2015).

Methods for modeling and supporting long-term tasks are in their infancy, but I expect that support for task continuation will also increase over time. One line of thinking suggests that systems could help searchers restore the state of their previous search (either for the searcher or for the system), offer task-relevant views on their search histories, or suggest future actions based on activities performed to date (Hassan et al., 2014). In Section 5.4.4 I discuss the various types of search support – implicit and explicit – that could be offered to help people engaging in long-running search tasks in more detail. Along similar lines, I expect that techniques to offer *strategic* search support will receive increased attention, and some progress has already been made in this area (e.g., Bhavnani et al., 2003), including for Web search (Singla et al., 2010; Capra et al., 2015).

2.2 Primary Actions

The primary means for people to interact with search engines is through query statements (Section 2.2.1) and search-result selections (Section 2.2.2). As mentioned already, in commercial search engines these searcher actions are recorded on the server side and used to characterize search behavior, improve models of interests and intentions, and evaluate system performance. They are especially important signals in the offline training of algorithms for applications, such as query suggestion or ranking, or online applications such as contextualization of search queries. With additional instrumentation effort and implementation cost, other search activity can be mined and made available, as discussed in more detail in Section 2.3.

2.2.1 Search Queries

The search queries that people issue to search systems are explicit, usually short, statements of search intent. Although short, they can reveal much (although obviously not everything) about searchers' interests and intentions and often include sufficient information to retrieve relevant content (especially when combined with other signals). Queries are used by search systems to decide which results to show. They can also contribute in other ways, such as filtering implicit feedback mined from click behavior to focusing on activity with a related search intent (e.g., those with the same query or within a certain edit distance of the query; see Joachims, 2002). One situation in which the queries themselves may be used as implicit feedback is in the generation of query recommendations, which can be mined from query log data (Jones et al., 2006). Similar principles of implicit feedback are also applied in query auto-completions, shown to searchers in drop-down lists below the query entry area. Auto-completion algorithms can account for temporal variations in searcher's interests (Shokouhi and Radinsky, 2012) or learn over time which completions to suggest based on how searchers responded to those presented to them on previous occasions (Shokouhi, 2013).

2.2.1.1 *Query Formulation*
The query formulation process involves the construction of query statements and has been studied in detail by information retrieval researchers and information scientists. The need for information seeking is understood to originate from the searcher's realization of a gap in their state of knowledge that the searcher seeks to close. This is referred

to as an *anomalous state of knowledge* (ASK) (Belkin, 1980). Other models have been founded on the principle of a gap – a cognitive gap in the case of sensemaking (Dervin, 1983) – that can be bridged with the addition of new information. Once the searcher recognizes the need for information, the information need can evolve through four stages (Taylor, 1968):

1. **Visceral:** The initial need for information, which may change as information is added.
2. **Conscious:** Searcher possesses an ambiguous mental description of the information being sought.
3. **Formalized:** The searcher is able to formulate a question, irrespective of whether the information system can answer his/her question.
4. **Compromised:** The level at which the question is formalized in the form of a query statement for presentation to the search system.

In search settings, including many online services, because the system can only observe the compromised information need, its performance is largely dependent on the information provided by the searcher in the query statement (the so-called quality-in, quality-out principle [Croft and Thompson, 1987]). The formulation of the query can be a challenging task, especially in domains in which the searcher may lack domain knowledge (e.g., in medicine, where complex, technical vocabulary is common [Stanton et al., 2014; Zuccon et al., 2015]). Although Taylor's model was developed in a reference library scenario, it is still applicable in many of today's search settings, research has shown that the queries resulting from such processes may be unsuccessful because the vocabulary used in queries may not match the vocabulary used by document authors (Furnas et al., 1987). Gomez et al. (1990) demonstrated the need for rich indexing if query interfaces are to support the effective formulation of more natural search queries.

In addition to disagreement between authors and searcher, there is also disagreement between searchers about how to express their needs. For example, Furnas et al. (1987) showed that the same search term was favored by multiple participants less than 20% of the time given the same search target, leading to search failures 80–90% of the time. This mirrored results from related studies (Saracevic and Kantor, 1988; Zhao and Callan, 2010). Such findings highlight the limitations of query text as the primary means of interacting with search systems, as well as limited input to methods to model and discover people's search intent (Ruotsalo et al., 2015). Beyond the query text, additional information about the context (Ingwersen and Järvelin, 2005) and the searcher (Pitkow et al., 2002) can be used to augment the search query and provide searchers with more accurate search results. Query expansion techniques (Efthimiadis, 1996) can also be used to improve the quality of the query itself, either automatically or as part of an interactive process.

2.2.1.2 Mining and Applying Search Queries

Mining aggregated search queries has utility for a range of applications, including spelling correction, generating related searches (query recommendations that in some way are related to the current query – for example, query term overlap, session co-occurrence), and the generation of query auto-completions to be shown to searchers in real time as they type queries. Sequences of queries appearing in the search engine

Figure 2.1. Example of query auto-completion. So far, the searcher has typed the string [is it true that babies] and the Google search engine has offered a range of possible query completions.

logs can help generate spelling corrections for misspelled queries (Cucerzan and Brill, 2004; Ahmad and Kondrak, 2005). These can be presented to searchers on the SERP or used to generate a new result set directly (with an appropriate recourse link to enable recovery from erroneous spelling corrections). Query auto-completions are presented to searchers at the time of query construction to support more rapid generation of queries (e.g., if the user types [ca], the search engine may populate a drop-down list with [**ca**rtoon network], [**ca**pital one], and [**ca**reerbuilder]). Query auto-completion methods are typically based on query frequency and methods have been developed for efficient lookups by prefix matching (e.g., Chaudhuri and Kaushik, 2009). Figure 2.1 presents an example of query auto-completion in action.

Figure 2.1 is interesting because it also shows an example of the types of questions that people ask on search engines and the support that search engines provide via auto-completion, but also the potential biases that their query formulations can introduce ([White, 2013; White and Hassan, 2014] e.g., a potential skew toward pages with positive answers with the formulations shown in the figure). Query auto-completion can also be personalized to consider search histories (Shokouhi, 2013), or to return completions based on temporal patterns (Shokouhi and Radinsky, 2012). White and Marchionini (2007) proposed a *real-time query expansion* model that generates new query expansion terms as the searcher types rather than offering completions based on historic data. The results of a user study showed that this method helped people form better queries (containing a broader range of terms), but the searches were also susceptible to query skew as searchers were not fully aware of the impact of their selections on the results generated.

Another important use of aggregate query data is the generation of query recommendations, sometimes called *related searches* or *query suggestions* – that is, queries that are in some way related to the current query and may be useful candidates for follow-on queries. Query suggestions can be useful in supporting exploration or may provide searchers with query statements that better express their information needs than the original query. In practice, these query suggestions are generated in a number of ways given search log data, including using queries that frequently follow the current query in a search session (Jones et al., 2006) or by clustering queries based on clicks on the same results (Beeferman and Berger, 2000; Craswell and Szummer, 2007). To generate suggestions that support exploration, features (such as the different aspects of a task) need to be automatically determined and applied during the generation phase (Lucchese et al., 2013a; Hassan et al., 2014).

2.2.2 Item Selection

Search systems return items, often in ranked lists, for consideration by searchers. Searchers may then examine these items, starting with surrogate representations (snippets) search-result captions. Transitioning from the surrogate representation on the SERP to the item involves a selection operation. The primary selection method is click-through using a mouse cursor.[5] There are various types of clicks (depending on the position, the mouse button used, and the functionality supported by the interface, e.g., right-click to open search result in new browser tab), but I focus on two types in this section: (1) *hyperlink clicks*, either on the results, advertisements, or additional search engine functionality such as pagination or query suggestions, and (2) *non-hyperlink clicks* on other (potentially non-active) parts of the display. Non-hyperlink clicks can be intentional (e.g., to restore focus on a document) or unintentional (e.g., expecting an interface item to be clickable, when in fact it is not).

Result clicks, on hyperlinks in the case of web search systems, have been used as implicit relevance feedback to train search result ranking algorithms. One of the earliest search engines to leverage clicks as implicit feedback was *DirectHit* (Culliss, 1999), which monitored the sites on which searchers dwelled, penalized the sites that were not selected, and rotated in new sites for review. The site used these data to learn from the search behavior of previous searchers. The rotation of new content is an important because machine-learned search engines ranking algorithms that learn from clicks may be subject to the effects of preferential attachment, where popular web pages are promoted and reinforced as part of a feedback loop (Cho and Roy, 2004; Chakrabarti et al., 2005).

2.2.2.1 Hyperlink Clicks

Clicks on hyperlinks on the result page serve to navigate searchers to another (distal) location or perform some other action, such as submitting a query suggestion or paginating through the available search results.

2.2.2.1.1 Result and Advertising Clicks

Clicks on search result hyperlinks transport searchers to the distal content linked to the result page. The decision to click is informed by a number of factors, including perceived relevance based on result captions. In a web search, captions are typically composed of titles, snippets, and URLs. Despite its importance in informing the results that people click (Clarke et al., 2007; Yue et al., 2010; White and Horvitz, 2013), there has been limited innovation on caption generation and presentation over the past few decades. The last significant advance that was adopted by all major search engines was the use of query-biased summarization techniques for caption generation (Tombros and Sanderson, 1998). Figure 2.2 shows captions for search results and advertisements displayed on a SERP.

Captions have been enhanced with visual summaries (Teevan et al., 2009a) to support better selection decisions. Progressive revealment strategies support fluid transitions between the SERP and the "landing pages" comprising the full-texts of the selected results (Paek et al., 2004; Feild et al., 2013). Both of these strategies, and others, are discussed as ways to support search interaction in more detail in Chapter 5.

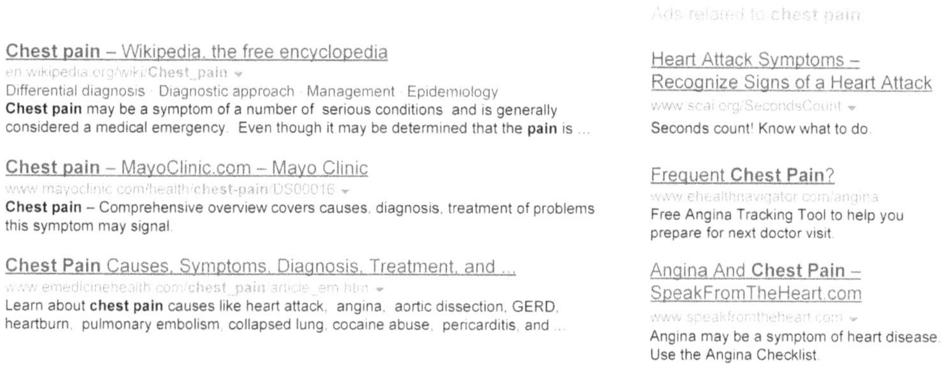

Figure 2.2. (a) Example result caption comprising title, snippet, and URL; and (b) Example advertisements.

Beyond the perceived relevance of the landing page from the caption, other factors – such as people's experience with the specific resource (Teevan et al., 2007), their general resource preferences (e.g., preferring wikipedia.org URLs over those from about.com; see Ieong et al. [2012]), and the position of the search result in the ranked list from the search system (Joachims et al., 2005) – can influence searchers' click-through decisions. Wu et al. (2014) performed a laboratory experiment in which they analyzed the effect of "information scent" present in the caption and the need for cognition (NFC)[6] on SERP click-through behavior. They showed that the presence of more relevant results led to more engagement and that the rank position of the relevant results affected the degree of engagement. They also showed that NFC affected pagination behavior and the position of result clicks (higher NFC meant less pagination and less exploration of lower ranked results). The interactions between these variables also affected behavior, including the time spent searching and searcher likelihood of abandoning the task. This clearly illustrates the importance of considering factors beyond relevance in designing and evaluating search systems (see Chapter 9).

2.2.2.1.2 Click Distributions

In addition to the clicks at the level of individual URLs, it is important to consider the *distribution* of clicks over the top-ranked results. Searchers have consistently been shown to examine the results from top to bottom, independent of query and the relevance of the search results (Joachims et al., 2005; Craswell et al., 2008). This results in click-through distributions heavily skewed to top-ranked positions (see top of Figure 2.3).

Although the distribution of clicks generally follows this predictable pattern, there can be exceptions for which the distribution is less consistent. Click-through *inversions* may result from the caption content leading to increases in click-through rate for lower-ranked search results (Clarke et al., 2007). These increases appear in the click-through curve as spikes, such as that shown in rank position two at the bottom of Figure 2.3.

The primary causes for these inversions are either relevance (search engine performing poorly ranking search results and forcing searchers to click lower in the ranked list to reach relevant results), or caption biases, where information is shown in the captions that attracts searcher attention independent of the relevance of the underlying

CTR
60%
50%
40%
30%
20%
10%
0%
CTR
50%
40%
30%
20%
10%
0%
1 2 3 4 5 6 7 8 9 10
Rank

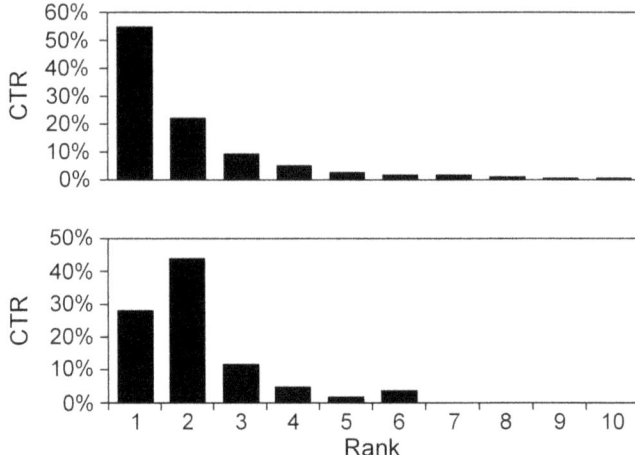

Figure 2.3. Click-through curves across the top-ten rank positions for all queries (top), and the symptom query [*stomach pain*] with click-through inversions at ranks two and six (bottom) (White and Horvitz, 2013).

document (e.g., the presence of terms such as "free" and "official" may attract undue attention to result captions (Clarke et al., 2007)); inversions may also be attributed to domain preferences, formatting (e.g., increased presence of boldfaced terms), or other factors. The presence of content with the potential to heighten searchers' levels of anxiety, such as that associated with serious medical conditions for symptom queries, may represent unexpressed fears and anxieties and result in increased click-through rates on these captions (White and Horvitz, 2013), as well as negatively impacting searchers' emotional state (Lauckner and Hsieh, 2013). Examples of such potentially alarming caption content are shown in Figure 2.4.

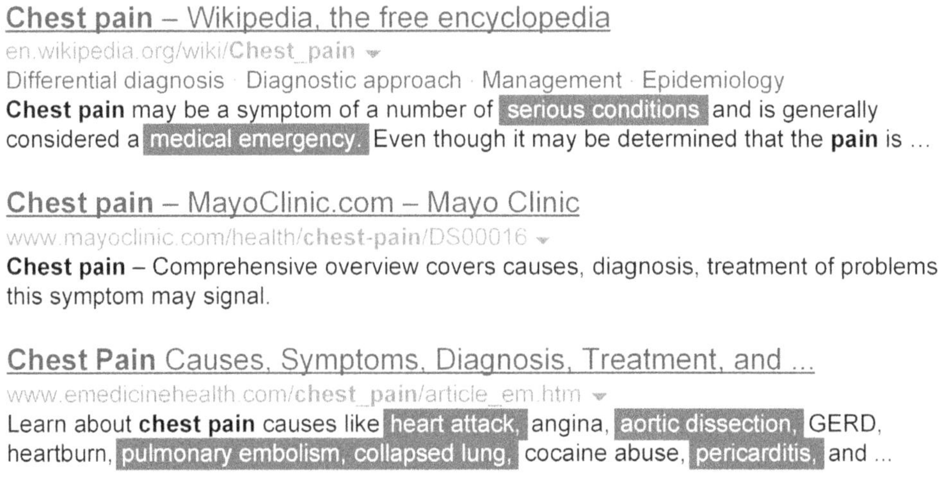

Chest pain – Wikipedia, the free encyclopedia
en.wikipedia.org/wiki/Chest_pain
Differential diagnosis · Diagnostic approach · Management · Epidemiology
Chest pain may be a symptom of a number of serious conditions and is generally considered a medical emergency. Even though it may be determined that the pain is ...
Chest pain – MayoClinic.com – Mayo Clinic
www.mayoclinic.com/health/chest-pain/DS00016
Chest pain – Comprehensive overview covers causes, diagnosis, treatment of problems this symptom may signal.
Chest Pain Causes, Symptoms, Diagnosis, Treatment, and ...
www.emedicinehealth.com/chest_pain/article_em.htm
Learn about chest pain causes like heart attack, angina, aortic dissection, GERD, heartburn, pulmonary embolism, collapsed lung, cocaine abuse, pericarditis, and ...

Figure 2.4. Captions for the top-three search results returned by a commercial web search engine for the query [*chest pain*]. Potentially-alarming caption content is highlighted (White and Horvitz, 2013a).

Given the presence of these factors that may affect click-through, models can be developed to predict the particular results that searchers will select. These models take into account caption content, as well as the position of results on the SERP and the likelihood that searchers will examine those results (Chapelle and Zhang, 2009; Yue et al., 2010; White and Horvitz, 2013). For example, Yue et al. (2010) showed that increased bolding of the terms in the title of search results is more likely to make a particular result be selected (and perhaps even remembered, given the Von Restorff effect [Hunt 1995; Teevan, 2006]). Beyond search results, similar models have been developed to predict click-through rates for unseen advertisements (Richardson et al., 2007), which contribute to algorithmic decisions about whether to display advertisement on SERPs, when combined with other signals such as a relevance/quality score.

2.2.2.1.3 Applying Clicks

As searchers explore a set of results, the results that they select can both reveal information about the relevance of the resource selected with respect to the query and provide indications on the relevance of SERP components (such as captions) on which searchers make the determination of which results to select. These clicks are logged by search engines and used in the sophisticated ranking algorithms that these engines employ to decide how to rank order search results (Joachims, 2002; Agichtein et al., 2006). Clicks can help resolve uncertainty for ambiguous queries and their use in ranking is based on the belief that the most popular result(s) will satisfy most people searching for a query – that is, the *dominant* search intent. Examples of queries for which this method works particularly well are navigational queries such as [facebook], [google], and so on – where the search goal is to reach a particular website and the most popular website is typically what is sought. Moving beyond aggregated search behavior, personalized navigational signals provide evidence pertaining to particular searcher's result preferences based on their own long-term click behavior (Dou et al., 2007; Teevan et al., 2011b). These signals highlight the resource preferences of an individual searcher, irrespective of what sites are popular overall. Research on re-finding that has shown that people frequently seek to re-find the same information (i.e., on average, approximately 40% of an individual's search queries are repeat queries [Teevan et al., 2007]), and are also likely to select the same results for repeat queries (Tyler and Teevan, 2010).

2.2.2.1.4 Functional Clicks

Functional clicks instruct the search engine to perform some action, such as retrieving the next page of results in ranked lists (so-called pagination or clicking the "Next" link on the SERP if available), or selecting a recommended query suggestion / related search. Although functional clicks are often ignored in published analyses of search behavior, they are important to search providers. There is utility in mining this activity for applications, such as query suggestion (e.g., learning connections between queries and selected query suggestions) and search quality estimation (e.g., identifying queries or query classes where people frequently paginate through search results without clicking on any results – an indicator of potential search dissatisfaction).

2.2.2.2 Non-Hyperlink Clicks

Searchers may also perform non-hyperlink clicks, where they click on the whitespace on the SERP or select items with the expectation that they are clickable. They may do this for a number of reasons, including accidentally, to restore focus to the page if they are using multiple applications, to place focus on particular areas (e.g., the search box), to cancel an interface presentation (e.g., a pop-up), or to mark the beginning of a related event (such as a text selection). These actions are not trackable using traditional click logging methods. However, such actions can be recorded by employing more sophisticated logging mechanisms (see Huang et al., 2011). Although they are difficult to interpret, non-hyperlink clicks have utility for search engines. For example, they can help identify usability issues (e.g., searchers clicking on non-selectable items), to identify text selections that can be used to generate better results (White and Buscher, 2012a), or to better understand SERP abandonment (Diriye et al., 2012).

2.3 Secondary Actions

Much of the research on search interaction has focused on interactions with SERPs. Researchers have considered how people create queries and select results. However, search activity is significantly more involved than that observed during interactions with search engines. Richer logging of search behavior at scale via client-side instrumentation enables systems to study the behavior of searchers once they depart from the search engine, as well as how behaviors are situated within broader information-seeking contexts (Ingwersen and Järvelin, 2005; Kumpulainen and Järvelin, 2010). This functionality can be integrated directly into Web browsers or it can be implemented as an optional add-on such as a Web browser toolbar. With searcher consent, these plugins can monitor not only queries but all resources that a searcher visits. This type of logging also enables competitive analysis that is not possible using server-side logging of interaction on a particular search system. In addition, competitive analysis can also be performed retrospectively by analyzing the activity of panels of individual searchers and households created by Web analytics companies such as comScore,[7] Nielsen,[8] and Experian HitWise.[9]

2.3.1 Trails

Analysis of recorded browsing patterns within a particular website can help researchers and search practitioners better understand searchers' needs and intentions. Consequently, this can inform the redesign of site structure, interface layout, and search support mechanisms, to make searches more effective. Browsing paths followed by human "trail blazers" (Bush, 1945) through information spaces can implicitly represent similarities and associations between visited items that can be incorporated in search and recommendation systems (Chalmers et al., 1998). Visited resources can be connected in a temporal sequence known as *trails*. The origin of a trail through collections of documents is found in the work of Vannevar Bush, especially in his seminal article "As We May Think" (Bush, 1945). Trails have since been studied extensively in the hypertext community (Reich et al., 1999) and more recently in other settings such as Web search (White and Drucker, 2007). Olston and Chi (2003) described the *ScentTrails* system that suggested paths through the Web based on estimates of the information scent in particular hyperlinks (i.e., an estimate of how much useful information they will encounter if they follow a particular path). Similarly, Pandit and Olston (2007) present an information-scent motivated model of navigation-aided retrieval based on a stochastic simulation of browsing behavior.

As an alternative to simulations, search providers and others with access to search logs can employ large datasets of anonymized searcher behavior collected from consenting individuals, directly leveraging the search and browsing history searcher populations to guide the actions of future searchers. Wexelblat and Maes (1999) described a system called *Footprints* to support within-domain navigation based on the browse trails of other users. In a search context, search providers are often not limited to data from a single site – the data available may be sourced from Web browser toolbars and other applications that provide visibility beyond the SERP and into interaction behaviors on any domain.

2.3.1.1 Web Trails

A trail comprises a temporally ordered sequence of items visited by searchers (Bilenko and White, 2008) or created manually as part of an explicit trailblazing process (Yuan and White, 2012). In a Web search context, trails can be initiated with a search query or a browsing event, and can span any number of subsequent queries and/or Web page views. Three types of search trails have been defined (White and Drucker, 2007):

- **Query trails** are initiated with a query and terminated with another query or any end-of-session event. These trails are typically short and the length of the post-query navigation trail may vary based on the type of query (navigational queries such as [facebook] might have a longer trail length) or on the searcher's level of satisfaction with the landing page and beyond (dissatisfaction may result in the searcher returning rapidly to the SERP to consider alternative results or issue revised search queries).
- **Session trails** are initiated with a search query and terminated with an end-of-session event, including session inactivity timeouts, off-task events such as checking email, or closing the Web browser window.
- **Browse trails** are initiated with a browsing event, such as visiting the searcher's Web browser homepage, and are terminated by a session inactivity timeout or other events such as Web browser close. Although browse trails may not be initiated by a search query, they may contain search trails and often contain important information-seeking behaviors such as Web browsing, which can be used for recommendation purposes (White et al., 2009), as well as other functions such as determining Web page quality independent of queries (Richardson et al., 2006).

2.3.1.2 Trail Termination

An important consideration in the design and application of search trails is the determination of the point at which the trail terminates. This endpoint can be defined in a

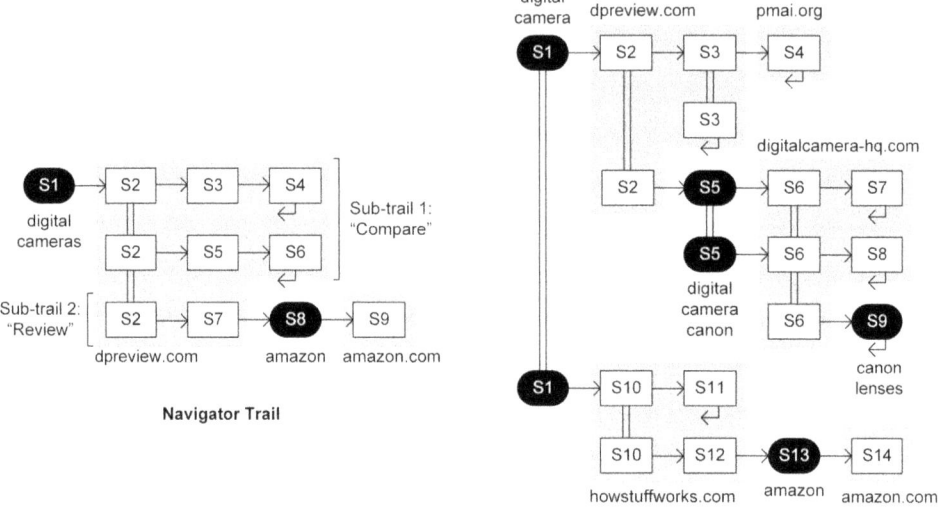

Figure 2.5. Examples of Web behavior graphs illustrating search trails for navigators and explorers (adapted from White and Drucker, 2007).

number of ways, including inactivity timeouts, visiting a homepage, or engaging in a task that is indicative of the current search being complete (e.g., checking email or visiting social networking site), all of which suggest that the active task is complete (White and Drucker, 2007). Destinations identified by using trail termination identification methods can be recommended to searchers (White et al., 2007) or applied in estimating search intent as part of an analysis of searcher goals (Downey et al., 2008).

2.3.1.3 Trail Visualization

The journey that searchers take on the trail may be as important as the destination (White and Huang, 2010; Eickhoff et al., 2014). Rather than only focusing on the destination, it is possible to visualize the search behavior graphically. Web behavior graphs provide a way of visualizing navigation patterns. Web behavior graphs are a variant of problem behavior graphs (Newell and Simon, 1972). These have been used to analyze both people's activity collected during information foraging experiments (Card et al., 2001) and in the analysis of behaviors from different classes of searchers (White and Drucker, 2007). Figure 2.5 presents examples of Web behavior graphs for two types of searcher, identified automatically via search log analysis: *navigators* (who tend to follow short, directed trails irrespective of the query) and *explorers* (whose trails are generally more exploratory, with more query reformulations and greater evidence of backtracking behavior to return to prior Web pages or queries in the session). In interpreting the figure, the behavior graphs representing the trails should be followed from left to right and top to bottom. Queries are shown as rounded dark rectangles. Web pages are white rectangles. Web domains are marked in gray, and backtracking is represented with a new row.

In Figure 2.5, both of the searchers are pursuing information related to the original search query, [digital cameras], and terminate their trail on the same Web page. As

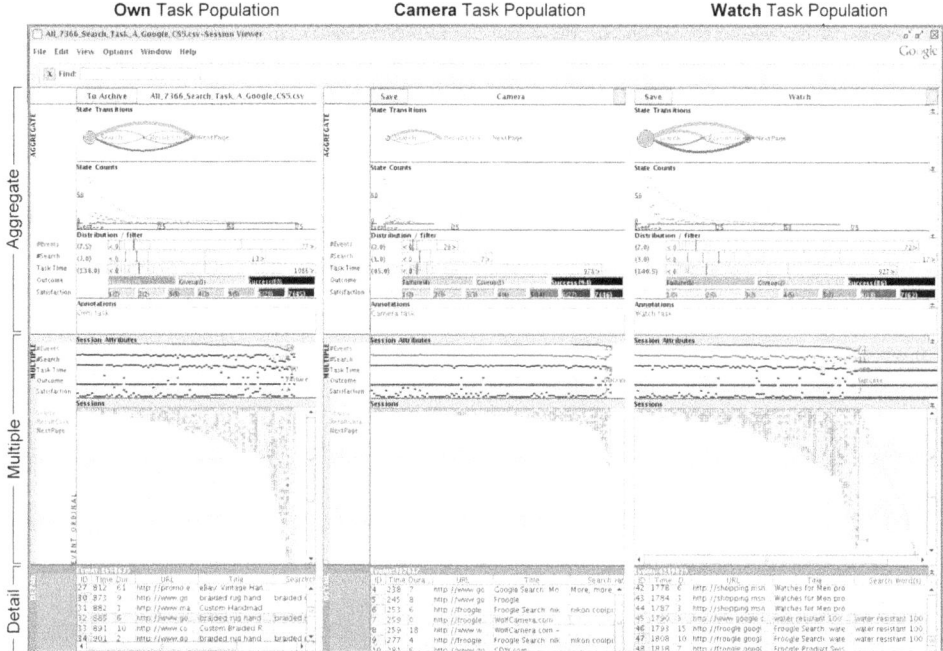

Figure 2.6. Displaying search sessions in the Google Session Viewer application (adapted from Lam et al., 2007). From left to right: The "Own" Task population with which participants performed their own self-created tasks; the Camera Task population with searches for a camera feature given brand and model; and the Watch Task population with searches to locate a watch based on given criteria. For each population, the session logs are shown in the Aggregate, the Multiple, and the Detail Panes. (See color plate 2.6.)

we can see, however, the two search behaviors are quite different. For example, the navigator searches within a single website with clearly defined steps. The explorer is much less focused and examines content from many websites via a range of different queries.

Behavior graphs can represent the search behavior in a compact form that facilities the review of the search behavior independent of the specific Web pages that were visited. However, because the focus is on presenting a single trail, there is no facility in this representation for aggregation across many searchers. Such aggregation can be useful in identifying trends in search behavior within a particular website or search query. Other representations of search behavior that display many trails simultaneously have been developed (see Figure 2.6), although it is still challenging to identify significant trends or patterns in the data because the trails are not properly aligned, other than on their start point (the query) and/or their destination.

Scaria et al. (2014) examined the differences between successful and abandoned navigation paths using data from an online game, Wikispeedia (West et al., 2009). They attempt to characterize what types of behavior are indicative of people abandoning their navigation tasks. They find that's searchers prefer backtracking to high-degree nodes that serve as landmarks and hubs for exploring the network of pages. Based on this analysis, the researchers developed statistical models for predicting whether searchers will successfully complete or abandon a search task. Kleinberg (2000) investigated the algorithmic aspects of the small-world problem, showing that efficient searching is only possible when the probability of a long-range link decays with a specific exponent. Downey et al. (2008) investigated the benefits of navigating versus querying further, finding that navigating is particularly useful when the information need is rare. West and Leskovec characterized human strategies in successful navigation tasks (2012a) and develop learned models capable of navigating automatically (2012b). In a similar way, Trattner et al. (2012) explored heuristic navigation algorithms based on hierarchical knowledge representations.

2.3.1.4 Trail Applications

One of the benefits of studying trail following behavior is the ability to identify pages or sub-trails that might be particularly relevant to searchers. Pages that many users end up at following the traversal of a search trail might have utility to searchers and search engines may wish to promote these pages or present these *popular destinations* (White et al., 2007) directly to searchers on SERPs as a way of helping them complete their tasks more efficiently. Of course, pointing searchers to destinations is only advisable if the information need can be satisfied with the content of a single page. In many exploratory searches (Marchionini, 2006a; White and Roth, 2009), as well as other dynamic search scenarios such as berrypicking (Bates, 1989) or orienteering (O'Day and Jeffries, 1993), the information encountered along the journey to the destination is as important as, if not more important than, locating a single page in supporting task completion, learning, and discovery.

White and Huang (2010) investigated this issue in the context of the Web search and showed that the journey has significant value over the destination in terms of metrics, including novelty, coverage, diversity, and relevance. This adds support to the integration of tours and trails directly into the search experience, while preserving the simplicity and ease of use of modern systems. One way to do this is to identify pages that derive particular value from following the trails, referred to as *waypoints*. White and Singla (2011) explored how different trail topologies (such a stars, trees, and linear chains) are observed in different search scenarios (informational versus navigational [Broder, 2002]). Examples of waypoints include bottleneck pages that searchers need to pass through to reach their goal and hub pages that people are frequently observed revisiting as they explore a particular domain or set of related websites. Rather than presenting the full trail to searchers, these waypoints could be identified and shown to searchers to supplement existing result lists as a way to promote progress toward search goals.

Trails are also used to identify particular Web pages that the search engine should promote (Agichtein et al., 2006; Bilenko and White, 2008). For example, if a particular Web page frequently resides on the click trail following the current query, then that page is likely to be relevant to the query and should be included in the result set and/or promoted ranked list. Machine-learned models employ these trail features for result ranking purposes. This way, trail-based signals are integrated into the existing query-response paradigm without the need for dedicated search support for trail analysis. The trails used for this purpose do not need to be limited to those starting with a search query. For example, trails may also start from, or comprise, browsed Web pages (White et al., 2009; Liebling et al., 2012; Ustinovsky and Serdyukov, 2013).

Mount Rainier National Park (U.S. National Park Service)
Government page about this volcano, environmental information and statistics.
http://nps.gov/mora → ../planyourvisit/things2know.htm → ../yoursafety.htm → ../wheretoeat.htm → ../directions.htm → ../hours.htm → ../feesandreservations.htm → ../educational-fee-waiver.htm

Mount Rainier – Wikipedia, the free encyclopedia
Mount Rainier is a large active stratovolcano (also know as a composite volcano) in Pierce County, Washington, USA, located 54 miles (87 km) southeast of Seattle.
http://en.wikipedia.org/wiki/Mount_Rainier → ./Peter_Rainier,_junior → ./Stratovolcano → ./Popocatepetl → ./List_of_volcanoes_in_Mexico → ./Paricutin → ./Monogenetic_volcano_field → ./Captain_from_Castle → ./Cinder_cone → ./Caldera

Figure 2.7. Example of trailfinding integration in the result page of a search system. Searchers are presented with a ranked list of results (trails), with the full steps of the trail also visible.

2.3.1.4.1 Trails as a Unit of Retrieval

For many search tasks, individual search results may represent only the starting point of search and exploration (Teevan et al., 2004). Once searchers select a result, they must then rely on their own skills in interpreting cues and information scent on items along the post-query navigation trail. The importance of post-query navigation has been highlighted in research on orienteering (O'Day and Jeffries, 1993; Teevan et al., 2004). To provide more complete support to searchers, trails can be integrated directly into the search experience as atomic units of retrieval (Bush, 1945; Teevan et al., 2004; Singla et al., 2010) or in the form of recommendations adjacent to search results (Capra et al., 2015). If there are common sequences of items that people with similar information needs follow, then those sequences may be identified using automatic or manual methods and presented to future searchers in their entirety as an alternative to ranked lists of documents (which are best viewed as potential starting points for post-query exploration).

The task of retrieving complete search trails is referred to as *trailfinding* (Singla et al., 2010). Found trails may provide guidance to future searchers about directions they should pursue and steps they should take to complete their search task. This is in contrast to existing search interaction models, which focus on returning a list of pages from which people can commence their information-seeking journey. Figure 2.7 shows an early example (from [Singla et al., 2010]) of how trails could be seamlessly integrated into existing search interfaces to direct searchers post-selection decisions.

Assuming an implementation similar to that shown in Figure 2.7, one challenge that would need to be addressed is how to direct searchers after they click on a particular search result, as any trail guidance on the SERP would likely disappear. Integrated support with client-side applications such as Web browser toolbars or the Web browser itself would allow that guidance to transition from the SERP to subsequent pages in the search session. In addition, there have been attempts to address this challenge by marking hyperlinks on navigated-to pages that searchers may benefit from selecting by building computational models of their interests and mapping those to the information found on distal hyperlinks. For example, both *ScentTrails* (Oltson and Chi, 2003) and *Volant* (Pandit and Olston, 2007) apply computational models of search intent to highlight hyperlinks on browsed-to pages that are of potential interest to searchers.

2.3.1.5 Trail Construction

In keeping with one of the themes of this book, I envisage that trails are created using automated mechanisms such as data mining. However, it is entirely possible that a hand-curated set of trails could be created for popular informational queries received by a search provider (Yuan and White, 2012). Bush (1945) envisaged trailblazing users (perhaps with subject-matter expertise within a domain of interest) forging paths through collections to be followed by future searchers. Directed paths (Zellweger, 1989) provide a means to guide readers as they traverse a sequence of connected components extracted from documents or from an existing hypertext network. Because these paths are comprised of document components, they are not required to follow the sequence order in which information is displayed in the document. Guided tours are a way in which people can manually create a sequence of items to assist others in completing a task or help them understand a new concept (Trigg, 1988). Although these tours are artifacts that can be created by anyone, they will have most value when created by those with expertise in the subject matter. Creating such a tour requires knowledge of connections between concepts and resources that may be unavailable to domain novices. Along these lines, Walden's Paths support learning by allowing teachers to create annotated linear sequences of Web-based information (with their own annotations and transitions) for consumption by students (Shipman et al., 2000). Other mechanisms – such as concept hierarchies – are also useful in creating tours derived from pages that are interrelated (Guinan and Smeaton, 1992).

Trails can also be observed in the paths that people elect to follow through websites (Wexelblat and Maes, 1999). Because trails are restricted to the pages in the website, the set of possible trails is limited, but there are still many opportunities to leverage trail following behavior to generate recommendations and support other tasks – for example, helping website designers understand how people traverse the pages in their site and make refinements to the website design if inefficiencies are detected (Wheeldon and Levene, 2003; Wexelblat and Maes, 1999). I discuss tours, trails, and related concepts, such as social navigation, in Chapter 6.

2.3.2 Page Examination

One of the most widely explored sources of implicit evidence about document relevance is dwell time – that is, the amount of time that people spend examining a particular page. Dwell time, also called viewing time, on a retrieved document may be a useful signal of document relevance. Research has suggested that a dwell time of thirty seconds is an appropriate threshold to use in determining searcher satisfaction with the content of a page (Fox et al., 2005), or the relevance of the content contained in the page (Kelly and Belkin, 2004). A dwell time that is significantly less thirty seconds (or to be more conservative, twenty seconds) is assumed to be associated with a non-relevant click and/or a dissatisfied searcher. That time was determined by deploying a pop-up survey to a sample of searchers and soliciting satisfaction ratings from them in situ. This information can then be compared against the amount of time that searchers spend on the page, and conclusions can be drawn about the thresholds for satisfaction or dissatisfaction. To provide more accurate models of dwell time, recent studies have shown that tracking cursor movements on landing pages (i.e., the pages reached by clicking on search result hyperlinks) can provide useful evidence about document relevance. This behavior must be tracked on landing pages using a browser toolbar, instrumented Wen browser, or client-side code injected directly into the pages themselves (Huang et al., 2011). Landing page examination signals have been shown to help enhance ranking algorithms (Guo and Agichtein, 2012).

2.3.2.1 Dwell Time Estimation

It can be difficult to estimate dwell times from data because doing so accurately depends on knowing when the page was in focus and the total amount of time that people spent actively examining page content. Also, because dwell time estimates rely on the difference between the page load times of subsequent pages, it can be challenging to estimate the dwell time of the last page in the session without richer logging. These pages are typically ignored in dwell time analysis – even though they may have special properties, such as containing the information that meets searchers' needs (Downey et al., 2008). Methods to provide accurate estimates of the dwell times on terminal pages are required.

Liu et al. (2010) applied Weibull analysis to estimate the underlying distributions of given dwell time data. They found that general Web browsing behavior follows "negative-aging" phenomenon – that is, the more time that searchers spend on a page during browsing, the less likely that searchers will depart the page. Recent work by Kim et al. (2014) explored various ways of estimating the dwell time on a page (client-side, using software installed on the searcher's machine [but only for those who have the software installed] versus server-side, where the time is estimated based on time away from the engine). This can be noisy since it is unclear what searchers are doing once they depart from the engine (e.g., whether they are actively examining the landing page, if they derive utility from it and find a link worth clicking, or if they get distracted or interrupted and pursue some other task). The researchers applied their findings to predict the degree of satisfaction associated with result clicks.

Being able to better label clicks as associated with searcher satisfaction can be useful for tasks such as result re-ranking (Xu et al., 2011) and query expansion (Buscher et al., 2009). More recently, Yin et al. (2013) applied dwell time to capture people's voting actions for recommending social media content. They interpreted longer dwell times on content as "pseudo votes," and improved recommendation performance by modeling the user's expectation levels that cause viewing and voting behaviors. Another method for estimating satisfaction labels for clicks included looking for the presence of query reformulation events immediately following the page visit, which may suggest that the searcher's needs are not being satisfied by the page content, even if the dwell time is high (Hassan, 2012).

In general, the application of implicit measures does not consider the characteristics of individual searchers. All searchers are assumed to exhibit stereotypical search behaviors around information that may be regarded as relevant. Although the most frequently used implicit feedback behavior is page dwell time, the amount of time a searcher spends on a page has been questioned for being too simplistic and ignoring other important factors, such as task, topic, and searcher characteristics (Kelly and

Belkin, 2001). Kelly and Cool (2002) found that as topic familiarity increased reading time decreased, and they proposed that as the searcher's state of knowledge increased their search behavior altered. Both Kelly and Belkin (2004) and White and Kelly (2006) identified individual and task differences in implicit feedback performance.

Feedback can be collected on document elements – such as subsections and paragraphs – rather than on entire documents. This allows for more accurate feedback by targeting the parts of the document that the searcher examines. The segmentation of documents can be performed in different ways, such as by using eye-gaze tracking in a laboratory setting (Brooks et al., 2006; Buscher et al., 2008). In the real world, mouse cursor behavior can be used a means of performing large-scale attention monitoring via server-side logging or client-side instrumentation. Viewport information (the dimensions and location of the visible portion of the screen that considers the zoom level) can also be captured for all devices, but could be especially useful as a proxy for searcher attention on mobile devices such as smartphones and tablets for which there are no cursor movements, but attention can be tracked by monitoring what parts of the page that people observe through viewport transitions (Huang and Diriye, 2012; Lagun et al., 2014). Research has demonstrated the effectiveness of using behavioral features (specifically dwell time, highlighting, copying, and link selections), at the passage level to identify relevant document segments (Buscher et al., 2009; Kong et al., 2013).

2.3.3 Tabbed Browsing and Multitasking

Searchers engaged in multiple tasks simultaneously (Spink et al., 2006) may want to examine multiple items or mitigate network constraints by requesting many items concurrently. Today's Web browsers support tabbed browsing, allowing people to navigate multiple Web pages simultaneously. Browsing flow within a single tab in a browser or browser window may be interrupted by switching to pages in other tabs and windows. This can be initiated by opening one or more pages from a single page; specifically, opening multiple links on a page in new windows or tabs. Figure 2.8 shows the transitions between up to four tabs within a single browser window. In interpreting logged search behavior, it is important to consider that search behavior can be interleaved between these tabs (Huang et al., 2012). Different tabs may be associated with different search tasks, making task-oriented behavior difficult to discern if there is no identifier in the search log associated with the web browser tab.

In Figure 2.8, we can see that the searcher has opened a number of new tabs at various points in the lifetime of the browser window. This activity is referred to as "branching" because the searcher is spawning a new browsing thread and can continue browsing on either thread.[10] Branching occurs when a searcher opens a link in a new tab or window. The figure shows the transitions between up to four tabs within a single browser window; the transition from page 2 to page 3 is an example of branching.

Branching can substitute for a classic browser feature – the Back button – which enables backtracking. Rather than sequentially viewing the interesting links on a page by clicking then tapping the Back button to return to the original page, users can simply open all the attractive links on a page in tabs to view later one by one. There are multiple benefits to this approach: opened pages will pre-load, shortening the wait time between

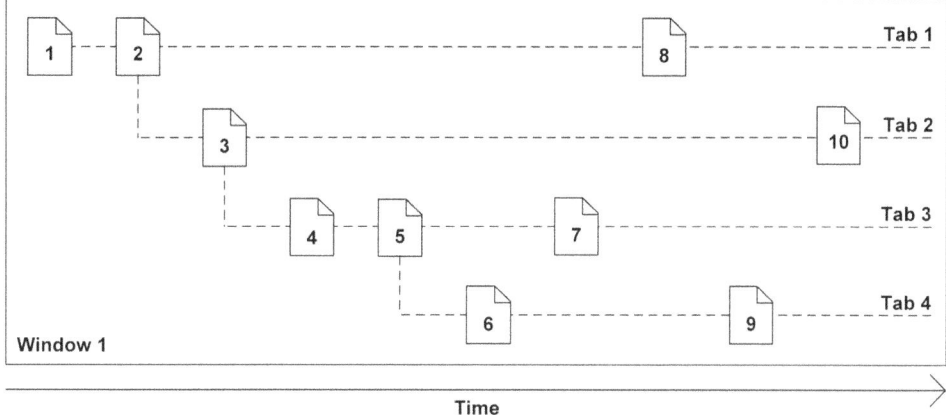

Figure 2.8. An example of a browsing session with multiple tabs over time. The user starts by viewing a single page and ultimately navigates to eleven pages across four browser tabs (adapted from Huang et al., 2012).

viewing pages; there is no risk of being unable to return to the originating page; and searchers may spend as much time on the originating page as desired without having to remember all of the links they were planning to view. Indeed, Weinreich et al. (2006) note that "the usage of multiple windows and tabs has partly replaced back button usage." Awareness of this behavior is important in interpreting behavior signals and extracting behaviors such as the construction of search trails and/or search sessions, which by default interpret contiguous sequential visits to Web pages as being part of the same task. However, studies of information-seeking behavior have shown that multitasking is common (e.g., Spink et al. [2006] showed that more than 80% of two-query sessions contained multiple topics), and large-scale analysis of search behavior needs to consider multitasking and multi-tabbing directly in behavioral modeling, especially in making sense of signals such as landing page dwell time. Because people often restrict each task to a small set of tabs (primarily one), it might be possible to model multitasking better by simply considering the identifier of the tab within which the behavior is observed. Automated methods have also been developed to identify tasks within search trails (Liao et al., 2012), based on features such as query overlap. The resultant task-specific trails can then be applied for tasks such as satisfaction estimation and ranking.

2.4 Beyond Queries and Clicks

Studies of online search behavior have shown that there are no search-result clicks for 30–40% of all queries (Li et al., 2009; Diriye et al., 2012). Therefore, there is a significant amount of training data that the search engine ranking algorithm does not have access to if it learns only from click-based features. As search engines push more content to searchers on the SERP, there will be a reduction in the need for searchers to click. As a result, there is a decrease in the utility of the click signal as an estimate for searcher attention. Large-scale attention monitoring via proxies for searcher attention – such as cursor movements and engagement with particular interface elements – enables analysts to move beyond tracking query statements and result click-through, and toward richer behavioral signals. Fine-grained search interactions in the desktop setting, such as mouse cursor movements and scrolling, have been shown to be valuable for understanding searcher intent, attention, and preferences for Web search results (Guo and Agichtein, 2010; Huang et al., 2011).

Featurizing cursor movements provides insight into how deeply in the ranking searchers examined results (max y-position; see Huang et al. [2011; 2012]), or offers more nuanced ranking features via cursor movement "motifs" (Lagun et al., 2014), leading to significant improvements in the relevance of search results. Cursor tracking can be useful in a range of retrospective analyses, including estimating the regions of Web pages that attracted searcher interest (Mueller and Lockerd, 2001; Guo and Agichtein, 2008). Monitoring these behaviors at scale enables more detailed tracking of searcher attention, including previously unavailable events such as caption hovers and scroll depth. The premise behind the monitoring of regions to which the searcher is attending is that the consideration of search results is still a useful indicator of searcher interest, even if there is no result click-through. Even without richer logging mechanisms, by analyzing the behavior preceding the click or the results surrounding the click (e.g., the position of the result in the list, and the results that appear directly above and below it [Joachims et al., 2005; Shokouhi et al., 2013]), search systems can better interpret observed click activity. In the remainder of this section, I discuss the collection and representation of signals gathered from other attention monitoring mechanisms, including eye-gaze tracking, large-scale cursor tracking, and touch interactions.

2.4.1 Eye-Gaze Tracking

Eye-gaze tracking technology that measure the point of gaze is used in research on the visual system in domains such as psychology, accessibility, advertising, health (e.g., gaze patterns for autism detection in children [Baron-Cohen et al., 1996]), security (e.g., using gaze patterns as passwords [Kumar et al., 2007]), cognitive linguistics, and product design. They have been used to support activities such as reading on desktop and mobile devices (Biedert et al., 2010; 2012) and in providing segment level implicit feedback based on results that searchers examine (Salojarvi et al., 2005; Brooks et al., 2006; Buscher et al., 2008). The cost of collecting gaze tracking data is falling and more accurate inferences about searcher attention are possible from relatively inexpensive eye-gaze trackers.

2.4.1.1 Types of Eye Movement
The neurology of eye movements has been studied in great detail; Leigh and Zee (1999) provide an excellent overview. Eye movements can be divided into *fixations* (when the eye gaze pauses in a certain position), *saccades* (when it moves to another position), and *smooth pursuit* (where the eye is closely tracking a moving object). Saccades and smooth pursuit are the two ways in which humans can voluntarily shift their gaze. Saccades are ballistic movements, meaning that once the movement has begun, it cannot be interrupted until completion. The resulting series of fixations and saccades

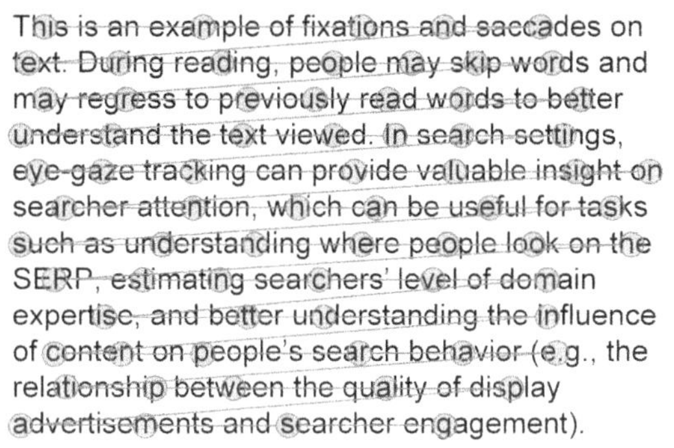

This is an example of fixations and saccades on text. During reading, people may skip words and may regress to previously read words to better understand the text viewed. In search settings, eye-gaze tracking can provide valuable insight on searcher attention, which can be useful for tasks such as understanding where people look on the SERP, estimating searchers' level of domain expertise, and better understanding the influence of content on people's search behavior (e.g., the relationship between the quality of display advertisements and searcher engagement).

Figure 2.9. Fixations and saccades as recorded by gaze tracking technology.

is called a scanpath. Figure 2.9 shows an example scanpath for a person reading text. Fixations and saccades are also marked in the figure.

Information from the eye is made available during a fixation, but not during a saccade. The central one or two degrees of the visual angle (the fovea) provide the bulk of visual information; the input from larger eccentricities (the periphery) is less informative. Hence, the locations of fixations along a scanpath show what information loci on the stimulus were processed during an eye tracking session. Fixation duration varies based on the nature of the content (e.g., approximately 250 milliseconds [ms] when reading linguistic text, 350 ms when viewing a scene [Rayner, 1998]). Rapid serial visual presentation (RSVP) provides a continuous presentation of words on the same part of the display, reducing saccade time (Potter, 1976; Chun and Potter, 1995). This has been shown to support significantly faster reading (up to twelve words per second) with no degradation in comprehension or task load (Wobbrock et al., 2002; Öquist and Goldstein, 2003). Smooth pursuit may not be entirely smooth. For example, the sustained pursuit of a rapidly moving object may require catch-up saccades (De Bouwer et al., 2002).

Detailed data collected by gaze tracking technology can be used to understand how searches examine search result lists (Joachims et al., 2007) or measure the value of new interface features (Feild et al., 2013). To develop models of implicit feedback at the passage level (Buscher et al., 2009), or to understand the effect of search-result and advertisement quality on examination behavior (Buscher et al., 2010). In the case of document examination, it is possible to capture implicit feedback at the sub-document level based on where on the page searcher attention appears to be focused (Brooks et al., 2006; Buscher et al., 2008).

When a sizeable amount of gaze tracking data is available, heatmaps that highlight regions of interest can be created. An example heatmap for a Google SERP is shown in Figure 2.10. The heatmap highlights what is commonly known as the "golden triangle," or "F" shape, where a lot of visual attention is focused on the top left hand side of page and on top three or four result snippets (Sherman, 2005; Lorigo et al., 2008).

Heatmap visualizations can be useful in determining where searchers allocate their attentional resources when examining search user interfaces. This can be useful from a design perspective, as well as obtaining a general understanding for what aspects of a presented page were considered by the searcher (e.g., how much attention was paid

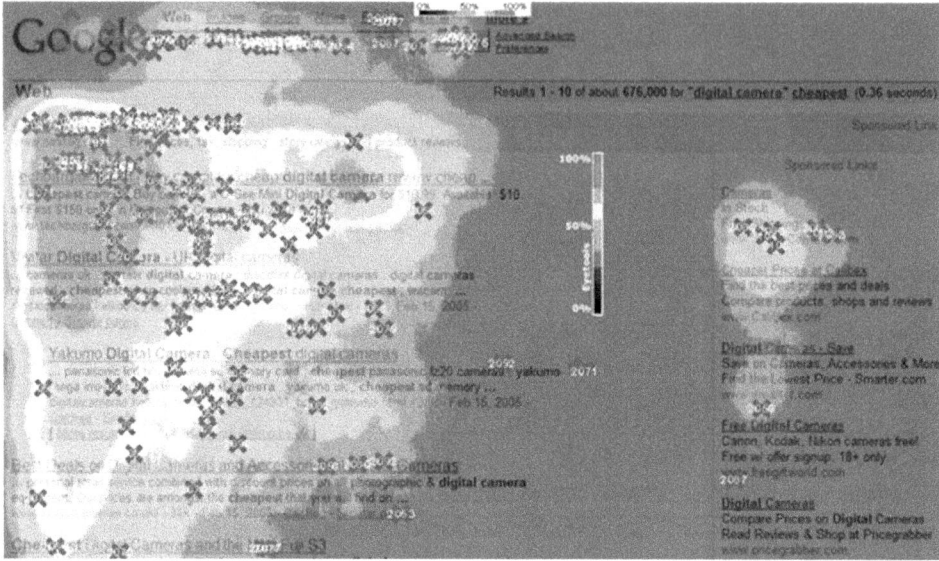

Figure 2.10. Example of a heatmap for eye gaze on a SERP. (See color plate 2.10.)

to the advertisements on the right rail) even if no clicks were observed (Buscher et al., 2010). Other aspects of eye movement can also be used to measure aspects of system performance. Pupil size can vary in response to different degrees of cognitive effort (Iqbal et al., 2004) or as an indication of interest level (Hess and Polt, 1960). Returning specifically to information seeking, pupillary response has been shown as an effective means of discriminating between relevant and non-relevant content (Oliveira et al., 2009; Gwizdka and Zhang, 2015).

2.4.1.2 Collection of Eye Movements

The collection of data on eye gaze requires special hardware. Eye gaze tracking setups can vary greatly; some are head-mounted, some enforce limited motion, and some function remotely and can compensate for head movements during tracking. Head-mounted gaze trackers can be more accurate, but also impede natural and free head movement. Historically, gaze trackers have required a subject's head be held perfectly still (usually via clamps or headrests) and for them to have uncorrected vision. Modern gaze trackers accurately track the gaze position of the eyes, and use that data to estimate the focus of visual attention even when the subject's head is moving and they are wearing eyeglasses or contact lenses.

In addition to mounting the eye-gaze tracker at or near the display, other ways of tracking gaze have been developed that have practical utility where there is no display for a searcher to review. For example, special glasses have been developed that allow gaze to be captured in settings such as shopping where store owners care about, say, which items are attracting consumer attention. Although 50/60 Hz is most common, many video-based eye trackers operate at 240, 350, or even 1000/1250 Hz, which is needed to capture the detail of the very rapid eye movement (or other ocular activity such as blinking) during reading, or during studies of neurology.

2.4.1.3 Mechanics of Gaze Tracking

The most widely used current designs are video-based eye trackers. A camera focuses on one or both eyes and records their movement as the viewer reviews an on-screen stimulus. Most modern eye-trackers use the center of the pupil and infrared / near-infrared non-collimated light to create corneal reflections. The vector between the pupil center and the corneal reflections can be used to compute the focal point on surface or the gaze direction. Calibration of the individual is usually needed before using the eye tracker, which can be cumbersome. Recently, methods have been proposed to make explicit personal calibration of eye-gaze trackers less tedious (Pfeuffer et al., 2013) or even perform calibration automatically (Chen and Ji, 2015). This allows the signals received by the system to be accurately mapped to coordinates on the screen being reviewed. Given the sporadic nature of gaze fixations, smoothing techniques such as fixation grouping (i.e., matching groups of fixations to page elements, such as a line of text [Beymer and Russell, 2005]), are necessary to resolve ambiguities associated with which element is being examined.

Two general types of eye gaze tracking can be used: *bright pupil* and *dark pupil*. The two approaches differ in terms of the location of the illumination source with respect to the optics. If the illumination is aligned with the optical path (from the display to the eye), then the light is reflected by the retina creating a bright pupil effect. This effect is similar to the red eye effect in photography. If the illumination source is offset from the optical path, then the pupil appears dark because the reflection from the retina is directed away from the camera. Bright pupil tracking creates a greater contrast between the iris and the pupil, leading to more robust gaze tracking that is less hindered by obscuring features such as eyelashes. Bright pupil tracking is less effective for applications where the eye gaze tracking occurs outdoors because extraneous infrared sources can interfere with monitoring.

2.4.1.4 Drawbacks of Gaze Tracking

Although the accuracy of gaze tracking technology is improving, highly accurate versions of the devices are still prohibitively expensive, with prices in the tens of thousands of dollars. Lower fidelity versions are now available for much less cost and may become more commonplace in computer systems given compelling usage scenarios. This technology may be useful for personalized applications whereby a system could monitor and learn from an individual's attentional patterns over time (perhaps important given individual differences in behavior that have already been noted [Aula et al., 2005b; Dumais et al., 2010]), but it is unavailable at the scale necessary to be useful for large-scale data mining. There are other non-search scenarios – such as supporting rapid selection of links, returning a "lost" mouse cursor to the current point of focus, or warping the mouse cursor to a hyperlink in advance of its selection (Zhai et al., 1999) – that may also have significant value for computer users.

2.4.2 Estimating Gaze Using Cursor Tracking

Because scale is important in learning generalizable models for ranking and other applications (applicable across many searchers and search scenarios), a means of estimating attention/eye-gaze is required.

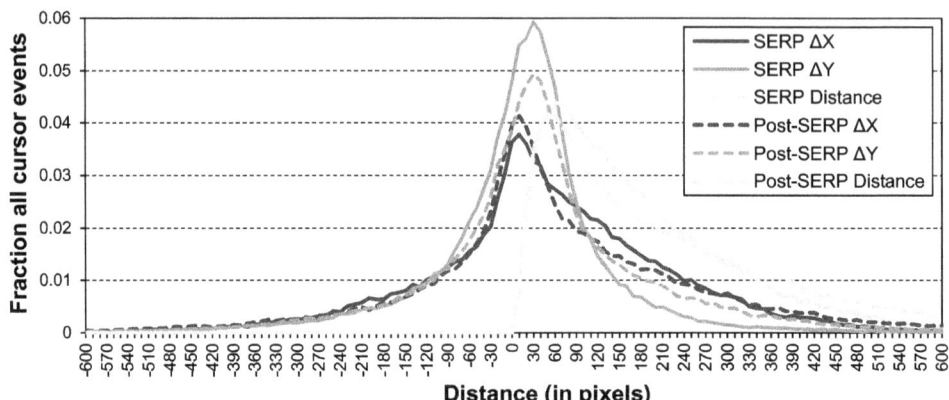

Figure 2.11. Euclidean distance between the mouse cursor position and the gaze position (Huang et al., 2011).

2.4.2.1 Cursor-Gaze Alignment

Movements of the mouse cursor have been shown to be an accurate way of estimating the point of regard at any point in time (Rodden et al., 2008; Guo and Agichtein, 2008; Huang et al., 2011). Figure 2.11 shows a plot of the frequencies with which the cursor resides at each distance from the gaze location on the screen.

The alignment between cursor and gaze has also been shown to vary with the activity that the searcher is performing, ranging from on average 75px in Euclidean distance at around the time of a mouse click, to around 150–200px at other times (Huang et al., 2012). This may be sufficient to estimate gaze as long as the cursor is moving; however, when the cursor is stationary (which it is around 60% of the time for most users during search result examination), alignment is at its worst. Accurate gaze trackers may someday be available generally in all devices – in which case, signals from those devices can leveraged for large-scale attention monitoring.

2.4.2.2 Tracking Cursor Activity

Tracking cursor activity and other interactions – such as scrolling and text highlighting – can generate a sizable amount of data. In studies, cursor position has been recorded at predetermined time intervals (e.g., every 100ms [Rodden et al., 2008]), which is impractical at large scale because of the significant data generated that must also be transmitted over the network to remote servers and stored/processed for millions of searchers. One alternative is to record events *only* when activity is observed, but this is still problematic because even a single cursor movement triggers many cursor events.

To address the challenges associated with capturing cursor movements at scale, Huang et al. (2011) devised a scalable cursor tracking approach by only recording cursor positions after a movement delay. They found that recording cursor positions only after a 40ms pause provided a reasonable tradeoff between data quantity and granularity of the recorded events. This approach recorded sufficient key points of cursor movement – for example, when the searcher moved the mouse cursor in a different direction or at endpoints before and after a cursor move. Occasionally, points within a longer movement were also captured if the searcher hesitated while moving.

```
onCursorMove:
     loc = getCursorPos()
     wait(40 milliseconds)
     if loc = = getCursorPos(): // cursor stable for
     40ms
          buffer.add(time,loc,getRegion(loc),"position")
onCursorClick:
     buffer.add(time,loc,getRegion(loc),"click")
onTick, onPageClose:
     send(buffer)
     clear(buffer)
```

Algorithm 2.1. Example of a large-scale cursor-tracking algorithm.

All mouse clicks were recorded because they were less frequent events. The events were buffered and sent to a remote server every two seconds and also when the user navigated away from the SERP through clicking on a hyperlink or closing the tab or browser. Using this approach, each recorded packet of cursor movements (in the buffer and sent to the server at any one time) is typically 1–3 kilobytes of data. The pseudocode in Algorithm 2.1 summarizes this logic. Although it may be infeasible to capture every movement of the mouse at scale, it is not clear that this is necessary to obtain a sense for where attention is focused on the SERP and use that as a sign of searcher examination behavior. For example, using the large-scale cursor tracking method, we can estimate which results searchers have considered via hover information (Huang et al., 2011). To increase confidence in such estimates, models of searcher attention can incorporate evidence of other behaviors, such as reading. This is apparent in situations for which searchers are observed moving the cursor in a zigzag pattern, from left to right and top to bottom as they examine text, following the text as though they were pointing to it with their finger as they read. On SERPs, this behavior is most likely to be observed in result snippets, where people inspect the snippet prior to making a decision about which result to visit. The presence of this cursor reading behavior has been verified via gaze tracking studies (Rodden et al., 2008). White and Buscher (2012a) showed that tracking text selections within SERP captions could improve their performance for subsequent queries by using terms that co-occurred in the snippet with the selected text. Although text selections are rare (only about 1% of queries have a text selection), effective utilization of the behavior can yield strong relevance gains.

The term *abandonment* has been used to describe a situation in which there are no clicks on the result hyperlinks on the result page. In such cases, it is difficult to understand whether people found the information they sought directly on the result page (e.g., in a direct answer on the result page or an answer present in the snippet text itself) or whether they were unhappy with the results. Research on good and bad abandonment aims to understand whether the lack of clicks on the SERP is attributable to the searcher receiving the information they seek from the SERP, which is *good* abandonment, or whether the SERP content failed to satisfy their information needs, which is *bad* abandonment (Li et al., 2009). A number of methods have been employed to explain this phenomenon, including third-party labeling of abandonment instances and in-situ labeling of abandonment by searchers. Predictive models have been developed showing that we can predict the abandonment rationale with reasonable accuracy (around 70%) by observing search behavior before and after the abandonment instance, including overlap with follow-on queries, as well as cursor interactions on the result page and the result page content – for example, whether certain types of instant answers that do not require a click were present (Diriye et al., 2012). Cursor information can also help develop predictive models of search interaction, because it allows for more accurate estimates of result examination (Huang et al., 2012), as well as other applications such as understanding search experiences resulting from Web page layout and advertisements (Navalpakkam and Churchill, 2012).

2.4.2.3 Drawbacks of Large-Scale Cursor Tracking

Although cursor tracking has a number of benefits, there are also drawbacks, including: (1) performance – although scripts can be efficiently written and compressed, it is still likely that there will be an increased page load time associated with the additional scripting (1–5% the experiments of Huang et al. [2011])[11]; (2) increased consumption of network bandwidth, which is finite and can be expensive; and (3) increased event callback loss owing to increased network contention for other events like clicks.

If the addition of cursor tracking is too costly, then alternatives can be employed. One approach is to monitor engagement with areas of interest (AOIs) via mouse cursor events such as those associated with entry and exit into the AOI, rather than tracking specific cursor coordinates. Edmonds et al. (2007) proposed this approach to collect engagement data from dynamic Web pages. Indeed, the specific Cartesian coordinates may be meaningless unless translated into AOIs. Focusing on engagement with AOIs is one way to reduce log volume, handle changes in page layout with page redesigns and different renderings in different browsers and devices, and also reduce the time required to process logs to match Cartesian coordinates to AOIs.

Another way in which the effect on page load time can be mitigated is by *lazy loading* the code required to track the cursor movements. This involves deferring the initialization of the code required to track cursor movements until after the page has loaded, perhaps using Asynchronous JavaScript and XML (AJAX). A drawback of this approach is that the first few movements of the mouse cursor following the page loading may be missed. However, these movements are often primarily reflective of the position of the clicked hyperlink on the referring page, rather than anything useful about searcher attention (Huang et al., 2012).

2.4.3 Visualizing Page Engagement

In both gaze tracking and cursor tracking an important consideration is how the collected data should be summarized for review. Scanpaths are useful for analyzing cognitive intent, interest, and salience. Clicks can be summarized using histograms depicting the frequency with which clicks occur on the various interface elements and rank positions (see Figure 2.13 in Section 2.4.4 for an example). Although cursor movements can be transformed into a similar representation using engagement with areas of interest, the data collected from these sensors is inherently noisier than that from clicks. There are a number of ways in which positional data can be presented graphically. There are

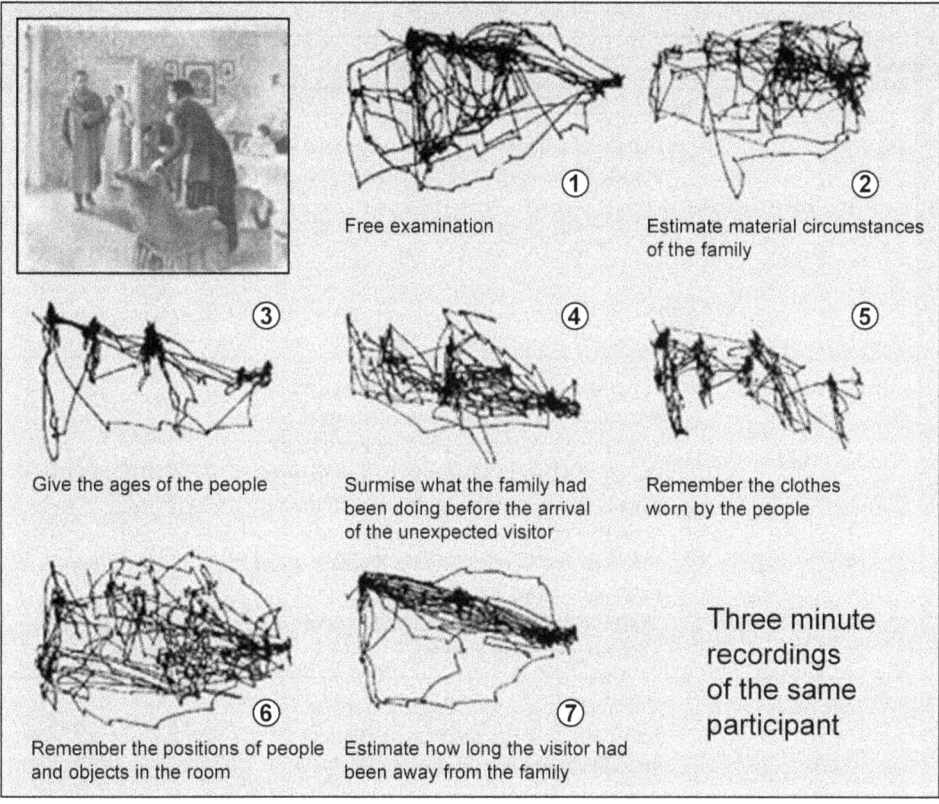

Figure 2.12. Examples of eye scanning records (adapted from Yarbus, 1967). The pattern of saccadic eye movements depends on the task. 1. Free examination. 2. Estimate material circumstances of family. 3. Give ages of people. 4. Surmise what the family members were doing before the visitor's arrival. 5. Remember the clothes worn by the people. 6. Remember the positions and objects in the room. 7. Estimate how long the "unexpected visitor" had been away.

two groups of visualization methods: static and dynamic. Static visualizations present a fixed representation of the underlying data, where dynamic visualizations present the cursor and gaze movements in an animated sequence at the individual and aggregate level. Table 2.2 provides examples of both static and dynamic visualization methods. These methods can be used to visualize individual and group inspection behaviors. Some of these presentation methods (e.g., heatmaps) are less useful for studying the search activity of individual searchers and alternatives (e.g., saccade patterns) may be difficult to interpret if multiple searchers' behaviors are shown in the presentation.

Visualization mechanisms can also be useful for understanding differences in how people consume content as a function of different underlying intentions. Research in this area extends well beyond examination of online content and predates the Web by some time. Yarbus (1967) studied differences in people's saccadic eye movements in reviewing an image, depending on the task that they were assigned. Assigned tasks ranged from free examination to memorization. Figure 2.12 shows the quite significant differences in how people studied the image in the upper left of the figure as a function of the search task.

Table 2.2. *Visualization methods for examining the results of eye-gaze tracking studies*

Name (type)	Description	Example
Saccade paths (static)	Temporally ordered connected graph comprising nodes and links, where the nodes are the fixations and the edges are saccades.	
Heatmaps (static)	Graphical representation where regions of a document that readers focus their gaze are represented as colors denoting examination intensity (darker means more examination). This is the most commonly used method to visualize eye-gaze tracking findings (Nielsen and Pernice, 2010). Unlike saccade paths, heatmaps are mainly used for the agglomerated analysis of many readers' visual exploration patterns.	
Blind zones maps (static)	This method is a simplified variant of heatmaps, where readers' visually less attended zones are displayed clearly. This supports an easier understanding of the regions that were not examined.	
Animated representations of point(s) on the interface (dynamic)	This method is used when the visual behavior is examined individually, indicating where readers focused their gaze in each moment, complemented with a path indicating the previous saccade movements.	
Bee swarm plots (dynamic)	Rather than visualizing the movements of individual readers, bee swarm plots allow the gaze patterns of multiple participants to be displayed and analyzed simultaneously. These plots represent the points of fixation in a stimulus that attract the most attention, allowing the comparison of different participants' reactions to a given stimulus.	

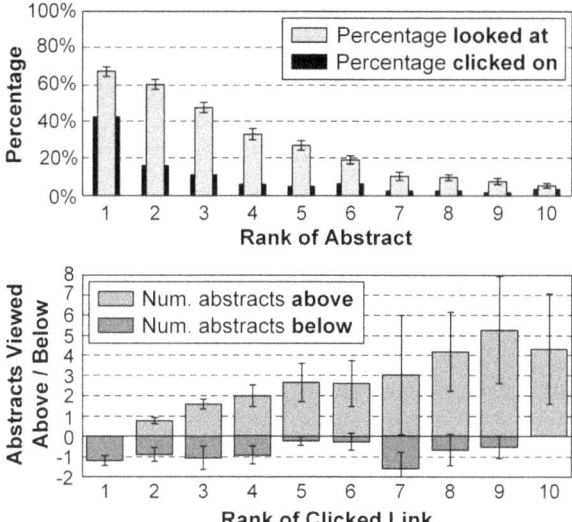

Figure 2.13. Fraction of results examined and clicked at each rank position, and the number of result captions viewed in relation to the position of the clicked result (both are adapted from Radlinski and Joachims, 2005).

The differences in the gaze patterns for the different tasks in Figure 2.12 clearly demonstrate the impact of the task on examination behavior. Differences in gaze examination behavior as a function of search intent (navigational versus informational) has also been noted in the context of search tasks (Cutrell and Guan, 2007). Cole et al. (2014) showed that a cognitive representation of page interactions, based on patterns of recorded eye movements during the reading process can help discriminate between tasks along a number of dimensions, including complexity, specificity, and the nature of the information product (intellectual or factual). Personalized and contextualized systems tailored to the searcher and their specific search situation (discussed in Chapter 9) can leverage this information to build models that adjust the search experience based on the type of task that people are engaged in.

2.4.4 Monitoring Examination and Attention

Examination strategies dictate the results that people consider and the order in which result examination occurs. Gaze tracking technology has been employed in a number of studies to investigate how people examine search results (Joachims et al., 2005; Lorigo et al., 2008). There is a sharp drop in the likelihood that people will examine the caption of search results with rank position. This trend is also evidenced in searchers' click-through behavior, independent of query; the top result receiving significantly more attention and is selected on significantly more frequently than the other search results (Joachims et al., 2005). Figure 2.13 shows examples of examination and click-through distributions across the top-ranked search results returned by a Web search system.

It is clear from Figure 2.13 that both eye-gaze distributions and click distributions decrease rapidly as a function of rank position. Searchers inspect many more results than they select. Searchers also generally view approximately one result below the rank of the result selected. This has been replicated in other studies (e.g., Cutrell and

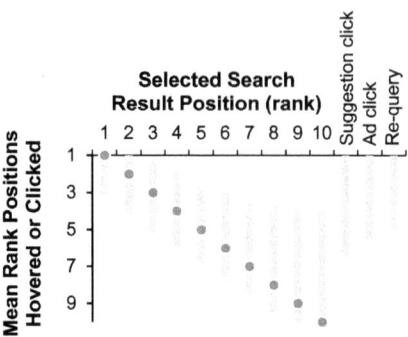

Figure 2.14. Mean number of search results hovered over before searchers clicked on a result (above and below that result). Result clicks are red circles, result hovers are blue lines (Huang et al., 2011).

Guan, 2007), including studies with large-scale cursor tracking (Huang et al., 2011) demonstrating the promise of this method as a proxy for eye gaze. Huang et al. (2011) examined which search results were hovered on before clicking on a result, re-querying, or clicking query suggestions or advertisements. This provided additional information about how searchers are employing their cursor during result examination, and it again allowed a comparison with prior research on gaze tracking (Cutrell and Guan, 2007). Figure 2.14 shows as blue lines the mean number of search results hovered on before a click, and clicks are shown as red circles. The data are broken down by result position (1–10), and separately for clicks on query suggestions, clicks on advertisements, and re-querying activity.

Figure 2.14 shows that prior to clicking on a search result, people consider the surrounding search results. For example, before clicking on result 1, people on average also hover on results 2 and 3; when they click on result 2 they also hover on results 1, 3, and 4; and so on. The findings are similar to those reported by Cutrell and Guan (2007), but differ in that the search result hovers do not appear to extend as far above the clicked search result in cases where a result is clicked on far down the list (in positions 6 through 10). This may be because queries for which low-ranked clicks are observed may have clearly irrelevant results in top ranks. By excluding hovers of less than 100ms (as was done in this analysis), Huang and colleagues missed rapid skims over such irrelevant results. This correlation with the findings of gaze tracking studies adds credence to the use of the cursor tracking as a proxy for searcher attention on SERPs; it also raises important questions about the consideration of additional examination behaviors, specifically skips and misses, in addition to click-through on search results. I now discuss these behaviors in some more detail.

2.4.4.1 Skips, Clicks, and Misses

In examining ranked lists of search results, searchers can interact with the results in a few key ways:

- **Click:** Click on a result link to visit the landing page.
- **Skip:** Not click the top result, but instead click at a lower rank (further down the list). Reaching results at lower ranks involves skipping over results positioned at higher ranks. This can signify that the skipped results are non-relevant.

- **Miss:** Not consider the result because it was visible and/or it was not noticed or because searcher did not scroll to a region of the SERP where he/she could consider it. Misses may be operationalized in log analysis as appearing below the lowest-ranked click (or perhaps more than one result below the lowest-ranked click, given the gaze tracking results in Figure 2.14). Alternatively, given access to log data containing viewport coordinates and dimensions, and the locations of results within the SERP, we can make accurate inferences about the results that searchers viewed (Buscher et al., 2012).

Some of these actions (skips and clicks) have been used in implicit feedback strategies for learning to rank (Radlinski and Joachims, 2005). Both the skip and the miss are dependent on the presence of at least one click, which provides strong evidence of the depth of exploration in search results. This makes assumptions about the nature of searchers' interactions with SERPs, some of which has been informed by gaze tracking studies (e.g., Joachims et al., 2007). By considering whether the searcher examined the search result, search engines can make decisions about how to interpret interactions toward it and whether to offer them in future queries in the search session or beyond (Radlinski and Joachims, 2005). Shokouhi et al. (2013) demonstrated that Web search engines frequently show the same documents repeatedly for different queries within the same search session (40% of multi-query sessions). Depending on historic searcher interactions with these repeated results, and the details of the session, the researchers showed that sometimes the repeated results should be promoted, while other times they should be demoted.

As the focus of search interaction expands beyond desktop search interactions to include other devices, we must also consider that results on tablets and smartphones may not be presented quite as they are on desktop machines or laptop computers (e.g., results may be shown horizontally or in grid format). The standard models of search result examination (e.g., the linear model proposed in Joachims et al. [2005] and validated at scale by Craswell et al. [2008]) may not apply to non-linear result arrangements. Research on the examination of nonstandard layout in search results is still in its infancy. Chierichetti et al. (2011) develop models of how searchers examine two-dimensional result arrangements that are common in image search SERPs. Diaz et al. (2013) built predictive models of search examination behavior trained on one-dimensional ranked lists, and demonstrated their applicability in predicting searcher engagement with multidimensional result layouts.

2.4.4.2 Viewport

The viewport represents the visible portion of the canvas. It has dimensions and it has a location, usually describing its position relative to the upper left-hand corner of the canvas. Through viewport data we can estimate which parts of the page searchers are reviewing at any given point in time and construct heatmaps reflecting the salient regions of pages based on popularity, dwell time, and/or degree of zoom, which has been shown to vary by page layout (Speicher, 2012) for use in tasks such as summarization or implicit feedback, as a proxy for attention. Huang and Diriye (2012) discussed the use of heatmaps from mobile device viewports as a way to measure page examination (Figure 2.15). While such analysis may not provide the fine-grained representation that is possible with gaze or cursor tracking, it still offers a useful signal of searcher

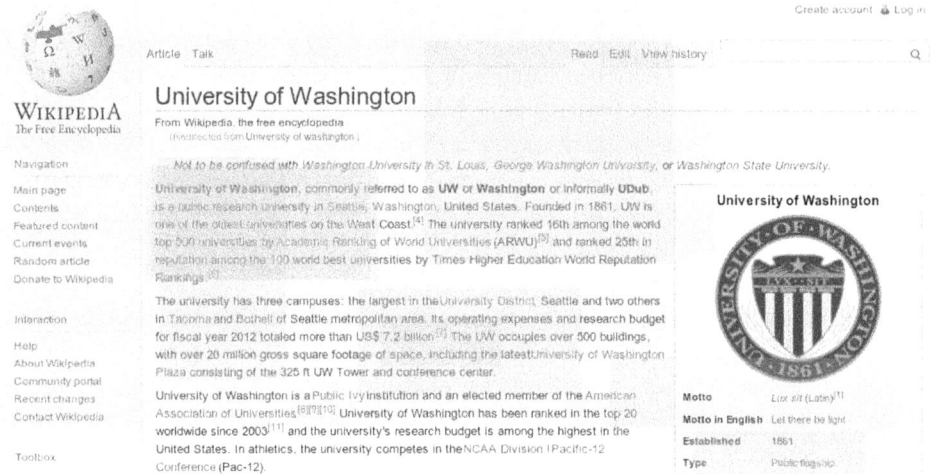

Figure 2.15. Heatmap based on viewport coordinates and dimensions (used with permission, Huang and Diriye, 2012).

attention that could be applied in a variety of contexts, such as improving mobile relevance. *ViewSer* (Lagun and Agichtein, 2011) restricts the viewport by blurring the page and un-blurring only the search result hovered over by the mouse cursor. An experiment showed that having searchers intentionally shift their viewports enabled them to determine snippet attractiveness and help re-rank search results in a way that improved result relevance. Similar principles can be applied when tracking the viewport on a device with smaller screen, substituting the un-blurred page region with the viewport on a small screen. There are some indications of the utility of such an approach in recent work in relevance and satisfaction modeling on mobile devices (Guo et al., 2013; Lagun et al., 2014). Lagun et al. (2014) found strong correlations between gaze duration and viewport duration on a per result basis, and that the average searcher attention is focused on the top half of the phone screen, suggesting that we may be able to scalably and reliably identify which specific result the searcher is considering given viewport data alone.

2.4.4.3 Scrolling

Scrolling provides functionality to navigate to content that is inaccessible in the current viewport via adjusting its horizontal or vertical position relative to the document. In a similar way to the viewport monitoring, tracking the scroll position, especially the y-max of the scrollbar, quantifies the examination depth in the SERP or within an item itself. Studies of website usability have shown that scrolling occurs infrequently (e.g., only 23% of searchers scroll on their first visit to a website [Nielsen and Loranger, 2006]). Studies of scrolling during SERP examination reveal that it occurs for just less than 30% of search queries (Huang et al., 2012). These queries may be difficult or informational in nature. The phrase "below the fold" (from the newspaper industry) refers to Web page content that searchers must scroll to reach. In SERP examination, the position of the fold can affect search-result click-through distributions – that is, results appearing below the fold receive lower click-through rates than those that are visible immediately when the page loads (Buscher et al., 2010).

As mentioned earlier, combining scrolling with viewport information and the location of AOIs allows us to determine exactly what the searcher could see at any given point in time. In the case of search result examination, this information assigns more accurate labels for skips and misses of results than is possible by considering click information alone. Given aggregated scrolling interactions, we can also visualize the regions of pages that attract most attention from searchers to guide future interactions (Hill and Hollan, 1992). Systems can also communicate relevance information for regions of examined documents (e.g., the *ProfileSkim* system [Harper et al., 2002] highlights parts of documents that match user profiles), as well directly on the scrollbar for lists of search results (e.g., the *ScrollTiles* system [White, 2004]).

2.4.4.4 Head Direction and Searcher Attention

Eye-gaze tracking technology is expensive, especially if the goal is to monitor attention at the resolution of specific text in documents or AOIs in SERPs. Less accurate gaze trackers are available for much lower cost (e.g., both EyeTribe and Tobii offer low-cost trackers with reasonable resolution), but it is also unclear what value these have in collecting and representing search behavior, where accuracy is important in distinguishing between items examined. Web cameras (or front-facing cameras on devices such as smartphones and tablets) have been proposed as low-cost alternatives to gaze tracking (e.g., Chau and Betke, 2005; Li et al., 2006; San Augustin et al., 2010). Such methods usually involve modification and special placement of the web camera in close proximity to the eye, which can be uncomfortable and hinder reading. There has been some limited success in applying machine learning to attain an accuracy of gaze tracking with web cameras to within 2 to 4 degrees (Sewell and Komogorstev, 2010) (in contrast to the < 1 degree accuracy attainable with dedicated eye-gaze tracking hardware). Although the granularity of these solutions does not allow for exact monitoring of the focus of searcher attention, these methods do provide the system with insight into whether the searcher is actively reading the content available on the display or which region of the page they are examining, which can be used to enable routine applications such as smart scrolling with a glance or as the searcher's eye gaze position approaches the page fold.

Beyond single monitors, early research on estimating attention coarsely on multiple monitors or different parts of the same large monitor or projected display also hold promise for behavioral analysis – not only to infer retrospectively from logged signals the regions of a page attended to, but also to leverage these signals in real time for attention-enhanced interaction. Head pose can be estimated using commodity technologies, including Web cameras and the Microsoft Kinect (Fanelli et al., 2011). Signals from these devices about the position of the head relative to the display can serve as an input for eye-gaze estimation (Funes Mora and Odobez, 2012).

2.4.5 Touch Interactions

To work well with smartphones and tablets, desktop interaction models must be adapted to handle touch interactions such as pinching and swiping, and to account for the

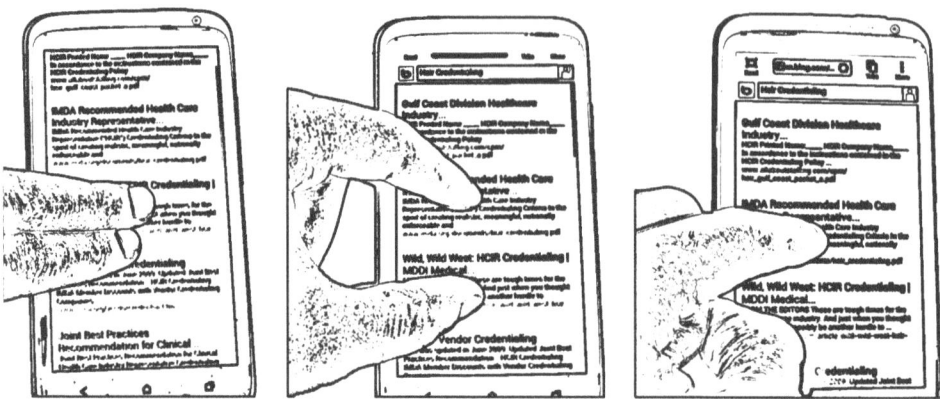

Figure 2.16. Examples of touch interactions with search results on a smartphone (used with permission, Huang and Diriye, 2012).

different device form factors (e.g., only a small number of result captions can be visible on a smartphone display at one time). As natural user interaction becomes prevalent, additional signals from touch devices, such as swipes and scrolls, offer searchers new ways to engage with search results and provide search engines with additional information about searcher attention and possible search relevance (Guo et al., 2013). Figure 2.16 presents some examples of how searchers use touch interactions to interact with search systems running on mobile devices, specifically item selection, zooming, and scrolling.

Touch interactions and supporting technologies have been discussed in the research literature for decades (Johnson, 1965; 1967). A growing number of devices now support touch interactions, and new interaction paradigms enable keyboard-mouse interactions to be replaced by touch interaction (Shneiderman, 1991). Interactions of this nature are important in next-generation searching, alongside other natural forms of search interaction such as spoken dialog and gesture, which are less widely deployed (Chapter 5).

2.4.5.1 Mechanics of Touch Monitoring

Although there are a number of different technologies that capture touch interactions, the three basic systems used to recognize touch are: (1) resistive, (2) capacitive, and (3) surface acoustic wave (Sears et al., 1990). The methods register different stimuli as touch events. A resistive system registers a touch as long as the two layers make contact, which means that the object used as a pointer is unimportant. A capacitive system, on the other hand, must have a conductive input, usually a finger, to register a touch. The surface acoustic wave system works much like the resistive system, allowing a touch with almost any object except hard and small objects such as pen tips. Interpreting multiple points of contact (or so-called "plural-point awareness") enables more advanced functionality such as pinch to zoom. The form factors for multi-touch ranges from handheld devices (in the case of the iPhone and other smartphones) to tabletop devices. Buxton (2007) provides an excellent overview of a range of different types of multi-touch devices.

One of the main disadvantages is that touch events have little or no support in Web browsers, which means that they cannot be tracked at scale. Other drawbacks include the inaccuracy of the selection, which can be challenging on densely packed displays, and there are also missing behaviors, such as hovering. Recent research has attempted to address challenges with selection and occlusion (Benko et al., 2006; Wigdor et al., 2007), as well as the detection of hover events on touch devices (e.g., Samsung's *Air View* system or *PreCursor* [Mistry and Wang, 2011]). Swipes are also captured and interpreted independent of position, thus the swiping signal is not used as an indication of interest in a particular region of the document. To the extent that swipes are used to rapidly reposition the viewport, however, swipes do have some utility in inferring interests, intentions, or motivations (e.g., rapid swiping could provide indications of negative interest in the content that is skipped). More broadly, further research is needed to understand the nature of touch interactions and identify specific patterns of interaction that signal relevance and search satisfaction, and can also transcend application boundaries.

2.4.5.2 Monitoring and Mining Touch at Scale

We can mine and model touch interactions in a similar way to other interaction behaviors. Touch can be instrumented in much the same way as interactions such as cursor tracking, but may require additional client-side code to capture. Aspects of the page layout and formatting can be automatically adjusted to handle touch interactions (Levia, 2011). The tracking of touch events such as *touchstart*, *touchmove*, and *touchend* requires special instrumentation (Carta et al., 2011). However, the adoption and analysis of touch events are set to become more widespread given forthcoming W3C standards;[12] although the community still depends on Web browser manufacturers to include support for these events in their applications. In the meantime, to track touch interactions, developers need to develop dedicated browsers or hack existing browsers. Guo et al. (2013) employed a specially instrumented Web browser to capture interaction data for their study. They evaluated a variety of touch interactions on a smartphone as implicit relevance feedback and demonstrated improvements to search ranking quality by mining touch data. Other research has explored the use of touch data to assess usability in information-seeking contexts (Lettner and Holzmann, 2012).

The efficient capture and transmission of touch behaviors remotely and at scale is important for improving search relevance both for individual searchers and for aggregate learning models of these behaviors across many searchers. Just as with the cursor tracking methods described earlier in this chapter, in collecting additional signals consideration needs to be given to important issues such as the impact on page weight and network bandwidth usage limitations. This also raises the important issue of the data collection strategy, which is discussed in more detail in the next section.

2.5 Collection Strategies

To learn about the search process from search behavior or to develop computational models of the process, search systems must be able to efficiently capture data on search activity and the context within which that activity was performed (physical, temporal, virtual [application context], etc.). For example, Web pages that utilize responsive Web design (Marcotte, 2011) will present an optimal (and importantly, *different*) viewing experience for each device in terms of ease of reading and navigation. That means that the specific layout of content on the current device needs to be recorded. Increasingly, interaction events will be stored in the cloud with searcher consent and appropriate consideration for searcher privacy by search providers. Embedded in the terms of use for many online services is the stipulation that the service provider be able to record interactions for service improvements. Interactions with online services are stored on remote servers and used both in the aggregate, for searcher's cohorts (e.g., searchers in the same location, with the same interests, and/or the same level of domain knowledge), and for the searcher alone, to better understand their interests and intentions. There are a number of ways in which behavioral data can be collected. The means by which this occurs depends largely on the situation at search time, including the type of device that the searcher is using, its nature (shared versus private), and constraints such as network bandwidth that might impact the type of data that can be collected and how quickly that data can be transmitted to remote servers for logging.

In the context of search behavior analysis, there is some core information that needs to be recorded irrespective of where the event is occurring: (1) the type of event (e.g., click, query); (2) a timestamp denoting the time that the event occurred and the nature of the event (including time zone information as appropriate); (3) a unique identifier for the event and for the searcher if permitted; and (4) the atomic information element that is being logged (e.g., URL or query text). Care needs to be taken on how these data are represented to minimize storage and overhead processing. A wealth of contextual information such as the device used, physical location, and abstract information about the event is also recordable given access to definitive signals or inferences from observed data. For example, it is often possible to distinguish a query from a non-query via URL patterns and the Web domain (e.g., the text attributed to the "q=" parameter in a google.com URL). This means queries do not need to be stored and logged separately from the URL of the Web page that is accessed, reducing the size of each log entry. Across billions of log entries such small savings are significant in terms of storage cost and log processing time.

There are two main contexts within which research in the area is conducted: (1) *en vitro*, which is a laboratory setting in which the experimenter may be able to control a number of different aspects of the experimental setup, and instrument and record rich data on a variety aspects of search interaction; and (2) *en vivo*, which is in a naturalistic setting (i.e., in the "wild") (either following deployment of a production system, or in large-scale testing [interleaving, flighting, etc.] as discussed in Chapter 10). In natural settings the data recording may be more limited but the diversity in terms of information goals and searchers is much greater, allowing for more generalizable claims to be made about the value of the method(s) evaluated.

2.5.1 Laboratory Settings

In laboratory settings, sophisticated logging can be employed to capture a broad range of aspects of people's search behavior. Richer logging of events – such as keystrokes and application accesses – can yield more complete insights about search behavior than what would be possible in remote settings. Beyond activity logging, complementary methods such as think-alouds and retrospective interviews can be used to understand rationales for observed behaviors. Participants in the laboratory may also be aware that their activity is being recorded and not feel that their privacy is being invaded (e.g., logging all keystrokes might not be acceptable remotely given concerns about password privacy, etc.). In addition, expensive dedicated eye-gaze tracking technology could also be employed in a laboratory setting that is not available in remote locations.

The ability to employ local logging also allows for the tracking of searcher activity beyond the confines of a particular application, as well as cross-application engagement (e.g., movement between applications as a function of the current search task). Tracking tasks beyond the confines of the search system and/or the Web browser is more difficult to do in the real world, given concerns about privacy and the issues with compatibility and completeness of recorded data between applications. Aspects of this tracking technology could also be deployed remotely, enabling the tracking of search behavior beyond laboratory settings. Fu (2010) investigated implicit feedback opportunities by matching search behaviors to queries. He created a corpus of underspecified queries, and captured the behaviors of searchers using a range of approaches, including transaction logs, gaze tracking, and video. Professional searchers (reference librarians) assessed the behaviors to infer interests, and used measures such as confidence variations over time to map behaviors to different states (search, select, examine, and retain).

Rather than deploying tracking software on one or more laboratory machines, experimenters can also develop specialized software that experimental participants can install to track their activity and upload it to a remote server for later analysis (e.g., Fox et al., 2005; Hassan et al., 2011; Diriye et al., 2012). This enables the study of search behavior in more natural settings, where the application can still assert some control over the experimental process in terms of the conditions in which it solicits responses from participants or the impact that it has on system operation. Depending on where the application resides, it can influence the types of information accessed to different degrees. For example, a plug-in that runs within a Web browser will not be able to observe activity in other applications, whereas one running inside the operating system could conceivably observe all searcher activity, enabling the tracking and analysis of information behavior across different applications. The role of searching within the broader ecosystem of application usage is not well understood and such low-level tracking would facilitate such studies.

2.5.2 Natural Settings

Collecting behavioral data in the wild faces a number of challenges that are not encountered by systems attempting to record data locally. Application designers need to make tradeoffs regarding the amount of data captured versus the amount of data that can be transmitted over the network without affecting system performance, while also considering other factors such as searcher privacy. Deciding which signals to record requires a degree of foresight about how the logged events will be used, which may not always be possible. Consulting with those who have experience with the studies of this nature is one way to inform reliable decision making. It is clear that it is worth logging core

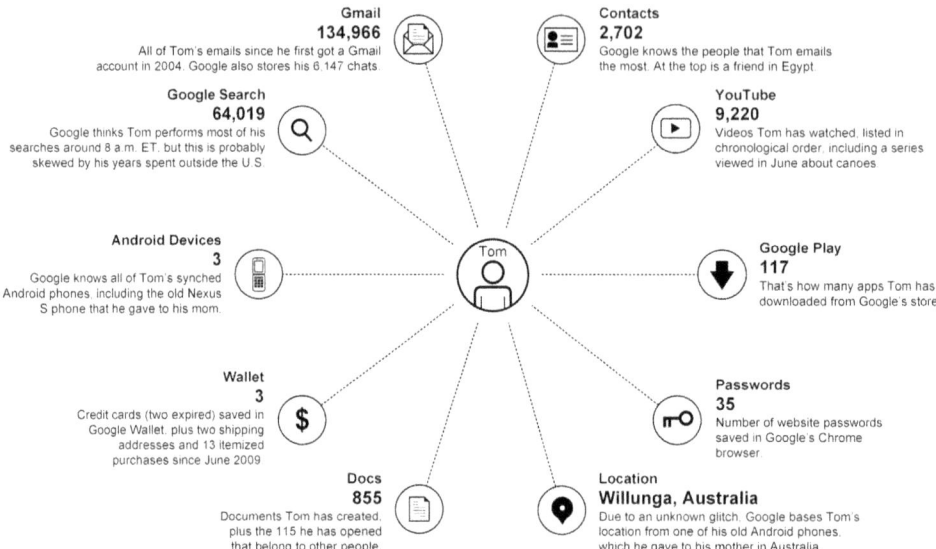

Figure 2.17. Information stored by Google about signed-in users of its online services, specifically in this case Wall Street Journal reporter Tom Gara (adapted from Gara, 2014).

activities such as queries and hyperlink clicks as they have demonstrated significant value in a range of previous studies of search behavior and resultant applications. However, there are other events, such as the currently open applications or the launch point of the query, for which the cost-benefit tradeoffs are less well understood.

Implicit feedback from gestural and voice interaction with search engines will also become more prevalent. Devices such as the Xbox and the accompanying Kinect enable different opportunities for collaborative search, richer sensing of searcher behavior (including physiological signals, useful for modeling searchers' affective state), and the integration of gestural feedback into search result examination, allowing searchers to fluidly explore result sets. To be used in ranking, select signals from this feedback will need to be shared with remote search providers. The physical search context, including the number of people present in the room as the search is being performed and their identities as inferred from facial recognition, enables richer representations of the searcher's situation which facilitates the provision of more accurate result sets. All of this information needs to be collected, stored, and shared in a way that allows multiple stakeholders to leverage the data to improve the search experience. There are significant challenges in developing data representations that can succinctly represent the complexities of this broad range of different interaction behavior, and the context within which they were performed.

Before concluding this discussion of data collection in natural settings, it is worth noting that commercial search engines already know a lot about their users, especially those who utilize various online services such as search, email, data storage, and entertainment. For example, for signed-in users, Google has access to all Web pages visited online, all search queries, all email sent and received, the physical locations searched for, instant messages, and videos watched (Gara, 2014). Figure 2.17 presents a visualization summarizing the information that Google stores about a particular individual (in this case, Wall Street Journal reporter Tom Gara), and surfaces to people on demand via a password-protected dashboard.[13]

While the wealth of information collected can be extremely useful in creating search experiences tailored to particular searchers' interests and preferences, there are also significant privacy concerns in having such long-term histories stored by a single corporate entity and accessed so readily online. Additionally, those with malicious or illegal intentions may seek out embarrassing searches or emails for public release or use in blackmail, or mine the private data for identity theft. I will discuss important issues surrounding searcher privacy in greater detail in Chapter 12.

2.6 Summary

In this chapter, I have described the various actions that are recorded by search engines, as well as new opportunities to develop richer models of searchers' interests and intentions using new signals. I focused mostly on modalities that have obtained mainstream adoption. There are others such as spoken dialog and gestural interactions for which the interaction models are still being defined. These and other emerging modalities are covered in more detail in Chapter 6. The availability of rich behavioral data across a range of modalities serves as an important foundation for next-generation search systems as they attempt to support searchers more completely across a wide span of search tasks. In the next chapter, I discuss modeling of interests and intentions, which can capitalize on richer and larger-scale data to improve the search experience, by (1) building systems that leverage the models, and (2) attaining more complete insights regarding system performance.

CHAPTER 3

Modeling Interests and Intentions

In this chapter, I discuss various aspects of the interactive search process, including next-generation search experiences and emerging trends (Section 3.1). I discuss various models of search interaction that have been developed for applications such as click prediction, satisfaction, and relevance (Section 3.2). I also enumerate some of the main components required for model building, including data, data mining, and machine learning (Section 3.3). From the breadth of the topics covered in this chapter, clear that many factors must be considered in modeling interests and intentions via interactions with search systems.

3.1 Modeling Next-Generation Search Interaction

Let us begin with a high-level model of next-generation search interaction that reflects emerging trends in the area, yet builds on much of the work on collecting and representing search interaction that was described in Chapter 2. The model is depicted visually in Figure 3.1. Although an interaction model is not strictly necessary for a discussion of progress in this area, it can be useful in framing many of the contributions that are mentioned in this book. I discuss emerging trends likely to affect search interaction, as well as other factors including the role of large-scale behavioral data in guiding effective decisions by future searchers and search providers; generic and personalized machine-learned models of searchers' interests, intentions, and search satisfaction levels; support for task completion; cloud-based application and storage (used to retain found information items that were found, generated by the searcher, or in the process of being generated (work in progress), as well as rapidly accessible profiles of searchers' long-term interests and intentions – reflecting completed and ongoing search tasks); and context of various forms, natural interaction with search systems, and ubiquitous search (through mobile computing and support for cross-device interactions). Core elements of next-generation search interactions are proactive and reactive experiences and intelligent personal assistants working in concert to surface relevant and useful information at an appropriate time.

3.1.1 Emerging Trends

There are a number of emerging trends in computer and information sciences, and in society more broadly, that search engine designers need to consider when designing next-generation search systems. These will influence the design of search technologies, how people interact with search systems, searcher experiences, and search system evaluation. Some of the main trends can be summarized as follows:

- **Mobile:** Mobile devices will soon be the primary means by which people access search technology. Mobile devices will soon surpass desktop computers as the primary means of accessing content online. Research into the development of different mechanisms for query entry (including spoken dialog queries) and result presentation will be important in helping searchers find information while mobile. These capabilities reduce the barrier to entry for search while mobile, but it can also be challenging to present many results on mobile displays. This limits the potential for exploration and serendipity on such devices because they cannot leverage the incredibly strong visual capacities of humans (Shneiderman, 1996). There is also the potential to leverage signals about the search setting – for example, utilization of a variety of contextual signals such as physical location and ambient noise.
- **Cloud Storage and Computation:** Cloud computing presents the opportunity to store, analyze, and access data from anywhere at any time. This has implications for search in areas such as personalization (where a person's search history could be accessed from any device) or personal information management (where content generated by the searcher at a previous time could be accessed from anywhere).
- **Big (and Small) Data:** Aggregated data about many people's interests and activities – known as "big data" – from a broad range of different sources, including online search and browsing are being mined and analyzed. Insights from these data can be used to improve online services, learn about the world, and inform decision making and action. Likewise, "small data" (rich, comprehensive data about individuals) is used for applications such as personalization, as well as in support of higher-level activities such as reflection and learning.
- **Natural User Interfaces:** Recent advances in technologies – such as touch, gesture, and speech recognition – enables people to interact with search systems in ways that are different from recent technology. Making search interaction more natural means that search technologies can be integrated more seamlessly into devices and services.
- **Social Computing:** Online social networks and social media have unlocked enormous potential to communicate ideas, get assistance with problems and recommendations, and learn about social interactions and dynamics. This potential can be unlocked for a wide range of search-related applications, including people finding and question answering.
- **Machine Learning and Artificial Intelligence:** Although these topics have been researched for some time and already have been integrated into search technology (e.g., in search engine ranking algorithms [Burges et al., 2005]), machine learning and artificial intelligence will be at the center of future advances in search interaction. Techniques from these areas are becoming more widely used and will be integrated into a broad range of different search applications, including proactive

search and recommendations, as well as intelligent agents capable of engaging in direct dialog with the searcher (e.g., Microsoft Cortana, Apple Siri) and learning their preferences over time.

These are all important themes that are central to the discussion in the remainder of this book. It is important to note that the associated ideas and technologies do not exist in isolation. They need to be combined to create compelling and generally useful search experiences. For example, machine learning algorithms require large amounts of data to perform effectively, and mobile computing relies on cloud storage of documents and profile information to serve information to searchers both proactively and reactively.

3.1.2 Next-Generation Search Interaction

Next-generation search systems will support and leverage the emerging trends while building on work in data mining, user modeling, and search interface design. Figure 3.1 summarizes many of these aspects in an illustration of next-generation search interaction. In this vision, search systems are personal assistants that sense and learn from a variety of signals from their environment to support the current searcher. The personal assistant can capitalize on many of the technological advances described thus far and operate alongside the searcher as a search companion. Assistants react to queries provided by the searcher, but importantly, they also anticipate future needs and make recommendations based on existing interests – both explicitly communicated by the searcher and inferred by the system based on people's activity.

The searcher is central to the search process. Search support in next-generation search interaction is situated with respect to the searcher and their current search situation. At any point in time, searchers are engaged in tasks and require support for task completion that the system can provide. The system has access to searchers' historic search profiles and can help them resume ongoing tasks (Kotov et al., 2011) or even help them complete tasks by leveraging the interactions of other searchers stored by the system from their previous searching (Hassan and White, 2012; White et al., 2013a). Mainstream search behaviors – such as queries and search click-through – still have relevance in these settings, but the current search ecosystem is significantly richer than what is typically considered in models constructed from queries and clicks alone. As can be seen in Figure 3.1, there is significant interplay between the various components that needs to be factored into the design of considered when designing search systems and the evaluation of these systems to support a range of information problems.

As search evolves to capitalize on new capabilities and shifting searcher expectations around how relevant a search should be and where it should be available, the following activities will become important in supporting people's interactions in pursuit of their information objectives:

- Natural interaction with the system, including speech, touch, gesture, and gaze; as well as combinations of these different information sources.
- Reactive support (acting *in response* to searcher queries) and proactive support (acting on behalf of the searcher without an explicit request to do so). The interplay between these types of support is also important (e.g., in using signals from

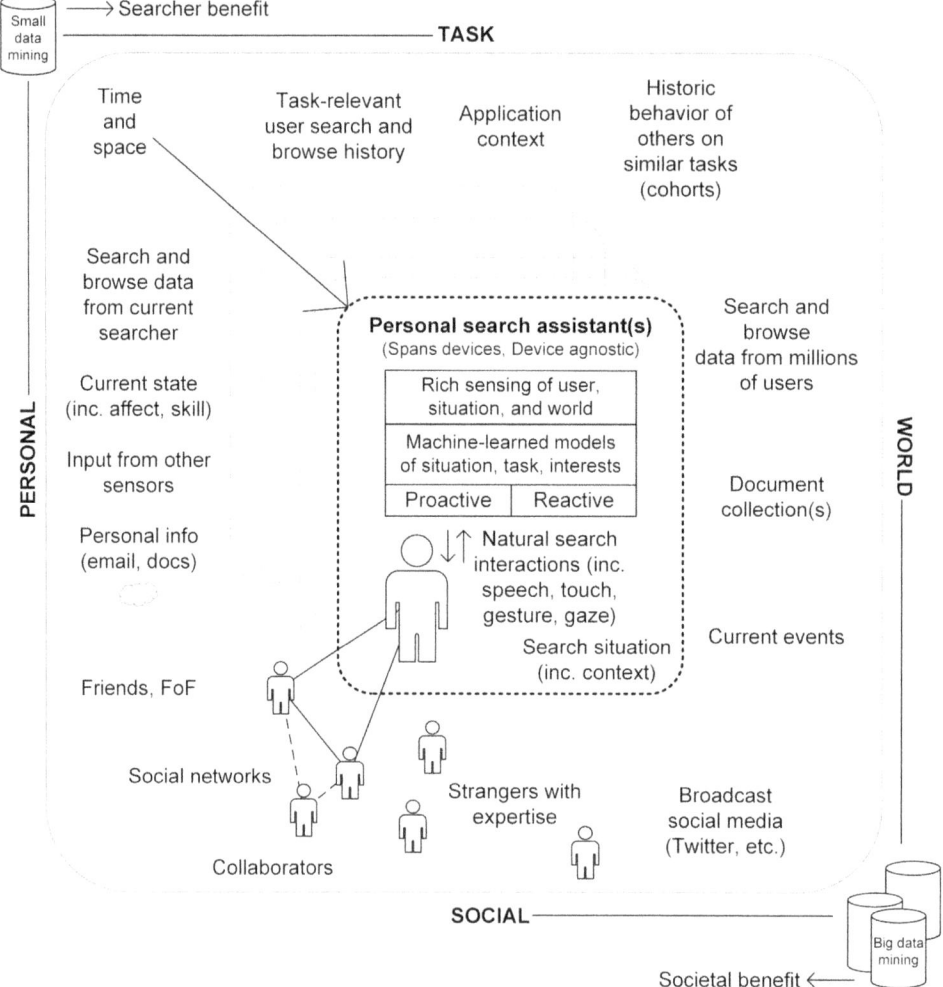

Figure 3.1. Next-generation search systems represented as personal assistants equipped with advanced sensing and modeling capabilities.

reactive search experiences to improve proactivity (Shokouhi and Guo, 2015), or deciding when to make recommendations versus when to wait for the searcher to initiate a search request).

- Search over time, devices, and applications, including predictions about task resumption. Access to a user profile from any device at any time could support the proactive retrieval of content that is appropriate for the current task as well as a range of compelling proactive search scenarios, such as slow searches and the resumption of long-term tasks.
- Cloud-based storage of "small data" from an individual collected from a wide array of sensors across their devices can facilitate user profile construction, personalization, and higher-order tasks such as reflection and learning. For example, Bateman et al. (2012) provided searchers with a dashboard describing aspects of their search activity over time (e.g., length of query) and facilitated comparisons of that activity with that of typical searchers and expert searchers.

- Support for different phases of tasks (e.g., guided tours to help searchers progress smoothly through the phases of a task [Trigg, 1988; Reich et al., 1999; Hassan and White, 2012]), targeting processes as well as task outcomes, using data mined from large-scale log data (e.g., search trails followed after a query has been issued [e.g., Singla et al., 2010], or generated automatically based on computational models of searchers' information needs (Olson and Chi, 2003; Pandit and Olson, 2007).
- Use of context, from searcher situation and more broadly (e.g., information about the task, the application(s) being used, physical location, time, etc. [Ingwersen and Järvelin, 2005]), as well as personal information about the searcher, including their level of subject-matter expertise (White et al., 2009). Richer modeling of searchers and their scenario allows systems to represent these factors internally and consider them when locating resources (e.g., find low-text documents if the search is urgent) and to better model searchers' learning processes over the course of a search session and longer term (Eickhoff et al., 2014) – so as to provide them with appropriate information for their current skill level and to help advance their skills to new levels.
- Consideration of how information is understood and used, and methods to support those processes in addition to information retrieval. This involves support for the collection and storage of found information, as well as the synthesis of that information, and the application of insights gleaned from it for other search tasks. This also has applications for the evaluation of systems, which need to consider the role that the systems play in affecting cognitive and emotional change, as well as fulfilling needs as part of broader informational work tasks and aspirational searcher goals.
- Activity on social networks. Through search engines that log search activity, people can also be connected via their behaviors (even in real-time, with searcher consent). Many of the existing models of information seeking involve searchers seeking information in isolation, but this is changing and support for collaborative search (explicit and implicit) is becoming more prevalent (Shah, 2010b; 2014). Moving forward, there needs to be more emphasis on searchers as active participants within their social environment, influencing others' searching and decision-making processes rather than only being passively impacted by others' demands and expectations, as has largely been the focus in search interaction to date.

When we move beyond the individual searcher, there is opportunity to learn about the world from insights gleaned from big data. This will require methods to handle data biases, such as only having access to the usage data from the users of a particular service, or only those who elect to query about a topic. Studies of biases have been conducted in social media (Kiciman, 2012), and in comparison between topics discussed on social media and those observed in search logs (De Choudhury et al., 2014). Methods have also been proposed to control for such biases during online experimentation (Eckles et al., 2015). Such studies and methods will become more important as search systems increasingly capitalize on large-scale usage data.

These are only some of the factors that need to be considered to support next-generation search interaction, but they highlight the enormous opportunity for research in this area. Many of the aspects of the model in Figure 3.1 are explored in detail in the remainder of the book. There has already been significant work on modeling aspects of search behavior and deploying such models in Web settings at scale to improve aspects of the search experience – primarily the improvement of search-result relevance. Given the central role of such modeling in the framework (in the "Machine-learned models of situation, tasks, interests" module in Figure 3.1), we begin by describing such models and their applications to better understand and improve the search experience.

3.2 Models of Searcher Behavior

Some of the most significant advances in Information Retrieval in the past decade have been made in the area of searcher behavior modeling[1] (e.g., Agichtein et al., 2006; White and Drucker, 2007; Dou et al., 2007; Chapelle and Zhang, 2009; Teevan et al., 2011b; Huang et al., 2011). Being able to accurately model searchers' information-seeking activities as they search and navigate through document collections has a range of applications, including better understanding the search process, estimating satisfaction, identifying connections between queries and/or URLs, and learning which results are relevant. The ability to make these predictions reliably requires significant quantities of behavioral data, coupled with algorithms that can learn effectively from that data.[2] I discuss the requirements for model building in Section 3.3. In the remainder of the current section, I discuss some of the popular types of searcher behavior models that have emerged from the research community over the past decade. These models will continue to be important in next-generation search systems, and their capabilities will be extended to integrate new and more voluminous data, as well as more sophisticated models of search interaction given new search experiences.

3.2.1 Examination

Accurately modeling the search process and predicting the results that searchers are going to click on is a well-studied research area (Chapelle and Zhang, 2009; Craswell et al., 2008; Zhang et al., 2010), that is important in understanding the effect of factors such as rank position, captions, and searcher preferences on engagement with search results. Models in this area are based on assumptions about how people examine SERPs. For example, in the cascade model, searchers are assumed to read the results from top to bottom and stop when they reach a relevant search result (Craswell et al., 2008). Although these models often do not impact result ranking directly, much of the motivation behind their development centers on the accurate prediction of how searchers inspect and select results, which we can then turn into relevance enhancements. The click prediction models consider factors such as whether searchers examine the captions and the order in which that examination occurs.

Armed with predictions on what results searchers are likely to select, prediction accuracy is measured using a set of queries and clicks as extracted log data. Generating labels for this task is easier than for the other modeling tasks described in this section, because a click is either observed or it is not; there is no subjectivity as there is for satisfaction or for relevance (discussed later in this chapter). As mentioned in Section 2.4.2, more recent research has considered mouse cursor activity as a proxy of searcher attention, facilitating the development of more accurate models of which result captions were considered during SERP examination (Huang et al., 2012). Click prediction models are also applied in online advertising, where the goal is to maximize revenue from searcher clicks, including for new advertisements for which behavioral data are missing (Richardson et al., 2007). The probability that an advertisement will be clicked is an important input to the algorithms that search providers utilize to determine which advertisements to display on SERPs. Cursor movement data can lead to more accurate predictive models (Huang et al., 2012), as can considering resource revisitation behavior (Xu et al., 2012).

One of the most common metrics for evaluating the performance of click prediction algorithms is *click perplexity*, which has been employed in a number of studies (Chapelle and Zhang, 2009; Guo et al., 2009; Zhang et al., 2010) as a measure of how effectively a click prediction models predicts click-through rates (i.e., the ratio of the number of times a document is selected for a query and the number of times that document is returned for a query). Click perplexity measures how "surprised" a click prediction model is after observing a click on a result (Dupret and Piwowarksi, 2008). The perplexity over a set of binary observations is estimated via the geometric average of the predicted probability of the observations. It reflects the average number of times that an experiment needs to be repeated to observe a correct prediction. As a result, the lowest attainable perplexity (of the perfect deterministic model) is one. This means that the trained model perfectly predicted the test data, while a larger perplexity means that the model was less accurate.

3.2.1.1 Behavioral Biases

Interpreting searcher behavior is not as straightforward as simply counting mouse hovers and hyperlink clicks. A number of biases in behavior have been observed in behavioral studies that can affect how searchers examine search results and hence the predictions obtained from click prediction models. The behavior is biased in a sense that it affects people's choices about whether to click on a particular result, and depends on a combination of at least document relevance and position in search results. We have covered at least one of these biases in our discussions of click-through distributions (Chapter 2). Identified biases include:

- **Position bias:** People consider search results from the top to bottom of the ranked list, irrespective of actual relevance (Joachims et al., 2005). Position bias describes a case in which a searcher's decision on which result to select is based on rank position of the search result rather than its relevance to the information need. This is also referred to as "trust bias" or "presentation bias," because searchers are observed trusting the presented ranking of the search engine, irrespective of the relevance of the search results or the performance of the search engine. This leads to the consistent click-through curves, such as that shown in Figure 2.14, which clearly demonstrate that searchers are much less likely to click on low-ranked results. These curves have been observed across a wide range of different search queries, and in a variety of different search settings. This bias pervades a broad range of information-seeking scenarios. From the searcher's perspective, this may be rational as the search engine may know more about the available content than the searcher does. Of course, this can be problematic if the engine itself is biased in how it interprets search queries or indexes Web content (White and Hassan, 2014). Beyond its implications for skewing models that learn from this behavior, position bias can also affect real-world decisions that searchers make (e.g., studies have shown that a significant fraction of searchers believe that the ranking of medical conditions for symptom queries reflect real-world likelihoods of occurrence [White and Horvitz, 2009]). As searchers rely increasingly on search engines for a broader range of search scenarios, aligning rank position with actual likelihoods may be important for consequential search tasks and/or those for which searchers may be most likely to trust the search engine (e.g., search tasks where subject matter expertise is important, such as those with a medical focus).

- **Caption bias:** Captions – typically comprising result title, snippet, and URL – are used by searchers to inform their search-result click decisions. Potential biases associated with these captions can be divided into at least two classes: (1) attractiveness bias, and (2) context bias. Attractiveness bias suggests that searchers are more likely to click on search results that attract their attention, such as captions that include particular words (e.g., "official" or "free" [Clarke et al., 2007]) or formatting (e.g., increased bolding of title terms [Yue et al., 2010]). The inclusion of thumbnail images in the captions (Woodruff et al., 2001; Teevan et al., 2009a; Muralidharan et al., 2012) also attracts attention to the caption, making it more likely to be examined, as does the presence of concerning content which may increase levels of anxiety (White and Horvitz, 2013). Context is also important. Proximal search results may affect the likelihood that people select a particular result. Searchers have been shown to make relative rather than holistic determinations about whether to click on a result; comparing the result to those near it in the result list rather than the full list (Radlinski and Joachims, 2005; Joachims et al., 2005; Shokouhi et al., 2013). The relative attractiveness of a result caption in comparison to its immediate neighbors in the result list can impact whether searchers decide to visit that result, irrespective of the content of the caption itself.

- **Resource bias:** People have been shown to exhibit preference for particular Web domains (e.g., preferring wikipedia.org over about.com; see Ieong et al. [2012]). This resource preference is observed in many other settings, including retail or entertainment, but its presence in the context of search interaction can significantly affect behavioral signals from which examination models are learned.

- **Cognitive bias:** Recent research has provided some evidence of cognitive bias in how people examine search results. In a study of Web search behavior for yes-no health questions, White (2013) demonstrated that people were significantly more likely to click on positive (yes-oriented content) than on negative (no-oriented) content, and that this held when controlling for rank position and the availability of these answers in the result set. Because cognitive biases (Tversky and Kahneman, 1974) have been shown to pervade many aspects of human behavior, it comes as no surprise that these biases appear in search interaction (White and Horvitz, 2009; White and Horvitz, 2015). What is surprising is that they have not (as yet) been studied sufficiently in the Information Retrieval or Information Science research community. I discuss cognitive biases and their implications for search interaction in more detail in Chapter 14.

3.2.1.2 Mitigating Biases

Separating biases from actual relevance or searcher intent, which is often the desired goal of using behavioral data, can be challenging, both practically and theoretically. Methods to counteract these biases have been actively explored in recent years. One way to address bias is to interpret searcher clicks as relative feedback about pairs of results (Joachims, 2002; Radlinski and Joachims, 2005). The main premise is that clicks should be interpreted as a *relative* statement that a particular result is likely more relevant than another result that has been skipped over. This compensates for the presentation order by considering the order that results are observed by searchers; however, the preference information gleaned from the application of this method always opposes the original rank ordering (e.g., presenting the results in reverse order is ideal), making it difficult to use this data for ranking purposes.

The *FairPairs* method (Radlinski and Joachims, 2006) modifies the presentation of the search results to collect cleaner training data, while minimizing the impact on the quality of the search results that are presented. Another similar approach is *interleaving* (Chapelle et al., 2012), which merges search results from multiple ranking algorithms. These methods operate under the assumption that the presentation of search results and other potential biases can be controlled in much the same way as other forms of experimentation (Hinkelmann and Kempthorne, 1994), where the goal in this case is to learn unbiased data for machine learning purposes. FairPairs flips adjacent pairs of results in the search engine ranking according to a randomized scheme. This allows for the capture of implicit feedback providing relevance judgments that are unaffected by presentation bias. However, this does rely on the randomization being performed online in the active search engine with real searchers. This method is not applicable retrospectively to historic log data, because it relies on being able to manipulate the ranking of the search results *at presentation time*. When we seek to remove bias from log data, one of the most effective methods is to focus solely on the top-ranked search result, which is assumed always to be considered by the searcher (an assumption that is validated by eye-gaze tracking studies [Joachims et al., 2007]). Other methods are emerging that allow for the removal of biases from historic logs using counterfactual analysis (Li et al., 2011), and these methods can have utility in the evaluation of online evaluation methods such as interleaving (Radlinski and Craswell, 2013), which are discussed in more detail in Chapter 10.

3.2.2 Satisfaction

Satisfaction is a personal belief that captures how positively searchers view their experience. The concept has been explored in a range of different domains, including marketing (Oliver, 2010) and psychology (Seligman and Csikszentmihalyi, 2000). Oliver et al. (1980) verified that post-purchase consumer satisfaction is a function of pre-purchase consumer expectation and the disconfirmation after purchase (the discrepancy between perceived and expected utility of the product). The disconfirmation factor suggests that we can explain searcher satisfaction by comparing actual search outcomes to expected search outcomes. Within information search, there is significant literature on estimating task success or failure from online search behavior. According to Su's review (Su, 1992), Cleverdon first proposed the use of satisfaction in a search content in the 1970s, as an alternative to system-oriented metrics. Kelly (2009) reviewed a definition: "satisfaction can be understood as the fulfillment of a specified desire or goal." When evaluating search systems, satisfaction can be determined regarding not only the holistic search experience but also some specific aspects (Su, 2003) – for example, the precision or completeness of the results, system response time, caption formatting, and general appearance of the interface. Although success and satisfaction may not always be correlated, an assumption that is often made is that if a searcher completes their task successfully, then they are likely to be satisfied. Being able to predict from search interaction behavior when searchers are either satisfied or successful is important for search providers in analyzing search system performance, and in particular, in identifying the specific circumstances (e.g., classes of queries, search topics, or types of search task) around which search engine performance can be improved via, for example, focused feature engineering or tailored interface enhancements.

People's satisfaction with generic information systems has been studied extensively in the context of management information systems. These studies focused on developing valid instruments (schemes of designing questionnaires) for measuring satisfaction. They usually adopted a factorized approach. For example, Bailey and Pearson (1983) and Ives et al. (1983) developed and validated an instrument involving thirty-nine factors. McKinney et al. (2002) developed an instrument for customer satisfaction in eCommerce with thirty-four factors related to information and system quality. These studies provide exhaustive enumerations of the factors that contribute to customer satisfaction, but still do not explain satisfaction in a principled way.

In economics, there is a close relationship between satisfaction and utility. For example, Mankiw (2010) introduced utility as "a person's subjective measure of well-being or satisfaction." Marshall (2009) equates both the utility of products and consumer's satisfaction with product purchases to the price that the consumer is willing to pay for the product. Satisfaction can therefore be defined in terms of utility. For example, Su (2003) defined utility as a measure of worth of search results versus time, physical effort, and mental effort expended. This suggests that searcher satisfaction as a compound measure of multiple factors, including search outcome and search effort (Jiang et al., 2015). Similarly, Yilmaz et al. (2014) also confirmed the impact of searcher effort on document relevance and utility.

Methods that have been used to measure satisfaction correlating search behavior, such as search-result clicks and dwell time for clicks, with either self-reported success or labels of success provided by expert judges. Fox et al. (2005) developed an instrumented browser to determine whether there was an association between explicit ratings of satisfaction and implicit measures of searcher interest and identified the measures that were most strongly associated with searcher satisfaction. They found that there was a relationship between search activity and search satisfaction ratings, and that search-result click-through, dwell time, and session termination activity combined to make good predictors of satisfaction for Web pages. In their study, Fox and colleagues also found that short dwell times and clicking many (four or more) search results for a query were both indicators of dissatisfaction.

Sequences of queries can be modeled at different levels of granularity, specifically at the level of search *sessions*, or search *tasks*, which are atomic information needs. Behavioral patterns can be used to predict searcher satisfaction for search sessions.

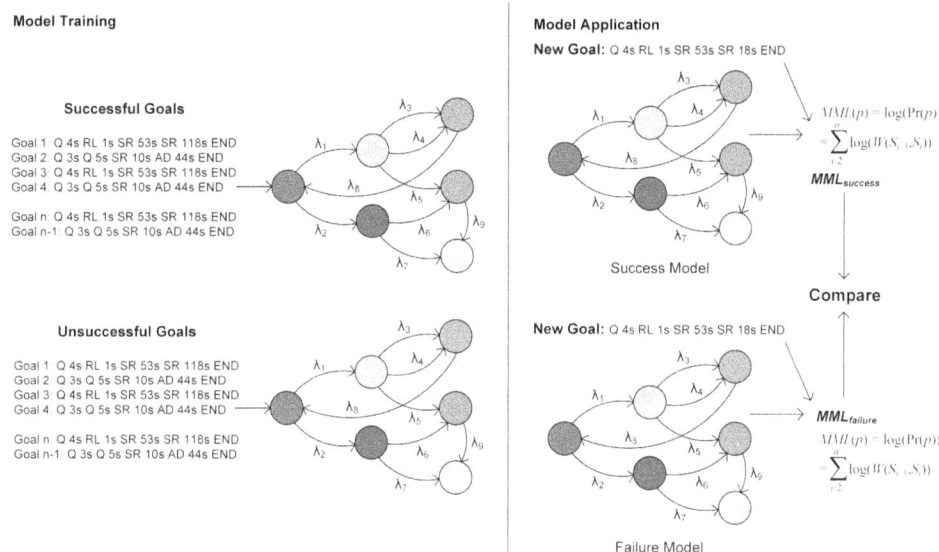

Figure 3.2. Hidden Markov Model representation of a satisfaction model. Based on models described in Hassan et al. (2010). Used with permission.

Huffman and Hochster (2007) found a relatively strong linear correlation between session satisfaction and the relevance of the first three results returned for the first query in a search task. Hassan et al. (2010) built models of searcher behavior to estimate search success on a session level independent of the relevance of documents retrieved by the search engine, considering inter-query relationships and other factors such as clicks during the course of the search session. We might expect to observe multiple queries with overlap in cases for which searchers are dissatisfied with the search experience and struggling to find the information that they seek.

Although tasks are potentially more coherent than sessions, they are more challenging to identify because they require more sophisticated modeling than is possible with the standard inactivity timeout. Figure 3.2 presents an example of a Hidden Markov Model from Hassan et al. (2010), where the nodes denote specific actions and the edges denote transition probabilities.

These models can be learned from labeled data captured in situ using browser toolbars, where volunteer searchers provide explicit data on their level of satisfaction at the termination of their search task (Hassan et al., 2011). Other mechanisms, such as online games, collect data at the coarse level of multiple actions (sessions) rather than individual actions (Ageev et al., 2011). One drawback of such methods is that they provide satisfaction labels at a high/abstract level (task or session), limiting the generalizability of the data collected to other scenarios in which task or multi-action sequences are being considered.

At the finer-grained level of individual actions, searcher satisfaction can be estimated through dwell time on landing pages, SERP click-through, re-querying immediately after visiting a search result (Hassan, 2012) or any action in the session (Wang et al., 2014b). Time spent on landing pages can be highly predictive of satisfaction. Short dwell times suggest that searchers are dissatisfied with the page. Empirical analysis has revealed that searchers can adopt a "screen and glean" approach, assessing the page content in less than five seconds (the screen phase), and sticking with the page for a longer time if the content appears to be of interest (the glean phase; see Liu et al., [2010]). Estimations of satisfaction levels do not need to be binary; they can be modeled as a likelihood (see, e.g., Hassan [2012]). Beyond desktop settings, research on satisfaction on mobile devices – such as smartphones – has emerged, capitalizing on signals including viewport coordinates and touch interactions (Guo et al., 2013; Lagun et al., 2014b). As search on mobile devices and across devices becomes more prevalent, interest in cross-device satisfaction modeling will increase. For example, Wang et al. (2014) found that many transitions (switches) from smartphones to mobile devices involved the same query on both devices and occurred within a short period of time, suggesting dissatisfaction with the search experience on mobile devices; a similar conclusion has also been reached in non-search settings (Karlson et al., 2010). Research on satisfaction modeling has also been expanded to non-search settings, such as the evaluation of intelligent personal assistants, specifically for Cortana, Microsoft's intelligent personal assistant (Jiang et al., 2015).

Despite the complexity, satisfaction has historically been modeled as a binary variable in its measurement within search systems. Jiang et al. (2015) present the first study of *graded* search satisfaction in the context of Web search. They analyze search sessions mined from search engine logs and annotated by third-party judges. Although the third-party annotation methodology is not ideal given the subjectivity of satisfaction (in situ judgments from searchers could be more accurate, but also more disruptive), it does offer a way for search engines to obtain labeled data. Jiang and colleagues observe clear differences in search behavior in sessions with different satisfaction levels. Given the presence of these differences, they built a predictive model to estimate graded search satisfaction more accurately than existing satisfaction modeling methods via search outcomes and searcher effort, both independently and in combination.

An important aspect of search satisfaction is the performance of the search engine. If the engine is performing poorly, then it is less likely that searchers will be satisfied with their experience. Engine performance can be assessed using traditional methods such as human relevance judgment (which has a long history in information retrieval [see Buckley and Voorhees, 2004]), but this can be costly at scale, and it is also difficult to cover a sufficiently broad range of information needs to allow meaningful metrics about the performance of search systems to be derived. Alternative methods of predicting query performance involve use of the query, the results, associated searcher behaviors, and other factors, such as the relatedness of the results, all of which are explored in more detail in Section 3.2.5.

3.2.2.1 Search Abandonment

Abandonment occurs when searchers do not click on any of the results returned by the search engine. It can be used as a measure of searcher satisfaction (Li et al., 2009; Diriye et al., 2012; Song et al., 2014). Defining abandonment can be difficult because there are many ways in which searchers can abandon a SERP: (1) clicking on a query suggestion; (2) closing the browser window; (3) clicking to another vertical (e.g., Images, News); or (4) an inactivity timeout, whereby the searcher does not engage with the SERP within a time window. Searchers may abandon the SERP because they are satisfied with the contents of the page (e.g., a direct answer on the SERP or an answer appearing on the text of the result snippet satisfied their needs directly); this is referred to as "good abandonment" (Li et al., 2009) and was found to be common in both desktop and mobile search. Huang et al. (2011) showed that there were differences in the mouse cursor movement patterns depending on whether or not the answer to a searcher's question appeared in the captions on the SERP. Cursor-based signals have been used as features in the development of learned models to accurately predict abandonment rationales (Diriye et al., 2012). Song et al. (2014) showed that abandonment rationales could transcend multiple queries (e.g., a query with bad abandonment, where searchers do not engage because they are dissatisfied with the search experience [Li et al., 2009] is likely to be preceded by another bad abandonment query). Abandonment signals can also be used for applications beyond satisfaction modeling, such as reducing anticipated future abandonment by learning to re-rank search results (Das Sarma et al., 2008).

3.2.2.2 Individualized Models

Personalized models of search satisfaction have been developed to capture differences between individuals or within searcher cohorts. Because satisfaction is a personal belief, it seems reasonable to build models for each person if possible, especially as there can be large individual differences in metrics used to estimate satisfaction, such as dwell time on landing pages (Hassan and White, 2013). Isolating the aspects of behavior that are associated with the individual rather than the search task (which has also been shown to contribute to behavioral differences [Byström and Järvelin, 1995; Thatcher, 2008; Liu et al., 2010]) is an important area of research that needs more attention. *Task-dependent* models of search satisfaction could lead to significant gains in estimates of satisfaction over global models and even personal models. Once behaviors and resources associated with satisfied outcomes are identified, search providers can apply those findings to identify failure cases, and even automatically improve the performance of the search engine for these underperforming queries (Hassan et al., 2013).

3.2.2.3 Search Frustration Models

Searchers experiencing difficulty in finding the information they seek may manifest *frustration* in their search behavior and other signals (including physiological indicators). Frustration is a negative emotional response related to anger and disappointment that arises from perceived resistance to the fulfillment of a goal. In search situations, this may be related to struggle in completing a particular search task. While satisfaction and frustration are closely related, they are distinct. Searchers may ultimately satisfy their information needs but still be frustrated in the process (Ceaparu et al., 2004). Frustration may therefore need to be considered separately in developing models of searcher behavior. With richer sensing (such as affective monitoring and feedback, discussed in Chapter 5), systems can also build models of other aspects of the search process that we might expect to vary more on an individual basis. Modeling frustration accurately may require physiological sensors, such as those used in affective models, to measure signals such as galvanic skin response and heart rate. Historically, these sensors have been costly and cumbersome to wear, impacting the experience for experimental participants and biasing experimental results. However, wearable devices such as the Microsoft Band[3] (pictured in Figure 3.3) can collect a range of physiological

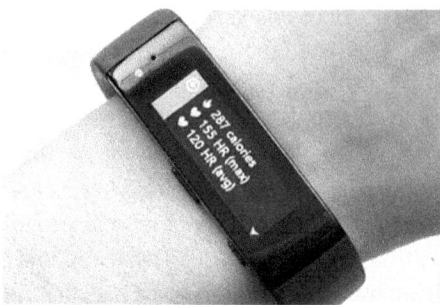

Figure 3.3. Microsoft Band wearable device worn on wrist. Illustration shows the heart rate of the user collected during activity, both maximum and average, as well as the total number of calories burned.

signals (such as heart rate, galvanic skin response, and skin temperature), and can gather and record these data with minimal annoyance to searchers and minimal interference with people's search activity.

Devices such as the Microsoft Band could be used by researchers during user studies as a low-cost, unobtrusive alternative to more sophisticated monitoring methods, and as a way to collect physiological signals during searching that could be shared with a search system to model frustration and other emotions in concert with behavioral signals such as queries and clicks.

Kanoulas et al. (2011) and Xie and Cool (2009) have studied frustration in information-seeking settings, but have not attempted to model frustration in a way that could be utilized directly by search engines. Feild et al. (2010) developed methods to predict searcher frustration from behavioral signals gathered during the search process. They assigned searchers difficult information-seeking tasks and monitored their degree of frustration via query logs and physiological sensors. Feild and colleagues found that behavioral features such as the total duration of the session and query complexity were effective predictors of searcher frustration. These aligned with features that were shown to be useful in predicting search engine switching – that is, the voluntary transition between different engines. White and Dumais (2009) (and others, e.g., [Heath and White, 2008; Laxman et al., 2008]) demonstrated that there are behavioral patterns – such as query sequences with no intervening clicks – that help predict search engine switches. Being able to estimate frustration from search activity alone is a promising direction, primarily because of the potential to scale models of frustration that are based on searcher activity well beyond the pool of searchers whose physiological state can be monitored in detail.

Care taken in interpreting behavioral signals for signs of frustration. Although issuing multiple similar queries can be a frustration signal, the searcher may also simply be exploring different aspects of a particular topic (Marchionini, 2006a). Distinguishing between different rationales embodied in similar information-seeking behaviors is important in interpreting behavioral data. Models capable of accurately distinguishing between contrasting explanations can be constructed by considering features such as the extent of the overlap between consecutive queries in the search session (Hassan Awadallah et al., 2014). By considering the motivation for the observed sequences

Table 3.1. *Data sources and applications for the relevance models. Surface ranking refers to the use of signals from interactions with SERPs. Deeper ranking describes the use of signals from result clicks* and *from subsequent search trails traversed by searchers post click*

	Trigger	
Source	*Query*	*Document*
Individual Web page	Surface ranking (result clicks only; improved precision in ranking already high-ranked results)	Page or website recommendation
Sequence of Web pages (trail)	Deeper ranking (result clicks plus other resources from trail; improved recall from finding new resources)	Guided navigation (pre-fetching, guided tours)

of queries with and without result click-through, more accurate models of search satisfaction can be developed.

3.2.3 Relevance

Relevance is a complex and multi-faceted concept that has been studied in detail in the information retrieval and information science communities (Saracevic, 1975; Schamber, 1994; Mizzaro, 1997). An important use of behavioral data is in the identification of relevant resources globally (Joachims, 2002; Agichtein et al., 2006) and individually (Tan et al., 2006; Dou et al., 2007). Aggregated and individual search behavior can be used to identify Web pages that are relevant for a particular query based on logged visits to those pages. Relevance models capture the resources that are relevant to a particular query. The most common way of doing this is to mine query-document pairs from the search logs, and order the URLs within the query based on their popularity. This can be an effective way of capturing the common intents that people may have when they issue particular queries (e.g., 95% of searchers who issue the query [facebook] want to log on to the facebook.com website; see White and Huang [2010]). Of course, the approach is ineffective if the searcher actually has a less dominant intent when issuing the query (e.g., for the searchers who query for [facebook] to learn more about the company or check the stock prices), and in these cases additional information about searchers and their context (e.g., their short- and long-term search histories) may be needed to disambiguate search intentions. If there is insufficient signal, searchers may need to re-query to perform the disambiguation. Because searchers tend to repeat their behaviors, long-term search histories might be a particularly useful signal in predicting which resources to suggest (Tyler and Teevan, 2010; Teevan et al., 2011b). Rather than relying solely on interactions on SERPs, search engines may also leverage the behavior of their searchers after they depart from the engine. As described in Chapter 2, client-side applications such as browser toolbars are needed to track searchers' behavior once they leave the search engine. Table 3.1 presents the various types of relevance model and the data sources that can populate the models in each case. There are two main types of trigger (i.e., the cue for the model to be applied): a query and a document. In this section, I focus on the query triggers and postpone discussion of resource triggered scenarios to Chapter 6. Searcher behavior pertaining to the results returned at high-ranked positions by the search engine, called surface-level ranking can be used to build relevance models, but the opportunity for the search system to identify new resources is limited by what is returned by the engine. Deeper ranking also considers the trails that people follow after examining the search results. This reduces the dependence on the original ranking of the search engine, mitigating some of the biases inherent in result click data (see Section 3.2.1.1), and creates opportunity for new results that searchers locate through their own navigation activity to be included in the ranking. These data also provide a way in which un-crawled content can be discovered by search engines (Bai et al., 2011) and Web page quality can be estimated independent of search queries (Richardson et al., 2006).

3.2.3.1 Query-Document Based

Click records from search engines provide weak indications of relevance. Many of the applications of behavioral data for relevance modeling have focused on query-document pairs (with documents represented by a unique identifier such as a URL), specifically on the number of visits that a particular document receives for a query. Query-document pairs have been used as training data for search engine ranking algorithms (Joachims et al., 2002; Agichtein et al., 2006), or to identify definitive search results (Agichtein and Zheng, 2006), and have also been combined with querying activity as query *chains* of related queries connected to the same terminal resource (Radlinski and Joachims, 2005). Query-click data to order search results has utility within intranet sites such as university search engines (Kemp and Ramamohanaroa, 2002), as well as in commercial search engines which receive significantly more usage. It also has utility for related retrieval scenarios, such as the ranking of human experts given search log data from enterprises (Macdonald and White, 2009).

There may be multiple intents associated with a query, meaning that any relevance signal for query may be directed at multiple documents. These queries are said to have a high click entropy (Dou et al., 2007). This is often the case for informational queries, which can require special treatment emphasizing diversity in the ranking such that multiple search intentions could be satisfied with the results retrieved. In such cases, methods to promote particular results for particular searchers are needed (e.g., personal navigation [Teevan et al., 2011b]). Despite these potential shortcomings, there are many frequently issued queries (navigational and otherwise) when search behavior effectively captures the dominant intent of the vast majority of searchers, and using aggregated query-documents evidence in those circumstances may be sufficient to satisfy most searchers' needs. In Chapter 9, I examine the *risks* involved in personalizing and contextualizing result ranking – a topic of increased interest and importance.

Strategies to expand the range of results that can be associated with a particular query include fuzzy matching to find similar search queries based on similarity measures such as Levenshtein distance or term overlap (Radlinski and Joachims, 2005; Hassan Awadallah et al., 2014), sophisticated task modeling to find other searchers attempting similar search tasks (Hassan et al., 2010; Lucchese et al., 2013a; Lucchese et al., 2013b; Liao et al., 2012; White et al., 2013a), and cohort identification (Teevan et al., 2009b; Yang et al., 2014). Clustering and random walks on the search engine click-through graph – the mapping from queries to result clicks that can be mined from log data – can be used to find alternative resources that have been visited by searchers issuing similar queries (Beeferman and Berger, 2000; Craswell and Szummer, 2007). Algorithms for such methods may include the following few steps:

1. Start with a seed query (or seed set of queries) of interest (Q).
2. Mine historic search log data and identify the clicked results for (Q).
3. Find other queries (Q') that also lead to clicks on the same set of results (sometimes referred to as "co clicks"). These associated queries are assumed to capture some aspects of the search intent as the original query. Stop here if the goal is to find similar queries, otherwise continue to step 4.
4. Identify the results that are clicked for (Q'). Stop here if the goal is to find an expanded set of results that are related (to varying degrees) to Q.

Beeferman and Berger (2000) employed agglomerative clustering, whereby the query-click graph is iteratively compressed, one query and clicked search result at a time. An advantage of this method is that it can discover related queries (pages) that are not necessarily connected by the same page (query). Rather than focusing on individual query-document pairs, the *query chains* method (Radlinski and Joachims, 2005) focuses on behavioral sequences within the same search session. The queries in the sequences that precede a URL visit can be associated with the destination document, and are applied to direct searchers who issue *any* of the queries in the chain to that terminal document, on the assumption that the searcher ultimately wanted to reach a particular result, and the intermediate, unsuccessful queries were all alternative representations of the same underlying intent. Other research has also assumed that terminal documents can reflect searchers' underlying information goals (Downey et al., 2008). The queries in the chain are those that are interrelated per various definitions of query similarity (term overlap, cosine distance, etc.). By considering all these variants in addition to the ultimate successful query, search engines can provide better quality ranking for a greater proportion of the search queries that they receive.

Such methods for fuzzy matching are related to the vocabulary problem (Furnas et al., 1987) in which people have difficulty in searching because they express their information needs in a way different than similar concepts are expressed in documents. This can happen for a number of reasons, including a lack of subject matter expertise. The problem has also been identified in domains outside search, including command line interfaces, where people may use different instructions to refer to the same machine operation. Reisner (1963; 1966) described the creation of an adaptive thesaurus, connecting terms and their synonyms. Extending this work to term-object pairs in computer systems, Furnas (1985) described an adaptive *index*, whereby terms map to particular objects – tailored to a particular application context that learned a mapping between variants (different language) and actual instructions. Analysis of query chains adopts a similar rationale, although the mapping is from query-{result} rather than query-query. I discuss applications of other similar ideas, such as document annotation and query suggestion, in Chapter 5.

3.2.3.2 Query-Trail Based

Studies of Web search behavior have shown that a significant fraction of search activity during search sessions involves content resident on Web pages accessed on the search trails that searchers traverse once they depart from the search engine (Teevan et al., 2004; White and Drucker, 2007; Bilenko and White, 2008). Implicit feedback algorithms that focus solely on search engine interactions miss out on this potentially valuable data source. Search interaction behavior along these trails can be used to identify potentially useful resources in several ways:

- **Reinforce existing (visited) results (improve precision):** Provide a more reliable estimate of the utility associated with a particular click based on searcher behavior after that click. For example, if we observe a searcher selecting a hyperlink on the page that he or she gets to, then we can more strongly weight interaction behavior pertaining to that result. Agichtein et al. (2006) used limited post-query browsing behavior to train a search engine ranking algorithm and showed that search effectiveness improved as a result.

- **Identify (new) relevant information sources (improve recall):** One significant drawback of many of the previous approaches is that they are mainly trying to learn behavior for *seen* (already observed) queries, rather than handling unseen (new) queries, which constitute a significant fraction (possibly more than half) of the traffic that search engines receive. Rather than reinforcing the result clicks, documents to which searchers browse can be mined to improve result ranking. Bilenko and White (2008) demonstrate that searchers' post-search browsing activity strongly reflects implicit endorsement of visited pages, which allows estimation of topical relevance of Web resources by mining large-scale data sets of search trails. They presented heuristic and probabilistic algorithms for suggesting authoritative websites for search queries. A detailed experimental evaluation shows that exploiting complete post-search browsing trails outperforms alternatives in isolation (e.g., click-through logs), and yields accuracy improvements when employed as a feature in learning to rank for Web search applications. Other research has leveraged searchers' recent browsing activity for personalization purposes (e.g., Liebling et al., 2012; Ustinovsky and Serdyukov, 2013).

Several algorithms based on automated machine learning methods have been proposed for creating adaptive ranking functions that combine many sources of evidence, including those provided by other rankers. Burges et al. (2005) developed a ranking algorithm based on neural networks (their seminal research is covered in more detail later in this chapter); Richardson et al. (2006) utilized many searchers' interactions with Web domains to improve their static rank (an assessment of the quality of the page used by search engine ranking algorithms in ranking results), independent of search queries or hyperlink structure; Agarwal et al. (2006) proposed the combination of random walks over the link graph with relevance feedback information; and Agichtein and Zheng (2006) used classification techniques and machine learning algorithms to incorporate click-through evidence into the selection of the top-ranked result. The top result has particular significance in SERP examination because results at that position are almost always considered by searchers when examining lists of results, irrespective of result relevance (Joachims et al., 2005).

It is possible to combine evidence from trails originating with queries with those originating from document visits (the right column in Table 3.1). In a similar way to how query chains connect queries based on query term overlap, salient Web resources can be identified using *resource overlap* between search and browse trails to extend search trails in multiple directions – effectively connecting a network of sites that were visited, or could have been visited, for each query. This improves trail coverage and also facilitates the application of trails in other applications such as recommendation, where credit may be given for the suggestion of surprising or interesting content.

Searchers' interaction behavior is sensitive to changes in the relevance of search results. Song et al. (2013) performed a longitudinal analysis of searcher engagement (e.g., average daily sessions per user, average queries per session, average query length, and average click-through rate) for two searcher groups: (1) a treatment group whose result relevance was intentionally degraded, and (2) a control group whose results were unchanged from the underlying ranker. The authors showed that there were differences in the short- and long-term behaviors of the two groups (e.g., engagement in the group with degraded relevance *increased* in the short-term because searching required more effort, but decreased in the long-term as searcher trust decreased). They also showed that these engagement signals could be used to learn predictive models to estimate the long-term impact of relevance degradation on searcher engagement.

Different searchers may have different conceptions of relevance given the same query (Pitkow et al., 2002; Teevan et al., 2005). User interest models can be personalized to particular searchers and their search situations to handle cases in which a searcher possesses non-dominant intent or for which the additional information available in short- and long-term search histories can further enhance search effectiveness beyond what is possible from popularity alone (Tan et al., 2006; Shen et al., 2005a). This can involve modeling the prior interactions with the search engine or even previous browsing data. These models can be based on the documents themselves, or there can be different levels of abstraction for example, considering the topic of the document allows for richer modeling of search interests (White et al., 2010; Bennett et al., 2010; 2012). Personalization (to the searcher, typically based on signals mined from their long-term search and browse history) and contextualization (to the current search situation, typically short term – focused on the current search query or the search session comprising recent interactions), is an important area of research that has received significant attention. I discuss personalization and contextualization in search engines in more detail in Chapter 9.

3.2.4 Re-finding and Revisitation

Search tasks can span multiple sessions and searcher interests can persist over time over time. Inspecting long-term search behavior shows that repeat queries are common (Aula et al., 2005a; Capra and Pérez-Quiñones, 2005; Teevan, 2007). For example, Teevan et al. (2007) showed that 33% of search queries have been issued previously by the same searcher. More generally, a number of studies have reported that re-accessing information is common. This analysis has been performed using a mixture of log studies (Cockburn and McKenzie, 2001; Herder, 2005; Obendorf et al., 2007; Tauscher and Greenberg, 1997) and survey analysis (Aula et al., 2005a; Kellar et al., 2007;

Sellen et al., 2002). Revisitation was found to occur frequently, with 50–80% of Web surfing involving revisitation to previously visited pages, even after a significant amount of time has passed between the visits (Obendorf et al., 2007). This has led to the development of taxonomies of searcher intentions, goals, and strategies associated with revisitation (Morrison et al., 2001; Kellar et al., 2007), and also a range of various types of support, which I discuss more later.

Two notable and recent large-scale studies of revisitation were performed by Adar et al. (2008), who analyzed large-scale revisitation behaviors using logs from a search engine toolbar. Through their analysis, the researchers identified twelve types of revisitation behavior, corresponding to four groups and based on the length of the time interval between revisits – that is, *fast* (<1 hour), *medium* (hourly or daily), *slow* (>1 day), and hybrid (similar to more than one group). They derived a number of design implications, including some specific to search engines – for example, emphasizing consistency in search results (Teevan, 2007). They also found that revisitation was correlated with the extent of the meaningful change in the page, with pages that changed in some significant way (e.g., news websites posting a new story) were likely to be revisited more frequently. In follow-up work, Adar et al. (2009) targeted the relationship between the dynamics of Web content and the frequency of revisitation. They showed that different revisitation patterns resonated with different kinds of changes.

3.2.5 Other Models

Turning attention to emerging trends in information-seeking research, search providers need to support both individual search queries (ad hoc retrieval), as well as search *tasks*. Search systems must support task completion, including modeling the search process within and between search sessions, and estimating the difficulty of search tasks.

3.2.5.1 Modeling Simple and Complex Search Tasks

The focus in search interaction modeling has been focused traditionally on activities occurring within the same search session. Sessions defined via inactivity timeouts (or in other ways) can be noisy. There has been a recent growth in interest in research on modeling coherent search tasks based on features such as overlap between queries (Radlinski and Joachims, 2005; Jones and Klinkner, 2008). Once the tasks have been identified then they can be used for a variety of the modeling activities already described in this chapter, including relevance modeling and satisfaction modeling (Hassan et al., 2010). Models of the current searcher's task and other people's tasks can be learned from search logs (White et al., 2013a). These models can be used to recommend relevant resources to others attempting the same task, leading to relevance gains over query-based systems that ignore the more complete task context.

Ingwersen and Järvelin (2005) defined models of tasks at varying levels of abstraction. The work task, viewed as the catalyst behind search activity, provides a problem context within which the searcher operates. Within the context of a single task, searchers perform sub-tasks, designed to reach their goals incrementally. As part of this process, they must divide their larger work tasks into smaller tasks and tackle each in sequence or, if possible, in parallel. The division of complex tasks into manageable sub-tasks has been referred to as "selfsourcing" (Teevan et al., 2014a), given its similarities to crowdsourcing, which assigns small subtasks to many individuals. For work tasks that are complex or poorly defined, however, it can be difficult for searchers to divide the task into manageable chunks, because the information required to accomplish that task cannot be determined in advance (Byström and Järvelin, 1995; Vakkari 1999). There are both simple and complex task models:

- **Simple task models (typically within-session):** Simple tasks are often performed within a single search session. The user can complete the task in this time and may well desire to do so. Session is used as a crude approximation for a search task in the absence of more sophisticated models. However, multi-tasking during search is common (Spink et al., 2006), and this can lead to interwoven task histories that are difficult to disentangle. Methods are emerging to tackle task segmentation, and – by using features such as query content – reasonable accuracy can be attained (e.g., Liao et al., 2012).
- **Complex task models (typically between-session):** There are some, usually complex tasks that persist over time. These tasks may span multiple search sessions and contain multiple aspects. These tasks present a challenge to users of search systems but also an opportunity to support users engaged in these tasks (Villa et al., 2009). Focusing on the temporal dimension more than complexity, support may be needed to help users resume these tasks, including pre-fetching relevant material on the same or different devices (Kotov et al., 2011; Wang et al., 2013). One of the important requirements in such resumption support is being able to predict that a searcher will resume a task at some point in the future. Research has shown that topic is important in deciding whether search tasks will be resumed at a later date (Agichtein et al., 2012). There is also the reverse problem (looking back in time rather than forward) of attributing historic search activity to the current search task – for example, which, if any, of the searcher's long-term search history pertains to the current task. This can be useful for applications such as search personalization, where personalization algorithms can perform better if they focus on the task-relevant subset of the searchers' long-term activity (White et al., 2013).

3.2.5.2 Modeling Task Difficulty

Earlier in this section, I discussed the related concepts of satisfaction and frustration. Both of these can be related to properties of the search task, specifically the difficulty of the task being attempted. As such, *task difficulty* has been a focus of research on search behavior. Aula et al. (2010) examined the behavior of searchers engaged in challenging closed informational search tasks for which the answer was difficult to find. They examined search behavior in two studies – a usability study and an online study – and showed that there were differences in search behavior when searchers were experiencing difficulty in finding related information. Specifically, in these difficult tasks, searchers applied more advanced operators, spent longer on the SERP (both on average in terms of maximum time, and overall in terms of proportion of their total time on task), and issued the longest search query toward the middle of the search session.

Other research on the effects of task difficulty on search behavior has shown that beyond queries, there are other behavioral signals that can correlate with task difficulty.

For example, as task difficulty increases, the number of results viewed increases and average dwell time pages also increases (Liu et al., 2010a), as does the number of pages retained for later inspection (e.g., via bookmarking [Kim, 2006]). Gwizdka and Spence (2006) showed that the number of the unique Web pages visited, the time spent on each page, the degree of deviation from the optimal path, and the degree of the navigation path's linearity, were good predictors of subjective task difficulty. Beyond evidence present in the search activity, studies have also shown that signals of task difficulty are mediated by domain knowledge, and that should be considered when interpreting those signals (Liu et al., 2012). Information about domain expertise is typically unavailable to search engines, but it could be approximated from searchers' topical interests and the estimates of the reading difficulty of the pages that they view (Kim et al., 2012).

3.2.5.3 Modeling Query Performance

Related to search task difficulty is the challenge of query performance prediction. The performance of the search system can have a large impact on search outcomes. Smith and Kantor (2008) experimented with intentionally degraded search systems and showed that searchers were just as successful as on the original system if they altered the search behavior to adapt to the poor system performance. The authors suggested that behavioral signals may provide insight into the performance of search systems. Others have performed comparisons between searcher and system-based query performance predictions, allowing them to understand query performance prediction from the searcher's perspective. Hauff et al. (2010) showed a low degree of correlation between raters' predictions about the likely performance of queries and predicted performance. Because query performance predictors can be based on intuitions about how searchers might rate queries, researchers argue that more work is needed to understand the mismatch between the searcher and the system performance predictions.

Rather than estimating the difficulty that a searcher will experience in completing a search task, query performance prediction estimates the difficulty that a search engine will experience in satisfying a particular query. Being able to anticipate the performance of the search engine for a query enables the search engine to decide whether it should suggest alternative queries or devote additional computational resources to handling the query. Query performance prediction (QPP) methods can be classified according to the time that they perform the prediction, either *pre-retrieval* (before the retrieval of results) or *post-retrieval* (after one or more retrieval stages). The main difference between these types of QPP methods is the information to which they have access at prediction time and the impact that they can have on how the prediction is employed (e.g., pre-retrieval predictions can inform the searcher about the prediction).

Pre-retrieval methods have traditionally employed heuristics requiring the use of collection statistics to estimate the specificity of the query (He and Ounis, 2004; Scholer et al., 2004), using external data sources or clustering to detect query ambiguity (He et al., 2008), relatedness of the query terms to detect well-formed queries (Hauff et al., 2008), and the ease with which the system will be able to process the query based on the distribution of query terms across a large set of documents (Zhao et al., 2008). In recent years, search interaction data capturing historic interactions for the same or similar search queries has been used to tackle the query performance prediction challenge.

The signals used range from historic click-through and search engine switching statistics (Guo et al., 2010), to more sophisticated association rules based on lexical and topical attributes of the query that have been shown to outperform more traditional click-through-based methods (Kim et al., 2013).

Post-retrieval methods are employed after one or more result sets have been retrieved by the search system. A number of methods have been employed for this purpose. In one approach, differences between the result distribution and the collection – that is, to calculate a clarity score based on homogeneity (higher is better; see Cronen-Townsend et al. [2002]). Other approaches involve comparing against other result lists and computing their overlap (Yom-Tov et al., 2005), where higher overlap is associated with better quality queries – also, the documents can be perturbed to analyze its stability (again, higher is better; see Zhou and Croft [2006]). Other metrics – such as the diversity of the search results (Diaz, 2007) and the distribution of retrieval scores assigned to the returned documents – can also help with the prediction of query performance (Shtok et al., 2009). Moving beyond distributions of search results, others have considered the relationship *between* search results, specifically their hyperlink structure, to estimate the quality of the search results returned for a query (Leskovec et al., 2007).

Searcher behavior has also been shown to be a useful indicator of query performance. Guo et al. (2010) utilized search activity for this purpose, and found that interaction features mined from logs can significantly improve prediction performance. Kim et al. (2013) proposed a method to generate association rules by combining topical and lexical features from the query, and showed that the generated rules are effective for predicting query performance. Continuing this line of work, Kim et al. (2014) use multiple query attributes and also page attributes with the new objective of building better models of click dwell time and predicting click-level search satisfaction rather than query performance.

3.2.6 External Effects

The models described in this section have assumed that the same principles can be applied across all situations. Differences in search behavior attributable to task effects (Byström and Järvelin, 1995; Thatcher, 2008; Liu et al., 2010), individual differences (Saracevic, 1991; Ford et al., 2005; Cole et al., 2011), and, recently, device effects (Wang et al., 2013; Montañez et al., 2014) mean that care needs to be taken in developing and applying models of search interaction behavior. The device effects are particularly relevant to the theme of next-generation search technology. As I discussed earlier in the book, there has been a shift in usage patterns toward mobile computing over the past decade, meaning that mobile searching is also more prevalent. As such, models like those described in this subsection need to be re-framed and re-purposed for those domains – and new models may be needed. There is also a range of various signals available from natural search interactions that provide rich information about search satisfaction levels and the relevance of information encountered during the search process. Nascent research in this area leverages eye-gaze data and other data sources such as viewport location (Guo et al., 2013; Lagun et al., 2014b) to model satisfaction, but more research is required.

3.3 Components for Model Building

Many of the models described in the previous section rely on being able to make inferences about searcher intentions from recorded interaction data, typically collected on a large scale so that insights can be generalized across a broad range of different searchers and different search situations.

3.3.1 Data Representation

The focus of "data" in this book is on behavioral search interaction data associated with the pursuit of information in online repositories such as the Web, but also other collections, such as digital libraries. However, data are being generated from a multitude of different providers, each with their own representation of activity and unique identifiers for searchers. The units of data in these logs are individual search events, often connected with a query identifier (to associate all events from the same query instance), a session identifier (to connect all events from the same session), and a searcher identifier. Timestamps are also included so that the chronological sequence of events can be determined, along with additional contextual information such as the geolocation and system information about the device (e.g., operating system and version, Web browser). Given the data collected in this form, interaction sequences are mined and applied to construct representations of the data, including transition probabilities between different activity states (e.g., *Query* $\rightarrow$ *Query*, *Query* $\rightarrow$ *Click* and *Query* $\rightarrow$ *End*).

As next-generation search systems move toward the storage and application of richer data beyond just queries and clicks (e.g., mouse interactions, touch interactions, attention estimates, etc.), representation searcher activity data becomes more important. This includes the granularity with which the data are collected from searchers and the associated costs in doing so at different granularities. For example, the costs of recording every action (e.g., every cursor movement) and transmitting this data over the network can be substantial. Decisions need to be made about which are the most salient movements to capture and apply in modeling tasks (e.g., cursor hovers on AOIs, changes in cursor direction). Because every action does not have equal value in characterizing and modeling, search behavior data compression methods can be utilized – for example, for applications such as reducing the size of cursor tracking logs (Leiva and Huang, 2015). Such compression methods will become useful as the richness of search activity logs increases. Additionally, it is often more useful (e.g., for applications of log data such as better understanding search behavior) to record all activity from a sizeable subset of searchers (say 100,000 individuals) than a subset of actions from all searchers.

3.3.2 Data Volume

The scale at which data is being produced has grown dramatically in recent years. The world's technological per capita capacity to store information has roughly doubled every forty months since the 1980s (Hilbert and Lopez, 2011); as of 2012, every day 2.5 exabytes (2.5×10^{18}) of data were created (IBM, 2013). This information explosion creates both a challenge and an opportunity for the designers of search engines, who must make decisions about which content to index. Search engines currently use only queries and clicks mined from search logs to model search behavior. However, search interaction will become much richer, and there is a need for richer interaction models that also model searcher attention via methods such as gaze tracking in laboratory settings (and increasingly in the wild in natural settings) and cursor tracking at scale, as well as interactions beyond the search engine, such as the navigation trails that searchers are observed to follow. Data from social networks is also increasing (e.g., Facebook has more than 1 billion members and Twitter users post more than 250 million messages each day) and has applications in improving search systems by connecting users, providing a medium for question asking, and generating insights about population dynamics, human behavior, and global/local events (e.g., see Chapter 8). Searchable content is dynamic and changing over time, and data such as statistics, multimedia, sensor streams and biochemical sequences are becoming searchable and present their own set of challenges (Marchionini, 2006b).

3.3.2.1 Storing Big Data in the Cloud

The data that is emerging from these processes is so large and complex that it is impossible to process using on-hand database management tools or traditional data processing applications. Given its scale, large volumes of data are colloquially referred to as *big data*. The challenges of big data include capture, curation, storage, search, sharing, transfer, analysis, and visualization. Processing large amounts of data requires massively parallel software running on thousands or tens of thousands of servers. The definition of big data varies depending on the capabilities of the organization managing the dataset, and on the capabilities of the applications that are used to process and analyze the data.

Scientists regularly encounter limitations owing to large data sets in many areas, including meteorology, genomics, connectomics, complex physics simulations, and biological and environmental research. The limitations also affect Web search and finance and business informatics. At the time of writing, data sets that are feasible to process in a reasonable amount of time are on the order of exabytes of data. Data is increasingly being gathered by a range of devices, including smartphones, cameras, and wireless networks. As mentioned previously, the logged data comprises information on the resources that people access, as well as other information regarding the context in which that access occurs (e.g., location [Bennett et al., 2011]). This data can be useful for a range of applications, including improving search-result ranking and selecting advertisements based on predicted click-through rates (Richardson et al., 2007). Indeed, predicted click-through plays an important role in the online auctions that determine the price of SERP display advertisements, in determining which advertisements should be shown for the query, and the order in which advertisements should be shown on SERPs.

Although the availability of large volumes of data about interests and intentions is attractive for a variety of applications, search-related and otherwise, the data are collected from searcher populations that potentially are affected by a range of different sampling biases, including the fact that searchers are associated with a restricted population who may choose to use a particular service. Biases of this nature have already been noted in online services such as Twitter, which may not be reflective the general population (Kiciman, 2012). This bias may not be significant because the data are being applied to model users of the service and/or improve the specific service. However, if the data are being used to better understand humans or the world holistically, then a more complete understanding of biases in the data and the development of methods to account for that bias in any analysis of the data are necessary.

Related biases have been studied in the context of experimentation within social networks, where peer affects or social interactions (Manski, 2000) create interference and affect the outcomes for experiments. In such cases, outcomes for a treatment group could be impacted by other connected members, some of whom may also be exposed to the treatment and some of who may not (Eckles et al., 2015). Eckles and colleagues proposed methods to reduce this bias in the design and analysis of experiments involving people in connected settings such as social networks via randomization methods linked to the network structure (e.g., graph cluster randomization), as well as analysis methods that also consider the treatment assignment of network neighbors.

3.3.2.2 Processing Big Data

Methods for efficiently storing and processing large amounts of data have emerged, allowing analysis, such as the computation of correlations, to be performed at a scale previously unimaginable. Large data centers have been constructed to enable large volumes of interaction data to be collected from users of online services and mined for behavioral insights, including, where systems are lacking, and to identify resources of interest. The reduction in the price of storage and the development of technologies for processing large volumes of data have been key enablers for this transformation, as has the realization that there is significant value in storing and mining the data from online services to improve customer experiences.

Beyond simply possessing large amounts of storage and processing power, new algorithms need to be developed to enable the efficient analysis of this data. Streaming over data on a single machine does not scale to petabytes of data. Algorithms for the distributed processing of large data volumes are therefore needed. One such algorithm is *MapReduce*, a programming model for processing large data sets with a parallel, distributed algorithm on a cluster containing many machines (Dean and Ghemawat, 2008). A MapReduce program comprises a Map() procedure that performs filtering and sorting (such as sorting students by first name into queues, one queue for each name) and a Reduce() procedure that performs a summary operation (such as counting the number of students in each queue, yielding name frequencies). MapReduce orchestrates by marshalling the distributed servers, running the various tasks in parallel, managing all communications and data transfers between the various parts of the system. Redundancy, fault tolerance, and overall job management are also typically handled during job execution (Figure 3.4).

Managing the distribution of workload to many machines manually is clearly not feasible. When these methods are applied, we are typically dealing with large quantities of data. To control the operations that are performed with the data, languages such as SCOPE from Microsoft have been developed to simplify the analysis for data scientists. SCOPE is an SQL-like language that abstracts away many of the complexities of distributed computation (Chaiken et al., 2008). Alternatives exist, including Pig, a

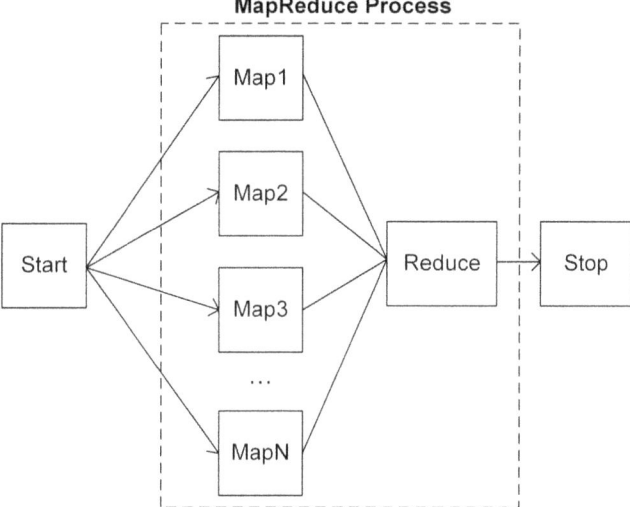

Figure 3.4. Schematic of the MapReduce process.

high-level platform for creating MapReduce programs with Hadoop, an open-source framework for storage and large-scale processing of data-sets on clusters of commodity hardware.

There are two main applications for the large volumes of data that can be collected and analyzed using these methods: data mining and machine learning.

- **Data mining** focuses on the discovery of unknown properties in data.
- **Machine learning** focuses on prediction, based on known properties learned from data.

The two areas overlap in many ways: data mining uses many machine learning methods, but with a different objective. Machine learning also employs data mining methods such as "unsupervised learning" or as a preprocessing step to improve learner accuracy, or to guide human intuition and inform feature generation. These are both very broad areas with highly active research communities. In the remainder of this section I touch on research in each of these areas, with a focus on their applications for the search domain, and in particular interactions with search systems.

3.3.3 Data Mining

Data mining, an interdisciplinary subfield of computer science, describes the computational process of discovering patterns in large data sets involving methods at the intersection of artificial intelligence, machine learning, statistics, and database systems. The overall goal of the data mining process is to extract information from a data set and transform it into an understandable structure for further use. Aside from the raw analysis step, it involves database and data management aspects, data pre-processing, model and inference considerations, interestingness metrics, complexity considerations, post-processing of discovered structures, visualization, and online updating. Broder et al.

(2014) identified three issues with the large volumes of data to which data mining can be applied, specifically: (1) many data points, (2) many dimensions, and (3) many clusters. These can be resolved via a number of different mechanisms, including sampling to handle data volume, dimensionality reduction to handle many dimensions, and efficient clustering algorithms. Many excellent summaries of data mining are available (Witten and Frank, 2005; Han et al., 2006).

3.3.3.1 Applications in Search

There are a number of applications of data mining in search systems. At a high level, search engines can mine the data collected from their users to better understand their search intentions and identify potential issues with their system. The following are two examples of how data mining techniques can be applied in the context of search to derive value from the behavioral data collected by search engines:

- **Problem identification:** Search engines can use data mining to identify salient patterns in user interaction behavior that can be indicative of a problem with the current system. For example, if a popular result has been inadvertently dropped from the search engine index, then we might observe an increase in engagement with other results. Click inversions, describing deviations from the standard click-through curve (covered in more detail later) can be used to identify issues with the search engine ranking algorithm. Inferences made from behavioral data could also be combined with feedback from other sources, such as the free-text feedback that some searchers elect provide to the search engine about its performance. An interesting area of future research is combining that free-form feedback with behavioral data to generate *actionable* insights about system performance, providing the search engine with the opportunity to improve its performance by understanding the *why* (from the feedback) in addition to the *what* (observed from behavior). Some progress has been made in the area of mining actionable insights from feedback data provided by search engine users (Dan et al., 2012).
- **Pattern mining:** Patterns of search interaction behavior that are observed to precede events of interest, such as engine switching (Laxman et al., 2008; White and Dumais, 2009), or be associated with particular searcher sentiments, such as satisfaction or frustration that can be used to inform the development of predictive models to anticipate these actions in real-time and be applied retrospectively on log data (Feild et al., 2010; Hassan et al., 2010). For example, if a search system could determine that searchers were more likely to switch to another engine given a particular sequence of interactions mined from the logs (e.g., a sequence of related queries with no result clicks), it could use that information to intervene proactively if that particular usage pattern is observed in real time in other searchers' interaction sequences.

Note that although large-scale data about searcher behavior can be used to compute metrics on search system performance (e.g., number of sessions per searcher per time period), this is not strictly data mining per the definition offered above because the metrics are known in advance and the data are only being used to populate the statistics in the metrics. However, data mining could be used earlier in the process to help analyze data streams and identify significant patterns of search behavior to inform the development of new metrics.

3.3.3.2 Best Practices for Log Mining

In mining large-scale behavioral data, data scientists need to make a number of decisions that can impact the outcomes of the data mining process. The methods used to mine logs in the context of search interaction depend largely on the application context, but a number of best practices should be followed to ensure that log-based insights are meaningful. These include:

- **Data source:** Consider the source of the data that is used and whether it provides access to the right type of signals for the analysis. If the interest is in monitoring queries and click-through, logs from a single search engine might be most appropriate – because it is likely that most or all of available search traffic will be recorded. In contrast, logs from client-side tools, such as browser toolbars, do capture behavior on a number of search engines, allowing both competitive analysis and analysis of browsing behavior to be performed, but the log data may be less complete (e.g., the data may be missing result lists and other information such as result content).
- **Bias:** Consider whether there are any biases in the data (all data sources are likely to have a bias of some sort), the extent to which the data are biased, and whether that bias affects the conclusions that can be drawn from the data. For example, the logs collected from a search engine toolbar might contain people who view a search engine's products more favorably, or who lack the technical skill or the willingness to uninstall that software. Those who use a particular browser may also represent a particular searcher cohort – which may in turn affect aspects of their online behavior, meaning that cohort is overly represented in the log data.
- **Market and vertical:** Consider the particular market and the vertical (Web, Images, News, etc.) to be analyzed. The market (e.g., the English United States locale) can be used to control for cultural and linguistic variations in search behavior. Additional classifiers can be applied to determine the language of the query text. Filtering to particular markets can help improve the efficiency of data processing jobs that stream through large quantities of data, because a large fraction of the data can be filtered out early in the analysis pipeline.
- **Data volume:** It is unlikely that all data from all logs is really necessary to draw reliable conclusions. Processing all queries takes additional time. Given millions or billions of records, it may be worth sampling a reasonable subset of the data that enables rapid processing on a distributed cluster, or even on a local machine. If some filtering is going to be performed, consider the expected number of matches and adjust the sample size accordingly. Sampling is particularly important during the development of analytical tools. Ideally the first phases of development would happen locally to allow for rapid iteration, before transitioning to a larger data set when working versions of analysis tools (e.g., scripts) are available.
- **Log duration:** Related to data volume is the duration of the log sample that is analyzed. Duration is dependent on overall usage of the service. However, one week of logs is the minimum amount required to perform meaningful analysis that factors out day-of-week effects For example, on weekends the search traffic may be lower and the search tasks may be different (e.g., more recreational). If longitudinal analysis is to be performed, then months of data may be needed, taking care to control for the impact of holidays, and external planned and unplanned

(e.g., news events) – events all of which will affect search behavior and subsequently, the findings of behavioral analysis. Ideally, for longitudinal studies, searchers would be aligned on a landmark query (e.g., their first search for a medication [White et al., 2014] or healthcare facility [White and Horvitz, 2014]) prior to further study. One advantage of this is that they can act as their own control in a contrastive analysis of pre- and post-landmark query search activity.

- **Externalities:** Following on from the previous point, care needs to be taken regarding the impact of external events on observed patterns in the search behavior. Media coverage can affect searching, which in turn can skew search behavior (Butler, 2013). Changes in the search engine ranking algorithms may also play a central role (Lazer et al., 2014).
- **Sampling:** There is a need to consider whether all interactions from a single searcher are important or whether multiple searchers' interactions for the same event are important. The former is important if we are performing longitudinal analysis of search behavior (and if we are, then per-searcher sampling and the log duration becomes critically important). The latter is important if we are considering different searchers' behaviors for the same query (e.g., in estimating click-through rate for a query, computing click-through entropy, etc.) or with the same resource.
- **Unit:** Sessions or impressions (i.e., queries plus associated clicks). Sessions can be identified using standard methods such as inactivity timeouts. In handling impressions, care needs to be taken to avoid over-counting. For example, user click results and then click backs might count as two queries, when it is just an artifact of the search interface. Other examples of such artifacts are pagination (clicking the "next" button), which is a function of how the system elects to present the results rather than a new query (there is likely a result-page number in the logs to allow these events to be filtered).
- **Searcher duration:** Related to the previous point, decisions need to be made about whether to limit analysis to independent queries, independent sessions or whether cross-session analysis is employed to track searchers longitudinally. Previous research has demonstrated the importance of longitudinal analysis, especially for tasks such as information maintenance (Kotov et al., 2011; Agichtein et al., 2012). Even once cross-session analysis has been selected, a decision still needs to be made about the duration of the active interrogation period, which may range from days to many months. Ultimately, this may be limited by the terms of use under which log data are retained.
- **Statistical testing:** Given the large sample sizes observed in logs, it is likely that even very small differences will be statistically significant. As has been noted in previous research, there is a difference between statistically significant differences and *meaningful* differences, and other measures – such as effect sizes (Cohen, 1988) – may be necessary to better understand those differences.

3.3.4 Machine Learning

Once the data has been mined and salient patterns have been extracted, the data can be applied for a range of applications. An easy way to do this is to manually formulate rules reflecting intuition about the nature of the patterns identified during data mining. For example, returning to my earlier discussion of searcher frustration, one might conjecture that a sequence of related queries with no intervening result selections is a strong indication that the searcher was frustrated with the search experience. Representing that pattern in a searchable form and identifying instances of its occurrence might be sufficient for some applications. For many cases, however, the rules are less apparent and it can be difficult to learn them manually. As such, *automated* learning methods need to be applied, falling under the broad label of machine learning.

Machine learning involves developing systems and algorithms capable of learning from data. It has been applied in a range of successful applications within the search domain, from learning to rank results by combining signals from multiple sources, including aggregate behavioral data, to modeling search satisfaction. Central to machine learning are representation and generalization. Representation of data instances and functions evaluated on these instances are part of all machine learning systems. Generalization is the property that the system will perform well on unseen data instances. Given the need to manage the uncertainty inherent in information seeking and use, I expect that the application of machine learning methods will play an important role in the future of search interaction beyond their application for search-result ranking that is their primary application at present.

The simplicity with which machine-learned models can be developed and applied using toolkits such as Weka[4] and Azure Machine Learning can fuel the integration of machine learning into a range of search-related applications. Much of the heavy lifting in this context lies in the generation of appropriate features and design of experiments to evaluate model performance (e.g., ensuring that we do not test on the training data). New machine learning algorithms in the context of search are fairly rare, although they can be impactful when they do emerge (Burges et al., 2005). A broad range of different learning algorithms have been developed, including logistic regression, support vector machines, and boosted regression trees. The specific model is often not hugely significant, although some models are inappropriate for the type of data studied, and some can better handle noisy or missing data. It is not my intention to provide a detailed description of machine learning methods in this book. For more detailed coverage of this topic, there are a number of excellent resources (Mitchell, 1997; Bishop, 2006; Murphy, 2012).

3.3.4.1 Feature Engineering

Often the most important parts of solving a problem using machine learning is developing effective features from which the system can learn (Domingos, 2012). Unlike the learning algorithms, feature engineering is domain specific, and the feature generation process must be performed manually. Although the generation process is manual, large numbers of features can be generated and the best performing subset of features can be automatically chosen for learning based on metrics such as information gain.

3.3.4.1.1 Feature Selection

The development of features is typically done by hand based on human intuition. Once a set of features has been established, the selection of a subset of those features can be performed automatically to remove redundant or irrelevant features. Feature selection – also known as variable selection, attribute selection, or variable subset selection – is the process of selecting a subset of relevant features for use in model construction. Redundant features are those that provide no more information than the currently selected features, and irrelevant features provide no useful information in any context. Feature selection techniques are often used in domains for which there are many features and comparatively few samples (or data points). There are a number of feature selection methods. The choice of evaluation metric heavily influences the algorithm, and it is these evaluation metrics which distinguish the three main categories of feature selection algorithms: (1) wrappers, (2) filters, and (3) embedded methods (Guyon and Elisseeff, 2003).

There are a number of benefits from using feature selection, including improved model interpretability, shorter training times, and enhanced generalization by reducing over-fitting to the training data. Feature selection is also useful as part of the data analysis process, because it reveals which features are important for prediction and how these features are related. This can be important in understanding the model that has been created by the training process, as well as developing compressed versions of more sophisticated versions of the model (fewer features) that are more suitable for deployment at scale. There are a number of valid reasons for going to production with simpler models, including reducing development costs, improving runtime efficiency, and better explicability of the predictions made, which is important in debugging its performance.

3.3.4.2 Learning Algorithms

There are a range of learning algorithms that can be applied to address challenges in next-generation search interaction. These are built around various sets of principles for how the models should learn. Many studies have shown little difference in the performance of these different algorithms. That said, because some models – such as multiple additive regression trees (MART; see Friedman [1999]) – are more robust to noisy data and are more efficient and easily distributable among many nodes, they are better suited for application in a distributed computing setting.

Learning algorithms can vary the type of input available during the training process, and can be grouped into three classes:

- **Supervised learning algorithms** are trained on labeled examples (i.e., input where the desired output is known). The supervised learning algorithm attempts to generalize a function or mapping from inputs to outputs which can then be used to speculatively generate an output for previously unseen inputs.
- **Unsupervised learning algorithms** operate on unlabeled examples (i.e., input where the desired output is unknown). In these algorithms, the objective is to discover structure in the data (e.g., through a cluster analysis), not to generalize a mapping from inputs to outputs.
- **Semi-supervised learning algorithms** combine *both* labeled and unlabeled examples to generate an appropriate function or classifier.

There are other types of machine learning algorithm that vary the nature of the learning task (e.g., transduction, reinforcement learning, etc.) that are not covered in detail in this book. The reader is advised to see the related literature for more details on these methods (Mitchell, 1997; Bishop, 2006; Murphy, 2012). Deep learning methods (e.g., Hinton and Salakhutdinov, 2006) model concepts at levels of abstraction different than traditional learning algorithms, leading to richer and more performant learned models.

Advances have been made in applying methods from deep learning to improve the search-result ranking globally for all searchers (Huang et al., 2013) and individually (Song et al., 2014).

Human intuition is essential to effectively guide the application of machine learning. Some machine learning systems attempt to eliminate the need for such intuition, while others adopt a collaborative approach. Human intuition cannot, however, be entirely eliminated from the learning process, because the system's designer must specify how the data is to be represented and what mechanisms will be used to search for a characterization of the data. Humans are therefore central to the learning process, even if they are not involved directly in the learning process (although there could be direct involvement in cases where *interactive* machine learning is practiced [Fogarty et al., 2008; Kapoor et al., 2010]).

3.3.4.3 Label Generation

The most commonly adopted learning method in search interaction involves supervised methods in which the desired output is known and it is the objective of the system to learn a generalizable model based on provided training data. A key aspect of the learning process is the generation of labeled training data, in particular, from where these data are sourced. The challenge of course is in obtaining reliable training data from which to learn models. Although the labels are traditionally provided by humans in many machine learning scenarios, this is not required; and, in some cases where it is likely that human judges would experience difficulty in performing the labeling, alternative sources for labeled data may be required. Generating labels based on implicit feedback is more scalable than manual labeling (e.g., positive cases are "satisfied" result clicks with dwell time of thirty seconds or more, and negative cases are "quickback" result clicks with short dwell times; for binary models, see, e.g., Bennett et al. [2011; 2012], Sontag et al. [2012], and Collins-Thompson et al. [2011]; for graded models, see, e.g., Ustinovskiy et al. [2015]). The disadvantage is that the quality of the judgments obtained has the potential to be lower and there is no control over the judgment process (i.e., it is impossible to define *a priori* what relevance means and have items labeled with per that definition – as would be the case in a human labeling effort). In addition, search behaviors can be affected by unforeseen effects and biases that can be difficult to account for when interpreting judgments (White, 2013).

Both judgment collection methods suffer drawbacks related to a lack of clarity in the information need. Human judges are often presented with a single query and need to make inferences about the relevance of pooled search results to those queries (where results are combined (pooled) across multiple search systems, see Section 3.3.4.3.1). This can be challenging if the search query is ambiguous. We see the queries and the clicks if behavioral data are used; but we still do not know the motivation behind the observed clicks, and the resource selected may be personal relevance to the searcher but not have the global relevance (for all or most searchers), which would be preferred for learning generic ranker. As I discuss later in the book (Chapter 9), personalized ranking models – trained to recognize contextual signals of particular use to the current searcher – may need to be developed. An advantage of machine-learned models is that once they are learned, their performance can be tuned to the particular application setting by varying the tradeoff between precision and recall. We can often improve the accuracy of a machine-learned model by sacrificing coverage of some search situations. For example, models of personal navigation (Dou et al., 2007; Teevan et al., 2011b) target specific situations in which people repeat the same query and click on the same result more than a few times in their search history. A machine-learned model can learn that if it sees that specific query again, that result should be promoted for that query. Although the coverage of this method is low (only a small fraction of search queries are covered), it is highly accurate. Live experiments have shown that searchers almost always select the personal-navigation result when it is promoted to the top of the ranked list.

3.3.4.3.1 Labels in Search

In search settings, training data consists of queries and documents matched with the relevance degree of each match. It may be prepared manually by human assessors, who examine search results for some queries and determine relevance of each result. It is not feasible to check the relevance of all documents for these queries, and it is not clear that this is necessary. Searchers typically only review the first page of results for a query and rarely paginate to other result pages (meaning that relevance metrics are typically not computed beyond the top ten rank positions, and are primarily in the top few results). Therefore, it is only really necessary to judge the top-n results, where n is set to something reasonable (such as fifty) to account for variations in ranking over time. To afford comparative judging between engines and reduce judging cost (no need to judge each engine separately), a technique called *pooling* is used (Spärck-Jones and Van Rijsbergen, 1976). In the case of Web search, pooling might involve retrieving the union of the top-ranked search results from various Web search engines and having human assessors label the relevance of those results to the query along some dimension, either binary or multi-level, as appropriate.

Human-labeled data has historically been expensive to collect, although costs are dropping with crowdsourcing, and can be unreliable because judgments are sourced from third-party assessors. Contextual information can and should be provided to judges to better understand the intention behind observed search interaction (Borlund and Ingwersen, 1998; Eickhoff et al., 2013). If appropriate behavioral sequences can be defined, interaction alone can be used to define labels within search settings or beyond (e.g., evidence of the searcher calling an emergency telephone number as a proxy for detecting an emergency situation [Mishra et al., 2014]). One example of a behavioral sequence with utility in this context is *query chains* (described earlier; see Radlinski and Joachims [2005]), which involve connecting all queries in a sequence to the terminal result clicks, increasing the volume of training data available to the machine-learned ranking algorithm, while addressing mismatches in vocabulary between content creators and consumers.

3.3.4.4 Application in Search: Learning to Rank

There have been a number of applications of machine learning in search systems, but perhaps the most significant has been its use in ranking search engine results. Learning to rank is a relatively new research area that has emerged in the past decade. Fuhr (1989) introduced the notion of machine-learned ranking, describing learning approaches in information retrieval as a generalization of parameter estimation. Fuhr focused on a specific variant of this approach, using polynomial regression. The challenge of learning to rank search results using relevance judgments has since received significant attention in machine learning community (e.g., Cohen et al., 1999; Chu and Keerthi, 2005; Yu et al., 2005).

Learning-to-rank or machine-learned ranking (MLR) is a type of supervised or semi-supervised machine learning problem in which the goal is to automatically construct a ranking model from training data (Pedersen, 2008). Training data consists of lists of items with some partial order specified between items in each list. This order is typically induced by giving a numerical or ordinal score or a binary judgment (e.g., "relevant" or "not relevant") for each item. The objective of the learned model is to rank (i.e., produce a permutation of items in new, unseen lists) in a way that is similar to the rankings in the training data.

Many of the standard content-based ranking models – such the vector space model or the Boolean model – have been superseded, at least in a Web search setting, by machine-learned models that integrate these matching algorithms as one of many features. This allows them to leverage the strengths of many features (including aggregated search behavior) and attain significant gains in retrieval effectiveness.[5] Although a combination of evidence methods such as Dempster-Shafer theory (Shafer, 1976) have been applied in retrieval settings (e.g., for image search [Jose et al., 1998] and for structured document retrieval [Lalmas and Ruthven, 1998]), the introduction of machine learning into ranking has led to significant improvements in result relevance, especially in commercial Web search engines. Search engines have been using machine-learning technology for many years, ever since the AltaVista search engine was one of the first to employ MLR. Other commercial search engines such as Microsoft Bing and the Russian search engine Yandex have also publically reported their utilization of MLR in ranking search results.

MLR methods can be grouped into three main categories (Liu, 2009):

- **Pointwise approach:** Each query-document pair in the training data has a numerical or ordinal score. Then learning-to-rank problem can be approximated by a regression problem; given a single query-document pair, its score is predicted. Supervised machine learning algorithms can be readily used for this purpose. Ordinal regression and classification algorithms can also be used in the pointwise approach when they are used to predict a score of a single query-document pair, as long as it assumes a small, finite number of values.
- **Pairwise approach:** In this approach, the learning-to-rank problem is approximated by a classification problem – learning a binary classifier that can tell which document is better in a given pair of documents. The goal is to minimize the average number of inversions in ranking.
- **Listwise approach:** These algorithms try to directly optimize the value of one of the above evaluation measures, averaged over all queries in the training data. This is difficult because as most evaluation measures are not continuous functions with respect to ranking model's parameters, continuous approximations or bounds on evaluation measures have to be used.

Following on from the earlier discussion of feature engineering in machine-learned applications, features are also incredibly important in the learning-to-rank space.

For the convenience of MLR algorithms, query-document pairs are usually represented by numerical vectors, which are called feature vectors. Such approach is sometimes called bag of features and is analogous to bag of words and vector space model (Salton et al., 1975). Components of such vectors are referred to as features, factors, or ranking signals. They may be divided into three groups (features from document retrieval are provided as examples):

- **Query features** depend only on the query – for example, the number of words in a query.
- **Query-independent or static features** depend only on the document, but not on the query – for example, PageRank (Brin and Page, 1998), HITS (Kleinberg, 1999), document length, or inverse document frequency of terms in the collection. Such features can be pre-computed in off-line mode during indexing. They may be used to compute document's static quality score (or static rank), which is often used to speed up search query evaluation.
- **Query-dependent or dynamic features** depend both on the contents of the document and the query, such as TF-IDF score or other non-machine-learned ranking functions.

Features derived from search interaction behavior are most commonly used in the derivation of *query-dependent* features (e.g., click-through rates on particular documents), because the focus in search is typically associated with a particular information need, rather than search behavior in general. However, there have been some successful attempts to use searcher behavior for computing static rank scores based on the popularity of particular Web pages or websites as a proxy for their quality (Richardson et al., 2006).

We have focused on the applications of machine learning for ranking search results because that is the most common application scenario in search systems at present. However, as search transitions from ranked results to applications in proactive search, recommendation, and spoken dialog, the role of machine learning in search interaction will continue to grow – covered later in the book. MLR may also be applied to personalized search given the availability of training data for the individual searcher. Although separate models may be learned for each searcher, the storage and training of individual models may not be practical; instead a single model that uses features of the search history and/or search context could be developed (Bennett et al., 2012), as could methods that adapt the weights in the global model to individual searchers (Wang et al., 2013).

3.3.4.5 Limitations of Machine Learning

Although there is significant promise in applying machine learning algorithms, there are also a number of potential drawbacks associated with automatically learned models. First, the models are only as good as the quality of the labels that they receive; this is the so-called garbage-in-garbage-out problem. The features that are created need to be representative of the types of problem that are being addressed, and as such, the problem formulation needs to be correct when training the models. There are also drawbacks associated with focusing on correlation between features and apparent relevance, rather than causation (i.e., the presence of particular attributes that cause a document to be relevant). Given the uncertainty associated with both relevance and behavioral analysis, focusing on correlation rather than causation may still be reasonable and the experience of the community has shown that this still allows for the development of practically useful retrieval algorithms.

3.3.5 Real-Time Application of Models

An important constraint in serving searchers using constructed models in online settings at scale is latency – that is, the speed with which the model can be executed and its output leveraged to improve some aspect of the search experience. The models that are learned through the processes described in this chapter often need to be applied in real time across millions of searchers. This means that they need to be compact and run efficiently in distributed systems.

3.3.5.1 Case Study: Page Load Time

Previous research has shown that page-load time (PLT) can have a significant effect on user perception of satisfaction. Intensive research and engineering efforts have focused on achieving low latency in large, complex computing systems such as search engines (Dean and Barroso, 2013). Since the early days of human computer interaction, researchers have studied the influence of system response time on the success, speed, and satisfaction of interactions (Shneiderman, 1984). In general, these studies have found that sub-second response times are preferred and can increase people's productivity.

Search engines in particular are designed to target speed. Modern Web search engines deliver results rapidly because searchers interact more with them than they do with slower results, and because fast results are perceived as being of higher quality. Maxwell and Azzopardi (2014) showed that searchers experiencing delays in both query processing and document selections viewed fewer documents but also marked a greater percentage of the documents that they viewed as relevant. Google conducted online experiments in which they intentionally injected server-side delays, ranging from 100 to 400 milliseconds, into the process of generating the search results to observe changes to people's behavior. They found that increasing the page load time of the SERP by as little as 100 milliseconds decreased the number of searches per person. These differences increased over time and persisted even after the experiment ended and there were no longer any delays (Shurman and Brutlag, 2009). In similar experiments, Bing added server delays ranging from 50 to 2,000 milliseconds. They observed decreases in queries and clicks, and an increase in time to click, with larger effects with more delay (Shurman and Brutlag, 2009). Recognizing the importance of speed to users, Google added site speed (i.e., how quickly a website responds to requests) as a relevance signal in search ranking. As testament to the perceived importance of retrieval latency to searchers, retrieval time is also highlighted by search engines, including Google, alongside other information (e.g., "About 13,000 results [0.29 seconds]").

Speed appears to be so important that even improvements to search engines that seem like they should unambiguously impact the search experience in a positive way can lead to negative outcomes if they increase latency. For example, when Google experimented with returning thirty results instead of ten, they found that traffic and revenue in the experimental group dropped significantly. One likely explanation is that the additional search results required an additional half-second to load (Faber, 2006). Arapakis et al. (2014) studied the interplay between the response latency of the Web search system and the search experience and showed that people who use a search system that responds quickly are more likely to notice delays than users of a slow search system, and that the latency becomes noticeable once they exceed one second. They also show that when controlling for result page content, SERPs that are displayed with less latency are more likely to receive more clicks. Others have shown that searchers are tolerant of delays until a "tipping point" after which their behaviors and their perceptions change (Taylor et al., 2013).

Application of machine-learned models at scale also necessitates rapid access to searcher data and efficient computation of feature values. Some contextual features can be computed offline, e.g., those related to the location of the searcher at query time, because they will not change dramatically between searcher cohorts. However, others are searcher-specific or context-specific and require rapid access to information about the searchers' recent and/or historic search activities. User profiles need to be accessed almost instantaneously at query time. As such, they need to be stored in memory on machines inside data centers, and the models therefore have to be compactly represented in efficient data structures. This means that they are usually based only on a fixed number of search queries or a pre-defined time-frame (e.g., the most recent four weeks of search history).

3.4 Summary

Technological advances and evolving social norms are creating new opportunities to better model the search process, including collecting more complete data from searchers about their information needs and leveraging social relationships to answer questions. Models such as those described in this chapter are now commonplace within search systems and will become even more central in next-generation search systems, especially as machine learning plays a more fundamental role. In the next chapter, I consider various models and frameworks that have been proposed in the Information Retrieval, Information Science, and Human-Computer Interaction communities to describe how people explore, seek, collect, and use information. These models were developed at a time before rich sensing of behavioral data at scale, natural searcher interaction, extensive utilization of mobile computing, and the consideration of social interactions in and around information seeking. Discussing the models is important to frame some of the discussions of interests and intentions in this chapter, and to ground some of our further discussions of search support and search algorithms as we move forward together in the book.

CHAPTER 4

Models and Frameworks for Information Seeking

The theory and practice of information seeking has been researched extensively in the Information Science and Information Retrieval (IR) research communities. Many of the models of interests and intentions described in the previous chapter have foundations in this literature. As such, it is worth reviewing the research in this area and how it applies to next-generation search systems. Many models of search behavior that have been proposed are based on observations of how people search on their own and how they interact with intermediaries, such as reference librarians, during the search process. Indeed, the reference librarian model (of a human search expert trying to satisfy a patron's information needs) remains the prevalent interaction model in many search systems, including commercial Web search engines. The primary difference is that in these systems human librarians have been largely replaced by automation in the retrieval process (including formulating effective queries via tools such as query auto-completion, query suggestion, and backend query alterations), and by the searcher themselves (for example, in decisions regarding the relevance, filtering, and synthesis of the retrieved items) to generate a set of relevant information items, and ultimately, one or more answers to the questions that motivated their search.

Information-seeking behavior forms part of the broader field of Information Behavior, which includes both intentional information seeking (such as querying or actively browsing for information), and unintentional behaviors (such as passively watching a television commercial; see Wilson [1999]). Models of information seeking are informative for the design of search interfaces and behavioral models (for tasks such as click prediction, satisfaction modeling, etc.) that meet searchers' needs and are representative of the types of actions that they perform. One such conceptualization involves different modes of information searching, reflecting different ways that people search for information. Table 4.1 summarizes these different modes as based on Wilson (1998) and Bates (2005), which varies how directed (goal-oriented) and how active the searcher will be during the information search process.

Research in areas such as exploratory search, information foraging, sensemaking, learning, creativity, and knowledge discovery, alongside more traditional models of information seeking (e.g., cognitive, strategic, process, episodic, and stratified models

Table 4.1. *Modes of information searching (adapted from Wilson [1997] and Bates [2005])*

	Active	Passive
Directed	**Searching:** Active searching directed to particular sources to answer specific questions.	**Monitoring:** Passive alertness, primed by interest, that enables an individual to notice information of interest
Undirected	**Browsing:** Active exploration/search without a clear goal, or for only loosely defined objectives.	**Awareness:** Passive, undirected absorption of experiences and learning.

of search interaction), have covered many of the modes highlighted in Table 4.1. There are a number of theories and frameworks that have contrasted searching and browsing (Belkin et al., 1993; Marchionini, 1995). Hearst (2009) suggested that one way to distinguish between searching and browsing is that queries produce ad hoc collections of items, whereas browsing follows predefined navigation trails laid out by others (for example, during the authorship of websites, where pages are connected by chains of hyperlinks and people traverse the hyperlink graph between pages during browsing). Predefined trails can be shortcut using search queries (White et al., 2007; White and Huang, 2010), or created on-the-fly during undirected exploration (Hertzum and Frokjaer, 1996), where activity may be associated with general interest rather than a focused information need present at the time of interaction. Another way to contrast these activities is in terms of the amount of cognitive effort required to fulfill the task. Aula et al. (2005a) suggest that querying is a more analytical and cognitively demanding mechanism for finding information than browsing. Querying involves many activities, including the formulation and execution of search statements, which is not required during browsing tasks. Browsing tasks are often recognition-oriented and driven by factors such as information scent (discussed in Section 4.3).

Information seeking is a fundamental human activity that provides many of the "raw materials" for planned behavior, decision making, and the production of new information products (Marchionini, 1995). The principles that underlie information-seeking activity have their origins in other aspects of people's behavior, including the act of foraging for food (Sandstrom, 1994; Pirolli and Card, 1995). Even though the process of searching for information can be conducted manually (and has been for millennia), recent advances in information technology have afforded the opportunity to use electronic information and compute cycles for human intelligence amplification (Ashby, 1956). There has been a significant amount of research and discussion on the augmentation of human intellect using technology (Bush, 1945; Licklider, 1960; Engelbart, 1962). Researchers have advocated for symbiotic relationships between humans and machines that involve changes in the ways that humans tackle complex problems. Subscribers to this vision believe that machines could be viewed as cognitive prosthetics, supplementing and enhancing human intelligence – and enabling people to solve more complex problems than could be tenable without search assistance. Technology is now sufficiently advanced that this vision can be realized, albeit accompanied by a need to address the information overload associated with allocating attentional resources appropriately when faced with a barrage of content (Simon, 1971). To handle this overload, humans and search systems need to focus on task-relevant information, and on acquiring and applying the information needed for task completion.

Wilson (1997) identified four categories of information seeking and acquisition that cover many of the types of information behavior discussed in this book: (1) *passive attention*, such as listening to the radio or watching television, where there is no explicit intent to acquire information, but it may happen regardless; (2) *passive search*, where searching for one object may lead to the acquisition of information that is useful for another task; (3) *active search*, where people actively seek information to satisfy their information need (this is the most commonly considered type of information seeking and acquisition both in the literature and in industry) and; (4) *ongoing search*, where active searching continues over time – a common activity for broad search intents such as information maintenance, undirected browsing, or transactions (Agichtein et al., 2012). The type of search support that is best suited to help searchers varies for each of these categories: in passive circumstances recommendations may be more appropriate, for active search effective query handling and suggestion becomes important, and for ongoing searches it is important to effectively support task resumption and the recommendation of next steps across devices, domains, applications, and over time.

The simple interaction model of the information retrieval process involving an isolated and singular query satisfied by a single result in a list of candidates is insufficient to represent the breadth of information tasks that searchers perform (Bates, 1989; O'Day and Jeffries, 1993). People are engaged in complex information-seeking scenarios with uncertain outcomes, and dynamic information needs and information environments. In addition, in comparison with early research in information retrieval, searchers now interact directly with the information while searching, rather than information surrogates such as bibliographic databases, where the information objects had to be sourced separately from the search process. Being able to engage and explore with resources during the search process has significant impact on how people search (e.g., greater interplay between content examination and query formulation [Eickhoff et al., 2015]), as well as how we design interactive search systems (e.g., to support transitions between SERPs and selected results [Feild et al., 2013] or result revisitation decisions [Teevan et al., 2007]). Proposed models of information seeking traditionally focus on the nature of the search process, the cognitive mechanics of searching, and the rationales behind observed search behaviors.

Many of the models of information searching were developed in an era preceding the Internet and before many technological innovations that shape how we engage with search systems at present and will do so in the future (e.g., mobile computing, mining of aggregated behavioral data, natural search interaction). Nonetheless, there is still significant value in these models; in a large part because there are aspects of information behavior, such as the uncertainty inherent in seeking solutions (Kuhlthau, 1991), that are associated with people and transcend technological advances. Aspects of these models are therefore still relevant in informing the design of information-seeking support systems (Marchionini and White, 2009) to support activities, including helping searchers clarify vague information needs, learn from information present in the collection, and investigate solutions to information problems. The validation and application of information-seeking models to large-scale behavioral data – which is a focus of this book – remains largely an open question. It is not entirely clear that the models obtained are a function of the experimental protocol (tasks, systems, etc.) under which the data were collected. That said, there has been some work, primarily on information scent and information foraging (Chi et al., 2005; Pirolli, 2007) that has validated the behavioral models at scale using website traffic, and demonstrated strong regularities in human navigation behavior (Huberman et al., 1998).

The discussion of models and frameworks is divided into four key areas: (1) the act of exploring, where the information objective may be unknown or not present; (2) seeking information, where there is a specific purpose to the information behavior and the focus of the models is on the pursuit of those aims; (3) gathering and organizing information, where the focus is on the collection and storage of information during the search process; and (4) using information, which involves the application of the information found.

4.1 Exploring

Let us first consider models of exploratory behavior and browsing. Information behavior encompasses intentional information seeking as well as unintentional information encounters (Case, 2002). By nature, humans seek to extend their knowledge by journeying beyond visible horizons. During exploration they gather information to develop complex intellectual skills such as comprehension, application, analysis, synthesis, and evaluation (Bloom et al., 1956). Support for browsing in information systems has traditionally relied on methods such as hyperlink navigation or embedded menus (Shneiderman, 1998). The need to consider combinations of search and browsing has been highlighted (Marchionini and Shneiderman, 1988) and further operationalized in systems for which queries and hyperlinks are synonymous (Golovchinsky, 1997a; Golovchinsky, 1997b).

A significant fraction of information-seeking activity occurs out of the view of search systems, either once searchers click on a result and navigate away from the system and out into the corpus, or when just browsing connected document collections such as the Web. This activity is commonly known as "browsing". Despite recent progress in satisfying information needs from search systems (e.g., Bernstein et al., 2012), browsing remains a core information-seeking activity and needs to be better understood and supported in next-generation-search systems. Carmel et al. (1992) identified three types of browsing: (1) *search-oriented browsing*, which is the process of locating information that is relevant to a fixed task; (2) *review browsing*, which is the process of scanning resources to find interesting information; and (3) *scan browsing*, where people scan to find information without reviewing or integrating that information. In reviewing research on browsing, Marchionini (1995) identified three similar types of browsing that vary based on the target of the search and the systematicity of the tactics employed: (1) *directed browsing*, which involves focused, systematic browsing in search of a known item); (2) *semi-directed browsing*, where the target is less well defined and less systematic strategies are used; and (3) *undirected browsing*, where there is no real purpose and little focus (e.g., flipping through a magazine, "channel-surfing" on a television or radio; see Choo et al. [1999]). Exploratory activities such as browsing create opportunity for systems to perform in situ recommendations of queries and resources to those engaged in these activities, building models of interests

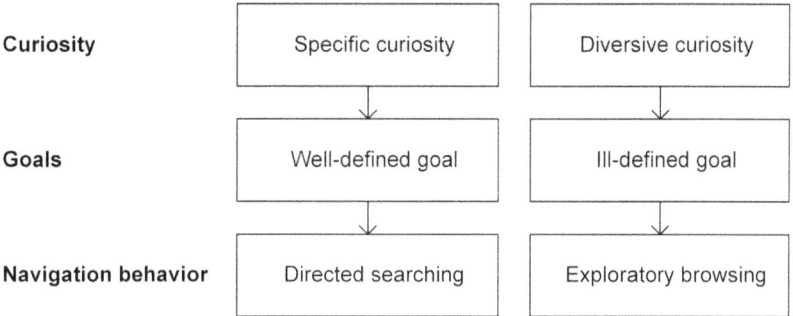

Figure 4.1. Variants of curiosity and their role in search (adapted from White and Roth, 2009).

and intentions based on recent activity or on the activities of others accessing similar resources.

Models of exploratory search behavior are frequently associated with curiosity, which causes natural inquisitive behavior such as exploration, investigation, and learning, evident by observation in many animal and human species. Berlyne (1960) proposed a categorization of curiosity based on the distinction between specific and diversive curiosity. Specific curiosity is the desire for a particular piece of information, as typified by an attempt to solve a problem or puzzle. Diversive curiosity is a more general seeking of stimulation or novelty, as typified by a bored television viewer flipping between channels. In information seeking, specific curiosity corresponds to well-defined goals and directed searching, while diversive curiosity corresponds to ill-defined goals and exploratory browsing. Figure 4.1 illustrates the variants of curiosity and their roles in searching. Although switching between the two types of navigational behavior is necessary for many search scenarios, this is not detailed in the figure. Other aspects – such as levels of concern and anxiety associated with temporal constraints associated with the task – direct the strategies employed by searchers (e.g., people are less likely to explore broadly if they are time constrained).

Berlyne (1960) also proposed three states of exploratory behavior: (1) *orienting* responses, (2) *locomotor* responses, and (3) *investigatory* responses. In terms of information seeking (in particular, exploratory search, which is discussed later in this chapter), these parallel: (a) obtaining overviews of the data, perhaps through information visualizations that highlight unseen parts of the information space and support connections with current knowledge, and surveying the information landscape for potential next steps; (b) focusing on a specific object, such as a potentially relevant or interesting document; and (c) examining that object. This aligns with Wolfe's model of visual search (1994), which postulates that people survey the available information initially, then target points of interest within the broader visual field for more complex interpretation and understanding. Tradeoffs between exploration and exploitation from reinforcement learning (see Auer, 2003) are also relevant, whereby learned models (of, say, search intent or result relevance) and the environment form an online loop, and the learning process involves balancing the presentation items that are most likely to be relevant (exploitation) against a broader analysis of the information space (exploration; see Ruotsalo et al. [2015]).

Hughes (1997) traces the history of the various theories developed to explain exploratory behavior. Hughes defines intrinsic exploration as involving "exploratory acts that are not instrumental in achieving any particular goal other than performance of the acts themselves." This is contrasted with extrinsic search, driven by a goal, such as the need to find food or shelter, or escape from danger. Many search tasks and processes are intrinsic in nature, including information foraging and many of the goal-directed tasks on which implicit feedback data are collected. More open-ended activities – such as exploratory search, berrypicking, and orienteering – are more closely related to intrinsic exploration, although there are often goal or task constraints that restrict these activities from being purely exploratory.

Supporting curiosity-driven exploration can lead to significant personal growth opportunities (Kashdan et al., 2004). Loewenstein (1994) posits a sensemaking theory to explain curiosity that is similar to work on information seeking (e.g., Belkin, 1978; Dervin, 1983). The theory states that in the animal kingdom, motile animals' exposures to new environments, stimuli, or information bring the possibility of discovering new food sources, mates and nesting or sleeping sites, or ways to escape predation. In these cases, exploration is valuable and often underappreciated, although too much exploration brings its own risks of death or a decline in reproduction (Bell, 1991). There is clearly not the same risk or competition for resources in the open Web. However, the benefits of exploration in terms of discovering new information and new pathways through the collection (that can be exploited repeatedly) are still apparent (White and Huang, 2010).

Bates (2007) suggests that browsing is a cognitive and behavioral expression of exploratory behavior, that she claims comprises four elements: (1) glimpse a scene; (2) target an element of a scene visually and/or physically (if multiple items are of interest, they are examined sequentially); (3) examine item(s) of interest; and (4) physically or conceptually acquire or abandon examined item(s). This sequence is repeated indefinitely as people explore to satisfy their curiosity. Systems to support exploratory behaviors in information collections should provide collection overviews (glimpses), the ability to traverse trails through the collection (exploratory browsing), including tools for isolating and comparing multiple items of interest, and support for document examination and retention. There are many search systems that perform one or more of these functions. Few systems, if any, offer all of this functionality. Systems that offer comprehensive search assistance would help people complete a broad range of information tasks.

4.2 Seeking

Information seeking typically assumes a model of the search process involving the initial recognition and specification of an information need, followed by the examination of search results, and repetition of the cycle until a satisfactory result set is located (Shneiderman et al., 1998; Marchionini and White, 2007). As mentioned earlier, a number of models of the information-seeking process and information-seeking behavior have been developed (e.g., Choo et al., 2000; Ellis, 1989; Kuhlthau, 1991; Marchionini, 1995; Wilson, 1997). The proposed models can be categorized based on their dominant themes: (1) *cognitive models* focus on the cognitive processes underlying search activity (Dervin and Nilan, 1986; Ingwersen, 1996); (2) *process models* are generally multi-stage representations of searchers' activities during the search process (Kuhlthau, 1991; Marchionini, 1995; Belkin et al., 1993; Belkin et al., 1995; Pharo, 1999); (3) *stratified models* represent search interaction as a set of strata on the searcher and the system, where each stratum influences searchers' interaction behavior (Saracevic, 1997); (4) *strategic models* focus on the strategies that searchers employ when searching for information (e.g., Bates, 1990), and (5) *economic models* focus on the application of insights from economic theory in information interaction (Birchler and Bütler, 2007; Azzopardi, 2011).

4.2.1 Cognitive Models

Cognitive models focus on individuals' complex psychological functions during the retrieval process, and these models can be derived from models of task performance (Norman, 1988), which provided an account of how people operate in the world independent of search. In one example of how such a model could be applied, Norman divides actions into doing (execution) and checking (evaluation) – allowing for the identification of various gaps (or gulfs) between intention and achievement, and determining whether goals have been met and focusing on information-seeking behavior. Information needs can be cast similarly, focusing on formulating needs as the goal, performing actions such as query formulation and navigation as execution, and the assessment of the content returned by the engine as evaluation (Hearst, 2009). Additional steps such as query reformulation may be required to bridge the gulf between the current state of the search (both systems and processes), and the current state of the world.

The ASK hypothesis states that there is a gap between what one knows and what one would like to know, and the need to fill the gap is what drives one to seek and retrieve information (Belkin et al., 1982). This information lack leads to the goal that is to be achieved as a result of the search process. Given this goal, one then decides on an action that he or she must take to meet that goal. A person's mental model is a dynamic, internal representation of a problematic situation or system which receives inputs from the world and returns predictions on the effects for those inputs (Marchionini, 1989). The mental model represents the search situation at the time of the search and uses that model to select the appropriate action. As I discuss later in this book, the situation may be influenced by a number of contextual factors, many of which are outside of a searchers' control – and understanding the impact of those factors is important in modeling the search process more fully – so as to offer the right type of assistance.

Building on earlier work (Ingwersen and Pejtersen, 1986; Ingwersen and Wormell, 1989), Ingwersen (1992) contributed to our understanding of search interaction with the cognitive model of information transfer (1992, 1996). The model integrated both systems-oriented information retrieval research and cognitive information retrieval research. Systems-oriented research includes authors' texts, text representation, retrieval techniques and queries. Cognitive information retrieval research includes the searcher's problem space, information problems, requests, interaction with intermediaries, and interface design. Ingwersen's model incorporates the context, or the socio-organizational environment, of the information seeker. To elaborate further, context includes the scientific or professional domains with information preferences, and

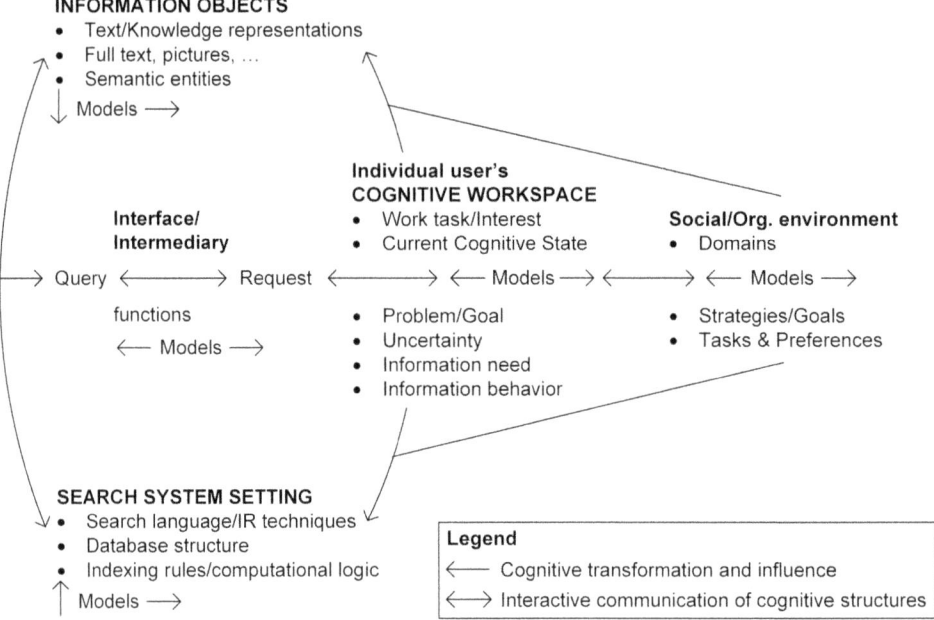

Figure 4.2. The cognitive model of information transfer (adapted from Ingwersen, 1992).

the strategies and work tasks that shape the searcher's awareness. In 1996, Ingwersen changed his model to include search interaction, adding the work task and corresponding situation, as perceived by the searcher. The model emphasizes the primary elements of information retrieval theory and the cognitive variation at any specific moment in time (found in documents, search systems, and in a searcher's cognitive space). Ingwersen's model not only considers particular instances of time, but it also demonstrates the influence of context on information and systems longitudinally. Longitudinal relevance also applies to Ingwersen's cognitive model in the social interaction between the work tasks and the searcher. Figure 4.2 illustrates the cognitive model where various cognitive elements are seen to interact.

To understand the cognitive aspects of information retrieval research, Wilson (1999) devised a model that summarized user-oriented (cognitive) information searching. The primary purpose of Wilson's model is to demonstrate the locality of the various elements of the search process; in particular, how they are nested. Wilson's model places information search in the innermost part of the model, followed by information-seeking behavior and information behavior, respectively. The model decreases in specificity as it moves outward; information-seeking behavior comprises a portion of information behavior, and information search is a specific type of information-seeking behavior.

Ingwersen (1992; 1994) and Pao (1993) developed the principle of polyrepresentation, whereby cognitive overlaps occur during information retrieval by different information structures (i.e., indexers versus citations). Polyrepresentation can be used as a means for precise retrieval and for the expansion of intellectual availability of subject matter. Ingwersen (1996; 2002) expanded the concept of polyrepresentation within a cognitive theory of search interaction that includes five major information structures: (1) citations, (2) author(s), (3) indexers, (4) selector(s), and (5) thesauri. All of these structures have some degree of cognitive overlap, which is important to recognize when considering search techniques. This overlap may also be useful for exploratory searchers, who may seek highly reliable information sources or wish to use overlap to broaden their topic knowledge. Overlap between different representations of the same information need has been shown to be useful in retrieval settings (Belkin et al., 1993), as well in the recommendation of content in Web-scale resource recommendation scenarios (White et al., 2009). Modern search engines may also blend the results of multiple queries expressing similar or complementary search intents with a view toward enriching the set of results retrieved (e.g., Sheldon et al., 2011). Kato et al. (2014) investigated searcher needs associated with the cognitive characteristics of documents (e.g., comprehensibility, subjectivity, and concreteness). The authors defined these as *cognitive search intents* (CSIs), and they developed machine-learned query expansion algorithms to improve the performance of search systems for some types of CSI, moving beyond topical relevance and utility as the main ranking criteria.

4.2.2 Process Models

Information seeking process models represent information searching as a multi-stage process through which people transition during the search process, with backtracking and iteration as required.

Kuhlthau (1991; 1993) developed a model of the information search process (ISP) that identifies and emphasizes the importance of the individual stages that learning tasks and problem solving involve. Kuhlthau (1991) proposed that the feelings of doubt, anxiety, and frustration are natural and play a role in information seeking. Occurrence of these feelings has already been studied (Ford, 1980; Mellon, 1986), and anxiety has usually been associated with a lack of knowledge of information sources and apparatus. Information seeking, by its very nature, causes anxiety because there is no guaranteed positive outcome to the search (i.e., the searcher can be unsuccessful in finding what they seek). Kuhlthau's research involved a series of longitudinal empirical studies conducted on students and library patrons. The information-search process model that she developed highlights the differences in feelings, thoughts, and actions that people experience during the search process. Changes in feelings, thoughts, and actions of the searcher are stage dependent, and each task is unique to the stage of the investigational process.

Kuhlthau's stages, as interpreted by Ingwersen and Järvelin (2005), include: (1) *initiation*: becoming aware of the need for information, when facing a problem; (2) *selection*: the general topic for seeking information is identified and selected; (3) *exploration*: seeking and investigating information on the general topic; (4) *focus formulation*: fixing and structuring of the problem to be solved; (5) *collection*: gathering pertinent information for the focused topic; and (6) *presentation*: completing seeking, reporting, and using the result of the task. There is an additional *assessment* phase at the end of the process, where people may reflect on the outcomes of the search, as well as the process undertaken to retrieve the sought information.

At the time, Kuhlthau's model was unique in incorporating psychological aspects of search into information seeking. Table 4.2 presents Kuhlthau's model of the information

Table 4.2. *Information Search Process (ISP) model (Kuhlthau, 1991)*

Model of the Information Search Process

	Initiation	Selection	Exploration	Formulation	Collection	Presentation	Assessment
Feelings (Affective)	Uncertainty	Optimization	Confusion Frustration Doubt	Clarity	Sense of direction/ Confidence	Satisfaction or Disappointment	Sense of accomplishment
Thoughts (Cognitive)	Vague —————————————————————→ Focused				Increased interest —————————→		Increased self-awareness
Actions (Physical)	Seeking relevant information ———————————————— Exploring				Seeking pertinent information ————————→ Documenting		

search process, as it focuses on affect, cognition, and search activity – all of which are important themes in this book. The model highlights exploration as one of the primary tasks that searchers conduct. Exploration, as interpreted in Kuhlthau's model, is an investigational stage of the information-seeking process. In the model, the actions of the searcher/actor transition from exploring to documenting during the search process. The central role of affect in Kuhlthau's model is important given the focus of this book. Richer sensing of affective, physiological, and behavioral signals allows search systems to estimate searchers' affective state directly during the search process and apply it as relevance feedback (Arapakis et al., 2008; Moshfeghi and Jose, 2013b). Understanding the nature of the affect at different times during the search session using models such as that proposed by Kuhlthau allows systems to also provide phase-appropriate support (e.g., assistance in query formulation to reduce initial uncertainty, or better exploration support to reduce confusion and frustration). As highlighted in Chapter 3, methods have also emerged to detect frustration and exploration from behavioral signals alone (Feild et al., 2010; Hassan et al., 2014). The predictions made by these models can be used to situate searchers at the correct stage within the information search process, which in turn can inform the types of support that systems offer (e.g., collection overviews or guidance from prior searchers, to support the reduction of uncertainty during the early stages of the search).

Ellis proposed a set of eight features that form a framework for information-seeking behavior (Ellis, 1989; Ellis et al., 1993; Ellis and Haugan, 1997). The feature set differentiates the various information-seeking patterns of scientists and engineers in their individual surroundings (Ellis and Haugan, 1997): (1) *starting*: activities such as the initial search for an overview of the literature or locating key people working in the field; (2) *chaining*: following footnotes and citations in known material or "forward" chaining from known items through citation indexes or proceeding in personal networks; (3) *browsing*: variably directed and structured scanning of primary and secondary sources; (4) *differentiating*: using known differences in information sources as a way of filtering the amount of information obtained; (5) *monitoring*: regularly following developments in a field through particular formal and informal channels and sources; (6) *extracting*: selectively identifying relevant material in an information source; (7) *verifying*: checking the accuracy of information; and (8) *finding*: activities actually finishing the information seeking process. Focusing more on searchers' internal *representations* of themselves and the objects with which they interact than their information seeking *behaviors*, Borgman (1984) examined the search process via searchers' mental models of the search system and the knowledge domain being searched. At the time, this complemented ongoing research on mental models within the human factors community (Norman, 1983; Carroll and Anderson, 1987) and more generally within psychology research (Johnson-Laird, 1983).

Most situations involving information seeking can be characterized by Ellis's model. However, the model does not capture the main aspects of exploratory search processes (Marchionini, 2006a; White and Roth, 2009). The feature set excludes external causative factors, and an individual is not guaranteed to undergo an identical information-seeking process as outlined in the model. In addition, the model does not support tasks or retrieval operations, and it is unidirectional; it does not analyze relationships among the features. Choo et al. (2000) developed a model of online information seeking that combines both browsing and searching. It suggests that much

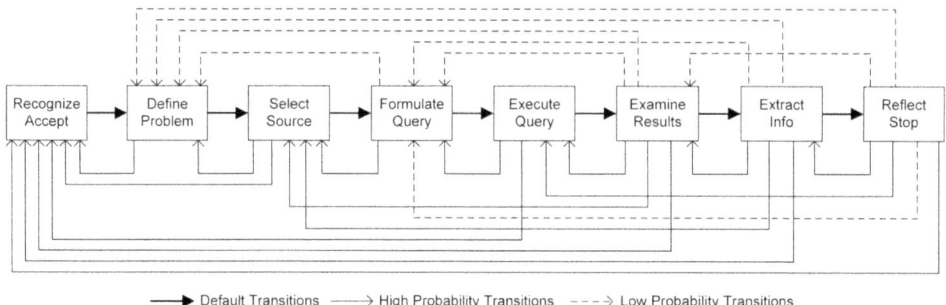

Figure 4.3. Information seeking process model (adapted from Marchionini, 1995).

of Ellis's model is already implemented by components currently available in Web browsers. Searchers can begin at a website (starting), follow links to information resources (chaining), bookmark pages (differentiating), subscribe to services that provide electronic mail alerts (monitoring), and search for information within sites or information sources (extracting).

Marchionini (1995) proposed another model of the information-seeking process, directed toward electronic environments. In his model, the information seeking process is composed of eight sub-processes which develop in parallel, potentially at different rates: (1) recognize and accept an information problem, (2) define and understand the problem, (3) choose a search system, (4) formulate a query statement, (5) execute a search, (6) examine the results, (7) extract information, and (8) reflect/iterate/stop. Figure 4.3 presents an illustration of the various stages between which information seekers transition.

This model defines the activities at each stage and is more suitable for electronic environments than Ellis's model. The information-seeking process model captures many important elements of information seeking, including aspects of collection exploration in examining results, and aspects of knowledge acquisition in extracting information. It is focused, however, on the search for information and does not consider learning and understanding, nor does it fully represent the search context or information use. At a time when personalization and contextualization of the search process are growing in importance, these are all important omissions from the model and limit its applicability beyond understanding search activities – and into higher-order activities that next-generation search systems will need to support in order help searchers tackle their information problems more completely (from conception to completion).

Wilson (1997) proposed that fields outside of information science – which include decision making, psychology, innovation, health communication, and consumer research – are vital to the advancement of information behavior analysis. He advised information scientists to expand the scope of their research to include more disciplines. As search technology becomes more pervasive, there is justification for this general argument. Wilson's model is a broad, static model that summarizes general information behavior, and it is not directly based on empirical findings. Wilson's model includes a "person in context" or a person with a particular task at hand for which information is required. His model shows that information-seeking behavior influences the person in context and their informational needs, which is also true of exploratory

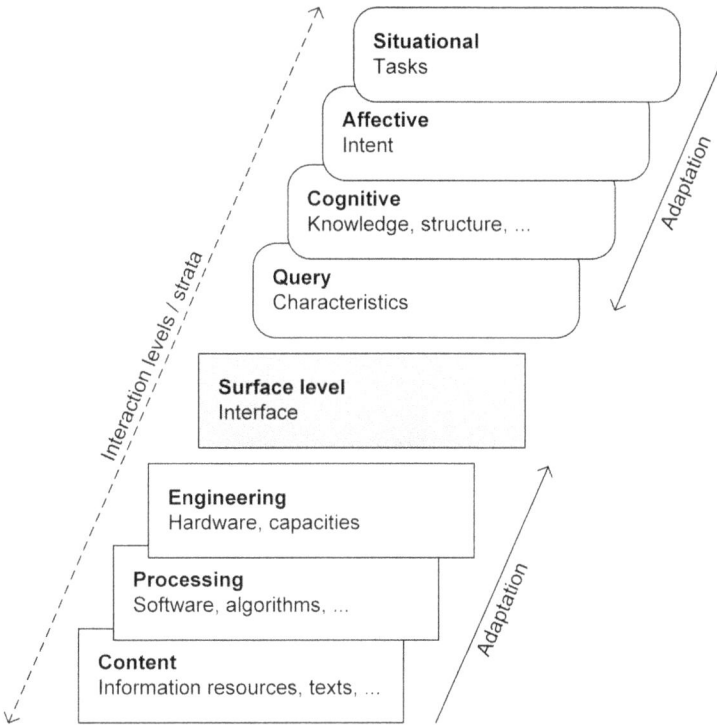

Figure 4.4. Stratified model of information retrieval interaction (adapted from Saracevic, 1996).

searching. In other words, as people search, they may decide to investigate information other than that which they were initially seeking. In exploratory search, the search process profoundly influences searchers' task perceptions. Wilson's model illustrates that intervening variables (e.g., cognitive abilities, demographics, task, and related environmental/situational constraints) can affect information-seeking behavior.

4.2.3 Stratified Models

Saracevic (1996) devised a model that also examined situational relevance, while examining the many types of relevance that are involved in search interaction. Stratified models help determine the range of abstraction levels that need to be considered when evaluating the effectiveness of a search system. Saracevic proposed a model of stratified interaction including hardware, software, searcher cognition, and situational levels, which suggests that the system and the searcher have equal influence on the outcome of the search (Saracevic, 1997). Any system involves hardware, processing, and data structures. For a given searcher, their interaction involves cognitive, affective, and situational levels, which represent their interpretation, motivation, and requirements, respectively. Figure 4.4 presents a visualization of the stratified model.

A core principle underlying the stratified model is that the search interaction is a dialog between the searcher and the search system at the surface level, with the expectation of merging and adaptation between the two agents over the course of the search process. The searcher (upper) side of the model represents many of the important factors affecting information behavior, including the search situation and searcher affect. The system (lower) side of the model was later extended by Spink et al. (1998), who added a graduated relevance dimension, and Bates (2002), who identified additional levels that interact and affect each other. The key point made by these stratified models is that even if an effective searching algorithm is implemented, or an intuitive user interface is designed, poor indexing or hardware can hinder the entire value of the system, acting as the weakest link in the chain. Similarly, a searcher's interpretation of results may seriously affect their success in achieving their goals with the system. By exposing the different layers, each can be individually checked for bottlenecks in performance.

4.2.4 Strategic Models

Strategic models define the different strategies and tactics that a user may employ when interacting with information, such as refining a search or returning to the beginning of a search session and beginning anew. Bates proposed a model containing four levels of search strategies: "move," "tactic," "stratagem," and "strategy" (Bates, 1979a; 1979b; 1990), as they applied to bibliographic and reference searches in manual and online search systems. A "move" is a single action performed by the searcher, either physically or mentally: mental actions may be deciding or reading. A "tactic" is a combination of moves, and there are endless combinations of moves that can be used to support a tactic, which depends on system implementations. Earlier in this book (see Table 2.1 and its discussion), I discussed tactics as they refer to search tasks and sessions during the collection and representation of search activity. Bates (1979a) defines thirty-two specific information search tactics, as listed in Table 4.3.

Perhaps the most important conclusion to draw from Table 4.3 is the broad range of possible tactics and the requirements that they place on search systems to be able to support these activities. They call for support in formulating search queries (*term* and *search formulation* tactics), but also higher-order activities such as ensuring the search remains on track (*monitoring* tactics), providing awareness of the collection context within which people are searching and navigating (*file structure* tactics), and providing support to searchers in overcoming difficulties in finding relevant information (*idea* tactics). It is worth noting that these specific search tactics were devised by Bates based on her own search experiences, as well as her interpretation of the literature and conversations with others. Access to large-scale search log data comprising searches on a broad range of information search tasks provides new opportunity for much richer characterizations of search tactics, in settings beyond bibliographic and reference searches. Early work on understanding Web search goals present in search logs has made some useful progress in this area (Broder, 2002; Rose and Levinson, 2004).

As noted earlier in the book (Chapter 2), "stratagems" as defined by Bates, are a larger combination of individual moves and tactics: some examples provided by the author include performing a citation search or following a footnote. In today's terms, such stratagems would be defined as missions or search sessions (Jones and Klinkner, 2008). "Strategies" are again higher and involve a combination of moves, tactics, and stratagems – such as finding relevant work for a research article – and depends heavily on what the searcher is currently working on. As highlighted earlier, these may reflect

Table 4.3. *Bates's 32 tactics and their definitions. See Bates (1979a) for full definitions of these tactics*

Tactic Category	Description	List of Tactics
Monitoring Tactics	Tactics to keep the search on track and efficient.	CHECK, WEIGH, PATTERN, CORRECT, RECORD
File Structure Tactics	Techniques for threading one's way through the file structure of the information facility to the desired file, source, or information within the source.	BIBBLE, SELECT, SURVEY, CUT, STRETCH, SCAFFOLD, CLEAVE
Search Formulation Tactics	Tactics to aid in the process of designing or redesigning the search formulation.	SPECIFY, EXHAUST, REDUCE, PARALLEL, PINPOINT, BLOCK
Term Tactics	Tactics to aid in the selection and revision of specific terms within the search formulation.	SUPER, SUB, RELATE, NEIGHBOR, TRACE, VARY, FIX, REARRANGE, CONTRARY, RESPELL, RESPACE
Idea Tactics	Tactics for getting ideas to help with stymied searches.	RESCUE, BREACH, FOCUS

complex search tasks that often span multiple search sessions (Kotov et al., 2011; Agichtein et al., 2012). Characterizing the various types of strategies that searchers employ during information seeking is essential in designing effective search support.

Cool et al. (1996) attempted to empirically identify different information-seeking strategies. They did this by first asking experimental participants how they would search for information on a particular problem in a specific type of database. They also studied the behaviors of people interacting with an experimental search system that lacked some common search functionality and provided some entirely new functionality. They identified a set of strategies that were similar to those identified by Bates, and also extended the set of strategies that were identified in the earlier study.

The episodic model (Belkin et al., 1995) defines the flow in scenarios of human-system interactions that overcomes some of the shortcomings of the stratified approach presented earlier. The flow definitions are called "scripts" that define the typical steps of interaction between a searcher and an information system, including multiple exit points for variances such as success or failure. To do this, Belkin and colleagues first highlight four binary dimensions that define sixteen unique Information-Seeking Strategies (ISS; see Belkin et al. [1993]). While the episodic model is connected to cognitive processes, it is based on more specific processes of searchers' information-seeking behavior. The model considers the sequence of interactions in an episode of information seeking and classifies search behavior along four dimensions:

- **Method of interaction:** This first dimension defines whether searchers seek a particular information object or scanning a set of information objects.
- **Goal of interaction:** The goal dimension defines what the searcher aims to get out of the interaction (to learn something or to select something). In analytic terms, the distinction might be between "find out what" and "find out why." As I discuss later

Table 4.4. *Information seeking strategies (Belkin et al., 1993)*

ISS	Method		Goal		Mode		Resource	
	Scan	Search	Learn	Select	Recognize	Specify	Information	Meta-information
ISS1	X		X		X		X	
ISS2	X		X		X			X
ISS3	X		X			X	X	
ISS4	X		X			X		X
ISS5	X			X	X		X	
ISS6	X			X	X			X
ISS7	X			X		X	X	
ISS8	X			X		X		X
ISS9		X	X		X		X	
ISS10		X	X		X			X
ISS11		X	X			X	X	
ISS12		X	X			X		X
ISS13		X		X	X		X	
ISS14		X		X	X			X
ISS15		X		X		X	X	
ISS16		X		X		X		X

in this chapter, learning is an important aspect of the search process, especially during more exploratory information-seeking episodes.
- **Mode of retrieval:** Searchers can be classified by the manner in which they seek satisfaction.
- **Resource considered:** This final dimension covers the strategy employed by searchers (e.g., reviewing data directly or relying on meta-data).

Each of the traditional search processes (enumerated in the model as REPRESENTATION, COMPARISON, SUMMARIZATION, NAVIGATION, and VISUALIZATION) can be instantiated in a variety of ways. The model shows that many of the same events in search interaction repeat themselves, and illustrate the cyclic, temporal nature of the search process (Robins, 2000). Searchers engage in different kinds of interactions, dependent on a number of factors, such as the task, history, type of information, and so on. The different kinds of interactions support different processes such as judgment, interpretation, modification, browsing, and so on. Table 4.4 describes the different information seeking strategies that can be represented by different combinations of the four dimensions listed above. For example, traditional Web search engines such as Google and Bing are best used for ISS15 (shown in Table 4.4), where the searcher is seeking (Method) to select (Goal) by specifying (Mode) attributes of a specific information object (Resource).

Consequently, traditional Web search engines least support searchers who are scanning (Method) to learn (Goal) by recognizing (Method) some metadata about an information object (Goal): this is ISS2. Faceted browsing, described in more detail later in the book, supports searchers by presenting all the meta-information to them in advance and letting them choose. Conversely, this best supports ISS2, but may inadequately support ISS15: useful meta-data can be embedded in long lists and it may require more effort to find them than to simply type them into a search box.

The ISS model has been applied to Web searching and navigation studies involving human participants (Belkin et al., 1995; Pharo, 1999), with findings suggesting that the model is insufficiently exhaustive and that there is a potential for interdependency between the method of searching and the mode of retrieval (Pharo, 1999). In an effort to address such concerns, Belkin and Cool (2002) extended the four dimensions in the episodic model to incorporate all possible interactions between people and information within five facets. Further research by Huvilla and Widen-Wulff (2006) suggested that the initial four dimensions are sufficiently expressive to classify seeking behaviors.

4.2.5 Economic Models

Recently, there has been much attention on the development on the role of economic theory in information interaction (Birchler and Bütler, 2007; Azzopardi, 2011). Cooper (1972) modeled trade-offs in time in terms of how long people should spend searching versus the amount of time that the system should spend searching. More broadly, the contributions that economics could make to search were outlined by Varian (1999) in the form of three primary directions: (1) obtain better estimates regarding the probability of relevance; (2) apply the theory of optimal search behavior (Stigler, 1961) in retrieval settings (e.g., to predict when a searcher should stop examining a ranked list of search results [Birchler and Bütler, 2007]); and (3) examine the economic value of information using consumer theory, where people are trying to maximize expected utility or minimize expected cost. Models have been developed that use portfolio theory (Wang and Zhu, 2009) and production theory (Azzopardi, 2011) to model the search process. Although there are some indications that these models may not fully represent the search process (Azzopardi et al., 2013), there have been recent indications that these models can be iteratively refined to produce models that more accurately represent and explain the behaviors of real searchers (Azzopardi, 2014). There are similarities between this work and research on information foraging theory, where the assumption is that searchers are rational agents seeking to maximize their rate of return on the decision to invest in foraging within an information patch (Pirolli, 2007). In years to come, there will be more emphasis on models that leverage economic principles and have computational foundations.

4.2.6 Discussion

While the models developed in this area provide a better understanding of how people search, it is not always clear how these models can be translated into actionable insights that inform system design. Recently, there has been heightened interest in connecting theory and practice (Russell-Rose and Tate, 2012). Wilson et al. (2010) proposed a combination of Bates's lower levels of search activity and Belkin's ISS model to produce a framework for the automated evaluation of advanced search interfaces. In this evaluation method, at any point in time, the searcher is viewing the search interface from one of the sixteen ISS conditions, and sees it in terms of the tactics they can employ at that time. The conditions and the tactics act as filters, restricting the space of possible interactions with the interface. The interface can be seen by each tactic in a different way, in terms of how easy it is to employ that tactic across its interactive features. Bates's "moves" are used as a speculative metric between the layers. So each tactic has a total score of how easily they can be applied with each part of a search interface. In turn, when a searcher looks at the potential tactics through one of the sixteen ISS conditions, they see how many moves they can make with each tactic. This is an example of how considering the *processes* involved in the search for information can yield improvements in system design. Understanding search processes also presents an opportunity to guide experimental decisions and the design of new experimental procedures such as sophisticated simulations of search behavior (White et al., 2005c; Lin and Smucker, 2008). I discuss simulations in Chapter 11.

Many of the models described thus far assume a linear relationship between search (directed searching) and browsing (undirected searching) activities. Others have proposed nonlinear (Foster, 2004) and multi-faceted (Chang and Rice, 1993) models. Going even further, research in "everyday-life" information seeking[1] (Savolainen, 1995; McKenzie, 2003) proposes a distinction between exploratory (high-level) and immersive (low-level) search activities. Transitions between these high- and low-level activities that may be common when people are exploring information spaces (White and Roth, 2009) are not well supported in existing search interfaces (Dörk et al., 2011) and need to be handled explicitly to help searchers successfully tackle a more comprehensive set of search tasks.

4.3 Gathering and Organizing

Models of information gathering and organizing are related to much of the previous work on information seeking, but often attempt to utilize metaphors based on how people collect and arrange objects in the real world. These models build on many of the factors of exploratory behavior and information seeking described in the preceding sections. They also have connections to information gain metrics that are used in the evaluation of search systems – for example, normalized discounted cumulative gain (NDCG; see Järvelin and Kekäläinen [2002]) for search results, and time-biased gain for search sessions (Smucker and Clarke, 2012a). The best-known models that fall into this category include information foraging, berrypicking, and orienteering.

4.3.1 Information Foraging

I first discuss optimal foraging theory and the foraging behavior on which it is based.

4.3.1.1 Foraging and Optimal Foraging

Optimal foraging theory (MacArthur and Pianka, 1966) has been developed by anthropologists and ecologists and is based on the study of foraging behavior. It states that organisms forage so as to maximize their net energy intake per unit time. MacArthur and Pianka also demonstrated that how food is distributed spatially (i.e., its "patchiness" over the landscape) impacts an animal's diet. They suggested that the time spent foraging for sustenance can be divided into two phases: (1) *search time*: time spent trying to locate its next prey item; and (2) *handling time*: time taken to pursue, capture, and consume a prey item once it is selected. The search time involves locating any number of prey items, whereas the handling time is focused on the time devoted to a single item once it has been chosen.

Optimal foraging theory suggests that the eating habits of animals centers around maximizing energy intake as a function of time. Therefore, for every predator, certain prey are worth pursuing (given the effort required to capture them and the reward attained if they are caught), while other prey would result in a net loss of energy. Similar principles can be applied to the search for information, with human searchers attempting to maximize their gain of relevant information during a search episode. Recently, information gain over time has received increased attention from the information retrieval research community (Smucker and Clarke, 2012a,b). Related concepts such as diet width (the number of different kinds of food items the animal is prepared to include in its diet) are affected by the abundance of prey and the cost of consumption.

Stephens and Krebs's (1986) work on optimality modeling serves as the basis for the research on foraging theory. They showed how optimality modeling can be applied to any situation where we want to understand decisions. They identified three key assumptions that are made in developing these models:

- **Decision assumption** refers to a specific aspect of an agent's behavior that requires a decision to be made. For example, in the marginal value theorem (Charnov, 1976), this is the decision of when to abandon a particular patch given that the rate of return of prey items within it decreases over time. This is regarded as an assumption given its reliance on the relationship between the decision of when to abandon a patch and energy acquisition.
- **Currency assumption** defines what is meant by good performance at the task at hand. In the marginal value theorem, this is associated with the energy gained from consuming prey. Similar ideas can be applied to information consumption, although there are other currencies such as novelty and diversity that are also important depending on the search task.
- **Constraint assumption** governs the limits and definition of the relationship between the currency and decision variables. That is, anything that is related to achieving the objectives of the other assumptions. Returning to the marginal value theorem, this could be the assumption that animals do not return to a previously foraged patch (which may not be true, especially over long periods of time, during which prey items within a patch may be replenished), and that the resources within a patch decrease as a function of foraging time (for some types of resource, such as information [the focus in this book] this may not always be the case).

Figure 4.5 graphically depicts the marginal value theorem, specifically the diminishing returns that may be obtained from additional time spent in a particular patch as prey becomes more difficult to locate (shown by the leveling off of the resource intake curve; see Krebs and Davies [1989]). Transit to the patch is also an important constraint given the time and energy expended (Sinervo, 1997). In this model, the net energy gain per unit time (the standard optimization currency in foraging models) is calculated from the slope of the diagonal line from the start of the transit time to the

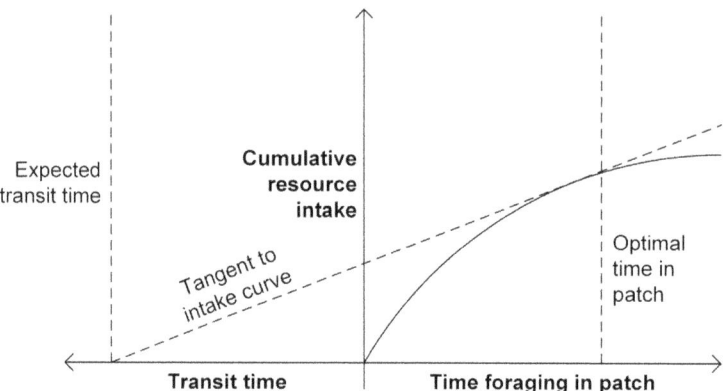

Figure 4.5. Graphical representation of the marginal value theorem.

intersection with the curve of diminishing returns (the solid line in Figure 4.5). To maximize the currency, the tangent line should have the greatest slope. The point of intersection of this tangent line is the optimal amount of time for the animal to remain in the current patch before transitioning to another patch.

Many of the principles from foraging theory transfer directly to information search behaviors. I now discuss information foraging and information scent in more detail.

4.3.1.2 Information Foraging

Sandstrom (1994), and to some extent Russell et al. (1993), applied principles from optimal foraging to information searching. They refer to this as *information foraging*. The conjecture is that mathematical models of optimal foraging behavior in animals could be applied to information behavior in humans. The currency of information is measured with respect to its novelty, with the goals of the search experience (at least in the case of the scholars) assumed to be in maximizing the novelty in the information that they examine. There are many ways in which information currency can be defined, many of which are covered in the description of evaluation measures found in Chapter 10. One attractive aspect of using novelty as the currency is that it provides a useful constraint assumption in models of information foraging behavior, allowing it to be mapped more easily to existing models from behavioral ecology. The core premise is that the citation of another paper loses its novelty over time as the paper receives more citations from other sources. This allows for the application of models associated with the consumption of food (a physical commodity that is depleted over time) and information (which is an abstract commodity that is largely constant over time; but the *value* of information is based on qualities ascribed by people and does change over time).

Pirolli and Card (1999) further developed these ideas and proposed *information foraging theory*, a scientific theory that applies the ideas from optimal foraging theory to understand how people search for information (casting human information interaction as a natural science). It covers how people will adapt to their information environments, and how these environments should be shaped to support effective searching. Moving beyond novelty as the currency (as assumed by Sandstrom in earlier work), Pirolli and Card use the *quality* of the information gathered during the search process. Because people cannot explore all of the information available to them (and indeed are limited in their cognitive capacity to only being able to process a few bits per second [Miller, 1956]), they need to make decisions about how to allocate their limited attentional resources efficiently (e.g., a "poverty of attention" is created by a glut of information (Simon, 1971; Davenport and Beck, 2013). People's attention is a scarce resource; and as computing resources are becoming commoditized, the focus should be on helping people manage their attention effectively. Information foraging theory is based on the assumption that, when searching for information, humans use the same innate foraging mechanisms that evolved to help our ancestors find food. Better understanding human search behavior can improve the usability of websites or other user interfaces.

Pirolli and Card's model of information foraging combines rational analysis and cognitive modeling after noticing similarities between searchers' information searching patterns and animal food foraging strategies. They noticed that as searchers examined resources (hyperlinks, etc.) they employed the same strategies as animals foraging for food. Humans are *informavores* (Miller, 1983), describing a human behavior whereby people adapt to the world by seeking and consuming information, much in the same way as animals seek sustenance, and use this information to support problem solving. As such, during information seeking, searchers are continually making decisions about the nature of the sought information, whether to continue to examine the current information resource and try to locate more information, or whether to move onto another resource, which path or link to following to get there, and when to terminate the search for information. The foraging metaphor highlights how information seekers can use cues left by previous visitors to find *patches* of information in a document collection and then consume information to satisfy their needs. There are clear applications for these ideas in systems that leverage historic data to support current searchers within specific domains (Wexelblat and Maes, 1999) or generally in Web search (Joachims, 2002; White et al., 2007).

A central concept in information foraging theory is information *scent*. Searchers assess the appropriateness of a particular trail by considering a representation, usually a textual description such as a search result caption or a thumbnail image, of the distal content. Furnas (1997) suggested that a representational object held a "residue" of the information item it represented. The concept of residue was further refined by Pirolli (1997) as information scent and defined by Card et al. (2001, p. 499) as a person's "(imperfect) perception of the value, cost, or access path of information sources obtained from proximal cues, such as WWW links." The profitability of an information source (Pirolli and Card, 1995; 1999) was defined in terms of the value of information gained per the unit cost of processing the information resource. Cost is defined in terms in terms of time spent, resources utilized, and opportunities lost when pursuing one particular search strategy instead of others (Russell et al., 1993).

On the Web, people navigate by information scent using proximal (local) cues such as visual and textual snippets (result captions in the case of SERPs), hyperlink text, or other types of cues such as enhanced thumbnails (Woodruff et al., 2001; Teevan et al., 2009a). This type of human information behavior is referred to as *navigation by information scent* (Pirolli, 1997). In a similar way to animals relying on chemical scents to indicate the chances of finding prey in their current location and to guide them to other promising patches, information seekers use cues in their information environment to guide them to content of interest and solutions to their information problems. Inside the Web browser, information scent can reside in, among other things, hyperlinks, search engine query auto-completion functionality, SERP captions, and previously visited hyperlinks that may be rendered in a different color to represent historic access. Beyond the Web browser, menus, commands, icons, and tooltips all provide information scent regarding the relevant functionality they offer to searchers.

During information foraging, humans make estimates about how much utility they are likely to obtain from the information viewed on a given path, and following the search for information they can compare their outcome with their predictions. Chi et al. (2005) developed information scent ideas and an algorithm to actually use these concepts in real interactive systems, including the modeling of online browsing behavior, the inference of information needs from Web visit log files, and the use of information scent concepts in reading and browsing interfaces. When the information scent starts to decrease (i.e., searchers experience diminishing marginal returns from additional search effort until they reach a point at which they no longer expect to find useful additional information), they may transition to another information source. Evidence of such behavior can be clearly observed in an analysis of Web behavior graphs, where people are frequently observed to terminate progress on a particular path and backtrack when they start to encounter non-relevant content (Card et al., 2001). Systems such as *ScentTrails* (Olston and Chi, 2003) can highlight hyperlinks on Web pages that have strong information scent (estimated according to a computational model) and are worth exploring. Empirical analysis has shown that such support can reduce the navigation costs to searchers associated with locating relevant hyperlinks (Woodruff et al., 2002).

Information is not evenly distributed across information collections; it is distributed in a patchy way. In addition to considering information scent, which may attract searchers to follow a particular path, we also need to consider the process by which people will leave a website. At some point, searchers make a decision that the expected utility of continuing to use this website is lower than a certain threshold, which is learned by searchers over time given their search experiences. Based on the marginal value theorem (Charnov, 1976) this decision would be made when the marginal capture rate of relevant information on the site drops below the average capture rate for the collection. Awareness of the average is searcher dependent, and some searchers may be unaware that there are other patches out there. It has been shown that computational models can predict with reasonable accuracy the hyperlinks that people will select and the lengths of the trails that people traverse within a given website before abandoning their searches (Pirolli and Fu, 2003; Fu and Pirolli, 2007). That said, there is limited support for helping searchers who may lack this experience, or may be unfamiliar with the current domain, make decisions about when they have exhausted an information patch (or at least depleted it to a level at which the marginal value is low), and when they should move elsewhere. More research is needed in developing decision support for this type of information patch foraging.

An interesting aspect of the model proposed by Pirolli and Card is the notion of patch enrichment, whereby people can modify the information patches to suit the needs of the current search task. Through a series of refinements as searchers isolate and synthesize relevant information, arrange it into sub-topics, and so on, the patches are transformed into new patches with higher rates of return of relevant information and lower search times, which helps the forager be more efficient in finding high quality information.

4.3.1.2.1 Computational Models of Information Foraging
Computational cognitive models of information foraging behavior (computer simulations) have been developed that incorporate principles from information scent to characterize information foraging behavior on the Web and make predictions about how they will react when they encounter particular information (e.g., SNIF-ACT [Pirolli, and Fu 2003; Fu and Pirolli, 2007]). These models, based on rational analysis (Anderson, 1990), associate information scent with relevance and assume that this relevance is a driver of their search interaction behavior. They capitalize on consistencies in online behavior (Huberman et al., 1998) and also relate closely to simulations of searcher behavior that are discussed in Chapter 11.

Mathematical models of spreading activation operate in a similar way to models of associative memory and have been used to perform this rational analysis of information scent. That is, ideas are connected in memory with various strengths, and then when something attracts a searcher's attention (e.g., reviewing a hyperlink on a Web page), it activates associated ideas, spreading the activation across the network. The amount of activation that accumulates on an information goal provides an indication for the degree of relevance associated with an item being examined (Anderson, 1983). Because the strength of association between concepts cannot be measured directly in these computational models, it is frequently estimated based on statistical techniques applied to natural language corpora, including the semantic relatedness of words (e.g., the pointwise mutual information of two terms co-occurring within a document in the collection). These weights can be fed into a cognitive model (such as ACT-R [Adaptive Control of Thought-Rational, Anderson and Lebiere, 1998], comprising a number of memory modules and if-then rules, which can effectively model human behavior) and can be used to simulate people on the Web. Adaptive control of thought in information foraging (ACT-IF, Pirolli, 1997) models optimal foraging behavior in large text collections using the Scatter/Gather search interface (Cutting et al., 1992). Inferring user needs by information scent (IUNIS) demonstrates that people can be clustered into types or profiles based on their surfing patterns (Chi et al., 2001; Heer and Chi, 2001). Collaborative filtering, discussed in Chapter 6, allows searchers to forage for information in groups much like the way a group of humans may collaborate to hunt for food when items in their diet are distributed sparsely in the environment. By ascribing usage histories to resources, people can benefit from the foraging behavior of others within a single domain (Wexelblat and Maes, 1999), but also in Web searches using trails mined from prior searchers (Agichtein et al., 2006; Bilenko and White, 2008; Capra et al., 2015) or created manually (Yuan and White, 2012).

Computational models of search behavior can be used for tasks such as predicting the resources that will be selected by searchers, given some context of links that they are considering (e.g., given a search engine result list, we can make predictions about which links will be selected). Of course, given large-scale search interaction data collected by search engines, we can observe searchers' information access patterns without needing to simulate search activity; but that only applies to the environment in which the data are collected. A significant advantage of the simulated model is that it could be applied to assess the usability of *unseen* websites and inform decisions around what changes in information scent could improve the navigability of the site (e.g., to reduce the need for as much backtracking on the site or show that a certain fraction of searchers are going to reach the particular content that they seek on the site, given information about the tasks that people are likely attempting). This requires a textual description of the task and the content of the site that is being analyzed (including the targets being sought).

Important future work in this area involves modeling the search behavior of searchers of different levels of expertise, other properties of the searcher, and other types of information-seeking behavior beyond focused exploration of a particular website, as well as understanding the effects of intrinsic and extrinsic motivators on search behavior. These and related issues are discussed later in the book (Chapter 11), when searcher simulations are covered. More recent work on information foraging has focused on social and cooperative knowledge production, social bookmarking, and wikis (Chi et al., 2007; Pirolli, 2009). This type of foraging behavior can be supported effectively by the Web, but is not a focus of this book. For more details on information foraging theory, see Pirolli (2007).

4.3.2 Berrypicking and Orienteering

Beyond information foraging, other analogies from the physical world have been employed to model how people search for information in an undirected manner, with an emphasis on browsing and exploration. Two of the most popular models are *berrypicking* (Bates, 1990) and *orienteering* (O'Day and Jeffries, 1993).

4.3.2.1 Berrypicking

Berrypicking assumes that interesting information is scattered throughout the collection like berries on bushes, and that people must pick the berries individually. In a similar way to information foraging (Pirolli and Card, 1995) and wayfinding (Lynch, 1960), this approach views the searcher as moving through an information space gathering fragments of information and seeking cues from the local context that inform future navigation decisions. However, unlike foraging, the focus is on the dynamics of the information need (and the resultant search queries and future resource selection decisions) rather than the exploitation-exploration tradeoffs and the act of search (foraging) that is targeted by information foraging research.

The berrypicking model assumes that the query is constantly shifting and that as searchers move between sources the new information they are exposed to can facilitate new ideas and new directions, including new conceptions of their query statements. Bates (1989) described this as an "evolving search," and as the search progresses, the desired outcome may also change. At each stage of the search, with each conception of the query, the searcher may identify useful information and references. Searchers' understanding of their information needs is enhanced as they encounter additional information during a search. Campbell (2000) suggested that this enhancement occurs to support or deny beliefs in various aspects of the need. The searcher revises their beliefs in what information is relevant until it reaches an end point of redundancy.

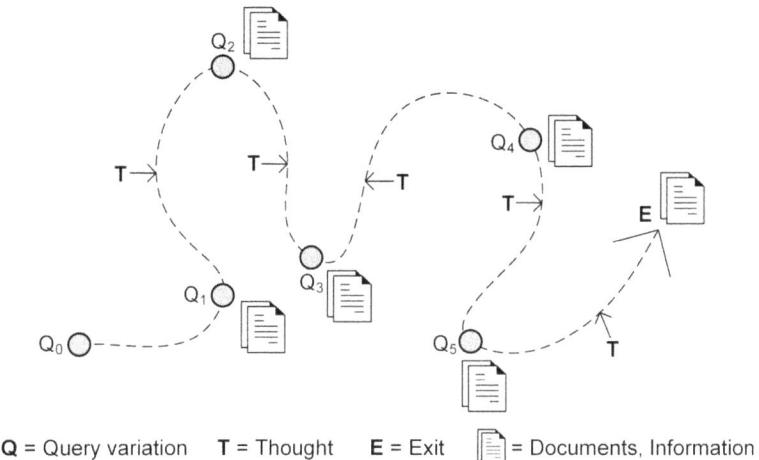

Figure 4.6. An evolving, berrypicking search (adapted from Bates, 1989).

Redundancy may arise because the information need has been satisfied or it no longer has importance to the searcher. Figure 4.6 shows an example of an evolving, berrypicking search. The path that the searcher takes through the collection is both winding and punctuated with new thoughts and document encounters as the search proceeds, which may lead to refined search queries and revisions to the information need.

The berrypicking model differs from the traditional lookup model (query-document matching) in two respects: (1) the query is evolving rather than solitary and unchanging, and (2) the nature of the search process follows a berrypicking pattern, instead of leading to a single best retrieved set. The berrypicking model also assumes that searchers are monitoring the progress of the search, and weighing the costs and benefits with a view to continuing down the current path or refining the search strategy in light of encountered information. This cost-benefit analysis has also been captured in work on sensemaking (Russell et al., 1993), which evolved into research on information foraging (discussed in Section 4.3.1). In that work, it was assumed that searchers continually perform cost structure analysis (or analysis of diminishing returns) to gauge their level of progress toward a particular goal. In effect, they view searchers as purely rational agents; always seeking to maximize their rate of return in pursuit of their information objectives.

Although needs *can* be largely static as people explore collections, it is the specific consideration of information need dynamics that is the defining characteristic of berrypicking models. In a similar way to many of the session- or task-based models of relevance or satisfaction developed for applications such as Web search, the assumption is that for many tasks, searchers' information goals are not satisfied by a single query, but rather a series of related queries and resources issued and examined during their information journey (White and Huang, 2010; Eickhoff et al., 2014).

Some recent research has shown that such trail-following behavior is common in Web search settings, and is especially evident when we consider the behaviors occurring beyond the search engine (White and Drucker, 2007). Analysis of the patterns of behavior allows researchers and search providers to identify classes of searchers and/or queries for which this behavior is noted. In prior work, I have quantified the value of the journey versus the start and end points, and defined a number of metrics for measuring the value derived from reviewing information (e.g., coverage, novelty, diversity; see White and Huang [2010]). Berrypicking has many implications for the design of search systems, including that systems should offer support for storing intermediate results (items gathered along the journey) and provide support for rehydrating previous states should a change in direction be unfruitful. The model also highlights difficulties with evaluating search scenarios in which people exhibit (or need to exhibit) such complex information search behaviors. Both Bates (1990) and Belkin (1993) proposed search interfaces that enabled searchers to modify and refine their queries as their needs evolve, thus modeling search as an information gathering activity.

4.3.2.2 Orienteering

The term orienteering most commonly refers to a class of recreational activities requiring the use of navigational skills and aids, including a map and a compass, to move between points in an unfamiliar terrain. Similar principles can be applied to information landscapes. O'Day and Jeffries (1993) proposed an orienteering analogy to understand searchers' information-seeking strategies. They contrasted two types of information seeking: *teleporting* and *orienteering*. In teleporting, searchers jump directly to the information of interest (per ad hoc searches), whereas with orienteering, searchers use local and contextual information to guide them in making decisions on a step-by-step basis as they proceed to their destination. Teleportation can be supported by a "perfect" search engine that fully understands searchers' well-specified information needs and returns only relevant items (Teevan et al., 2004), but there are circumstances in which searchers are unable to specify their information needs at a level to make search systems effective. Support for orienteering requires a broad range of tools to support different phases of the search process, including support for the search, browsing, query refinement, and re-finding. Teleportation may be an aspirational goal for search engines (e.g., Google's "I'm feeling lucky" button is one example), but in reality search systems are actually supporting orientation. They provide searchers with a set of starting points (result hyperlinks and associated information such as captions and URLs) from which to explore the information space on their own, relying on searchers' recall and recognition skills to locate relevant information in the subset of the collection to which the search system directs them.

Post-query navigation trails extracted from search logs have been shown to exhibit traits of orienteering behavior (White and Drucker, 2007). Presenting ranked lists of likely starting points is an effective strategy for mitigating risk in the ranking process; the search engine does not fully understand the intent of the searcher and it would be risky to present a single result (hence the emphasis on chance in the "I'm feeling lucky" functionality). Searchers have adapted to this results-presentation strategy and do not expect a single result in response to their queries. There are other advantages for orienteering, including increased confidence in the information that has been found, learning about the context for future searches, and an ability to backtrack if a seemingly erroneous trail is followed.

Web browsers already support some aspects of orienteering, by allowing searchers to follow links, backtrack, and revisit previous pages, and by providing direct access to search engines from within the browser. Such support can have utility in helping people orienteer effectively. For example, scratchpads and other custom views on search histories (Morris and Horvitz, 2007; Morris et al., 2008; Donato et al., 2010) can help people store information obtained during searching and browsing. Other systems can alert people to content on revisited resources that have changed since their last visit (Teevan et al., 2010). Using browsing data from instrumented Web browsers to model the orienteering behavior of the general population of Web users provides information on popular trails and resources that are not evident in search click data alone. Of course, the trail does not need to be browse-based. Trails of connected search queries may also be effective in supporting orienteering behavior – by directing searchers to future queries to fulfill aspects of their needs – and this is an area for which search sessions mined from search logs could be useful (Jones et al., 2006; White et al., 2007; Hassan Awadallah et al., 2014).

O'Day and Jeffries demonstrated the benefit of considering the entirety of searchers' trails, especially interconnected but diverse searches on a topic of a single problem-based theme, over time. They defined three main search types: (1) monitoring a well-known topic over time; (2) following a plan to perform some function (e.g., improve a business process); and (3) exploratory, whereby searchers explore a topic in an undirected fashion, such as learning about an unfamiliar topic. As part of their analysis of the behavior of professional intermediaries (financial analysts, statistician, etc.) they observed that people employed at least two of these search types and that each stage of search was preceded by the reading, assimilation, and analysis of found material. O'Day and Jeffries verified the predictions of Bates's berrypicking model, especially those involving the dynamics of information needs, including that searches tend to trigger new directions and that context from previous searches are carried to the next stage of the search process. Importantly, the findings of the O'Day and Jeffries analysis show that the value resides in the accumulation of information encountered during the search process, not just the final result set.

O'Day and Jeffries also identified two factors that influence information gathering strategies: triggers and stop conditions. Triggers serve as motivation to transition between strategies, including: (1) pursuing the next logical step in a plan, (2) encountering something interesting, (3) explaining change, and (4) finding missing pieces. Stop conditions determine when people will terminate searches. Although the stop conditions were not as clearly defined as the triggers, there were some noteworthy explanations such as the lack of compelling triggers, a belief that the searchers had performed sufficient searching for the task, some inhibiting factor, or diminishing marginal returns. The last explanations is particularly relevant to the research on information foraging described in the previous section, which explicitly models this effect. More recent work has demonstrated the need for orienteering (Teevan et al., 2004) since it enables searchers to be less specific about their information needs at the outset of their search – both to conserve time in specifying the query and in supporting searchers in situations where they may be unable to articulate their information needs – and provided a context by which to frame and interpret the results. Situated navigation (Suchman, 1987) describes a similar process by which people navigate with respect to their current context.

Once information of interest has been located, it needs to be analyzed and synthesized. O'Day and Jefferies also identified a number of post-search behaviors that were observed as part of the orienteering process. These could be grouped into "read" and "annotate," plus six analytical categories: (1) identifying trends in the data, (2) performing comparisons between the resources found, (3) aggregating and scaling, (4) identifying an important subset of the data encountered, (5) assessing the information along a number of different dimensions, and (6) interpreting the information found. Although many of these tasks represent common uses for the data collected, there is little explicit support for the transition between information seeking and information use. Information use involving the analysis and synthesis of search results is an important, and often overlooked, aspect of the search process. Information use is discussed in more detail later in this chapter (Section 4.4).

4.3.3 Organizing and Sharing

Once information has been collected from multiple places, it needs to be combined and organized for future application. An important part of gathering information is to organize it in meaningful ways and share it with others to facilitate collaboration and peer review.

As discussed earlier, document retention is a useful signal for implicit feedback in search systems (Kelly and Teevan, 2003). There are a number of retention activities that are possible during the course of searching, including bookmarking, printing, and saving encountered documents. Bookmarks are a popular way to create personal information workspaces of Web resources. Lists of bookmarks comprise lists of resource identifiers (e.g., URLs) or page titles, and can be organized into a hierarchical category structure. Studies of how people use bookmarks (e.g., Abrams et al., 1998) have observed numerous strategies, but also ways in which bookmarks could be improved. Within the search community, research on this area has focused on the development of scratchpads and related tools to let people retain their state when they terminate a search episode and also store the information that they have gathered during their searches (Morris and Horvitz, 2007; Morris et al., 2008; Donato et al., 2010). Beyond storing full information items, methods have been developed to facilitate the retention of information fragments extracted from documents (e.g., snippets of text) and to mark-up documents to identify the most salient parts. It is likely that only aspects of results are relevant to searchers, and they may only want to retain these fragments rather than the full text of the document, especially if documents are complex or lengthy, and navigating within them or retracing steps can be problematic.[2] Research has considered how and why scraps of information are not stored effectively, although those are typically generated outside of search (Bernstein et al., 2008).

Card et al. (1991; 1996) introduced the concept of information workspaces to describe environments within which information items can be stored and manipulated. They employed a book metaphor to group collections of related Web pages. Mackinlay et al. (1995) proposed a system for accessing articles in a citation database, and represented each document as a "butterfly" with inlinks and outlinks to that document depicted visually. They found that this representation helps people explore related articles, group articles, and generate queries based on the current article. *Data Mountain* (Robertson et al., 1998) provides three-dimensional support for the spatial representation and manipulation of items that can be useful in organizing and surveying information once it is found. *TopicShop* (Amento et al., 2000) helps people gather, evaluate, and organize collections of websites by presenting them with information automatically extracted from those sites. TopicShop could be enhanced to support task interleaving, whereby people combine the task of organizing found items with other related activities, such as exploring, or with entirely different tasks.

The pile metaphor (Mander et al., 1992) lets searchers manage information objects via piles on a virtual desktop. These piles support a range of grouping and browsing methods informed by real-world document handling. For example, searchers can pull documents out of the pile, group documents in semantically coherent piles, or spread out pile items using simple mouse gestures. Rose et al. (1993) applied the piles in a search application, including methods to automatically and manually create piles and sub-piles based on content. More sophisticated pile representations have employed physics simulations that enabled more realistic interaction with such a system (Agarawala and Balakrishnan, 2006). Pile visualizations have also been applied in other contexts, such as social navigation and security (DiGioia and Dourish, 2005).

Moving beyond the collection and organization of items by searchers, spatial hypertext allows authors to organize their content so as to express relationships among nodes in the network using spatial and visual cues such as proximity, alignment, and graphical similarity. Marshall et al. (1994) created a spatial hypertext system called *VIKI* that leverages the power of the human perceptual system, spatial and geographic memory, and – more generally – spatial intelligence. Users of the system employed the spatial representation to read documents in context accompanied by an awareness of proximal, related nodes. Rather than relying on authors to group pages effectively (which many authors may be unwilling or unable to do), Pirolli et al. (1996) experimented with link-based algorithms for clustering and categorizing Web pages.

Once workspaces such as those described in this section have been created over the course of the search, searchers may wish to share the byproducts of this process with others in support of decision processes and other related activities. Awareness of group activities has been explored in the computer-supported collaborative work (CSCW) community (Dourish and Bellotti, 1992; Grudin, 1994), but research in the use of shared workspaces in the context of information seeking has been somewhat lacking. Research on information sharing (Talja and Hansen, 2006) and collaborative information retrieval highlights the need to support communication and awareness during the search process (Hansen and Järvelin, 2000; Shah and Marchionini, 2010; Morris and Horvitz, 2007; Twidale et al., 1997). Recent research on collaborative searching has focused on the involvement of others (strangers or friends) to help resolve information challenges (Morris et al., 2010). The collaborative search process is discussed in more detail in Chapter 8.

4.4 Using

The models described thus far separate the process of finding information from the integration of that knowledge and the application of the knowledge to create artifacts and inform future activity. In this section, models are covered that consider such applications, beginning with sensemaking.

4.4.1 Sensemaking

Sensemaking is the creation of situational awareness and understanding in situations of high complexity or uncertainty in order to make decisions. It is "a motivated, continuous effort to understand connections (which can be among people, places, and events) in order to anticipate their trajectories and act effectively" (Klein et al., 2006, p. 71). It is the process of encoding retrieved information to answer task-specific questions. People may engage in sensemaking tasks frequently, and it is an "anytime" activity, meaning that a workable solution is available at any point in the process (although more time and more properties is likely to result in a better quality solution). Sensemaking generally involves five steps identified through observation and cognitive task analysis (Pirolli and Card, 2005): (1) knowledge gap recognition; (2) generation of an initial structure or model of the knowledge needed to complete the task – concepts, relationships, and hypotheses; (3) search for information; (4) analysis and synthesis of information to create insight and understanding; and (5) creation of a knowledge product or direct action based on the insight or understanding. These steps can be summarized as first combined internal cognitive resources and external cognitive resources.

Sensemaking typically involves a series of continuing gap-defining and gap-bridging activities between situations (Dervin, 1992; 1998). It is an active two-way process of fitting data into a frame (mental model) and fitting a frame around the data. These processes occur simultaneously; data evoke frames, and frames select and connect data. When there is no adequate fit, the data may be reconsidered or an existing frame may be revised (Klein et al., 2006).

Research in cognition, learning, and task-based information seeking and use provides important insights for understanding sensemaking. Researchers have proposed several models to capture the processes involved in sensemaking (Dervin, 1992, 1998; Dervin and Nilan, 1986; Pirolli and Card, 2005; Qu and Furnas, 2008; Russell et al., 1993). Dervin and colleagues (1986; 1992; 1998) focused on developing sensemaking theories underlying the "cognitive gap" that individuals experience when attempting to make sense of observed data (e.g., Dervin and Nilan, 1986). In the model, searchers that have a particular task and situation encounter a trouble spot or a "gap" that impedes their progress. The searcher must overcome the gap by finding help or making sense of the current situation to attain their desired outcome. Figure 4.7 denotes the sensemaking process, resulting in a bridge that spans the gap impeding searchers' progress.

In this model, Dervin and Nilan regard information seeking as a situation-sensitive sensemaking process. They suggest that information seeking should be holistic and focus on subjective information constructed by human actors, constructive actors with internal (or cognitive) conceptions as opposed to passive receivers of information, and situations within which actors act (including preceding and following information system use; see Ingwersen and Järvelin [2005]).

Russell et al. (1993, p. 269) described sensemaking as "the process of encoding retrieved information to answer task-specific questions." They defined a sensemaking model comprising four main processes: (1) *searching for representation (structure)*: the

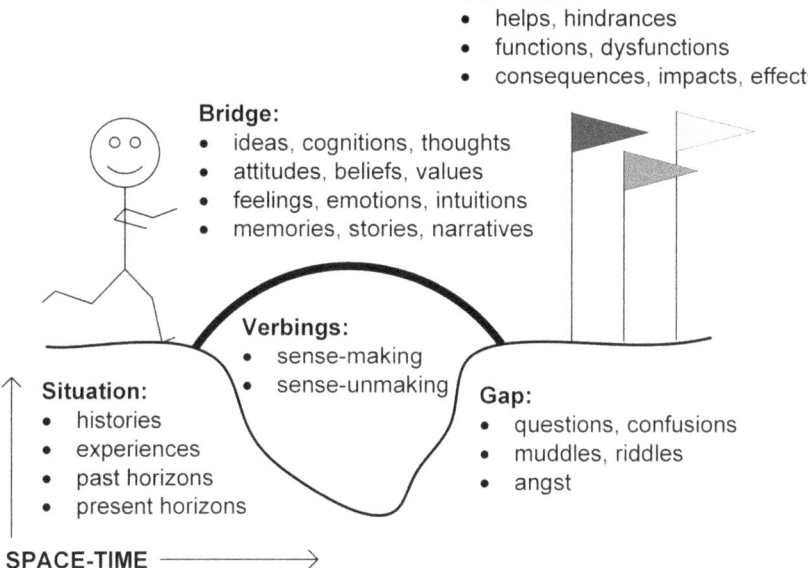

Figure 4.7. Sensemaking process during search (adapted from Dervin, 1983).

sensemaker creates representations to capture salient patterns of data; (2) *creating instances of representations*: the sensemaker identifies information of interest and encodes it in the representation; (3) *modifying representation*: representations are modified during sensemaking when data is ill-fitted or missing in the representation; and (4) *consuming instantiated representations*: the sensemaker consumes the instantiated representation and uses it in performing the task. Russell's model indicates the iterative nature of sensemaking. The processes may be followed for several iterations until the sensemaking is successful. Qu and Furnas (2007) separate the search for structures from the search for data in the sensemaking process. They also integrate the two processes and emphasize the bidirectional relationship between search and representation construction (Zhang et al., 2008).

Pirolli and Card (2005) conducted a cognitive task analysis and identified two loops of sensemaking activities: (1) an information foraging loop that involves searching for information, filtering it, and reading and extracting information into some schema; and (2) a sensemaking loop that involves iterative development of a mental model (a conceptualization) from the schema that best fits the evidence. A variety of conceptual changes can happen to the mental representation of knowledge as a sensemaker learns about the task, problem, or situation. Researchers have identified various degrees of change, ranging on a continuum from the addition of facts, weak revision, or radical restructuring (Vosniadou and Brewer, 1987). Piaget (1978) recognized two types of conceptual change in knowledge acquisition: (1) *assimilation*: the addition of information to existing knowledge structures; and (2) *accommodation*: the modification or change of existing knowledge structures.

Information processing is driven by inductive processes (from data to theory) or structure (from theory to data). The foraging loop is a trade-off among three kinds of processes (1): information exploration, (2) information enrichment, and (3) information exploitation (e.g., reading information obtained in a particular part of the information space).[3] Typically, searchers cannot explore all documents, and must forego coverage in order to enrich and exploit the information. The sensemaking loop involves substantial problem structuring (the generation, exploration, and management of hypotheses), evidentiary reasoning (marshalling evidence to support or disconfirm hypotheses), and decision making (choosing a prediction or course of action from the set of alternatives). These processes are affected by established cognitive limitations and biases (Pirolli, 2009).

Among several task characteristics recognized by Kim and Soergel (2005), the tasks that require at least some degree of sensemaking often involve: (1) new situations or problems; (2) complex, less structured situations or problems; (3) a new domain; and (4) an unclear information need. There is an overlap between such situations and exploratory searching discussed in the next subsection. Searchers engaged in exploratory and other types of complex search tasks are constantly engaged in sensemaking activities as they move through the information space. These movements are interrupted when a gap is encountered that requires information to be bridged. Sensemaking is an individual process of *construction*, not a process of utilizing existing information. However, the construction process involves the application of the found information. Exploratory and complex searches typically involve a prolonged engagement in which individuals iteratively look up and learn new concepts and facts. The knowledge acquisition causes the searchers to dynamically change and refine their information goals, and to ask more informed questions that probe deeper into the problems and the information space.

Overall, the sensemaking process involves the assimilation of new knowledge to enhance a person's previous state of knowledge, yielding a better understanding of a particular topic. This process may also generate information artifacts that can be shared broadly between individuals.

4.4.1.1 Social Sensemaking

Increased connectedness between individuals, facilitated by services such as social networks, has been accompanied by the opportunity for *social* sensemaking. During this process, people synthesize new information through, or following, social interactions or inputs. This could involve synthesizing disparate pieces of information that have been shared by many people (and the individual makes sense of that information), or it could describe a collaborative process whereby groups of people attempt to make sense of information collaboratively. The former may take place on the Web (the collaboratively edited online encyclopedia Wikipedia (wikipedia.org) is a good example of this), as are other sources such as forums and social media. The latter may take place as joint decision making within organizations, where the objective is to reach decisions that guide future action based on available information. Research in this area has targeted the development of tools to help perform these tasks (Convertino et al., 2009).

With increased connectivity between individuals, there is now a greater opportunity than ever for the views and insights of others to shape people's beliefs and perspectives on the world. Social inputs can be attained through explicit, collocated interactions (e.g., talking with friends in a coffee shop) or implicit, remote, and asynchronous interactions (e.g., reviewing a social media posting). The challenge for people in operating in these information environments is in knowing which information can be trusted (credibility assessment), how to overcome their own biases in how information presented is perceived and acted on, and how to decide which communities offer the best return on investment (social interactions frequently have associated costs in the noise, social interference, and so on [Knight, 1924; Thibaut and Kelly, 1959]). Also important in this area is how easily knowledge produced by one person transfers to others, and other effects associated with social capital, such as brokerage (i.e., the interactions between people at the intersection of social worlds [Burt, 2005]).

4.4.2 Exploratory Search

Exploratory search can be used to describe both an information-seeking problem context that is open-ended, persistent, and multi-faceted, and an information-seeking process that is opportunistic, iterative, and multi-tactical. In the first sense, exploratory search is commonly used in scientific discovery, learning, and decision-making contexts. In the second sense, exploratory tactics are used in all manner of information seeking, and reflect seeker preferences and experiences as much as the search goals (Marchionini, 2006a). Exploratory searches can span multiple queries and/or sessions. They are often curiosity driven and emphasize learning and investigation. Although almost all searches are in some way exploratory, it is not only the act of exploration that makes a search exploratory; the search must also include complex cognitive activities associated with knowledge acquisition and the development of cognitive skills (White and Roth, 2009).

In a similar way to orienteering, in exploratory search, people usually submit a tentative query to navigate proximal to relevant documents in the collection, then explore the environment to better understand how to exploit it, selectively seeking and passively obtaining cues about their next steps (White et al., 2006a). Information exploration is a broad class of activities in which new information is sought in a defined conceptual area. Exploratory search can be considered a specialization of information exploration; exploratory data analysis (Tukey, 1977) is another such specialization. In exploratory searches, the answer may only emerge after analysis of the information gathered during one's journey (sometimes spanning multiple days, weeks, or even months). Exploratory searches can have a profound impact on searchers' personal development, because they reflect the pursuit of higher-level learning objectives.

Learning is a critical component in exploratory search. Learning associated with exploratory search systems is subtly different. Rather than searching to close a gap in one's knowledge (where the gap may be known or its presence at least identified to the user at the outset of the search; see Belkin et al. [1982]), the goal in exploratory searches may be less clearly defined; learning in exploratory search is not only about memorization of salient facts, but rather the development of higher-level intellectual capabilities (e.g., application, synthesis, evaluation). The overarching goal of exploratory search is typically to create a knowledge product (e.g., a research paper) or shape an action (e.g., choosing a medical treatment; see Pirolli [2009]).

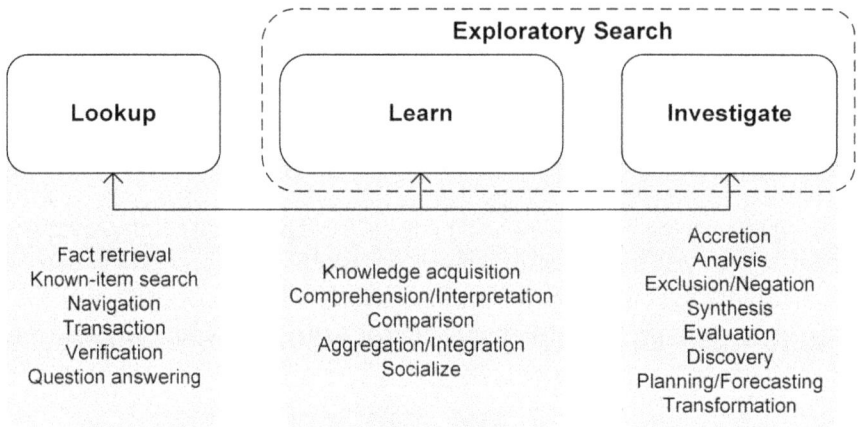

Figure 4.8. Exploratory search activities (adapted from Marchionini, 2006a).

Marchionini (2006a) proposed a set of search activities associated with an exploratory search process and separated the activities related to exploration from lookup searches, handled by traditional search technologies such as Web search engines. Figure 4.8 illustrates these activities.

Although the activities are shown separately in Figure 4.8, there is interplay between them (e.g., lookup searches are embedded in learning or investigation, learning is an important part of investigation). Lookup searches generally involve the retrieval of single answers (e.g., a single piece of information satisfies a known item search, fact retrieval, or question answering; a single Web page satisfies a navigational query submitted to a Web search engine), as seen in Figure 4.8. The majority of today's search systems handle lookup searches well, given the significant investment in ranking technologies and instant answers (e.g., weather forecasts or stock quotes) by search providers. However, activities associated with exploratory searches require more involvement from the searcher, more synergy between searcher and search system, and more functionality from the system, extending beyond just query specification and result presentation. Even in the absence of dedicated support for exploratory searching, evidence of searcher learning can be observed over the course of search sessions (Eickhoff et al., 2014) and longer term over weeks and months (White et al., 2009).

Exploratory search shares connections with many of the models and methods already described in this chapter. It may be similar to berrypicking and information foraging in a behavioral sense, but it is more likely to be driven by curiosity rather than a desire to fulfill an information need. The target of the search is likely to change throughout the search as information needs evolve, but it is likely that it was not well defined at the outset of the search. The goal may not be to maximize the rate of information gain. For example, searchers may be observed to employ seemingly irrational search strategies (e.g., retracing their steps through the information space to revisit a branching point or reading redundant information to confirm a hypothesis) to help them acquire the knowledge that they seek and understand the information that they encounter.

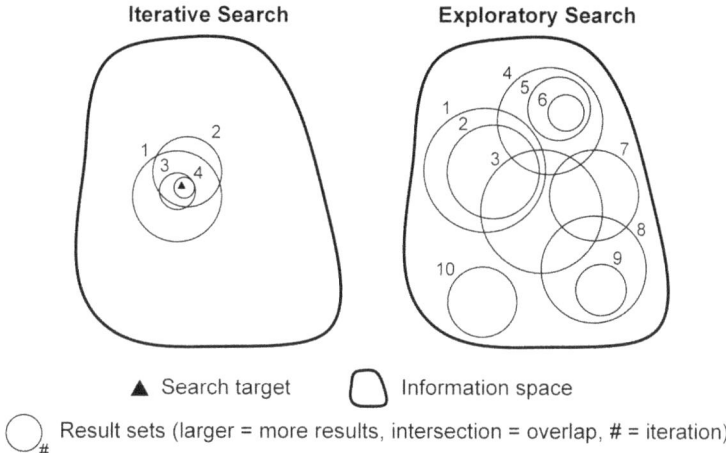

Figure 4.9. Iterative search versus exploratory search strategies (adapted from White and Roth, 2009).

4.4.2.1 Exploratory Search Behaviors

The interaction behaviors observed during an exploratory search are generally a combination of browsing and focused searching, with more emphasis on the former. People use browsing as a way to resolve the uncertainty and confusion that can occur as new information is encountered. Exploratory search is also different from more traditional models of iterative search behavior (e.g., iterative query refinement [Belkin et al., 2001]). The emphasis in exploratory search is on learning about the topic of the search, understanding collection content, and capitalizing on serendipitous opportunities to pursue particular directions when they emerge. Figure 4.9 compares and contrasts the iterative and exploratory search strategies.

The exploratory and iterative search strategies differ in how the searcher traverses the information space and in knowledge of the destination. In the iterative search strategy, the target of the search is typically known, and the search task is to find the target. Iterative search strategies can involve the consultation of thesauri before the search, the use of query recommendations offered by commercial search engines, and the systematic refinement of query statements (Marchionini and Shneiderman, 1988). In a user study of a search engine interface enhancement known as popular destinations (i.e., domains where the majority of searchers ended up after issuing a search query, as determined from search logs), White et al. (2007) found that query suggestions were generally most useful for refining the system's representation of the searcher's need, rather than initiating new directions for the searcher to investigate. Because the problem context may be open-ended or multifaceted in exploratory searches, a single target answer may not exist. In such situations, information novelty and information coverage are important aspects, as well as situational relevance (Saracevic, 2007). Some metrics can capture aspects of the exploratory search process by analyzing search activity (White and Huang, 2010).

During exploratory searching, searchers visit more of the information space, and many search targets may be present, each corresponding to an aspect of the task. Within exploration, there may be some degree of progressive narrowing as part of the exploration-enrichment-exploration trade-off (Patterson et al., 2001). Search under this model begins with the retrieval of a broad set of documents, such as one retrieved by a high-recall/low-precision query, then proceeds with narrowing that set to progressively smaller, higher-precision result sets, before reading the documents and extracting the information. This behavior is observed in Figure 4.9, between Exploratory Search query iterations 4–6.

Notably, there is a lack of formal models on exploratory search behavior. This may be expected given the dynamic and subjective nature of the exploration and learning process. However, some degree of formality could be useful. Formal models of how people engage in exploratory search could inform the design of search systems (e.g., in optimizing result presentation to maximize gain during exploratory search), as well as to support the development of measurement and simulation methods in much the same way as has been accomplished in research on information foraging. These models could be informed by available search log data, and could be based on existing representations of search and browsing activity (Downey et al., 2007). Some progress has been made in this area, targeting the development of frameworks to evaluate exploratory search systems using signals such as search action sequences (Hendahewa and Shah, 2015).

4.4.3 Problem Solving

Searches are performed within a context of broader situations, driven by information problems. Beyond simply finding information, search systems also help people solve these problems. Problem solving – an active research area that has been studied extensively – is regarded as a higher-order cognitive process and is the most complex of all intellectual functions (Goldstein and Levin, 1987). A detailed discussion of general problem solving is beyond the scope of this book; Newell and Simon (1972) offer an excellent summary.

Within the context of information behavior, models of information problem solving have been proposed, primarily in the educational literature (Eisenberg and Berkowitz, 1990, 1992; Moore, 1995; 1997). The models focus on the six stages necessary to build information problem-solving skills, specifically: (1) task definition, (2) information-seeking strategies, (3) location and access, (4) use of information, (5) synthesis, and (6) evaluation, although the higher-order cognitive processes underrepresented in the model have also been proposed (Brand-Gruwel et al., 2005).

The process and outcomes of information finding can be affected by a number of factors, including the computer skill level of the searcher (Marchionini, 1995). Although subject matter expertise is important in solving problems, metacognitive knowledge and skills (i.e., knowledge of when and how to use particular strategies for learning and problem solving [Metcalfe and Shimamura, 1994]) can compensate for a lack of subject-matter expertise (Land and Greene, 2000; Moore, 1995). Sperber and Wilson (1995) argued that problem solving does not apply to all information searching situations, but that there are some tasks for which the procedures, outcomes, and applications of the found information are extremely well defined.

There are two phases of the problem-solving process that I focus on in this discussion: (1) the *definition and elicitation* of the problem, and (2) the *process* by which people find solutions. It is the focus on solutions that differentiates the problem solving models from traditional models on information seeking.

4.4.3.1 Problem Definition and Elicitation

Before proceeding, the searcher must first understand their information problem in a similar way to other models of information seeking. During this phase, prior knowledge may be important in grounding and interpreting the information encountered (Hill, 1999; Moore, 1995). Once the problem is understood, active searching can begin.

A key to supporting problem solving is understanding the problematic *situation* of the searcher at the time of the search. When the searcher is engaging directly with another human (e.g., reference librarian or subject matter expert), the problematic situation can be elicited directly from the searcher and used by the intermediary to find relevant information. Human intermediaries have been shown to bring their own challenges to the retrieval process and the importance of interaction between searcher and intermediary has been highlighted as important for cognitive model construction (Belkin, 1984). In online settings at scale, however, there is a reliance on the search system to implicitly comprehend the information needs of the searcher and the interaction is in the pursuit of information rather than to communicate needs and preferences during a dedicated reference interview. Intelligent personal assistants can engage in rich dialog with searchers to better understand their information needs and surface more relevant content.

Evidence from a number of studies of information-seeking behavior (Harter, 1992; Spink et al., 1998; Tang and Solomon, 1998) has shown that information needs are transient and developing. There may also be periods of heightened uncertainty and confusion as people discover new information and assimilate knowledge. In information seeking, complex situations or tasks are often framed as wider information tasks involving problem solving (Attfield et al., 2003; Byström and Järvelin, 1995; Kuhlthau, 1993; Vakkari, 1999; Wilson, 1999). For anything other than well-defined tasks, the problem context often can be ill-structured, and people require additional information from external sources to clarify their goals and actions. People engaged in exploratory searches or complex search tasks are engaged in weak problem solving (Newell and Simon, 1972) with a lack of prior domain knowledge and/or unclear or unsystematic steps through the information space. During such searches, it is likely that the problem context will become better understood by the searcher, allowing them to make more informed decisions about interaction or information use. Hendry and Harper (1997) introduce an informal information-seeking environment called *SketchTrieve*, which helped searchers seek information and solve problems by spatially managing representations of the search process. As part of their study, they used the cognitive dimensions framework (Green, 1991) to map the design space for their information-seeking environments. This included aspects such as the closeness of the mapping of the displayed elements to the searcher's problem domain and the viscosity (i.e., how easily can one action be changed into another).

There are many ways to model the information needs of searchers, including implicitly modeling their interests and intentions based on their search behavior. Search systems can also ask them directly by providing interface capabilities that can solicit more verbose descriptions of information needs (Kelly et al., 2005). Traditionally, descriptions of information needs would be provided to human intermediaries – such as reference librarians – who would engage in a dialog with the searcher to clarify their information needs (e.g., Taylor, 1968; Belkin, 1990). This is currently not possible at scale, at least not at present, although this may change through the reinstatement of people as expert intermediaries in the search process (e.g., websites such as ChaCha [chacha.com] that offer search experts, and services such as *IM-an-Expert* [White et al., 2011], *Aardvark* [Horowitz and Kamvar, 2010], and *Google Helpouts* offer instant access to subject matter experts via modalities such as instant messaging and video chat).

There are other salient issues, such as the ways in which people can be encouraged to provide a description of their information needs. This is important since they need to perceive benefit from this approach before they expend the effort. A tighter coupling is needed between the expended effort and system response. This is similar to what is found in systems that implement rapid feedback loops (Ahlberg and Shneiderman, 1994; Glowacka et al., 2013) that allow searchers to fluidly control attributes of the search query and have the search system respond to their needs directly and immediately. These systems support searchers in making sense of the information retrieved in response to an initial query. Searchers have become accustomed to issuing short queries and search engines may struggle with longer queries (which can often yield no results; see Bendersky and Croft [2009]). There may also be challenges in providing verbose descriptions of needs on devices with limited textual input capabilities such as smartphones, where the provision of anything more than a couple of query terms may be hindered by the form factor. Advances in speech recognition now allow people to convey their information needs via spoken dialog to an intelligent assistant, or to another human with expertise in search systems or the task domain.

4.4.3.2 Finding Solutions

Once the information problem has been modeled appropriately, it can be tackled using a search system. During this process, the information encountered is combined with prior knowledge to reach a deeper understanding of the problem and solution alternatives (Schmeck and Geisler-Brenstein, 1989). The problem solution can be constructed from information within relevant documents and knowledge accumulated during the search process, including the examination of partially relevant and irrelevant documents. The information product (i.e., the solution) that emerges from this process may assume different forms including reports, articles, and presentations.

An important aspect of information problem solving is regulation. This involves the coordination of the information problem-solving process and directly impacts the effectiveness and efficiency of that process (Hill, 1999; Hill and Hannafin, 1997; Marchionini, 1995). Searcher skills (prior knowledge and competencies), actions, and outcomes are evaluated and refined during the process to optimize for successful outcomes (De Jong and Simons, 1988). This evaluation can be formative (i.e., conducted during the performance of the task) or summative (i.e., based on task outcomes). In Chapter 10 and 11, I discuss evaluation methodologies and metrics, including those focused on process and those focused on outcomes.

4.4.3.3 Understanding Problems

Solving information problems involves a structured, iterative process of organizing and correcting information that spans many actions and possibly multiple search sessions. During the problem-solving process, the information need derived from the problem is prone to change and evolve from an initial, vague state into one known and understood by the searcher (Ingwersen, 1994). As the information need changes, the searcher's ability to articulate query statements and identify relevant information improves based on their heightened level of problem comprehension (Belkin, 2000).

During such problem solving, executive functions responsible for a managing cognitive processes associated with goal-directed action (Elliot, 2003; Monsell, 2003; Chan et al., 2008) handles phases such as problem representation, planning and selecting strategies, maintaining the strategies in short-term memory to perform them by certain rules, and then evaluating the results with appropriate consideration of errors (Zelazo et al., 1997). Earlier in this book (Chapter 2) I discussed Web behavior graphs, a variant of problem behavior graphs (Newell and Simon, 1972), as an effective means of visualizing the trails that people follow when engaged in information search behavior (Card et al., 2001). Problem behavior graphs are normally constructed using verbal protocol analysis or videotaped analysis of a person working with information systems to solve an information problem. Given access to records of the specific actions that people perform when engaged in information seeking, we can study search behavior directly (White and Drucker, 2007). This allows researchers and search providers to perform more rapid codification and mining of observed behaviors to identify salient patterns for use in searcher/query clustering or predicting next actions, as well as the comparison and aggregation of task processes. Basing the graphs on fine-grained activity streams reduces the generalizability of the claims that can be made, unless there are attempts to cluster search sequences of search topics (Cadez et al., 2003) or represent the actions that searchers perform in a more abstract manner (e.g., as motifs representing action types [Fox et al., 2005]), whereby sequences are used to denote search activity (e.g., qR^* for a query followed by multiple result selections [Downey et al., 2007]).

4.4.4 Creativity

Searching and information seeking can be creative processes. Creativity is an application of the information found during searching. The outcomes of information seeking and information gathering described thus far in this chapter feed directly into the creative process. Creativity has been discussed in models of information seeking, especially during topic exploration and formation (Kuhlthau, 1992). The desire to be creative may be a useful driver of information searching, but the act of being creative is an example of information *use*, meaning that it is appropriate for inclusion in this section. Dörk et al. (2011) described the *information flaneur*, a curious, creative, and critical searcher persona, which emphasizes positive information experiences (rather than negative experiences associated with information needs and information problems; see Kari and Hartel [2007]).

4.4.4.1 Defining Creativity

Creativity has been explored in many ways, but the consensus appears to be that it not only involves the production of novel, useful products (Mumford, 2003), but can also be focused on the process of producing something – initially an idea, but eventually a virtual or physical artifact – that is original and valuable or is characterized by originality, expressively, and imagination. Creativity has been explored in detail in psychology research (Sternberg, 1999; Mayer, 1999; Csikszentmihalyi, 1997) and can be viewed along many different dimensions, including as properties of people, products, and the set of cognitive processes, and as a personal, social, and cultural phenomenon (adding some novel and valuable to the individual, as well as to the culture). Some have questioned the need for creativity to have social confirmation, and have argued that a novel product from the individual's perspective is sufficient (Boden, 2004). In measuring the creativity of an individual, interesting dimensions to consider include the frequency with which creativity occurs, its degree of domain dependence, and whether it is quantitative (objectively measurable) or qualitative (subjectively measurable).

Creativity has been explored directly in information science. Bawden (1986) described four types of information that could be useful in supporting creative process and unconventional thinking: interdisciplinary, peripheral, speculative, and exceptions and inconsistencies. Building on this work, Kules (2005) suggested that creative searches can embody (at least) four characteristics: (1) have generative goals (e.g., learn about a topic area or generate ideas); (2) be cross-context (e.g., searches could extend across domains or collections); (3) be exploratory and iterative (e.g., searches exhibit exploratory properties such as those described earlier in this chapter); and (4) encourage serendipity and be non-linear (e.g., contain a lot of branching – also observed in the search trails of subject matter experts [White et al., 2009]).

The related concept of serendipity has also been discussed in the research literature, with an emphasis on learning information without activity seeking it (Williamson, 1998) and chance encounters with information stimulating creative processes (Toms, 2000b; André et al., 2009). People may also take steps to increase the likelihood of serendipitous information encounters (Ross, 1999). Traditional keyword search methods have been identified as a potential threat to serendipity as they may overly constrict the result space to exact term matches (Foster and Ford, 2003; schraefel, 2009). These could be implemented in search systems using a variety of mechanisms, such as randomly selecting information or purposely using sub-standard similarity measures to generate anomalies and exceptions. Other proposals have included modeling preparedness (Toms, 2000b) or open-mindedness (Foster and Ford, 2003) as ways to be more receptive to new information when it arrives. Although the operationalization of preparedness and open-mindedness in search systems is less clear, it does share some traits with novelty. Support such as similarity-based suggestions (Toms, 2000a) or visual information surrogates (Kerne et al., 2008) may be useful in promoting serendipity within systems (Dörk et al., 2011). More recently, information-based ideation

(Kerne et al., 2014) has emerged as a paradigm for investigating open-ended tasks and activities where searchers develop new ideas during the search process.

4.4.4.2 Supporting Creativity

Definitions and taxonomies of creativity are useful for informing the design of search systems. The dimensions identified during their development have important implications for tools to support creativity during the search process. For example, the importance of the social aspect of creativity suggests that the outcomes of the creative process need to be shareable, with potentially novel contributions clearly outlined.

Research on the development of creativity support tools seeks to foster innovation through access to information (Shneiderman, 2000; 2002). The output of these systems can range from information artifacts, to generated hypotheses, and the discovery of new insights about data. Some outcomes may be ephemeral and difficult to measure. Creativity support tools support the easy exploration of multiple alternatives as well as mechanisms for storing states and histories and allowing actions to be easily undone. Backtracking support is important since searchers may pursue a number of avenues as part of resolving their problem (including following unfruitful trails), and being able to return to a previous state if a trail was not fruitful is important. As computing becomes more social, the role of groups in creativity-oriented search processes (such as collaborative brainstorming) will increase in importance.

Within search settings, there are a number of systems that leverage new interaction paradigms to help information seekers be more creative. Given characteristics such as those in the previous section, search systems can be designed to foster creativity by providing, for example, overviews, visualizations, and support for storing and managing information, as well as suspending and rehydrating states over time. Systems such as *Scatter-Gather* (Cutting et al., 1992) and *Cat-a-Cone* (Hearst and Karadi, 1997) purposely support browsing and exploration of information spaces, which can be useful in fostering creativity (O'Connor, 1988). Beyond interactive support, others have suggested that search systems need to consider creativity explicitly as part of their retrieval processes – for example, by employing fuzzy matching techniques to retrieve results that may be only somewhat related to the search queries (Ford, 1999), or through more expressive query statements (Shneiderman, 2007). Such methods enable searchers to retrieve diverse information and facilitate both divergent and convergent idea generation. Given the importance of being able to measure creativity (e.g., to assess system performance in supporting this important task goal), there is a more detailed discussion of the *measurement* of creativity in Chapter 10.

4.5 Summary

In this chapter, I have presented a number of models for exploring, gathering, and applying retrieved information. These models capture many different aspects of information seeking and use. Each of the aspects is important in its own right, but many of the models have a singular focus, on just one aspect of information seeking and use (e.g., analyzing the search process but not how the information is used once it is found), and ignoring others and the connections/transitions between them (e.g., exploring document collections, but not how this exploration informs subsequent searching for more specific content and ultimately the application of that information and its synthesis with other found items). The models should not be considered in isolation; there are benefits of combining different models to conceptualize search interaction behavior. For example, Wilson et al. (2010) demonstrated the utility of combining multiple models of the information seeking process for the offline evaluation of interfaces to search systems.

Many of the models described in this chapter have also largely been conceived, evaluated, and applied in library settings, restricted domains or websites, or digital libraries. While these environments remain a critical setting for information seeking, much of the general population performs their electronic searching via generic Web search engines. The models also ignore a range of issues that affect how people find and use information in the real world, including the role of factors such as domain knowledge (White et al., 2009), demographics (Weber and Castillo, 2010), or physical location (Bennett et al., 2011) in influencing how people seek and consume content. Human information behavior has also been shown to be remarkably consistent across a variety of search settings, and many of the core principles emphasized by these models can and should influence the design of search support in online services and retrospective analyses of logged behavioral signals. However, there has been little research on *validating* many of these models at scale in naturalistic search settings (e.g., although some of the research on information foraging is a notable exception [Pirolli and Fu, 2003; Fu and Pirolli, 2007]), and such studies are necessary to truly understand the applicability of these models in modern-day search settings, "in the wild" beyond restricted domains. Specialized search services are also emerging rapidly within mobile applications and in focused search domains, and there is a need to better understand the applicability of the generic models of information behavior to these specialized settings.

Many of the models described in this chapter rely on signals about searchers' cognitive processes (e.g., problem identification or learning) that may be difficult to observe from search activity alone. At scale, the support that has been offered (and the retrospective analysis that has been performed) has primarily been limited to information finding activities such as query formulation and search-result click-through. Support for the higher-order cognitive search functions has largely not been transferred into search systems, but this needs to happen in order to support more complex search activities. Although some progress has been made in this area (e.g., Eickhoff et al. [2014] mined search logs for evidence of short- and long-term learning, and Hassan et al. [2014] sought evidence of exploration, both via retrospective analysis of search log data), more work is needed to more fully understand how such activities occur using existing search technologies. In the next chapter, I consider some of the existing methods deployed within search systems, and how new technologies are emerging to help amplify people's search capabilities, advance their intellect, enhance their task productivity, and make search systems engaging and pleasurable to use.

PART II
System Support

This part of the book describes how the methods, principles, and models described in the previous chapter can be applied to build systems capable of supporting people's search-related interactions. I discuss both the current state-of-the-art in supporting searching, and anticipated advances in search systems in light of newly emerging technologies. Examples of existing search systems are included as appropriate.

CHAPTER 5

Helping People Search

The previous chapters have targeted actions that are useful as signals in models of relevance and satisfaction, as well as models of information seeking and use that have been developed to better understand the search process. One of the largest changes in information systems over the past few decades has been the transformation of search systems from tools that are used only by trained experts (such as reference librarians) to applications and services for the general population. In the early 1980s, researchers argued that information retrieval may become an elite activity unless search interfaces became easier for novices to use (Ingwersen, 1984). Supporting searching by the general populace involves both the simplification of query construction and result examination, as well as the introduction of tools to help people build queries and consider the results returned. In this chapter, I turn my attention to the mechanisms that have been developed to help people search. I focus on the search experience and searcher-facing components in particular, rather than the sophisticated methods employed during crawling, indexing, and ranking. Ranking algorithms and other backend components have been covered at length by other scholars (e.g., Manning et al., 2008; Croft et al., 2010); however, much still remains to be learned about the complexity of various interactive processes in search, and particularly about the effects of the variables involved (Belkin and Croft, 1992). Others provide excellent summaries of the history of search interfaces; both up to the end of past century (Marchionini and Komlodi, 1998; Shneiderman et al., 1999), and more recently (Hearst, 2009).

Emerging interest in areas such as human-computer information retrieval (HCIR) (Marchionini, 2006b) has directed attention toward the need to support users engaged in complex tasks and support more than simply information finding tasks. Information finding is handled well by existing search technologies. One of the central tenets of the design of search systems has been the need for searchers to assume control and responsibility over the search process. Search systems can offer assistance to searchers in performing their search tasks, but to benefit most from the search process, searchers must be engaged in the process and be responsible for their actions and the outcomes of the search. Control over the search process can be exercised in many ways, including through traditional search support tools such as relevance feedback, query suggestion, query expansion, or more novel methods that move beyond the turn-taking model such as dynamic queries and agile views, and other more recent advances such as gesture and voice control enable fluid and natural interactions between searchers and machines. The more recent enhancements create a wealth of opportunity to help searchers engage with search systems more effectively, and capitalize on some of the opportunities at the intersection of natural user interaction and information retrieval (i.e., nascent research in *natural-user information retrieval* [NUIR]).[1] There can be both functional and non-functional motivations for this. For example, speech input may be more convenient to searchers in a situation in which they are unable to touch the device (e.g., while driving or engaged in exercise); immersive and gesture-based environments may be more engaging and pleasurable to use than text-based counterparts, or better suited to co-located collaborative settings (Morris et al., 2006; Jones et al., 2014).

This chapter includes a discussion of various mechanisms that search systems offer to help searchers pursue their information goals, including some emerging technologies. There are different ways that search systems can support search interaction, many of which are application dependent. For example, faceted search interfaces (Tunkelang, 2009) may only be appropriate in situations for which search results can be easily represented by metadata, as may be the case in electronic commerce. Much like information visualization, discussed in more detail in Section 6.3, search interfaces assume many forms; some are generic, but most are custom-tailored for a particular search task or problem domain.

Let us begin by describing recent research on understanding current search practices, many of which will likely be supported in future search systems.

5.1 Understanding Current Search Practices

An important aspect of providing search support is to understand current search practices. Over the past several decades, there have a number of characterizations of search behavior with the intention of understanding search activity in more detail. Some studies have focused on characterizing how people search (e.g., the length of the queries that they issue to search engines [Silverstein et al., 1999; Jansen et al., 2000]). These studies are primarily observational and descriptive (e.g., Broder, 2002; Rose and Levinson, 2004; Jansen et al., 2000; Kellar et al., 2006; White and Drucker, 2007). Broder (2002) devised a tripartite taxonomy of Web search intentions based on a survey and an analysis of search queries. He identified three types of search intentions: (1) *navigational*: immediate intent is to visit a particular site; immediate is important here because, once the searcher reaches the target website, their task may be refined; (2) *informational*: intent to acquire information present in one or more Web pages; and (3) *transactional*: intent to perform some Web-mediated activity. Although this taxonomy was refined by Rose and Levinson (2004) on the basis of the various intents within a single category (e.g., informational directed and informational undirected to reflect subtle differences in the nature of the informational goals), it was still built around the same framework.

Moving beyond classifying queries, Kellar et al. (2006) used data collected from an instrumented browser on a small sample of twenty-one participants to generate a task taxonomy containing five categories: (1) *fact finding*: pursuing or items to assist in completion of within-session search tasks; (2) *information gathering*: collecting information, often from multiple sources, that can span multiple search sessions; (3) *browsing*: open-ended tasks with no particular goal; (4) *transactions*: performing actions online (e.g., banking, commerce, email); and (5) *other*: other activities, such as maintaining a website. White and Drucker (2007) identified different classes of searchers – navigators and explorers – based on those searchers' information access patterns observed in large-scale search logs. Navigators were shown to follow focused search trails with little deviation. In contrast, explorers' search trails contained more branches than navigators; they tended to explore the information space in more detail, irrespective of the nature of their search task. Individual differences in behavior have also been noted in more fine-grained search interactions such as eye gaze (Aula et al., 2005b; Dumais et al., 2010), and similar patterns were recently noted in result examination behavior is large-scale cursor tracking (Buscher et al., 2012).

Important lessons can be learned from mining online behavior that can directly inform the design of retrieval algorithms. For example, research on revisitation and re-finding revealed that people often issue the same search queries and return to the same results over time (Teevan et al., 2007; Tyler and Teevan, 2010). Building on these insights, by considering the fraction of the time that people revisit the same resource for the same query, we can develop algorithms such as personal navigation that identify and promote specific results that are frequently re-accessed by searchers (Dou et al., 2007; Teevan et al., 2011b).

The studies needed to attain these insights can be small- or large-scale, with different methodologies and opportunities for analyzing observed behaviors in each case. Small-scale studies may involve the observation of a small groups of searchers over a prolonged period of time, supported by interviews, stimulated recall, and other methods to allow a richer analysis of information needs than is possible from observing search activity alone (Kelly, 2004; Kellar et al., 2006). Large-scale studies are primarily log-based (they may be supported by surveys, but perhaps not involving the same cohort in light of privacy concerns with connecting multiple data sources and personally identifiable information that may be at risk as a result), and involve inferences about the nature of the observed queries or search tasks given search behaviors.

The central point is that characterizations of search behavior presents the possibility of providing clear insight into the nature of the types of search tasks that people are attempting, which can be used to inform the design of search systems. In utilizing such analysis to inform design decisions, care must be taken to avoid a circular relationship between what is possible on an interface and what searchers are observed doing via search log data. This may lead to the design of systems that place too much emphasis on supporting entrenched behaviors and insufficient focus on the newly emerging or uncommon tasks (e.g., time-critical searches for which where people have urgent information needs [Mishra et al., 2014], discussed in Chapter 9) may not occur frequently but may warrant special support given their criticality to searchers when they do. This makes it more important to understand search intentions from different perspectives and employ a variety of methods to triangulate current search practices and also solicit ideas for system improvement from different sources.

5.2 Current Search Support

Search systems already support many aspects of search interaction, including the examination of search results through ranking, the provision of search-result captions to support result selection decisions, and support for selecting query terms popular with others or known to have high discriminative power. There are four main classes of activities that have been supported in previous research: (1) creating search queries through automatic or user-controlled query expansion (e.g., Mitra et al., 1998); (2) supporting result selection decisions through the presentation of summaries (e.g., Clarke et al., 2007); (3) indicating relevance via systems that can capture and leverage searchers' relevance feedback (e.g., Salton and Buckley, 1990); and (4) making search decisions through direct searcher assistance (e.g., Meadow et al., 1979). The third class was covered earlier in the book. In this section, I focus on the other three aspects.

5.2.1 Informing Search Result Clicks

In modern search systems, result clicks are motivated by the captions (titles, snippets, and URLs) presented by search engines and shown directly on SERPs (Clarke et al., 2007). For reference, Figure 2.2 presents examples of result captions.

Where appropriate given the nature of the query or the results, these captions can also contain additional information about the document, such as thumbnails and review ratings. Although research into caption development has shown the benefits of biasing summaries toward searcher-specified query terms (Tombros and Sanderson, 1998), such summaries may not be fully representative of the content of the document, sometimes leading to erroneous visits to landing pages. Research on the impact of caption content on search behavior has shown that there are particular terms (e.g., "free," "official") that can attract searcher attention irrespective of relevance (Clarke et al., 2007). Indeed, even term bolding has been shown to attract user attention (Yue et al., 2010). Other factors – such as the presence of potentially alarming content (White and Horvitz, 2013) or results from favored domains (Ieong et al., 2012) – have been shown to affect search-result selection decisions. Evaluation methods such as click inversions (Clarke et al. [2007]; where click-through rates do not decrease with rank position), or interleaving (Chapelle et al. [2012]; where results from two search engines are interwoven on the SERP to help control for positional biases) can help study these effects at scale.

Recent research has attempted to better inform result selection decisions and postsearch navigation using taxonomy data to show child nodes of linked documents in the presentation of search results (Keller et al., 2013). Captions support gisting whereby searchers can attain a sense for document meaning (versus sensemaking, which requires more information from the text of one or more documents), when combined with searcher knowledge and experience (Spence, 2002; Marchionini et al., 2009).

Textual snippets are usually short; there are other representations of results that can be leveraged to support selection decisions. Visualizations of search results have been developed to help inform result selection decisions. Research on subtopic structuring (Hearst and Plaunt, 1993) and text tiling (Hearst, 1997) has shown that structure

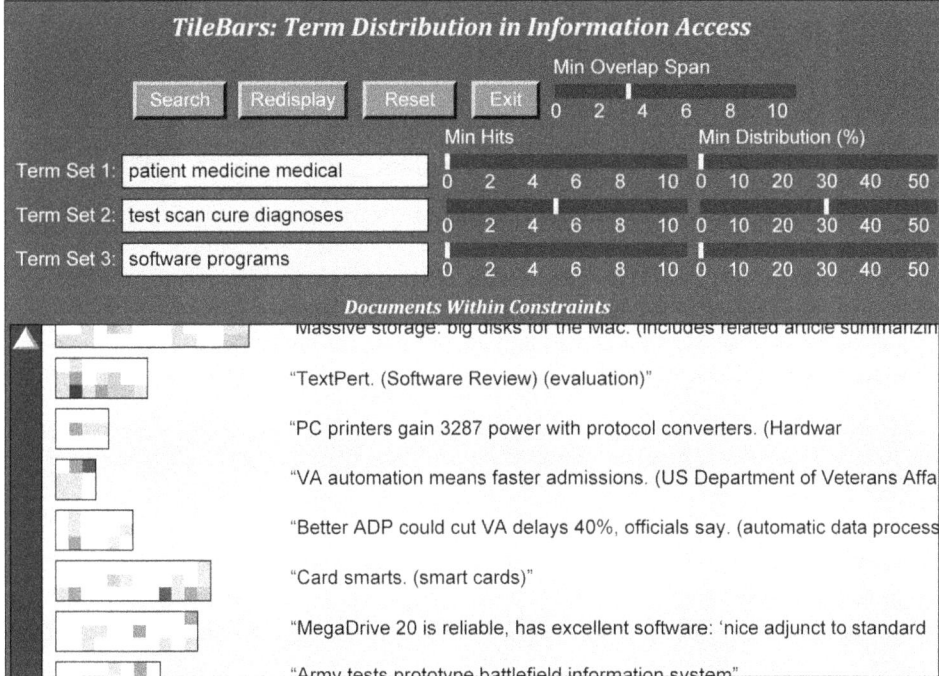

Figure 5.1. Example of *TileBars* interface where term sets within documents are highlighted (adapted from Hearst, 1995).

can be imposed on full-texts of documents, so that topically coherent units of text can be defined. These tiles can then be highlighted to searchers interactively. In one instantiation, *TileBars* (Hearst, 1995) simultaneously and compactly indicates relative document length, query term frequency, and query term distribution. These are shown as a column on the result page adjacent to the results. The patterns in a *TileBars* column can be quickly scanned and deciphered, aiding searchers in making judgments about potential result relevance and support (albeit to a limited extent) orientation within the chosen search result post selection. Figure 5.1 presents an example of *TileBars* shown to the left of each result.

TileBars is not alone in graphically representing the connection between user-selected attributes and document content. Other systems such as *InfoCrystal* (Spoerri, 1993) and *VIBE* (Korfhage, 1991), developed at around a similar time, also illustrate this relationship. Although they are visually appealing and may have some utility in locating relevant content inside documents, *TileBars* may also be difficult for regular searchers to interpret (e.g., given their horizontal orientation) and transfer into the selected document as the highlighting of salient regions does not occur within the document itself (just on the SERP). Later in this chapter (Section 5.2.1.1) I discuss methods to support orientation within the target search result.

Thumbnails have also been examined to provide additional information about the content of landing pages. Woodruff et al. (2001) studied the use of text snippets, unaltered thumbnails, and enhanced thumbnails of landing pages. The enhanced thumbnails, including various treatments such as highlighting and magnifying keywords, led

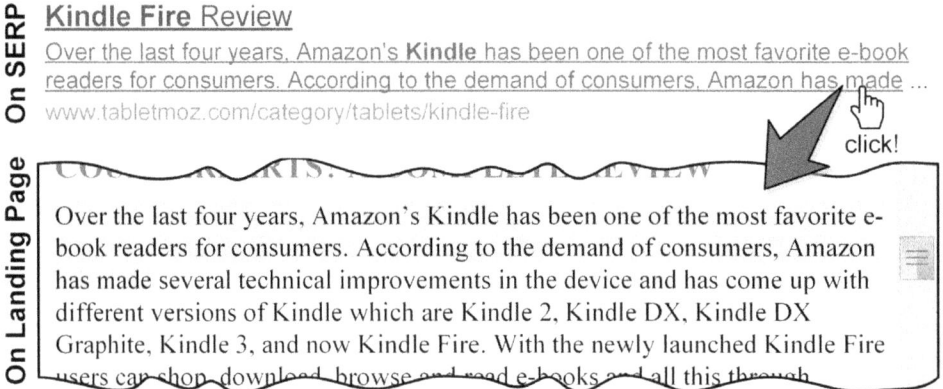

Figure 5.2. Schematic illustrating the interaction flow in clickable snippets (Feild et al. [2013]). Searchers click on the snippet text to be taken directly to that text in the source document.

to faster search completion times across several task categories. Teevan et al. (2009) examined how different representations of Web pages affected people's ability to recognize new relevant Web content and return to previously viewed Web pages. Their findings suggested that text snippets help find unseen pages and thumbnails help re-find pages for which searchers have seen the thumbnail. Aula et al. (2010b) showed that thumbnails add information about the relevance of Web pages that is not available in their textual summaries. However, showing only thumbnails, with no text information, resulted in poorer performance than showing only textual summaries.

5.2.1.1 Supporting Transitions

In addition to informing result selection decisions, systems should also directly support the *transition* between SERPs and the results. In current mainstream search systems, once the searcher selects a result and visits the document, they need to make their own decisions about where to locate the information they seek. That is, searchers require support in orienting themselves within landing pages. Few people know about or utilize find-in-page functionality (Ctrl-F; see Buchanan and Loizides [2007]; Loizides and Buchanan [2008]). This means that once people make the decisions to select a result, they must then use inefficient strategies such as skimming and scanning to locate that information within landing page.

Some recent research has attempted to better support searchers in orienting within documents post-selection. Feild et al. (2013) presented *clickable snippets*, which provide a way for searchers to navigate directly to those parts of the Web page that were mentioned directly in the snippet text on the result page. Figure 5.2 illustrates the interaction flow in clickable snippets.

In a search system implementing clickable snippets, searchers can click directly on the text in the snippet and will be transported (with appropriate transition support such as fades and scrolling) directly to the corresponding part of the Web page. This saves the searcher time in orienting themselves on the page, specifically in locating the text from the snippet that may have driven the selection decision. Other approaches have dynamically expanded the caption on the SERP (Paek et al., 2004), or have offered thumbnail previews of the content on the SERP directly (sometimes with the location of the caption in the summary highlighted; as described in the previous subsection). Beyond search, Zellweger et al. (2000) proposed *fluid documents* that display additional information about the content of embedded hyperlinks on a page when hovered over. The fluid documents system does not provide any support to searchers once they select a particular result and navigate to the document. Others have focused on the application of term/passage highlighting as a way to focus searcher attention once they click through to the landing page (e.g., [Chi et al., 2005]), or ways to navigate to salient regions of the landing page (Harper et al., 2004; Caracciolo and de Rijke, 2006).

5.2.2 Creating and Reformulating Queries

Searchers are traditionally responsible for modifying their own query statements. However, as suggested in Chapter 2, this process of query formulation can be problematic if people have insufficient knowledge of the domain, search system, or vocabulary used to index documents to create well-formed queries. Various studies of search engine logs (Jansen et al., 2000) and comparisons of mediated and unmediated searches (Spink et al., 1996) indicate that assistance given to searchers during query formulation (and reformulation) is an important determinant of search success. There has been relevant related work on query refinement and the discovery of semantically similar queries especially in a Web search setting. Beeferman and Berger (2000) proposed an approach that exploits search engine click-through data, in which they represented search queries and visited search results as a bipartite graph and applied an agglomerative clustering technique to identify related queries and Web pages. Cui et al. (2002) showed that the lexical features of the query space and the Web document space are different, and investigated the mapping between query words and the words in visited search results to perform query expansion. Daumé and Brill (2004) extracted suggestions based on document clusters that have common top-ranked documents. Various other sources of information have been investigated, such as pre-computed document abstracts (Billerbeck and Zobel, 2004), temporal query patterns (Vlachos et al., 2004), and query substitutions (Jones et al., 2006).

Alternative query formulations, known as query suggestions, can be offered to searchers following an initial query, allowing them to improve the formalized specification of their needs presented as queries to the search system. The recent popularity of Web search engines and associated search log analysis methods has facilitated the development query suggestion algorithms that draw on the query reformulation behavior of many searchers to make query recommendations based on previous searcher interactions (Jones et al., 2006). Figure 5.3 shows an example of these suggestions in the left-rail of a SERP.

These suggestions are useful for *refining* an existing query, but not necessarily for suggesting new directions that searchers should follow, or the steps required to complete complex (multi-step) or exploratory (multi-aspect) search tasks. Hassan Awadallah et al. (2014) presented methods to recommend queries that are more exploratory in nature, to help people tackle complex search tasks.

Researchers have studied the utility of query suggestions via user studies. White et al. (2007) compared query suggestions against the suggestion of links to resources

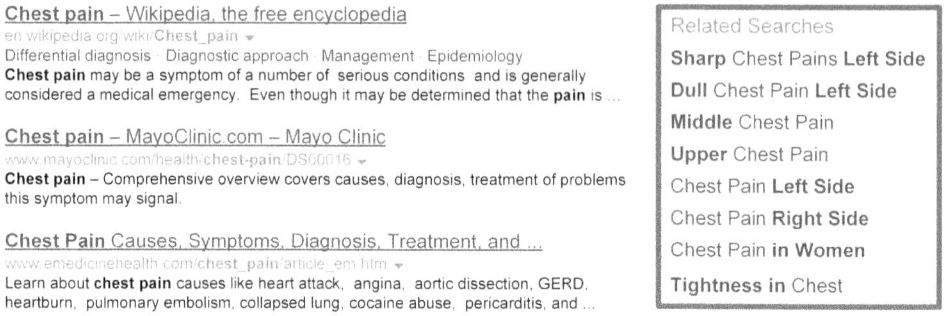

```
Chest pain – Wikipedia, the free encyclopedia
en.wikipedia.org/wiki/Chest_pain
Differential diagnosis · Diagnostic approach · Management · Epidemiology
Chest pain may be a symptom of a number of serious conditions and is generally
considered a medical emergency. Even though it may be determined that the pain is ...

Chest pain – MayoClinic.com – Mayo Clinic
www.mayoclinic.com/health/chest-pain/DS00016
Chest pain – Comprehensive overview covers causes, diagnosis, treatment of problems
this symptom may signal.

Chest Pain Causes, Symptoms, Diagnosis, Treatment, and ...
www.emedicinehealth.com/chest_pain/article_em.htm
Learn about chest pain causes like heart attack, angina, aortic dissection, GERD,
heartburn, pulmonary embolism, collapsed lung, cocaine abuse, pericarditis, and ...
```

```
Related Searches
Sharp Chest Pains Left Side
Dull Chest Pain Left Side
Middle Chest Pain
Upper Chest Pain
Chest Pain Left Side
Chest Pain Right Side
Chest Pain in Women
Tightness in Chest
```

Figure 5.3. Query suggestions (referred to as "Related Searches," highlighted) on a SERP.

frequently visited by past searchers with similar information needs. A user study revealed that systems suggesting query refinements were preferred for known-item tasks, and systems offering popular destinations were preferred for exploratory search tasks. Overall, popular destination suggestions strategically influenced searches in a way not achievable by query suggestion approaches by offering direct access to salient resources. Kelly et al. (2010) performed a user study to examine the effects of query suggestion quality and popularity on the usage of information search activities. Study findings showed that subjects could distinguish between high and low quality queries and were not influenced by the usage information. Qualitative data revealed that participants viewed the suggestions favorably, but that usage information was less important for the search task used in this study.

One way that search systems can assist the query creation process is by suggesting additional query terms for query modification (Efthimiadis, 1996). This modification can occur interactively with searcher participation (i.e., interactive query expansion [IQE]), or automatically without searcher involvement (i.e., automatic query expansion [AQE]). The process up-weights terms occurring in relevant documents and down-weights those in non-relevant documents. The terms chosen by the search system are typically those that discriminate the most between the documents marked and those that are unmarked.

IQE is thought to be advantageous because searchers have control over query modifications (Belkin et al., 2001; Koenemann and Belkin, 1996; Ruthven, 2003), but it also creates a burden. User studies (Koenemann and Belkin, 1996; Beaulieu, 1997) have shown that although terms selected during AQE benefit from the presence of statistical information inaccessible to searchers, searchers would still like to be in control of query expansion decisions. Koenemann and Belkin (1996) investigated the use and effectiveness of different levels of relevance feedback (RF) and query expansion with three experimental systems, ranging from "opaque" (an AQE system in which term selection is hidden from the searcher), through "transparent" (an AQE system in which terms are visible but not selectable by searchers), to "penetrable" (an IQE system in which terms are visible and selectable by searchers). Their findings show that increasing the level of searcher control over query expansion term selection improves search effectiveness. Beaulieu (1997) investigated three interfaces for search systems: one offered AQE, and two offered IQE. All systems were used as an interface to a university library catalog. Beaulieu's findings show that, although an improved interface can increase the amount

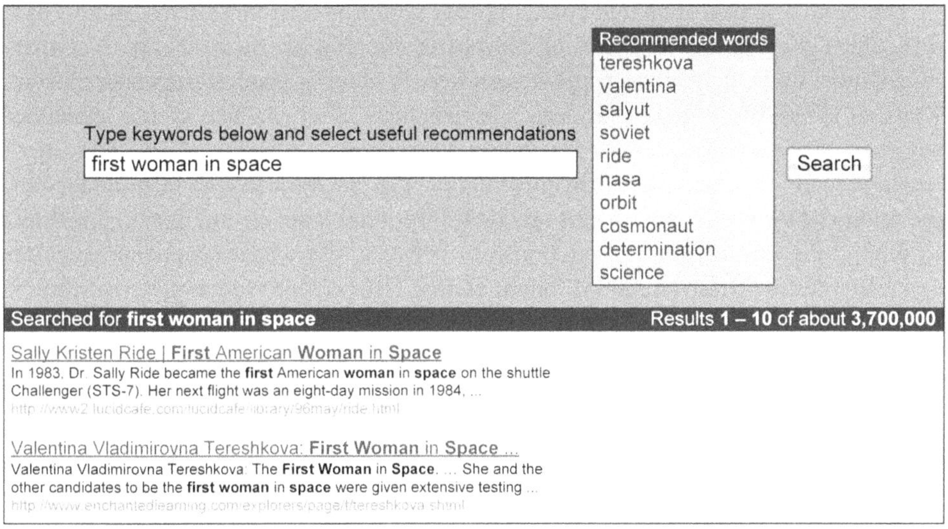

CURRENT SEARCH SUPPORT 149

Figure 5.4. Real-time query expansion (adapted from White and Marchionini, 2007).

of utilization of IQE and the effectiveness of term selection, the retrieval effectiveness did not surpass AQE.

Anick (2003) has demonstrated that although progress was made in promoting IQE, it remains a problem how to get searchers to consistently employ IQE in operational environments. Two possible explanations for this are that IQE is generally not integrated into searchers' established information-seeking behaviors (e.g., examining lists of documents), and it may not be offered at a time in the search when it is needed most (i.e., during the initial query formulation). These challenges can be addressed by coupling IQE more closely with familiar search activities, rather than as a separate functionality that searchers must learn. White and Marchionini (2007) introduce a variant of IQE known as *real-time query expansion* (RTQE), which has informed recent work on query auto-completion and instant search (where the search engine retrieves search results directly as searchers type). As a searcher enters their query in a text box at the interface, RTQE provides a list of suggested additional query terms to augment the current query, in effect offering query expansion options (based on pseudo-relevance feedback of the top-ranked documents) during query composition. Figure 5.4 shows an example of RTQE in action for the query [first woman in space].

White and Marchionini conducted a user study comparing three search systems: (1) a baseline with no query expansion support; (2) a search system that provides expansion options during query entry; and (3) a system that provides query expansion suggestions after queries have been submitted. The results show that offering RTQE leads to better quality initial queries, more engagement in the search, and an increase in the uptake of query expansion. However, the results also highlighted that the technique could also lead searchers in the wrong direction, especially when the subject matter of the search is unfamiliar. Because searchers were not able to predict the effect of adding an expansion term and are not able to preview the documents that would be generated, they could add erroneous terms to their initial query.

Therefore, it appears that IQE could improve search effectiveness, but searchers have difficulties in exploiting its potential. Simple term-listing interfaces that present terms in isolation are inadequate to support searchers in making good expansion decisions. Kelly et al. (2009) argued that searchers are more likely to use system-generated suggestions if they are presented as query suggestions rather than term suggestions because searchers seek additional information that allows them to fully understand the relationships between the terms and their information needs. Interfaces should aim to support the identification of relationships between relevant material and suggested expansion terms (Ruthven, 2003). Sahib et al. (2010) offered functional visibility, in line with the suggestions of Beaulieu and Jones (1998), by making searchers aware of the potential impact of the term selections.

Rather than relying on the system to recommend terms, it is also possible to get users to communicate richer representations of their information needs. Belkin et al. (2003) tried to improve search effectiveness by encouraging searchers to produce more complete initial queries by providing more space for query entry or asking searchers to more fully describe their information problem. Kelly et al. (2005) investigated the effectiveness of a document-independent technique for eliciting feedback from searchers about their information problems. They designed a feedback form to obtain additional information from searchers, administered the form to searchers after initial querying, and ran a series of offline ranking experiments based on the information from the form. Their results demonstrated that the form was successful at eliciting more information and that this information significantly improved retrieval effectiveness.

5.2.2.1 Relevance Feedback

One of the core principles of gathering and using search interaction data is the provision of relevance feedback (RF). This feedback can be either implicit or explicit. Searchers can provide implicit feedback about their interests and preferences by passively observing their interactions with the SERP during information access. In contrast, explicit feedback is collected directly from searchers (e.g., via relevance feedback, or "more like this," capabilities on SERPs).

5.2.2.1.1 Explicit Relevance Feedback

Explicit feedback can also be captured direct from searchers using purpose-built interfaces that can record searcher preferences associated with the full-text of documents or fragments associated with the documents, such as titles and query-biased summaries (White et al., 2005b). Feedback provision facilities usually assumes the form of checkboxes that people can select to explicitly indicate their preference for particular documents. Explicit feedback has been shown to be effective in non-interactive experimental environments (e.g., Salton and Buckley, 1990) and to a limited extent in interactive retrieval (Beaulieu, 1997). Traditionally, it is assumed that the results that are not selected are non-relevant, but by supporting explicit feedback the system is able to consider the information (or the *type* of information) that the searcher is not interested in. Spink and Losee (1996) provided a substantial review of relevance feedback.

5.2.2.1.1.1 Challenges
Despite the potential benefits of explicit relevance feedback, there are also a number of challenges faced by searchers when using systems that offer it (based on White, 2011):

- **Cognitive load:** Searchers may lack the cognitive resources to effectively manage the additional requirements of marking documents while trying to complete their search task. The process of indicating which information is relevant is unfamiliar to searchers, and is adjunct to the activity of locating relevant information. Beaulieu and Jones (1998) suggested that increased feedback and searcher control over query operations may increase cognitive load and that more control will not necessarily improve retrieval effectiveness.
- **Additional effort:** While relevance feedback is conceptually simple, it does not provide support for the search strategies and tactics employed by searchers (Bates, 1990). The feedback mechanism is not implemented as part of routine search activity; searchers may forget to use the feature or find it too onerous (Furnas, 2002). There is a trade-off between searchers visiting documents because the system expects them to (i.e., to gauge their relevance) and searchers visiting documents because they genuinely want to (i.e., they are interested in the content). In operational environments searchers may be unable or unwilling to visit documents to assess their relevance.
- **Failure to handle complex documents:** Relevance feedback systems can suffer badly if the corpus consists of a large number of multi-topic or partially relevant documents. In such documents, it is more likely that the relevant parts will contain the appropriate potential query modification terms, and terms in the remainder of the document may be erroneous, irrelevant, and inappropriate. However, relevance feedback systems treat documents as single entities with an inherent notion of relevance and non-relevance encompassing the whole entity, not the constituent parts. The techniques used to represent the document at the interface are also important for the use of relevance feedback. Janes (1991) and Barry (1998) demonstrated in two separate investigations that the use of different document representations (e.g., title, abstract, and full-text) can affect relevance assessments. For this reason, researchers have studied basing relevance feedback only on query-relevant parts of documents (Salton et al., 1993; Callan, 1994; Allan, 1995; Lam-Adesina and Jones, 2001; White et al., 2003) – in a similar way to that discussed earlier in the context of eye-gaze tracking (Buscher et al., 2008).
- **Nature of relevance judgments:** Relevance assessments are usually binary in nature (i.e., a document is either relevant or it is not) and partial relevance is seldom considered. One exception is the work of Ruthven et al. (2002), who offered searchers a sliding scale that allowed them to indicate the extent to which a document was relevant. Previous studies have shown that the number of partially relevant documents in a retrieved set of documents is correlated with changes in the search topic or relevance criteria (Spink et al., 1998). Potentially relevant documents are therefore useful drivers for the search process or for changing the scope of the search. The order in which relevance assessments are made can also affect searchers' feelings of satisfaction with the feedback system

(Tianmiyu and Ajiferuke, 1988). Order effects during relevance assessment have also been observed in other tasks, such as with the provision of third-party relevance judgments used in the assessment of search systems (Scholer et al., 2013; Shokouhi et al., 2015).

- **Reliance on initial result ranking:** Searchers are only able to judge the relevance of the documents that are presented to them. If a small number of relevant documents are retrieved, then the ability of the system to approximate a searcher's information need (via modified queries taken from searchers' relevance judgments) can be adversely affected.
- **Needs large quantities of feedback:** The underlying query modification algorithms need a lot of relevance information to operate effectively (Rocchio, 1971). The current design of explicit RF interfaces does not fit well with this requirement, and despite the simplicity of these interfaces, searchers have shown a reluctance to provide relevance assessments.
- **Searchers assess documents individually:** Feedback is typically treated as a batch process for which searchers provide feedback on the relevance of a number of documents and request support in query formulation. This may not be the best approach, because in interactive environments searchers assess documents individually, not as a batch. Incremental feedback (Aalbersberg, 1992) requires searchers to assess documents individually; searchers are asked about the relevance of a document before being shown the next document. Through this feedback process the query is iteratively modified. The method does not force searchers to use RF, although it does force them to provide feedback and may hinder their abilities to make relative relevance assessments between documents (Florance and Marchionini, 1995).

On the Web, search systems such as Google have offered relevance feedback by letting searchers request "Similar Pages" to retrieve related documents. Studies by Spink and Saracevic (1997) and Jansen et al. (2000) have shown that explicit feedback on the Web is used around half often as in non-Web settings, perhaps given the lack of training offered to searchers and unclear communication of its potential benefit. Therefore, the design of explicit feedback techniques for search systems operating in Web settings needs to be more carefully approached than in other settings.

To be truly useful, searcher-system dialog must have a perceived benefit to the searcher. If this benefit cannot be guaranteed, feedback approaches based on passive observational evidence (i.e., feedback mechanisms for which searchers have no preconceived expectations of its performance) are more appropriate.

5.2.2.1.2 Implicit Relevance Feedback

Implicit feedback has been explored at length in the information retrieval community to identify interests pertaining to a particular searcher, and more recently by search engines to identify aggregate interests. Early research in this area within the retrieval community, and some on recommender systems, focused on the use of document retention events such as bookmarking and printing, as well as document dwell time to provide estimates of searcher interests from their search behaviors over the course of a session or longitudinally. Models constructed from these behaviors could be used to enhance the search experience by, for example, training generic machine-learned ranking models (Joachims, 2002), re-ranking search results provided by the search engine, or generating related searches that can be used to augment or replace the current search query.

Many researchers have provided conceptual classifications of potential behavioral sources of implicit feedback (Nichols [1997]; Oard and Kim [2001]; Claypool, et al. [2001]; Kelly and Teevan [2003]). Nichols (1997) categorized the actions that a searcher might be observed performing during information seeking and discussed the costs and benefits of using implicit ratings in information seeking. Claypool et al. (2001) carried out such an evaluation and showed that certain implicit indicators could be used to infer searcher interests. Oard and Kim (2001) built on the work of Nichols by categorizing implicit ratings into four main types based on the underlying intent of the observed behavior: examine, retain, reference, and annotate. "Examine" is when a searcher studies a document; examples of such behavior are view (e.g., reading time), listen, and select. "Retain" is when a searcher saves a document for later use; examples include bookmark, save, and print. "Reference" behaviors involve users linking all or part of a document to another document; examples include reply, link, and cite. "Annotate" refers to those behaviors that the searcher engages in to intentionally add personal value to an information object, such as marking-up, rating, and organizing documents. Kelly and Teevan (2003) classified implicit feedback research and added another behavior category of "Create," which describes the behaviors typically associated with the creation of original information. Only the "Examine" and "Retain" categories are appropriate to the behavior of online searchers because the "Reference," "Annotate," and "Create" categories all require control over documents and inter-document relationships. Claypool et al. (2001) categorized a series of different interest indicators and proposed a set of observable behaviors for use as implicit measures of interest. Dwell time, mouse clicks, and scrolling on pages during general Web browsing were all recorded along with implicit ratings. Claypool et al. found a strong positive correlation between dwell time and scrolling behaviors and explicit ratings.

There has been recent research on the use of eye-gaze tracking to identify salient regions of documents and use that information for implicit feedback (Brooks et al., 2006; Buscher et al., 2008). Brooks and colleagues performed a comparative study of topical similarity between material included in a brief written report and eye-gaze behavior patterns for task modeling, and showed that eye-tracking can be as effective as lexical overlap. Buscher and colleagues examined the effect of incorporating gaze-based attention feedback associated with document sub-components for personalizing the search process. They used this information on the subdocument level as implicit feedback for query expansion and search-result re-ranking. They showed that considering reading behavior as implicit feedback yields improvements in search result accuracy of around 30% in the general case. However, the extent of the improvements varies depending on the internal structure of the viewed documents and the nature of the information need. Golovchinsky (1997) used clicked hyperlinks as indications that words in the anchor text of the hyperlink were relevant. Campbell (1999) used browse

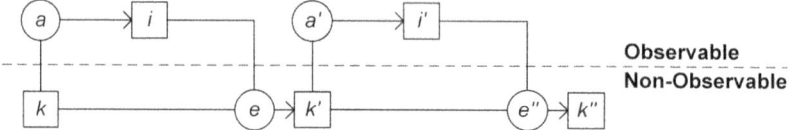

Figure 5.5. Updating of the knowledge state based on selection and exposure to information, connected over time in a sequence to reveal the observable and non-observable states (adapted from Campbell and Van Rijsbergen, 1996).

paths between retrieved documents to implicitly infer information needs based on the principles of *ostension*.

5.2.2.1.2.1 Ostension

Ostension refers to the explanation of a term by pointing at or otherwise indicating one or more objects to which it applies. Campbell and Van Rijsbergen (1996) proposed an ostensive model of developing information needs. The model recognizes the developmental nature of needs (in line with Bates [1989]), while also recognizing that information needs themselves may be inaccessible; and the model relies on the assumption (supported in much of the literature on implicit feedback, discussed earlier in this book), that evidence about the nature of those needs is observable in people's information-seeking behaviors.

Ostension can be used in many scenarios when the searched concept is difficult to define explicitly, either because the words will not be understood (as with children or new speakers of a language), or because of the nature of the concept (such as colors or sensations). For example, we can define "red" by pointing out red objects – apples, stop signs, or roses – rather than describing the color in terms of hue or combinations of other colors. Implicit in this definition, and common in fuller expositions of ostension (e.g., [Quine, 1953; Quine, 1969]), is the assumption that evidence contributing to an ostensive definition are purposeful acts of communication. Such acts are the basis for conventional relevance feedback.

The ostensive model recognizes the changing uncertainty inherent in searchers' cognition of their information needs,[2] and centers around the collection and combination of ostensive evidence based on what the system can observe as the searcher pursues information objectives. The model captures the impact that exposure to information has on the knowledge state of the searcher and how this knowledge state updates with exposure to information (say, by reading content retrieved by the search system) (e). Figure 5.5 graphically illustrates the revision of a knowledge state (k) through the selection of, and subsequent exposure (via actions, labeled a) to, information (i), which can be connected over time as the searcher performs more actions and can be divided into observable and non-observable states based on whether they can be seen by the search system.

The relationship between the observable and non-observable aspects is the fundamental assumption behind implicit feedback and has led to the development of many models of implicit feedback, for which the goal was to replace intentional communicative acts between the searcher and the search system with those based on observational evidence. Through this iterative search process, the system can resolve uncertainty about the nature of the information being sought by the searcher.

5.2.2.1.2.2 Challenges

Just as there are challenges associated with the application of explicit feedback, there are also challenges in the use of implicit feedback. Because the feedback is collected passively from search behavior, the activity being logged and how it is applied may not be apparent. This may raise concerns about searcher control over the search process, including the extent to which the system is operating on searchers' behalf rather than under their control (Bates, 1990; White and Ruthven, 2007). In addition, not all of the activity observed by the system is relevant, and ways to provide more focused means of collecting implicit feedback need to be explored (e.g., at the sub-document level [White et al., 2005b; Buscher et al., 2008]). The activity that is used by the system to model search relevance is dependent on the nature of the search interface and the information surfaced by the engine. This may lead to issues of preferential attachment (also known as the "rich get richer" phenomenon), which can be a concern within Web search ranking (Cho and Roy, 2004) since popular pages may never leave the top-ranked search results.

5.2.2.1.3 Comparing Explicit and Implicit Feedback

In one of the few comparative studies of explicit and implicit relevance feedback, White et al. (2005) answered questions about factors that may affect the provision and usefulness of implicit feedback: search task complexity, the searcher's level of search experience, and the stage in the search. They concluded that: (1) implicit feedback is generally more useful than explicit feedback for complex search tasks, when searchers want to focus on the search task and get new ideas for their search from the system; (2) implicit feedback is preferred to explicit feedback overall and generally preferred by inexperienced searchers wanting to reduce the burden of providing feedback; and (3) within a single search session, implicit feedback is affected by temporal location in a search (i.e., it is used in the middle, not the beginning or end) and task complexity. White et al. (2002) also compared explicit feedback and implicit feedback, using dwell time on pop-up summaries as the implicit feedback signal, and showed no discernable difference in performance between the two feedback mechanisms.

5.2.2.1.4 Alternative Forms of Relevance Feedback

Feedback mechanisms other than explicit and implicit feedback have been proposed and evaluated. Belkin et al. (2001) showed that systems suggesting terms for query expansion based on explicit feedback provided to the system were useful for searchers. However, a system implementing pseudo-relevance feedback (that simply assumes that all of the top-ranked documents are relevant [Buckley et al., 1992]) was better received, leading to improved search performance and searcher satisfaction. The nature of the feedback was the only difference from the traditional explicit relevance feedback system, and the pseudo-relevance feedback system removed the burden of having to interact with the search system or mark search results as relevant. Another potential application of RF techniques is in negative relevance feedback, for which the important terms in non-relevant documents are de-emphasized or removed completely from the query. This approach may improve searching behavior when used in interactive search systems (Belkin et al., 1996a; 1998). In these studies it was suggested that the technique was difficult to use, it was not helpful, and its effectiveness was dependent on the search topic. As with many search interface enhancements, this may be because of how the facility to provide negative relevance feedback was offered at the interface. Other interaction metaphors, such as Rodden's use of a bookshelf to represent the current search context (Rodden, 1998), have also been employed to help searchers utilize relevance feedback systems, and communicate the use and impact of relevance feedback in an understandable way.

5.2.2.2 Instant Results Provision

In addition to providing results directly on the homepage, search engines can also offer recommendations as searchers start to enter their query. Alternatives include enhanced query suggestion that could present summaries of the results and relevant entities inline as the query is being formulated, rather than having to wait for a query to be issued and a set of search results to be retrieved. Although this may have an effect on metrics, such as query share that may be important to search engines (depending on how queries are counted by Internet analytics companies such as comScore), it also provides searchers with a more efficient search experience by furnishing required resources in less time.

Typically search support on query entry is reserved for query completions (or query expansions [White and Marchionini, 2007]), but we also provided results directly in the auto-completion drop-down, saving searchers the effort of examining the SERP if the search engine can be confident that the searcher's need can be met with the result link shown. The Google "I'm feeling lucky" button is similar in some ways, but directs searchers to the top result only after they have finished typing; providing the support as they type, this gives searchers more control and may save them the effort of typing additional query terms that may be unnecessary to disambiguate their search intentions. *Google Instant*, a feature that displays suggested results while searchers type (blurring the boundary between query formulation and the retrieval of search results), was introduced in late 2010. At the time of the announcement, Google expected Instant to save searchers two to five seconds in every search; collectively, approximately 11 million seconds per hour. One of the most remarkable aspects of *Google Instant* is the server-side technology required to serve search results in this way *at scale*: the search engine needs to perform a query after each keystroke, although the results for popular queries can be cached to reduce the server load. This approach still requires that searchers review the search results after each keystroke, which may in fact slow query entry, and the experience of having the user interface update so dramatically after every keystroke could be disconcerting for some searchers.

5.2.3 Making Search Decisions

Advances in search technology have meant that search systems can now offer assistance to searchers beyond retrieving a set of documents. For example, search systems can now recommend search strategies and are capable of automatically reorganizing results to help searchers explore more effectively.

Search systems operating on behalf of searchers raises questions regarding searcher control. Bates (1990) presented a framework for envisioning search system design that related system involvement in the search process and the search activities that systems directly support. System involvement ranges from Level 0 (i.e., no involvement) to

Level 4b (i.e., complete system involvement with no searcher notification). Search activities include moves (identifiable thoughts or actions that are part of information seeking), tactics (one or more moves made to further a search), stratagems (large/complex sets of moves/tactics), and overall strategy that determines the direction of the search. Marchionini (2006a) noted a series of exploratory search activities that could be considered as stratagems (e.g., comparison, discovery, synthesis). Strategies involve a combination of moves, tactics, and stratagems. Strategies depend heavily on the current task context, such as finding pertinent research for a journal article.

Berrypicking (Bates, 1984; and discussed in Chapter 4) could be considered a complex combination of tactics and moves, whereas a simple lookup could be a basic set of tactics and moves. Information viewed by the searcher is used to inform subsequent moves and tactics, such as the queries to issue or documents to examine. In exploratory searches, encountered knowledge will be transformational, and it will create significant changes in terms of new stratagems and strategies. Searchers may decide to search within a new domain, use a different search system or interface, or adopt a different search strategy, perhaps involving collaborations with other searchers.

Meadow (1979) showed that it was problematic for systems to suggest moves as they may not be in line with the overall goals of the search. In a related study, Beaulieu and Jones (1998) investigated three factors that affect interaction with search systems – functional visibility, cognitive load, and balance of control between the searcher and system – and related them to a previous set of experiments. The functional visibility – providing the searcher more information on how the system functions – was found to be important on two levels. Not only must the searcher be aware of what options are available at any stage but they must also be aware of the effect of these options. The study by Beaulieu and Jones demonstrated that separate query modification and relevance assessment, can be more cognitively demanding for searchers. White and Ruthven (2007) demonstrated an inverse relationship between the severity of an action's outcome and the willingness of searchers to delegate control of that action to the system. That is, searchers wanted control of the actions that had significant impact (e.g., issuing a new query), but were willing to delegate responsibility for less significant actions (e.g., re-ranking the top search results) to the system. Such findings make us consider the degree of control associated with particular kinds of interaction and develop systems with mixed control.

Systems such as THOMAS (Oddy, 1977) and Grundy (Rich, 1979; Rich, 1983) tried to infer user preferences by characterizing search behavior, using stereotypes to personalize retrieval. To address the problems of user modeling based on stereotypical representations of their users, systems such as IR-NLI II (Brajnik et al., 1987) and FIRE (Brajnik et al., 1996) individuate the user modeling process using long-term search histories to personalize retrieval. Systems such as PLEXUS (Vickery and Brooks, 1987) and I^3R (Croft and Thompson, 1987) used different methods to improve query formulation and select appropriate retrieval strategies. PLEXUS simulated a reference librarian and asked a series of questions to build a more reliable user model. I^3R used multiple retrieval techniques to form a better model of the searcher's information needs. White et al. (2005) presented a search interface that recommended a search strategy (e.g., re-ranking search results or issuing a new query), based on the estimated degree of change in searchers' information needs during a search session.

Attentive systems accompany the searcher during their information seeking journey, and they can model searcher interests by observing searchers' behaviors. Letizia (Lieberman, 1995), for example, learns searchers' current interests and can recommend nearby pages by doing a look-ahead search (i.e., predicting what searchers may be interested in the future, based on inference history). *PowerScout* (Lieberman et al., 2001) uses a model of searcher interests to construct a new complex query and search the Web for documents semantically similar to the last relevant document. In a similar way, *WebWatcher* (Armstrong et al., 1995) accompanies people as they browse, but in addition to passively observing their search behavior, *WebWatcher* also acts as a learning apprentice. *Suitor* (Maglio et al., 2000) tracks computer users through multiple channels – gaze, Web browsing, and application focus – to determine their interests. *Watson* (Budzik and Hammond, 2000), uses contextual information, in the form of text in the active document, and uses this information to proactively retrieve resources from distributed information repositories by devising a new query.

As well as observing a particular searcher's activities and context, it is also possible to use others' previous interactions to assist with decision making. Currently, search engines employ data mining techniques to identify popular landing pages or popular destinations across all sites (Agichtein et al., 2006; White et al., 2007) on the SERP. Recent developments in large-scale log analysis have meant that search engines can select the multi-page trails followed by searchers, or present full trails to others issuing the same query. In *As We May Think* (Bush, 1945), Vannevar Bush envisioned using trails marked and willingly shared by trailblazing searchers to guide others. Joachims et al. (1997) suggested that in many cases, only a sequence of pages and the knowledge about how they relate can satisfy a searcher's information need. Trails can be selected based on popularity, diversity, query relevance, and similar factors (Singla et al., 2010). Leveraging previous search behaviors in this way may help future searchers with similar information needs make decisions about which resources to consider or steps to take, expediting task completion. Computational models use "information scent" (Olston and Chi, 2003) and searcher interests (Pandit and Olson, 2007) to help searchers decide which items to visit.

5.3 Search Interface Design

Beyond the simple types of support described thus far in this chapter, there has been a significant amount of research on the design of search user interfaces to help people perform a broad range of search tasks that extend beyond lookup scenarios. In this section, I will briefly touch on some of the research in this area.

5.3.1 Interface Methods

There has been a large amount of research on the design and development search interfaces to handle a range of aspects of the search process. Support has been developed to help people store their search histories, support the entire process, and make sense of the information that is gathered. Hearst (2009) provided an excellent summary of historic and recent developments in search user interfaces. As an example of the important role of interface methods in search interaction, I present a case study of a particularly powerful interface method: faceted navigation (Hearst, 2000).

Information seekers often express a desire for interfaces that organize search results into meaningful groups and to help make sense of the results and decide on actions (Hearst, 2006). There are many different views that can be used for the results, including result properties (e.g., categorical overviews [Dumais et al., 2001]) or tables of contents laying out where the components appear (Egan et al., 1989; Landauer et al., 1993). Both of these approaches create categorical views of the data. Clustering is an alternative to categorization that is performed automatically based on automatically-identified groups of similar items. These groups are generated on the basis of the content of information items rather than relying on metadata, as is evidenced in the *Scatter/Gather* system (Cutting et al., 1992). Clustering can be automated and is useful in detecting subtle nuances present in both the query and the retrieved items. In contrast, categorization may return more easily interpretable labels and make it easier for searchers to navigate the collection. Categorization has been repeatedly shown to be preferable over clustering in the design of search interfaces (Rodden et al., 2001; Pratt et al., 1999), and can be particularly useful for searchers engaged in exploratory or undirected search tasks (Kaki, 2005).

5.3.1.1 Case Study Example: Faceted Navigation

Traditionally, categorization methods describe documents using a single category that is reachable by a single path in the hierarchy. Alternatively, it is possible to associate many categories with those results in an attempt to help searchers reach their destination documents in many different ways. Faceted navigation (Hearst, 2000; Hearst et al., 2002) involves the creation of sets of categories that capture various aspects of the information items, each of which corresponds to a different facet relevant to the collection that is being navigated. Items in the collection are then assigned to one or more facet labels, allowing them to be reached in many ways (rather than just a singular path through the hierarchy, which may be difficult to find). Searchers engaged in complex search scenarios can benefit from structured overviews of the facets of a search topic. Faceted search interfaces provide this option via a presentation of the elements of the data being explored, allowing searchers to filter by one or more attributes of interest. *Flamenco* (Yee et al., 2003) offered search interfaces for flexible searching on a variety of orthogonal properties (facets) to provide rapid exploration and query iteration based on the interests of the searcher. Figure 5.6 presents a screenshot of *Flamenco* in action for images in the Thinker collection of the Fine Arts Museum of San Francisco, with facet values "Asia" and "fabrics" specified.

The faceted navigation approach is widely used in many websites, including electronic commerce sites such as Amazon.com. The facets for the category "Home Appliances" might include Brand, Color, Energy Efficiency, Dimensions, Review Score, and Price. Many facets depend on the nature of the product, but some apply to all offerings (e.g., the Review Score and Price may be made available for all items).

The faceted interface presentation style gives searchers the opportunity to evaluate and manipulate the result set, usually to narrow its scope. It enables flexible ways to

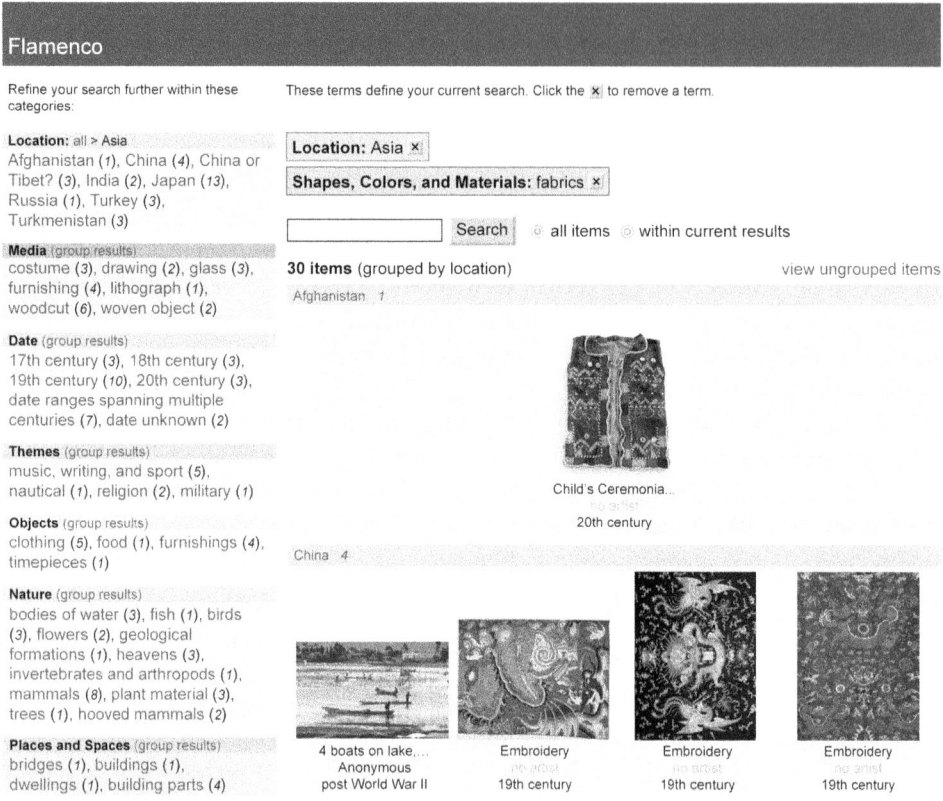

Figure 5.6. *Flamenco* interface with facets selected (adapted from Yee et al., 2003).

access the collection contents. Navigating within the hierarchy builds up a complex query over sub-hierarchies. The approach reduces mental workload by promoting recognition over recall and suggesting logical but perhaps unexpected alternatives, while avoiding empty results sets. Meaningful categories support learning, reflection, discovery, and information finding (Kwasnik, 1999; Soergel, 1999). A drawback of faceted navigation interfaces is the need for the manual creation of category hierarchies. There has been some progress in this regard via semi-supervised methods (Stoica and Hearst, 2004). Another drawback is that facets impose additional structure on the information space that may constrain freeform exploration.

Research on the design of search user interfaces has been fairly extensive, but progress has slowed in recent years as attention has turned to how people interact with existing search technologies (primarily query formulation and result examination). It is somewhat surprising that, despite of all of the research on search interaction, the standard presentation approach of a ranked list of ten search result captions has outlasted attempts to radically change how we interact with search results (e.g., via cartographic maps with the kartoo.com search engine). The reasons for this include its simplicity, familiarity among searchers, and generalizability of the result presentation method to a range of search contexts. Many other solutions to the challenge of developing search interfaces are only effective when content of a particular type is available or when the searcher is attempting a particular task, or when they have involved sophisticated visualizations that are unfamiliar to searchers or impractical to distribute broadly given their complexity and challenges in bandwidth consumption.

5.3.2 Interface Technology

Search interfaces such as those already described in this section can be offered via client-side applications that generally need to be downloaded and installed on the local machine or via Web services which provide an interactive search experience to searchers at scale. Searchers may be reluctant to install special software, although the move toward dedicated task-specific applications (discussed in more detail later) may lead to the increased adoption, especially in mobile computing environments. Developing engaging search experiences for Web browsers involves uses of client- and server-side scripting languages such as HTML and ASP.NET. To support more complete search experiences for the browser client, designers can develop rich internet applications (RIAs) that exhibit many of the characteristics of a desktop application using frameworks such as Adobe Flash. As Web traffic increasingly moves mobile, bandwidth constraints and the reduced display dimensions become ever more important factors in designing next-generation search interfaces. There also need to be multiple means of interacting with these systems, which will vary depending on interaction constraints. Support for natural interaction, primarily spoken dialog (both input to the system *and* output from it), will become increasingly important in designing support for interactions with search systems.

5.3.3 Impact of Interface Design

The design of the interface can have a significant impact on various aspects of the search process. Understanding this effect on performance is beneficial in designing effective search systems. Task analysis methods are useful in identifying searchers' needs and building principles for design. Methods such as cognitive engineering (e.g., Goals, Operators, Methods, and Selection [GOMS] rules) have utility for predicting searcher performance (Card et al., 1983), and scenario-based design and user testing (Carroll and Rosson, 1992). Running many variations of different search interfaces with different components, layouts, and so on in laboratory experiments can be costly and time-consuming. Techniques are emerging for the evaluation of these systems using established models of information seeking, such as those mentioned in the previous chapter (Wilson et al., 2010). Other simulations of search behavior could also be constructed to evaluate aspects of the search experience, such as implicit feedback algorithms (White et al., 2005c), usability (Chi et al., 2005), and interface design (White, 2006). These simulations have enormous potential, but still offer no insight into how a search interface could be *perceived* by searchers. Focusing only on matters such as utility and usability, however, they do help narrow the space of alternatives to be considered in direct consultation with human participants, and could help streamline the evaluation process by reducing the number of human-subjects studies that are required. The impact of other factors, such as individual differences between searchers should also be considered in the design of search interfaces, and the design of user interfaces more generally (Dillon and Watson, 1996).

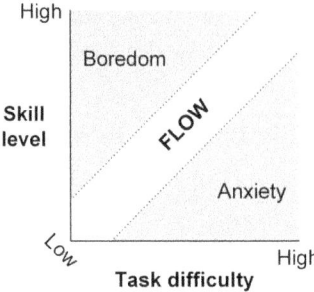

Figure 5.7. Skill level and task difficulty, and their impact on flow (adapted from Csikszentmihalyi, 1990).

5.3.3.1 Importance of Cognitive Flow

In his seminal work on cognitive flow, Csikszentmihalyi (1990) outlined his theory that people are happiest when they are in a state of concentration or complete absorption with the activity at hand and the situation. It is a state in which people are so involved in an activity that they lack self-consciousness, a sense of their surroundings, or awareness of the passage of time.[3] Csikszentmihalyi found that a person's skill and the difficulty of a task interact to result in different cognitive and emotional states. When the skill level is too low and the task is too difficult, levels of anxiety are elevated. Alternatively, if the task is too easy and skill level is too high, people become bored. However, when skill level and difficulty are roughly proportional, people enter flow states. Figure 5.7 illustrates the relative positioning of flow in relation to skill and difficulty, and its association with boredom and anxiety.

Flow is important in a number of search activities, including sensemaking, where people need to be immersed and engaged in the process to truly derive value from the system output. Task difficulty and domain expertise already have been explored in detail (Liu et al., 2010; White et al., 2009). While searchers' skill levels and their search tasks are beyond the control of the search system, systems can be designed to keep searchers in a state of flow by offering a number of capabilities. These include: (1) providing content tailored to their estimated skill level; (2) remove friction associated with executing system commands; (3) provide scent about next steps (queries to issue, results to select); (4) help searchers orient within document collections; and (5) offer fast system response times (Hearst, 2014b). Designing search systems to maximize flow is an intriguing proposition that may have significant payoffs in terms of satisfaction, enjoyment, learning, and creativity, all of which are important products of interactions with search systems.

5.3.4 Searcher Enhancements

Latency in gaining access to content can interrupt flow. Online systems are distributed, meaning that there is some latency between the selection of a hyperlink and the page content being loaded in a Web browser. This delay affects both pages and resources such as JavaScript, images, and so on, and is exacerbated by the inclusion of rich content on Web pages and lower bandwidth connections such as those available on mobile devices. As described earlier, latency in page load time can have a significant impact on the search experience; even only small increases in the amount of time taken by the search engine to provide responses to searcher queries has been shown to be negatively correlated with searcher satisfaction. As discussed in Chapter 3, latency in result provision is an area of great focus for search providers. New Web browser infrastructure also enables search engines to further reduce latencies beyond those associated with result presentation. The content of pages that are assumed to be visited by searchers can be downloaded in the background as the searcher is examining the current page, utilizing idle time to obtain documents that a searcher may visit in the near future. Continual computation methods (Horvitz, 1997; 1998) can be applied to decide which pages, or even segments of pages, to pre-fetch on limited bandwidth networks based on estimates of searcher utility from their content. Such technology can work in concert with background query systems or reconnaissance agents such as *Letizia* (Lieberman, 1995) or *WebWatcher* (Joachims et al., 1997) which attempt to download relevant content, but may not explicitly consider the cost-benefit tradeoffs involved in performing these actions. Using cursor movement data, accurate predictions can also be made about which resources searchers are planning on visiting, as they move their mouse pointer, with intentionality, toward a particular hyperlink.

To speed up the retrieval of search results in a search engine context, search engines can pre-render landing pages in the background that they suspect searchers will visit. Support for this has recently been added to Web browsers, allowing them to pre-fetch and pre-render content when instructed by the page author. This can also be performed client side via the Web browser. The Mozilla Firefox extension *Fasterfox*[4] has the option to pre-fetch all of the links on a Web page in the background, reducing the load time if one of the links is selected by the user. Predictive modeling could also be used (based on historic activity data, real-time cursor movements and/or real-time viewport data) to decide the order in which hyperlinks should be downloaded on a Web page, or decide which subset of the hyperlinks to pre-fetch.

5.4 Additional Search Support

Search support for complex situations is particularly important. Engelbart (1962) advocated for human–machine symbiosis during the resolution of complex situations and emphasized that this should not involve "isolated clever tricks that help in particular situations," but instead, "a way of life in an integrated domain where hunches, cut-and-try, intangibles, and the human 'feel for a situation' usefully coexist with powerful concepts, streamlined terminology and notation, sophisticated methods, and high-powered electronic aids." Systems can help searchers get closer to that vision via additional search support. There are a few useful ways in which systems can offer such support.

5.4.1 Richer Query Specification

Search systems provide ways in which searchers can custom tailor the results provided by the search engine by using special syntax or interacting with the specialized search interface designed to assist with the formulation of query statements.

5.4.1.1 Natural Language Queries

The standard way in which queries are expressed is via keywords comprising one or more words or phrases meant to capture the meaning of the searcher's search request; however, query statements can be represented in a number of ways, including as natural language queries. This may be more intuitive than entering keyword queries, especially to new searchers such as children (Marchionini, 1989b; Bilal, 2000). Search engines such as Ask.com have claimed to be able to handle natural language questions. Natural language questions can also be easily understood by other people who may be called on to interpret and respond to searcher questions in other systems, such as ChaCha.com. Beyond human-powered question answering, research on automatically answering questions has also been tackled in the TREC question-answering track (Voorhees, 1999) or on the Web more generally (Dumais et al., 2002).

5.4.1.2 Verbose Queries

The amount of space that a searcher is provided to specify their query has an effect on the length of the query provided (Franzen and Karlgren, 2000). Researchers have also experimented with varying richness of the query captured by the system to allow for the provision of different aspects of the information need (Kelly et al., 2005), and have experimented with the wording of the query instructions in an attempt to solicit richer queries (e.g., "Query Terms" versus "Please describe your information problem in detail, the more you say, the better the results are likely to be"; see Belkin et al. [2003]). Of course, providing more information to the search engine may not always be the best approach. One consideration in offering this type of support for search engines is that they may not perform well on long queries (Kumaran and Carvalho, 2009). Verbose queries can also take longer to type, especially on smartphones and tablets where the keyboard is not conducive to providing large amounts of text. In such modalities, spoken language queries will become increasingly important as a way to convey rich query statements. The system will then need ways of handling long queries that do not involve truncating the query once a particular token length limit is reached. At present, commercial search engines do not handle extremely long queries effectively (Bailey et al., 2010). They truncate long queries once a fixed limit of, say, 10 terms is reached, and return fewer search results overall as query length increases.

5.4.1.3 Advanced Search Syntax

Specialist searchers – such as those in the legal domain or reference librarians – often use advanced operators, often in the form of Boolean queries, to tailor their query statements. Search engines can interpret sophisticated queries that use query operators – such as plus/minus to enforce the inclusion/exclusion of a term in the returned result set, double quotes to enforce phrases, and site – to query for results within a particular site. Although this type of syntax used sparingly in query statements (one study of large-scale searching reported 1.1% of queries, 8.7% of searchers), research has shown that searchers who use these operators are more successful in their searching (White and Morris [2007]; and also exhibited other differences in their search behaviors). White and Morris used operators as a sign of search expertise and divided searchers into experts and non-experts based on their use of the syntax. Others have also found that the use of query operators was a strong indicator of search expertise (Aula and Siirtola, 2005). It is important to note that search expertise is not the same as domain expertise. Search expertise describes a level of general search skill, which may span multiple search topics. Navarro-Prieto et al. (1999) compared the cognitive strategies of high- and low-experienced Web searchers and found that, unlike experts, novices do not create search plans and strategies; they instead rely heavily on the results retrieved by search systems.

It is important also to note that the advanced search functionality of search engines may not be immediately apparent to searchers, especially novices. Advanced features are usually exposed on a separate interface and advanced functionality is available through specific query syntax. To address this issue, the search engine can offer interactive support (e.g., in the form of sliders) that can be transformed into advanced operators internally by the search engine and used for query alteration purposes, without searcher knowledge. This has the positive effect of generating better quality search results, but unfortunately it does not educate searchers on how best to formulate query statements for future retrieval tasks.

Training searchers to be more effective is an important responsibility for search engines and will lead to better quality searches and more satisfying search experiences in the long term. Recent work in this area has tackled both of these issues (e.g., by using hints and tips [Moraveji et al., 2011a; Savenkov and Agichtein, 2014] or social learning (whereby people acquire Web search skills by observing peer behavior) [Moraveji et al., 2011b]). Methods for empowering searchers with the skills they need to search more effectively will be discussed in more detail in Chapter 7, when I cover learning and information use.

5.4.1.4 Query Transparency

Formulating effective query statements relies on an understanding of how these queries will be interpreted by search systems. Mental models of search systems can play an important role in using queries effectively. Efthimiadis and Hendry (2005) explored laypeople's conceptual understanding of search engine operation by asking study participants to create sketches of how search engines operate. These sketches were then hand-coded by a panel of judges. While queries and results emerged as the most common concepts, many others – including matching, indexing, and crawling – also were referenced frequently. Focusing specifically on queries, Borgman (1985; 1996) explicitly studied the mental models of searchers on Boolean retrieval systems. She noted that many systems implicitly apply a default connective operator (AND or OR), and she concluded that this implicit choice can be problematic and confusing for the naïve searcher. Muramatsu and Pratt (2001) found that people often have erroneous mental models of how search engines transform queries internally (e.g., how they interpret Boolean operators or how they may automatically add expansion terms), and that this impacts their ability to interpret and make sense of search results. Others have demonstrated the variability in people's understanding of how search systems function more generally, beyond how they handle queries (Efthimiadis and Hendry, 2005).

Research has suggested that search systems should provide informative feedback about their operation (Shneiderman et al., 1997). Indeed, Anick and Tipirneni (1999) found that visible query transformations simplified query reformulation and increased searcher confidence in the results attained from their search. As discussed earlier, Koenemann and Belkin (1996) studied the degree of visibility and interactivity within the context of a relevance feedback system. The three levels of interactivity they proposed – opaque, transparent, and penetrable – reflect different degrees of openness about the underlying query transformations that the search engines may apply. Building on this research, *transparent queries* (TQ) (Muramatsu and Pratt 2001) uses lightweight visualization mechanisms to provide the missing feedback about query operations. TQ makes the normally opaque transformations and processing of a searcher's query more transparent by illustrating the transformations in a visually annotated presentation of the query. User studies show that when applied to different search engines, TQ helps searchers learn about the differences in how search engines process queries and also discover inconsistencies in their mental models of how search engines operate in practice. Despite its benefits, it is worth noting that the provision of increased functional visibility and control can increase searchers' cognitive load (Beaulieu and Jones, 1998) – which is problematic since cognitive resources are finite and there are limited resources for other tasks. Careful design and selective application of search system transparency is needed to realize its potential benefits while controlling costs.

5.4.1.5 Negative Search

The focus in this section thus far has been on the provision of terms to find matching documents. The general model that is assumed is that searchers seek a maximally relevant set of results, and they want the result set to be non-zero in set. However, in some cases searchers also may seek the discovery of gaps in existing knowledge so that new research ground can be forged or unpromising directions can be avoided. For example, Garfield (1970) proposed the concept of a "negative search," where the failure to retrieve results for a search query may actually be a positive outcome if the goal is to propose a new solution or a new problem, as is common practice in the scientific community. The challenge in pursuing this objective is how this support would be operationalized. This is a case in which a search system may want to pull from multiple sources and perform query expansion to increase the confidence that the lack of a match was not caused by missing vocabulary, as may be observed frequently when searchers are unfamiliar with a domain (Furnas et al., 1987; White et al., 2009b). Along similar lines, it will be useful for searchers to be told early in the search process that the information that they seek is unlikely to be available through the current search engine – saving them from wasted time and effort.

5.4.2 Surfacing Collective Behaviors

As discussed already in this book, there has been a large amount of work on mining large volumes of data patterns of search interaction and evidence regarding the relevance or utility of particular information resources. These results are typically integrated into the learned models of search result ranking and the connections back to the

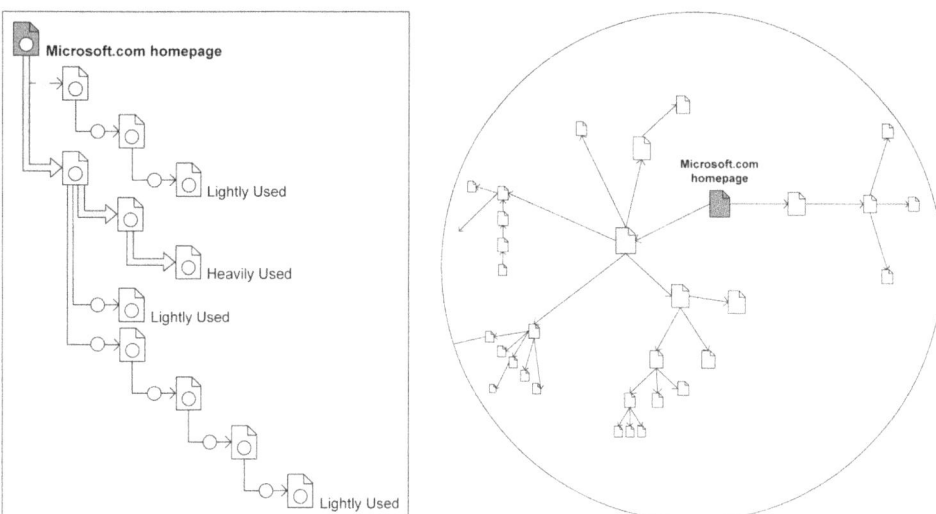

Figure 5.8. Interfaces to the path and site maps on the Footprints system (adapted from Wexelblat and Maes, 1999).

originating data is lost, at least to the searcher who may derive value from exploring some of the (perhaps more fruitful) trails that others have followed (Bush, 1945; Singla et al., 2010; Capra et al., 2015). Rather than only sharing the by-products of mining these collective data, the search activity can be mined, summarized, and presented directly to searchers to guide future decisions and actions. Although these tours and trails can be manually generated (Trigg, 1988; Yuan and White, 2012), mining and summarizing sequences from data as part of an automated process is a more scalable solution.

To realize this opportunity, behavioral data may be directly integrated into the search system. Many systems have attempted to integrate these signals to guide future action: *Footprints* (Wexelblat and Maes, 1999) mined trails from a particular web domain and used those to direct future users of the system to pages of interest within the website. Figure 5.8 presents screenshots of the footprints interface, showing two views to support navigation through the website: the *path* map (sequences of Web pages, with line thickness denoting the popularity) and the *site* map (transitions between pages, with size denoting transition popularity). It is important to note that because all page accesses are tracked (including clicks, typed URLs, and bookmark selections), links on the maps do not always correspond directly to embedded hyperlinks.

Beyond developing the systems, Wexelblat and Maes showed that the patterns conveyed in the maps and paths are an externalization of searchers' mental models. Interestingly, these visualizations were preferred by experimental participants who were more familiar with the domain. Novices may not understand the information presented in these visualizations and may not know how to apply them effectively. Freyne et al. (2007) added a second dimension to *Footprints* by displaying links to offer visual cues to the searchers. These are gathered from past searchers, and include popularity, recency, and user-generated annotations.

Other methods have been developed to support resource selection. White et al. (2007) recommended *popular destinations* that many searchers issuing the same query reached at the end of their post-query navigation trails. Amazon.com recommends products that other visitors have viewed. Edit and read wear (Hill et al., 1992; Hill and Hollan, 1994) highlights the parts of the documents that readers have examined or edited. *Knowledge Sea II* (Brusilovsky et al., 2004) supports learning by highlighting the parts of textbooks that other students have read and rated. Similarly, *AntWorld* (Kantor et al., 1999) presents resources to future searchers that others have reviewed and rated. While examples of successful interactions may be useful, there may also be benefit from exposing unsuccessful queries or trails, so as to help searchers decide what actions *not to take* – that is to avoid "dead ends" or parts of a collection that yielded little information value to past searchers with similar search intents.

In surfacing behavioral data for others to review, privacy concerns are paramount. Although only aggregated data should be shared publically, the granularity of the aggregation remains an open question (e.g., all searchers or only searchers from a particular location). While this depends on the application, the task, or the domain, it also depends on data volumes at each of the granularity levels (Singla et al., 2014a). Even data from a single machine may reflect the collective search behaviors of multiple searchers (White et al., 2014b), and as such may pose a significant privacy risks to those using the machine (e.g., the leakage of histories between searchers).

5.4.3 Specialized Applications

The growth in the usage of mobile devices,[5] in particular the smartphone and tablet revolution, has led to a large increase in the number of specialized applications – known as *apps*, *mobile apps*, or *mobile applications* – that can be used to perform very particular functions. Users can download/purchase these applications from online stores. The current search engine apps generally mirror the generic experience of online search engines, providing result lists and support for query formulation. However, there are also many specialized applications to support a broad range of information-seeking activities, including recommendations, location-based services such as maps and directions, and the provision of focused information (e.g., weather information, stock quotes, etc.), in much the same way that directed answers for queries of this type are supported by search engines. While specialized applications may be effective in helping people perform particular search tasks, there is limited interoperability between apps, meaning that behaviors and preferences in one application cannot be shared with another. Cloud-based storage of user profile information could help build connections between these applications. Mining cross-application usage logs may be useful for building user profiles for personalization and recommendation (Elkahky et al., 2015) and in identifying clusters of applications that frequently co-occur within the context of the same task (similar to *task tours* in Web search [Hassan and White, 2013]). These collections of applications could be recommended to searchers interactively, given signals about their likely intent.

5.4.4 Supporting Resuming and Re-finding

Search engines can expose search histories of queries and search result clicks to searchers with a view to supporting the types of re-finding and revisitation activities described in Chapter 3, and more broadly, addressing the challenge of search task *resumption* (Donato et al., 2010; Kotov et al., 2011).

5.4.4.1 Search Histories and Task Resumption

In the domain of Web search, there has been little research into what, and how, data should be displayed in search histories. In one study of personal and shared Web activity, participants found views containing the data of others to be more useful (Van Kleek et al., 2010). Both the Google and Bing search engines provide search history functionality that allows users to review past queries (google.com/history and bing.com/profile/history). Such systems have been shown to improve performance in re-finding and resuming search tasks (Morris et al., 2010). Re-finding can be a frustrating experience (Obendorf et al., 2007), even if only a short time has passed since the information was accessed (Teevan et al., 2007). Google's search history includes "Trends," which displays a searcher's most-frequent queries, most-visited sites, most-often clicked search results, and the total number of searches executed over various time frames. While search engines have recognized some value in presenting summaries of behavior, there is little information about what data should be presented and what effect it might have on user attitudes and behavior (Bateman et al., 2012). Komlodi et al. (2006) studied history tools in the legal domain and showed that although direct search history displays are the simplest to implement, history-based tools (such as scratchpads) are most useful to searchers, especially if they proactively capture information (e.g., based on the automatic identification of research missions [Donato et al., 2010]). Forecasting task resumption is useful to search engines in making decisions about whether to proactively fetch potentially useful task-relevant content (Kotov et al., 2011). An important aspect of such prefetching is the amount of time that the system has to seek information on the searchers' behalf. If search systems can accurately predict time until task resumption, they can make decisions about which resources to use, e.g., whether to pursue algorithmically generated (fast, inexpensive, low-moderate quality) or manually generated (slow, expensive, moderate high quality) solutions. An ability to discriminate between persistent topical interests from ongoing active tasks is also an important requirement in supporting searchers over time.

Even though tasks persist across time, activity that occurred in the distant past is less likely to be related to current information needs than recent activity. This temporal variance can be modeled using a number of different decay functions, including linear decay, exponential decay, and even no decay (Campbell and Van Rijsbergen, 1996; Bennett et al., 2012). The choice of function depends on a number of factors, including the length of the searcher's search history and the relatedness between historic behavior and the current search activity. For tasks that change substantially over time, an application may want to focus primarily on current search activity. Such uncertainty was a central component of the ostensive model described earlier (Campbell and

Van Rijsbergen, 1996), which explicitly considers temporal evidential uncertainty as part of the model. The model asserts that as the age of an information item increases, the uncertainty attached to inferences made on it about the current knowledge state will increase. This temporal decay in the relevance of an item can be communicated to searchers interactively in a number of ways, including decreasing the size of the item (Urban et al., 2006), or using dynamic overlays such as afterglow effects (Baudisch et al., 2006), which gradually disappear over time.

5.4.4.2 Re-finding and Revisitation

During re-finding activities, the process followed to find this information is important in returning to the previous state (Teevan et al., 2004; Capra and Pérez-Quiñones, 2005). Hearst (1999) suggested that search interfaces should show the steps taken in the past, including the short- and long-term search strategies that searchers had followed. Many of the systems to support re-finding (e.g., *Stuff I've Seen* [Dumais et al., 2003]) do not provide such navigation support, making it difficult for searchers to rehydrate their previous search state. Teevan et al. (2007) found that 27% of repeat searches had hyperlink clicks on new results as well as previously visited results, suggesting that searchers required support for both finding and re-finding search results, sometimes simultaneously. They also showed that people took longer to click on search results if the result list had changed from one instance of the query to the next; others (e.g., White et al., 2002a; White et al., 2002b) have shown that searchers experience difficulty in adapting to dynamism in lists of information items. As a result, Teevan (2007) presented a system called the *Re: Search Engine* that addresses this in results by maintained *perceived* consistency (by keeping memorable results in the same place in the ranked list), while inserting new results at locations in the list in which users may miss changes. Memorability was largely based on the rank position of clicked results. To support result selections, Teevan et al. (2009) added visual representations of pages to captions to support both search-related decisions (first-time visits) and revisitation by promoting salient text and images that are likely to be recalled in thumbnail captions.

There has been related research on refinding and revisitation beyond search systems, instead focusing on browser functionality such as more sophisticated back buttons (Greenberg and Cockburn, 1999; Milic-Frayling et al., 2004) or better history/bookmarking support (Ayers and Stasko, 1995; Kaasten and Greenberg, 2000; Takano and Winograd, 1998). Systems have emerged to monitor online content for changes and the notification of subscribers if changes are detected. *ChangeDetect* (changedetect.com) monitors web pages on behalf of its users and notifies them via electronic mail if the content of those pages changes. *Google Trends* offers a similar service where it will alert those who subscribe to a particular query if that term appears in the online news media. Rather than being passive recipients of change notifications, users can also receive notifications in situ. Teevan et al. (2010) introduced *DiffIE* as a browser plugin that highlights changes on pages that searchers were revisiting, with a view to supporting a focused examination of the page content. Figure 5.9 provides a screenshot of the *DiffIE* toolbar highlighting changes on a Web page.

Highlighting such as that shown in Figure 5.9 can be useful in focusing searcher attention on particular parts of the page. This may be especially useful for resources

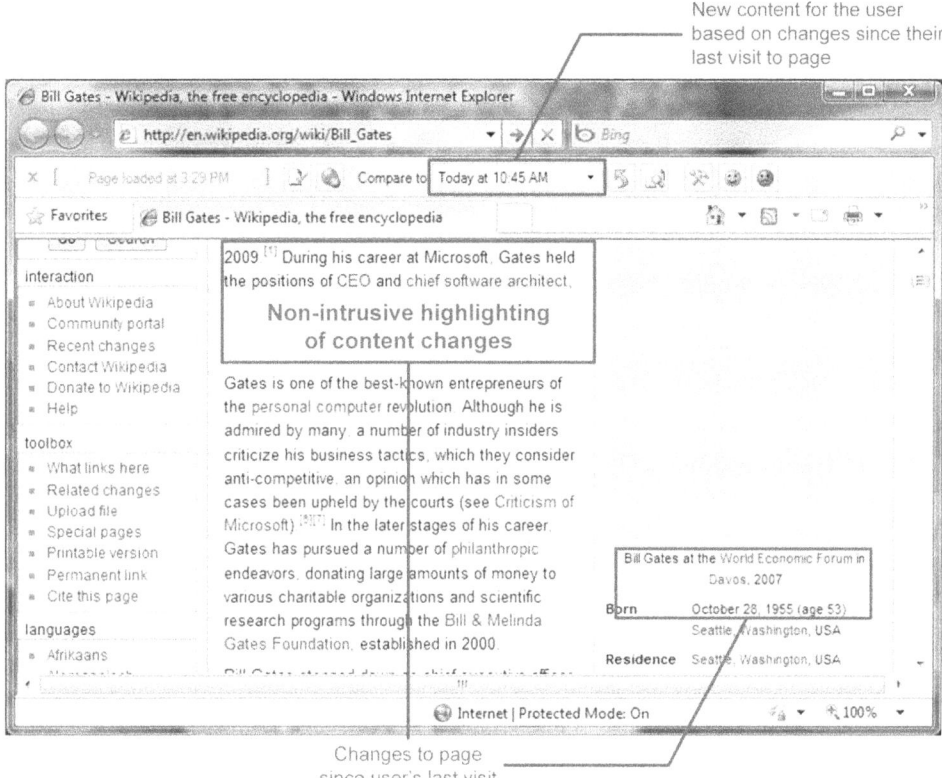

Figure 5.9. Screenshot of the *DiffIE* toolbar in action. Page changes since the last visit by the searcher are highlighted on the page for their reference.

that are highly dynamic (such as news websites) or long/content-rich pages on which changes may be difficult to identify. Beyond interactive search support, studies of re-finding can also provide guidance about which pages should be crawled based on an estimate of whether observed changes in content is meaningful (Adar et al., 2009).

5.5 New Methods and Modalities

Many of the additions presented in the previous section could be introduced into search systems with little investment, largely because they build on presently deployed methods or leverage already existing data sources. There is also a range of new methods and methodologies that are emerging to expand the range of possibility within search interaction. Research at the intersection of natural user interaction and search will continue to grow in importance and prominence over the coming decades. Hearst (2011) suggested that the availability of natural modes of interaction with computers, through spoken dialog, natural language, and collaboration with others, will affect how we interact with search systems and the world around us. I foresee that interactions with search systems will become more seamless, powered by a range of new methods and modalities. Research in related areas such as aesthetics in both human-computer interaction (Udsen and Jorgensen, 2005) and information visualization (Pousman et al., 2007) suggest that additional factors – such as experience, imagination, and reflection – will be important in the design of interfaces to support information seeking (Dörk et al., 2011). In the remainder of this section I discuss some of the methods and modalities that are emerging that will change the nature of search interaction.

5.5.1 Gaze-Enhanced Interaction

One way in which natural user interaction methods could be employed that is gaining in popularity is eye-gaze interaction. The price of gaze tracking technology continues to fall, and other technologies such as web cameras and motion sensors can be used to approximate aspects of expensive gaze trackers on large displays or multi-monitor setups (Hutchinson et al., 1989; Sibert and Jacob, 2000). Gaze-based interfaces may grow in popularity, but there are significant challenges in using gaze as a control mechanism. Applications that leverage this information are primarily using it as a substitute for utilizing pointing devices such as mice, but ultimately new interaction paradigms will emerge that can leverage gaze in ways beyond what is possible with a mouse pointer alone (e.g., to provide attention-aware search experiences). Devices such as the Microsoft HoloLens leverage gaze interaction to decide how to render holographic images in the user's field of view from within the display.

Eye gaze can be used in two main ways during human-computer interaction, either (a) as an effector to change something about the display based on where searcher attention is at a particular time, or (b) to inform the system of where searcher attention is focused at any point in time. Applications of eye gaze include eye typing, where fixations on onscreen keyboards are interpreted as keystrokes for able bodied and disabled people alike (Majaranta and Räihä, 2002; MacKenzie and Zhang, 2008). Because the eye is typically not used as an effector in everyday life, it may be difficult to leverage it for this purpose in computer systems, as much of our vision is undirected. This can lead to the so-called "Midas touch"[6] problem whereby the act of inspecting the display causes unwanted actions (Jacob, 1990). Using the eyes as input sensor and output effector could lead to conflicts (Zhai et al., 1999), but there has been some fairly recent progress on interacting with computers using gaze gestures (e.g., Drewes and Schmidt, 2007; Wobbrock et al., 2008). Because the cues in a gaze-based interaction system are implicit (although explicit audio cues could help improve accuracy) care is needed when interpreting eye-gaze position.

Eye-gaze position provides some useful signals about where people are attending that could be useful in developing information systems that are attention sensitive, as well support for basic interaction operations such as reducing mouse movement time, removing the need to look at the target, or even removing the need to click (with or without the needing to move the eye). Schemes such as instantaneous saccade (Komogorstev et al., 2009) allow for a target on the interface to be selected at the onset of a saccade. More traditionally, because gaze leads interaction (Huang et al., 2012), search systems can capitalize on the fact that searchers attend to a particular part of the screen *prior to* moving their mouse to that location to proactively reposition the mouse pointer (Zhai et al., 1999). This eliminates the need for cumbersome orientation of the pointer to a region on the page, which can be particularly challenging if the display is large and/or the target is small (a combination which has been explored in detail in research on Fitts's law [Fitts, 1954; MacKenzie, 1992]). When people are assumed to be reading a document (e.g., based on inferences about their reading patterns from eye movements [Rodden et al., 1998]), the system can remove the need for users to explicitly scroll through selected content by updating the displayed content dynamically on the basis of user gaze position as they reach the page fold. Individual differences in eye movements, already noted in a number of studies (Aula et al., 2005b; Dumais et al., 2010) suggests that tailored interfaces designed to support and react to how people examine information may also be useful to support more effective information interaction.

Tobii and other companies have recently released commodity gaze trackers (e.g., Tobii Rex, Eye Tribe) that allow gaze-tracking capabilities to be added to any search interface for low cost. These devices have a small form factor and can be placed on a monitor or laptop screen to measure in real time where on the screen the user is looking with reasonable accuracy that is quite sufficient for monitoring approximate gaze position on a display. Mobile and stationary devices will soon possess attention monitoring hardware and software in much the same way as webcams and microphones are commonplace in these devices today. This interaction modality may be particularly attractive in scenarios where searchers are unable to use their hands either through limitations of the current task that they are performing or because of a disability that limits the use of other modes of interaction. That said, the most effective application of gaze may well be as an estimate for searcher attention on the display.

Given the capability to track searcher attention without depending on their intentional use of an input device, a number of applications could be developed that include those to enhance search interaction directly. Dwell time can be used to identify intentionality to some degree (e.g., staring a point on the screen for a fraction of a second to activate it), although significant tuning may be required to account for individual differences in gaze-based interaction patterns. Systems such as *WaveLens* (Paek et al., 2004) offered an expanding result caption that increased in length as searchers hovered their mouse cursor over it. Such progressive revealment affordances could be enhanced via gaze-based interaction, where the caption would dynamically increase in size to accommodate fixation duration. The challenge in designing such support for exploration is to implement it in such a way that it is predictable and easily controllable by searchers. Overall, eye gaze might be better used to support more efficient selection (e.g., warping the cursor to regions that are likely to be clicked) and disambiguation (e.g., for text to speech translation).

Additional features – such as angles between saccades – can be used as a measure of scatter in people's viewing patterns, and used internally by the search to model factors such as engagement or frustration. Being able to understand the extent to which interactions are focused can be an important aspect of designing systems capable of performing interventions at the appropriate time. It is unlikely that a user would want to be interrupted at a time when they were in a highly engaged state, and previous research on interruptions supports this conjecture (Czerwinski et al., 2004). It is therefore important to be able to accurately reason about searcher attention, using signals such as face recognition (Horvitz and Apacible, 2003) that can be collected at scale using Web cameras, or cursor movement data (Huang et al., 2011).

5.5.2 Touch

Touch devices provide searchers with a more natural means of interacting with the devices and reduce the reliance on external keyboards, allowing the full device to be used to display content. Touch interactions with search systems or resources can be mined to infer satisfaction or relevance (e.g., Guo et al., 2011; Guo et al., 2013). At present, touch is generally mapped to click events, so the selection of results, scrolling, zooming, and so on can be performed using this mechanism. Multi-touch-enabled devices support a richer gesture vocabulary for interacting with search systems, including performing multiple actions simultaneously, such as selecting while zooming. Systems such as *LucidTouch* (Wigdor et al., 2007) allow people to control handheld devices by touching the back of the device, addressing issues with occlusion of graphical elements by fingers on small displays.

Regions surrounding the touchscreen can be used to provide additional touch interactions even though the searcher may not touch the screen directly. Mouse cursor interactions allow different levels of commitment associated with different cursor events: hover, single-click, and double-click. This is not available on touch screen displays at present. *PreCursor* (Mistry and Wang, 2011) allows searchers to both hover *and* click on touch devices, an affordance that is not possible with traditional monitoring of touch interactions. The *PreCursor* system uses an infrared laser to create an invisible layer in the front of a touchscreen with cameras sensing when the finger has broken the layer; and based on the illumination from the light, the position of the finger with respect to the screen can be computed, and a hover command is executed in the same way as it would be if the mouse pointer hovered on an icon. Other approaches have used the regions surrounding devices for near-surface interactions, including menu selections (Guimbretière and Nguyen, 2012) and expanding the usable interaction space more generally (Butler et al., 2008).

5.5.2.1 Interpreting Touch

Despite the attractiveness of touch technology, the role of touch interaction in the search process has been limited, although there are signs that this is changing (e.g., Guo et al. [2013]). We are observing a translation of functions such as result selection and scrolling from other form factors into the space of touch interactions on devices such as smartphones and tablets. Table 5.1 lists the main single- and multi-touch gestures along with examples of how these gestures are or could be used in search interfaces. The most useful touch gestures in a search context are likely to be the tap, flick, drag, and pinch/spread commands. These can be used to navigate through search results and zoom in or out of particular content as required. The drag and pinch/spread commands have a direct impact on the viewport coordinates (drag) and dimensions (pinch/spread), which can be useful for estimating attention, as mentioned earlier.

Table 5.1. *Touch gestures (adapted from http://static.lukew.com/TouchGestureGuide.pdf)*

Name	Picture of action being performed	Description	Current or possible use in search applications
Tap		Briefly touch surface with fingertip	Selecting result or highlighting result so that another action can be performed
Double tap		Rapidly touch surface twice with fingertip	Selecting result
Drag		Move fingertip over surface	Panning in cases where the visible document is zoomed
Flick		Quickly brush surface with fingertip	Forward and backward navigation, similar to the forward/back buttons in a Web browser
Pinch		Touch surface with two fingers and bring them closer together	Zoom out as with maps or in document examination
Spread		Touch surface with two fingers and move them apart	Zoom in as with maps or during inspection of document content
Press		Touch surface for extended period of time	Progressive revealment of content (as in *WaveLens* [Paek et al., 2004]), or in initiating additional menu functionality.
Press and tap		Press surface with one finger and briefly touch surface with second finger	Perform an additional action pertaining to a result; first select the result and then click the other action, such as save, print, or share
Press and drag		Press surface with one finger and move second finger over surface without losing contact	Scroll or step through a list of search results (swipe left/right to move between results), or horizontal/vertical navigation on landing pages
Rotate		Touch surface with two fingers and move them clockwise or counterclockwise	Rotate multi-dimensional content (e.g., maps) or multi-media content such as images during examination

Rather than re-implementing existing search interfaces so that they support touch interactions, the real value in using touch in searching comes from the broad range of new interaction capabilities that it provides, e.g., the ability to "press and tap" or "rotate" as shown in Table 5.1 (and combinations of these with other touch gestures). The vocabulary of touch gestures is plentiful and can even be defined by device users (Wobbrock et al., 2009). More nascent technologies, such as Apple's "Force Touch" functionality uses force sensors and haptic feedback to interpret the amount pressure applied when performing a touch interaction and simulate a click on a physical device. This has utility for a range of applications, including offering different views of a result depending on force of the click, or rapidly navigating a long document, lengthy media content, or a map given variations in pressure to scroll, fast-forward, or zoom.

In touch applications, systems lack access to hover over events because the movements between coordinates are not visible to the application (i.e., people's fingers are above the screen). Although there are new hardware capabilities that allow devices to track whether a finger is hovering over the screen (e.g., Samsung's "Air View," which implements gestures and other functionality – such as previewing images or messages – by holding or swiping a hand or finger slightly above the screen), it is not clear that people will use hover functionality in the same way as they do with a mouse cursor, where hovers are suggestive of consideration (e.g., before making a decision to select a result in the case of search-result examination; see Huang et al. [2012]). Swipes are also captured and interpreted independent of position. As such, the swiping signal cannot be used as an indication of interest in a particular region of the document. To the extent that swipes are used to rapidly reposition the viewport, however, they do have some utility in inferring interests or intentions (e.g., rapid swiping could provide indications of low interest in skipped content).

5.5.3 Gesture-Based Interaction

People perform gestures in everyday communication. Hand, arm, and body movements are commonplace during the interactions between humans. All physical actions require a person to perform a gesture of some sort. Kurtenbach and Hulteen (1990) claimed that a gesture "is a motion of the body that contains information." Until recently, machines have been focused on the consequence of the gesture (e.g., whether some action was taken) and have acted accordingly. Search systems will become more aware of their surroundings through more accurate sensing and more complete modeling of search situations. Given this enhanced understanding, search systems will be able to better interpret gestures to understand subtle nuances in how the interaction is performed (e.g., speedy or jerky motions may be indicative of impatience).

There are two main types of gesture: (1) *naturally occurring* gestures, and (2) *fixed vocabulary* gestures. Naturally occurring gestures typically occur during human–human interaction, but given advances in affective computing (see Section 5.5.6), computer systems are becoming more capable of interpreting these gestures in a similar way to humans. Fixed vocabulary gestures typically involve a set of constrained actions reserved for interaction with a system in cases where fine-grained, local interactions are infeasible (e.g., pointing interactions with projected displays [Bolt, 1980]).

5.5.3.1 Nature of Gestures

People use a broad range of gestures in everyday communication, and the choice of gesture is highly context- and culture-dependent (Morris et al., 1980). As discussed earlier when I covered affect, gestures are part of body language that describes various forms of nonverbal communication that reveal intentions or feelings. Body language includes behaviors other than gestures, including posture and facial expressions that can provide clues about to the attitude or state of mind of a person that can be difficult to discern otherwise. Gestural signals could be combined with other signals – such as affective feedback (Picard, 2000) – to construct a more detailed model of the searcher and their current situation.

Gestures are innate and humans often perform them even when they are not visible to the intended recipient, if there is one. One of the clues about the importance of the gesture in communication is that people are just as likely to gesture while talking on the phone as they are when they are engaged in a face–to-face conversation (Rimé, 1982). As far back as the 1960s, there was significant interest in using behavioral signals to develop interactive and adaptive computer systems (Pease, 2004). Many gestures such as pointing, touching, or moving objects are universal. Cadoz (1994) classified gestures into three groups according to their function: (1) *semiotic* gestures are used to communicate meaningful information; (2) *ergotic* gestures are used to manipulate the physical world and create artifacts; and (3) *epistemic* gestures are those used to learn from the environment through tactile or haptic exploration. Within these high-level categories a number of other classifications of gesture are possible. Mulder (1996) provided a good summary of various classifications.

The focus of this book is on the use of gestures to communicate with machines, and as such as we are mostly concerned with empty-handed semiotic gestures.[7] Within this class of gesture, taxonomies such as that proposed by Rimé and Schiaratura (1991) can be developed to include gestures such as symbolic (single meaning within a culture), deictic (pointing gestures, directing attention to specific events or objects in the environment), iconic (convey information about the size, shape, or orientation of the object of discourse), and pantomimic (demonstrating movement of an invisible tool or object). Of these four sub-classes of empty-handed semiotic gesture, the deictic class is most familiar to the human factors community. That said, there have been attempts to use other types of gesture. For example, Holz and Wilson (2011) presented *data miming*, an approach that required people to perform iconic gestures could be recognized by a system as real-world objects (chairs, tables, etc.) based on the degree of similarity match.

5.5.3.2 Gesture Vocabularies

Although there is a rich gestural taxonomy, there has been limited progress in the integration of gestures into human interactions with computers. Ideally gestures for the computer would mirror the kinds of gestures that people are familiar with naturally. The dominant current paradigm is direct manipulation (point and click), but given the unnatural manner in which people must interact with these systems, there is room for improvement. Standard gesture actions that exploit the ergotic function of hand movements have been explored in detail in the human factors community (e.g., Mulder

Table 5.2. *Examples of actions and possible gestures in search settings*

Action	Description	Possible Gesture
Selecting links and buttons	Focusing attention on a particular information item, such as a hyperlink. This could involve direct interaction where the user attempts to move an on-screen cursor to the part of the display containing the object to be selected, or a method whereby the focus is moved between different items in the available set.	Open palm hover over link or rapid up/down movements of extended fingers (as palm) to tab through the selectable items on a page.
Initiating actions	Beyond focusing on a particular item, such as a result link, the user needs a way to perform an action on that item, such as clicking through.	Clench fist or hover for N secs delay
Navigating forward and backward	Once a resource has been selected and is visible, functionality needs to be offered to move forward or backward through the space.	When document zoomed to 100%: Swipe to the left (move forward); swipe to the right (move backward).
Zooming	To review the content of a resource, the searcher may wish to zoom in on a particular part of the page to view it in more detail. Zooming outside the scope of the document could also be supported, enabling the user to assume a holistic view on the site, clusters of related pages, and so on.	Bring hands together (zoom out). Move hands apart (zoom in).
Scrolling and panning	Based on the zoom level and what content is visible, the system may need to support users in adjusting the coordinates of the viewport to examine different regions of the document.	Depending on viewport overflow, swipe hands vertically or horizontally.

[1996]). A gestural vocabulary has yet to emerge for search systems, largely because search interaction continues to be performed proximal to the searcher. However, moving forward there will need to be actions for at least the operations described in Table 5.2, which cover some examples of the core functions in interactions with search systems.

The search gesture taxonomy presented in Table 5.2 assumes that the content available from the device is similar in format to that already available to searchers through other devices (websites, etc.). However, it is likely that some content will be created to be more easily navigable on gesture-based systems and visible from a distance on large displays. It is also assumed that query input will be through spoken dialog, although corrections may need to be made using on-screen keyboards. This also assumes that the searcher is only going to passively review the content that is retrieved by the system, rather than purposely rearranging or organizing content as part of the search process.

Gesture recognition also has applications for domains beyond controlling machines, where, for example, sign language could be interpreted by a system with a view to mediating communication between people rather than trying to convey some information to the system directly. This can be done by using purpose-built gloves (e.g., the *GloveTalk* system [Fels and Hinton, 1993]) or using camera-based tracking of hand movements using *Kinect* devices (Chen et al., 2013).

5.5.3.3 Gesture Tracking Technologies

Previous research involved the use of gloves and other cumbersome input mechanism to recognize gestural interactions (Fels and Hinton, 1993; Zimmerman et al., 1987; Liang and Ouhyoung, 1998). Recent technological advances have enabled the consumerization of gestural technologies. One of the challenges in a move toward gestural interaction is the widespread adoption of direct manipulation. Two situations in which such interactions can be leveraged by computer systems: close proximity to the computer with fine-grained control (using only hands) and far from the machine, with a range of motion, including full-body gestures (in a living room). There are consumer technologies in both realms.

5.5.3.3.1 Proximal Control

The *Leap Motion* controller is a small peripheral device designed to be placed on a physical desktop, facing upward. Using two cameras and three infrared light emitting diodes, the device observes a roughly hemispherical area, to a distance of about one meter (three feet). The *Leap* is designed to track fingers (or similar items such as a pen) that cross into the observed area, to a spatial precision of about 0.01 millimeters. The smaller observation area and higher resolution of the device differentiates the product from devices that track the entire body, such as the *Kinect*, which is more suitable for whole-body tracking in a space the size of a living room. The *Leap* has been shown to perform tasks such as navigating a website, pinch-to-zoom gestures on maps, high-precision drawing, and manipulating complex three-dimensional data visualizations.

5.5.3.3.2 Distal Control

There are a number of consumer devices that employ motion sensing to enable distal control over computing devices using gesture recognition. That is, the searcher does not have to be positioned close to the computer system in the same way as they would with a mouse or keyboard. Some of these systems operate using cameras that monitor gestures, whereas others monitor the movement of hand-held devices through accelerometer and optical sensor technology. They use these signals to interact with and manipulate items on the screen.

Good examples of distal control over computer systems can be found in gaming consoles. The *Kinect* is a motion sensing input device by Microsoft for the Xbox video game console and Windows PCs. Based around a webcam-style add-on peripheral for the Xbox console, it enables users to control and interact with the Xbox without the need to touch a game controller, through a natural user interface using gestures and spoken commands. Newer versions of the *Kinect* also enable the tracking of physiological signals, specifically a player's heart rate and facial expression, twenty-five individual joints (even thumbs) and the precise rotation of such joints, the weight put on each limb, the speed of movements, and track gestures performed with a standard controller. The Sony PlayStation device also has a camera which supports motion sensing standard cameras (with the associated limitations on light levels by which the infra-red based *Kinect* camera is unaffected). The inclusion of cameras supports searcher recognition and profile loading, which has applications in personalizing search experiences. The Nintendo Wii gaming console comes with the Wii Remote that is capable of sensing acceleration along three axes using an accelerometer. The remote also uses an optimal sensor to determine where the remote is pointing by sensing infrared light from the sensor bar, allowing it to operate consistently independent of display dimensions. Through sensing and triangulation, the console computes distance between the controller and the sensor bar.

5.5.3.4 Gesture-Based Systems

Gesture based systems that have been developed fall into three categories: gesture only interfaces, gesture and speech interfaces, and conversational interfaces:

- **Gesture only (least natural):** These are interfaces for which the only means of interacting with the system is via gestures. Many of the gesture-based systems being introduced in the market recently take this form. Although they also process speech, they do not do so in *combination* with the gestures.
- **Gesture and speech:** By combining gestural and speech interaction modalities, systems can improve the reliability of their recognition methods and create an interface that is more powerful than either method alone. The combination facilitates ease of expression, enabling commands that are easy to execute, while retaining a large command vocabulary. Multimodal systems can be very powerful because the speech input can enhance the gesture with contextual understanding, by which user actions can be better interpreted, e.g., "Put that (pointing to an object) there"; "Make that red" (Bolt, 1980).
- **Conversational (most natural):** Involving a dialog between the system and the user, whereby both machine and humans interact as they would in a human–human interaction. An important difference between conversational systems and the gesture and speech is that there is a direct attempt to understand interactional cues. A number of interfaces of this nature have been proposed (Maes, 1994; Thorisson, 1996).

Overall, it is clear that there is both a range of gesture mechanisms and a significant opportunity to enhance the space of search interactions using gestures. Despite the promise, a compelling search application has not been developed to leverage gestures, and researchers have not embraced gesture as a viable interaction modality for search. Perhaps, the most compelling scenarios for gesture-based search interfaces lie in the *collaborative* information-seeking tasks, whereby: (1) people may be in settings in which they are naturally co-located with other searchers, (2) there is space for multiple people to engage in the task, and (3) technology already exists to recognize and track the interactions of multiple participants simultaneously.

5.5.4 Wearable and Augmented Reality

Rather than having the information projected on a dedicated screen and interacting via gestures, the physical world can be augmented with this information and people can interact with it using natural gestures. By using a camera and projection technology, virtually any surface can be turned in a medium for exploring information and providing input to the system. This removes the dependency on having a device and turns any surface into a means of input and output. Augmented reality has been studied in a range of different application contexts, including printer repair (Feiner et al., 1993) and trauma care (Horvitz and Shwe, 1995). *SixthSense* (Mistry and Maes 2009) is a wearable gestural interface that augments the physical world around us with digital information and lets us use natural hand gestures to interact with that information. The system attempts to free information from its confines (a computer display) by seamlessly integrating it with reality, and thus making the entire world an interface to computer systems. Technology such as *Google Glass* allows searchers to actively engage with search engines or passively receive recommendations while they are performing other tasks.

One of the most recent emerging trends in search technology has been wearable devices. Unlike devices such as smartphones and tablets, these devices are worn on the body for much of the day, allowing them to sense and acquire data on different aspects of people's search situation as well as other signals (e.g., physiological, consumption, location, performance). Research in quantified self (Wolf, 2010) and life logging (Mann, 1997; Gemmell et al., 2006) studies the acquisition and application of such rich data about people, largely via an array of wearable sensors. Supporting reflection on past behavior can help to guide behavioral changes (Bateman et al., 2012), but also reflect on our lives to search and organize past experiences (Czerwinski et al., 2006). However, the total capture of personally relevant data streams has been criticized (Sellen and Whittaker, 2010), with researchers arguing that tools that consider the psychological basis of human memory would be preferable (e.g., targeting items most likely to be forgotten rather than recording everything, capturing memory cues that can trigger memories rather than capturing the experiences directly). Beyond sensing and recording data about people's activities, wearable devices can also provide searchers with information proactively as it arrives. For example, *Google Glass* offers recommendations or advertisements to wearers in the periphery of their view, and smart watches can provide recommendations based on time or events (e.g., an incoming email in the Microsoft Band or Apple Watch).

Mobile phone cameras provide a valuable lens on the world through which image queries can be issued to identify unknown places or translate foreign language text – such as street signs – in real time (Watanabe et al., 1998; Yang et al., 1999). Figure 5.10 presents an example of augmented reality translation from French (on the left) to English (on the right) using *Word Lens*, shown in the original context.

Pictures of products, their unique identifying information (e.g., ISBNs, barcodes), provides a way in which people can retrieve information on products without having

Figure 5.10. Translation of a street sign from French to English using the *Word Lens* application from Quest Visual (now part of Google).

to enter the name of the product directly. This may be important given that these are all examples of ways in which search technology (combined with advances in computer vision and machine translation) is powering novel experiences that empower searchers as they interact with an unfamiliar world around them and seek to learn more. Wearable devices such as *Google Glass* provide a means for searchers to receive recommendations based on their current physical context, while also offering a seamless way to navigate, take a picture or video, or learn more about local history given their current location. Mobile devices may also house digital assistants that can interact with searchers to understand their needs in more detail (via combinations of context, dialog, and histories) and support them in completing particular search tasks.

5.5.5 Spoken Dialog

As speech recognition technology improves, the range of possibilities with this form of input will also expand (Hearst, 2011). A recent Google survey[8] shows that 55% teens and 41% adults use voice search more than once per day while multi-tasking, hanging out with friends, cooking, watching television, or exercising. Advances in speech recognition, artificial intelligence, and personalization will provide search systems with the ability to engage in realistic dialog with searchers to better understand their needs and communicate results and/or task progress. The focus in search systems has been largely on processing spoken dialog *input* (e.g., natural language queries communicated to a device through its microphone). Systems that can converse with searchers can offer more seamless interaction experiences that are especially useful for scenarios in which searchers may be unable to view SERPs (e.g., while in control of an automobile). Doing this effectively may involve the application of other technologies (such as summarization) to minimize the amount of information that has to be communicated to the searcher through the audio *output* channel, which is has much lower fidelity than visual mechanisms.

5.5.5.1 Input

One obvious way that spoken dialog will become part of searching is through speech input, which will rely heavily on the effectiveness of speech recognition technology. Technology in this area continues to improve in accuracy (and accuracy continues to improve via multimodal input signals methods such as automated lip reading (Petajan et al., 1988) and more recently gaze tracking). Searchers can currently communicate with search systems by talking to their devices, and this trend will continue into other applications settings, such as in automobiles. However, there are environments where speech input may not be the most efficient means of communicating an information need to a search system. In noisy environments such sporting events and concerts, it can be difficult for automatic speech recognition to distinguish between the searcher's query and the background noise. Similarly, in quite environments (for example, in libraries), as speaking at a volume where a device is able to comprehend spoken dialog may be disruptive to other patrons. Regardless, there are still many locations in which searchers can effectively utilize speech input, saving typing time in devices for which keystrokes can be difficult (Henze et al., 2012). Correcting mistakes made by speech recognition during query input may also be challenging (especially for homophones such as "wales" and "whales"), and may lead to searcher frustration. Historic logs can be mined for evidence of keyboard based query refinements after sequences of unsuccessful attempts at query entry via spoken dialog. Offering interfaces that combine multiple modalities (e.g., speech and touch) may be beneficial to searchers facing such difficulties. Systems may also use signals (or even simple auto-completions in the case of frequently provided information, in the case of online forms, or issued queries, in the case of re-finding) based on individual histories and the search context to facilitate more accurate understanding in a similar way to that attainable by humans.

In addition to detecting the query text from the spoken input of the searcher, the search engine could also use additional signals present in the auditory input to enhance search relevance. The system could learn from the level of background noise detected in the query signal. The background noise provides additional context that the search engine could use to make inferences about the nature of the searcher's situation. In a more advanced conception, the search engine may be able to "overhear" information in the background that could be relevant to the current search query (e.g., announcements over a loudspeaker). Similar features have been studied in terms of the "cocktail party effect" (Bronkhorst, 2000), which is the phenomenon of being able to focus one's auditory attention on a particular stimulus while filtering out a range of other stimuli, much the same way that a partygoer can focus on a single conversation in a noisy room. This effect is what allows most people to "tune into" a single voice and "tune out" all others. It may also describe a similar phenomenon that occurs when one may immediately detect words of importance originating from unattended stimuli, such as hearing one's name in another conversation. As a stretch goal, if the search system could identify a subset of the words being spoken in the background, it could even use that information as additional context. Other possible features include the tone of the spoken query, the speed, intonation, and so on, which could be used to provide emotional signals containing additional information such as the searcher's anxiety level and the urgency of the information need. Access to such data also facilitates a better understanding of voice query reformulation (Hassan Awadallah et al., 2015).

5.5.5.2 Output

Providing audio output for describing search results is challenging, but there are cases for which this can be particularly useful, such as when searchers are unable to attend to a screen to examine results directly. For example, a searcher driving an automobile may wish the system to communicate search results with them in a form other than visual format, which could be distracting.[9] Research in the human-computer interaction community has studied associated issues (e.g., the development of earcons [Blattner et al., 1989; Brewster et al., 1993; 1994] capable of sonifying user interfaces to communicate complex information using sound). However, as the ways in which we consume information from digital devices expands, we need to consider how to represent the results from search systems in ways that are consumable audibly. For factoid searching, this may be trivial; the real challenge arises when search systems must support the sonification of complex sets of search results (e.g., through initial summarization of the retrieved results and progressive exposure to content). It is likely that initial efforts to support audio output will need to focus on cases for which the information content can be easily summarized in a short response for queries for which the dominant search intent can be easily inferred(e.g., in terms of factual answers, definitions, calculations). This may also be appropriate in situations when searchers want to bypass rich SERPs or remove the need to click, scroll, or consume large amounts of content on small screens (e.g., smartphone or wearable device).

There are also interesting hardware challenges around how to communicate the audio signal to searchers. Broadcasting the signal is appropriate in one-on-one, quiet settings, such as during driving. However, this may not be an appropriate method if there is a lot of background noise or the results are in some way sensitive. Earbuds offer an interesting alternative, as they can communicate information unobtrusively. This could be a useful way for intelligent agents to communicate search results or context-dependent information (e.g., quietly whisper information about a past acquaintance prior to meeting them again, or interrupt a social encounter to inform both parties that at least one of them is expected at a meeting elsewhere).

In cases for which there is no results display, or when the results display is much larger than that currently supported, more work is needed on designing the search interface and interaction paradigms. For example, we may want to employ a progressive revealment strategy whereby only the minimum number of results needed is shown (if there is a clear match or direct answer), provide that and allow searchers to explore further if needed. Other desirable properties include providing easy switching of the search context to different result sets and providing direct support for the interplay between content finding and content generation, and leveraging the application context to interpret the query, and making exploration, retention, and application of potentially useful results as efficiently as technology, searcher, and environmental constraints allow.

5.5.6 Affective Monitoring and Feedback

Affective computing is the study and development of systems and devices that can recognize, interpret, process, and simulate human affect (Picard, 1995; Picard, 1997).

The basis for research in this area is to empower machines with the ability to simulate empathy, allowing the system to interpret a human emotional state and act accordingly. The aspirational goal of this technology is to improve the quality of the interaction between the human and the machine, and to facilitate the construction of more complete models of the current search situation, focused around the primary actor, the searcher. Noninvasive sensors on the skin are used to measure sweat or electrical impulses in the muscles. Observations from afar via cameras can also afford accurate predictions of affective state. Such methods can be especially useful for modeling aspects of search (such as frustration), but we are only just beginning this journey in the search community, and models are slowly creeping into the literature (e.g., Feild et al. [2010]). Ultimately, these methods may help systems better understand searchers' emotional states in ways that may not be possible through the observable search behaviors that are typically examined in behavioral data mining and modeling.

Affective input is gaining in popularity in search settings and there are some emerging applications such as e-learning, when the system could build a responsive automated tutor to help guide the student and react to their responses (e.g., bored, engaged, etc.; see Kapoor et al. [2001]; Sidney et al. [2005]) or to detect seizures (Poh et al., 2012). Affective monitoring applications that can help people act more rationally at times of emotional imbalance (e.g., road rage during driving or anger when feeling slighted). There is also a growing interest in employing affective signals to enhance the performance of search systems (Lopatovska and Arapakis, 2011). Affective feedback (Arapakis et al., 2008) can help systems present searchers with better quality results. Current feedback techniques determine content relevance with respect to the cognitive and situational levels of interaction between the searcher and the retrieval system. Searchers interact with intentions, motivations, and feelings, all of which are critical aspects of cognition and decision making. Arapakis and colleagues explored of the role of emotions in the information-seeking process. They showed that emotions interweave with different physiological, psychological, and cognitive processes, but also form distinctive patterns, according to specific task and/or specific searcher.

Poddar and Ruthven (2010) examined how participants' emotional responses are affected by the nature of the search task. The results of their study suggest that artificial tasks have higher uncertainty and less sense of ownership than genuine search tasks, and more complex search tasks have lower positive emotions and more uncertainty before and after searching. Similar findings were reported earlier also by Arapakis et al. (2008) in an information-seeking activity. They concluded that searchers' emotions transition from positive to negative valence as task difficulty increases. They also found that emotions both interweave with different physiological, psychological, and cognitive processes during an information-seeking process and form distinctive patterns according to specific tasks. These patterns can be used as feedback for the system in identifying searchers' emotional states. Although affective and physiological signals may show promise for use in relevance feedback, their accuracy is insufficient for application on their own. Moshfeghi and Jose (2013b) explored the use of these signals as a compliment to established behavioral signals such as document dwell time. They showed that implicit feedback methods can be enhanced through the inclusion of affective and physiological signals, and that the effectiveness of these signals various across intentions.

5.5.6.1 Methods for Capturing Affect

There are a number of methods for measuring affect in people as they engage with their environment, primarily based on passive sensors capturing signals assumed to be connected to emotional cues:

- **Emotional speech:** Variations in speech can occur with changes in the automatic nervous system, and this information can be used to produce systems capable of recognizing affect based on extracted features. For example, the pitch, volume, and enunciation of a speaker's voice may alter as a result of a change in affective state. These changes in speech patterns may be detectable algorithmically, with reasonable success rates in predicting affective state (Picard, 2000).
- **Facial affect:** This involves development of models to automatically identify facial expressions, using one or more modalities (a number of methods for doing this have been proposed). Facial recognition is different from facial affect recognition; the former is aimed at identifying known faces, whereas the latter focuses on inferring affective state from images or video. Multimodal methods (e.g., combining facial expressions and speech, or expressions and gestures) provide a more robust estimate of people's emotional state. Work in this area has focused on coding facial expressions into different emotions (e.g., anger, disgust, fear, happiness, sadness, and surprise) using so-called action units (Ekman and Friesen, 1976). These units are defined as a contraction or a relaxation of one or more muscles. These muscle movements can be used in defining a complex and objective emotional interpretation system.
- **Body gesture:** Gesture could be combined with other signals from speech and facial recognition. Three-dimensional models of the position and orientation of various limbs and joints can be developed. Real-time models of gesture are already being extensively used in natural user interaction contexts, enabled by devices such as the Microsoft *Kinect*, which can monitor many aspects of searchers' body positions and movements as they interact with the system. The methods available in this space can be characterized as *appearance based* or *three-dimensional model based* (Pavlovic et al., 1997). The former operates directly on still images of the surroundings, whereas the latter operates on models developed based on the position of body parts and their spatial movement.
- **Physiological indicators:** Physiological signs can reveal a lot about a person's current affective state (Picard, 1995; Picard, 1997). A number of methods have been developed to estimate emotional state from these signals. The application of these methods for computational modeling in search systems is a nascent research area, but the three primary signal sources that have received most attention are:
  - **Blood volume pulse:** The amount of infrared light reflected back through the skin is measured to estimate the rate at which blood is flowing (heart pulse rate). Because hemoglobin absorbs light, this can be used to identify cases in which the heart rate has changed. When a person is in an aroused state, the amplitude of their cardiac cycle may increase. The disadvantages of this

method include that it can be cumbersome to wear the sensing device, and also that variations in blood flow can be caused by a number of factors unrelated to arousal, including body temperature at measurement time and actions such as stretching.
- **Galvanic skin response (GSR):** Skin conductivity provides an indicator of the amount of moisture in the skin. Because the sweat glands that produce this moisture are controlled by the central nervous system, there is a positive correlation between the arousal state of the body and skin conductivity (Pavlovic et al., 1997). GSR sensors can be placed on the feet or the wrist. Basing the sensor on the wrist may interfere with important interactions involving the keyboard and mouse, although wearable devices such as the Microsoft Band (discussed in Section 3.2.2.3) offer lightweight ways to capture and stream/store GSR data.
- **Facial electromyography (fEMG):** This method measures electrical activity in facial muscles, by amplifying the electrical impulses associated with muscle contractions. Two muscles are of particular interest in fEMG: (1) those that associated with frowning (corrugator supercilii) for testing negative responses, and (2) those that connected with smiling (zygomaticus) for testing for positive responses (Larsen et al., 2003). The sensors detect small changes in the electrical impulses in those muscles and use that information to generate labels with positive or negative affect. A drawback of the technique for measuring affect during search interaction is that measuring these pulses requires electrodes directly on the face, which is both intrusive and may alter natural expression. Other methods such as cameras and other sensors can perform the remote estimation of affect, without the intrusion of fEMG (Kapoor and Picard, 2005; Madsen et al., 2008).

For all of these signals, a normal (baseline) value must be established for the searcher. This allows deviations from that baseline to be detected and associated with aspects of the search process, such as periods of intensive engagement or periods of frustration. To obtain accurate measurements, these individualized baselines must be established for each searcher at the outset of the measurement period. It is easier to develop baselines for some affective signals than others; for example, smiles and variations in speech may be consistent across searchers, but heart rate could vary based on many factors. In addition, it can be difficult to ensure realism in studies that utilize these measurement methods systems given the potential anxiety associated with artificial experimental settings or the general environment in which the readings are taken (e.g., physician's office).

Beyond physiological sensing, research in psychology has shown that mental processes connected with cognitive decision making can be captured by standard cursor movements (Spivey et al., 2005; Yamauchi et al., 2007). Theories such as embodied cognition (Wilson, 2002; Anderson, 2003) suggest that mental activities are reflected in states of the body, including posture, arm movements, and facial expression (and vice versa), which can be monitored by motion-sensing devices such as the *Kinect*. In light of this, it seems reasonable to assume that the use of the mouse cursor can reveal something about searchers' emotional states. Studies of arousal and valence have demonstrated a relationship with mouse activity such as total duration of all mouse movements and the number of velocity changes (Zimmermann et al., 2003). Kapoor et al. (2007) used a pressure-sensitive mouse to detect searcher frustration levels. Azcarraga and Suarez (2012) used features of mouse activity (number of clicks, distance that the cursor has traveled, click duration) to predict emotions during the use of an intelligent tutoring system. Yamauchi (2013) showed that mouse trajectory features such as velocity and direct changes were useful in predicting anxiety levels. In a complementary context to the search interaction that I target in this book – computer gaming – mouse click activity has also been shown to predict levels of gamer frustration (Scheirer et al., 2002).

Machine learning techniques can be applied to the combination of all of these inputs to produce either categorical labels (e.g., confused) or coordinates in the valence-arousal space (Calvo and D'Mello, 2010; Tao and Tan, 2005). Valence refers to the intrinsic degree of attractiveness (positive valence) or aversiveness (negative valence) of an event, object, or situation. Facial tracking of affect enables the tracking methods to be deployed online and facial expressions to be captured with consent from volunteer participants (e.g., via a Web camera as they watch a video). The current state-of-the-art models can achieve strong accuracy in predicting the emotional state of a person from facial signals (Madsen et al., 2008). Importantly, this enables the collection of large volumes of data about emotional states (billions of frames) that can be used to train predictive models of facial affect recognition for application in a many settings where affective modeling is important. This can be useful for a range of settings where emotive responses are critical. For example, applying an approach like this in the context of advertising, one can quickly obtain data on how different cohorts perceive television advertisements prior to their broadcast.

Given the intrinsically subjective nature of emotion, the development of accurate models of affect can be difficult. The facial recognition models that have been developed are insufficiently accurate to permit their widespread adoption, in part because they are developed and tested in artificial environments and their lack of robustness to changes in head rotation. Many of the sensors employed are noisy and the signals that are mined from these sensors may not be consistent across different searchers. To attain usable levels of efficacy, models need to be developed that are tailored to each searcher (which raises issues in the scalability of such models in practice, as highlighted earlier in Chapter 3). In addition, doing this involves calibration and often physical contact with the searcher. The methods that are used to capture these signals can also be intrusive (e.g., measuring GSR involves wearing a device that is pressed against the skin), and such signals may not be easily obtained at scale without the broad availability of low-cost commodity hardware for collecting such signals. Despite the challenges, there has been some progress in this area. For example, the Microsoft Band provides output from a number of sensors, include heart rate, GSR, and skin temperature. The high resolution camera in the Microsoft *Kinect 2.0* device enables applications that utilize it to monitor heart rate from changes in skin color (Wu et al., 2012) and estimate people's emotional state via facial affect detection models, similar to those described earlier. It is quite likely that such pervasive monitoring and application of signals concerning searcher affect will be commonplace in next-generation search systems.

There are clear privacy concerns surrounding the recording of detailed information about a person's physiological function, especially over time – as would be needed for applications such as personalization. Indeed, at some point, the affective information collected may actually equate to personal health information, and be subject to strict legal requirements in terms of how such sensitive data can be stored, accessed, and applied. Care needs to be taken to seek appropriate consent from searchers in order for such tracking to be performed, as well as to clearly establish expectations for important issues such as data ownership, privacy, and security. An additional challenge in a retrieval setting is to assign affect labels to resources, so that once searchers' affective state has been estimated, appropriate search results can be retrieved to reinforce the current state or to attempt to change the state if deemed appropriate.

5.5.6.2 Calibration of Affective Models

There are large individual differences in how people react to different situations that need to be considered in models of affective state. An important aspect of affective monitoring is calibrating the signals so that we can accurately model what is normal for each person and recognize significant positive or negative shifts from that baseline value. This may require observing behavior over some time (a baseline measurement phase) before a searcher is exposed to a stimulus of interest.

5.5.6.3 Applications of Affective Models

As search systems move closer to understanding searcher affect, they can apply that knowledge to benefit searchers. Mood has been shown to be important in shaping interests (e.g., in recommendation tasks such as the Netflix movie recommendation challenge described in Chapter 12), but it is also important in many other ways, such as influencing search behavior and ultimately the search itself. If the system can interpret the emotional state of the searcher in real-time, it can provide support for preserving a particular mood (e.g., keeping a searcher in a happy state) or changing the mood if desired (e.g., making the searcher happier). Beyond an individual's interactions with the search system, applications of affect modeling may be important when search involves interactions with others in collaborative settings. In social search, the *nature* of social interactions can be considered by search systems (e.g., by applying content analysis on exchanged messages) in more fully modeling the search situation and surfacing affect-appropriate results.

5.5.7 Multimodal

The emphasis thus far in this chapter has been on describing different emerging methods for interacting with devices. Although the methods have been described in isolation, the reality is that by *combining* multiple interaction methods, future search systems will support a broad range of activities and more accurately interpret searcher intentions. It will also allow them to offset some of the weaknesses in their methods (e.g., the lack of intentionality in gaze-based interaction or the absence of events such as hover in touch devices) by considering additional evidence from other inputs such as spoken dialog and gesture.

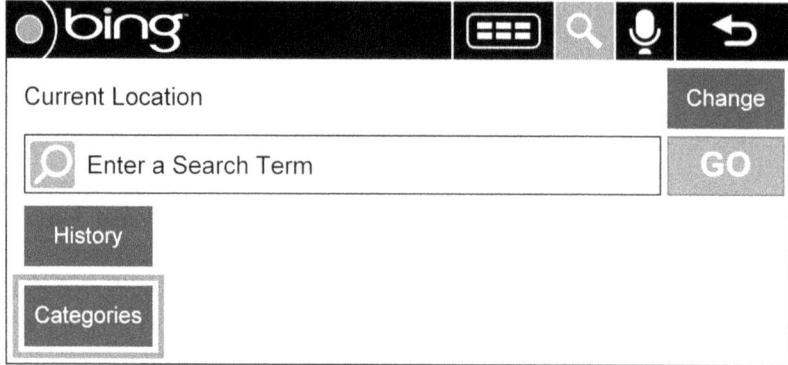

Figure 5.11. Schematic of the homepage of the Microsoft *Bing* search engine on the Lexus RX 350 automobile. The interface is shown in a display embedded in the dashboard of the car.

In addition to searcher and system benefit, the various modalities are also inherently related in a number of ways. For example, gesture is intimately connected to speech, both in terms of its reliance on speech to facilitate interpretation of the gestures, but also because it shares some attributes of speech. Only symbolic gestures can be interpreted without additional context (although these have their own challenges with factors such as cultural variance). In systems, because this context is provided by the application, there is no explicit need for speech input in many situations. Because searchers will have their own preferences about how they interact with search systems, providing them with control and learning their preferences will lead to better and richer search experiences. Providing searchers with the ability to engage with search systems in multiple ways is important in facilitating more effective search interactions.

5.5.8 Ubiquitous Search

Next-generation search systems will offer ubiquitous access to search technologies from any application, in any environment. Ubiquitous computing and pervasive computing, where computing technologies are available in everyday objects (such as refrigerators or automobiles; see Weiser [1993]; Abowd and Mynatt [2000]; Satyanarayanan [2001]), along with the increased usage of mobile devices such as smartphones, tablets, and slates, mean that the environments in which people interact with search systems will be more varied than the traditional personal computer.

Search is available as a dedicated application on a range of devices, including gaming consoles and from within high-end automobiles, allowing people to find information while in transit. In these cases, searchers interact with systems via speech recognition technology, which raises its own challenges for how to communicate queries and also the search results to searchers in a way that does not interfere with their ability to drive safely. Figure 5.11 shows an example of the existing interface to the Microsoft Bing search engine from a Lexus automobile, where queries can be entered via a remote touch controller or through voice entry.

There are also challenges associated with conveying search results audibly while driving or engaged in other activities where the computer display is out of sight.

For example, dictating long lists of results to the searcher may not be feasible in these situations, and further investigation of alternative presentation methods may be required. In particular, speech- and audio-based interfaces need be designed with speech behavior in mind, rather than trying to translate graphical solutions into audio interfaces (Yankelovich et al., 1995). There has been research on the navigation of common audio dialogue structures such as menus, lists, and forms on mobile devices (Resnick and Virzi, 1995), but little or no attention has been paid to how such support can be offered to users of search systems. Marchionini and Komlodi (1998) predicted a trend toward research in this area in the search community, but this has not emerged as rapidly as expected; that may change soon.

Other devices – such as fitness monitors or smart watches – have access to additional information (e.g., physiological signals) that can be a useful source of affective feedback to enrich personalized and contextual models. There is also increasing interest and opportunity in moving toward larger form factors than those visible through a phone, such as projected displays and large displays that can present search interfaces on large screens found in a range of venues from the conference room to living rooms, but also *around* those displays to provide additional context (Jones et al., 2013). These allow people to engage with search results in a range of new ways that were not possible previously, utilizing voice and gestural input to search engines in ways that were hitherto impossible. In doing so, attention needs to be paid to carefully designing the user experience given the distance between users and the screen (e.g., fine-grained actions such as checkbox selections are likely impossible without a redesign of the interface), rather than adjacent to the screen as is common practice in current search engines. Some of the discussion from Section 5.5.3 around different gestures for search is relevant here, although more attention needs to be given to the experience of presenting and reviewing search results from a distance. *Google Glass* provides a head-mounted display that allows searchers to perform everyday tasks but also invoke search through voice commands and display results within the visual view of the searcher. However, the need to wear this device limited the situations within which it is employed and has raised privacy concerns (Hong, 2013).

There are some scenarios, such as collaborative searching in a living room environment or in a conference room with multiple attendees, where people should be able to interact directly with search results (perhaps even the same search results, simultaneously) even though they are co-located (Morris, 2012). Collaborative searching in these settings has traditionally been challenging, but these settings are appealing for the design of collaborative search technologies given searcher co-presence and high likelihood of sharing consistent information goals. The nature of the coordination and the role of search engines in facilitating interaction with information and its usage within co-located search environments are both important.

5.5.9 Productivity Applications

One of the goals of next-generation search systems is to empower people to be more productive by surfacing task-relevant information at the right time, integrated within broader applications such as office suites. For many searchers, especially information workers, productivity involves the use of search systems in tandem with other applications, such as productivity applications (e.g., word processors, spreadsheets, and electronic mail clients). Content generation in productivity applications – such as word processing software – is an area in which search has the potential to be incredibly useful and is currently under-supported. Previous work has shown that Web searching only comprises a small fraction of time spent on information tasks and that there is significant interplay between different applications during task completion (Kumpulainen and Järvelin, 2010). As such, support for searching in these settings needs to facilitate fluid transitions between applications and the transfer of salient data (e.g., information fragments) between applications to support content creation.

There has been limited work in this area through scratchpads and other applications (Morris et al., 2008; Donato et al., 2010), even though these systems keep content within a single application (namely the Web browser or the search engine), systems must facilitate the synthesis of content collected from multiple applications. In an important step in this direction, Fourney et al. (2014) described *InterTwine*, a system that creates inter-application histories (in that case between a Web browser and an image processing application) to help people re-find information in both applications. The system offers three types of inter-application information scent: (1) application bridges that connect features of the currently open applications; (2) history snippets that communicate information about the context surrounding the past use of a command; and (3) history digests that provide context-dependent summaries of how an application was used with respect to a Web page. Given the synergies between many different applications, this type of cross-application support is badly needed. For example, the relationship between Web browsers and dedicated applications for tasks such as programming has been explored. Computer programmers make extensive use of online resources when writing code (Brandt et al., 2009) and when answering technical questions in online forums (Fourney and Morris, 2013).

There have a few attempts to support people's information seeking and use activities from within productivity applications such as email clients (Dumais et al., 2004) or even when searching personal information more generally (Dumais et al., 2003; Cutrell et al., 2006). Interactions with productivity applications provide useful clues about searcher intentions at a particular point in time, and can serve as useful context for applications to facilitate both just-in-time information access (Budzik and Hammond, 2000) and associative memory (Rhodes and Starner, 1996). Within the context of document creation, research on recommending citations to authors of research papers may be particularly relevant to the readership of this book (He et al., 2011; Livne et al., 2014), and clearly demonstrates the value of search-related technology as a service within applications that extend beyond basic document retrieval.

There may also be value in leveraging information retrieval methods to provide an alternative form of support – specifically, recommendations for other documents that might be relevant to the current content of interest. Proactive search systems such as *Implicit Query* (Cutrell et al., 2004) and others such as *WebWatcher* (Joachims et al., 1997) mine situational context (as observable by the application) to provide recommendations tailored to the current situation. The implicit query system automatically generates context-sensitive searches based on a person's current computing activities (e.g., reading or composing email). In the system, queries are automatically generated

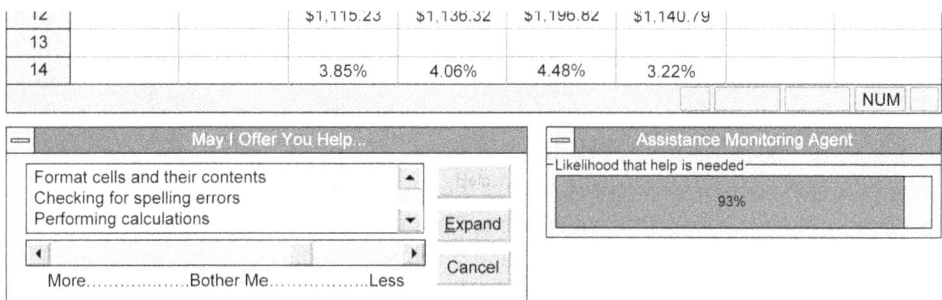

Figure 5.12. Screenshot of the *Lumière* system offering recommendations given a high likelihood (93%) that the user requires assistance at the current time.

by analyzing the current electronic mail message, and results are presented in a small pane adjacent to the current window to provide peripheral awareness of related information. This information can be useful during document composition, such as pulling together information fragments from disparate resources. Because this system is only making recommendations about on-topic content, there is not the same level of expectation as there might be for an assistant who is offering help in completing a specific named *task* (such as writing a letter), where it is important to understand task intent.

Rather than focusing on knowledge discovery, there is also a need to find and re-use previous content, either that generated by the author or that generated by others and received via means such as email (and also in the context of search via the re-issuance of search queries/revisitation to URLs [Teevan et al., 2007; Adar et al., 2008], as discussed earlier in the book). Systems such as *Stuff I've Seen* (Dumais et al., 2003) and *Phlat* (Cutrell et al., 2006) facilitates information re-use by providing a unified index of information that a person has encountered on their machine and providing different ways for people to re-access that information, including the assignment of tags to items and browsing. Improvements in search technology in systems such as Phlat, have meant that people no longer need to actively manage and organize their content by placing it directly in folders (Cutrell et al., 2006). This has implications for strategies used in personal information management (Malone, 1983; Whittaker and Sidner, 1996).

Lumière (Horvitz et al., 1998) is centered on harnessing probability and utility to provide assistance to computer software users. The project built Bayesian models for reasoning about the time-varying goals of computer users from their observed actions and queries, gaining access to a stream of events from software applications, developing (1) a language for transforming system events into observational variables represented in Bayesian user models, (2) persistent profiles to capture changes in a person's expertise, and (3) an overall architecture for an intelligent user interface. *Lumière* prototypes served as the basis for the animated Office Assistant in the early versions of the Microsoft Office suite of productivity applications. The assistant assumed an anthropomorphic presence, ranging from a genie to a genius. Figure 5.12 shows an example of the assistant in action, offering to help a person compose a letter. Such mixed initiative interfaces (Horvitz, 1998) support the coupling of automated assistance with direct manipulation in different contexts (e.g., scheduling/meeting management systems).

Patterns of work are also changing; with increasing frequency, people are working remotely, either at home or during travel (Olson, 1983; Dix and Beale, 1996; Churchill and Munro, 2001; Butler et al., 2007; Kaplan, 2014). To be effective at assisting searchers, personalization algorithms and intelligent agents need access to searchers' profile information irrespective of the device from which the query is issued. This is not possible if profiles are siloed on individual machines (as in client-side personalization [Teevan et al., 2005]). To be useful, profiles need to be stored remotely in the cloud and may be in tension with searchers' privacy expectations. Searchers can manually sign in to rehydrate their profile on a particular device, or they can be identified automatically (Carmagnola and Cena, 2009). Systems need to communicate the benefits to their users of sharing their profile information, and also limit shared information to only that necessary for the specific application scenario (e.g., sharing a vector of term weights rather than the content itself; see Kobsa [2007]; Krause and Horvitz [2008]).

5.5.10 Other

There are other capabilities that next-generation search systems will need to possess. One of the most pressing areas is in the realm of cross-device and cross-application activity, in particular supporting search tasks as they transcend time and people's movements around physical and virtual spaces, and hence, frequently, device and application boundaries. Cross device transitions are likely for tasks that require searchers to change physical location, and hence move away from a static device on which salient profile building content and/or search histories may be stored. Supporting cross-device searching requires ways of storing and resuming state between devices, and leveraging downtime between devices to find relevant and device-appropriate content (Wang et al., 2013; Montañez et al., 2014).

5.5.10.1 Cross-Device

Search tasks are not constrained by device boundaries and some people wish to resume tasks from any device, anywhere. Successful task completion, for some tasks (especially those involving exploration or planning in the virtual world, and execution on the move in the physical world – for example, restaurant selection), requires searchers to utilize multiple devices as they move around the physical world. Search tasks that once existed solely on a single device, now span multiple devices such as desktops, tablets, smartphones, and gaming consoles. Figure 5.13 presents an example of a single searcher's search activity across four types of device (desktop or laptop computer (referred to as "PC" in the figure), smartphone, tablet, and gaming console) within a single day. This example is drawn from the logs of the Microsoft Bing search engine analyzed by Montañez et al. (2014), but query text is replaced with similar alternatives to preserve anonymity. The analysis also showed that at least 5% of searchers are multi-device users, with queries from such searchers accounting for 16% of search volume on the engine studied (i.e., such searchers are highly engaged).

Reflecting on Figure 5.13, there are different topical patterns and different temporal patterns. For this searcher on this day, the PC and the gaming console are used in the

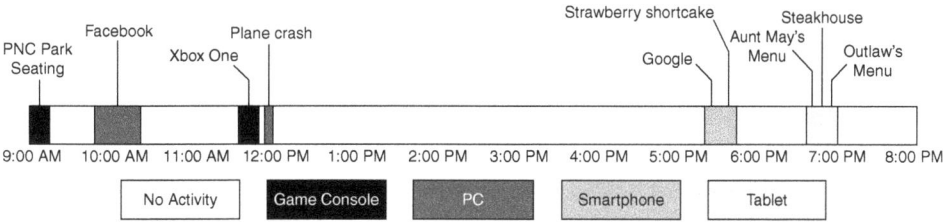

Figure 5.13. Fictionalized searcher timeline for one day, based on log data. Queries of interest on each of the four devices of interest is marked (adapted from Montañez et al., 2014).

morning (perhaps when they are at home), and the smartphone and tablet are used in the evening (when they may be at work or commuting). The morning activity involves planning future events and staying updated on events in social and news media. In the evening, we also observe a longer-running search task between smartphone and tablet for dining related topics; the topic and the mobile nature of the devices used suggest that the searcher may not be at home. Recent work has shown that the nature of the current location can be estimated using geolocation data (Krumm and Rouhana, 2013). Figure 5.13 also suggests some predictability in usage patterns. Aside from the time of day that the devices are utilized, gaming console usage precedes PC usage in both instances. All that being said, this represents only one searcher's (fictionalized) activity on one day. Improving the experience for all searchers as they transition between devices requires a better understanding of multi-device usage patterns over many searchers and queries.

Existing solutions to improving the search experience using personal data have been restricted to a single machine such as the desktop computer (e.g., using all data from a searcher's machine [Teevan et al., 2005]). However, as more user-generated content moves into the cloud via services such as Microsoft *OneDrive* and Google *Drive*, there is not only a need to support search over personal content stored in the cloud, but also an opportunity to apply the content stored in cloud repositories to enable cross-device search experiences that are not dependent on siloed data stored on a single device. Because stored data will likely cover a range of topics, to help ensure model quality it will be necessary to filter content so that only task-relevant content is used.

Beyond simply surfacing the right information at the right time, we also need to consider the device that will be used to serve that information to searchers. If search systems can perform predictions about whether searchers will resume an ongoing task on another device and which particular device they will use next (desktop computer, laptop, tablet, smartphone, or gaming console), they can pre-fetch the content so that when searchers resume their task, the information is ready for them (Montañez et al., 2014). Other related prediction tasks include predicting the device to which searchers will switch and the amount of time until the switch occurs. Accurately predicting the target device facilitates the provision of device-appropriate information (e.g., low-text content for delivery on a smartphone) for the target device. Being able to accurately predict *when* the task will be resumed is important because it helps the engine to understand how much time they have to act on the searcher's behalf. If they have a lot of time, the search engine may consult human experts and get them to provide answers to the task. In contrast, if time is more limited, search providers could issue a set of concurrent queries and blend the results.

Utilizing downtime between searcher actions has been discussed for some time in the context of automated reconnaissance agents (e.g., Lieberman, 1995; Lieberman, 2001) and recently in the context of slow search, where crowdworkers could be employed to assist with the search task in real time (Teevan et al., 2013). The challenge in doing this is that it is not always clear what action to take on behalf of the searcher or how methods such as crowdsourcing will scale to large query volumes. However, rather than performing an action on behalf of the searcher, the systems can better equip searchers to restart their tasks by providing a way to restore search state and suggest next steps based on the aggregated search behavior of others attempting the same or similar tasks (White et al., 2013a). The *S3* (Storable, Shareable Search) system (Morris and Horvitz, 2007) implicitly captured the process and products of exploratory Web searches (referred to as "investigations" by the authors), involving multiple queries. The persistent representation allows for the rehydration of search states during the continuation of search tasks over time. *S3* also supports the sharing and augmentation of investigations by collaborators, as well as being used as a standing query to retrieve relevant information that can be pushed to the searcher proactively or when they resume the investigation. Other systems such as *SearchBar* (Morris et al., 2008) and *ActionShot* (Li et al., 2010) automatically store information about the state of search episodes over time, to help searchers retrace their steps during their prior search episodes.

5.5.10.2 Storing Search State in Physical Form

One focus in this chapter has been on methods representing and supporting search interactions. Large aspects of user profiles may be persistent over time; but these profiles may not be accessible to all search systems that a searcher may use, and assuming that all search systems will be interoperable seems infeasible, at least in the short term in light of the limited view on data and search histories that each of these search systems currently has. Given the recent explosion in three-dimensional printing, providing searchers with a way to create a multidimensional representation of their search interests – a tangible search artifact – that could be carried with them and presented to any search system (and read with a depth camera) as an efficient way to store and restore complex information seeking state and persistent preferences. Assuming that these artifacts are interpretable by humans as well as machines, they can also serve as potentially useful memory aids; this is a topic that has been examined in detail in experimental psychology (see Intons-Peterson and Fournier [1986] for a useful summary).

5.5.10.3 Searching the Physical World

Another focus in this chapter has been on methods to support the search and retrieval of content from the digital world. However, given enhanced sensing technology and real-time tracking of objects (including inventory in retail settings), next generation search systems will help people to search the physical world of objects for items of interest. Situations where this is useful include locating personal items that may have been misplaced (e.g., car keys, remote controls, or spectacles) or items hidden from view by other items (e.g., an important document located deep in a paper pile). While the value of these methods is clear, there are also significant practical challenges in realizing this vision, both in terms of monitoring the state of an unstructured physical space such as a desktop (e.g., through cameras, tags, and sensors), identifying and indexing objects in that space such that their location at any given time is retrievable by a search system, and communicating that information back to a searcher (e.g., one option includes using a map to indicate the location of the information, illuminating the location of the item of interest in the physical space using spotlights or even lasers to guide the way). Recent advances in areas such as three-dimensional modeling on handheld devices could enable the modeling and searching of physical spaces.

Rather than relying on devices to model the environment, the environment itself could have some limited awareness (e.g., objects using embedded RFID tags allowing them to be easily located; see Want et al. [1992] and Wang et al. [2008]). For example, the *MAX* system allows users to search for a known object with a sensor attached and receive hints about its location (e.g., "top shelf of the third room,"), but it is only an exact match and does not support the retrieval of related objects (Yap et al., 2005). Infrared sensors can be attached to objects and people, supporting browsing and task completion via natural movement and examination gestures (e.g., in settings such as automobile repair and retail; see Merrill and Maes [1997]).

Within large indoor spaces such as department stores, knowledge of availability of inventory, store layout, and the current location of the searcher, can help systems direct users of smartphone applications or wearable devices to find sought products. Moving beyond locating objects, there are other ways in which searching the physical world can be supported, such as helping with wayfinding or revisitation in physical environments (I discuss that in more detail in Chapter 9), and the recognition of physical objects, using image features (Lowe, 1999) or other methods. As an example of recent advances in this area, the startup *Consumer Physics*[10] offers a way for searchers to identify items of interest (or find similar items) based on an object's molecular makeup. They have developed a miniature spectrometer and algorithms to match its output with databases of known items.

5.5.10.4 *Virtual Reality*

Moving beyond the limitations of the physical world, a type of immersive experience that has untapped potential is *virtual reality* (Rheingold, 1991; Brudea and Coiffet, 2003). Virtual reality simulates physical presence in virtual environments, usually through head-mounted displays. The technology has been researched and discussed for decades, and applied to many settings, including gaming, therapy, and training. The technology has also been studied within the context of information seeking and retrieval, with applications including collaborative search (Benford et al., 1995), content-based image retrieval (Nakazato and Huang, 2001), and geographic retrieval (Brown, 1999). The prospect of situating searchers within virtual environments is intriguing, and could have value for a range of exploratory and collaborative search scenarios. Until recently, the cost of virtual reality devices has been prohibitively high. There are signs that this is changing. Devices such as the *Oculus Rift*[11] bring immersive multimedia to the mass market, albeit with an initial focus on gaming. This means that it is now viable for search providers to design next-generation search systems comprising immersive search experiences, perhaps starting with specialized domains where technology has most utility (e.g., collaborative search).

5.6 Logging Richer Search Behavior

Many of the methods described thus far in the book rely on mining search behavior. It is clear that there is a lot that searchers and search systems can learn from the historic activity of the current searcher and other searchers. These interactions involve simple, well-defined, intentional events, such as queries and items selections that can be identified easily in mining search logs, allowing inferences to be made based about relevance and satisfaction on patterns of interaction. Jansen (2006a) provided a good description of the processes and procedures involved in analyzing search logs collected under this standard paradigm. As we move toward richer interactions between systems and machines (e.g., to identify common patterns in cursor activity and use these patterns to improve Web search engine ranking [Lagun et al., 2014a]), there are many challenges associated with recording and using activity in next-generation search systems:

- **Context dependence:** Many of the richer forms of interaction described in this chapter are highly dependent on the context in which the information is accessed, especially situational factors that affect needs and interests at the time that the query is issued. Recording the salient aspects of this context in addition to the actions performed by the searcher seems important in framing the search interaction appropriately. Because the range of contextual factors is infinite, difficult decisions need to be made regarding which contextual signals to record given their value in supporting envisaged scenarios and their prospective value in supporting applications of the future (i.e., highest general utility).
- **Missing interactions:** There are some characteristics of cursor-based interactions that have been shown to be useful that are not present in new modalities. One of the most important is the lack of hover interactions on touch devices, although (as described earlier) there is some research on methods to address this shortcoming by sensing when the finger is *above* the display (Mistry and Wang, 2011). Because hovers can provide clues about when people are considering an item, without that additional information, we have less insight into what people have examined. Missing information about how people interact with machines is important because it limits the systems understanding of searcher behaviors and intentions. Combinations of different signals from other available sources, such as eye-gaze tracking estimates, time between clicks, and rank positions of different clicks could be useful in handling these data, allowing for accurate inferences to be made even without strong evidence.
- **Data volume:** Richer interaction paradigms generate a large amount of data on searcher interactions, including eye-gaze coordinates, hand/head positions, and so on, which are sampled frequently to accurately represent the observed activity, as well as more traditional signals such as queries and clicks. Data that are generated

by these methods can be impractical to send to remote servers owing to bandwidth constraints. Compression techniques, including sampling the collected data on the client (after it has been collected) or limiting the information that is collected at the source, may be needed to throttle the amount of data that is transmitted remotely to the server.

- **Page latency:** Adding more tracking logic to the SERP increases the size of the page, which may have an impact on page load time latency. As stated earlier, page load time significant impacts searcher engagement (Shurman and Brutlag, 2009; Arapakis et al., 2014). Alternatives to the standard synchronous loading strategy include asynchronous lazy loading for which the tracking code is loaded in the background once the remainder of the page appears. In practice, this means that the first few interactions with the page might be missed, but engagement would be less affected because the page load time is unchanged; this may be preferable for a search provider.
- **Persistent identifiers:** The ability to learn from cross-device behaviors requires tracking searchers, with consent, as they transition between devices. Long-lived identifiers are needed to associate observed interactions with the correct searcher, and characterize transitions appropriately. Cookie-based identifiers may not be sufficiently persistent (e.g., searchers may clear their cookies), although research has shown that it may be possible to fairly reliably merge different cookie-based identifiers into a single identifier (Dasgupta et al., 2012).
- **Privacy considerations:** Logging search behavior more completely means that search providers have ever greater insight into the activities of their users. Many of the new signals that are collected, such as gestural sequences or mouse cursor trails, do not contain personally identifiable information. There may still be concerns from searchers about increased data logging and potential for unforeseen applications of these data, either in isolation or in combination with other data sources, where their privacy may be in particular jeopardy. Search providers should clearly communicate what information is being recorded and the potential benefits in doing so in the aggregate and individual levels (Horvitz and Mulligan, 2015). They may also want to offer searchers the option to opt-out of richer logging of search behavior (or even specific data streams), or compensate them for taking the risk that their log data could be sampled from a broader population of users of a service (Singla et al., 2014a).

An important challenge in making decisions regarding behavioral logging lies in predicting future uses for the data that are recorded. In making determinations, cost-benefit analysis and high-priority use cases are needed from stakeholders in close consultation with those with experience in leveraging such data for a range of different scenarios.

5.7 Summary

In this chapter, I have considered different existing methods for helping people search information spaces and have covered a large number of methods, including those for informing interaction decisions, devising query statements, and supporting decision making. I also described existing approaches for supporting search interactively, and additional methods that could be considered for inclusion in search systems. Importantly, I also discussed new methods and modalities that are emerging, some subset of which will transform how people seek information, and mechanisms in which search interactions with these interfaces will be recorded for later analysis and application. Irrespective of the methods employed, to be successful, additional search support needs to address real problems that searchers may encounter during the search process. The focus in this chapter has largely been on supporting search given the existence of a defined information need, but there are other ways in which search-related interaction could be supported in areas for which information is not so directly sought (e.g., in exploratory search settings; see Marchionini [2006a] and White et al. [2006]). In the next chapter, I consider how search systems support exploration and discovery.

CHAPTER 6

Exploration, Complexity, and Discovery

As the range of search tasks that people perform on search engines increases, supporting searchers in examining results, exploring result spaces, and discovering new insights from data will become key requirements in the design of search systems. An important part of providing this support is to identify when searchers are exploring and to design search interfaces to support exploratory activities.

In Chapter 5, I mainly focused on searching for information as an activity that search systems should support directly, and I discussed some of the existing and emerging techniques to support searchers in performing those searches. The focus for much of the work covered were cases for which the target of the search is known. Although search engines continue to improve how they handle lookup-based searches (assisted to a large extent by the availability of behavioral data), support for ill-defined, exploratory scenarios needs to be expanded. There is a range of information tasks for which information goals are less clearly defined; those tasks are built around searchers' desires to explore (e.g., Marchionini 2006a; White and Roth, 2009). As discussed in detail in Chapter 4, exploration is an important aspect of information behavior that can be motivated by intrinsic and extrinsic motivations (Berlyne, 1960). The exploration of information spaces can yield key new insights and advances, promote serendipity, and foster creativity. Exploration is central in activities such as learning, understanding, and decision making. All of these outcomes may occur during the search for known items, but the attainment of such goals is not a primary objective in traditional search systems. However, searchers' expectations are evolving and next-generation search system designers need to consider exploration and discovery as central elements of the search process.

In this chapter, I focus on both exploratory and complex search tasks, which have many of the following characteristics:

- Emphasis on learning and discovery, driven by task requirements and/or a desire to learn;
- Ill-defined and multi-aspect;

- Require both search and browsing;
- Higher-level goals beyond finding, such as enhanced understanding and decision-support; and
- Long-term (searches over multiple sessions) and persistent (even if searcher is not actively searching).

Exploration can range from general exploratory behavior (as defined in Section 4.1) to behavior associated with exploratory or complex search tasks, which is a more directed action (Marchionini, 1995). Tasks that are exploratory in nature include those in which the goal is explicitly to learn (Marchionini, 2006a) and tasks that are intrinsically complex (e.g., tasks that comprise multiple steps or multiple aspects; see Hassan and White [2012]; Hassan Awadallah et al. [2014]). In such cases, searchers' goals may include learning (both generally, about the content of the collection, and about themselves via reflection about their historic search activity [Bateman et al., 2012]), as well as formulating and testing hypotheses against data. Tools to support information visualization and visual analytics, as well as highly interactive searcher interfaces (including those leveraging touch, gesture, and spoken dialog input), may be useful in support of exploration and discovery.

Complex tasks involve multiple steps or multiple aspects. Supporting these tasks includes identifying task aspects, learning from other searchers who have attempted the same tasks, and supporting tasks across session boundaries. In leveraging the collective activity of others pursuing similar information objectives, being able to retain, learn from, and retrieve the processes by which searches are conducted is important. This is in addition to the use of artifacts (e.g., Web pages selected by many searchers with similar information needs) that are commonly employed in search systems. Even though exploration is an undirected process, people can still benefit from the cues and experiences of others to enhance their exploration activity. This may involve (re)constructing representations of tasks from seemingly disconnected interaction events (e.g., a series of isolated queries occurring in a particular sequence over a course of time) may reveal something about the phases that searchers progress through as they tackle a complex task such as planning a wedding, finding a job, or handling a complex medical diagnosis. Each of these has a number of aspects. For example, planning a wedding is a complex and stressful task that spans many months and sometimes years, and involves a broad range of activities, including: (1) selecting a venue for ceremony and/or reception; (2) choosing a date; (3) sending both save-the-dates and formal invitations; (4) creating a wedding website; (5) arranging catering; (6) booking entertainment (band, disc jockey, etc.); (7) booking a photographer/videographer; (8) booking an officiant; (9) determining the guest list and seating plans; (10) selecting flowers; (11) purchasing wedding rings; (12) choosing the wedding party; (13) deciding on attire (including the wedding dress); (14) arranging transportation to and from the venue; (15) procuring marriage licenses; (16) populating one or more wedding registries; and (17) making arrangements for the honeymoon (to name but a few of the subtasks involved). Recent research with longitudinal search log data has examined the nature of long-term search tasks (Kotov et al., 2011; Agichtein et al., 2012), and has provided evidence of temporal relationships between different aspects of the search task (e.g., people searching for "resume" then for "moving" at some later date; see Richardson [2008]). More recent research has sought evidence of causal connections between people's actions and outcomes from longitudinal data (Kiciman and Richardson, 2015).

In the remainder of this chapter, I describe research on identifying when searchers are engaged in exploratory activity, as well as the design of search support for exploration and discovery.

6.1 Identifying Exploration

Models of exploration and exploratory behavior were already discussed in Section 4.1. Support for exploration can be requested directly by the searcher if they believe that such support is necessary to assist them with their search tasks. Alternatively, search systems can proactively help searchers perform such exploratory activities. If they are going to be proactive, then systems need to automatically discern when a searcher is engaged in an exploration activity or are likely to be responsive to the receipt of recommendations given their current task. Support for exploration can be offered in real time to provide assistance to the searcher instantly or analyzed retrospectively on collective logs to understand the nature of searchers' information needs, and use that to inform the design of future iterations of search systems.

One of the challenges faced in automatically identifying the nature of the search behavior lies in generating labels describing the nature of the task, especially because the signals can look similar depending on the context. For example, it may not be clear whether the searcher is exploring the result space or is struggling to find the information that they seek. Recent research has studied user behavior when searchers are experiencing difficulty in finding relevant information (Aula et al., 2010), and also sought to distinguish between searchers struggling and exploring in search environments (Hassan et al., 2014). Web searchers often exhibit directed search behavior such as navigating to a particular website. In many circumstances, however, searchers may exhibit seemingly undirected behavior such as issuing many queries in sequence and visiting many results. In such cases, it is not clear whether their behavior is related to intentionally exploring the results or struggling to find the information that they seek. Figure 6.1 presents examples of a struggling session (Figure 6.1a) and an exploring session (Figure 6.1b), both based on search log data.

In Figure 6.1a, we can see that the searcher issued many related queries and clicked on many results (four queries and five results in total), providing some evidence that they are exploring. However, the queries are closely related, and the inter-query time is relatively short for some queries (suggesting impatience). This provides stronger evidence that the searcher is in fact struggling to find relevant information pertaining to the annual purchase of specific tax software. In Figure 6.1b, we see an example of a searcher exploring different aspects of a topic "career development," and issuing multiple queries with multiple clicks. While the difference between the two types of sessions may be discernible to human judges, existing automatic methods may be unable to perform this distinction using limited information such as the number of queries in the session or session duration.

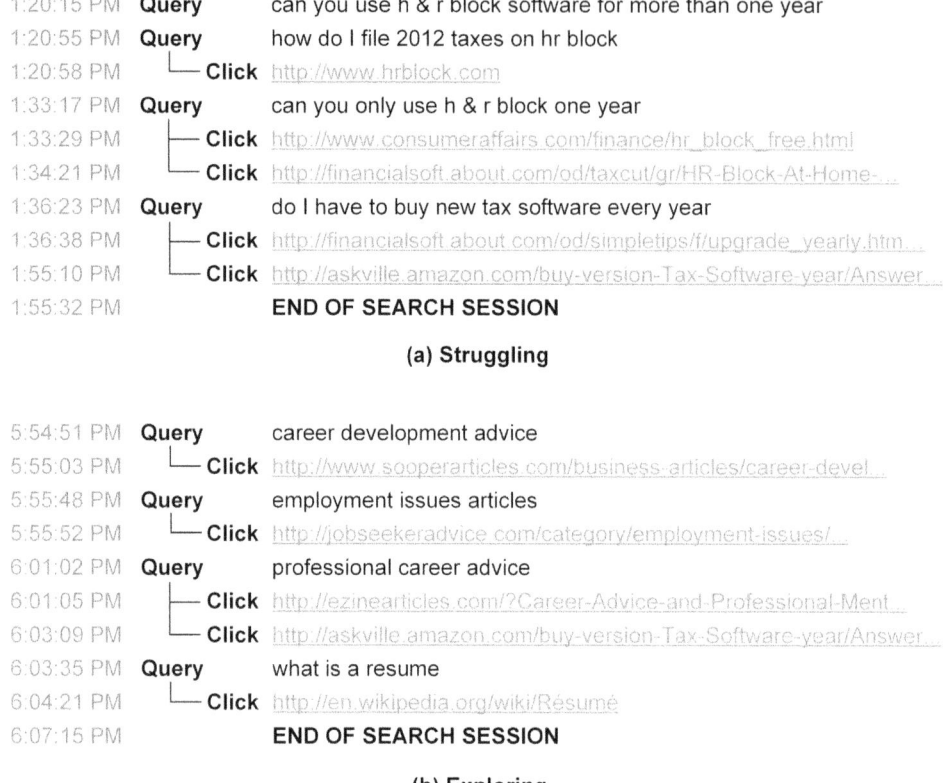

Figure 6.1. Examples of struggling and exploring sessions (adapted from Hassan et al., 2014).

Being able to disambiguate between struggling and exploring is vital for search systems both in performing retrospective analysis to understand search success, and in developing real-time support to assist searchers at query time. As can be seen in the examples just mentioned, many of the characteristics of exploration (e.g., multiple queries, long duration) are also observed in sessions in which people are struggling. Hassan et al. (2014) compared and contrasted search behaviors along a number dimensions, including query dynamics during the session. They found that there are some features that may be predictive of struggling, such as a low amount of similarity between consecutive queries, more clicks per query, as well as differences in the nature of the reformulation patterns (i.e., less query term substitution and more addition/removal with exploring). Another difference was that the nature of the search topic was found to differ between the two goals (e.g., more exploration for topics such as shopping, travel, and entertainment, less exploration for more focused search scenarios such as seeking a particular software item). Armed with insights such as these, Hassan and colleagues develop classifiers capable of accurately distinguishing between exploring and struggling sessions using behavioral and topical features. As mentioned earlier, being able to estimate when a searcher is engaging in exploratory behavior creates significant opportunity. For example, search engines can use this as an additional signal to inform satisfaction models that predict whether searchers are satisfied with their search outcomes, such as those discussed earlier in Chapter 3 (Hassan et al., 2010).

6.2 Supporting Exploration

Given that a search system can accurately estimate when a searcher is exploring, it is important to discuss the types of search support that could be provided. There are a number of options. The system could search proactively for related resources, or it could offer holistic support when it surfaces various aspects of the task (in visualizations such as guided tours [Trigg, 1988], trails [Bush, 1945], maps [Shahaf et al., 2012], and so on), and the searcher can select the path to take or a particular node of interest. An alternative is to support searchers in a stepwise manner, as the system recommends Web pages or search queries based on the searcher's current situation (e.g., highlighting hyperlinks that could be of interest to the searcher, or suggesting queries that could assist with exploration; see Chi et al. [2003]).

6.2.1 Exploratory Search Systems

Tools to support exploratory searching should help searchers define the problem, make sense of encountered information throughout the current session and across multiple sessions, and handle uncertainty and confusion by providing progress updates, explanations for system actions, and summaries of major themes present in encountered information (Marchionini, 2006a; White and Roth, 2009). The information needs of people grappling with chronic illness, work teams creating complex solutions or products, learners studying complex material over time, people making long-term plans, scientists investigating complex phenomena, and hobbyists tracking developments over a life time are well-served at only the most superficial levels by existing Web search engines (Marchionini and White, 2009). Exploratory search systems (ESSs) address this shortcoming by providing search solutions that empower people to move beyond single-session lookup tasks.

The unique nature of searches for which the target is unknown calls for new system designs to help searchers. White and Roth (2009) proposed the following eight requirements for ESSs:

1. Support the construction of search queries, including rapid query refinement (Chapter 5).
2. Leverage the search context to improve the relevance of search results and the quality of system recommendations (Chapter 10).
3. Offer facets and metadata-based result filtering (Chapter 5).
4. Offer rich information visualizations to support insight and decision making (Chapter 6).
5. Support learning and understanding, including estimating the current search state of the searcher and changes in that state within the search session and across search sessions (Eickhoff et al., 2014; see Chapter 7 in this book).
6. Facilitate collaboration between individuals, such as those working together on a specific task, in co-located and remote collaboration scenarios (Chapter 8).
7. Offer search histories, workspaces, and project updates (Chapter 6).
8. Support task management, for example, by allowing searchers to save and rehydrate their search state (Morris et al., 2008) and split tasks into manageable chunks (Teevan et al., 2014a; see Chapter 3 in this book).

Systems that support search exploration are a vital and a missing part of mainstream search technology. Many existing search systems only meet the first two requirements in this list. These and many of the other requirements are reflected in the discussions throughout this book (chapter numbers are provided with the requirements in the list), as are central aspects of next-generation search technologies.

Examples of ESSs include information visualization systems, document clustering and browsing systems, and intelligent content summarization systems. ESSs go beyond returning a single document or answer in response to a query and instead aim to instigate significant cognitive change through learning and improved understanding. Through relevance feedback and scratchpads to retain information as it is encountered, ESSs help people gather information in chunks rather than in a single result set. For example, browsing is a serendipitous activity that can yield benefit from extraneous information (Marchionini and Shneiderman, 1988). ESSs help searchers engaged in browsing to maximize their rate of information gain, make decisions about which navigational paths to follow, and understand the information that they encounter. Examples of the type of support that has been proposed includes new search interfaces to help media studies researchers refine their research questions and explore diverse topics (Bron et al., 2012), and interfaces to support complex tasks (Villa et al., 2009).

Through interface features such as dynamic queries (Ahlberg et al., 1992), ESSs can help searchers visualize the immediate impact of their refinement decisions on their views of the data such as starfield displays, cartograms, and histograms. The tight coupling between queries and results is also observed in other techniques such as *Magic Lenses* (Bier et al., 1993), and is especially valuable for exploration. In these scenarios, high-level overviews of collections and rapid previews of objects help people understand data structures and infer relationships among concepts. The ability to rapidly manipulate the data on a number of dimensions simultaneously is critical to the hypothesis generation and information need clarification that occurs in exploratory searches. As searchers form concrete hypotheses and information needs, uncertainty is reduced and their search behavior may pivot from exploratory browsing (emphasis on discovery, learning, and investigation) to focused searching and browsing (emphasis on query (re)formulation, result examination, and information extraction; see White and Roth [2009]).

6.2.1.1 Search Histories, Workspaces, and Progress Updates

Many of the exploratory search tasks that next-generation search systems will support the examination of multiple information sources and transcend multiple search sessions. Searchers require tools that allow them to easily revisit previously encountered items and to store potentially useful information for later use. Knowledge of how much of the information space has been explored on a topic and what remains to be seen, is useful for exploratory searchers (White and Roth, 2009). Systems to support this type of exploratory searching should: (1) offer a smart and structured history, a record the path a user followed to get to findings, and easy revisitation of results; (2) contain "workspaces" to support a spectrum of activities, from unstructured note-taking to integrated authoring environments; and (3) keep track of progress (and alert searchers if they are straying [and even support such deviations in the interests of serendipity]), remember dead ends, and record what has already been seen so that novel information or updates can be provided.

Systems have already been developed that offer elements of histories, workspaces, and progress updates. *Hunter Gatherer* (schraefel et al., 2002) is an interface that lets Web users perform three primary tasks: (1) collect components from within Web pages; (2) represent those components in a collection; (3) edit those component collections. *InkSeine* (Hinckley et al., 2007) is a tablet computer search application that enables its users to store a pointer to a search via a breadcrumb object intermixed with their handwritten notes. Dontcheva and colleagues (2006) developed a system for summarizing personal Web browsing sessions that allows searchers to define patterns for extracting structured information from a set of Web pages. The same authors introduced *Scrapbook*, a system that facilitates the creation of automatic patterns of content extraction spanning pages with similar document object models (Dontcheva et al., 2007). *SearchPad* (Bharat, 2000) allows users to explicitly flag a Web page for inclusion in a workspace to help the searcher maintain context during complex search tasks. Google's *Notebook* application[1] allows searchers to collect snippets of content from several Web pages and combine them in a single document.

6.2.2 Proactive Search and Recommendation

Much of the research on developing search systems has centered on reactive scenarios that respond to search demands expressed as a search query (a "pull" approach). A recent report summarizing strategic directions in information retrieval (Allan et al., 2012) has suggested that next-generation systems need to be both context-aware and able to make recommendations about appropriate content without requiring a query. The report also suggested that these systems need to be open domain (unlike traditional recommender systems, also discussed in this chapter, which tend to focus on a single domain), and synthesize information from multiple sources on the searcher's behalf. This includes proactive assistance prior to issuing a query, as they are formulating queries (e.g., in query auto-completion or real-time query expansion), as they browse content on the Web, or before they realize that they have the information need. In the research community, the Contextual Suggestion Track at the Text Retrieval Conference (TREC; see Dean-Hall et al. [2013]) has provided a vehicle by which research groups can experiment with various approaches for making context-sensitive recommendations.

6.2.2.1 Homepage and Page-Zero Experiences

One way in which search systems can help searchers is by providing them with useful experiences when they first approach the search system (i.e., on the homepage or on *page-zero experiences* containing dynamic result elements that can be populated as searchers type their search queries). Some query behavior, especially for repeat queries, might be sufficiently predictable to generate queries, answers, or results for homepage presentation without requiring explicit queries (Teevan et al., 2007). Personalized behavioral patterns can be mined for each searcher and used to identify frequent search habits (e.g., searching for news at the start of each day) that could be used to provide specific recommendations based on the search context (temporal cues in this case). Alternatively, search systems could proactively recommend content of potential interest to searchers given their specific interests, or provide them with the opportunity to resume a long-running task.

There has been recent research on the detection of long-running search tasks and the prediction of associated future interests (Kotov et al., 2011; Wang et al., 2013) that could have practical utility in this context. The system could also use the time between sessions on the same task to proactively retrieve content of potential interest to the searcher. A reconnaissance agent could operate on the searcher's behalf during the inter-search downtime to find information relevant to searcher's persistent tasks. This may also be useful in cross-device scenarios (or other slow searches [Teevan et al., 2013]), where considering the amount of time that has elapsed between activity on a search task could be useful for generating predictions regarding the ongoing level of interest from the searcher in the search task (e.g., whether they have abandoned the task, or whether it is still active).

6.2.2.2 *Standing Queries*

As part of supporting general exploration, a search engine may allow searchers to provide standing queries that can be issued periodically, and the results collated and presented to the searcher as electronic mail alerts (e.g., Google *Alerts* that can crawl online resources such as news stories, watching for mention of particular concepts) or on a personalized homepage as mentioned earlier. Standing queries provide support for information filtering (Allan, 1996) or cases for which people continue the same tasks over time (Morris and Horvitz, 2007). These queries may represent long-running searchers' interests that may be more likely to be exploratory in nature. Adopting standing queries for this task may also be more reliable than requiring that the search engine automatically identify exploratory interests. However, coverage of this approach is likely to be low, and current implementations place a burden on searchers to explicitly describe their long-lived interests, although these could be inferred from long-term search behavior.

6.2.2.3 *Proactive Search*

Research in this area focuses on anticipating searcher needs and the sometimes passive delivery of information that the system estimates matches searcher interests. These methods can learn from the search habits of individuals, and also consider interaction patterns observed across a broad set of searchers. Models can be constructed from a variety of difference sources, including previous queries and pages to which the searcher has browsed irrespective of their explicit usage of search engines to reach those resources. A goal in such proactive systems is to reduce the number of explicitly issued queries. Recent work has leveraged pre-search browsing context to predict/recommend future queries (Liebling et al., 2012) or for personalization purposes (Ustinovsky and Serdyukov, 2013). Once these models have been constructed, recommendations can be made regarding future pages (Dupret and Piwoworksi, 2008; White et al., 2009a) that are likely to interest searchers or queries that may support the retrieval of resources that align with their future interests (White et al., 2010).

This is also related to work on query-less searching, for which the goal is to furnish search results without requiring that the searcher provide a search query. Proactive search systems may do this on visits to a search engine homepage, as the searcher browses the Web (proactively identifying candidate next steps, as is the case with the ostensive browser described earlier; see Campbell and Van Rijsbergen [1996]). There are a number of scenarios in which predicting the next query or the next action could be useful, including simply saving the searcher time, or presenting them with serendipitous information that may be of general interest. The models need to be highly accurate and care needs to be taken in how recommendations are communicated to searchers, given that unnecessary notifications can cause frustration and disruption to their flow. To help better decide when to make such notifications, this could be coupled with methods for interruption management (Horvitz and Apacible, 2005).

6.2.2.4 Page Recommendations

Web browsers and operating systems represent the primary access points to search systems. The focus in this book has largely been on interactions with search technologies accessed via Web browsers. Current versions of Web browsers provide a way to request search results from anywhere on the Web by supporting the entry of query statements in the address bar or in a dedicated search box as part of the Web browser chrome. Moving forward, the browsers will increase their focus on recommendations based on page content and the historic search activity of the current searcher and those in the same cohorts (Lieberman, 1995; Wexelblat and Maes, 1999; Fu et al., 2000).

Early research on the development of social information filtering systems (Shardanand and Maes, 1995) proposed the generation of personalized recommendation from any type of database based on inter-searcher similarity. In the context of the Web, there has been some progress on the development of page prediction models (e.g., White et al., 2009a), which leverage large-scale data mining methods to look for access patterns pages visited by millions of Web surfers to predict the pages that people will visit next. In anticipation of these visits, the browser can pre-fetch content. The "Flip Ahead" feature in the Microsoft Internet Explorer browser supports this by predicting the page that Web users will visit next. Predictions are generated by mining browsing patterns, people's browsing habits, and common cues in Web pages, such as "next" links and pagination activities through multi-page Websites.

In addition to predicting the next page that a searcher will visit, usually within the same website, we can also suggest content that might be of interest to people as they browse the Web. In one instantiation of this idea, the "Suggested Sites" feature in Internet Explorer records interactions with user consent and uses those interactions to generate a set of recommended pages based on the currently viewed website as well as searcher's recent interaction history (White et al., 2009a). The service generates the suggestions based on the aggregated search and browsing data from other searchers (e.g., searchers who visited the current site, visited related sites within the same search or browsing session). One drawback of the implementation of suggested sites is that searchers need to explicitly request the assistance from the system. Other services, such as the discovery engine *StumbleUpon* (stumbleupon.com), provide similar solutions, but leverage a more proactive approach by highlighting recommendations to searchers when they are available and allow searchers to tailor the received recommendations. *StumbleUpon* finds and recommends Web content to its users, allowing them to discover and rate Web pages, photos, and videos that are personalized to their tastes and interests using peer-sourcing and social-networking principles.

6.2.2.5 Attentive Systems

In operational environments, attentive systems use unobtrusive methods to infer interests. Attentive systems accompany the searcher during their information-seeking journey, and model people's interests by observing search behavior (and other behaviors in inter-modal systems). These systems observe people via their interactions with computer applications, model the user based on these interactions, and anticipate user needs based on the model they develop. In attentive systems, the responsibility for monitoring this interaction is usually assigned to an external agent or assistant. This assistant can act based on inferences made from observing search behavior, or in response to an external event that might increase the priority of the information given the searcher's current context, as with traffic alerts in the case of intelligent personal assistants such as Google *Now* and Microsoft *Cortana*.

6.2.2.5.1 Recommendations during Consumption

Attentive information systems can be distinguished by a few main characteristics. They are capable of gathering information on people's behavior from a number of sources, even across multiple modalities. When only a single source is used, the probability of making incorrect inference of user intentions is high. Multiple sources of evidence (e.g., the set of applications open at present) can reduce ambiguity, allowing for a more accurate user model to be constructed. Attentive information systems learn from each person's activity stream to improve both the relevance and timeliness of the actions it performs. Unless urgent, suggestions should be shown unobtrusively, either selecting opportune moments of prolonged inactivity or in the periphery of the current, active task. These concepts are embodied by systems with a just-in-time (JIT) information infrastructure, where information is brought to users just as they need it, without requiring explicit requests (Budzik and Hammond, 2000). Such systems automatically search information repositories for searchers, and provide explicit, query-entry interfaces. I touch on two examples:

- **Behavior-Based Agents:** Behavior-based interface agents (Maes, 1994; Lashkari et al., 1994) develop and enhance their knowledge of the current domain incrementally from inferences made about user interaction. Systems of this type typically adopt a strategy that lies midway between information retrieval and information filtering (Sheth and Maes, 1993). In retrieval settings, a searcher actively queries a base of mostly irrelevant knowledge in the hopes of extracting a small amount of relevant information. In filtering settings, the searcher is the passive target of a stream of mostly relevant information, and the task is to remove or de-emphasize less relevant or completely irrelevant material (Belkin and Croft, 1992).

- **Reconnaissance Agents:** Reconnaissance agents look ahead in the searcher's browsing activities and act as an "advance scout" to save the searcher needless seeking by recommending the best paths to follow (Lieberman et al., 2001). These agents also infer individual preferences and interests by tracking long-term interactions between the searcher and the machine, and constructing rich profiles that reflect their interests and intentions irrespective of *where* the interaction occurs (e.g., in a search setting, during content creation, or during content consumption).

Examples of reconnaissance agents include *Lira* (Balabanovic and Shoham, 1995), *WebWatcher* (Armstrong et al., 1995), *Suitor* (Maglio et al., 2000), *Watson* (Budzik and Hammond, 2000), *PowerScout* (Lieberman et al., 2001), and *Letizia* (Lieberman, 1995). These systems typically operate on a restricted document domain or on the Web. The methods used to capture this interest and present system suggestions differ from system to system. *Letizia* (Lieberman, 1995), for example, learns its users' current interests and – by performing a look-ahead search (i.e., predicting what searchers may be interested in the future, based on inference history) – can recommend nearby pages. *PowerScout* (Lieberman et al., 2001) uses a model of user interests to construct a new complex query and search the Web for documents semantically similar to the last relevant document. *WebWatcher* (Armstrong et al., 1995), in a similar way, accompanies its users as they browse; but while it observes, *WebWatcher* also acts as a learning apprentice (Mitchell et al., 1994). Over time the system learns to acquire greater expertise for the parts of the Web that it has visited previously and for the topics in which previous visitors have had an interest. *Suitor* (Maglio et al., 2000) tracks computer users through multiple channels (e.g., eye-gaze, Web browsing, and application focus) to determine their interests. *Watson* (Budzik and Hammond, 2000) uses contextual information, in the form of text in the active document, to proactively retrieve documents from distributed information repositories by devising a new query.

6.2.2.5.2 Recommendations during Creation

Thus far in the chapter, I have focused on scenarios in which systems can make recommendations based on the content they are examining. Review of content is only one of many possible user activities. People may also benefit from recommendations made during the *creation* of content. In this setting, search systems surface content relevant to the document currently being edited. Recommendations during the creation of content has been explored in a number of contexts, including during the construction of electronic emails (where related documents from the author's machine can be recommended [Dumais et al., 2004]) and recently during authoring of research articles (where related citations can be recommended to authors [Livne et al., 2014]). This illustrates how search technology can be used in applications beyond directed searching to offer the types of in-situ support during content creation and use that will continue to grow in prominence.

6.2.2.5.3 Drawbacks of Attentive Systems

Despite the promise of these attentive systems, the issue of user control is still somewhat contentious. There is tension between intelligent agents that operate on behalf of the user but independent of their control (e.g., Web-based reconnaissance agents) and rich direct manipulation interfaces under strict user control (e.g., dynamic queries; see Belkin [1996] and Shneiderman and Maes [1997]). Despite the promise of automated systems capable of attending to searcher needs, these systems are difficult to build. There are also privacy concerns associated with the collection and triangulation of data from multiple sources. Ideally we would provide searchers both with cognitive prosthetics to amplify intelligence (Bush, 1945; Licklider, 1960; Engelbart, 1962) and with full control over all cooperative activity (Marchionini and Komlodi, 1999; Marchionini 2006b).

6.2.2.6 Recommender Systems

Recommender systems (see Konstan and Riedl, 2012) should also be discussed in the context of supporting exploration and discovery. Recommender systems are a subclass of information filtering systems that seek to predict the preference or rating that a person would give to an item. Recommender systems add items to the information streams that flows toward a user from external sources, and produce a ranked list of recommendations from these streams where the most relevant content is suggested. Although the focus of recommender systems is accuracy (i.e., suggestions that people will want to select), there are other desirable outcomes such as engendering trust in the information selected (Montaner et al., 2002) or improving serendipity by surfacing surprising or marginally related content (Ricci et al., 2011).

Recommendations are generated principally via two techniques: *collaborative filtering* and *content-based filtering*:

- **Collaborative filtering (CF)** approaches build a model from users' historic behavior, activities, or preferences (items previously purchased or selected and/or numerical ratings given to those items), as well as similar decisions made by other users; and then use that model to predict items (or ratings for items) in which the person may have an interest (Breese et al., 1998). Collaborative filtering approaches are desirable because they do not depend on being able to understand the content of the items in the collection; that is, they are based on user behavior or preferences pertaining to a particular document. Perhaps the most famous examples of this type of CF is item-to-item collaborative filtering ("people who buy x also buy y"), made popular by the Amazon.com recommender system. Because collaborative filtering methods rely on access to a large amount of information about the user to make accurate recommendations, they may be affected by the cold start problem (Schein et al., 2002). They may also require significant computational resources to perform effectively because they need to analyze all pairs; and they may suffer from issues of data sparsity because very few of the millions of items available will have ratings data.
- **Content-based filtering** approaches utilize a series of discrete characteristics of an item to recommend additional items with similar properties (Balabanović and Shoham, 1997; Basu et al., 1998; Melville et al., 2002). Content-based methods rely on being able to construct descriptions for the items in the collection and profile for the user preferences. Given this information, these algorithms try to recommend items that are similar to those that a user liked previously. The similarities between information filtering and information retrieval were discussed in

earlier work (Belkin and Croft, 1992), and methods from information retrieval (such as TF.IDF [Spärck-Jones, 1972]) can be applied in this context. Beyond the representations, there are similarities between this and applications in retrieval such as search personalization, whereby user profiles can be used to find similar items. Recommender systems are also a useful alternative to search algorithms because these systems can help searchers find information items that they may not have found via directed searching. Content-based recommender systems may be limited by the requirement that the recommended content be similar to the seed provided by the searcher, and they may be dependent on the type of information recommended by the system (e.g., they may not be able to apply recommendations built on news articles to other media).

There have been many applications of both of these methods in a variety of Web contexts (e.g., Pandora radio), but the applications to search directly have been limited. As a community, we have seen some attempts to recommend queries (Zaiane and Strillets, 2002), social tags (Song et al., 2008), or Web pages (Almeida and Almeida, 2004; Sun et al., 2005) based on aggregated behavioral data. Recent research on methods such as nuclear norm minimization and compressed sensing theory have gained attention from researchers in the machine-learning community, and has yielded some promising performance improvements (Jaggi and Sulovsk, 2010; Plan, 2011).

Collaborative and content-based filtering methods are often combined in the form of hybrid recommender systems (Burke, 2002). In these systems, the two algorithms can be applied separately and then combined, or they can be combined by adding content-based capabilities to the collaborative filtering approach (or vice versa). The combination of the two methods can help recommender systems overcome some of their drawbacks, especially those associated with a lack of data. *Netflix* is an example of such a system: *Netflix* makes recommendations based on the searching and watching habits of similar users, but also based on matching using characteristics of movies and television shows that the current user has rated highly. Interactively (at the interface, rather than deep in the recommendation algorithm), the line between search and recommender systems is becoming blurred (Chi, 2012) as recommender systems are offering search functionality in addition to their traditional recommendations, and vice versa.

6.2.2.6.1 Challenges and Opportunities

There are a number of challenges and opportunities in recommender systems research, especially from the perspective of applying the findings from academic research in industrial settings (Lebanon, 2014):

- The mismatch between the rating prediction task, which is the focus on many academic studies, and engagement prediction, which is more important in real-world recommendation settings.
- Real-world recommendation settings have more information about users and items than is available in any public dataset (e.g., user profile, demographics, location information, historic activity), which are removed from public datasets for privacy reasons.
- Real-world recommendation scenarios using implicit binary ratings (e.g., impressions, purchases) generated based on the passive observation of user behavior.

In explicit ratings, training data consists of both positive and negative feedback, while all training data is positive in implicit ratings.
- Few public datasets, which are much smaller in size than industrial data. This limits the nature of the research that can be conducted outside of industry and also the applicability of the findings from academia in industrial settings.

While there are challenges in this area, there are also opportunities. For example, an area of growing interest within recommender systems research is mobile recommender systems (Ge et al., 2010). There are interesting constraints on these algorithms, such as the requirement to have low computation and energy requirements, because they must be used on handheld or embedded devices, which can be severely resource constrained.

6.2.3 Guiding Search and Navigation

In response to received queries, search systems deposit searchers into a particular part of the information space, often with little context beyond the set of search results offered to them at retrieval time. Search systems could do a much better job in helping searchers make decisions about what paths to initiate (search results to select) and in making decisions once they depart from the search engine. Guided tours and other mechanisms exist for doing this in the hypertext community and it likely that lessons learned from there could be applied effectively in other contexts. Bush (1945) envisioned the *memex*, a proto-hypertext system to extend human memory and containing trails marked and willingly shared by trailblazing users to guide other people in future information-seeking episodes. Bush foresaw "a profession of trail blazers, those who find delight in the task of establishing useful trails through the enormous mass of the common record." More recently, others have reached similar conclusions in the context of hypertext and the Web. In an early paper on supporting information seeking on the Web, Chalmers et al. (1998) suggested that searchers may benefit from the experiences of others and presented a system whereby people (referred to as "recommenders") can manually construct Web navigation paths and then share these paths with others. Joachims et al. (1997) suggested that in many cases, only a *sequence* of pages and knowledge about how they relate can satisfy a person's information needs. This is in contrast to the ordered sequence of individual pages that is often presented to searchers, from which the searcher is expected to select results depending on level of interest and orienteer to their search target (O'Day and Jeffries, 1993; Teevan et al., 2004).

Procedural search knowledge has been shown to be important when searching for comprehensive information about a particular topic (Kirk, 1974; Bhavnani, 2002). For example, Bhavnani (2002) described the three-step process that an expert health seeker followed when searching for flu shot information: (1) access a reliable healthcare portal such as MEDLINEplus to identify sources for flu-shot; (2) access a high-quality source of information to retrieve general flu shot information; and (3) verify the information by visiting the website of a pharmaceutical company that sells the vaccine. This three-step process combining navigation, search, and verification is markedly different than that employed by domain novices, who may simply turn to general purpose search engines. Experts may have awareness of high-quality resources (Shute and Smith, 1993), but Bhavnani et al. (2003) suggested that they may also have

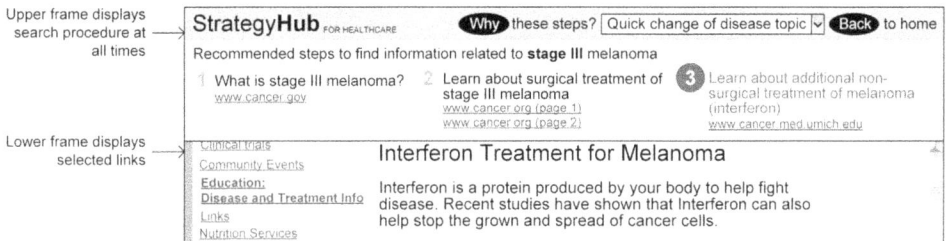

Figure 6.2. The Strategy Hub system (adapted from Bhavnani, 2003) displaying the recommended steps of a search procedure in the upper frame, with reliable links for each step. When a link is selected, the associated page is displayed in the lower frame.

procedural search knowledge pertaining to sub-goals, sequence ordering, and matching of resources to sub-goals. Such differences would be noted even if novice and expert searchers had similar search objectives (Yuan and White, 2012). Bhavnani et al. (2003) suggested that helping searchers formulate appropriately ordered sub-goals was especially important for unfamiliar domains, and devised strategy hubs to suggest search procedures and high-quality links to help searchers navigate unfamiliar information environments. The procedures were derived from a taxonomy of real-life questions created by domain experts (in this case skin cancer) and contained sub-goals such as "Learn about melanoma prevention," "Learn about melanoma risk factors," and "Estimate your risk of melanoma," all for a question associated with the risk and prevention of melanoma. These are shown to searchers in a separate frame, as in Figure 6.2.

User studies of this approach suggest that making such recommendations for procedural search actions can improve efficiency, effectiveness, and satisfaction for both domain novices and domain experts. The challenge is in creating such procedures for many different domains, and progress on the development of templates may be useful in those contexts. Systems to provide strategic search support based on user modeling methods have also been developed (Croft and Thompson, 1987; Manglano et al., 1998; Brajnik et al., 2002).

6.2.3.1 Social Navigation

Searchers can also learn from the logged behavior of other searchers; a means of mining the collective intelligence of the search population (Kantor et al., 2000). Social navigation (Dourish and Chalmers, 1994; Benyon, 1999; Dieberger et al., 2000) attempts to harness the collective knowledge of user communities to support information navigation. In introducing the concept, Dourish and Chalmers (1994, p. 1) described it as "moving 'towards' a cluster of other people, or selecting objects because others have been examining them." Systems have been developed that can use traces of user activity to support people in following in paths of others (Dieberger, 1997; Wexelblat and Maes, 1999). Beyond website traversal, this concept has been applied successfully in domains such as e-learning (Brusilovsky et al., 2004) and to support within-document navigation (Hill and Hollan, 1994). Figure 6.3 shows the interface to the *Knowledge Sea II* system, which is designed to help searchers navigate from lectures to relevant online tutorials in a map-based horizontal navigation format. Every cell of the *KnowledgeSea* map includes links to online materials that are related to keyword on the cell.

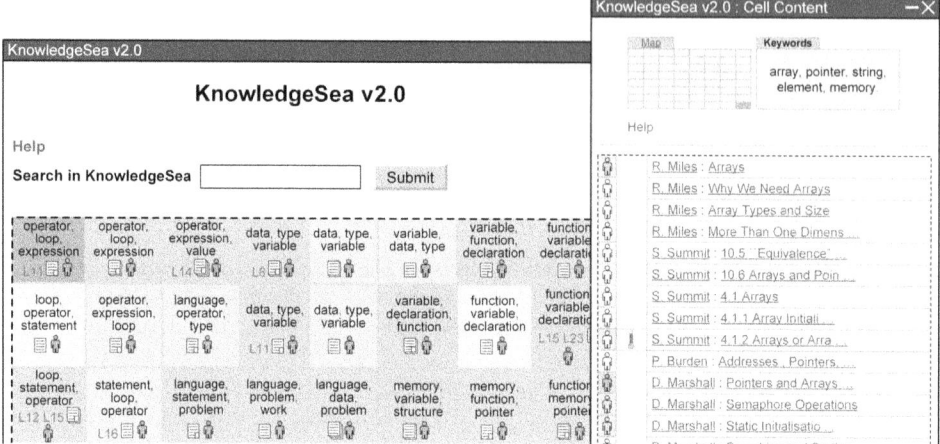

Figure 6.3. Interface to the *KnowledgeSea II* interface, which provides links to online course materials. Darker cells are most frequently visited, providing social navigation cues (adapted from Brusilovsky et al., 2004). (See color plate 6.3.)

Adjacent cells present similar material. The most important feature of the system is facilitating navigation by providing traffic-based and annotation-based social navigation support.

In the context of digital libraries, but also applicable in other domains, Brusilovsky et al. (2010) characterized the techniques employed by these systems in terms of: (1) the nature of the behavior; (2) how the data are combined to generate collective knowledge; and (3) how this collective knowledge is applied to the benefit of other users of the system in terms of supporting information access. *AntWorld* (Kantor et al., 1999) suggests resources to future users based on the collective search activity and explicit feedback of prior searchers. Freyne et al. (2007) combined social search and social navigation, allowing people to seamlessly initiate new searches as they navigate through the collection. The *Sociable Web* (Donath and Robertson, 1994), for example, allows a user to see that others are currently viewing the same Web page and to communicate with those people. Millen and Feinberg (2006) describe a social bookmarking system called *DogEar* that allows users to bookmark resources and use the bookmarks of other users to explore the collection. This explicit support for social navigation activities is typical of social bookmarking systems, but different from traditional social navigation methods that rely on implicit signals, primarily based on usage information. *WebTagger* (Keller et al., 1997), the system of Wittenburg et al. (1995), and the commercial site del.icio.us[2] all offer similar functionality.

6.2.3.2 Tours and Trails

In this subsection, I focus on a variety of methods to support the multi-step interaction of searchers. Many current search methods provide searchers with a ranked list of starting points from which to start their investigation, but once the searcher makes the decision about which result to select the searcher is largely on their own. Teevan et al. (2004) discussed the phenomenon of teleportation as it applies to information seeking, and White et al. (2007) presented a method to direct people to the terminal pages, which could be useful for some tasks. Researchers have shown that trails (Agichtein et al., 2006; Bilenko and White, 2008) mined from browsing logs are used as endorsements for trail pages that are useful for learning to rank search results more effectively. There can be significant searcher value from the search trail itself in terms of metrics such as coverage and diversity of the information that people are exposed to, versus just transporting them to the terminal page in the trail (White and Huang, 2010). Because there is value in the *journey* as well as the destination, next-generation search systems need to support such multi-step search strategies directly, with a view toward helping people expand their understanding of a topic beyond the factoid that they may seek at a particular time.

Much of the early work in this area was conducted within the hypertext community. Reich et al. (1999) discussed tours and trails as tools for helping hypertext users by highlighting where others have gone. They suggest that tours and trails differ in that trails are marked by searchers at each step of their information journey, whereas tours are constructed beforehand and may have a hierarchical structure. Reich and colleagues also suggested that by following searchers with similar needs as they move around the collection systems can use knowledge gained from the resources that they visit to help future information seekers.

6.2.3.2.1 Guided Tours

The hypertext community has explored the concept of guided tours through hypertext collections to ease problems with user disorientation (e.g., Trigg [1988]; Hammond and Allison [1988]). In the hypertext instantiation, these are manually curated sequences of hypertext cards that enable a reader to explore a particular topic. The order in which pages appeared on the tour is typically meaningful (e.g., basic, fundamental concepts may be explained before complex concepts are introduced) and the order in which people can access the stops on a tour could be enforced by the system to help ensure that they understand one concept before progressing to the next one. In some tour arrangements, searchers can branch to different stops, and deviate from the tour if a particular concept interests them in more detail, with the option to resume the tour at any point. To do this, the system must have a way for people to retain state as well as providing a way for them to effectively resume the tour at any point in time. One way to accomplish this is by using a toolbar or other visual representation of the tour (e.g., a browser frame or as a browser plugin). Zellweger (1989) introduced scripted documents, which are more dynamic than guided tours because they have conditional and programmable paths, automated playback, and active entries. Yuan and White (2012) studied the trailblazing activities of novice and expert searchers (where trails were created to help others), and showed large differences in the nature of the trails that each group created.

6.2.3.2.2 Task Tours

There has been some progress on the development of automatic methods to support sequences of interaction on the Web, either within particular websites or across the open Web. Guinan and Smeaton (1993) generated a tour for a given query based on term matching for node selection and inter-node relationships (e.g., "is_a" or "precedes") for node ordering. In a user study using a collection of lecture materials, they found that searchers followed these trails closely; 40% of the time, subjects did not deviate from the proposed trail. Hassan and White (2012) mined Web browsing logs to identify multi-step task-tours, sequences of topics (which could be translated into sites) that are found to co-occur frequently in the completion of a search task. These are designed to help searchers perform complex search tasks by suggesting the key activities (subtasks) that searchers should perform when attempting a search task. For example, for the query [buying a home], the task tour generated by their algorithm is: *Real Estate Search* (the trigger task on which the rest of the tour is shown if detected), *Find a Realtor*, *Financial Services*, *Online Maps*, and *Public Education*. These are many of the tasks that are required when purchasing a new residence, and the task names are derived from publically available sources such as the *Open Directory Project*, although they could be crowdsourced or assigned by an editorial team. Clough et al. (2011) proposed mechanisms for personalizing paths through digital cultural heritage collections based on the requirements of particular users and the groups to which they belonged (e.g., students/teachers, archivists, and historians/scholars).

6.2.3.2.3 Topic Maps

The need for guided tours to be constructed manually helps to ensure that the tours are of high quality, but also severely limits their scalability. Some recent work on the automatic development of zoom-able metro maps (Shahaf et al., 2012) created a concise structured set of documents that allow people to explore complex information spaces by maximizing the coverage of salient pieces of information concerning a topic, especially the evolution of complex news events over time. These events may be nonlinear and contain a large number of branches, side stories, and so on, making a map a suitable visualization for exploring this space. Figure 6.4 shows an example of a simplified metro map generated automatically for the debt crisis in Greece. Each line in the map follows a coherent narrative thread and different lines focus on different aspects of the story. The middle line details the chain of events from Greece's debt junk status to the Greek bailout. The L-shaped line covers strikes and riots in Greece. Both lines intersect at an article about the austerity plan, because it plays an important role in both storylines: it was a precondition for the bailout, but also triggered many strikes.

Metro maps visualize the relationships among retrieved pieces of information in a way that captures story development. It is possible to formulate the construction of these maps as an optimization problem and provide theoretical guarantees for efficiently generating the maps from data. Users can also interact with the system to generate maps that are more attuned to their own interests. Because news stories emerge over time, they are conducive to this type of visualization. If we are to employ these methods to help people explore information spaces such as the Web, then we need ways to measure the coherence, coverage, and connectivity of the graphs.

6.2.3.2.4 Supporting Website Navigation

Additional support can also be offered to information seekers as they move within an individual site. Wheeldon and Levene (2003) proposed an algorithm for automatically generating trails to assist in website navigation based on page similarity. They define trails as trees and expand them from the root node using the expected information gain as the probability of expansion. This gain is based on the term frequency of the

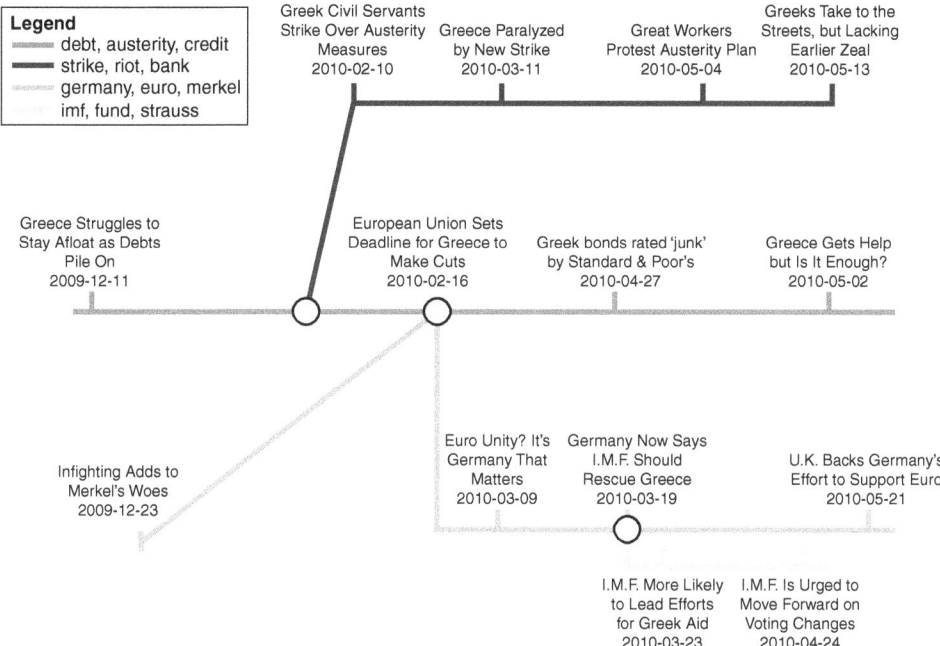

Figure 6.4. Example metro map generated for the debt crisis in Greece (adapted from Shahaf et al., 2012).

query in the document, with a penalty for duplicate documents. They presented trails using an interface attached to the browser. The resultant trails were shown to visitors to a particular website as a way to assist in navigation. A user study performed to evaluate the effectiveness of this method found that seeing the relationship between links helped, and that trails were a useful navigational aid. The *Footprints* system (Wexelblat and Maes, 1999; and described in Section 5.4.2) also provides evidence of previous interactions with online resources to support the navigation of future searchers.

Much of this research on supporting website navigation, and – more generally – on collecting and applying interaction histories covered throughout this book, has its roots in work in history-rich digital objects (Hill et al., 1992; Hill and Hollan, 1994), whereby digital objects (such as documents) retain and reveal their usage histories in much the same way as physical objects (such as books) do. Applying this analogy, search systems with functionality based on "wear" (e.g., edit wear reflecting content changes, read wear reflecting user examination) would likely be useful for focusing searcher attention on particular parts of documents.

6.2.2.2.5 Trailfinding

Trails reflecting post-query information seeking activity can also be constructed and retrieved in a similar way to Web pages (the so-called trailfinding challenge [Singla et al., 2010]). These trails can comprise popular sequences of pages or Web domains connected most frequently by hyperlinks, but other navigation actions such as entering the URL of the site into the address bar may also apply, although will not occur all that often. An example of trails presented at the search interface is found earlier in this book (Figure 2.8). In that example, the trails are connected to their originating pages in the search result.

6.2.3.3 Single-Step Suggestions

The approaches described in the previous section offer a holistic view of the tours and trails that searchers could follow to explore the search space. This is beneficial because it provides an overview of the space of topics and does not impose constraints on the sequence order in which pages are accessed; it also contextualizes the interactions with content. However, searchers may be unwilling to completely alter the ways in which they browse document collections or follow rigid trails based on others' implicit or explicit recommendations. The traditional method of exploring large collections of connected documents is via selecting hyperlinks. As discussed in Chapter 4, selection decisions are driven by many factors, including information scent (Chi et al., 2001), that can be estimated computationally (Chi et al., 2000).

Some of the systems discussed earlier in this chapter (e.g., *WebWatcher* [Joachims et al., 2007]), as well as other systems such as *ScentTrails* (Olston and Chi, 2003) and *Volant* (Pandit and Olston, 2007) highlight candidate pages based on models of information needs or user interests. The system can highlight links on the page based on the strength of the information scent, among other metrics, to estimate user interest level. Studies of these systems have shown that they can improve search speed and search success. Highlighted pages form a trail over time as people traverse hyperlinks, but the link-at-a-time approach does not expose the user to much needed initial context (Joachims et al., 2007). Rather than marking up the Web pages with additional content, similar functionality could be deployed within browser toolbars or the browser directly, for recommendation or pre-fetching purposes.

Beyond resource recommendation, we can also support searchers via query suggestions specifically designed to support exploration. Query suggestions can offer *idea tactics* (Bates, 1979b) to help generate new ideas or solutions to information problems. Recent research has also examined the intrinsically diverse nature of some information-seeking tasks. Such tasks typically require multiple queries on different aspects of the same information need (Raman et al., 2013). Raman and colleagues proposed an approach to alter the result rankings and also provide searchers with information regarding aspects of the task that they are likely to search for in the future. This relates to the aspectual retrieval task of the TREC Interactive Track (Voorhees and Harman, 2009). The task goal was for searchers to identify the various aspects or instances of a given topic.

Others have studied the generation of so-called exploration suggestions (Hassan Awadallah et al., 2014) that can be offered to searchers as a way to support them in completing their search tasks. Devising these suggestions involves mining behavioral data to identify the different aspects of search tasks, using a similar approach to that identified in the task tours research described earlier in this section. Figure 6.5 shows an example of the suggestions generated using this method for the query [*grand cayman car rental*] versus those presented by the related-search method of a commercial Web search engine. Others have proposed methods for identifying and clustering search tasks, also in the form of task graphs, as a way to provide support to searchers through task recommendations (Lucchese et al., 2013a; Lucchese et al., 2013b).

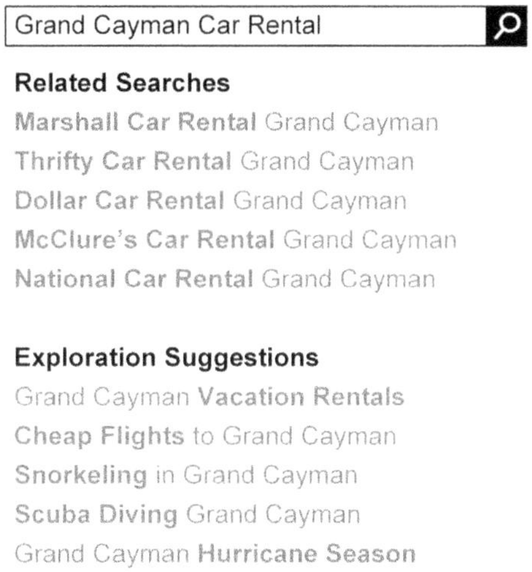

```
Grand Cayman Car Rental                🔍
```

Related Searches
Marshall Car Rental Grand Cayman
Thrifty Car Rental Grand Cayman
Dollar Car Rental Grand Cayman
McClure's Car Rental Grand Cayman
National Car Rental Grand Cayman

Exploration Suggestions
Grand Cayman Vacation Rentals
Cheap Flights to Grand Cayman
Snorkeling in Grand Cayman
Scuba Diving Grand Cayman
Grand Cayman Hurricane Season

Figure 6.5. Examples of suggestions from the related searches of a commercial Web search engine and suggestions produced by our method. Related searches offer different refinements to the current query while our method provides suggestion for future queries (beyond the current-query refinements) (adapted from Hassan Awadallah et al., 2014).

The related search suggestions are all very specific to the current query and involve refining the phrase "car rental" with specific car rental companies. The main objective of related searches is to help users refine their current query (Jones et al., 2006), and the suggestions shown fulfill that function well. Studies that delve deeper into how people employ suggestions (Kelly et al., 2010; Niu and Kelly, 2014) have shown that the suggestions provide support in cases for which people have less search expertise and greater difficulty searching, or at specific times during the search (i.e., toward the end; see Niu and Kelly [2014]), and showed that people were able to distinguish between high- and low-quality suggestions (Kelly et al., 2010).

Exploration suggestions are designed to help searchers explore new aspects of their current search task in future queries. This is evident in Figure 6.5: the exploration suggestions cover more distinct aspects of the task, rather than simply helping the searcher refine their current information need. The exploration suggestions generated from a graph of task aspects, defined as components or subtasks, of a broader information search task. In addition to using the aspect graph to generate suggestions that are generally applicable across searchers, other methods could identify potentially useful future queries (e.g., personalized variants based on searchers' interaction histories; see White et al. [2010]).

One challenge in generating these suggestions is that presenting them on the SERP may be distracting to searchers attempting to complete a particular aspect of their search task, when their focus may be more likely to be on refining their current searches. It may be more appropriate to display these suggestions in a dedicated part of the search engine homepage, or in the browser/toolbar, offering support for exploration when they are more likely to be in an exploratory frame of mind. In addition, because they are designed to support exploration, consideration needs to be given of the content that the searcher has already reviewed. Therefore, personalization of these suggestions, considering prior search activity may also be necessary.

6.2.3.4 Serendipity

In all of the solutions described in this section thus far, an important aspect of supporting exploration is the act of encountering information unexpectedly – that is, serendipity. Serendipity has long been identified as valuable, both as a pleasure in itself and as part of task-focused problem solving (Andre et al., 2009). It has been described as an event involving both unexpectedness and mental connection (McCay-Peet and Toms [2010]), while also requiring that people are prepared to observe the cues associated with the serendipitous event (Rubin et al., 2011). Several research efforts have sought to characterize, understand, and support serendipity in Web search. For example, André et al. (2009) studied whether search-result personalization could reduce the potential for serendipitous information discoveries (e.g., by creating a filter bubble). They found that personalization does not harm serendipity and may in fact be useful for supporting serendipity. Serendipity has also been considered in the context of collaborative filtering where interesting content is identified by matching individuals with similar interests. Previous work on collaborative filtering has considered promoting novelty and serendipity by helping searchers to uncover less popular and more diverse items (Ziegler et al., 2005). Intelligent agents such as *Letizia* (Lieberman et al., 1995) and *WebWatcher* (Joachims et al., 1997) promote serendipity by suggesting potentially interesting content to searchers that is related to their current activities.

6.3 Intelligent Assistants

Accompanying the growth of mobile devices has been the increased interest in digital personal assistants, software agents that are armed with knowledge about the searcher's situation and preferences and capable of helping them find information, complete tasks, and manage their life more effectively (Kozierok and Maes, 1993; Maes, 1994). It has long been argued that intelligent agents powered by sophisticated learning models to use search engine knowledge will fundamentally alter the way that people find and understand information (Mitchell et al., 1994).

Digital assistants such as Microsoft *Cortana*[3] and Google *Now*[4] (currently both proactive *and* reactive, i.e., making recommendations and responding to requests, respectively), and Apple *Siri*[5] (currently reactive only) support a rich, primarily spoken, dialog between the searcher and application. They can all field voice questions. These assistants access multiple online data sources (including Web search engines, social networks, and real-time feeds of traffic reports, news, weather, stock, etc.), leverage explicitly stated searcher preferences regarding their interests, and mine personal information stored locally on the device, including email and calendaring data. Google *Now* focuses on recommendations and proactive experience, *Siri* targets responses to questions, and *Cortana* targets reminders based on time, people, and places (including geo-fenced reminders that alert people when they reach a location, e.g., "Pick up milk and bread when I'm next at the grocery store").

The availability of these data provides a wealth of opportunity for richer modeling of computer usage and support for higher order activities, including tasks and task management. Given aggregated, anonymized data on the types of tasks that many people encounter (e.g., commitments that they make to others and requests that they receive),

Figure 6.6. Screenshots of three popular digital assistants available on smartphones and other devices.

assistants can help remind people to complete their tasks, learn task characteristics (e.g., duration of the task based on reminder data and likelihood of engagement with other individuals), predict task completion, and perform prioritization of tasks. Figure 6.6 shows screenshots of the three personal assistants currently offered by Google (*Now*), Apple (*Siri*), and Microsoft (*Cortana*).

Importantly, information about searchers' personal preferences, including preferred contacts, location preferences, and privacy settings, can be captured and stored on the device and used in a range of search settings, including proactive and reactive information seeking scenarios. The agent will also have additional information about social relationships (people who are important to the user) and ownership of products, to contextualize future activities (e.g., to distinguish searches for accessories for an owned product from those for a new product or a gift for someone else). Being able to retain and update user preferences, relationships, and personal inventories of items owned and gifted, over time (leveraging both implicit and explicit signals) also enables the system to support searchers in their pursuit of long-term search tasks, including creating standing queries and polling for updates based on incoming information or changes in the search setting (e.g., searching from a new location). Intelligent assistants may also offer explanations for the actions that they perform on behalf of their users (Billsus and Pazzani, 1999). Explanations are discussed in more detail in Section 9.3.

Importantly, agents may provide a single location from which to perform searches and accomplish search tasks. Given access to rich signals, some of which may be unseen by the searcher, assistants may become more capable of performing searches than the searcher themselves. Despite the attractiveness of this in terms of reduced searcher overhead, searchers may still want to adjust aspects of the queries or verify that they meet their needs. Providing interface support for representing and manipulating complex search queries in ways that are understandable to searchers of all skill levels is a

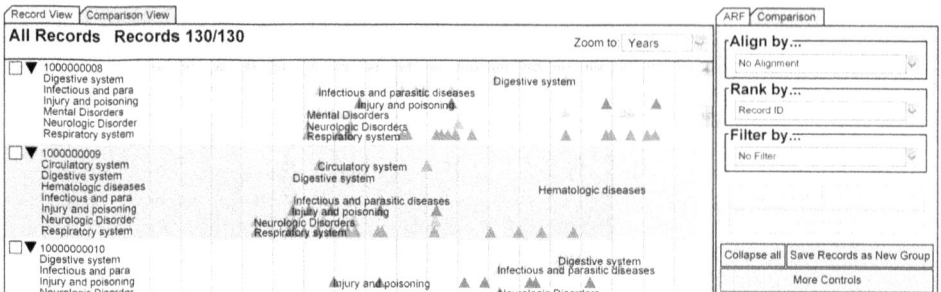

Figure 6.7. Interface to *Lifelines2* with recorded incidences marked. Human–Computer Interaction Laboratory, University of Maryland, www.cs.umd.edu/hcil/lifelines2. (See color plate 6.7.)

challenging research problem, although some progress has been made via visualization methods (e.g., Bier et al., 1993; Spoerri et al., 1993).

6.4 Discovering Insights

Searchers may often wish to use the outcomes of the search process to generate insights and inform action in the real world. Information visualization techniques, and even the standard methods for presenting search results, offer a way in which to accomplish this. Information visualization describes the study of visual representations of data – in pictorial or graphical format – to reinforce human cognition. A variety of information visualization methods have been proposed, including network diagrams, timelines (Plaisant et al., 1996), hierarchical representations such as *TreeMaps* (Shneiderman, 1992), and multidimensional displays of different types such as *Table Lens* (Rao and Card, 1994). Users can interact with these visualizations to better understand the data and explore parts of the space. There has also been success in applying methods from information visualization to support more effective information seeking (Williams et al., 1995). For example, dynamic queries may help people filter the data being shown instantly through direct-manipulation operations, allowing a deeper dive on particular aspects of interest (Ahlberg et al., 1992; Shneiderman, 1994). Projects such as *Lifelines2* (Wang et al., 2008) have used larger sets of data from patients' electronic health records and medical test results, enabling medical professionals to align-rank and sort them according to the attributes available on the data. *Lifelines2* enables discovery and exploration of patterns across these records to support hypothesis generation, and find cause-and-effect relationships in a population. *Lifelines2* enables dynamic exploration of many "what if" scenarios and new discoveries through correlations to be made. Figure 6.7 shows *Lifelines2* with recorded incidences of conditions marked.

LifeFlow (Wongsuphasawat et al., 2011) and *EventFlow* (Monroe et al., 2013) continue the same line of research, providing researchers and practitioners with important tools to analyze and understand data, including transfers within hospitals and traffic accident response logs, to identify best practices. There continues to be significant value in such interactive visualization systems to explore event sequences and identify salient temporal patterns worthy of further investigation. There is significant utility for such tools in healthcare applications (Shneiderman et al., 2013), where rich and voluminous patient information from sources such as electronic health records and claims reports enable sophisticated temporal analyses of individual patients and patient populations.

As an increasing volume of data is collected from a variety of different sources, being able to visualize the data in aggregate form, can help identify salient patterns, and communicate concepts and hypotheses to others. Companies such as *SAP* (sap.com) and *Spotfire* (spotfire.com) have developed applications to process business intelligence data and help data analysts draw reasonable inferences. IBM's *manyEyes* (Viégas et al., 2007) shows the value of being able to share visualizations of data, by adding facets onto the visualization. manyEyes uses information visualization as a catalyst for discussion and collective insight about data. Data analysis involves studying and summarizing data with the intention of extracting useful information to develop conclusions. The primary goal of data visualization is to communicate attributes of the underlying data clearly and effectively through graphical means. In doing so, data visualization methods need to balance both form and function, while considering their primary objective – communicating information to inform action. The visualizations can be static (such that they can be inspected but do not respond to queries), or they can be interactive (where they change in response to user input, allowing users to drill down into charts and graphs, and immediately change the data seen and how it is processed). As I describe later in this section, the interactive filtering of data using these methods has direct implications for the design of search systems.

Data (and information) visualization has emerged from a convergence of research in a number of areas, including human–computer interaction, computer graphics, and psychology. These visualizations provide an overview of the data and allow analysts both to understand behavioral patterns (e.g., traffic through a website) and to make improvements to the design of these sites based on inferences about usage. They allow insights that can be difficult or impossible for people to discover from looking at the raw data, which may be comprised of millions or billions of individual rows in the case of search logs, making patterns almost impossible to discern through direct inspection of the data. The visual representation of data capitalizes on humans' ability to visually process, explore, and understand large amounts of information. Such visualizations are an important part of applied research and problem solving. For readers interested specifically in information visualization, there are some excellent resources available (e.g., Card et al., 1999; Fayyad et al., 2002; Hearst, 2009).

6.4.1 Types of Data Visualization

There are a number of different types of data visualization, including histograms, scatter plots, surface plots, tree maps, network diagrams, and so on. The choice of method depends on a number of factors, such as the nature of the data and including the intended audience of the visualization. In addition to visualization, there are other data analysis methods – primarily statistics, data mining, and machine learning. However, visualization requires the most human involvement; it is most reliant on cognitive skills of analysts, but also supports the discovery of unstructured actionable insights. Visualizations also support the generation of hypotheses that can be further tested by more analytical or formal analysis, such as statistical hypothesis testing. There is no need for analysts to learn sophisticated methods to interpret the visualizations. Indeed, the best visualizations are highly intuitive, communicate their point clearly, and viewers do not need additional training to understand their meaning. They also stimulate viewer engagement and attention.

6.4.2 Visualization Activities

Data visualization can be an important part of data analysis and is connected to data mining. The focus in the data analysis task, however, tends to be more closely connected to making inferences than in data mining, and it works with data that may have been collected for this purpose, rather than working with large volumes of data which may have been collected for a different purpose (e.g., to evaluate the performance of a system), as is common practice in data mining. The types of tasks for which visualization methods can be applied include identifying areas in need of improvement, understanding factors affecting search behavior, and understanding the flow of activity through a particular website or the search process more generally.

There are a number of activities that people may wish to perform during data analysis. Shneiderman (1996) provided a task taxonomy of information visualization methods, comprising the following aspects:

- **Overview:** Gain an overview of the collection
- **Zoom:** Zoom in on particular items of interest
- **Filter:** Filter out uninteresting items to focus user attention
- **Details-On-Demand:** Select an item or group and get details when needed
- **Relate:** View relationships among items
- **History:** Retain a history of actions to support undo, replay, and progressive refinement
- **Extract:** Allow extraction of sub-collections of the data, and also of the query parameters (so that the query can be re-run elsewhere if needed)

Sets of requirements such as these can be used during the setting of requirements for a particular visualization project or during the evaluation of an existing data visualization technique. Many existing solutions support only a subset of these tasks, and to be generally useful, systems need to support a broad set of different task activities. This is of course not the only grouping. There are other groupings of activities that visualizations should support. For example, Amar et al. (2005) proposed the following three core tasks: (1) retrieving values; (2) finding data points; and (3) arranging data points (e.g., sorting, correlating, clustering, and characterizing). Some of these activities (e.g., retrieving values) are focused on cases for which there is a known hypothesis or specific question, and the data must be analyzed in a certain way to obtain an answer or supporting evidence. One thing that is not captured within these actions is the activity of exploring the data to find candidate hypotheses.

Data analysis can be divided into descriptive statistics, exploratory data analysis, and inferential statistics. Exploratory data analysis (Tukey, 1977) is an approach to analyzing data in which the objective is to formulate hypotheses that are worth testing.

This complements the tools in conventional (inferential) statistics that are focused on testing hypotheses. Given the raw data from a source such as search logs, the first step would be to create an appropriate visualization. Then we could review the visualization to formulate hypotheses about, say, differences in people's behavior between different populations or cohorts, or between websites. These hypotheses could then be tested using confirmatory data analysis (i.e., with statistical testing).

Beyond analyzing large volumes of numerical data, there are other types of data analysis such as qualitative research, which often involves the manual coding of data collected using methods such as interviews and open questions in surveys. This is a highly labor intensive task, but may yield valuable insights on participant perceptions that are not available as response options or not captured on numerical scales.

6.4.2.1 Locus of Control

Beyond the appropriateness of the visualization technique for the problem at hand, there are other factors – such as personality traits – that can impact the success of visualization techniques in helping people explore and learn. Locus of control is a theory used in personality psychology that refers to causation as perceived by individuals in response to personal outcomes or other events (Rotter, 1954). A person's "locus" is conceptualized as either internal (the person believes they can control their life) or external (meaning they believe that their decisions and life are controlled by environmental factors they cannot influence). Individuals with a high internal locus of control believe that events in their life derive primarily from their own actions; for example, if a person with an internal locus of control does not perform as well as they wanted to on a test, they would blame it on lack of preparedness on their part. This is relevant in the design of systems to support exploration because it affects searchers' willingness to adapt to a novel externalization of information (Ziemkiewicz et al., 2011).

6.4.3 Visualizations at Scale

Visualizing big data is challenging given large volumes, different varieties, and varying velocities. One of the main challenges with visualization methods is to convert the data into a manageable format that can be consumed by visualization methods. There are at least two elements of this: (1) reformatting the data so that it is in a form that the visualization software expects; and (2) compressing and aggregating the data where needed so that it is manageable, and so that visualizations that are generated have meaning. In performing this aggregation, the cardinality of the data (the uniqueness of the data values in a column) plays an important role in determining the efficacy of the system. When the data are extremely large (terabytes, petabytes, exabytes, and beyond – depending on how the visualization method is implemented and where it is executed [client or server]), visualizing all of the data points becomes impractical, and the data need to be aggregated and/or subsampled. This can happen prior to generating the visualization or during the generation of the visualization if searchers can control the information being displayed dynamically and stop the process when sufficient information is presented. Real-time manipulations of visualizations can be compelling but need to be implemented carefully, because they can quickly consume machine resources if searchers wish to do more than just basic filtering. In Chapter 12, I discuss *scalable* visualization tools, designed to handle large volumes of data.

6.4.4 Search Visualization

The methods described thus far have focused on data visualization from the analyst's perspective – enhancing their ability to make decisions by providing additional perspectives on the data (effectively acting as a cognitive prosthetic). A series of interfaces were proposed that employed a three-dimensional perspective to all users to visualize large document spaces, as well as a variety of methods such as cones, trees, and hyperbolic browser interfaces that allow searchers to visualize and directly manipulate large sets of information objects (Card et al., 1991).

From an end-user's perspective, the benefit that they can obtain from sophisticated information visualization methods is less clear as there may often be insufficient data from their own histories to populate these visualizations to such an extent that they become useful. Examples of this in the context of search may include tag clouds, which are visual representations of text data used to denote the importance of particular terms or phrases in a corpus using font size or color. Such support could help searchers in application settings such as selecting expansion terms. Interactive support – such as dynamic queries (Williamson and Shneiderman, 1992) – allows searchers to fluidly filter results using pre-defined attributes simultaneously and monitor the impact of these changes on the result set in real-time. This is particularly useful when the data can be easily represented visually, such that the effect of any changes in the query on the result set is immediately (or almost immediately, depending on the specific implementation) apparent.

Dynamic query systems also typically offer a graphical visualization of the request – for example, sliders to allow searchers to adjust the values of various parameters as well as visualize the limits on the query attributes as they pertain to the data being searched (minimum and maximum permissible values). This support can be useful especially to beginners, who can search the data without the need to learn the query specification. Such methods have utility in helping searchers explore unfamiliar information spaces, or by providing an overview of document collections and/or user activity within these collections, to support search-related decision making and guide exploration. An alternative to dynamic queries are *Magic Lenses* (Stone et al., 1994), which provide a way in which people can smoothly apply multiple filters to information in the collection. They are implemented as a transparent or semi-transparent user interface element that can be overlaid to filter content shown in the visualization. Figure 6.8 shows an example of *Magic Lenses* in action as part of a visualization tool for the specification of Boolean queries (Fishkin and Stone, 1995).

In the interface shown in Figure 6.8, text queries can be associated with a lens. When that lens is placed over the items in the collection (represented with icons in the figure), those that do not match the queries are filtered out. Boolean queries can be created by overlaying multiple lenses and selecting the appropriate operators and filters. For example, Figure 6.8 shows a disjunctive query that finds cities with relatively low housing prices or high annual salaries. Other tools allow people to control

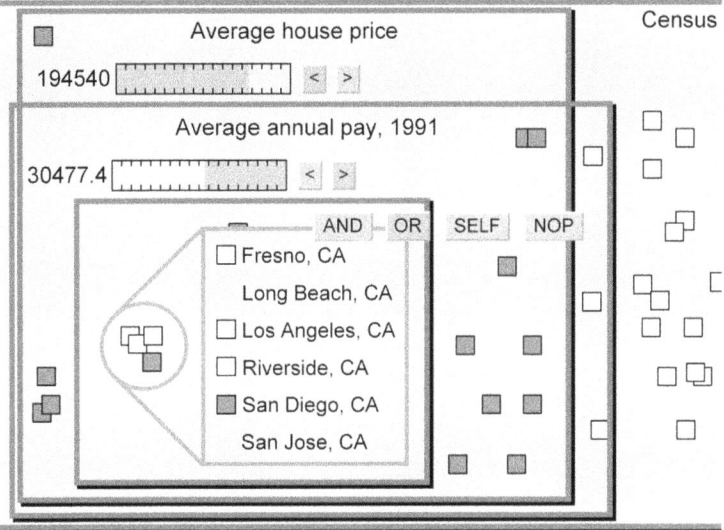

Figure 6.8. *Magic Lenses* for query specification (adapted from Fishkin and Stone, 1995).

the granularity of the information content that they review via zooming and panning (e.g., Bederson and Hollan, 1994).

6.5 Summary

In this chapter, I examined methods to support exploration and discovery during search interaction. The methods that were described covered cases in which the system provided support when intentionally sought by searchers, as well as cases in which support was offered to searchers passively when they were engaged in other search tasks such as Web browsing or the authoring of content (e.g., electronic mail, reports, research articles). Emerging next-generation search platforms – such as intelligent personal assistants – will also play an important role in surfacing the right information at the right time (similar to "just in time" information access [Budzik and Hammond, 2000]). I also discussed research on information visualization and informing decisions based on the insights gleaned from the document collection. In the next chapter, I focus in more detail on how acquired information can be used to inform action (information use) and help searchers learn both directly through the information/insights provided by the system, and by example through the historic behavior of other searchers.

CHAPTER 7

Learning and Use

Learning involves the acquisition of new, or the modification of existing, knowledge, skills, and behaviors. This chapter focuses on the use of search systems to support learning-related activities. I discuss aspects of the psychology of learning, and how people apply what they have learned during the information-seeking process. Modeling and supporting learning is essential in next-generation search technology. Support for learning will become an important aspect of how we design search systems, as well as how we evaluate these systems to understand their utility. Search systems can help people learn new content and also be reminded about content accessed historically. Providing the context of previous learning episodes and helping restore searcher state and refresh their understanding of the current search topic, if it is not in a subject area reflective of their regular interests.

Searching is similar in many ways to learning (Schmeck, 1988; Davis and Palladino, 1995). Previous work has provided some basis for a strong connection between searching and learning based on the construction of enhanced knowledge structures as a person assimilates new information attained during the search process with existing knowledge (Wittrock, 1974; Yankelovich et al., 1985). Case (2002) states that sense-making (such as that described in Chapter 4) is theoretically grounded in the constructivist learning theories of Dewey (1933), who in turn argued that learning can only occur through the activity of problem solving. The psychology community has explored learning in detail (e.g., Piaget [1952] and Vygotsky [1962] studied learning in the context of childhood development). Systems such as *SuperBook* (Egan et al., 1989) and *SuperManual* (Folz and Landauer, 2007) have improved the usability of existing content, books and manuals respectively, via computer-based enhancements such as rich indexing (to help address the vocabulary mismatch problem) and fisheye visualizations (Furnas, 1986) (to help people navigate and orient within text). Such enhancements can help people better comprehend text and generate better quality information artifacts in composition tasks. In creating systems where the focus is on learning, lessons can be drawn from the e-learning and intelligent tutoring communities (Corbett et al., 1997), such that searchers can be purposely engaged in sustained reasoning activities during browsing. Related work in the hypertext community, including research on the creation of guided

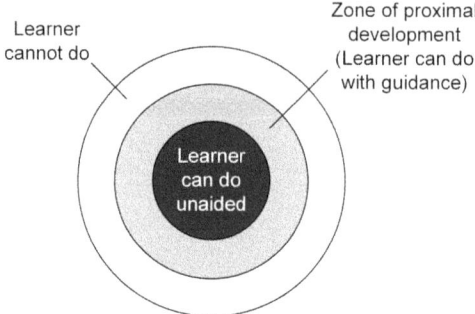

Figure 7.1. Zone of proximal development (adapted from Vygotsky, 1978).

tours (Trigg, 1988) through document collections, may also help people in support of learning and understanding.

Learning has been studied in detail and a substantial literature of on relevant concepts and frameworks of learning (e.g., Bloom et al., 1956; Kaptelenin and Nardi, 2006; Kintsch, 1998). Learning is often attained through guided instruction in classrooms or other instructional settings. There are even more opportunities for pursue independent learning opportunities through recognized educational establishments with the growth of massive open online courses (Martin, 2012; Vardi, 2012). This also creates interesting opportunities to analyze how people engage in learning at scale (Anderson et al., 2014). Learning is characterized in a number of different ways, including learning as knowledge acquisition, sensemaking, interpreting, and synthesizing (Saljo, 1979).

Learning is an important mental function reliant on the acquisition of knowledge and supported by perceived information. It leads to the development of new capacities, skills, values, understanding, and preferences. Once a person has acquired information and internalized it, such that they understand its meaning, translation, interpolation, and interpretation, he or she may then apply that knowledge in new domains and pursue higher-order learning activities such as analysis, synthesis, and evaluation (Anderson et al., 2001; Bloom et al., 1956). Searching to learn includes decision making and professional and life-long learning, as well as social searching to find communities of interest (e.g., social networks; see Marchionini [2006a]).

Search engines help people utilizing the information in massive collections to acquire new skills and knowledge. These systems need to be able to help searchers who teach in their own zone of proximal development (ZPD), an area of learning that occurs when a person is assisted by a teacher or peer with a higher skill set of the subject (Vygotsky, 1978). Figure 7.1 visualizes the ZPD with respect to both what the person can do unaided and what they cannot do with their current skills. In an information-seeking context, the role of teacher or peer can be fulfilled by a search system, one or more human experts, or a combination of the two agents (Chapter 8).

Rather than just helping searchers *locate* the information to satisfy information needs, search systems need to support intelligence amplification, knowledge building, and then synthesize that information and knowledge gained in tasks such as decision making (Marchionini and Shneiderman, 1988; Marchionini, 2006a). Given that searchers may often possess some idea of where to start or the resources to employ when faced with a search goal, the system can help by providing them with guidance in the form of pointers – that is, additional resources to consider or strategic support regarding how information should be located for tasks of this nature. The goal of this support is to both help searchers solve their current problem (unachievable without assistance), but also advance their skills so that they can tackle aspects of this and similar information search tasks with less direct assistance in the future (i.e., making searchers more skilled and self-sufficient).

Research on learning during searching has been limited. There are multiple ways in which a person can learn as they search and many ways in which systems can help people learn more effectively. Problem solving and learning have been connected to the information-seeking process (Marchionini, 1995); others in the information science community have related learning to notions of sensemaking (Dervin, 1983), exploration of new information spaces (White and Roth, 2009), or decision making (Klein et al., 1993). There are only a few studies to date that have explicitly considered search as a learning activity (Jansen et al., 2009; Wilson and Wilson, 2013). The focus in the design of search systems has traditionally been on efficiency and satisfying frequent requests (Agosti et al., 2014). However, the importance of learning during searching is being increasingly acknowledged (Jansen et al., 2009; Allan et al., 2012).

In this chapter I discuss the importance of supporting learning and information use, and how search technologies can be employed to assist with the learning process. There are important issues in addressing this challenge, such as how learning occurs in the context of information seeking, how we support learning, and how we know when systems have been successful at supporting learning. The final issue is important given that search providers may want to measure this at scale without being able to evaluate changes in searchers' subject matter expertise directly (e.g., via pre-search and post-search testing), as is traditionally done to measure learning. I discuss the assessment of learning in more detail in Chapter 11.

7.1 Learning

Let us consider two main aspects of learning: (1) taxonomies of learning as established by the educational literature; and (2) learning as a core part of the search process.

7.1.1 Taxonomies

Many methods for teaching and learning have been proposed, including behavioral learning (Skinner, 1974), active learning (Bonwell and Eison, 1991), and discovery learning (Bruner, 1961). Bloom's taxonomy of learning is relevant to the focus of this book (Bloom et al., 1956), as it describes a number of different levels of stages of learning, and classifies six levels of complexity in cognitive thinking. The taxonomy is structured in a hierarchical nature so that any person functioning on a higher level will have also mastered the levels below. This taxonomy was revised to make it more applicable to modern pedagogical practices, and to consider how the taxonomy intersects and acts upon different types and levels of knowledge (Anderson and Krathwohl, 2001). Figure 7.2 shows the revised version of the taxonomy.

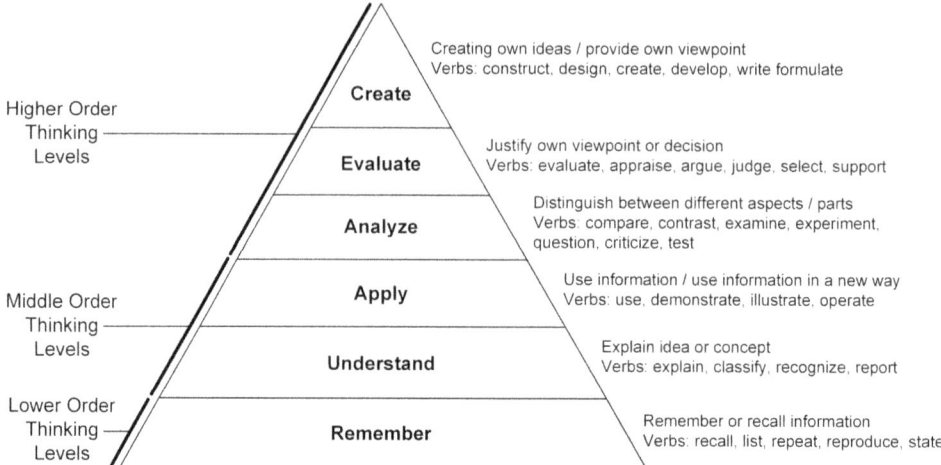

Figure 7.2. Anderson and Krathwohl taxonomy of learning objectives (adapted from Anderson and Krathwohl, 2001).

While the six levels of the taxonomy represent growing cognitive complexity, they are divided into two tiers: (1) lower order and middle order levels of thinking and (2) higher order levels of thinking, with three levels in each. The lowest and most basic level of the taxonomy is "remembering," which is simply the recall of relevant knowledge from long-term memory but does not require the construction of any new knowledge structures. Personalized search systems and intelligent agents can retain a perfect memory of the information accessed and aspects of the context at the time this occurred. Surfacing representations of these data at search time can be useful in refreshing the searcher's memory and in expediting future learning. "Understanding" occurs when the learner constructs meaning through several methods of interpretation including summarizing, comparing, and explaining. "Applying" is the third level in the taxonomy, and the highest of the lower tier and involves the learner carrying out or using a procedure through executing or implementing. The activities in the higher order tiers of learning begin with "analyzing," where organizing and differentiating allows the learner to break apart information and determine how the parts are related to one another as well as the overall structure. The next level, "evaluating," includes making judgments based on checking and critiquing. Finally, the highest level of learning is "creating," which allows the learner to generate, combine, and reorganize elements of information to create a coherent whole. In Bloom's original taxonomy "creating" was known as synthesis and "evaluating" was considered the highest level, preceded by "creating." "evaluating" and "creating" were reordered in Anderson's revision to create a more logical process in which one cannot effectively create without first evaluating the subject. Krathwohl (2002) revised Bloom's cognitive domain by separating two dimensions: knowledge and cognitive processing.

7.1.2 Information Seeking

Learning involves the acquisition and development of knowledge. Descriptions of information seeking as a process by which information needs are resolved do not

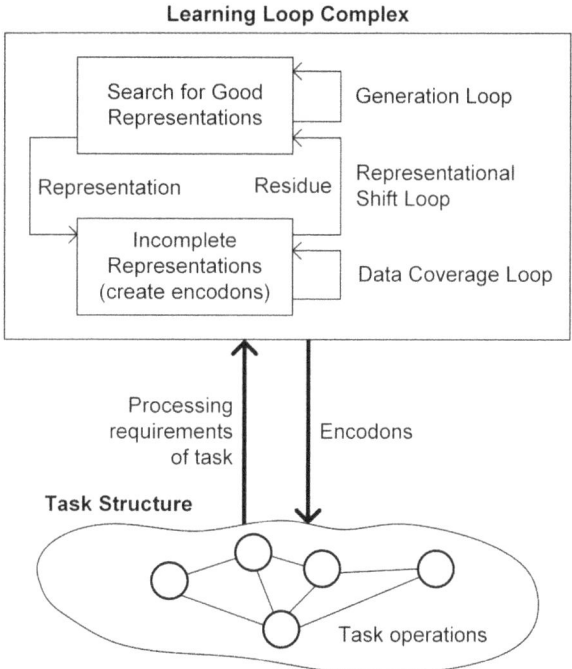

Figure 7.3. Interactions between the learning loop complex and task structure as part of the sensemaking process (adapted from Russell et al., 1993).

necessarily consider learning directly (Marchionini, 1995). Addressing a gap in one's knowledge has been established as an important motivator behind information-seeking activities (e.g., Belkin, 1982; Mackay, 1960; Taylor, 1968; Dervin, 1983). Belkin (1980) described search as being motivated by an anomalous state of knowledge (ASK) and explained how this lack of knowledge, depending on its size, may mean that searchers also cannot easily define or describe their information needs, possibly only recognizing it when their ASK is resolved. Dervin (1983) described the sensemaking problem in terms of searchers bridging that knowledge gap. Finding or building a bridge involves probing and testing information as possible sources of solutions. Both Belkin and Dervin's research on sensemaking identifies the process as containing a need for information (gap) and a method of finding information that attempts to fill this need. Russell et al. (1993) later defined sensemaking as "the process of encoding retrieved information to answer task-specific questions" and went on to define what they call a "learning loop complex." The learning loop complex is a multi-stage process in which searchers gather found information and encode it into representations that are applicable for the given situation (Figure 7.3).

Figure 7.3 shows that there is an interplay between the task and the learning process, resulting in the generation of internal representation of the task and a set of encodons. The encodons that are generated during the sensemaking process are used to perform some task-specific information processing step. They can guide searchers in terms of what to look for in the data, what questions they should ask, and how the answers to the questions should be organized. As Wilson and Wilson (2013) noted, the notion of a learning loop complex is similar to that of frames, as originally described by Piaget.

Other models include learning as part of the model. For example, in the berrypicking model (Bates, 1989) learning is reflected in query dynamics over the course of the search session. That is, the submitted queries will change based on changes in searchers' state of knowledge. Similarly, Kuhlthau's (1991) information seeking process – based on Kelly's "theory of learning" (Kelly, 1963) – includes a significant learning component, the beginning of which is uncertainty arising from a conflict between new information and previously held constructs. This uncertainty is a natural aspect of the learning process. Marchionini (2006a) elaborates on the learning elements inherent in information searching by describing searching to learn as increasingly viable in content rich, online environments. He conjectures that searching can be a learning process requiring multiple iterations and cognitive evaluation of retrieved results. Much of the time and effort in search tasks with a learning focus is devoted to examining and comparing search results, as well as reformulating queries to discover the boundaries of key concept definitions.

Learning search tasks are best suited to combinations of browsing and analytical strategies (Marchionini and Shneiderman, 1988), with lookup searches performed in order to find the correct neighborhood from which semi-directed browsing can proceed. Researchers have investigated learning strategies during interactions with hypermedia systems or learning environments (Hill and Hannafin, 1997; Budhu and Coleman, 2002; Tsai and Tsai, 2003), others have focused on query construction as a learning process (Zhang et al., 2006).

7.2 Modeling Searcher Knowledge Level

Search systems need to model searcher's current levels of knowledge and the information they have encountered and assimilated over time. This allows them to surface information that can stretch their knowledge level but not overreach and confuse the searcher. Research in learning theory (e.g., Jarvis et al., 2003) is relevant here since it suggests that people need to be shown content appropriate for their current state and their learning goals. Also relevant is work on expertise, which describes the extent of specialist knowledge within a particular area that an individual possesses (Ericsson and Smith, 1991; Chi et al., 2014).

An important prerequisite of being able to help searchers explore and learn during interactions with search systems is the ability to estimate their knowledge level at the time of their search, and model it in a way that can be consumed by the search system. Estimates of searchers' knowledge level can be made based on observations from a variety of sources, including their subject matter expertise from the queries that they issue (e.g., their complexity as estimated from the presence of technical vocabulary in their queries) and the nature of resources that they visit. For example, subject matter experts in medicine may be more likely to read articles in medical journals or use medical terminology in their queries.

Expertise has been studied in a variety of contexts (e.g., skill acquisition in playing chess [Chase and Simon, 1973]), mainly focusing on skill acquisition whereby deliberate practice is an effective predictor of expertise (Ericsson et al., 1993). The core assumption in this research is that task performance within a domain is directly connected to training and extended experience (Ericsson, 2006). However, studies have also shown that in some cases novices can make decisions of similar quality to experts if they are provided with simple tools (Camerer and Johnson, 1991; Bolger and Wright, 1992). In this section, I focus on modeling knowledge in an information seeking context, and discuss expertise enhancement later in this chapter.

The choice of methods varies to a large extent based on the scale at which the data are gathered – this governs the type of information that can be collected and the nature and sophistication of the models developed. For example, in online services, search providers may only have access to observational data about searcher activity, and perhaps a limited user profile with demographic and interests data. This supports a different (more limited) construction of an individual's learning profile than is possible via direct engagement of an individual over time (via surveys, interviews, tests, *and* behavioral analysis).

7.2.1 Laboratory Scale

There are many data collection methods from different disciplines – including log processing, gaze tracking, think alouds, observation, self-reports, and interviews – that are used to make determinations of expertise given unfettered access to the searcher. For example, in a laboratory study, Zhang et al. (2011) found that features such as document retention, query length, and the average rank of results selected could be predictive of domain expertise. Duggan and Payne (2008) showed that level of topic knowledge predicted answer accuracy and aspects of the search process, including reducing dwell times, more rapid abandonment of lines of inquiry, and shorter search queries. Liu et al. (2012) studied changes in searcher knowledge over the course of multiple search sessions, and showed that knowledge increased with each successive search session. Wildemuth (2004) showed that novices converge toward the same search patterns as experts as they are exposed to a topic and learn more about it. Methods from the learning sciences may also be appropriate to modeling levels of user knowledge, including testing strategies, comprehension tests, and text understanding methods. At scale, however, many of these methods are inapplicable because searchers cannot communicate their opinions or take tests to gauge their level of expertise. Cole et al. (2011; 2013) showed that eye-gaze patterns could be used to predict an individual's level of domain expertise using estimates of cognitive effort associated with reading. All of these methods rely on the searcher participating in a controlled laboratory setting. Although eye-gaze tracking is typically only available in laboratory settings, as mentioned in Chapters 3 and 5, commodity gaze-tracking technology is becoming more widely available and proxies such as cursor tracking also offer insights into how searchers are consuming content in ways that may reasonably approximate eye gaze. This has implications for better understanding when people are engaged in activities such as reading (Rodden et al., 2008), an important pre-requisite for learning.

7.2.2 Web-Scale

Recent work on large-scale log analysis suggests that there may be evidence of learning in search interactions (White et al., 2009b; Collins-Thompson et al., 2011;

Tan et al., 2012; Kim et al., 2012; Eickhoff et al., 2014). White et al. (2009b) discovered differences in the search behavior of domain experts and novices, including the query terms selected, the breadth of sites visited, and the search strategies employed. Zhang et al. (2011) also showed that they could predict domain expertise from search behavior. Moving toward applications, steps have been taken to tailor presented content to particular searchers depending on their estimated level of domain expertise. Tan et al. (2012) used the measured reading level and comprehensibility of content accessed by users of Yahoo! *Answers* to estimate this level of domain expertise and ranked answers accordingly (e.g., low expertise meant simpler answers were ranked higher). In the context of personalized Web searching, Collins-Thompson et al. (2011) modeled searcher knowledge based on the reading level of the documents that they viewed. These methods take the queries that searchers submit and the documents that they access and attempt to build models of their knowledge level using that data. The reading level estimates can be based on vocabularies that may vary in sophistication with age of knowledge acquisition. For example, in one recent instantiation, the U.S. school grade levels (1–12) were used as the basis for searcher expertise estimates. The searcher and readability information can be intersected with topical classifications of the pages that searchers visit so as better model subject matter expertise, as well as model activities such as stretch reading whereby searchers are observed reading content significantly above the estimated level of expertise (e.g., in learning about a medical diagnosis, completing tax returns; see Kim et al. [2012]).

Eickhoff et al. (2014) examined within-session learning, the development of expertise over the course of a search session by using features of search behavior such as vocabulary usage in query statements and the nature of the content reviewed over the course of the session. They also show that there are attributes of the pages that contribute to the change, and that the changes persist across session boundaries. This builds on earlier work by White et al. (2009b) that presented evidence of long-term learning given changes in the complexity of search queries within professional domains over multiple months. Such signals have utility in applications such as personalization for tasks such as facilitating a more nuanced content selection based on expertise and changes in that expertise over time. Advances in online education at a massive scale (i.e., massive open online courses [MOOCs]) are also facilitating advances in Web-scale analysis of the learning process (e.g., Anderson et al., 2014).

7.2.3 Types of Expertise

Before proceeding, it is worth considering three types of expertise that are particularly relevant in information seeking settings: (1) *domain or subject-matter expertise*; (2) *search expertise*; and (3) *task expertise*. Modeling these three types of searcher expertise accurately is important for search systems, but is also challenging, especially at scale given limited information on which to base expertise estimates. Although described separately, there are clear interactions and dependencies between the different types of expertise. For example, the development of expertise in performing a particular task that could be transferred to other domains will likely emerge from a familiarity within a particular domain and subject matter.

Table 7.1. *Levels of increasing skill and interaction search support appropriate at each level*

Novice	Advanced Beginner	Competent	Proficient	Expert
• Generic search support (e.g., search engines) • Guidelines, rules, and plans	• Generic search support • Situational information • Lists of work items and guidance with sequencing	• Both generic *and* specialized search support (e.g., domain-specific search system) • Planning and note taking • Collection and synthesis of information	• Both generic *and* specialized search support • Overviews and visualizations • Dynamically querying data • Detection and understanding of outliers	• Both generic *and* specialized search support • Overviews and visualizations • Dynamically querying data • Creativity and problem solving • Generalization and transfer of learning into other domains
➔ **Adv. beginner** • Situational information about task etc.	➔ **Competent** • Task planning (e.g., identifying subtasks)	➔ **Proficient** • Prioritizing task activities	➔ **Expert** • Trailblazing for other searchers • Pivots and restructuring visualizations	

7.2.3.1 Domain or Subject Matter Expertise

Domain or subject matter expertise describes people's knowledge in a specialized subject area such as a domain of interest. As suggested earlier in the chapter, there has been significant research in this area in the context of search that has highlighted differences in information seeking and resources sought as a function of differences in expertise (Bhavnani, 2002; Wildemuth, 2004; White et al., 2009b). There are also different levels of expertise. An attorney would be regarded as a having a high level of domain expertise in legal matters, whereas a paralegal may be less skilled in the subject matter. The challenge of modeling expertise level is important, as is providing search experiences that are tuned to a particular expertise level. One might foresee providing broad support (such as general purpose search engines) for novices and specialist search support and specific online legal research services for experts (e.g., Westlaw, providing access to case law, court documents, publications, etc.). However, expertise is a continuous and dynamic attribute; there are many levels of domain expertise that evolve for specific searchers as new skills are acquired over time. Table 7.1 describes five expertise levels and the types of search support that may be appropriate at each stage. This builds on the five-stage representation of skill acquisition proposed by Dreyfus and Dreyfus (1980). Over time, searchers progress from left to right. The rate of the progress and the point of termination (how expert they become) will vary individually. Table 7.1 shows that there should be differences in the types of support that are offered to searchers depending on their level of domain knowledge. All searchers need access to general search tools, but the additional support that search systems provide may vary as a function of the expertise level. Note that the support as described in Table 7.1 is designed to support searchers in their current level of expertise given their demands at that level. Different types of support may be required to transition searchers between levels. For example, because novice and advanced beginners may have difficulty in prioritizing work items (Eraut, 1994), support could be made available *before* there is an acknowledged need with a view to transitioning searchers to the next level. Each of the "non-expert" cells in Table 7.1 provides examples of the types of support that could be offered to help people advance their skill level.

7.2.3.2 Search Expertise

It is important to discuss people's skill level at performing information-seeking activities, both in a Web search setting and in other settings such as specialized domains. White and Morris (2007) showed that search experts (identified via their use of specialized query syntax such as quotation marks) were more likely to be successful in their searching than those without this expertise. Moraveji et al. (2011a) identified several factors that affect an individual's search performance, including knowledge of search engine features (Holscher and Strube, 2000; Moraveji et al., 2011a) and the resources being sought (White et al., 2007), topical expertise (White et al., 2009b), level of general literacy (Kodagoda and Wong, 2008), and differences between task types (Aula et al., 2010). Hsieh-Yee (1993) showed that search experience affected searchers' use of many search tactics, and domain expertise was only a factor once searchers had at least a fair amount of search experience.

There has been much work in characterizing the differences between search experts and novices, and in identifying characteristics that predict search performance. Several studies have used different searcher characteristics to determine who is an expert, including: having more than fifty hours of web experience (Lazonder et al., 2000), browsing the Web more than five hours/week (Khan and Locatis, 1998), and performing searches as part of a job for at least three years (Holscher and Strube, 2000). Behavioral differences have also been noted between novices and experts, where experts tend to take more (Brand-Gruwel et al., 2005) or less time (Saito and Miwa, 2001) to complete tasks, use more query terms (Holscher and Strube, 2000; White and Morris, 2007), use advanced operators (Aula et al., 2005a), and have higher (Khan and Locatis, 1998; Lazonder et al., 2000) or comparable performance (Brand-Gruwel et al., 2005).

To encourage searchers to learn better search skills, *A Google A Day* (agoogleaday.com) helps searchers to practice searching by providing daily questions. Searchers race against a timer to search for an answer, and if they reach a state where they are no longer making progress, they receive a hint query that will lead to the correct answer. Analysis of the data generated from this approach can be useful in understanding how people are searching, in identifying the strategies employed by the most effective searchers, and – perhaps most importantly for a search system – in identifying the cases in which people are struggling with search tasks, so as to inform the design of search support to help them.

Although significant search expertise may be desirable, there are also some negative implications of being too familiar with the search system being used. One of the most significant of these negative implications is *functional fixedness*, which is a cognitive bias that limits a person to using an object only in the way that it is traditionally used (Duncker, 1945). In search interaction, this may mean that search experts are overly constrained by their experience of what a search system can handle as query input.

7.2.3.3 Task Expertise

Task expertise describes people's expertise in performing particular search tasks, potentially independent of domain. Knowledge attained in one context could be easily transferred to another context, referred to as the transfer of learning (Thorndike and Woodworth, 1901; Ellis, 1965). For example, learning how to drive a car may help someone learn more quickly to drive a truck, or some of the skills acquired in tackling exploratory search tasks with unclear goals may apply to a broad range of search tasks, no matter the specific topic of the task. Transfer has been studied in detail by the psychology community and there are many different types of transfer, which vary based on factors such as how the knowledge from the source is transformed when it is applied in the target scenario and the impact that it has (Schunk, 2004).

7.2.3.4 Summary

Effectively modeling different types of expertise is central in developing search systems to help people learn appropriately. Although we have considered the different types of expertise distinctly, the boundaries between them are quite blurred. In each of these areas, the difference between experts and their counterparts is not only the quantity and complexity of the knowledge they have amassed; there are also qualitative differences in the organization of knowledge and its representation (Chi et al. [1982]; e.g., expert knowledge is encoded around domain-related concepts facilitating rapid retrieval from memory when relevant). As a way of supporting learning, searchers may benefit from greater searching (especially engaging in challenging search tasks, such as those promoted by *A Google A Day*) or by being exposed to additional search engine functionality (such as advanced query operators such as "site:," quotes, plus/minus) that may not be in their searching vocabulary. In addition, there may also be benefit from observing actions and strategies of those who possess a higher skill level (likely retrospectively, via visualizations of recorded activity [e.g., Bhavnani et al., 2003]), performing comparisons along meaningful dimensions such as the number of distinct resources accessed, the examination depth on SERPs, or the time spent examining resources after selection. This is explored in more depth in the next section.

7.3 Learning from Oneself and Others

Most searchers do not know how to use search systems as effectively as they might. This is, in part, because search systems do not provide sufficient feedback about how search behavior can be improved. There are a number of ways that people can learn from other individuals, either through the knowledge captured in authored documents or by observing the actions that others perform and, more broadly, their strategies.

7.3.1 Learning from Content

A different form of learning that is not based on the enhancement of people's information search skills relates to changes in knowledge associated with encountered content. As described in the previous section, models of search behavior can be built and those models can be used to select content to present to the searcher appropriate for their current level of understanding, and also with the goal of expanding their understanding by presenting them with new knowledge tailored to their current skill level. The nature of the content presented can be tuned over time so as to actively help searchers improve their knowledge levels. Searchers' demands for knowledge may also evolve over the course of the search session and beyond as they are exposed to information (Bates, 1989).

7.3.1.1 Developing Domain Knowledge

Although learning can be difficult to measure, it is possible to quantify these developments to some degree based only on changes in search behavior, at least within the context of two fundamental types of knowledge: *procedural* knowledge, which is how to do something, and *declarative* knowledge, which is knowledge about something (Anderson, 1976). Eickhoff et al. (2014) presented an in-depth analysis of search sessions in which people explicitly search for new knowledge on the Web using Bing search logs. They investigated within-session and cross-session developments of expertise, focusing on how the language and search behavior of a user on a topic evolves over time. In this way, the authors identify those sessions and page visits that appear to significantly boost the learning process. They show a strong connection between click-through and several metrics related to expertise. Based on models of the searcher and their specific context, Eickhoff and colleagues devise a model to predict, with good accuracy, which clicks will lead to enhanced learning. Their findings showed how search systems might better help people learn as they search (e.g., by predicting the knowledge acquisition potential of Web pages for a given searcher). This can help search systems rank search results in a way that is more appropriate for the current searcher, given their knowledge state and acquisition intent.

7.3.1.2 Developing Search Expertise

Rather than learning about a topic of interest, searchers can also learn how to be more effective *searchers* (Moraveji et al., 2011a; Moraveji et al., 2011b). Search technologies and interfaces are in constant flux, and these fluctuations alter both the types of questions that we can ask search systems and how we ask our questions. Russell (2010) claimed that searchers are continually faced with challenges in how to present their queries and how to interpret and locate desired information from search results. He suggested that researchers need to identify the strategies used by successful searchers and work to not only support, but also to teach these strategies when searchers interact with a search interface. Russell also described strategies for educating searchers about search features using both in-person instruction and offering interface elements that provide hints and tips at points of need. Specifically, he argued that teaching meta-skills for search was an effective strategy and outlined five important meta-skills: (1) how to learn (selecting new query terms, judging the salience of result snippets and content); (2) how to manage attention; (3) how to do research; (4) how to search first (i.e., to give the search system the opportunity to assist before pursuing other means); and (5) how to assess credibility of online content.

When faced with challenging searches, searchers have been found to be unsure about how to change strategies to leverage advanced search system functionality that could help them (Aula et al., 2010; Nielsen, 2011). This means that they largely employ the same strategies regardless of the situation or their level of search success, which can be an ineffective approach. Because attributes of search behavior, such as query length, can be predictive of search success (Aula and Nordhausen, 2006; White and Morris, 2007), searchers who know more about how to use search systems could be more successful. Search engines such as ChaCha.com employ search experts to assist searchers in finding the information that they need. However, such systems only offer a temporary solution and, as mentioned earlier in this chapter, attaining sustainable development in people's search skills that can be transferred to other search scenarios is an important objective.

The best way to help people develop search skills is unclear. Research in education and in persuading people to adopt new behaviors have both highlighted the importance of feedback on personal behavior for reflection and learning (Boud et al., 1985; Lazonder et al., 2000). Additionally, observing other skilled practitioners can improve learning (Bandura, 1986; Moraveji et al., 2011a), and knowing what others do can lead to positive choices (Thaler and Sunstein, 2008). Although search engines do not typically provide feedback, recent research has suggested that there is significant benefit from providing feedback to searchers on their attitudes and behaviors (Bateman et al., 2012). I now consider reflection and comparison as two ways in which people's search behavior can be positively influenced by their interactions with search systems.

7.3.2 Learning by Reflection and Persuasion

Personal area of personal informatics aims to design systems that help people learn about and understand their own behavior, with the goal of providing new insights, increasing self-control, and promoting the acquisition and maintenance of desirable behavior (Li et al., 2010). Persuasive technologies are designed to change behavior or attitudes, without the use of coercion (Fogg, 2002). Personal informatics and persuasive systems have been created for the purpose of reflecting on past behavior and promoting behavior change in several domains including physical activity (Consolvo et al., 2009), environmental impact (Froehlich et al., 2010), and Web page visitation (Van Kleek et al., 2010).

Theories of learning have promoted reflection as an essential part of learning (Boud et al., 1985; Collins et al., 1989). Reflection is the process "in which people recapture their experience, think about it mull it over and evaluate it... [it is] this working with experience that is important in learning" (Boud et al., 1985, p. 19). Other theories also highlight the social nature of learning, where learning occurs through observing and imitating skilled practitioners (Bandura, 1986; Moraveji et al., 2011a); and in so doing, learners can derive the thought process of others (Collins et al., 1989). Others have shown that providing descriptions of what other people do can "nudge" people toward particular decisions (Thaler and Sunstein, 2008).

In the domain of Web search, there has been little research into what and how usage data should be displayed for feedback to searchers. In one study of personal and shared

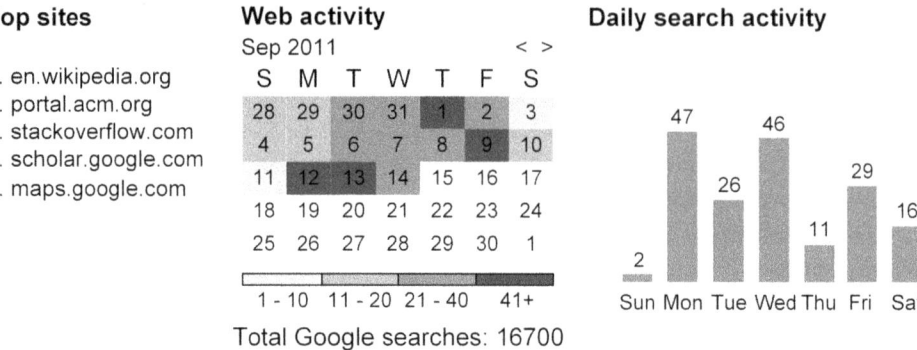

Figure 7.4. The search activity of a particular searcher in Google *Trends* (adapted from Bateman et al., 2012).

Web activity, participants found views containing the data of others to be more useful (Van Kleek et al., 2010). The Google and Bing search engines offer "Search History" functionality that lets searchers review their own past queries (google.com/history; bing.com/profile/history). Such systems have been shown to improve performance in re-finding and resuming search tasks (Morris et al., 2008), but it is unclear whether they would be effective tools for reflection because the data are not usually visualized and/or summarized in ways that are conducive to extracting patterns or insights. Google's search history includes *Trends*, which displays a searcher's most-frequent queries, most-visited sites, most-often clicked search results, and the total number of searches executed over different time frames (see Figure 7.4). While search engines have recognized some value in presenting summaries of search activity, little is known about what information is useful to searchers, and what effect the information presented to searchers might have on their attitudes and behavior.

7.3.3 Learning by Comparison

Observational learning occurs through observing the behavior of others (Bandura, 1971; 1986). It is a useful tool in helping people, especially children, acquire new responses. Search is traditionally a solitary activity, but in the context of the Web there is the opportunity to capitalize on the activity of others to improve search skills (assuming appropriate consent and anonymization of the sensitive log data). Note that these other searchers do not need to be experts in the subject or the use of search technologies, they could simply have traversed a trail through the document collection that is potentially valuable to the current searcher (e.g., as facilitated by *Footprints* (Wexelblat and Maes, 1999) or research on edit and read wear [Hill and Hollan, 1994]). As such, these searchers may have experience that the current searcher does not have (e.g., about queries that were successful, resources that were useful), and the current searcher could learn from those experiences to make their search more effective.

The specific resources selected may have some utility, although they may also only have value for the current search task. While the resources themselves might not be useful, searchers may be able to learn from the *strategies* that others employ to enhance their retrieval performance (Bhavnani et al., 2003; Bateman et al., 2012). As noted earlier in this chapter, this is essential in knowing what to look for in others' online activity and in identifying ways to extract salient behaviors that may benefit others. It is insufficient to simply instruct a searcher to employ experts' strategies. This is best illustrated by way of example. Imagine that experts issue longer queries than novices. Queries can be increased in length by simply adding stopwords such as "of" and "the," but those terms are often ignored by search systems. Telling novices that they should issue longer queries is only useful if it is accompanied by more information about the nature of these queries and the situations where longer queries might be beneficial. Providing this additional information provides instructional context that enables searcher to learn in ways that could be applied across the different task scenarios.

To explore how viewing the data of others might improve reflection on personal data, and to study if and how people make use of this new type of information, Bateman et al. (2012) created the *Search Dashboard*, an interface for reflection and comparison of personal search behavior. The dashboard aggregates and presents an individual's search history and provides comparisons with that of archetypal expert profiles. Bateman and colleagues performed a five-week study with ninety volunteer searchers and found that searchers are able to change aspects of their behavior to be more in line with that of the presented experts. The authors also show that reflection can be beneficial, even without comparison, by changing participants' views about their own search skills, what is possible with search, and what aspects of their behavior may influence search success. Their findings demonstrate a new way for search engines to help searchers modify their search behavior to maximize positive outcomes. There are interesting further directions in this area, such as exploring the other representations of skill level to support reflection and persuasion (e.g., Malacria et al., 2013 proposed "skillometers" – widgets that report user performance and promote behavioral change).

7.3.4 Limitations

Offering facility for their users to learn from experts is a commendable aspirational goal for search providers. While it may be attractive to learn from those with greater knowledge, there are limitations in doing so. One of these is that the content accessed by subject matter experts may not be understandable or useful to those with less domain knowledge. These experts may be accessing the content for a very particular purpose and the goals of their searching could be highly specific, and suited primarily to an audience of other experts. Methods such as instructional scaffolding describe the learning process and promote better learning as searchers construct new knowledge (Ninio and Bruner, 1978; scaffolding is derived from the zone of proximal development [Vygotsky, 1978]). However, this is often a gradual process that occurs over time (weeks, months, and years), and evidence of the learning process can be observed in signals derived from search data (White et al., 2009b; Eickhoff et al., 2014). Being able to accurately model the level of expertise of the current searcher involves taking a snapshot of their knowledge level at a particular time, but that can still be useful in that it allows for more nuanced matching by finding others who are similar along one or more dimensions (e.g., have similar levels of domain knowledge such that resources identified have relevance and are understandable for the current searcher).

Moving beyond the constraints associated with differences in relative expertise, there are also drawbacks associated with learning from those with significant domain and search system knowledge. As mentioned earlier, those possessing search expertise may be affected by functional fixedness (Duncker, 1945), where they adopt particular strategies to find information, but their engrained mental models of how search engines operate (e.g., in terms of the types of search queries that search engines can handle), can limit their ability for lateral thinking in solving certain complex search problems (Blair, 1980). Russell (2010) described a successful search using the query [*oh oh oh oh*] and the real-time search completions offered by Web search engines to find a song played at Stanford basketball games with those same lyrics. Experienced searchers may well discount the effectiveness of a query such as [*oh oh oh oh*] and not even try to submit it, and be less successful in searching as a result. Functional fixedness can also reduce the likelihood of encountering diverse and novel information, an important aspect of exploration, discovery, and learning (Marchionini, 2006a). Novice searchers may not experience such limitations in query formulation, and hence, they may be more successful in this task, especially if other searchers are asking similar types of questions and the search engine learns to map these "curious" formulations to relevant results (as was the case with the basketball example cited previously).

7.4 Intelligent Tutors

Beyond search, there are other domains where learning is particularly important, especially in education. There has been significant research in the intelligent tutoring community on the development of methods to foster learning and evaluate how people have learned using laboratory studies. An intelligent tutoring system (ITS) is an automated system that aims to offer immediate, tailored instruction or feedback to learners, usually without intervention from a human teacher (Psotka and Mutter, 1988). The goal of these systems is to facilitate learning in a meaningful and effective manner by using a variety of computing technologies. There are many examples of ITSs being used in both formal education and professional settings in which they have demonstrated their capabilities and limitations. There is a close relationship between intelligent tutoring, cognitive learning theories, and design; and there is ongoing research to improve the effectiveness of ITS. Concepts and ideas from that community can be brought to bear inside search systems to enhance how we think about learning in areas such as coached problem solving, detecting high and low learners and providing assistance, and searcher confusion detection.

7.5 Applying Knowledge

In addition to considering how people learn from information and the activities of others, it is also important to consider how information and knowledge once attained can be applied. The *use* of information may be the eventual goal of many search episodes, but it is an important aspect of search interaction that is often ignored.[1] A common assumption is that once a searcher has obtained information pertaining to their information needs, the role of the search system (and the need for search interaction) terminates. The process is much more fluid in reality, however, and there may be a continual interplay between search and information use after relevant information has been found by the searcher and system working synergistically together. Systems have been developed to better bridge the gap between information search and information use. *SketchTrieve* (Hendry and Harper, 1997) moves beyond exploration to support information processing activities such as annotating and linking documents. Although this supports the tighter integration of search and related applications such as Web browsers (thereby letting people *reach* search systems more easily), there is also a need to help searchers use the information that they encounter when it is found. Supporting information use involves the accurate representation of a searcher's task so that determinations of utility can be made accurately. Related research on the reliability of content (e.g., Schwarz and Morris, 2011) are also important in this context, since searchers need to make decisions about whether found information can be trusted sufficiently to use as the basis for decisions and actions.

Information and knowledge attained during search is applied as part of some broader task, including playing a role in decision making and learning, as described already in this chapter. Search systems should offer support for the application of knowledge and the visualization and representation of the information found to support decision making and action in the world. Searchers may collect many fragments of information as they search. To use this information to generate new knowledge, searchers should have a way to summarize the information encountered and synthesize that information to form knowledge. The current accepted role of search engines is that they support the *retrieval* of information, but not information *use*. Even in the retrieval aspects, the systems hedge their bets and provide searchers with a set of documents from which to start or continue their investigation, but little additional support is provided on how the information residing in those results could be used for task completion. An important aspect of such support is representations of the goals and outcomes of the search task. Utility-focused ranking or summary generation (targeting the potential uses of the information resident inside documents with respect to those goals) can help people make more informed selection decisions about which pages to review, and also help systems make ranking decisions. For example, awareness that the goal of the task is to learn a new skill allows the systems to favor pages with numbered lists, or call out the presence of such lists in result captions presented on SERPs. Visual clues could also be provided on how documents in a result list are complementary or can be combined to help people complete search tasks (e.g., the likely contributions of a particular result to a broader task; whether the information is redundant given other information in the list; or the correct sequencing of the results to facilitate optimal learning).

7.6 Summary

In this chapter, I discussed how learning is modeled and studied in search, and how search systems can assist in the development of expertise through methods such as reflection and comparison with other searchers. Learning does not have to be a mundane activity (e.g., research on "serious fun" has shown that making tasks fun can assist with learning, especially for children [Schulz and Bonawitz, 2007; Hirsh-Pasek et al., 2008]). I discussed three types of expertise – search, domain, and task – and how they could be modeled in search settings, especially at scale when searcher data are often limited.

Learning is an important aspect of the search process that should better understood and supported in an information-seeking context. To develop search systems that foster learning, and to measure the performance of existing systems in supporting learning, search providers need to be able to measure system performance in this regard. I return to the important issue of evaluating system support for learning in Chapter 11, alongside a broad range of different evaluation metrics associated with the search process and outcomes. As the range of tasks that searchers perform increases over time and tasks become more complex, next-generation search systems will consider learning as a first order task outcome, and tasks that extend beyond the basic retrieval of basic facts. To improve over time, system performance on these more complex tasks needs to be directly measurable. I discuss measurement in more detail in Chapter 10.

CHAPTER 8
Interaction Beyond the Individual

People are important recipients and consumers of search outcomes, and can also be important participants in the search process – pursuing common search objectives and helping searchers answer questions. Many search systems model information seeking as a solitary process comprising interaction between human and machine. However, interactive searching occurs within a social context (Ingwersen and Järvelin, 2005). Frequently, the outcomes of searches are meant to inform interactions with others or to create resources that influence or are used by other people. In addition, searchers can benefit from other people's expertise and experiences. Conversations between individuals can assist with developing a plan and help searchers crystalize their thinking about a path forward.

As the world becomes more connected, interactions with other people are going to play an increasingly important role in search interaction. Search systems can play a central role in facilitating interpersonal interactions, both in terms of connecting people and in mediating their dialogs. They can connect strangers pursuing the same task at the same time (Bateman et al., 2012; González-Ibáñez et al., 2015), and facilitate co-searching between friends and colleagues alike (Morris and Horvitz, 2007; Amershi and Morris, 2008). The strangers may be search experts who can provide guidance on search strategies that would help people locate their information faster by better understanding how best to query, and/or they could be subject matter experts with the domain knowledge to answer searcher questions directly via synchronous or asynchronous communication channels without requiring further engagement with the search system (Adamic et al., 2008).

Social information can be employed by search systems in a number of ways, including: (1) asking others (e.g., social question and answer, where experts can help searchers answer questions); (2) working together (e.g., collaborative information seeking – including cases for which the collaboration may be initiated by the search system (González-Ibáñez et al. [2012]); (3) learning from the behavior of others in the aggregate (e.g., trails extracted from search logs can provide guidance on where searchers should go next; see Wexelblat and Maes [1999] and Joachims [2002]); (4) learning from link creation (e.g., hyperlink analysis of resources explicitly connected by document authors; see Brin and Page [1998] and Kleinberg [1999]), and; (5) explicit recommendations (e.g., recommender systems [see Konstan and Riedl, 2012]). Points (3), (4), and (5) are covered elsewhere in the book. As such, the focus in this chapter is mainly on collaborative information seeking and engaging with others to solve ongoing problems. Returning to the theme of learning that was discussed in the previous chapter, involving others in the search process is one way that people can learn, i.e., through direct communication with individuals with greater expertise or passive observation of their search activities.

Collaborative searching it typically intentional. Searchers purposely engage with others known to them in the pursuit of a common goal (Shah, 2010a). Beyond friends, family, and acquaintances, there may also be significant benefit in interacting with strangers given the opportunity to obtain different perspectives (Whittaker, 1996). Both the specific role of the human in such collaboration and the demands on the system depend in large part on the speed with which a response is required. If a delay is acceptable, the question could be handled asynchronously, during which time an answer could be crafted, as is common in community question-answering scenarios (Liu et al., 2008), and more recently the manual creation of answers for rare, but specific information needs (Bernstein et al., 2012) and slow search (Teevan et al., 2013). Integrating people other than the searcher directly into the search process could fulfill two functions: (1) better understanding of information needs as expressed in queries (which are notoriously difficult for search engines to comprehend automatically from short keyword queries); and (2) crafting better responses for presentation to searchers.

The humans involved in the search process could be expert searchers and/or domain experts, capable of assisting the searcher in finding useful information. For example, if the system was to support dialog with the searcher (as is the case in the *IM-an-Expert* system [White et al., 2011]), then a human answerer could use the iterative nature of the dialog to more fully understand the searcher's (or asker's) information needs. Alternatively, if the answerer was an expert searcher, he/she could formulate search queries in ways that would help the searcher find the most relevant information resources. There is the issue of whether expertise matters – that is, whether any other people (who could have any level of expertise) can assist searchers with comprehending information needs versus a crowd of experts who are fully qualified and capable of answering. Involving experts may not only be costly financially, it also creates challenges associated with establishing a common ground between novices and experts. The need for common ground has been well documented in the literature on communication theory (Clark and Brennan, 1991). It could be addressed in the context of question answering by considering *relative* expertise of searchers and experts during question matching (White and Richardson, 2012). White and Richardson proposed that in selecting experts, search systems should model *both* the asker's level of expertise and the answerer's level of expertise, and it should consider the *difference* between these expertise levels in the selection of candidate experts (i.e., an answerer with only slightly more expertise than the asker may be sufficient). From the search providers' perspective, there are interesting load balancing challenges involving preserving the most qualified answerers for the most qualified askers, given that expert in this context is a relative concept (i.e., more knowledgeable than the asker) and the risk of overwhelming highly-qualified answerers with many questions.

Once an answerer has been connected with the initial asker of the question, they can engage with the asker in a number of ways, including low fidelity communication media such as instant messaging (as was the case with the *Aardvark* system [Horowitz and Kamvar, 2010]) and higher fidelity methods such as audio and/or video (e.g., Skype or Google Helpouts). It is still unclear whether there really is value from the higher bandwidth communication methods for question-answering support, but there may be some tasks when being able to see the answerer could be useful in explaining how to solve a problem (e.g., changing a bicycle tire) or in engendering trust in the answer and the answerer (Bos et al., 2002). As with any solution, there are still challenges that need to be addressed, including the costs of collaboration, both in terms of incentives for answerers (Twidale and Nichols, 1996) and coordinating activities between individuals during collaborative processes (Gray, 1989; London, 1995), including collaborative searching (Shah, 2010a).

8.1 Collaborative Searching

Although motivated by task definitions that emerge from broader contexts, including social contexts, people frequently pursue their search objectives individually. Recently there has been a growing interest in supporting explicit collaboration between searchers in the context of information seeking. Researchers have argued that collaboration could facilitate more enhanced information exploration, in part by exploiting the different skills and experiences of collaborators (Hyldegård, 2006; Hyldegård, 2009; Shah, 2010b; Shah and González-Ibáñez, 2011; Twidale, Nichols, and Paice, 1997). For instance, a subject specialist (e.g., an attorney) and a search specialist (e.g., a legal librarian) could collaborate to retrieve better results and deeper understanding of the material and its sources. This would allow searchers to find information that people may find challenging to synthesize individually (Pickens et al., 2008). While collaboration may increase the likelihood of finding relevant information, collaboration may also help boost novelty and diversity in the information retrieved during the search process (Shah et al., 2010).

Despite some good progress in the design of collaborative search systems, there is still quite some way to go in developing systems capable of supporting effective intentional collaborative searching. In a recent survey, Morris (2013) found that while people were satisfied with their most recent collaborative search, there was still room for improvement in areas such as improving awareness of others' activities on the system, directly compare search results retrieved, and reduce redundancy. Although systems such as *Coagmento* (Shah, 2013) and *SearchTogether* (Morris and Horvitz, 2007) already offer this functionality (e.g., *Coagmento* provides visibility into collaborators' search histories), there is a need for availability of such functionality in collaborative search systems more broadly. Other issues – such as the friction involved in moving between tools to perform collaborative searching (Morris and Horvitz, 2007) – may also contribute to the slow uptake of specialized collaborative search systems. There are of course scenarios in which collaboration is important. Hearst (2014) recently proposed a set of three such scenarios for which intentional collaboration could be helpful: (1) *one from many*: select one option from a number of different but similar alternatives (especially when the searchers are the stakeholders in the decisions that result from the searching); (2) *topic coverage*: fully cover a topic space (e.g., perhaps using a "divide-and-conquer" approach where each searcher covers some aspect); and (3) *information novelty*: finding new or unknown information (e.g., in the case of the DARPA Red Balloon Challenge [Tang, 2011; Hearst, 2014], a competition to most rapidly locate red balloons situated around the U.S.).

Research on collaborative information retrieval has focused primarily on explicit/intentional forms of collaboration in which the participants are purposely engaged in collaborative activity (Fidel et al., 2000; 2004; Golovchinsky et al., 2008; Morris, 2008; Shah, 2010a). Conversely, research on implicit/unintentional forms of collaboration such as collaborative filtering (Resnick and Varian, 1997, discussed in Chapter 6) has targeted methods capable of exploiting individual behaviors on a population to assist members of the population and new members of the population. As highlighted throughout the book thus far, searchers' aggregated on-task behavior can be mined at scale from the logs of behavioral data collected by search systems, both at the query level (Joachims 2002; Agichtein et al., 2006), and across multiple queries/tasks (Radlinski and Joachims, 2005; White et al., 2013a). These methods leverage the aggregated historic behavior of many searchers to identify resources of interest to the current searcher given their task. The implicit/unintentional forms of collaboration are based on retrospective analyses of search behavior, meaning that they cannot support the initiation of synchronous collaborations between searchers actively engaged in the same search task. Such support was proposed in research on so-called "collabportunities," which describe opportunities for collaboration that may be missed if a search system cannot connect searchers with common interests (González-Ibáñez et al., 2012).

Research on explicit/intentional collaboration in information search targets behaviors and collaborative practices that can be supported with technology. This can be grouped into the following two categories based on the nature of the mediation that forms part of the collaboration (Pickens et al., 2008):

- **System or algorithmically mediated:** The system acts as an active agent and provides mediation among the collaborators to enhance their productivity and experience. Example systems include *Cerchiamo* (Golovchinsky et al., 2008) and *Querium* (Golovchinsky et al., 2012).
- **User or interface mediated:** The control lies with the human collaborators, with the system serving as a passive component. Searchers drive the collaboration, and the system primarily provides various functions on the interface level. Examples include *Ariadne* (Twidale and Nichols, 1996), *SearchTogether* (Morris and Horvitz, 2007), and *Coagmento* (Shah, 2010a).

In both cases it is assumed that the collaboration occurs as a part of a larger ongoing collaborative project among participants. *Querium* (Golovchinsky et al., 2012) supports and mediates explicit collaboration among searchers. It does so by providing specialized tools that provide searchers with control to perform actions such as information sharing and communication. In addition, the tool incorporates algorithmic mediation that is system driven and does not require explicit searcher intervention. In systems such as *SearchTogether* (Morris and Horvitz, 2007) and *Coagmento* (Shah, 2010a), searchers have complete control over a set of features that support the collaborative search process. However, unlike *Querium*, collaboration in these systems depends uniquely on explicit actions from searchers. Collaborative retrieval systems differ from synchronous social question-answering systems, such as *IM-an-Expert* (White et al., 2011), *Aardvark* (Horowitz and Kamvar, 2010), IBM *Community Tools* (Weisz et al., 2006), and others in which people pose questions to others via synchronous communication channels such as instant messaging. They assume that dialog participants have clearly defined roles (an asker with a question and an answerer with the knowledge to answer the question or provide an informed recommendation). In contrast, in collaborative information seeking, searchers are peers and contribute to the pursuit of their shared information goals.

8.1.1 Co-Located Collaborative Search

Much of the emphasis in this section has been on collaboration between remote parties, separated by physical distance (and potentially also time) in the case of asynchronous communications. It is commonly thought that this type of synchronous and asynchronous collaboration could benefit from search support. However, there is also emerging interest in the development of tools to support *co-located* collaborative search, which is a surprisingly common practice. Morris (2008) found that close to 90% of searchers reported having engaged in a "backseat driving" practice of watching another person search, and suggesting queries or resources to select. Methods to support such a practice using additional input mechanisms such as gesture or spoken dialog, could be valuable in next-generation search systems. Other studies have shown that searching together with multiple phones is also a common practice – for example, to find a restaurant (Morris, 2013) – and applications are emerging to support that type of coordination activity (Teevan et al., 2014b).

Switching to system support, there has been related work in collaboratively searching a digital photo collection using an interactive tabletop display (Morris et al., 2006), and dividing a Web page into multiple components for review by a group on handheld devices (Maekawa et al., 2006). More recently, support for co-located Web search and task planning have emerged (Amershi and Morris, 2008; Teevan et al., 2014b). *CoSearch* (Amershi and Morris, 2008) provides each searcher with their own pointing device (mouse) from which they can engage with the system, although they still need to take turns with the shared keyboard. The opportunities for such shared experiences are greatly enhanced with today's search technologies, whereby gesture and speech could be used to engage in co-located searching. Teevan et al. (2014) describes *O-SNAP* (Orchestrating Search Negotiations Among People), which allows co-located mobile searchers to signal that they are ready to collaborate with each other. As mobile devices become more aware of their surroundings (including proximal devices and people), many interesting applications will emerge that allow tasks to be divided and opinions collected.

8.2 Seeking Help from Others

Many systems now provide a functionality through which people can request help from others, including even directly from search engines (Hecht et al., 2012). Many systems have been developed to support collaborative question answering, including databases of questions and their associated answers (Ackerman and McDonald, 1996), forums, list servers, and chat systems that distribute instant messages to groups of people with registered interest in the topic of the question (Singley et al., 2008). Web question-and-answer (Q&A) sites, where askers pose questions and others answer them, are popular and can provide quality answers (Harper et al., 2008), but can have high latency even when the number of users is large (Hsieh and Counts, 2009). Mailing lists broadcast questions to all members of the list, potentially interrupting and overloading all recipients and requiring that they adopt strategies to manage discussion threads (e.g., by directing incoming email to folders, increasing time to response; see Ludford et al. [2004]).

8.2.1 Communication

An important aspect in designing systems capable of supporting search via collaboration is the means by which the dialog occurs. There are two main methods: (1) *synchronous* collaboration in which the asker and the answerer are engaged in a real-time dialog via a platform such as instant messaging or higher fidelity mechanisms such as voice or video calling; and (2) *asynchronous* collaboration for which the dialog occurs via a medium such as a website (such as Yahoo! *Answers*, *Quora*, or *Stack Overflow*), or social networks such as *Facebook*. The differences between the two communication methods are summarized in detail in the following sections. Synchronous methods interrupt fewer answerers, but they also rely on being able to accurately identify those answerers, which can be challenging if limited information is available about their interests and expertise.

8.2.1.1 Synchronous

Synchronous communication allows for both parties to contribute simultaneously to the answer discussion. Groupware systems have been developed that facilitate synchronous communication between individuals, normally using instant messaging (IM; see Jensen et al. [2000]). IM, typically used through a client-side application, allows users to exchange short textual messages with others with extremely low latency. Synchronous communications can also be performed using higher fidelity methods such as telephone or video calling. The nature of the medium can be determined by the nature of the task (e.g., whether the asker needs to observe the answerer performing some action when particular steps are required, or whether the information need is ill-defined and requires clarification). Also, the different forms of communication may facilitate different degrees of multitasking by the answerer; those conversing via instant messaging can handle numerous conversations simultaneously, whereas those employing higher fidelity methods such as telephone or video can only participate in a single conversation at a time. This has consequences for remuneration in situations for which more answers equates to more revenue. Parties may also be updated on the status of the other person, including their availability to answer questions and even whether they are actively typing on their keyboard during the dialog via "person is typing" messages. This can help maintain the connection between the asker and the answerer, and reduce dialog abandonment rates and improve

Figure 8.1. Synchronous social question-answering in the *Aardvark* system (adapted from vark.com).

conversation flow because searchers know that others are actively composing a message.

Instant messaging (IM) is popular in virtual communities, and despite its drawbacks for archiving and navigation, IM is informal and provides instant support for negotiation of meaning (Nardi et al., 2000; Ribak et al., 2002), which are characteristics needed for free flow and sharing of tacit knowledge. Among other things, researchers have studied the role of responsiveness in IM communication (Avrahami et al., 2008), the support for multitasking during communication that IM provides (Isaacs et al., 2002), and the effect of task type on IM interruptions (Czerwinski et al., 2000). *ReachOut* (Ribak et al., 2002) combines publish/subscribe technology from a listserv with narrowly focused topics to help reduce information overload. It uses IM for awareness, but has persistence and sup-ports question/user targeting. Systems such as *Babble* (Bradner et al., 1999) and *Well* (Rheingold, 2000) also use chat to facilitate collaboration. The *IM-an-Expert* system (White et al., 2011) uses estimates of prospective answerers' expertise with respect to the question in making a decision about who to ask. This can be done using a range of methods, including basic keyword matching between terms in the question and those in the searcher's profile (described in Section 8.2.2.2).

Moving beyond enterprise settings to the open Web, *Aardvark* (Horowitz and Kamvar, 2010) was an IM-based synchronous social Q&A system purchased by Google that removes the need for askers to select the target of the question prior to asking. Instead, Aardvark automatically routes incoming questions to the asker's social network. Questions were submitted via different entry points (including the *Aardvark* website, email, or instant messaging), and *Aardvark* identified and facilitated a live chat or email conversation with one or more topic experts in the asker's extended social network. Figure 8.1 illustrates the three phases of the question-answering process in the *Aardvark* system. In an analysis of *Aardvark* usage, Horowitz and Kamvar (2010) showed that its primary use was subjective questions for which human judgment or recommendation was sought (drawing on the experiences of others who are close to them in their social network; e.g., what is a good Italian restaurant in Manhattan?). The service was also used extensively for technical support questions. Horowitz and Kamvar (2010) also reported that answerers are usually within one to two "hops" on the asker's social network (i.e., they were using friends of the asker or friends of the asker's friends).

Because synchronous methods facilitate direct dialog between askers and answerers, the ability of askers and answerers to converse with each other effectively may also affect the outcome. Indeed, psychologists and human-computer interaction researchers have shown that expertise differences can hinder dialog between domain novices and experts (Isaacs and Clark, 1987; Pollack, 1985) and that IM is a difficult medium for establishing the common ground that is important in successful dialog (McCarthy et al., 1991). Research on initial interactions (Svennevig, 2000) has studied both how people become acquainted and how support for conversations between strangers has been developed (Ofek et al., 2013). However, such support may not be as necessary in question-answering settings because the dialog purpose is known to both parties.

8.2.1.2 Asynchronous

In asynchronous forms of communication, participants take turns asking and answering questions and are mediated by an external service. Messages are exchanged using a website such as Yahoo! *Answers* or *StackOverflow*, via electronic mail, or other media. There have been a number of studies of different methods for asynchronous communication (Horowitz and Kamvar, 2010; Morris et al., 2010; White et al., 2011). Individual messages might be longer than those sent via IM and the timespan between messages also may be longer, in part because of the extended length and also because of lower expectations about response time for emails, meaning that people may be less likely to hurry with a response. The introduction of a delay removes the need for answerers to be on retainer to answer questions at the time the question is posed and allows them to answer at their own pace. The dynamics of email handling and response times already have been studied (e.g., Tyler and Tang, 2003). Another important dimension is managing asker expectations about when an answer will be received given the medium employed by the system. Wait times can vary based on a number of factors, especially time of day. As in customer service scenarios, the expected wait time needs to be communicated *before* askers invest time in formalizing and submitting their question.

8.2.2 Distribution

To distribute questions from askers to potential answerers, a number of strategies have been employed, ranging from broadcasting messages widely, and even in public forums, to targeting individual users who may have the interest or expertise to answer (see Ribak et al., 2002); I discuss both broadcast and targeted approaches in this section. Note that the means in which the question is distributed is different from the nature of the answer dialog (e.g., it is possible for the broadcast methods to use synchronous channels such as chat rooms) and for asynchronous methods to be targeted (e.g., directing electronic mails to likely respondents). Table 8.1 summarizes the types of technology and question-answering support for combinations of various distribution and communication methods.

Table 8.1. *Different communication and distribution channels*

		Communication method	
		Synchronous	*Asynchronous*
Distribution method	*Targeted*	• Instant messaging • In person meetings • Phone	• Electronic mail • Text messaging
	Broadcast	• Chat rooms • Conference calls • Group meetings	• Forums • Social networks • Distribution lists

8.2.2.1 Broadcast

The ways in which people get help can also vary to include cases in which people broadcast a request for help broadly to a large set of users, perhaps via a website such as Yahoo! *Answers*, or by posting on the wall of their social network (e.g., *Facebook*). These posts will be seen by other people who are monitoring the site, who can then make decisions about whether they wish to answer the question. *Mimir* (Hsieh and Counts, 2009), a market-based question-and-answer service, employs a strategy of broadcasting all questions to all users that is similar to an email distribution list, and they do not filter question recipients based on personalization. Some sites offer functionality whereby answerers can be alerted to incoming questions on topics of their interest. In a similar way, askers of the question can be notified when an answer is received, meaning that they do not need to check back with the website periodically to determine whether an answer was received. The way in which questions are worded in these circumstances can have a large effect on answer likelihoods. In a study of question-asking on *Facebook*, Morris et al. (2010) showed that question wording and even the inclusion of punctuation such as question marks was important in determining the number and quality of answers received. Research has also explored the prediction on answer likelihood and answer quality in community question-answering (CQA) settings such as Yahoo! *Answers* (Liu et al., 2008; Shah and Pomerantz, 2010). Researchers have also examined how questions posed on such sites evolve from failing search queries using retrospective analysis of log data containing both queries and questions (Liu et al., 2012). The data collected on the activity of many users of question-answering sites can also be used for the identification of authorities (i.e., people with expertise in a particular subject area; see Jurczyk and Agichtein [2007]), who can be targeted to help answer questions.

8.2.2.2 Targeted

Rather than broadcasting questions and depending on others to notice them and respond, an alternative solution involves the system sending targeted requests to specific answerers asking them if they are willing to answer the question.[1] This involves being able to accurately identify experts. These candidate answerers can be ranked on estimates of their expertise with respect to the question using simple keyword match algorithms such as TF.IDF (Spärck-Jones, 1972), or with more sophisticated formal models designed specifically for the challenge of expert finding (e.g., Balog et al., 2006). Other methods that leverage signals such as the profiles of peers in the organization (Karimzadehgan et al., 2009), may also be useful in identifying experts.

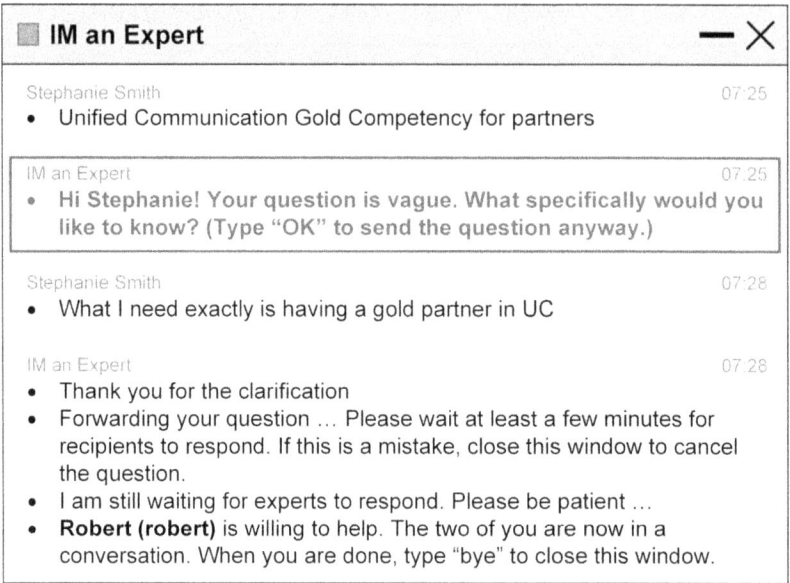

Figure 8.2. A screenshot of *IM-an-Expert* system with clarification request support (highlighted; adapted from Kato et al., 2013).

Understanding the effect of expertise differences can help in designing better social search systems, perhaps by including relative expertise when selecting candidate answerers (Smirnova and Balog, 2011), or providing support to help ground the Q&A dialog. White and Richardson (2012) showed that people were more satisfied with answers from people with greater expertise than them and that satisfaction plateaued beyond a certain different in expertise level, but there were still differences in the nature of the dialog. Additionally, research is needed on predicting dialog outcomes by encouraging askers to reformulate questions before it is dispatched to candidate answerers (Kato et al., 2013; an example is shown in Figure 8.2), as well as automatically identifying answers in dialogs (Cong et al., 2008).

Expertise location systems help find people with specific, desired knowledge (Ackerman and McDonald, 1998). These systems harness technology to locate people and engage with them to benefit from their knowledge. Such systems are becoming very popular in both research (Kautz et al., 1997; McDonald and Ackerman, 2000; Singley et al., 2008, White et al., 2011) and enterprises. *ReferralWeb* (Kautz et al., 1997) and *Expertise Recommender* (McDonald and Ackerman, 2000) leverage two types of profiles, one concerning expertise and the other concerning social relations. Both systems obtain expertise information by data mining. *ReferralWeb* mines public Web documents for knowledge about potential experts through content analysis to identify salient topics and social relationships. *Expertise Recommender* mines work products and byproducts such as software source control systems and technical support databases. *ReferralWeb* does not provide any explicit support for the interaction process; seekers are expected to use whatever means they find appropriate to communicate with the experts. *Expertise Recommender* provides a simple IM system for users logged into the system

(McDonald and Ackerman, 2000), one of many ways to communicate in an organizational setting. *BlueReach* (Singley et al., 2008) is a real-time expertise sharing and capture application that connects an asker to another individual who can provide the answer. *BlueReach* provides a browse-able directory of expertise categories and subcategories to allow users to locate the right expert and initiate an IM dialog, while safeguarding experts' time. Expertise location systems still assume that answers should come from experts – often experts whose role is to help others – and use previously created content to reduce their workload. *IM-an-Expert* (White et al., 2011) utilizes content both explicitly provided by experts (keywords and URLs of pages describing their expertise and interests) and implicitly (documents that they have authored, emails sent to distribution lists, previously-answered questions). Within an enterprise setting there may be a significant amount of information available about each person on which askers can base determinations of expertise. In contrast, in settings such as the Web, such a determination may not be as straightforward because there may be less information available about askers and answers. There are also important confidentiality and ethical factors that must be considered when crawling online content about individuals for use in search applications.

Two recent examples of leveraging people power to support information search at scale on the Web are *Aardvark* and *Helpouts* (helpouts.google.com). *Aardvark* was described in Section 8.2.1.1. More recently, Google proposed a service called *Helpouts*, which involves live video chat with experts. *Helpouts* is a way to connect people who need help with people who can give help, in real time, over live video. With *Helpouts*, people can get help whenever it is needed and from wherever they are. The service includes experts from teachers, counselors, doctors, home repair experts, personal trainers, hobby enthusiasts, and more. People will be able to choose who to get help from based on qualifications, availability, ratings, and reviews. Scheduling and paying for help will be easy, and *Helpouts* will be accessible from any device. Two drawbacks of *Helpouts* were (1) the need for financial remuneration (justified by the cost involved in using domain experts in real time) and (2) that assistance may not be rendered at question time, often when searchers need it most. Instead, askers and answerers needed to schedule a mutually convenient appointment to meet with the expert at a later time or date. While there are advantages to such a service over IM-based solutions such as *Aardvark* and *IM-an-Expert* (primarily the video chat and the provision of financial remuneration to experts [important in incentivizing participation in the absence of other motivators such as social ties]), the fact that askers had to schedule assistance and had to pay for its receipt, may have negatively impacted usage.

8.2.2.2.1 Issues in Targeting
For the answerer, targeted distribution of questions may mean more direct interruptions, which could overwhelm experts and lead them to leave the service. Research in the human factors community has shown that it can take people can take a considerable time (many minutes) to recover from an interruption to their task flow (Iqbal and Horvitz, 2007). This may be particularly important for experts with extensive profiles, which may match against a wide array of questions and may in fact serve as a disincentive to

providing detailed profile information. This could be handled by controls that would allow answerers to specify their preferences regarding the number of questions that they wish to receive per day and even specific times when they are available to answer (as in IM-an-Expert [Richardson and White, 2011]). In addition, the system could also take into account the total number of questions that expert has received recently and their current status (e.g., "Away," "In a meeting," etc.), and use that additional information as part of the decision process in balancing the distribution of questions among candidate answerers.

Many expert-finding systems rely on question askers to identify knowledgeable answerers (Singley et al., 2008; Shami et al., 2008) given a subset of the potential answerers selected from a pool by the search system. When ranked lists of experts are shown to searchers, research has shown that rank order and social connection information displayed in snippets of search results can significantly predict whether a searcher considers a particular expert (Shami et al., 2008). Manually selecting and contacting candidate experts adds social awkwardness, and is time consuming for both parties. Systems that mediate the matching process, managing the selection and invitation of candidate answerers on the asker's behalf, may be particularly powerful.

By focusing on identifying experts, all of these systems ignore the powerful concept of peer-support (Greer et al., 1998), and the advantages that sharing needs and conducting public discussions have for enhancing community cohesion. Of course, peer support has challenges around incentivizing participation and load balancing. Researchers have theorized about the impact of community size and other factors on member contributions (Ludford et al., 2004; Oliver and Marwell, 1998; Williams and Karau, 1991), but a key difference in targeted question-answering is that searchers are not aware of other community activity, potentially reducing reputation effects and potentially reducing the number of members who contribute to the process. White et al. (2011) conducted a large user study the impact of community size and contact rate (the number of searchers contacted at each round of question-answering) on the effectiveness of synchronous social question answering. Their findings suggest that to maximally satisfy both askers and answerers, such systems should use low contact rates and build large communities of expertise.

8.3 Recipients

There are two main groups of people who are the potential recipients of these questions are (1) friends, or those in the askers social network, either directly or some number of hops away on the social network graph (friends of friends [FoF], etc.); and (2) subject matter experts (often strangers), or those with sufficient knowledge of the question topic. Similar expertise measures for each of the groups (although some questions – e.g., recommendations – may be better suited to friends), but their recruitment and incentives may be radically different given different underlying motivations. In addition to these human groups, machines will play an increasingly important role in answering questions directly and in brokering the question-answer process between social networks and other (potentially even automated) answering methods (Hecht et al., 2012).

8.3.1 Friends or Acquaintances

One of the primary sources of information about the strength of ties between individuals is social networks. Social networks are social structures that comprise a set of social actors (such as individuals or organizations) and a set of the dyadic ties between them. Social network research provides a set of methods for analyzing the structure of whole social entities as well as a variety of theories explaining the patterns observed in these structures (Wasserman, 1994; Carrington et al., 2005). Social network analysis can be used to identify local and global patterns, locate influential entities, and examine network dynamics. Networks can be useful channels for disseminating information and expertise within organizations and beyond (Granovetter, 1973; Watts and Strogatz, 1998). There are also important issues (such as trust) that can be modeled within social networks, and leveraged to support enhanced personalization and recommendation (Goldbeck, 2005).

Social networking websites such as *Facebook* provide people with an easy way to manage and grow their networks, and also communicate with others in those networks via public broadcasts or private messages. These networks are explicitly defined and formed by their members. For social networks that are not explicitly defined, systems such as *ReferralWeb* (Kautz et al., 1997) can be useful in creating such networks from publically available information from these systems online (e.g., hyperlinks between homepages, archived forum exchanges) that can provide additional signals for expert finding algorithms (Kautz et al., 1996).

Social networking sites provide a way to easily identify communities of friends, who can be defined as those proximal to the searcher in their social network: either those directly connected to the searcher or those who are friends of the searcher's friends. Friends of the asker may also make good answerers for many of their questions, especially those that have experience related to a searcher's past activities, such as visiting a restaurant (rather than expertise based knowledge). Friends may share interests, expectations, and demographic attributes with the asker, and may be better placed than a stranger to provide advice related to the asker's preferences. As such, friends may be particularly useful in recommendation scenarios such as what is the best X in Y. This "friendsourcing" has been applied to describe such cases where friends can help others perform tasks (Bernstein et al., 2010). In doing so, care needs to be taken to consider the costs (e.g., social capital, discussed in Section 4.4.1.1) involved in leveraging these social relationships, as well as the impact of other factors such as the nature of the task being attempted on people's behavior (e.g., people are more likely to friendsource if the answer is difficult to attain; see Rzeszotarski and Morris [2014]). For other questions, specialist domain knowledge may be required and askers may need to engage directly with subject matter experts to get their questions answered. Question-answering systems can help mediate the identification and pursuit of help from domain experts.

8.3.2 Experts (Usually Strangers)

Beyond friends, family, and acquaintances, there may also be significant benefit in interacting with strangers given the availability of different perspectives (Whittaker, 1996).

Advances in machine translation and speech recognition mean that asker and answerer may be able to converse directly via phone or video chat to solve an information problem without speaking a shared language. Experts may have familiarity in a particular area or may have specialist knowledge of search systems, allowing them to help searchers locate useful resources, but not offer direct advice themselves. As mentioned earlier in this chapter, expertise location – the task of matching a received question to one or more candidate answerers – has been studied extensively in the information retrieval community (e.g., Balog et al., 2006), including limited studies on the application of large-scale behavioral data to the challenge (Macdonald and White, 2009). Beyond matching, there are a number of issues in the involvement of experts in the retrieval process: (1) expert recruitment; (2) the creation of profiles describing their interests and expertise; and (3) the incentivization of experts to continue to answer questions over time.

8.3.2.1 Recruitment

A challenge in using experts to answer questions lies in finding and recruiting these experts to a search system. A range of tactics can be employed to alert potential answerers to the service (e.g., search and social media advertisements, announcements on the search engine homepage). The broader question is to define which people or groups of people (cohorts) to target during the recruitment process. In one approach, a small set of experts on a range of topics – perhaps even the designers of the system, at least initially – could be recruited and the system could be deployed externally. Analysis of the type of questions that are asked could lead to insights about focus areas for expert recruitment, highlight missing areas of expertise, as well as the expertise levels of the askers. Armed with this knowledge, search providers can solicit involvement from groups who possess expertise in the topic(s) of interest (e.g., from owners of websites or weblogs on a topic of interest) at the appropriate level.

8.3.2.2 Profile Creation

Experts can be encouraged to create user profiles describing their interests or expertise. It is in their interest to provide a detailed description and/or pointers to other sites, to reduce irrelevant interruptions from questions on topics unrelated to their topics of interest. However, studies have shown that experts are unlikely to explicitly describe their interests to the system through explicit keywords or pointers to resources such as homepages (e.g., around half of the subscribed experts in a recent study of an enterprise search system did not provide profile data [Serdyukov et al., 2011]).

A number of strategies can be used to address challenges in profile generation. These include:

- **Leverage implicit information about the expert:** In addition to gathering this information explicitly from searchers, we can also utilize implicit sources of expertise information such as documents and emails that they have authored. If such information is missing for an individual, the only information that the system has in answering questions is the content of questions previously answered. While methods may exist to generate profiles based on implicit sources, such information may be missing and what is attainable may be of low quality.
- **Simplify profile generation:** Keywords can be recommended to searchers at profile generation time. The automatic generation of explicit user profiles can

be a valuable resource for expert finding and has received some recent attention from the research community (Balog and De Rijke, 2007; Serdyukov et al., 2011).

- **Use information from others who share similar attributes:** One way to build profiles is to propagate expertise information from those proximal to that individual in the organization (e.g., peers and managers, or other people networks; see Karimzadehgan et al. [2009]). It is assumed that such searchers possess similar knowledge, as assertion supported by the study from Karimzadehgan and colleagues. This could lead to improvements in the quality of the experts found, as well as increasing the size of expert pool, thereby increasing the chances of finding an answerer (this is particularly important in synchronous question-answer settings).

These strategies can be employed in isolation or combined as ways to help expert-finding systems better understand their experts and better match questions to answerers.

8.3.2.3 Incentivization

Motivation is an important issue for both friends and experts. Friends or colleagues may feel more of a social obligation to assist questioners, whereas strangers may need to be encouraged through intrinsic incentives and extrinsic incentives (Shapira et al., 2001). There are a number of ways in which this can be accomplished, including monetary and virtual rewards in the form of points (which can be converted to physical goods) or reputation within the system and beyond (e.g., the Microsoft "most valuable professional" [MVP] program, which recognizes those who evangelize and share knowledge of Microsoft products). Careful attention is needed regarding about incentivization schemes so as to encourage appropriate types of participation to maintain participation in the long term across many questions.

8.3.2.3.1 Rewards

There has been significant research in different types of economic incentives in participating in social question answering (e.g., Edelman, 2004; Harper et al., 2008; Rafaeli et al., 2007), which have shown that non-monetary, intrinsic motivations are important in this process (e.g., altruism and expected reciprocity). Research in psychology and experimental economics has shown that monetary incentives may overwhelm other motivations (Deci et al., 1999), even though social and psychological motivators have been shown to be important in determining online contributions (Ling et al., 2005; Burke et al., 2009; Burke et al., 2011). Chawla et al. (2012) explored the idea of using crowd-sourced contests as a way to encourage high-quality contributions. Badges reward searchers for their achievements and incentivize them to contribute more to online communities (Singer, 2012). Badges have been used in a number of offline domains, ranging from educational settings (Bishop, 1989) to customer retention (Kopalle and Neslin, 2004; Lewis, 2004), as a way to reward desired behavior. Antin and Churchill (2011) offer a conceptual organization for different types of badges, based on – among other things – the underlying social-psychological motivations. Anderson et al. (2013) showed that badges may be useful in steering human behavior in online settings and presented formal models for reasoning about the impact that badges have on human behavior. This has utility for assessing the impact of badges in the design of social systems.

8.3.3 Machines

Automatic question-answering methods can be applied in addition to human question answering methods, either as an alternative to employing human labor or to complement the use of humans – allowing experts to focus on more challenging questions. If there are factoid questions that could be answered by a machine, this could reduce the overhead on human answerers, allowing them to focus on questions that are difficult to answer in a single answer or where more information or dialog are required to make progress. These systems could work by leveraging vast repositories of knowledge such as that available on the Web and beyond (e.g., *AskMSR* [Banko et al., 2002)]; *Watson* [Ferruci et al., 2010]). Moving beyond the machine-only approach, systems such as *SearchBuddies* (Hecht et al., 2012) provide direct connections between the human and machine Q&A. These systems first try to answer the question automatically using search engine technology, while also engaging social network contacts if an answer cannot be furnished by the system, or enrich an already-provided system answer with additional human perspectives.

8.4 Archiving Answers and Supporting Future Searching

Archiving the question-answering dialogs enables their use in creating knowledge bases and help future searchers while reducing the load on others and reducing answerer wait times. If an asker poses a question that has been asked on the system previously, that answer can be shown to the asker before the question is dispatched to recipients or while they wait for answers from humans (and askers can cancel the process of question distribution if they find the answer). This is common practice in systems such as Yahoo *Answers* (answers.yahoo.com), and other solutions such as *AnswerGarden* (Ackerman and McDonald, 1996). If the asker agrees that the archived dialog answers their question, then the question no longer needs to be distributed in real time to live experts. Doing this effectively requires that there be a way of accurately matching an incoming question against previously answered questions – including question semantics, which may be difficult to discern automatically. Because questions will likely be phrased as natural language, sophisticated matching algorithms that consider question semantics and the meaning of the answers that are provided are necessary. These stored dialogs also have utility in conversational understanding systems that can learn from dialogs and use this information to better respond automatically, and naturally, to human questions (Allen et al., 2001).

In addition, at question time, the asker can provide a rating on the quality of the answer (e.g., on a five-point scale from *not helpful* to *helpful*), and the answerer may wish to mark the location of the answer in the dialog and provide semantic tags for the dialog to support future retrieval by other searchers (Richardson and White, 2011). The answer ratings provided by askers can be reported to summarize system performance, but they can also be used to dynamically modify the ranking algorithm to better target questions to experts. For example, if an answerer frequently accepts questions on a particular topic but also receives low answer ratings signaling poor answer quality, then the system may not send such questions to those potential answerers in the future.

Rather than having humans involved in answering questions that are posed by searchers directly, there is also the opportunity for humans to be used in extracting factoid answerers from web pages that can be used to support future searching. Search engines now offer support directly on the search result page for a broad range of queries that extends beyond ranked lists of Web documents. Queries associated with topics such as weather, definitions, and movies may return "direct" or "instant" answers that can resolve a searcher's information need without any additional interaction (although this creates its own set of challenges regarding metrics; see my earlier discussion on good or bad abandonment [Chapter 3]). Despite the usefulness of answers, they are limited to popular needs because each answer type is manually authored by employees of the search engine, and resources are limited. Bernstein et al. (2012) introduced "tail answers" to cover long-tail needs such as the average body temperature for a dog, substitutes for molasses, and the keyboard shortcut for a right-click. Bernstein and colleagues employed a combination of search log mining and paid crowdsourcing techniques to create such answers, to help searchers with similar information needs, and extend the range of queries that search systems support directly.

8.5 Summary

I have discussed the role of collaboration in the search process, and the support for search using input from those known to the asker and outside their social network. Given that broad range of interests and expertise in online communities, this expertise may be leveraged to support searchers in both expressing their information needs and in resolving them through dialog (either synchronous or asynchronous). When involving external experts in the search process (who are often strangers be unknown to the asker), motivations such as reciprocity or altruism may be less effective, and other incentives become important. Monetary incentives may not be effective in the long term, primarily because answerers are motivated by factors beyond financial gain (Ling et al., 2005). Non-monetary reward mechanisms (such as badges to publically recognize answerers' skills) are often used to motivate answerers to participate, and importantly, maintain participation over time. Given scaling issues, there are also concerns about whether it is possible to offer real-time support to large volumes of searchers versus providing asynchronous support such as that available via question-answering Websites at which people are able to answer in their own time.

For real-time systems for which support is expected to be offered the moment that the searcher makes his/her request, there may be high costs involved in retaining a pool of answerers who are ready to furnish an answer or engage in follow-up dialog at a moment's notice. In addition, in developing the support in which we expect people to use new methods to locate search assistance (in this case other people), it is important that we integrate this support with existing systems (e.g., surfaced in response to complex queries or when searchers appear to be struggling). Too many collaborative search systems have been developed as standalone solutions that are forgotten about when they could be most useful. As a result, people often resort to tackling problems independently. Next-generation versions of these systems will need to be more closely coupled with existing search, productivity, and leisure applications for their potential value to searchers to be realized.

CHAPTER 9

Personalization and Contextualization

Earlier in the book, I discussed modeling various aspects of search behavior, such as the relevance of search results or searcher satisfaction with search systems. In this chapter, the focus turns to the process of modeling searchers' long-term interests (via personalization) and their current search situation (via contextualization). The personalization and contextualization of the user experience are increasingly important in search and recommendation systems, and enriching queries with this information facilitates the provision of individualized and situation-dependent experiences that will be commonplace in next-generation search systems, and are increasingly evident in today's search systems.

Information about searcher's interests and intentions can be used to tailor the search experience to individual searchers and to those in similar situations. Although limited to what situational information is visible to the search engine and affected by other limitations (such as profile size and log volume), rich models of search interests and their search situations can still be developed. In this chapter, I cover both personalization and contextualization; these concepts are often conflated in the research literature, they are but they are in fact quite different. I distinguish between them primarily in terms of the nature of the data used for model construction. Specifically, I define personalization and contextualization as follows:

- **Personalization:** Tailored to the individual searcher. Search systems may not be representative of individual searcher's information needs (Teevan et al., 2010), and personalization can help address this issue. Methods to support personalization are usually developed by modeling the *long-term* activity of individual searchers (e.g., search queries and clicks over a period of thirty days or more) to truly understand their interests. It is only by monitoring search behavior longitudinally that a truly individualized user profile can be constructed. Although some authors have regarded using within-session behavior as personalization (Daoud et al., 2009; Sriram et al., 2004), the data are often too sparse (just a few queries and document selections), and too task-specific, to adequately represent the searcher so that the search experience can be tailored to them. Because they rely on short-term interaction histories, such session-based models cannot impact the first query in the session (Bennett et el., 2012). Personalized models can be based on people's online activity over time, or other sources of data, such as files on the searcher's machine. Given the complexity and diversity of information needs, monitoring searches over such a long period means that any profile created will be unique and individualized to the current searcher. That is, it is highly unlikely that another searcher will issue the same queries in the same sequence and have an identical profile. If there is insufficient information about searcher interests, data from cohorts of similar searchers based on location, interests, or expertise can be used to address issues in data sparseness (White et al., 2013a; Yan et al., 2014). Data sparseness is directly related to the cold-start problem in recommender systems, where limited information is available to the system initially (Schein et al., 2002).

- **Contextualization:** Tailored to the search situation. Search systems may not adequately represent the context within which searches are performed, which is important in shaping search interaction (Ingwersen and Järvelin, 2005). Contextualization of information needs can help enhance the system representation of search intent beyond evidence gathered from queries and click data alone. Methods to support contextualization are usually developed via additional signals that are available to the search engine at query time. These include geographic location, time, and recent interaction behavior (representing the searcher's task-relevant interests). I choose to regard *recent* interactions as a contextualization signal rather than a personalization signal because the use of these signals is deterministic (i.e., anyone with the same preceding interactions will have the same tailored experience, and it is much more likely that many people could have an identical short-term interaction history than would share an identical long-term profile). Long-term profiles are likely to be distinct between searchers and reflect the interests and intentions of individuals. These long-term profiles are more appropriately viewed as a data source for personalization purposes.

Similar distinctions between contextualized and individualized signals have been observed elsewhere. For example, the *Outride* client distinguished between conditions occurring within the active search task (contextualization) and the characteristics that distinguish an individual searcher (personalization; see Pitkow et al. [2002]).

As a demonstration of the importance of these methods. Several mainstream Web search engines (Google, Yahoo!, Bing) have announced the application of personalization and contextualization of search results and search experiences more generally (e.g., personalized query suggestions [Shokouhi, 2013] and personalized advertising [Bilenko and Richardson, 2011]). As part of the efforts to introduce personalization into commercial search engines, there have been attempts to allow searchers to specify their interests directly to the search engine. Google *Personalized Search* allows searchers to explicitly describe their interests by selecting from a set of pre-defined topics. This information is used to promote pages related to those topics. *My Yahoo!* search provides searchers with the ability to save websites they like and exclude the sites that they explicitly dislike. Start-ups such as *SurfCanyon*[1] tailor Web search results and advertisements using Web browser plugins to adjust the results post retrieval.

In the remainder of this chapter, I discuss personalization and contextualization in detail, including describing the various processes involved in developing such models on both the client and server sides. The chapter concludes by discussing the need to consider explanations for what actions can be taken by the system on their behalf (e.g., reordering the top results) and user control (e.g., with recourse links).

9.1 Personalization

As described in the Introduction, personalization has the objective of individualizing the search experience to a particular searcher. This is important because different people have been shown to expect different results for the same queries (Teevan et al., 2005). Personalization requires tracking long-term behavior; it requires sufficient evidence of the *person's* interests to develop an individualized profile for them. Profiles can be based on their search history or other resources such as documents stored on the user's computer. I begin by covering some of the main personalization methods and research on understanding personalization efficacy, building profiles, improving data quality, and handling data sparseness. Although it is possible to build profiles based on explicit feedback about which items are personally relevant, I focus primarily on methods to infer personal relevance automatically given its general applicability and searchers' reluctance to provide feedback, for which there are many reasons, as discussed earlier in the book (Chapter 3). Although personalization is typically performed within a single search system or Web domain, personalization models that span multiple domains have also been developed (Low et al., 2011).

9.1.1 Potential for Personalization

The promise of personalization is search experiences tailored toward individual searchers' interests and intentions. The potential gains from personalization may not always be clear. Teevan et al. (2010) explored the *potential for personalization* – that is, the performance gap between returning results to satisfy an individual and how well they currently perform by returning results designed to satisfy everyone. They used three data sources: explicit relevance judgments, clicks on search results, and content-based signals from local documents. Using the explicit relevance judgments, they computed the performance in terms of normalized discounted cumulative gain (NDCG; see Järvelin and Kekäläinen [2002]) for results tailored to the individual, the group of participants in the study, and Web search generally (no personalization). The NDCG values of given different group sizes are shown in Figure 9.1. The potential for personalization – the gap between individual and group-based ranking – is also marked on the figure for reference.

The figure shows that with perfect personalization, the average NDCG for an individual is one. As more people's interests are considered in generating a ranking, the average NDCG for each individual drops for the ideal group ranking. The gap represents the potential value to be gained by personalizing the search results. There is also a gap between the current NDCG for the Web results and the best group ranking, which represents the potential improvement to be gained merely by improving results without

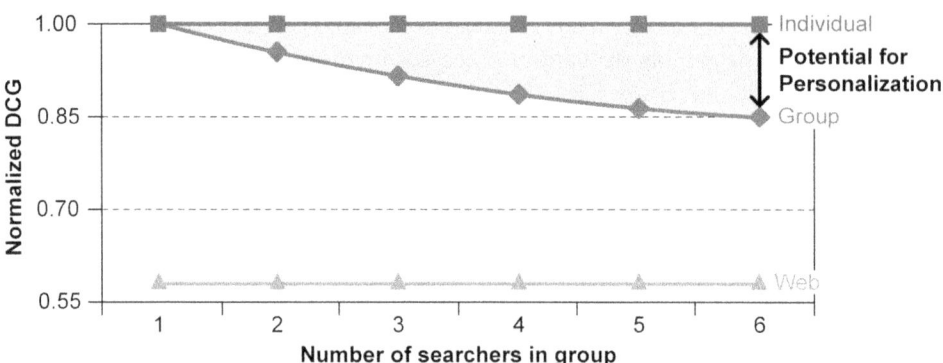

Figure 9.1. Variations in the search engine performance given different numbers of searchers' interests (adapted from Teevan et al., 2010).

consideration of the individual. It is clear from this important analysis that there is significant opportunity to improve the search experience through personalization.

9.1.2 Methods

Various personalization methods have been proposed. I present here some approaches grouped by the source of the searcher representation that they adopt, specifically: (1) document content; (2) queries and result selections; and (3) concepts or categories. It is important to note that, given our definition of personalization, research on leveraging *short-term* browsing context to improve search engine performance (e.g., Liebling et al., 2012; Ustinovsky and Serdyukov, 2013) is considered to be a contextualization signal and is discussed later in the chapter when interaction context is covered. As noted earlier, short-term behaviors are insufficient to represent the characteristics of the searcher, something that is required to individualize the search experience.

9.1.2.1 Document Content

Content-based methods rely on the extraction of terms from documents deemed relevant to the current searcher (e.g., files on the local machine) represented as weighted vectors. Because they rely on access to data of this type, content-based methods traditionally leverage client-side implementations. Teevan et al. (2005) explored the effectiveness of a personalized method using data stored on a searcher's local machine (documents, emails, etc.) and previous search interactions (queries and visited Web pages). Terms extracted from these files were deemed more personally relevant, and were used to re-rank the top-retrieved Web search results using standard retrieval methods (e.g., Okapi BM25 [Spärck-Jones et al., 2000]). Matthijs and Radlinski (2011) developed a Web browser plug-in to monitor Web browsing activity and deployed it to a group of technology specialists. They collected develop searcher interest profiles using keywords from titles of visited pages, as well as the body text, and metadata fields. Matthijs and Radlinski used this information to construct user profiles that could re-rank the top results from the search engine so as to promote the most relevant pages. These are just two examples of how document content can be used in personalization. Beyond documents, searches, and browsing activity (all considered traditional sources of evidence for personalization purposes), data from other sources can be used. For example, intelligent personal assistants such as Microsoft *Cortana* or Google *Now* also have access to information about a person's activities and interests via their calendar, electronic mails, and reminders – as well as inferences made about places of interest and their movement patterns (e.g., when they commute to work). Because such information is highly sensitive, most content-based personalization that leverages these and similar signals will occur on the client side, with only a minimal amount of anonymized data being sent to remote servers as required to serve search personalized results and retain search state over time, and across devices, domains, and applications.

Desktop search technology allows people to search over their own content, including Web browser histories, electronic mail archives, text documents, and multimedia content. Searching occurs using locally stored and generated indices of local files (filenames, metadata, and content in the case of supported file formats). There are a number of desktop search applications, including Google *Desktop Search*,[2] Windows *Search* (based on the *Stuff I've Seen* system [Dumais et al., 2003]), Apple *Spotlight Search*,[3] and *Beagle* for Linux.[4] There is also a tighter coupling between search and the operating system. Operating systems from companies such as Google and Microsoft allow searchers to engage with search providers via a number of modalities from anywhere on the operating system. This can be done reactively at the searcher's request, or proactively to surface content based on current/recent behavior or persistent interests. Such client-side search technology creates opportunities for the use of application context to model the current search situation in more detail, and for issuing search queries across documents, allowing for a much richer and more cohesive search experience. This contrasts with the status quo in search interaction and information use, where searchers frequently need to transition between applications, typically a Web browser or dedicated search application, to perform a search.

9.1.2.2 Queries and Result Selections

When personalization is performed remotely on the server it typically relies on behaviors observable to the search engine (e.g., historic queries and search-result clicks). A number of methods have been proposed that focus only on representing users in terms of their historic search behaviors (e.g., Sugiyama et al., 2004; Shen et al., 2005b; Sun et al., 2005; Dou et al., 2007; Teevan et al., 2011b). Shen et al. (2005) proposed a method to perform query expansion and result re-ranking based on implicit feedback collected from historic click-through from the same searcher. Terms for the query expansion process are derived from the captions of clicked results. Sun et al. (2005) presented an approach for handling the sparseness of click-through data by considering the relationships between searchers, queries, and documents; and the researchers applied a singular value decomposition to represent their associations. Dou et al. (2007) proposed *P-Click*, a method which which promotes the results previously visited by the same searcher for the same query. Teevan et al. (2011) proposed *personal navigation*, involving the promotion of documents visited multiple times by individual searchers for the same query. Although the query coverage of the personal navigation method is moderate, the method is also highly precise. The personal navigation method was inspired by re-finding research (as described earlier) and other related work on repeat

Table 9.1. *Interaction between repeat and new queries and result selection*

	Row Total	Repeat Selection	New Selection
Repeat query	33%	29%	4%
New query	67%	10%	57%
Column Total		39%	61%

searching and visitation to particular resources (e.g., Wedig and Madani, 2006; Teevan et al., 2007; Adar et al., 2008; Tyler and Teevan, 2010). Table 9.1 presents the interaction between repeated and new queries and clicks, derived from large-scale log analyses. The table shows that re-finding is common: 33% of queries are repeat queries, 39% of clicks are repeat clicks, and (importantly for applications such as personal navigation) 29% of clicks are on a previously clicked document for a prior query.

Moving beyond queries and clicks, Sugiyama et al. (2004) utilized searchers' full browsing history for personalization purposes. However, unlike the earlier work of Matthijs and Radlinski (2011), the research used the URLs of the pages accessed rather than the page content, meaning that the solution is more applicable at Web scale. Other research on resource preferences has shown that there can be other reasons, such as preference for particular domains (Ieong et al., 2012; Tyler et al., 2015), that drives searchers' decisions to select particular results from available alternatives.

9.1.2.3 Concepts and Categories

Rather than representing information needs based on the terms used to describe them, these can also be represented at higher levels of abstraction, such as concepts, ontologies, or categorical representations. These approaches typically convert the long-term search behavior of searchers into conceptual and/or categorical representations, improving coverage of personalization methods and facilitating fuzzy matching between queries, user profiles, and search results. The topicality of pages and queries can be automatically assigned using methods such as those proposed by Bennett et al. (2010). Such approaches have modeled people by classifying their previously visited Web pages in terms of sets of concepts (Liu et al., 2004), ontologies or topic hierarchies (Pretschner and Gauch, 1999; Gauch et al., 2003; Sieg et al., 2007; Speretta and Gauch, 2005; Qiu and Cho, 2006) or matching hierarchical category representations with their corresponding keywords (Liu et al., 2002; Chirita et al., 2005). Recent work has explored the application of these methods on large-scale data collected from search engines to build topical representations of searchers' long-term interests (e.g., Sontag et al., 2012; Bennett et al., 2012). Many of these methods leverage categorical representations such as the Open Directory Project (ODP)[5] to represent search interests, although other representations, such as entities from knowledge bases including Wikipedia[6] or Freebase[7] can be employed.

Beyond focusing only on search topical interests, it is possible to represent searchers in other ways that could be useful for building profiles for personalization. Estimates of searchers skill level as reading level (Collins-Thompson et al., 2011; Tan et al., 2012), domain expertise and topic familiarity (Kumaran et al., 2005; White et al., 2009b; Kim et al., 2012), and general search expertise (White and Morris, 2007) are all useful in this regard. In addition, rather than recommending content that the searcher may have previously considered (which has limited value for some types of task, such as those focused on discovery or exploration), knowledge of the historic context facilitates the provision of recommendations for novel content that the searcher may not have examined or used previously (i.e., helping the searcher find new information in addition to information with historic utility).

9.1.3 Application of Personalized Models

These different ways of representing long-term searcher interests are then used to tailor the search experience to the current searcher. In a retrieval setting, such as a search engine, there are two main applications: (1) re-rank the top-n search results based on the representation of interests, so as to promote documents that better match their interests; and (2) re-run the query over all the documents and employ the representation of searcher interests as part of the ranking algorithm to generate a new ranked list biased toward the individual searcher's interests.

Re-ranking is more conservative because it is a reshuffling of the top-ranked search results (which are presumably already highly relevant, at least topically). Because people inspect search results from top-to-bottom, even small modifications to the result lists may have a significant impact on task performance. The re-ranking can be performed on the client side (Sugiyama et al., 2004; Teevan et al., 2005) or the server side within the search engine (Sontag et al., 2012). As I describe later, re-ranking can also be used as part of a strategy to evaluate the performance of personalization algorithms offline, prior to deployment in a search engine. However, re-ranking has the quite significant drawback that result diversity – important in tailoring results to individual preferences – may be low. The second strategy described earlier – a new set of results are retrieved based on a combination of the current query and the personalized signal – is one way to increase result diversity.

Diversity and personalization are different ways to address the challenge of ambiguity in search queries (i.e., focus on a single intent [personalization] versus covering a range of different intents [diversification]). However, diversity also contributes to search personalization, and some progress has been made in this area, including the use of different query reformulation strategies (Radlinski and Dumais, 2006) or explicitly modeling searchers in existing result diversification methods (Vallet and Castells, 2012). Re-running a query (after personalized behavioral signals have been incorporated) can yield greater diversity of search results, but also more risk of non-relevance. This also requires the personalization to be more tightly connected to the ranking algorithm, which makes it more difficult to decouple and improve independently.

9.1.4 Beyond the Searcher Identifier

A central competency in any personalized experience is being able to associate the current and historic search activity with the correct person. This can be especially difficult on shared devices for which the actions of multiple searchers may be interwoven in the construction of user profiles. In online services, searchers are typically represented by a unique identifier associated with the Web browser or machine that they are using to access the service (e.g., based on IP address or Web browser cookie), allowing the remote system to tailor the search experience to individual searchers. However, shared machine usage is common (recent statistics suggest that 75% of U.S. households have a computer and in most homes that machine is shared between family members [File, 2013]), meaning that the search history of a single machine identifier may actually comprise the search histories of multiple searchers. This can be problematic for personalization because it results in the combination of multiple profiles when ideally we would be able to isolate individuals' search behavior. Recent work on activity attribution in the search domain (White et al., 2014b) has shown that it is possible to accurately attribute observed search behavior to the correct searcher and apply those models to enhance personalization performance (Singla et al., 2014b). More generally, it has been shown that attribution-based methods have the potential to significantly enhance personalization effectiveness (White and Hassan Awadallah, 2015).

9.1.4.1 Activity Attribution

There is scope for the development of algorithms to correctly attribute queries to searchers and improve personalized search and advertising through more accurate targeting (Singla et al., 2014b; White and Hassan Awadallah, 2015). The development of such models could involve clustering techniques to combine interactions from the same searcher and quantify the number of searchers utilizing a machine. White et al. (2014b) addressed three prediction tasks that could have significant utility for search systems in this area: (1) determining whether there are multiple users behind a single identifier, which could help decide whether it is worth employing potentially computationally expensive techniques to count the number of searchers querying from a particular identifier; (2) determining how many searchers there are connected to that identifier; and (3) assigning an incoming action to the correct searcher or searcher profile, allowing for more accurate utilization of their particular long-term search behavior for personalization (providing a cleaner signal than what is available from the full identifier alone). Being able to disentangle histories of queries allows systems to perform more focused personalization of search results or advertisements, among other applications. This could also help preserve searcher privacy, because it could limit the leakage of profile information (including query and browse histories) between searchers. The activity attribution process (as applied for personalization) is summarized in Figure 9.2.

Research on the attribution of search interaction shares some characteristics with research in other domains, specifically signal processing, acoustics, and language analysis. In fraud detection, the goal is to identify suspicious changes in a person's behavior, where observed activity may not be representative of their typical actions (Fawcett and Provost, 1997). In signal processing, blind signal separation (Amari et al., 1996; Cardoso, 1998) and instantiations such as independent component analysis (Comon, 1994) involve separating source signals from observed mixtures, typically the output of an array of sensors. Blind signal separation has been successfully applied in communication research (Anand et al., 1995), as well as in medicine (MacQueen, 1967). Rather than automatically attributing activity, the system can solicit confirmation

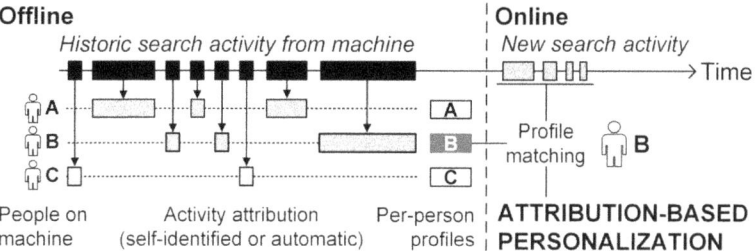

Figure 9.2. Personalization based on search activity attribution (adapted from White and Hassan Awadallah, 2015).

about the current searcher's identity if the confidence level in the attribution prediction is low. The attribution challenge is also evident in other domains such as on-demand movie recommendation, which can be made more challenging if profiles represent the combined interests of many viewers in the same household. Services such as Netflix use a profile for each viewer and require that each viewer sign in when they accessing the service. This is cumbersome and methods to automatically attribute activity to individuals is preferable.

9.1.4.2 Attribution for Personalization

Current applications of personalization assume a direct mapping between the observed behaviors on the searcher's machine and the current searcher (or at least that machine activity will be somewhat representative of the needs of the current searcher). The ability to more accurately attribute search activity to the correct *person* who is performing the searches at any point in time, can lead to more accurate personalization (White and Hassan Awadallah, 2015). However, in remote settings it may not be clear who is performing a search at a particular time, especially if the machine is shared between the activity of multiple people. At scale, current practice is to use unique identifiers assigned to the machine rather than the searcher to tailor the search experience. However, this may create noisy signals for applications such as personalization and tailored advertising. Previous work by White et al. (2014b) showed that when considering approximately two years' of search logs, more than half (56%) of the machine identifiers comprise multiple people.[8] Given activity attribution, search engines can individualize the search experience. Featurizing historic search activity at the person-level and the machine-level, and combining the two representations, has been shown to yields slight but significant improvements in personalization (Singla et al., 2014b).

9.1.4.3 Personas

Even within an individual searcher there could be differences in their preferences depending on their context of use. In different situations, people assume different personas depicting how individuals present themselves to the world (Jung, 1953). Searchers at work or at home may have dramatically different guises, which could affect how they present themselves to the search engine. In one example, physical location might be a good proxy for the different personas (e.g., home versus work [Nippert-Eng, 2008]). Traditionally, work is performed in a particular place (e.g., the office) and location labels can be estimated from patterns of geographic data (Krumm and Rouhana, 2013). In the current trend of remote work, however, search engines may need to complement location data with task information to decide when to apply particular personas. From a search system perspective, representing these personas in more detail facilitates a more accurate personalization by tailoring the search experience to a particular aspect of their searcher's profile.

9.1.4.4 Connecting Machine Identifiers

A challenge related in the activity attribution space is the transient nature of the machine identifiers used by search providers to develop profiles over time. These identifiers are often assigned based on Web browser cookies and deletions of those cookies (so-called cookie churn) over time can create challenges for personalization. Cookies can be cleared for a number of reasons: some Web browsers will clear cookies when the browser is closed, some users will delete cookies manually (to preserve privacy), and other cookies expire after a certain amount of time. A number of studies have shown that this affects a significant portion of online traffic, totaling around 30%.[9] In light of the value that access to longer-term profiles can provide for building models about individuals' interests and preferences, there have been successful attempts to associate multiple browser cookies with a single searcher, using methods such as graph coloring (Dasgupta et al., 2012). While this can lead to gains in personalization performance by providing more evidence about searchers' interests, their privacy preferences should also be respected; they may not want their long-term behaviors to be connected across identifiers if they took steps to explicitly disassociate themselves (e.g., by intentionally clearing their cookies).

9.1.5 Assessing the Value of Personalization

Methods to evaluate the performance of the personalization involve human labeling of a small set of queries (Teevan et al., 2005), utilizing the TREC query and document collection to simulate the personalized search setting, retrospective log analysis of clicks on search results (Dou et al., 2007; Gao et al., 2009; Bennett et al., 2012), or interleaving (Matthijs and Radlinski, 2011). Research into the potential for personalization (Teevan et al., 2005; 2010; discussed in Section 9.1.1) studied differences in explicit relevance judgments for the same query by different searchers, and showed that there was a large gap between how well search engines perform when trying to satisfy everyone versus tailoring the search experience to individual searchers. Building on this work, personalization has also been shown to perform particularly well for queries with high degrees of variation in their degree of repetition within a single searcher, as well as the nature of their search intentions, primarily operationalized in terms of result selection entropy (Dou et al., 2007; Teevan et al., 2008).

9.1.6 Beyond Topical Interests and Resource Preferences

The focus, thus far has been on personalization based on adapting to the topical interests of searchers and favoring resources that they have accessed previously. However, there are other ways in which search systems can tailor the search experience to the interests of particular searchers. This includes modeling searcher beliefs and applying those models to make determinations about which information to share. For example, search engines could favor information that supports a searcher's beliefs (e.g., offers a Democrat or Republican slant in response to queries on politically-sensitive issues), versus simply being topically relevant to their search request (e.g., on political issues in this case). Recent discussions on the so-called filter bubble have suggested that search engines may skew search results to particular perspectives, irrespective of reality (Pariser, 2011); an assertion supported by follow-on research (White and Hassan, 2014).

Search engine rankings also have political or social ramifications (Goldman, 2008). Research on biases in information retrieval (White, 2013; 2014) suggest that searchers' beliefs in outcomes should be factored into personalization, both as a way for search systems to validate their beliefs by providing supporting information, and as a way for these systems to direct searchers to the correct answers (i.e., emphasize veracity). The tradeoff between satisfaction and accuracy has been studied in psychology (Hart et al., 2009), but more work is needed on this tradeoff in retrieval settings. This also involves developing ways to model searchers beliefs as well as their interests, summarizing how information relates to their beliefs, and providing them with control over how the personalization algorithm balances veracity and belief validation during the search process. Related research in areas such as persuasion (Fogg, 2002) may also be useful in shifting searcher beliefs in some circumstances. One such case is when searchers may believe something that is known to be factually inaccurate (e.g., that vaccines cause autism). Given the prevalence of such issues, this raises a broad array of interesting and important questions about the role that search engines play in influencing people's beliefs, and the directions and views of society generally. For example, Epstein and Robertson (2015) showed that commercial search engines could manipulate their search results to influence the outcomes of elections. They presented biased search rankings (shown in such a way that searchers were unaware of the manipulation) that had a significant impact (a shift of 20% or more) on the voting preferences of undecided voters.

9.1.7 Balancing Risk and Reward

Personalization methods have focused on improving average effectiveness over generic baseline models that are applied across all searchers. These approaches typically improve average performance of search results relative to simple baselines, but they often ignore the important issue of robustness. That is, although achieving an average gain overall, the new models often hurt performance on many queries. Gains from personalization for some searchers and some queries, can be offset by losses for others. Search systems may wish to minimize the negative experiences that their users have, so this can limit the application of personalization operationally. Search systems need to consider the tradeoff between risk and reward to understand the costs and benefits of personalization. This is measured via metrics that gauge variance in search system effectiveness and can be depicted graphically in win-loss or risk-reward curves (Collins-Thompson, 2009). Figure 9.3 presents a win-loss histogram for a personalization method, in this case based on content complexity and searcher reading level (Collins-Thompson et al., 2011). On the x-axis, the histogram shows the number of positions that the single relevant result was moved because of personalization-based result re-ranking. "Hurt" means that the relevant result was demoted and "Helped"

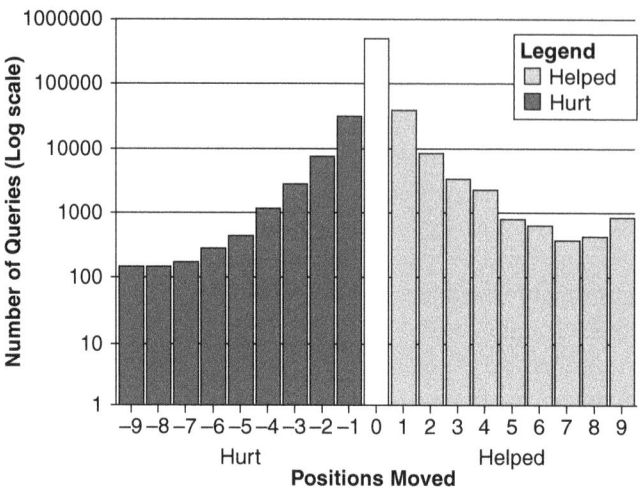

Figure 9.3. Histogram showing the variance of losses (left tail) and gains (right tail) using re-ranking by reading level. The loss or gain in rank position of the last satisfied click in the session (used as a relevance judgment) appears on the *x*-axis. The *y*-axis denotes the number of queries (note the log scale; adapted from Collins-Thompson et al., 2011).

means that result was promoted. The figure shows that the performance on most of the queries (82.7%) was unchanged, whereas the performance on 9.4% of queries was improved by personalization, whereas the performance on 7.8% of queries was degraded by personalization. This method yields a net positive gain, and performs well when re-ranking by six or more positions, with the ratio of helped being more than twice that of hurt in those occasions. A robust ranking algorithm is one that is able to achieve good average results, while having a minimal failure profile – measured in terms of the number of queries where re-ranking negatively impacts performance.

Mitigating risk in personalization is important. If a net-positive personalization method improves the ranking for 10% of queries by a large margin, then an experimenter may be fooled into believing that the model is performing well. However, if it is hurting the other 90% of queries (albeit by a much smaller margin – it would need to result in an overall improvement), then we would need to consider the viability of the method. To address the challenge of balancing risk and reward as part of the ranking process, Wang et al. (2012) devised a unified framework for jointly optimizing effectiveness and robustness. They proposed an objective that captures the tradeoff between these two competing measures and demonstrated that they are able to jointly optimize for these two measures in a principled learning framework. They showed through experiments that ranking models learned this way significantly decreased the worst ranking failures while maintaining strong average effectiveness on par with current state-of-the-art models. Beyond personalization, risk and reward can also be considered in a number of other settings, including in search engine evaluation (whereby a determination can be made about whether a search system exhibits risk and then identify the contributing topics; see Dincer et al. [2014]), during query expansion (Collins-Thompson, 2009), or search engine vertical selection (e.g., choosing between specialized search support such as news, images, and videos, or traditional search results; see Zhou et al. [2012]).

9.1.8 Searcher Cohorts

One significant drawback of personalization is that it relies on access to significant information about the searcher's interests, usually collected over a period of time either from their search behavior or from the contents of documents stored on their local machine (Teevan et al., 2005). If there is insufficient data available to represent search interests, then personalization may underperform given limited insight into that which searchers are interested. One way to address this challenge is by using *cohorts* of similar searchers. Cohorts in this context comprise groups of searchers who are similar to the current searcher along some dimensions. The value of cohorts for personalization has been demonstrated in small- and large-scale studies of search personalization (Dou et al., 2007; Teevan et al., 2011b; White et al., 2013a). Cohorts can be defined in a number of ways, and similar to the current searcher can be represented along one or more dimensions, including the queries that they issue and the Web sites that they visit. Teevan et al. (2009) explored the similarity of query selection, desktop information, and explicit relevance judgments across a small group of work colleagues grouped along two dimensions: (1) the longevity of their personal relationship; and (2) how explicitly the group was formed. They found that some groupings provide insight into what members considered relevant to queries related to the group focus, but that it can be challenging to identify valuable groups implicitly. White et al. (2013) addressed this issue by implicitly modeling the search task of the searcher, finding others who have attempted a similar task historically, and using their on-task behavior to enhance relevance. Although they used cohorts (location, topic expertise, and search engine entry point [i.e., the portal through which the searcher issued the query]) as part of their ranking experiments, they observed limited gain in their experimental setting and how they chose to model and integrate cohorts.

Data from the cohort can be combined with data that are available from the searcher and used broaden the range of different searchers for whom tailored search results can be offered. There are interesting challenges in how to combine data from the current searcher, that searcher's cohorts, and the generic ranking model (applied to all searchers). It may not always be the case that we want to apply the cohort models, because there may be cases in which we have sufficient information on a user's interests (e.g., in the case of personal navigation [Teevan et al., 2011b]) or in the case in which their interests are best represented by the dominant intentions of all searchers (e.g., queries with a very clear dominant intent) rather than specific subsets of the searchers, which may just fragment the document selection signals and reduce its reliability. Wang et al. (2014) described methods to automatically identify latent searcher groups and utilize different ranking features for each group. This builds on earlier research that automatically clustered queries and estimated independent ranking models for each of the query clusters (Giannopolous et al., 2011). Yan et al. (2014) devised methods to automatically identify cohorts of searchers. They used the result selection data from those in these cohorts to improve personalization.

As Yan et al. (2014) suggested, there are many ways in which cohorts can be modeled (people can be similar along a number of dimensions), including: (1) *topical interests*: searchers in topical interest cohorts may share similar interests (the topical interests can be determined in a number of ways, including using category classification); (2) *domain expertise*: searchers with similar levels of subject matter expertise within the same topic may be interested in the same resources; and (3) *search task*: people who have attempted similar tasks may belong in the same cohort, others may be able to learn from their on-task behavior at both the resource level (pages that people can access) and the strategic level (the techniques that other searchers employed to find relevant information). Mei and Church (2008) proposed the use of IP address as a way to personalize searching. That is, the system should back-off to the searcher's IP address if there is insufficient profile data. This works well if individuals are accessing the Web via an organizational proxy, assuming of course that people in the same organization have similar interests and expertise. The communication of strategies in a way that other searchers can comprehend is a challenging endeavor, although some research in this area has shown that it is possible to change user behavior by providing them with insights about how their search activity relates to other searchers, either search experts or the typical (average) searcher (Bateman et al., 2012). Irrespective of the specific cohort(s) adopted by a search system, the core principal is that systems find searchers who are *substitutable* for the current searcher in the absence of data from them, and *complementary* to the current searcher in the cases for which we have some data but a richer user profile with more comprehensive evidence could be applied.

9.2 Contextualization

Contextualization is closely related to personalization, but is tailored to the searcher's *situation* rather than the searcher themselves. That is, different searchers who are situated within the same context (e.g., issue the same queries and click on the same set of results over the course of a search session) experience the same contextualization irrespective of their long-term search history. The distinction between contextualization and personalization is often blurred in the research literature on mining and modeling search behavior. Contextualization occurs on a level that is invariant between searchers (e.g., location from which a query is issued, time at which the action occurs, and recent search interactions). As a result, all searchers with the same context should be presented with the same search experience; and it is quite feasible that many searchers will share such contexts, even those based on recent interactions. In contrast, personalization involves tailoring the search experience to an individual searcher and requires significant additional evidence of that particular searcher's interests and intentions, collected implicitly over a prolonged period of time (or explicitly in less time, should searchers be willing to be burdened with providing such information to the system and the system is able to collect, represent, and leverage that additional data effectively).

Historically, information-seeking behavior has largely been modeled in a context-free manner (Ingwersen and Järvelin, 2005). However, the relevance of such information depends on time, place, history of interaction, task in hand, and a range of other factors that are not given explicitly but are implicit in the interaction and ambient

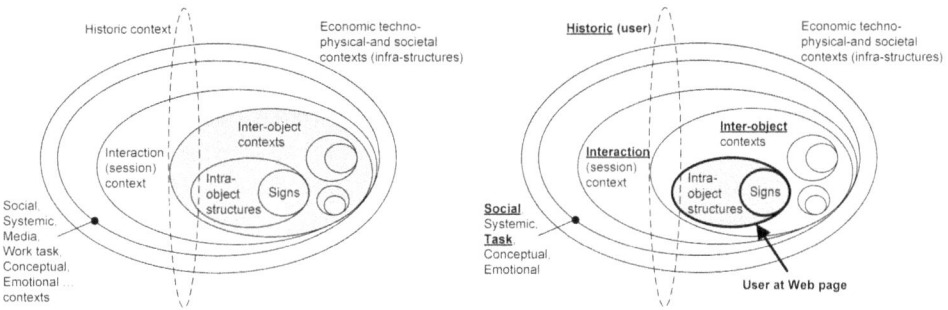

Figure 9.4. Nested model of context stratification for search (adapted from Ingwersen and Järvelin, 2005). The original model is shown, as is a modified version for the recommendation example from White et al., 2009a).

environment (namely, the context). Such contextual data can be used effectively to constrain retrieval of information, thereby reducing the complexity of the retrieval process.

Ingwersen and Järvelin (2005) proposed a nested model of context. The dimensions of the nested model represent the main contextual influences affecting people engaged in information behavior: (1) *object structures*: signs (i.e., discrete units of meaning), page features, and cognitive structures (searcher); (2) *inter-object contexts or structures*: between-object relations such as hyperlinks or citations; (3) *interaction context*: evidence of interaction behavior during the search session; (4) *social, systemic, domain-work task context*: peer group (social context), retrieval system (systemic), real work or daily-life tasks (task context); (5) *economic techno-, physical-, and societal context*: prevailing infrastructures that influence all elements in the nested model of context; and (6) *historic context*: the experiences of the cognitive actor (searcher) that affect how they perceive and interpret situations. Figure 9.4 visualizes the stratification of contexts, depicting the relationships between the different aspects. Such strata range from the traditional content features of and between information objects, such as words nested in paragraphs and hyperlinks, over eye-gaze and cursor movements during the search task, into the searcher's current work or daily-life task situation of which it forms part. The underlying hypothesis (and belief) is that by considering the context, a new generation of search systems, that are dependent on models of context, can be created, designed and developed, delivering performance exceeding that of context-insensitive search systems. Also shown in Figure 9.4 is a version of the context stratification adapted to a recommendation context (White et al., 2009a). In this example, the individual is visiting a Web page u_t, and the goal of the recommendation system is to present recommendations by utilizing contextual signals.

Much of the historic work in the area of context in search is theoretical, although there was some early attempt to capture and characterize contextual signals empirically (Cool, 2001; Cool and Spink, 2002). Contextual signals interact and it may require machine-learned models of the how different signals contribute and impact on one another to leverage them simultaneously. Recently, the pace and breadth of research in this area has quickened, focused on the development of context-sensitive models for both retrieval and recommendation (White et al., 2010; Bennett et al., 2011; Bennett et al., 2012). Retrieval operations are usually performed *reactively*, when a searcher specifies a query and the search engine can use information about the search situation to improve the search process. The latter is applied *proactively*, such as during Web browsing, where context can inform recommendations about other related resources or related actions.

I now describe some of the contexts leveraged in today's search systems. There are a number of other models of context, including those associated with searchers' cognitive and affective states, or infrastructures, that may be more difficult to model at scale, primarily given the limited data to which people have access.

9.2.1 Social Context

As discussed in Chapter 8, information seeking is rarely performed in complete isolation. While others may not be part of the search process directly, they are often involved in setting the objectives for the information search task as well as being the intended recipients for the information discovered, and decisions that have been made from it. Other people can also play a vital role in supporting searchers in completing their search task, through collaborative search activities or through traces of their behaviors and/or explicit ratings that can provide pointers to resources of interest, as is the case with search engines and recommender systems. The social context within which people perform their searches can have a significant impact on their search performance and can be a critical determinant of search success. As mentioned earlier, signals can be derived from searcher cohorts with similar interests, domain knowledge, or other attributes such as their location. Once these searchers have been identified and the cohort(s) for the current searcher identified, the social context can be filtered to only include similar searchers and apply the model for applications such as search engine ranking (e.g., White et al., 2013a). Given a document of interest, the social context can be operationalized as the combination of user profiles of all searchers who also visit that page, filtered to similar searchers if appropriate (White et al., 2009a).

9.2.2 Document Context

The document context can be interpreted in at least two ways: (1) the content of a document being examined by the searcher; or (2) the collections of documents within which the information is being sought. The content of the document currently being examined by the searcher provides useful insight into their interests and intentions, and can serve as a springboard for future queries. The content of these documents has been shown to influence future queries in predictable ways.

The collection can be heterogeneous or homogeneous, referring to the diversity of the types and content covered. The nature of the documents in the collection and their relationships to each other can play an important role in governing how people engage with that information and the types of information needs that people have when searching the collection. For example, people are likely to behave differently when searching a video or music collection than if they were searching a collection of free text or newswire documents. The relationships between documents can also be important in supporting navigation between pages (ranging from presenting hyperlinks to highlighting/prefetching next steps), quantifying the extent of the relationship between documents, and in determining which documents and/or document authors should be regarded as authoritative. The document context can be operationalized as the pages that link to that page (i.e., the external resources which implicitly endorse the page by creating a link from their resource to another). The documents that refer to the document being examined are often related to it. They can reinforce the ideas presented in the current document and provide additional relevant content to enrich the contextual signal.

9.2.2.1 Hyperlink Analysis

The hyperlink structure of the Web (and other large collections, such as organizational intranets) is incredibly complex and dynamic. The Web comprises billions of interconnected pages created and linked together, over time. The hyperlink structure of the Web has been analyzed in detail to understand its structure and a variety of other issues (Henzinger, 2001). Among the practical uses of the Web graph, a number of algorithms have been proposed to leverage the links between pages and use them to estimate the quality of pages on the Web, independent of query statements, including *PageRank* (Page and Brin, 1998) and *HITS* (Kleinberg, 1999). These algorithms regard the hyperlinks created between pages as implicit endorsements for those pages by the authors, and gives strong weight to landing pages that receive a large number of links from other pages when also considering the quality of those links, especially those links originating in a different Web domain, and considering issues such as reciprocity.[10] These methods focus on links generated by human authors of pages, rather than those generated by algorithms (e.g., in a SERP or other dynamically-generated content). The links are an important aspect of the Web search interaction experience, because they connect distal resources and provide a means by which people can traverse online content (e.g., following trails as described earlier in the book) and move rapidly between resources. The quality estimates for search results are used by search engines as query-independent *static rank* scores. In contrast, *dynamic rank* scores describe the strength of the match between queries and content, which are used as the basis for the query-dependent ranking of search results.

Additional information associated with the hyperlink, in particular the *anchor text* (i.e., the phrases on which people click, and potentially some of the content from before and after the link on the page) can be used as additional content labels for the target pages. Terms are chosen by the authors of pages and have been shown to succinctly reflect the concepts expressed in the pages and can therefore be useful metadata for ranking, but can also be abused, as examples of so-called "Google bombing" have shown. In these cases, large numbers of inward links with off-topic keywords have been created to point to specific sites for comical or satirical purposes. As discussed in Chapter 4, people navigating the Web also use the anchor text as cues (information scent [Chi et al., 2001]) for hyperlink click-through decisions, and support can be provided to help people decide which hyperlinks to select when navigating collections (Olston and Chi, 2003).

9.2.3 Task Context

The task that the searcher is performing is broader than simply the query that is being entered. That said, the query statement is often all that the search system sees about the task. Given this limited knowledge the system must make inferences about searcher intentions (e.g., assuming the dominant search intent in the absence of additional personal or contextual signals). One data source that has been proven to be useful are the resources accessed by others attempting the same search task, where task can be represented in terms of the search queries issued (Joachims et al., 2002; Agichtein et al., 2006) or more richly (e.g., in terms of domains, topical categories, and queries [White et al., 2013a]).

There are a number of ways in which the pages encountered by searchers attempting similar tasks are identified. White et al. (2009a) used co-clicked results to construct task models. This approach is useful for other tasks such as query suggestion (Beeferman and Berger, 2000; Craswell and Szummer, 2007). Related queries identified via this mechanism represent interests of those engaged in similar tasks, hence it could help the current searcher identify task-relevant resources.

Rich models of the search context can be developed, allowing search systems to compare the search tasks attempted by different searchers and find others who have attempted similar tasks based on similarity between resources accessed and even between search behaviors (if the goal is to find searchers attempting similar search tasks, irrespective of the topic of the search; as mentioned in the discussion of task expertise in Chapter 7). White et al. (2013) modeled search tasks based on features of the queries and resources accessed, including their topical characteristics. Task models are built from the current searcher's activity and other searchers' activity; the latter is mined from search engine log data. Model similarity can be used to find situations where people are attempting similar search tasks and use their on-task behavior to improve relevance. Because the matching is performed based on task models (which include the domains of resources accessed, as well as topical categorizations of those resources) rather than query text, these methods offer better coverage of the range of information needs than the traditional query-based methods (e.g., Joachims, 2002; Agichtein et al., 2006) alone. More generally, tasks can be extracted from other sources (such as electronic email communications) in which people may make requests or commitments to perform some action (Corston-Oliver et al., 2004).

Although the task models covered in this section contain the search topic as a central element in the similarity matching. However, it is feasible that some aspects of task knowledge are transferrable across the different subject areas (e.g., strategies employed in tackling task A in subject area Y could be applied when attempting the same task in subject area Z). Mining these strategies from log data requires topic agnostic representations of search activity. String representations of activity sequences (sometimes referred to as "motifs") have been used in a number of related studies to depict search activity more generally (Fox et al., 2005; White et al., 2007; Downey et al., 2007; Lagun et al., 2014). This facilitates the identification of salient sequences of search interaction behavior using methods such as clustering (Cadez et al., 2003) and more sophisticated sequence mining techniques (Laxman et al., 2008). Clusters can then be used to group searchers based on the search strategies that they employ (e.g., into groups of navigators, explorers, and other searchers [White et al., 2007]).

9.2.4 Interaction Context

The interaction context contains the previous interactions from the current searcher, typically from within the current search session, although the time frame could be longer or could be more tightly focused (e.g., for the current *task* rather than the current session; see Lucchese et al. [2013b] and Liao et al. [2012]). The interaction events often comprise queries and result selections, although additional information such as browsing behavior can also be used, depending on what is available to the system at recommendation time.

There are two main types of pre-search interaction context: (1) *search context*, and (2) *browsing context*.

9.2.4.1 Search Context

The search context comprises interactions with the search system directly, including queries, result clicks, and other functional interactions such a paginations and quick-backs (some of which may be indicative of searcher dissatisfaction). This information can be used to generate new result sets or alternative query statements based on topical interests expressed in the prior queries and resources visited. There has been a significant amount of research, with a focus on using recent interactions for applications such as contextualizing the search experience (Xiang et al., 2010; Bennett et al., 2012). Xiang et al. (2010) developed heuristics to promote search results with the same topical category if successive queries in a search session were related by general similarity and were not specializations, generalizations, or reformulations. Bennett et al. (2012) studied the tradeoff between using short- and long-term activity data to tailor the search experience to the search situation and the searcher specifically. Figure 9.5 illustrates some of the findings from their study, specifically variations in the performance (reported in terms of gain in mean average precision over a commercial search engine ranking algorithm) by featurizing aspects of the observed search activity in different ways: session, historic (i.e., before the current session), aggregate (session+historic), and union (session+historic+aggregate). Figure 9.5a shows that the more information you have about a searcher's on-topic interests, the better the system can perform (increase in the mean average precision gain over baseline from left to right). Figure 9.5b shows that the utility of long-term information (historic) decreases as the number of queries in a session incease.

Many search engines store recent queries, allowing them to perform offline analysis of search sessions, identify candidate query suggestions, improve search-result ranking by considering query chains, and so on. Session information, even just the previous query and its associated clicks, can be useful in building more complete models of search intentions than the current query alone. This information can then be used to improve the relevance of search results and inform recommendations, and has recently been explored in depth (e.g., Bennett et al., 2012; Shokouhi et al., 2013). Tasks such

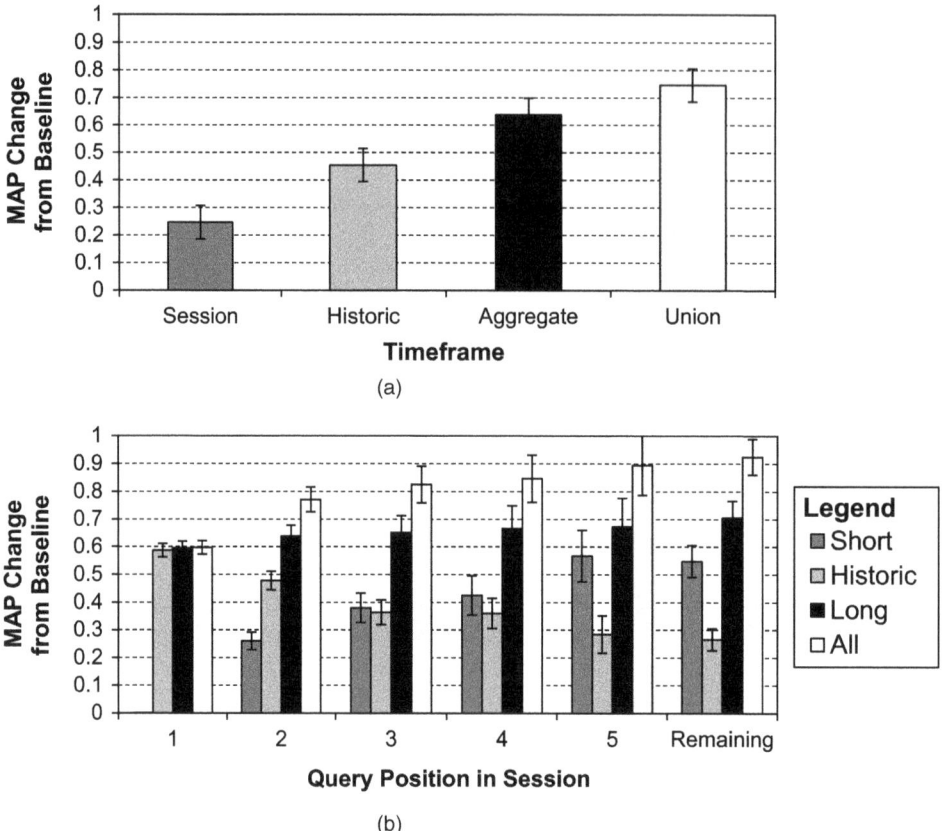

Figure 9.5. (a) Gain over non-personalized baseline for contextualization based on features generated at different temporal granularities. (b) Variations in performance of the models depending on the query position within the session (adapted from Bennett et al., 2012).

as improving the relevance of search results by considering previous queries in the session or predicting future interests at different levels of temporal granularity (next hour, next day, and so on). Some of the core ideas in modeling intentions involve representing search activity in a way that is comparable between searchers, to facilitate the development of models that can learn to contextualize.

Location and temporal information are available for the current query at minimal expense to the search engine. However, leveraging search histories are more costly. This requires the engine to be able to locate the history for the specific searcher in a few milliseconds following receipt when the query. Practically, this requires that searchers' profiles be compact and be stored in memory on servers or in rapid access data stores (such as Berkeley DBs [Olson et al., 1999]). Given large numbers of searchers, there may be a strict limit on the amount of information about individual searchers histories that search engines can store and serve for use in tailoring the search experience at query time (e.g., the last 200 queries or activity from the last 28 days). Search providers need to function within these and similar operational constraints, and yet still serve large numbers of searchers in a fraction of a second. This demonstrates the significant challenges associated with developing search systems for deployment at scale.

9.2.4.2 Browsing Context

There are three types of browsing context that all of particular interest: (1) *pre-search* browsing context; (2) *post-search* browsing context; and (3) *general* browsing context.

- **Pre-search browsing context:** Browsing activity in the time immediately preceding engagement with a search engine. This could be the page immediately before the search engine query (Liebling et al., 2012) or the sequence of pages that come before the query (Ustinovsky and Serdyukov, 2013). This could be monitored by the search engine using a toolbar plugin or by monitoring the referrer document (if available) to learn which resource that the searcher visited prior to visiting the search system. If the pre-search page is available, then its content can have utility in augmenting the current query and help better model searcher interests.
- **Post-search browsing context:** Browsing occurring after a query can be contextualized by both the preceding documents and the preceding query statements.
- **General browsing context:** The browsing context can be used to generate output for prospective recommendations at any point, irrespective of whether they are engaging directly with a search engine. Rather than relying on the presence of a query, recommendations can be made based on browsing context alone. In this case, the recommendations may be applied to the recommendation of alternative information resources rather than directly impacting the search experience, as would be the case with result re-ranking or query suggestion. Two examples of this in practice are the Internet Explorer (IE) "Suggested Sites" feature (which recommends websites of potential interest to searchers, supporting them as they explore and learn about a topic of interest) and the IE "Flip Ahead" feature (which pre-fetches Web pages that people are likely to visit next, reducing page load times associated with network latency and improving the navigation experience).

Although the focus has been on search queries and hyperlink clicks, *any* recent interactions can form the interaction context for the current search query, including swipes and scrolls on touch-enabled devices, spoken dialog, and gestural interactions. The challenge lies in (1) interpreting interaction signals in a meaningful and useful way, and (2) decoupling the signals connected to search intentions from those connected with specific interface affordances such as pressing the "Next" button, which is artefact of how the search systems choose to present search results but reveals little about search intentions (except perhaps that the intention may be difficult to satisfy and offers insight about the performance of the result ranking algorithm).

9.2.5 Physical Context

Intentions can vary with physical location. To support searching in settings for which location matters, search systems can leverage searcher location in selecting and re-ranking search results. The utility of this approach depends on geographic locations also being associated with particular search results, and the distance between the searcher's location and the results can be used as a ranking feature. Alternatively, people can explicitly express their location preferences in query statements (e.g., [*pizza new york*]), providing a reference point from which locations in documents can be determined. The locations associated with documents can be computed in a number

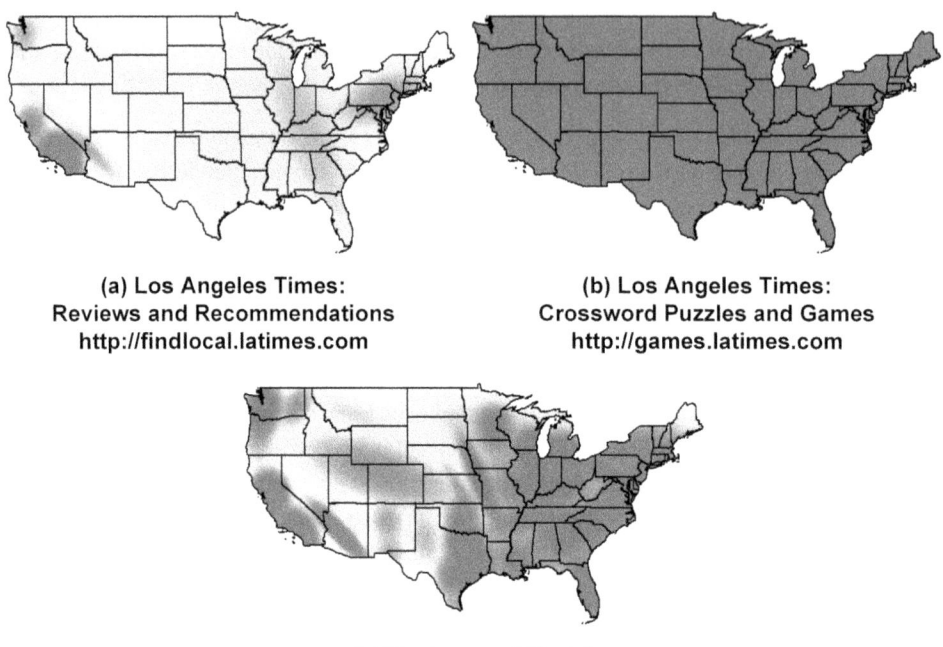

Figure 9.6. Example of location density estimates: red indicates higher density, orange and yellow indicate lower densities. For two results returned for the query [*la times*] and the population background model (adapted from Bennett et al., 2011). (See color plate 9.6.)

of ways, including identifying locations from the page content (Martins et al., 2010), assigning documents to geographic scopes (Amitay et al., 2004), and considering geographic relevance (Andrade and Silva, 2006; Jones et al., 2008). Recently, there has been significant research on large-scale usage data containing the locations of searchers who are accessing those documents (Mei et al., 2006; Zhuang et al., 2008; Bennett et al., 2011; Lymberopoulos et al., 2011). Incorporating location (even simply a U.S. state rather than the entire country), or distance between the searcher and the business can significantly improve the accuracy of result click-through predictions (Lymberopoulos et al., 2011), and that the distance between the current location and a business, can affect click-through rate in local search (Lv et al., 2012).

The location of searchers of an online service can be determined using a variety of mechanisms, including Global Positioning System (GPS) coordinates for mobile devices, and reverse IP lookups. This allows the computation of a measure of location interest for each document, which can be valuable because not all documents related to a specific location are equally location sensitive (e.g., people searching for [*picturehouse cinemas*] are likely to be interested in the closest such location, whereas those searching for [*disneyland*] may not necessarily be interested in the closest Disneyland theme park). Such usage information is used to compute probability distributions for query-document pairs similar to that shown in Figure 9.6. The figure shows that probability that searchers in different locations are interested in different sections of the Los

Angeles Times newspaper. Figure 9.6 shows that the local news section is of interest primarily to people in the greater Los Angeles area, but the crossword section of the newspaper is frequently accessed by users from across the United States. This suggests that a searcher in Miami issuing the query [*la times*] is relatively more likely to be seeking the crossword section than the local news section desired by a searcher in Los Angeles. Distributions such as this can also provide utility for other purposes such as identifying the nature of the service areas for websites of interest. Such distributions can be applied for the purpose of contextualizing the query given the searcher's physical location at query time (Bennett et al., 2011).

Other research has also studied the connection between location and interest. Mei et al. (2006) used the geography of Weblog authors to model spatial patterns of news topics. Wang et al. (2005) presented a method to automatically determine the dominant locations of search queries by mining the top-ranked search results and/or query logs. They tackled the problem of detecting provider, content, and serving location based on content features of Web pages, hyperlinks, and queries. Mei and Church (2008) used IP addresses to group searchers, and locations associated with IP addresses are frequently used for geocoding.

The location at the time of searching provides an important contextual signal. Location can be studied at the town or city level (as in [Bennett et al., 2011]), but can also be examined based on the nature of the location (e.g., the type of facility at which the searcher is located at query time). Examples of this include home versus elsewhere (West et al., 2013b; Krumm and Rouhana, 2013) or at or near a medical facility (Hong-Yang et al., 2013; White and Horvitz, 2013b). In these studies, the nature of the location was shown to impact search behavior. The studies revealed patterns such as: searchers were more likely to search for adult material while at home and were more likely to search for medical information while at a medical facility.

Much of the information about exact location relies on GPS coordinates from the phone. Other inferences can be made about the nature of the location without relying on mobile search logs encoded with GPS information. For example, based only on time of day and day of week, and observed patterns in the aggregated search behavior of many searchers, we can make inferences about whether a user is at home or at work at the time a query is received (e.g., if a query is made between Monday and Friday and between 9 AM and 5 PM, it is more likely to be received from an office location). This additional information on queries' potential locations could be used to custom tailor the results that users receive. This demonstrates the importance of considering not only the geographic location, but also the types of locations within which searchers may reside at the time the query is issued. Other location context information, such as the searchers with whom they are co-located at search time, may also reveal important details on the search task (Reis and Church, 2013; Teevan et al., 2014b).

Search can be affected by many aspects of the physical environment. Given the potential for this context to change quite dramatically in mobile settings, mobile search is particularly affected by the physical environment. The situation at the instant that the query is received, coupled with movement information (e.g., speed or direction of travel) can impact search behavior. In considering the role of physical context, we need to move beyond interactions with search system to also consider decisions and actions in the real world. Many searches are performed to inform choices that people make and real world actions that they perform – that is, the search itself is not the intended goal (although there are exceptions, e.g., recent work on "casual leisure search" [Elsweiler et al., 2011]).

Recent research in health information seeking (White and Horvitz, 2010) has demonstrated that people will quite often transition from searching the Web on a health topic to the pursuit of professional care. In doing so, they will issue queries designed to locate in-world medical resources (e.g., [*cardiologist 98072*]). White and Horvitz referred to these as healthcare utilization intentions (HUIs). These and similar transitions will become increasingly important as more of search is performed is situ on mobile devices (e.g., as seen earlier when I discussed cross-device search). Understanding the nature of these transitions and building tools to support them can enable a range of different services. West et al. (2013) used geotagged query log data (specifically address searches) to show that a search system can predict with high accuracy that a searcher is going to visit a particular business. With this capability, search systems can help searchers be more efficient in their daily lives. For example, given a high-confidence prediction that the searcher will visit a particular location, the system can create a virtual list of action items to perform at nearby businesses (e.g., a prediction that a searcher will visit a bank can be accompanied by recommendations to visit the grocery store across the street to pick up milk, and mail a letter at the post office next door). This relies on having access to information about pending events from which to compose such a list. Next-generation search systems, especially intelligent personal assistants, already have access to information about pending tasks and calendar appointments that could be combined with these predictions. Systems such as *Predestination* (Krumm and Horvitz, 2006) and *FarOut* (Sadilek and Krumm, 2012) make predictions about people's intended destinations based on short- and long-term movement trajectories and historic mobility data. Combining models of human motion with models of intention from queries will undoubtedly lead to better predictions about future behaviors.

Beyond the current geographic location of the device, there are other aspects of the physical context that may have utility for searching. If the searcher is traveling at the time that they engage with the search system, then they may well be seeking information pertaining to their planned destination (Teevan et al., 2011a). The proximity of the device to other search-enabled devices may reveal something about the likelihood of switching devices (Montañez et al., 2014). Other information, such as long-term location preferences, can be used to estimate the likelihood of them visiting locations visited previously, but more interestingly, the likelihood of them visiting new destinations based on trends in the data and location properties (Krumm and Horvitz, 2006). The nature of the current destination can also be inferred from diary data (e.g., home versus work [Krumm and Rouhana, 2013]). Recent work on automatically labeling the ambience of locations (Wang et al., 2014a) points toward the provision of richer signaling about the nature of the environment in which the search is being performed, which can be used to classify the type of business (e.g., mall vs. coffee shop; see Chon et al. [2012]), and for localization purposes (Azizyan et al., 2009).

9.2.5.1 Leveraging Resource Locations

Location information assigned to documents by automated processes can be useful. The location information can be used in other ways to identify instances of travel or to find regions of interest in or around particular locations.

9.2.5.1.1 Remote Location

The focus in this chapter has been on leveraging the location of the searchers to tailor online experiences to their needs. The searcher, however, might not always be searching from the location in which they are interested. For example, they may be planning an upcoming trip and wish to favor locations pertaining to a distal location, or they may be on a trip and wish to favor resources related to their designated home. By leveraging resource geotagging we can learn about the remote location that the searcher is interested in at a particular time using selected resources, and tailor the presented information to that location. Tracking such remote locations over time allows search systems to generate models of travel preferences that inform other aspects, including recommendations for events and activities in frequent destinations for the searcher.

9.2.5.1.2 Personal Location Preferences

As discussed earlier, location information determined using reverse IP lookups can be inaccurate. There are a number of reasons for this, including inaccuracies in the lookup database and the size of the city in which the searcher resides (for larger cities, the latitude and longitude of the city center may be a less useful proxy for the searcher's current location in the absence of more accurate location data). If search systems observe the searcher at the same location repeatedly we can build a profile of their location preferences (e.g., a particular borough of a city of interest) based on their behavior and use that information to provide a revised location estimate that is more accurate than that available from IP address alone. Such *personal location preferences* could be useful for a number of applications where there is significant uncertainty in location data.

9.2.5.2 Knowledge of Surroundings

Rather than focusing on the geolocation of searchers at query time, knowledge of their immediate surroundings may also serve as useful information to contextualize searches. Mobile systems can use this information to guide searchers' movements through physical spaces (e.g., as a tour guide for tourists [Abowd et al., 1997; Cheverst et al., 2000]). Within fixed settings such as a meeting rooms or homes, search systems can leverage additional information about the nature of the setting to tailor the search experience. In one application, *Kinect*-enabled devices could observe the room in which the search is being performed and apply facial recognition to identify other people in the room or apply optical character recognition to recognize visible text (e.g., the spines of books on bookshelves) to serve as additional context for the current search activity. Smartphones are now equipped with similar capabilities: they can recognize and translate text (Petter et al., 2011; as discussed in Chapter 5), and construct three-dimensional models of their environment for use in applications such as navigation, gaming, and construction (e.g., easily obtaining room dimensions for a home remodeling project;

Figure 9.7. Modeling indoor environments using a Google *Tango* device. (See color plate 9.7.)

see Sankar and Seitz [2012]). If the data is tagged with room information (e.g., living room, kitchen), it can be used in richer models of search context and search intentions.

Recent research has examined spatial mobility (Biczok et al., 2014) and the influence of indoor spatial context (e.g., location within large indoor spaces and similar indoor locations) on information seeking (Ren et al., 2014). There should be much more research in this area. The mobility of smartphones also allows peoples' trails through indoor spaces to be recorded, allowing them to retrace their steps through unfamiliar environments, be aggregated across many searchers to understand the geometry of buildings and construct accurate indoor maps of buildings across the world (e.g., to provide more complete travel directions that extend beyond the street level currently supported in many mapping applications; see Gao et al. [2014]), or support object detection and search (Heitz and Koller, 2008). Figure 9.7 shows an example of indoor modeling using a Google *Tango* device that can share human sense of space and movement, and that understands and perceives the world the same way as humans. Related research in the area of *active badges* (Want et al., 1992) is also relevant, but is primarily focused on locating people rather than leveraging their situational context to enhance search performance.

9.2.5.3 *Local Knowledge*

Local knowledge describes an understanding of a particular location gained through experience with it. A national U.S. survey showed that people spend more than two hours per day in everyday places in their vicinity, including restaurants, malls, and health clubs (Klepis et al., 2001), affording ample opportunity to gain experiences that are useful in both identifying candidate places and distinguishing between places

(Ludford et al., 2007). Antin et al. (2012) showed that more than half of the respondents to an online survey claimed to have both local knowledge and personal investment in their local area. Research has focused on finding general topic experts in forums, question answering sites, and online communities (Zhang et al., 2007; Liu et al., 2005; Chi, 2012). However, because studies have shown that one quarter of Web search queries have local intent (Himmelstein, 2005), people's local experiences may also bring significant benefit to others searching for local information or afford search personalization based on search engine estimates of a searcher's local know-how. Despite the potential benefit of local knowledge to non-locals, it may be tacit and undocumented, and therefore challenging for search systems derive practical value from, unless they can involve local experts directly in the search process to answer queries for which there is little or no information available in other sources. Such human-in-the-loop systems were discussed in Chapter 8. One example of such a system is *Aardvark* (Horowitz and Kamvar, 2010), which fielded a large number of questions related to local recommendations, a subject that local experts may be skilled at handling.

There has been research on capturing and leveraging local knowledge. Wu et al. (2011) mined Google *MyMaps* data and found that locals and non-locals referred to different landmarks in New York City when creating personalized city maps. Locals focused on daily life activities and newly blooming neighborhoods whereas non-locals focused on tourist destinations and activities. The authors also presented promising early findings from using collaborative filtering to generate recommendations via map co-occurrence. Ludford et al. (2007) created a location-based reminder system, *Place-Mail*. The authors identified the heuristics that people use when deciding which place information to share and how these findings relate to the design of local knowledge sharing systems, and they identified new uses of place information. White and Buscher (2012b) mined aggregate search log data to identify locals and non-locals. Locals were defined as those for whom all of their page visits in a one-month period came from a single geographic location. Their analyses revealed differences in the interests and intentions of the two groups, and these differences were more pronounced when the distance from home location was considered. The authors also showed that locals made different resource consumption decisions, in the context of restaurant visitations: selecting restaurants that were more highly rated than those chosen by non-locals. Beyond search logs, local knowledge has also been mined from social media data using the spread and focus-based proximity of the core audience for their social media postings (Cheng et al., 2014).

Given access to signals regarding local knowledge at an individual or aggregate level, systems can take action to enhance the search experience, including:

- **Personalizing to local interests:** Because locals and non-locals frequently seek different information about the same location. Search and recommendation systems could be personalized based on whether a user is a local, perhaps by applying a ranking algorithm giving differential weight to tourist sites. Differences in searchers' interests per their distance from the target location, means that search systems could also leverage distance between a searcher's primary (not

necessarily current) location and the target as a ranking feature or as a trigger for showing local event information or social recommendations (e.g., local friends' suggestions).
- **Leveraging local knowledge:** The lower quality ratings for the restaurants that non-locals intend to visit underscore the need for better support for non-locals' selection of local venues and activities. To help, we could highlight local favorites to non-locals directly on SERPs for local queries or leverage the search behavior of locals mined from search log data to improve the quality of the results returned for local queries.

Beyond technological augmentations, there are also important social implications from leveraging local knowledge that must be considered. For example, directing non-locals to popular local attractions may turn local gems into tourist hotspots, reducing their appeal over time. It is arguable whether search systems need to consider such factors when designing their algorithms, but more broadly, search providers need to be cognizant of the impact of their systems on the physical world and work with stakeholders to address any relevant concerns.

9.2.6 Application Context

As mentioned earlier, the act of searching is often associated with other applications linked to the creation or use of content. Next-generation search systems will have an awareness of this context. That is, search systems will have knowledge that it is running alongside other applications and be able to use that information as context to enhance the current search experience. Another example of where the context surrounding search will become important is its use in supporting other applications such a productivity suites. The application context within which search is initiated – be it a word processing application, a Web browser, or a dedicated search application – reveals some information about the interests and intentions of the searcher at that point in time. A similar model could be applied for the device that is currently being used. The fidelity of this information could vary dramatically from information about which applications are running, total usage time, and time of last access, to the specific content of the documents that are being composed at the time that the search is performed. If any sensitive information is shared remotely then appropriate privacy safeguards are required and searcher consent is needed.

Rather than relying on client-side software to capture application context, a contextual signal could be derived from content stored in the cloud. People may be observed switching between Web applications, invoking the search from inside an application, or copying the output of a search to another application. Beyond searching for an information fragment to support knowledge creation, the integration of search with other activities, even just managing personal information in email inboxes has changed how information is retained and largely removed the need for the explicit practice of personal information management (Cutrell et al., 2006; Jones, 2007). System awareness of the context of use may also help. A common example is when a searcher is turning to a search engine during a presentation or sharing their screen with other searchers. In such cases, the system may benefit from knowledge about the context of use (e.g., in presentation mode and sharing), and exclude features such as searcher's query and click history, which could be considered a privacy risk, especially if shared broadly in a public forum.

9.2.7 Temporal Context

Time-aware information access is emerging as an important area of research in the search and data mining communities. Research in this area has focused on a number of temporal aspects, including behavioral dynamics of populations of searchers over time (Radinsky et al., 2013), with applications for tasks such as query auto-completion (Shokouhi and Radinsky, 2012). Trend analysis of Web searches have shown both an overall popularity of particular resources, and a shift in how frequently people look for online information (Sellen, et al., 2002). Studying longitudinal trends in online search behavior within and between users can be useful for understanding searchers' in-world activities (Richardson, 2008; Choi and Varian, 2012), with applications in healthcare at both the population level (Ginsberg et al., 2009) and the individual level (e.g., in dealing with recent diagnoses [Schwartz et al., 2006]). Other data sources, such as long-term news corpora, can be used effectively to predict future events (Radinsky and Horvitz, 2013). Time is also an important aspect of evaluation, with emerging methods focused on information gained over the course of the search session (Järvelin et al., 2008; Smucker and Clarke, 2012). Urgency may also affect relevance (Saracevic, 1997), but these evaluation metrics do not consider urgency directly.

Time has been discussed as a fundamental attribute of the situation or context in information seeking, a qualifier of access to information (in terms of constraints such as urgency), and an indicator of the information-seeking process (in terms of stages or cycles; see Savolainen [2006]). Time is an important *contextual* factor in searching for a number of reasons. Because all queries received by the search engine, and all logged queries, will have an associated timestamp, time awareness is less expensive to attain than other contextual factors. Until recently, the importance of time in retrieval systems has been underappreciated. However, both document collections (especially collections of social media content, but also other content on the Web such as news articles), and information needs are dynamic, changing at different levels of temporal granularity as people are exposed to content or as their task requirements alter in light of external factors (Elsas and Dumais, 2010; Kulkarni et al., 2011). Previous work has shown that the content of most Web pages changes over time (Adar et al., 2008). The results that a person receives may only have value if they are found within a particular time (e.g., when the searcher is under time constraints), or if results pertaining to a particular time are returned (results have temporal relevance).

9.2.7.1 Freshness

Freshness describes the recency of the content presented to searchers during the search process. There is a need to consider both freshness *and* relevance when considering the effect of time in result ranking (and perhaps even jointly optimized for these as part of the ranking procedure). Freshness is important for some time-sensitive queries that are linked to annual events such as scientific conferences, award shows (Oscars, Grammys, etc.), or sporting events (Superbowl, March Madness). When searchers query for these events without specifying the date explicitly in the query (which is the most common scenario observed in search engine logs) they expect the search engine to return the *most recent* results (pertaining to the current year in the case of an event) at or near the top of the ranked list. Dong et al. (2010) proposed a classifier to detect recency-sensitive queries. Others have proposed temporal document selection features that capture a spiking interest in a query (result set) pair (Inagaki et al., 2010). Research on *concept drift* seeks to detect changes in search behavior associated changes in the intent connected to a search query over time (e.g., searchers seeking information on a conference will be less satisfied with the previous year's website when the next year comes around; see Kiseleva et al. [2014]). Accurate detection of such situations has applications in areas such as search satisfaction modeling, query auto-completion, and recency ranking. Achieving this involves a combination of factors, including crawling and indexing strategies employed by the search engine, to ensure that the latest content is retrievable, and perhaps manual intervention for particular results as needed to ensure that popular, recent needs are correctly served.

9.2.7.2 Appropriateness

Alternatively, the intentions behind the same query may vary depending on the time of year at which the query is issued. For example, interest in for sporting events such as the U.S. Open varies with the time of year and there are multiple events which bear the same name. A query for [*us open*] in August or September more likely refers to the U.S. Open Tennis Championships, whereas the same query issued in mid-June more likely refers to the U.S. Open Championship golf tournament (and other sports-related intentions in the areas of bowling, badminton, cycling, and so on, all occurring at different times of the year are also possible). Similarly, a query for the Olympic Games will have a different intention depending on when it is issued (sometimes it will refer to the summer games, sometimes it will refer to the winter games). When examining search activity recorded in search engine log data, we can observe patterns that reflect these temporal dynamics. That is, documents are differentially accessed for the same query depending on the time of year that the query is issued (Radinsky et al., 2013). By considering the time at which the query is received, and correlating that query with external events (e.g., combining temporal signals from news streams and query streams), user intentions can be disambiguated. Beyond considering ranking, there is a need to develop evaluation methodologies tailored to time-sensitive tasks, including the availability of publically available dynamic collections such as Twitter, Wikipedia edits, and news streams. Although not strictly related to contextualization, there are opportunities to develop of time-sensitive summaries and sparklines/timelines (similar to that shown in Figure 9.8) that allow people to visualize changes pertaining to a query and/or a page over time. Fourney et al. (2015) used such visualizations to represent temporal changes in search behavior associated with pregnancy searching over the duration of the pregnancy, from searchers who self-identified as being pregnant via first-person declarations of pregnancy (e.g., [*I am N weeks pregnant*]). Figure 9.9 illustrates the temporal dynamics of pregnancy-related query bigrams over time. Methods have also been developed to help searchers identify changes in pages since their last visit to that page, simply by highlighting the text that has changed (Teevan et al., 2010). Beyond supporting search interactions, temporal search data can also be used for a range of other applications,

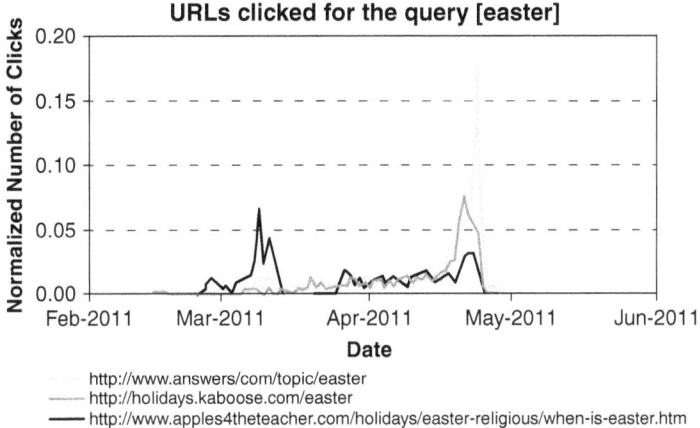

Figure 9.8. Example of temporally dependent access of Web pages (URLs) for same query (adapted from Radinsky et al., 2013).

such as predicting future events in the world, including disease outbreaks, deaths, and riots (Radinsky and Horvitz, 2013).

Irrespective of the topic, there are also clear cycles in information access patterns across days and weeks (Mei and Church, 2008). There are peak times at which we see greater query volume (middle of the day), and searching may be more frequent on weekdays versus weekends. This has implications for load balancing on search engine servers, which is an important topic in the systems community (e.g., Barroso et al., 2003). In addition to fluctuations in query volume, we can also observe changes in topical interests as a function of time. For example, searches for sports-related content might be higher on the weekend, whereas finance-related searches might be more frequent during the work week.

9.2.7.3 Urgency

Search may be performed in the context of pressing, time-constrained situations where information is urgently needed (McKenzie and Davies, 2002; Savolainen, 2006; Crescenzi et al., 2013; Mishra et al., 2014). This could be in the context of natural disasters or to assist those with acute medical concerns. Events such as fainting, seizures, bleeding, broken bones, numbness, vertigo, and pain may lead to the urgent pursuit of medical information in support of timely action. In time-critical situations, the value of retrieved information diminishes with delays in action informed by the information (Horvitz and Rutledge, 1991). Urgency of action has largely been ignored in search interaction. There is some limited support available in search engines for particular queries (e.g., searching for poison or suicide on Google will return hotline telephone numbers ([Cohen, 2010]). Others have conducted research on crisis informatics (Palen et al., 2007), including the role of social media in these settings (Palen, 2008). Guo et al. (2013) proposed methods to update people about natural disasters, a more widespread event than a particular medical emergency, by making decisions about which information to share, considering attributes such as accuracy.

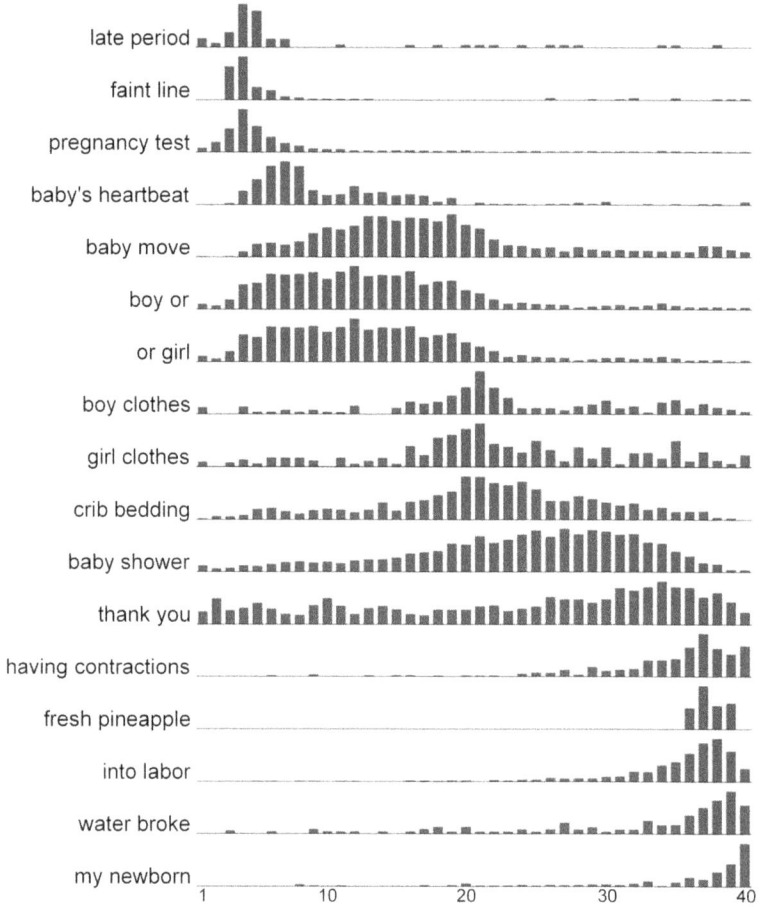

Figure 9.9. Histograms of query bigrams over forty weeks of gestation. Time-dependent query volumes of each bigram (left) are displayed by gestational week for searchers who self-identified as pregnant (n = 13,030 searchers). Each bar represents the proportion of searchers who searched at least once for bigram of interest in the corresponding gestational week. Histograms are normalized with respect to the maxima of each bigram (adapted from Fourney et al., 2015).

Given the availability of tools to model information needs and interests sophisticated methods could be developed. If search systems could estimate the urgency of searchers' information needs at query time, they could favor content that assists searchers in performing urgent tasks. Surfacing content which has time-critical relevance could help people, with taking timely action in acute, life-threatening situations. One such situation is the pursuit of information about how to treat an urgent medical condition in the face of a health emergency. Time-criticality has been studied in domains beyond search and researchers have examined time-utility tradeoffs in settings such as trauma care (Horvitz and Seiver, 1997), emergency medicine (Horvitz and Rutledge, 1991; Landgren 2006), aerospace (Horvitz and Barry, 1995), and communications (Horvitz et al., 1999). Beyond applications, the work has explored key principles of time-critical decisions in light of computational and cognitive overload (Horvitz, 2001). Such careful exploration of the tradeoffs between time and utility could enable search engines to consider urgency. Psychologists have also examined the measurement and impact of time urgency on human behavior (Landy et al., 1991) and work task performance (Bingham and Hailey, 1989).

Mishra et al. (2014) showed that people turn to search engines with urgent information needs, and they developed machine-learned classifiers capable of estimating the urgency of observed queries given a range of features. The set of features representing the current situation of the searcher, including location, altitude, proximity to specific sites and resources, and time of day, were all useful in developing predictive models of the urgency of search sessions. These predictions can be used by search systems to determine whether specialized ranking or interface support should be offered. Studies have shown that results returned by search systems for urgent health scenarios are irrelevant, inaccurate, and do not consider the influence of cognitive load on people facing emergency situations (Horvitz and Barry, 1995; Murugiah et al., 2011). Given an estimate of urgency, search systems could favor particular types of content (e.g., how-to pages) or display instant answers comprising graphics or videos to guide people in taking action quickly. The results most appropriate for urgent situations might not be ideal for more relaxed settings. For example, the best material for reviewing cardiopulmonary resuscitation (CPR) during a course on advanced cardiac life support would be quite different than content displayed to frenetic searchers trying to determine a course of action when an elderly relative is suddenly unresponsive and no heartbeat is detected.

9.2.7.4 Memorable Events

Time is an important aspect when people are seeking to find information in their own personal histories. Research on personal information management has led to the development of systems to support finding information (e.g., *Stuff I've Seen* [Dumais et al., 2003], *MyLifeBits* [Gemmell et al., 2002], and *Phlat* [Cutrell et al., 2006]). *LifeBrowser* (Horvitz et al., 2004) is based on statistical modeling of the likelihoods that particular events would be memory landmarks. The researchers suggested that the new classes of support for activities that span the realms of both digital work and digital life (e.g., predicting meeting attendance [Horvitz et al., 1999; Mynatt and Tullio, 2001]; identifying images of landmark events from personal image collections [Platt, 2000]). Many of these systems rely on being able to identify some aspect of the task around which the information is sought. Czerwinski and Horvitz (2002) showed that people forgot a significant number of computing tasks they had performed one month in the past, but were able to recall more effectively when prompted with videos and photographs of their work at the time; human memory depends on the relationship between encoded content and the cues and context associated with that content (Tulving and Thompson, 1973; Davies and Thompson, 1988). Research also suggests that people use routine or extraordinary events as "anchors" when trying to reconstruct memories of the past (Smith et al., 1978).

Many systems have been developed that explicitly exploit time to help people search over personal content. *Lifestreams* (Fertig et al., 1996) enables searching for personal content with an emphasis on time and the visual nature of electronic documents. *LifeLines* (Plaisant et al., 1996) leverages the time-based structure of human memory with a view toward displaying personal histories on a timeline representation.

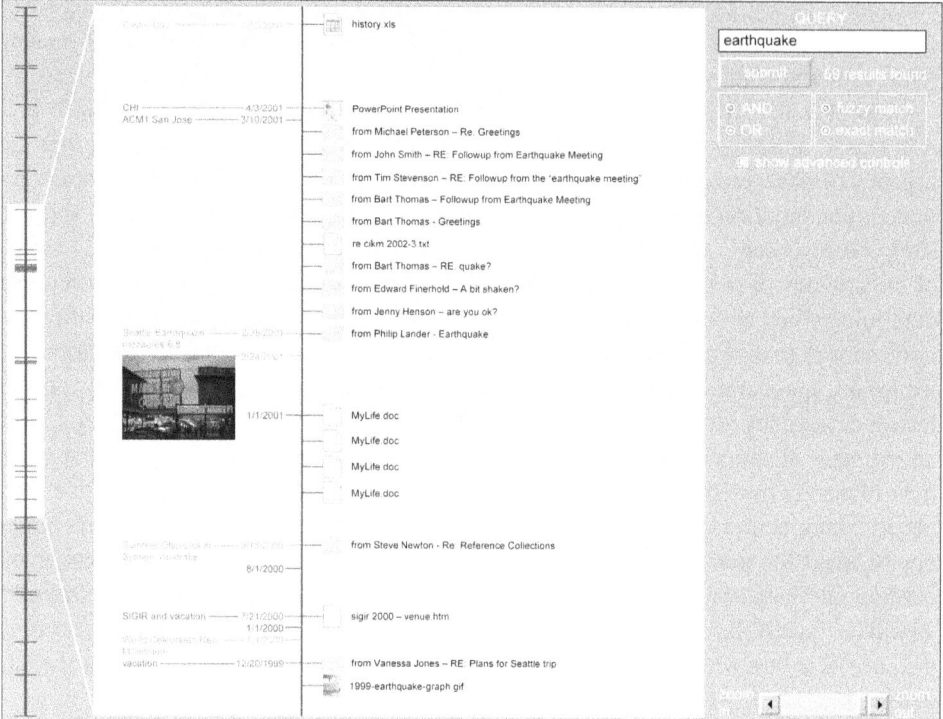

Figure 9.10. Screenshot of timeline visualization from *Stuff I've Seen* (adapted from Ringel et al., 2003).

Kumar et al. (1998) used timelines to visualize topics such as world history and stock prices, as well as metadata about documents in digital libraries, such as publication date. Memory landmarks (Ringel et al., 2003) demonstrated the value of timelines containing both personal and public temporal landmarks as navigation cues for guiding search over subsets of personal content. Results of searches are presented with an overview-plus-detail timeline visualization (Figure 9.10). In a large-scale study, users of the *Stuff I've Seen* desktop search system (Dumais et al., 2003) exhibited a strong preference for temporal ordering, which was remembered by participants, rather than best match, which is based on estimated relevance to the search query.

9.2.8 Summary

It is clear that there are many sources of contextual information from which both existing and next-generation search systems can draw to refine their representations of searcher needs and enhance the search experience. Many of these are available using existing sensing technologies (e.g., time, location), but the more sophisticated or nuanced aspects (e.g., urgency, indoor context, or surroundings) require more complete modeling and enhanced sensing of searchers' situations. Developments in computing technology, specifically around sensing and reasoning under uncertainty will make such advances possible. Moving forward, context will play an increasingly important role in search interaction and in tailoring the search experience to searchers' specific situations in both proactive and reactive search scenarios.

9.3 Explanations and Searcher Control

As described in this section so far, search systems can leverage additional personal and contextual cues to tailor the search experience. The system, however, should provide searchers with a sense of the nature of the action that it is performing, as well as offering searchers control (e.g., the option to reverse the action or prevent the system from performing the action for future queries).

9.3.1 Explanations

There are a number of ways in which the models constructed via personalization or contextualization can be employed in search systems. The most common usage for these models is to re-order the original, non-personalized ranking retrieved by the search engine so as to promote pages of likely interest to the current searcher and/or their situation to higher-rank positions. There may be circumstances in which searchers do not want the system to personalize or contextualize the results (e.g., some searchers may have privacy concerns associated with using data beyond their search query). Systems should provide searchers with control over if and how the additional information is collected and employed by the system. If actions are taken by the system on behalf of searchers, they should be clearly explained and be reversible.

Although searchers may have grown accustomed to some noise in search system output, surprising results (good or bad) may require an explanation. Possible reasons could include the result being visited many times by the same searcher in their (recent) search history, with or without a query dependency, it being popular with others in the searcher's current location, or social explanations suggested as related to the preferences of other known or similar individuals (e.g., "X, Y, and 5 other friends visited this link"; see Herlocker et al. [2000] and Sharma and Cosley [2013]). Explanations have been considered as a way to help people understand the benefit of providing relevance feedback (Ruthven, 2002) or longer search queries (Belkin et al., 2003). However, here I focus on the role of providing explanations to system output, rather than any action that the searcher can perform to improve the search process. Explanations can be textual or graphical, but whichever medium is selected, they should be designed to convey to the searcher in simple terms why particular action has been taken (e.g., "You visited this page many times in the past month" or "This is popular with other people in your location"). Explanations are usually associated with either particular items on the SERP, or are included generally to cover all of the top-ranked results. They have also been studied within the context of recommender systems as a way to explain why the recommendations were generated (Tintarev and Masthoff, 2007). Because such recommendations may be made proactively, without any explicit request from searchers, explanations for their predictions may be necessary.

Explanations may create potential privacy concerns because they prominently display aspects of the search history on the interface or may reveal aspects of others' search behaviors when social information is used. This is problematic for shared computers, as more than one person may view the explanation and be able to make inferences about previous activities. Searchers may not feel comfortable with their history being so directly visible to others. Mechanisms such as the activity attribution, discussed earlier in this chapter and in detail in previous work (White et al., 2014b; White and Hassan Awadallah, 2015), or manual searcher logins can be used to lessen the privacy risks, such that it is more likely that searchers will be presented with their own data only. Such privacy dangers can never be completely eliminated from the process.

As well as offering searchers an explanation for *why* particular results appeared, search systems can also use the explanations as a way to instruct searchers about how they can assume control over system operation (e.g., to find other similar results using relevance feedback; as described in Chapter 3), provide a way to remove a particular item from a search history, disable a type of personalization, or disable all future personalization. The explanations are an important part of the interaction between humans and search systems, allowing searchers to make more informed decisions about how search systems should act on their behalf. They form an important part of the dialog between searchers and search systems, and help searchers better understand system functionality and better trust the actions that systems take on searcher's behalf.

9.3.2 Searcher Control

One of the most important aspects in next-generation search systems is control over aspects of the search process (Marchionini, 2006b). That control is only useful if searchers can apply it effectively. For example, searchers may lack knowledge about the distribution of terms or phrases in the document collection that makes the selection of query expansion terms potentially problematic. In situations in which people struggle to exercise this control effectively, they may want to delegate responsibility for aspects of the search process to the system (Bates, 1990). Beaulieu and Jones (1998) argued that it is therefore vital for the search system to determine when to assume control for search engine operations, and when the user should be involved. This control can manifest in search systems by providing searchers with input on decisions such as whether to include particular query expansion terms (Koenemann and Belkin, 1996), re-ranking results (White and Ruthven, 2007), and offering recourse links to reverse system actions such as automatically correcting a detected spelling error. White and Marchionini (2007) proposed a slightly different technique to allow searchers to control the application of relevance feedback. In their setting, searchers were able to choose a list of suggested additional query terms while the query is formulated. Their results show that the real-time query expansion technique (RTQE) is more useful for exploratory search tasks, especially early in a search task when searchers' needs may be most uncertain and they may benefit from support in selecting appropriate terms. However, they also acknowledged that RTQE techniques can cause query skew because searchers have insufficient information regarding the impact of their selections on the results generated.

In the advanced settings of the search system, searchers may also be provided with control about whether to personalize or contextualize the results for all of their queries. Research on the development of searcher controllable models for personalized search has examined the strengths and weaknesses of these methods. Wærn (2004) studied the issue of mixed control within information filtering tasks and showed that profiles generated explicitly by searchers was effective even after a significant amount of additional training. However, she also showed that searchers could not accurately determine profile utility for this task nor improve existing profiles that had already been created and used for learning. Despite the potential gains in search relevance, some users may be reluctant to enable personalization given significant concerns about their privacy (Kobsa, 2007; Krause and Horvitz, 2008).

Open user models have been proposed in the area of adaptive educational systems that model the knowledge, difficulties, and misconceptions of the individual (Bull, 2004; Kay, 2006). Open and editable user models have been less common in information access settings, although they have been proposed in some recommendation contexts (Baudisch and Brueckner, 2002). Studies of such profiles in the context of adaptive news access have met with limited success, in part because they did not show the impact of the profile change on the search results immediately, but largely because searchers were unable to distinguish good and bad profiles (Wærn 2004). In the same setting, Ahn et al. (2007) showed that the capability to edit user profiles should be applied with caution; they even found a negative correlation between the amount of searcher interference with the profile and the recommendation performance of the system.

9.4 Summary

In this chapter, I focused on methods for the personalization and contextualization of the search process, whereby the search system may augment a presented search query with additional information about the searcher and/or their search situation. Many aspects of personalization and a broad range of different search contexts can be applied by search systems to enhance the search process. Trends suggest that next-generation search systems will be highly adaptive to the searcher and their situation. They will pull data from the environment to better respond to searcher requests, whilst also proactively identifying and *pushing* content of potential interest to searchers. For example, *infoFACTORY* (Mizarro and Tasso, 2002) recommended relevant content as soon as it is published on the Web, without the need for searchers to query for that content directly. Other methods predict searchers' future goals and actions, so that a system may work proactively on their behalf (Joachims et al., 1997; Zukerman and Albrecht, 2001; Lieberman et al., 2001). Because integrating personal and contextual signals may alter the search engine output, the experience may be disconcerting for searchers and even "creepy," depending on the particular inferences made and how they are employed by the search system (Battelle, 2005). Informative explanations can help searchers to understand why system operations occurred. By allowing searchers to control aspects of the search process through recourse functionality (to undo system operations) and explicit settings for contextualization and personalization, search systems can deliver custom-tailored search experiences while also placing searchers in control.

PART III
Evaluation

I now turn to how interactive search systems should be evaluated, including the measures that should be employed, the methodologies, and the data and tools that are needed to perform these evaluations. This is particularly important if systems are being compared across multiple experimental sites and systems are being tested at scale with millions of searchers. Web search providers need to understand the performance of their systems at scale, across a diverse set of information needs and large populations. As a result, methods to understand searcher preferences solely via the retrospective analysis of logged search activity (e.g., which results or interface items receive the most attention given variations in ranking and/or interface presentation) are particularly attractive. More sophisticated experimental apparatuses allow different measures of systems performance to be computed and a more complete sense of searcher performance to be attained. There are also a number of alternatives to computing metrics from behavior, such as capturing labels directly from searchers directly (in situ) at search time, and measuring signals such as cognitive load and affect to enrich signals based only on the explicit actions that searchers perform.

CHAPTER 10
Evaluation Measures

Measuring the performance of search systems is essential in improving their effectiveness. Computing measures (or metrics, used synonymously in this chapter) lets search providers benchmark current performance, as well as quantify the impact of any changes. Some measures target the outcomes of the search process (e.g., the relevance of the found items), while some are more focused on the search process itself (e.g., the efficiency or cognitive load of the search process). Although numerous measures of search system performance have been proposed, none can fully evaluate search systems from all perspectives. As search systems become more sophisticated and support a broader range of tasks, new evaluation metrics and metric combinations will be needed.

Engelbart (1962, p. 1) suggested that the increased capability attributable to augmenting human intellect would likely lead to: "more-rapid comprehension, better comprehension, the possibility of gaining a useful degree of comprehension in a situation that previously was too complex, speedier solutions, better solutions, and the possibility of finding solutions to problems that could not previously be solved." Systems that offer such opportunities cannot simply be evaluated using traditional retrieval measures such as precision and recall, which only consider the relevance of the found content and how much of the relevant content is found. In this case, we would need metrics that assess the quality of the solution and assess the impact of the search process on people's understanding of the subject matter.

There are two groups of metrics considered in this chapter: (1) those that assess the search *process* in which the searcher was engaged; and (2) those that target the *outcomes* attained as a result of that process. For completeness, I cover some of the traditional metrics, but many of those discussed draw on research in other communities, such as psychology. Irrespective of the target for the metric computation, with enhancements in next-generation search systems, evaluation metrics (and methods, discussed in the Chapter 11) need to cater to a diverse range of searchers, tasks, and interactivity.

Traditionally, the unit of retrieval evaluation is the search query. Next-generation search systems, however, place an emphasis on supporting the completion of complete search tasks end-to-end (rather than considering queries independently and satisfying

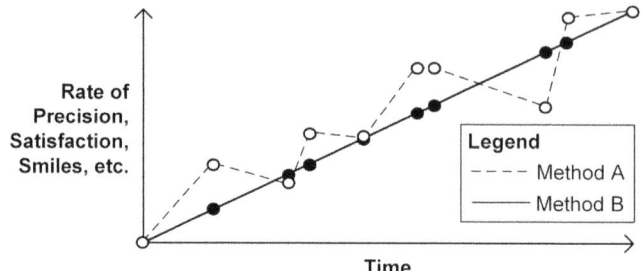

Figure 10.1. Various search experiences (based on Marchionini, 2011).

task-relevant information needs one query at a time). A related question is how to evaluate search systems holistically (e.g., based on the sum total of the information they encounter over the search episode). There has been some work to develop metrics that can handle system performance during a search session (Huffman and Hochster, 2007; Järvelin et al., 2008; Smucker and Clarke, 2012). Before proceeding, it is worth considering the search experience visually depicted in Figure 10.1, which illustrates two multi-query search episodes over time and the values of some metric of choice during that time, where the metric could be one of many, including any of those described later in this chapter.

One of the lines in Figure 10.1 shows steady progress from lower-left to upper-right, while the other takes a more erratic route between the same starting and ending points. The open question is which line represents better, or perhaps more desirable, system performance from a searcher's perspective. There are benefits associated with the predictability of steady progress, but there are also benefits associated with the more erratic line, including relieving frustration though surprise (e.g., the sharp upward spikes of the erratic line) and achieving strong search performance, if only for a short time. The erratic line is more likely to reflect a learning process that is characteristic of exploratory searching (Marchionini, 2006a; White and Roth, 2009). This example illustrates the need to consider aspects of the search *process* in addition to point-based measures connected with particular task outcomes or individual search queries.

This chapter focuses on various measures that can be used to understand the performance of search systems. Although usability is important, that is not a considered specifically; the topic has been covered extensively in the human factors and psychology (Card et al., 1983; Gould and Lewis, 1985; Landauer, 1996; Dumas and Redish, 1999; Nielsen and Norman, 2000). Not all measures are appropriate for all systems. Measure appropriateness varies depending on factors such as the intended purpose of the system (e.g., supporting exploration and discovery versus keyword retrieval) and its operating environment (mobile versus desktop, general purpose versus domain specific, etc.). If new metrics are proposed, they need to be validated, and where possible, mixed method approaches should be employed to improve the reliability of analysis.

As search expands beyond rudimentary document retrieval, alternative performance measures need to be adopted. Measures that model rates of learning, mental load, and engagement, as well as more traditional metrics such satisfaction and relevance are needed. In addition to assessing the information gained, or how the search process makes people feel, we also need to consider the role of search systems in helping searchers be productive and attaining their information objectives. Experimenters can focus on task relevance (Reid, 2000) or frame search within a broader work task (Borlund, 2003); there will be an increased emphasis on the latter as support for end-to-end task completion becomes more widespread.

Many of these new metrics need to be personalized and calibrated to individual searchers to adequately represent their search situation. People may exhibit individual learning styles when they learn and process information (Kolb, 1985), and it is important to consider these differences during evaluation. It is important to consider how these metrics will be operationalized in various settings, especially at scale when direct contact with the searcher may be impractical. Result click-through data from individual searchers has been proposed as ground truth to train and evaluate personalization algorithms (Dou et al., 2007; Gao et al., 2009; Bennett et al., 2011). Leveraging clicks in this way yields information about which results returned for each query were relevant *for the current searcher*. In cases in which information needs may vary between people then personalized judgments such as this can be more accurate than those associated with the overall topical relevance of the content attained via third-party judges. Personalized judgments are discussed in more detail in Section 10.2.1.4.

As well as considering clicks on results for the current query, personalized measures can also consider search behavior for future queries in the session, so that if a click is not observed on a result in the current query, there is still a chance that the relevance of that result to the searcher's request will be discovered via search activity (e.g., clicks, dwell times, result skips) later in the search session.

In outlining some of the metrics that need to be discussed in evaluating next-generation search systems, let us consider two main dimensions:

- The **measurement of the search process** is based on the value of the process that searchers engage in to meet their information objectives.
- The **measurement of search outcomes** is based on the relevance/accuracy/benefit of the resources/answers gained as a result of searching.

Dividing metrics in this way helps frame thinking regarding the scenarios in which metrics in each of the classes should be employed. Existing metrics are also discussed, including their relationship with each other. The measures discussed in this chapter are by definition quantitative in nature. There is also value in qualitative assessment of search system performance using mechanisms such as think-alouds and stimulated recall. Qualitative methods are discussed in more detail in Chapter 11.

10.1 Process-Oriented Measures

These are measures that are calculated based on the search process. These metrics can be based only on behavioral traces or – if user study data are collected – additional information can be captured about the process, including asking searchers to describe their rationale as the process is unfolding (e.g., via think-alouds) or once the search task is complete (e.g., using stimulated recall). Less attention has been paid to such process-oriented measures in information retrieval evaluation, but they provide useful insight into the nature of the search process.

10.1.1 Learning

As described in Chapter 7, learning involves acquiring new, or modifying and reinforcing, existing knowledge, behaviors, skills, values, or preferences, and may involve synthesizing different types of information. As described earlier in the book, various taxonomies of learning have been proposed (e.g., Bloom et al., 1956), and learning has also been studied extensively by cognitive psychologists (e.g., Landauer, 2002). However, subject-matter learning may be a viable way in which to evaluate the performance of search systems, as a function of the amount of time spent and effort expended.

While it can be clearly observed that a searcher has encountered a particular information item, it is the *impact* of that encounter on their knowledge state and level of domain understanding that is much more challenging to measure. Support for more-rapid learning across a number of searchers and a range of tasks is indicative of a system that is more effective at supporting exploratory search activities. For example, in the evaluation of *Scatter/Gather*, an interface designed to support search result exploration through text clustering, Pirolli et al. (1996b) defined learning and understanding in terms of topic structure and query formulation capabilities at various points during subject interaction with the system. Compared with a control group that performed the same tasks using a standard search engine, *Scatter/Gather* users showed larger gains in understanding the underlying topic structure and in formulating effective queries.

The need to consider learning as a metric for evaluation has re-emerged recently number of recent workshops in the Information Retrieval community (Agosti et al., 2014; White et al., 2006b), and has been identified as a pressing need by researchers (Marchionini, 2006a; White and Roth, 2009). Learning does not happen all at once. Instead, it builds on and is shaped by what people already know. Learning is best viewed as a process, rather than a collection of factual and procedural knowledge. Effectively estimating learning within and across sessions requires collecting, representing, and contrasting information about a searcher's state of knowledge at different stages in the information search process.

Measurement of learning can be difficult for a number of reasons, mainly because it is an internal process that it is susceptible to significant variation between searchers (Wilson and Wilson, 2013). To measure learning in a laboratory setting, researchers can assess the attainment of learning outcomes (e.g., comprehension test scores) or the richness/completeness of the post-exploration perspective on the topic of the search compared with the searcher's pre-search perspective that is captured through methods such as interviews or assignments (Kim et al., 2009; Kammerer et al., 2009). Just as there are individual differences in terms of the efficacy of learning, learning is also most likely to occur in informational search tasks (Broder, 2002), where searchers may be purposely seeking new knowledge. Conversely, learning is less likely to occur during re-finding tasks where people revisit previously examined resources (Teevan et al., 2007), unless there are significant changes in that content that may lead to new insights (Adar et al., 2008; 2009).

Learning can be assessed across the search process at a variety of levels, ranging from individual actions – such as queries – to evidence of lifelong learning (Ingwersen and Järvelin, 2005). Assessing knowledge before and after the task can be particularly

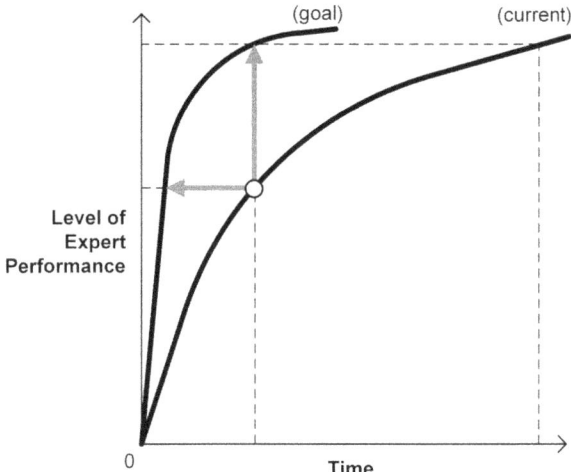

Figure 10.2. Measuring performance relative to the optimal (adapted from White and Roth, 2009).

useful for cases in which it is not possible to compute a goal for the search task (e.g., for open-ended, exploratory tasks) and hence not possible to objectively measure performance against learning outcomes. Returning to the earlier discussion of transfer of learning (Thorndike and Woodworth, 1901; Ellis, 1965), experimenters may also assess whether knowledge gained during the search process could be applied in tasks related to that tested during the experiment.

To target learning, experimenters can monitor how much subject-matter learning occurs as a function of exploration time. Progress over time toward task goals can be depicted visually in the form of learning curves. *Table Lens* (Rao and Card, 1994) is an information visualization tool that supports sensemaking from large tables or spreadsheets. Pirolli and Rao (1996) showed that participants grasped properties or variables and relationships among variables at a faster rate when using *Table Lens* compared to a standard table representation. Pirolli (2007) suggested that search systems could be evaluated through a cost structure analysis by finding metrics of learning or expertise and then comparing how information-seeking on one system versus another produces better or worse gains against those metrics. Figure 10.2 presents a visual representation of the measurement of the level of expert performance relative to the optimal level of performance.

Measuring learning as a function of time is attractive because it facilitates comparability between participants in ways that is otherwise difficult to attain. Researchers working in this area must measure the depth and effectiveness of learning rather than focus on efficiency, especially for exploratory tasks in which longer task completion times may signal more engagement (traditionally considered to be a positive indicator of system performance).

Jansen et al. (2009) performed a user study with searching scenarios generated to correspond to the different levels of Anderson and Krathwohl's (2001) taxonomy from the cognitive learning domain. They found that there are searching characteristics that are specific to each of the six categories in the taxonomy (e.g., that applying and analyzing require the most searching effort in terms of queries per session and total time spent searching). Interestingly, they showed similarities in search behavior between the two lowest categories (remembering and understanding) and the two highest categories (evaluating and creating), suggesting that determining the cognitive complexity of learning objectives from search behavior alone may be problematic. Wilson and Wilson (2013) evaluated various approaches for analyzing the degree of learning noted in written summaries (fact and statement counting, topic coverage, and a novel approach based on Bloom's taxonomy) from domain novices and experts for learning-style work tasks. They showed that measuring learning using these methods can be affected by factors such as summary length, which could lead to overestimation of count-based learning metrics.

The focus thus far has been on individuals learning during searches performed on their own. People can also learn during explicit or implicit collaboration with others (Bruffee, 1993). Populations of searchers can learn through group mechanisms, (Chen and Chiu, 2008), and analysis of traffic on particular groups on social networks might be useful indicators of shared learning activities.

While it is unlikely that learning can be fully measured in remote settings outside of a laboratory environment, there are ways in which remote observers could infer changes in knowledge state to estimate that learning has occurred as a result of system usage. They could look for evidence that new knowledge is being applied, for example in query statements with more technical, domain-specific vocabulary, or they could look for indications that searchers are examining more complex and/or specialist content. As suggested in Chapter 7, search providers may observe signals indicative of possible learning by considering, among other things, increases in the sophistication of the language used in queries both over the short term and the long term (White et al., 2009b; Eickhoff et al., 2014). Beyond changes in subject matter expertise, others have considered changes in search expertise over time, via social learning (Moraveji et al., 2011a), as searchers are exposed to hints and tips that provide guidance on how to search (Moraveji et al., 2011b), or to reflect on their own search behaviors in comparison with the behaviors of search experts (Bateman et al., 2012).

10.1.2 Efficiency

Efficiency measures the amount of useful effort during a search process. Previous research has studied search efficiency directly as part of evaluating search systems with human participants (Zamir and Etzioni, 1999; Goldberg et al., 2002; Gwizdka, 2008; Moraveji et al., 2011b). The primary measure of efficiency is the amount of time required to meet a state of task completeness, usually determined by the searcher based on perceptions of progress. As discussed earlier in the chapter, time may be more appropriate for known-item searching rather than exploration-related activities where more time may in fact signal satisfaction and increased engagement. Xu and Mease (2009) demonstrated that total task completion time is correlated with searcher satisfaction for difficult tasks, and that variation in time between searchers is greater than within searchers. Task time can include the total time spent on the task, the time that is spent considering relevant and non-relevant documents, and the proportion of time spent engaged in certain activities of interest (e.g., the amount of time spent querying versus browsing). Measuring how quickly searchers attain a level of knowledge may contradict other measures of system performance such as engagement, enjoyment, and learning, which may increase with time spent on a task. In such cases, it may be in the interests of searchers to maximize rather than minimize time on task. Other measures of efficiency can also be used, such as the total number of actions performed during the task or the amount of backtracking (i.e., retracing one's steps through a document collection). Time may be applicable if it is used to normalize other metrics to compute rates (e.g., the rate of accumulation of relevant content).

10.1.3 Cognitive Load

The cognitive load is the amount of cognitive effort that searchers need to expend to perform the search. As described in Chapter 4, cognition plays an important part in the search process and interactions with computers generally (Card et al., 1983; Ingwersen, 1996). The term *cognitive load* is used in cognitive psychology to illustrate the load related to the executive control of working memory. Cognitive load can have a significant impact on the search process, including decisions about whether to engage with particular features (e.g., Back and Oppenheim, 2001). Being able to measure levels of mental effort is important for understanding the cognitive demands imposed on searchers by tasks, interfaces, and information displays, and to devise mechanisms that consider cognitive load (e.g., notification delivery design [Adamcyz and Bailey, 2004]) or to lower the cognitive load required for effective search interaction. A high cognitive load is not always a negative indicator; it could be necessary given the nature of the task or the current stage (Sweller et al., 1998). I focus on measurement in this section, but a good summary on cognitive load more generally from an information science perspective, and the impact of task effects, is provided by Gwizdka (2010).

There are a number of ways in which to classify the methods used to measure cognitive load, but the most common breakdown is in terms of performance, subjective, and physiological measures (Cegarra and Chevalier, 2008). The methods that I focus on in this book are empirical, involving the direct measurement of cognitive load in participants. Analytical methods form another group, and include methods such as expert opinion, task analysis, and simulation (Card et al., 1983).

10.1.3.1 Subjective

In subjective measures, participants in studies provide their perceptions of cognitive load. These measures provide insight into the cognitive state of the searcher and are important for assessing their perceptions of the search task and the search system. Examples of these methods include self-rating scales, think-aloud protocols, and post-task interviews. The most famous and best known method is the NASA Task Load Index (TLX; see Hart and Staveland [1988]). Subjective measures are usually collected after the task is complete. As such, they do not provide insight into the changes in the cognitive load over the course of a task.

10.1.3.2 Performance

These measures include performance on the primary task and performance on the secondary task. Participant performance is measured objectively on the primary task.

Measures selected for this purpose include the number of errors, the time to complete search tasks, and task completion time (relative to population and to ideal). Although time may be an appropriate measure for cases in which the cadence is controlled externally, as mentioned in the previous subsection, there can be many reasons beyond higher cognitive load that a search proceeds slowly. When a secondary task is included, these are referred to as "dual-task techniques" (Brunken et al., 2002; Cegarra and Chevalier, 2008). The application of the second task assumes that there are finite cognitive resources that need to be split between tasks (Wickens, 2002). The performance of the two tasks is linked so that as the performance of the primary task improves, the performance on the secondary task degrades (and vice versa). The secondary task often involves the monitoring of external events delivered periodically through the visual or auditory channel, depending on the nature of the primary task (e.g., pressing a button when an audible alert is provided). Experimenters measure metrics such as the reaction time to secondary task events and the number of misses of these events. Care should be taken to set the frequency of secondary events to a level that is sufficiently large to affect performance, but still allows near-normal performance on the primary task. Other methods have involved measuring cognitive load via the difficulty associated with providing a relevance judgment, in the form of relevance feedback (Back and Oppenheim, 2001).

10.1.3.3 Physiological
There are also physiological signals that may indicate the level of cognitive load. These measures are objective and can be captured using a number of sensing methods, including electro-encephalography (EEG), functional near infrared spectroscopy (fNIRS; see Hirshfield, et al. [2009]), and eye-gaze tracking. For eye-gaze tracking, changes in pupil diameter can help assess mental load in studies in information science and human-computer interaction (e.g., Iqbal et al., 2004; Tungare and Pérez-Quinones, 2009).

The dual-task and physiological methods for measuring cognitive load have the advantage that they support real-time collection of data during the course of the task. This allows for analysis of how cognitive load changes during interaction. Physiological measures can be difficult to interpret, and require calibration for each participant as well as the use of expensive and cumbersome hardware. The dual-task method is the most commonly used method because it supports inexpensive and objective assessment of primary task performance.

Within the context of information search, a number of studies have examined cognitive load. These have focused on the effects of factors such as: (1) visual complexity of content (Gwizdka and Spence, 2007; Rosenholtz et al., 2007); (2) general task effects, with load measured using changes in pupil size (Iqbal et al., 2004); and (3) search task stages, using dual-task methods (Kim and Rieh, 2005; Dennis et al., 1998; 2002; Gwizdka, 2010). Kim and Rieh (2005) used a dual-task method to measure cognitive load in Web search. They found different degrees of cognitive load – measured in terms of the number of misses on the secondary task – depending on the nature of task. Searchers had less load during result list examination and higher load during document examination, reflecting the care with which they consider the two information sources. Dennis et al. (1998; 2002) also employed dual-task methods and found lower cognitive load during query refinement on the *Excite* search engine compared with result list examination on the same engine. They also experimented with a different search interface (the *Hyper Index Browser*) that allowed searchers to view results at a more abstract level and offered query refinements. They compared this interface with a standard Google SERP and found differences in the cognitive load, primarily that the new interface required more mental effort (although a lack of familiarity with the interface and the introduction of a new query refinement method likely also contributed). Gwizdka (2010) found that cognitive load is sensitive to dynamic changes in task demands, such as various task stages. Cognitive load was much higher during query formulation and providing explicit relevance feedback compared to examining search results and viewing individual results.

Moshfeghi et al. (2013) used functional magnetic resonance imaging (fMRI) to better understand relevance by connecting it directly with brain activity. They showed that different regions of the brain performed differently when processing relevant and non-relevant documents. Eugster et al. (2014) employed EEG sensing to quantify neural activity and predict the relevance of terms 17% better than the marginal distribution. Because the method is based on changes in specific brain areas, it does not require calibration. The researchers created an application whereby a term set can be constructed for an unknown topic of interest based on brain signals alone. EEG signals may serve as a useful complement to existing implicit feedback signals such as dwell time or click-through. Although it is unclear how these methods could be applied at scale given the cost and nature of the technology, this research still represents important progress in better measuring factors such as relevance that are typically latent. Recent advances in brain sensing hardware has also led to the development and application lower-cost methods such as fNIRS to measure hemodynamic response (blood delivery to active neuronal tissues; see Major et al. [2014]), allowing the researchers to objectively measure cognitive workload in interactive search settings. In addition to evaluation, such sensing can also be used to detect cognitive overload during multitasking, prompting system support (e.g., in prioritizing tasks; see Solovey et al. [2012]).

10.1.4 Serendipity

Serendipity describes "fortunate mistakes" (Van Andel, 1994; Barber and Merton, 2006) whereby people encounter information that affects them positively. Measuring serendipity may be important in search systems that support exploration and discovery. There are two aspects: (1) the delight and accidental nature of the discovery; and (2) utilizing that discovery for some productive purpose (e.g., in the advancement of science; see Kohn [1989] and Roberts [1989]). There have been a number of attempts to consider the role of serendipity in computer systems (Lieberman, 1995; Beale, 2007), many with a specific focus on search (Marchionini and Shneiderman, 1988; Foster and Ford, 2003; André et al., 2009; Toms, 2000). In the context of search, the traditional focus has been the nature of the information encountered (relevant versus non-relevant) and the type of information activity being performed (directed browsing, non-directed browsing, none; see André et al. [2009b]). In information-seeking contexts, serendipity can be associated both with an information item or information fragment that is deemed to be surprisingly relevant, interesting, or useful while not specifically searching for it, and with the effect that information has on user understanding and the resultant generation of insight(s). This may happen during searching or more likely, it may be recommendations are made to the searchers as they are examining other content. Serendipity is similar to novelty, but emphasizes personal pleasure or surprisingness in addition to exposure to new information.

Serendipity is difficult to measure and can be difficult to induce experimentally (Erdelez, 2004; André et al., 2009a; André et al., 2009b). In the scientific community, longer term analysis of the impact of the discovery may be apparent, allowing the retrospective assessment of the value of a chance encounter. Studies in information seeking generally rely on self-reported data, especially interviews (Erdelez, 1999; Foster and Ford, 2003; André et al., 2009a), which may not be as revealing. Indeed, André et al. (2009a) noted that while study participants were happy to discuss serendipitous encounters, the identification of specific instances was more challenging. Toms (2000a) manipulated tasks (goal directed and not goal directed) and observed differences in the search behavior depending on the nature of the task. Specifically, she found that participants without a goal were more focused on coverage and exploration, whereas those with a goal were more interested in meaningful content.

Spink et al. (1998) showed that "partially relevant" results could lead to the generation of new ideas and directions. Building on this earlier work, André et al. (2009b) identified some features that could be used to identify potentially serendipitous search queries. These include whether the query was informational versus. navigational, work related versus not, or contained a person's name versus not. Click entropy, capturing variations in the results selected for a query in the aggregate across many searchers (Dou et al., 2007), was also found to be related to serendipity (i.e., entropy was positively correlated with the number of potentially serendipitous results). André et al. also found that the degree of personal relevance of a page (based on content and behavioral features) could help identify potentially serendipitous pages. Analyzing search logs for instances of these queries or results could facilitate the discovery of serendipitous encounters at scale. Understanding how these encounters occur can help inform the design of search systems to increase the likelihood of serendipity occurring. Other approaches could involve mining search log data for large deviations in search behavior or interests following a search query or a visit to an information resource. If data is available on subsequent information use, that could strengthen claims about serendipity by allowing the impact of the information on decision making and action to be considered. Research on methods to measure creativity may also be relevant to our discussion of measuring serendipity (Guilford, 1967; Sternberg and Lubart, 1999; Sternberg et al., 2002; Gladwell, 2008), although these methods typically focus on individual characteristics rather than those of particular situations.

10.1.5 Enjoyment, Happiness, and Pleasure

There has been a significant amount of research into the pleasure that people obtain when interacting with computers (Ghani and Deshpande, 1994; Malone, 1981; Turkle, 1984; Carroll and Thomas, 1988), including related research on aspects of positive psychology, such as cognitive flow (Csikszentmihalyi, 1990), which was discussed in Chapter 5. Rushinek and Rushinek (1986) found that a sense of control was an important factor in making computer use pleasurable. In information seeking, people can derive pleasure from the information revealed by the search system or the search experience more generally. White et al. (2006) argued for the inclusion of pleasure in the evaluation of exploratory search systems, and others have argued that pleasure and affect are an important part of the search process more generally (Kuhlthau, 1991; Marchionini, 2006b; Belkin, 2008). Beyond other more traditional measures of search effectiveness are measures related to searcher enjoyment and pleasure from using the system. In addition to utility, which is an important requirement of all search systems, these systems should also be delightful to use. Searcher delight can be regarded as a useful tie-breaker when comparing systems with equivalent performance characteristics in terms of relevance and utility.

Progress on measuring enjoyment and pleasure in search systems has been limited. Sun and Zhang (2006) studied the causal relationship between perceived enjoyment and perceived ease of use in information systems. In the human factors community, researchers have devised semantic differentials that can be used to probe for positive affect retrospectively (e.g., Ghani et al., 1991). However, this does not facilitate direct measurement during the search, and doing so would be intrusive. Measurement of enjoyment could be achieved in a similar way to that of affective feedback described earlier, whereby physiological sensors are employed. Software can be deployed to interpret images from front-facing cameras to identify when facial expressions change and interpret these expressions during the search process (Moshfeghi and Jose, 2013a). There has been some work in this area, including the development of relevance feedback algorithms that use affective cues (Arapakis et al., 2008; Arapakis et al., 2009).

10.1.6 Frustration

Searchers may be impeded in the search process, resulting in their frustration. Frustration has been studied broadly in domains such as intelligent tutoring systems (discussed in Chapter 7; see Cooper et al. [2009] and Kapoor et al. [2007]), but is starting to gain traction in the search community with recent user studies conducted on its role in the search process (Xie and Cool, 2009; Feild et al., 2010), as well as broader discussions of its impact on information seeking generally (Kuhlthau, 1991). Xie and Cool (2009) studied help-seeking activities in digital libraries and constructed a model of the factors that contribute to these situations from the individual, task, and interaction perspective. Feild et al. (2010) studied frustration within Web search using behavioral analysis and physical sensing via a mental state camera, a pressure sensitive mouse, and a pressure sensitive chair. They found that the behavioral features (e.g., chains of queries with no result clicks) were more predictive of frustration levels than the physical sensors.

Research on struggling behavior has shown that there are common patterns that people employ (e.g., increasing query lengths in the middle of session; see Aula et al. [2010]), and recent research has shown that struggling behavior can be predicted from search data (Hassan et al., 2014). It may also be linked to other activities, such as search engine switching (White and Dumais, 2009), which is mostly, although not always, associated with frustration and dissatisfaction. Note that researchers regard frustration as a process-oriented measure because it is likely that searchers will continue to search even if frustrated, and they can be satisfied while still being frustrated (Ceaparu et al., 2004). Beyond queries and clicks, there may be other behavioral features such as cursor movements, attributes of touch interactions (e.g., pressure and touch size [Guo et al., 2013]), eye-gaze tracking, or richer affect detection from front-facing cameras that could help measure frustration more accurately than query and selection behaviors alone. In measurement tasks, frustration can also be induced using methods such as slow system operation (e.g., Scheirer et al., 2002) or less relevant results, with a view to understanding the impact on searcher perceptions, actions, and outcomes.

10.1.7 Engagement

Searcher engagement is a complex construct that emphasizes the positive aspects of interaction (O'Brien and Toms, 2010; Lehmann et al., 2012). One definition of engagement that is particularly relevant to the goals of this book is "a user's response to an interaction that gains, maintains, and encourages their attention, particularly when they are intrinsically motivated" (Jacques, 1996). There are other related concepts such as being captivated by the technology used. Overall, engagement refers to the emotional, cognitive, and behavioral connections that exists at any point in time and over time, between a searcher and a technological resource. The goal in this section is not to define engagement (that has been done well in other venues; see e.g., O'Brien and Toms [2008]), but rather to discuss how engagement can be measured during interactions with search systems.

Many of the methods introduced earlier in this book can be viewed as a way to measure engagement, including methods for attention and interaction tracking. On the Web, analytics companies such as ClickTale (clicktale.com) can estimate engagement with a website this through a variety of mechanisms, including click trails and cursor movements. More generally, engagement can be measured using three main methods: (1) self-reports; (2) cognitive analysis; or (3) interaction monitoring.

10.1.7.1 Self-Reported Engagement

Self-reported engagement tools include questionnaires, interviews, think-alouds (or think after/stimulated recall; see Sauro and Dumas [2009], O'Brien and Toms [2010], and Webster and Ho [1997]), which can provide subjective data on respondents' attitudes, feelings, beliefs, or knowledge about a subject or situation that is often collected on a fairly small scale. The data captured from searchers' subjective experiences and can be rich, especially if open-ended questions or interviews are included, which can be costly to code and transcribe. Metrics that employ self-reporting to focus specifically on engagement include: (1) focused attention, which measures the degree to which attention was focused on the system under consideration at the expense of other peripheral information; and (2) positive affect, where people report on their feelings at search time. Self-reporting methods have well-known drawbacks, such as their subjective nature (Slater, 2010) and demand characteristics (Orne, 1962; 1969).

10.1.7.2 Cognitive Engagement

Task-based methods (such as the dual-task methods described in our earlier discussions of cognitive load) include neurological methods (e.g., EEG), physiological measures (e.g., gaze tracking and mouse tracking; see Ehmke and Wilson [2007] and Huang et al. [2011]), and provide objective data that can be captured at both small and large scales in the laboratory and in the field, and can yield large quantities of data about how people interact. The two main categories of cognitive engagement measures are:

- **Physiological measures** include involuntary body responses, including gaze behavior, mouse gestures, biometrics (e.g., skin conductance, respiration, brain waves, body temperature, blood volume pulse), and facial expression analysis. Experiments involving these measures can be difficult and expensive to setup, and intrusive to run, especially because it is not always clear that there is a direct correspondence between physiological measures and specific behaviors; and it may also not be clear how to interpret these signals.
- **Perceptual measures** include follow-on task performance and the subjective perception of time. The former involves assessing how a person performs on a task immediately following a period of engaged interaction. The latter requires asking searchers to make some estimation of the passage of time during an activity (Czerwinski et al., 2001; O'Brien and Toms, 2010).

10.1.7.3 Interaction Engagement

Web analytic methods, including metrics and models, provide objective insight into how people engage with search systems at scale in naturalistic settings (Yom-Tov et al., 2012). Examples of metrics that fall into this category include click-through rate, total queries per searcher, sessions per unique searcher, number of return visits and/or active days, and search engine switching (as a measure of loyalty; covered in Section 11.2.6). These may have clearly defined goals, such as a target click-through rate for different aspects of the search experience, or the total number of sessions per searcher over time.

10.1.7.4 Summary of Engagement Measures

Although the measures of engagement are described separately here, a combination of the approaches can be used to devise reliable signals of engagement. If multiple signals agree, it is likely that the searcher is truly engaged. One of the challenges in performing this combination of multiple signals in this way is to ensure that the capture of one signal does not unduly interfere with another. For example, the capture of data using a think-aloud protocol is likely to influence people's search behaviors as they will need to verbalize the rationale for their actions as they occur. Care needs to be taken to not let such cross method effects skew the data collected or the conclusions reached. In the case of think-alouds, it likely makes most sense to not also analyze the behavioral data collected with that methodology, at least not for evidence of behaviors on which generalizable claims will be made. There has also been recent interest in the standardization of user engagement (O'Brien and Toms, 2013) and how it should be measured that will allow cross-system comparisons of metrics and tracking of engagement over time (Lalmas et al., 2014).

Attention now turns to the outcome-oriented measures that are more focused on the products or perceptions of the search process rather than the process itself.

10.2 Outcome-Oriented Measures

The following measures reflect search outcomes, and are typically computed after the search process is complete.

10.2.1 Relevance

The relevance of information objects to information needs is central to information retrieval. The concept of relevance has been explored in detail by the information retrieval community and it has been defined in a number of different ways, including *topical* relevance (reflecting the extent to which an information object is on the same topic as the query) and *utility* (reflecting the usefulness of the document for helping searchers perform their task). The concept of relevance is complex and multi-faceted, and a detailed treatment of relevance is beyond the scope of this book. There are some excellent reviews and discussions on this topic (e.g., Schamber, 1994; Saracevic, 1996; Mizzaro, 1997). A challenge in the assessment of relevance has been the cost of judging results (e.g., even small changes in metrics such as a shift from mean average precision to the more user-focused precision, as ten retrieved documents require larger topic sets for similar levels of confidence; see Voorhees [2009]). Many metrics have been developed to quantify the relevance of results to searchers' information needs. There is also a more recent trend toward computing *personalized* relevance estimates based on inferences made from searcher behavior (e.g., White et al., 2010; Teevan et al., 2011b; Bennett et al., 2012). These metrics are important in evaluating contextualization and personalization algorithms for which there is no substitute for relevance judgments direct from the individual searcher.

10.2.1.1 Metrics

A broad range of metrics have been proposed for evaluating the relevance of results returned by search systems. These include Mean Average Precision (MAP), Mean Reciprocal Rank (MRR), Rank Biased Precision (RBP; see Moffat and Zobel [2008]), Normalized Discounted Cumulative Gain (NDCG; see Järvelin and Kekäläinen [2002], mentioned in Chapter 9), and Binary Preference (BPref; see Buckley and Voorhees [2004]), which handles incomplete judgment data better than average precision. Behind all of these metrics lies a user model describing how searchers examine the results and the impact of search engine actions, such as poor ordering of those results, on outcome such as the amount of user effort and information gained per rank position. Central to the design of this model is experimenter intuition about how people behave when interacting with the search system and what goals the systems should have; the metric then becomes about satisfying those goals. Given a ranked list of search results as an input, many of these metrics model the effort that a searcher has to expend to obtain relevant information (typically as the depth in the result list that they need to reach in order to obtain relevant information) and the gain to searchers from examining documents in the list in descending rank order. In the case of NDCG, this gain is then compared against the ideal gain (the best attainable with the collection of documents, and the retrieval performance of the system can be computed. In my discussion, I focus on three popular relevance metrics: (1) precision and recall; (2) mean reciprocal rank; and (3) discounted cumulative gain.

10.2.1.1.1 Precision and Recall

In information retrieval, precision (also called positive predictive value) is the fraction of retrieved instances that are relevant, whereas recall (also known as sensitivity) is the fraction of relevant instances that are retrieved. Both precision and recall are therefore based on an understanding and measure of relevance and are typically averaged across all queries (Baeza-Yates and Ribeiro-Neto, 1999).

- **Precision:** The fraction of retrieved documents that is relevant to the search. Precision takes all retrieved documents into account, but it can also be evaluated at a given cut-off rank, considering only the topmost results returned by the system. This measure is called precision at rank position n or $P@n$. For example for a text search on a set of documents precision is the number of correct results divided by the number of results up to a defined rank.
- **Recall:** The fraction of the documents that is relevant to the query that are successfully retrieved. For a text search on a set of documents, for example, recall is the number of correct results divided by the number of results that should have been returned. In binary classification, because recall is called sensitivity, it can be looked at as the probability that a relevant document is retrieved by the query. Recall is important in a number of settings, such as legal retrieval. Recall is a fundamental issue in a number of application domains, especially patent or medical retrieval, when missing information is not tolerable. In a seminal study, Blair and Maron (1985) questioned the viability of search systems for recalling relevant results and showed that searchers overestimated the recall of a legal search system (thinking that they attained 75% when they actually only found 20%), even though they employed iterative approaches where they reviewed returned results. Maron (1988) suggested that to be effective, searchers need to be able to predict and utilize discriminatory terms, which can be challenging.

It is trivial to achieve perfect recall by returning all documents in response to any query. Therefore, recall alone may be a necessary component of evaluating search systems, but it is not sufficient. The number of non-relevant documents should also be considered, by computing the precision. The two measures are often combined to compute the F_1 score (or F-measure) to provide a single measurement of the performance of a system from the harmonic mean of precision and recall (i.e., $2 \times (P \times R)/(P + R)$; see Jardine and Van Rijsbergen [1971]). Other commonly used measures are F_2, which weights recall higher than precision, and $F_{0.5}$, which weights precision higher than recall. The decision about which F-measure to apply lies in the specific application – that is, when precision outweighs recall (e.g., in engine switch prediction [Guo et al., 2011]), $F_{0.5}$ will often be used as the evaluation metric.

10.2.1.1.2 Mean Reciprocal Rank

Measures such as precision and recall consider all relevant items up to a particular rank position. However, in cases for which there may only be a single answer (e.g., in question-answering scenarios) we require a measure of how effectively the system finds that particular answer. The mean reciprocal rank (MRR) (Voorhees, 1999) is the multiplicative inverse of the *rank* of the first relevant result (or correct answer), averaged across all queries under consideration. The MRR is defined over a set of queries Q is defined as $\frac{1}{|Q|} \sum_{i=1}^{|Q|} \frac{1}{rank_i}$. If multiple relevant results appear in the ranked list, the search engine only receives credit for the first item.

10.2.1.1.3 Discounted Cumulative Gain

Precision, recall, and MRR all assume binary relevance labels (relevant or not relevant). However, relevance is multidimensional (Barry, 1994; Saracevic, 1975) and different aspects of relevance have been recognized (Cosijn and Ingwersen, 2000; Schamber et al., 1990). As such, graded relevance judgments may more accurately reflect the continuous nature of relevance (Robertson, 1977) and has been shown to lead to different rank orderings of the search results (Kekäläinen, 2005).

Discounted cumulative gain (DCG) is a measure of search engine effectiveness. Unlike the models described thus far, DCG uses a graded relevance scale of documents in a search engine result set, and it measures the usefulness, or gain, of a document based on its position in the result list. The gain is accumulated from the top to the bottom of the result list, with the gain of each result discounted at lower ranks. Two assumptions are central to the metric: (1) highly relevant documents are more useful when appearing earlier in a search engine result list (have higher ranks); and (2) highly relevant documents are more useful than marginally relevant documents, which are in turn more useful than irrelevant documents. DCG originates from an earlier, more primitive, measure called cumulative gain (CG), which focuses on the accumulation of value during the examination of a result list, irrespective of the rank order in which those results are returned by the search engine for the query. The CG_p at rank p is defined as $\sum_{i=1}^{p} rel_i$. Where rel_i is the graded relevance of the result at position i. Importantly, CG is not affected by changes in the ordering of search results. The metric therefore has limited utility for search engine evaluation as a variant that discounts the gain as a function of rank position is needed. This is known as discounted cumulative gain (DCG). This discount reflects the reduced value to searchers from presenting a relevant result at a low rank.

The premise of DCG is that highly relevant documents appearing lower in a search result list should be penalized as the graded relevance value is reduced logarithmically proportional to the position of the result. The DCG accumulated at rank p (DCG_p) can be defined as $rel_1 + \sum_{i=2}^{p} (rel_i / \log_2(i))$ or $\sum_{i=1}^{p} ((2^{rel_i} - 1)/(\log_2(i + 1)))$, with the latter placing more emphasis on retrieving relevant documents. Because DCG does not allow for the consistent comparison of search engines between queries (e.g., given differences in the length of result lists depending on the query), the DCG value needs to be normalized. This is achieved by sorting the documents in the result list for a query by their relevance score, irrespective of the actual order in which they were retrieved by the engine. This is best attainable DCG with the results retrieved, known as the ideal DCG (IDCG) at a given rank position. This allows us to compute the normalized discounted cumulative gain ($NDCG_p$) for a query as $DCG_p/IDCG_p$. The NDCG value is between 0.0 and 1.0, inclusive, and is therefore comparable between queries. In a perfect ranking algorithm, the DCG_p will equal the $IDCG_p$, resulting in an NDCG value of 1.0. The NDCG values can be averaged across all queries in the test set to compute the average performance of a ranking algorithm. One way to construct an accurate ideal result set is to pool results for the same query from different search providers and have the relevance of those results judged by human assessors.

Although NDCG has been adopted for a range of ranking applications, including in the evaluation of commercial search engines (Burges et al., 2005), there are some drawbacks. The metric does not penalize a search engine for the retrieval of bad results beyond a particular rank position or for missing results (e.g., the metric only assesses the gain relative to what was retrieved, not to what could have been retrieved). As such, it is more appropriate for evaluation settings in which there is an emphasis on precision, as is the case with Web search ranking. There are ways around these shortcomings (e.g., by adding penalty functions for results that we want to penalize or adding low relevance scores at the rank positions of the relevant documents). Other shortcomings that apply to this and other metrics is that they only assess what is returned to the search engine up to a particular rank, and do not give the search system credit for results that are retrieved beyond that rank, even if they are of reasonable quality.

Note that the set of metrics is not exhaustive, but it does highlight some of the more commonly used metrics in evaluating search systems. Many other metrics have been proposed, all of which attempt to capture some notion of relevance or utility as users inspect result lists (for a more complete review of measures of retrieval effectiveness, see Croft et al. [2010]). All of these metrics rely on the availability of judgments of query-document relevance, but are agnostic to the source of the judgment. Judgments can be obtained explicitly (as described later), or implicitly via careful mining of search activity. Both of these methods support the creation of personalized judgments, although the latter is more conducive to this because required data can be collected passively without interrupting searchers directly.

Relevance metrics rely on the availability of judgments on the documents with respect to a query. These are collected using a Cranfield methodology – judgments are collected based on pooling the results of the different search systems being compared and assigning those results to external judges for labeling.[1] Given a large number of such query-document pairings, metrics such as average precision and recall can then be computed to assess the performance of the system. Given these ratings across a diverse set of representative queries that the system could likely encounter, we can estimate the overall performance of the system using metrics such as mean average precision. These judgments can be binary (e.g., relevant or not relevant), or multi-level (e.g., a six-point scale such as: *bad*, *poor*, *fair*, *good*, *excellent*, and *perfect*), depending on the nature of the evaluation task. Multi-level judgments can also be converted to binary judgments by thresholding the value of the multi-level judgment (e.g., all query-document pairs with a value of *fair* or higher could be assigned a rating of "relevant" and everything else would receive a rating of "non-relevant"). Metrics designed to handle binary relevance judgments could then be applied as before.

10.2.1.1.3.1 Session-Level Measures

The methods described thus far have focused on the relevance of single queries. However, as mentioned earlier, there is a growing interest in evaluating retrieval performance over a full session (Järvelin et al., 2008; Kanoulas et al., 2011; Jiang et al., 2012). Järvelin et al. (2008) developed measures such as session-based cumulative gain to summarize search performance across multiple queries within a search task. Kanoulas et al. (2011) utilized TREC data, including data from the TREC 2010 Session Track (Kanoulas et al., 2010), to evaluate groups of measures: (1) those that make no assumptions about searcher behavior; and (2) those that make some simple assumptions. They showed that they can generalize existing metrics (such as mean average precision) to a multi-query setting. Jiang et al. (2012) developed a method to simulate query reformulations in the context of a search session to estimate document utility. Focusing on sessions allows metrics to better represent the dynamic process of searching (Bates, 1989), especially because in many information-seeking tasks there may be no definite solution. The process may be just as important in these tasks, if not more important, than the destination (the final state). Metrics must therefore consider the attainment of relevant content over time, and the dynamic nature of relevance (which may also shift during the task in line with changes in information needs), rather than system performance at a particular time. Although the focus is on topical relevance thus far in this chapter, other types of relevance, including situational, cognitive, and motivational are also important in search evaluation (Saracevic, 2007). The objective, topical relevance benchmarks traditionally used in the evaluation of search systems do not generalize across searchers, and it is difficult to create benchmark judgments based on other types of relevance, because they are more likely to vary by individual. That said, progress has been made on developing personalized relevance measures.

10.2.1.2 Agreement with Searchers

Evaluation measures are meant to reflect searcher preferences. Ideally a ranking of systems by a metric would match the ranking of the same systems by preference. There have been studies of the alignment of metrics and those related to searcher preferences revealed explicitly in user studies or implicitly in search logs (Sanderson et al., 2010; Turpin and Hersh, 2001; 2002; Smucker and Jethani, 2010). Agreement has been measured in terms of: (1) agreement between measures and explicit ratings/search outcomes; and (2) agreement between measures and searcher behavior.

10.2.1.2.1 Ratings and Outcomes

Studies by Hersh et al. (2000) and Turpin and Hersh (2001) examined the alignment between test collections and evaluation measures, and the outcomes of user studies with the same systems. Although the offline evaluation revealed a difference in retrieval performance between the systems, this finding was not repeated in either of the online evaluations. Other studies have experimented with artificial document rankings with controlled levels of effectiveness, and found that there was a correlation between the outcomes of offline and online studies but only for large differences in offline measures (Allan et al., 2005; Turpin and Scholer, 2006), including additional measures such as searcher satisfaction (Al-Maskari et al., 2008). Thomas and Hawking (2006) employed a side-by-side preference methodology where they presented participants with the top ten results from Google on one side, and lower ranked results (e.g., from twenty-one to thirty) on the other side, which were presumed to be of lower quality given the rank differences. They found a strong preference for the higher-ranked results.

These studies have shown that the Cranfield-style metrics can have low predictive power about the performance of search systems. One explanation for the lack of difference between the online and offline settings is that searchers have been shown to adapt their search strategies when faced with a poorly performing system (e.g., issuing more queries to find more relevant information than was attainable with a single query; see Smith and Kantor [2008]). Another explanation is that the offline evaluation settings lack realism – that is, they do not attempt to model a searcher or the interface with which they are engaging at query time (Smucker and Jethani, 2010). The same authors showed that as the search interface became more complex, offline measures such as precision become less predictive of user performance. Beyond laboratory settings, a long tradition of studies have examined the relationship between satisfaction and system performance and showed little evidence of a connection between effectiveness measures and satisfaction (Tagliacozzo, 1977; Su, 1992).

10.2.1.2.2 Searcher Behavior

A number of studies have examined the relationship between search activity (primarily document selection decisions) and relevance metrics (absolute or relative [preference-based]) in uncontrolled experimental settings (Agichtein et al., 2006; Fox et al., 2005; Carterette and Jones, 2007). It is possible to evaluate the relationship with a controlled experimental design if certain behavioral biases are considered. As noted earlier, there is a strong positional bias in how searchers examine search results irrespective of relevance (Joachims et al., 2005). Research into methods such as interleaving (Joachims, 2002) has shown that by merging the results from two different rankers, interactions can form a blind preference judgment between pairs of results. Results of such analysis on live search systems have shown that searchers more frequently select results that originate from the ranking algorithm with better performance (Joachims, 2002). Others results have been found when providing users combined rankings search results and observing their click preferences (Radlinski et al., 2008). Ali and Chang (2006) showed that click-through rate is associated with relevance, and it is weaker than expected (40, likely because clicks are motivated by factors beyond relevance (such as curiosity and surprise). They found that document selections may be the most useful predictor for navigational and single-word queries. In considering longer-term preferences, Hu et al. (2011) found a relationship between search engine satisfaction and long-term reuse, but that it was engine dependent (e.g., not apparent for the dominant search engine, but clear for others).

10.2.1.3 Time and Effort

The metrics described earlier assume that people examine the search result list at a constant speed, carefully examining each of the search results. However, observational studies of search behavior clearly show that these assumptions do not reflect reality. Variance between searchers in terms of how they inspect the result lists and examine documents post selection is high (driven by different needs and intentions, as well as different traits and interaction styles), and this needs to be reflected in the metrics that are used for evaluation purposes. In addition to searcher and task effects, properties of the content itself (e.g., document length and the presence of duplicates in the result list) may also influence the amount of effort that searchers must expend seeking information. Smucker and Clarke (2012) introduced a measure known as time-biased gain, which considers temporal effects during the search process. These are currently ignored by existing metrics such as those described earlier. This builds on a range of previous research in this area. Expected search length (ESL; see Cooper [1968]) provides a measure of searcher effort by predicting the expected number of documents that a searcher must read before finding a desired number of relevant documents. Expected search duration (Dunlop, 1997) extends the ESL metric to predict the amount of time needed to process the results retrieved. De Vries et al. (2004) extended the research by Cooper and Dunlop to address situations in which the systems being evaluated do not retrieve fixed, predefined retrieval units, creating the potential for issues associated with overlap in search result content. Other research has utilized time as a way to represent the cost of interaction (Pirolli et al., 1996; Baskaya et al., 2012, 2013).

10.2.1.4 Personalized Relevance Measurement

Many of the metrics that have been described in this section rely on the presence of relevance judgments for query-document pairs provided by third-party judges. However, in settings sensitive to the search situation (e.g., when personalization or contextualization are employed), it is not always clear that judgments from other searchers will accurately capture the interests and intentions of the current searcher at the time of their search. Ideally, in such circumstances we would like to be able to elicit relevance judgments direct from the searchers as they perform their search task. However, it is impractical to capture explicit judgments directly from searchers in this way. The cost to searchers in terms of interruptions to provide relevance assessments is too great, and it may affect their associated search behaviors in ways that make them unusable for learning.

One method that has been used successfully in recent work on large-scale personalization and contextualization research is leveraging behavioral data to provide implicit judgments on clicked documents in the top-n ranked results (Dou et al., 2007; Gao et al., 2009; Bennett et al., 2011). Given a searcher, their short- and long-term search behavior (as a source of data for building models), and their future behavior (at least their behavior for the current query), we can formulate an evaluation task whereby given the clicks on the search results, the goal of the personalization is to reorder the top-n search results to promote the pages that received the clicks in the ranked list. Rather than using all clicks, it may be preferable to focus only on those clicks where the searcher appeared to be especially satisfied with the outcome (e.g., those "satisfied" clicks with a dwell time exceeding a thirty-second threshold or were the last clicks observed in the session). The assumption is that these were the pages that met *that particular searcher's* needs and that by promoting those results in the ranking the search provider create a better a search experience.

Using this methodology we can use search behavior to generate binary relevance judgments and apply metrics such as MAP or MRR, described previously, or perform a more nuanced inspection of the search behavior to generate multi-level judgments appropriate for metrics such as NDCG. The advantage of MAP over MRR is that it can handle multiple judgments, allowing for more complete judgments in the case of informational queries where multiple clicks are more likely (Teevan et al., 2008).

To infer multi-level judgments from behavior, result selections (or lack thereof) needs to be interpreted based on subsequent search behavior. For example, the amount of time that a searcher spends on the landing page following a click could provide insight into some insight into the utility of that page (Liu et al., 2010). In one such scheme, results with no click could be assigned a rating of 0, those with any click could get a rating of 1, and those with a satisfied click (dwell time exceeding a threshold such as thirty seconds [Fox et al., 2005]) could receive a rating of 2. Established metrics for handling judgments of this nature, such as NDCG, could then be applied. Special consideration may be given to results that lie below the lowest-ranked click, since it is not clear that searchers considered those results in making their selection decisions (Shokouhi et al., 2013). The recent Yandex personalization challenge employed multi-level personalized relevance judgments from log data.[2] Research connected to that challenge showed that in that setting better retrieval performance was attained from training a machine-learned ranking algorithm using graded personalized implicit relevance judgments (Ustinovskiy et al., 2015).

10.2.2 Novelty and Diversity

There are aspects of results beyond relevance that need to be considered when evaluating retrieval systems. Two of these are novelty and diversity, and there are measures of the effect of these in search. In computing these metrics, they can be viewed from the perspective of the search engine (Clarke et al., 2008) or from the perspective of the searcher (White and Huang, 2010; Singla et al., 2010). The work of Clarke et al., which builds on the work of many others (e.g., Goffman, 1964; Boyce, 1982; Carbonell and Goldstein, 1998), specifically focuses focused on addressing redundancy (with increased novelty) and ambiguity (with more or less diversity, depending on whether the focus is on accommodating multiple information needs [Spärck-Jones et al., 2007]). Clarke et al. accomplished this using informational nuggets extracted from documents that can be compared to represent properties of the documents and the results, and hence can be used to compute the metrics. They also considered how documents in the result list are related, a factor that is usually ignored in offline evaluation. Many others have since explored the diversification of search results (e.g., Wang and Zhu, 2009; Agrawal et al., 2009; Santos et al., 2011).

As an alternative to modeling novelty and diversity within the results of the search system, other research has focused on novelty and diversity from the searcher's perspective (e.g., Xu and Yin, 2008). In these terms, novelty can be defined as the presence of information that is new to the searcher, and diversity can be defined in terms of the presence of information on different aspects of the search topic that the searcher is exposed to by the search system or through their own selection decisions. It is important to note that novelty is a personal construct and will vary by searcher. In contrast, because it is task-dependent, diversity is less likely to vary by individual, although there may be individual preferences regarding the degree of focus in the information they encounter. Novelty and diversity can be described in more detail as:

- **Novelty:** Modeling novelty requires access to information about the searcher's long-term search behavior so as to build a model of their knowledge before the query or search session. Novelty is important in certain search tasks, and is closely associated with learning as described earlier in this chapter. There are also challenges associated with a high degree of novelty, including difficulty in interpreting content when searchers lack subject-matter expertise.
- **Diversity:** This covers the range of *different* items or topics that were encountered during the search process, but is independent of the searcher's knowledge level before the task. There are likely a range of subtopics within a subject area. Diversity measures the extent to which people are presented with, review, or attain knowledge on each of those areas from searching. For example, if a topic has five known aspects and a searcher learns about two of them with one system and four with a different system, then the second system is more performant, at least along this dimension.

Applying these metrics at scale can be difficult since search providers are often unable to ask searchers about novelty or diversity directly. One way to do this is to build representations of each of the metrics above using data to which we do have access (e.g., topical categories assigned the queries that searchers issue and the pages that they visit). In previous research (White et al., 2009a; White et al., 2010; Singla et al., 2010), distributions of the Open Directory Project (ODP, dmoz.org) categories have been used to represent topical interests, and have been used to measure novelty and diversity from the searcher's perspective from search log data alone (White and Huang, 2010).

10.2.3 Success

Search success measures the extent to which a person completes their search task. This can be measured in a number of different ways, and can be both subjective and objective. In the subjective definition, searchers define their own success (even if the outcome may be objectively assessed as incorrect – e.g., they found a factually incorrect answer to the question – as long as they believe that they are successful, then that is sufficient). The objective definition focuses on a searcher-independent definition of success and could be assessed using criteria employed by third parties (such as human assessors judging relevance or teachers grading assignments), including factual correctness. Hassan et al. (2010) showed that behavioral signals yielded more accurate assessments of search success (from the searcher's perspective) than more traditional metrics such as DCG. They modeled task success and found that sequences of actions, as well as the time between the actions, are good predictors of search success.

Explicit estimation of overall time by participants has been used as an estimator of success in usability settings (Czerwinski et al., 2001). Research in psychology has focused on time estimation (Van Bergen, 1968; Weybrew 1984), which was itself related to earlier work by Ziegarnik (1927), who showed that people were more likely to freely recall uncompleted tasks than those completed successfully. Such implicit probes can be preferable to explicit reporting because they address some of the biases in self-reporting, where people can exhibit a bias toward positive responses (Nielsen and Levy, 1994).

10.2.4 Satisfaction

Satisfaction it typically measured at the end of search sessions rather than on a per-action basis. It is not the same as success, in that people can be dissatisfied with the search process but still meet their information objectives. Satisfaction is an emotional response. It has been studied extensively in a number of areas, such as psychology (Lopez and Snyder, 2011) and commerce (Oliver, 2010). Recently, there has been a significant amount of research on developing models of search satisfaction from behavioral data. Research by Fox et al. (2005) blazed a trail for much of the work in this area by showing that behavioral signals can be correlated with explicit ratings provided by assessors. Satisfaction modeling, typically at the session level, is based on inferences from interaction behavior. Traditionally, long dwell times (e.g., thirty seconds or more) have been used to predict satisfaction with a particular result click (Fox et al., 2005). Click-through rate represents the frequency with which a searchers clicks on a particular result, or any result, for given queries or overall, divided by the frequency with which that result is presented. This can be a useful measure of satisfaction, but there are cases for which click-through rate is not always a useful indicator of satisfaction (e.g., where good abandonment is observed [Li et al., 2009]).

The dwell time for a document relates to a number of factors, including the content of the document and its complexity (e.g., Liu et al., 2010; Kim et al., 2014). Rather than focusing on individual actions such as clicks, we can also study levels of satisfaction associated with a full search session. Fox et al. (2005) attempt to predict user-annotated levels of satisfaction using a variety of implicit measures derived from search behavior. For example, they propose the gene patterns (also called "motifs") to summarize the sequences of search behavior observed in the search logs. Huffman and Hochster (2007) predicted session satisfaction using a regression model incorporating the relevance of the top three results returned for the first query, the type of information need, and the number of actions in the session. Hassan et al. (2011) captured satisfaction ratings from searchers in-situ at the termination of their search tasks, and used these labels to train models that were capable of identifying instances of search satisfaction.

More sophisticated satisfaction models are emerging that also consider behavior before and after result clicks (e.g., if the dwell is immediately followed by a related query reformulation, it is unlikely that the click was satisfied, even if the observed dwell time had a long duration; see Hassan [2012] and Kim et al. [2014]), or attributing satisfaction at the action level, albeit while still capturing satisfaction labels at the task level (Ageev et al., 2011). Emerging methods for estimating searcher satisfaction can be quite sophisticated and consider historic interactions from within the current search session and even personalized to the individual searcher (Hassan and White, 2013). The long-term effects of search satisfaction are also interesting to explore, because they may affect long-term usage patterns on search engines (Hu et al., 2011; Song et al., 2013). A challenge in developing and applying these complete metrics is their understandability; it is difficult for search providers to completely trust inferences and conclusions that they cannot completely explain. More elegant variants of sophisticated models that utilize easy-to-explain and easy-to-implement criteria, such as post-dwell reformulations (Hassan, 2012), may be preferable for search practitioners.

10.2.5 Ideation and Creativity

Creativity is often a desired outcome of the search process, especially when searches are more exploratory. Behavioral science researchers have attempted to measure creativity in a number of ways, including psychometric methods such as psychological tests and other methods (e.g., behavioral, biographical, biological [brain activity]; see Mayer [1999] and Cropely [2000]). Measuring these attributes is difficult in a laboratory setting in much the same way as exist for other types of experimental research. One particularly important drawback is that the measures focus on the creativity of *individuals* rather than the artifacts created during searching. In these cases, benchmarks include famous artists, performers, or scientists who have gained recognition for their creativity.

In search settings, researchers and search providers may be interested in measuring any amplification in creativity afforded by the search system, with the unaided searcher as a baseline. It is challenging to measure the performance of systems unless there are observable, measurable elements that can be compared across searchers and systems. An important aspect of the creative process is the generation of new ideas that are intelligible to the creator and understood in terms of prior knowledge (Boden, 1996).

In terms of evaluating systems designed to support creativity, experiments can study the process (e.g., the number of unique alternatives attempted, the time to devise solutions), the uptake of the system (e.g., the number of searchers, etc.) while also focusing on the nature of the solutions themselves, including their value to stakeholders (the searcher included) and their quality, as well as what contribution they make toward broader goals. In online services, discussed frequently in this book, many of these attributes may not be visible to system designers when analyzing data remotely and retrospectively; therefore, attention needs to be focused on observable measures, such as the resources accessed, the content generated, and importantly, the reaction that the content receives if posted in a public forum (the social confirmation step). Beyond support for search, highlighting connections between research communities (via their publications) can have significant societal implications. For example, Swanson's discovery of previously unknown connections between migraines and magnesium was made via a citation analysis and a manual review of terms in both literatures (Swanson, 1988). More recent examples of such systems (e.g., *LitLinker*; see Pratt and Yetisgen-Yildiz [2003]) provide a way to interactively explore scientific literature within a domain by following potential links, paving the way for similar kinds of scientific discovery and innovation. Kerne et al. (2014) proposed the use of elemental and holistic metrics to evaluate ideation. Elemental metrics evaluate creativity within found objects, and concern such things as fluency (e.g., number of elements generated or discovered), flexibility (e.g., the amount of diversity of the ideas), and novelty (i.e., the rareness of an idea). Holistic metrics cover how a curation compiles the items that are found, including the visual presentation, exposition (written presentation), and relevance, which may serve as a more traditional baseline.

10.2.6 Adoption and Retention

A strong signal that searchers are dissatisfied with a search system lies whether they stick with that engine over time. Retention has been studied in the search community via search engine switching, describing voluntary transitions between search engines (Telang et al., 1999; Juan and Chang, 2005; White and Dumais, 2009; Guo et al., 2011). Searchers transition for a number of reasons (dissatisfaction, but also curiosity and verification). The duration of switches also ranges from a single query (followed by a return to the source engine) to permanent defection to the destination engine.

10.2.6.1 Within-Session Switching

Researchers have studied switching rationales in situ surveys and using retrospective surveys, and showed that the two methods attained similar conclusions. White and Dumais (2009) performed a retrospective analysis of switching behavior through a survey and log analysis, and developed models to predict switching events. They showed that switching was somewhat rare (only around 1% of search sessions), and that searchers can transition for a number of reasons, primarily dissatisfaction with the results provided by the search engine, but also other factors such as a desire to review information available of that other search engine (coverage) or general preferences (e.g., returning to their default search engine). Guo et al. (2011) performed a follow-on study in which they captured switching rationales in situ using a browser plug-in, and showed that they could accurately predict why people switch between search engines. For reference, a pie chart showing the switching rationales gathered through the retrospective survey is presented in Figure 10.3.

Researchers have also developed models to predict the timing of search engine switches within search sessions and to estimate the rationale for an observed switch (Laxman et al., 2008; Guo et al., 2011). The former can help design interventions to provide additional support to a searcher who looks likely to leave a search system for a competitor. Different search interfaces or additional computational resources could be devoted to these searchers to improve their likelihood of search success. They may be offered the opportunity for dialog with a search or domain expert, who could help them in their search. Being able to predict *why* a searcher switched engines may have particular utility if applied retrospectively over search logs, allowing a search engine to identify the instances in which searchers were dissatisfied and focus on those examples for further investigation. Given that the switching event may not be observable to the search engine (i.e., the engine can only observe actions on the engine itself), recent research has focused on the development of methods to predict whether switches have occurred. For example, within the context of a recent Yandex data challenge, Savenkov et al. (2013) developed models to detect the occurrence of engine switches using data about personal preferences and behavioral patterns *on a single engine*. Switches can be

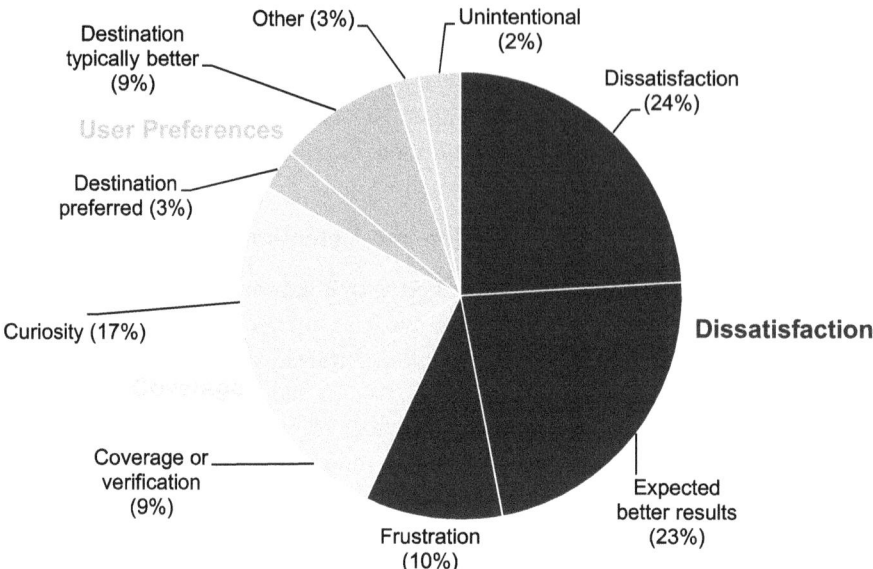

Figure 10.3. Switching rationales collected via retrospective surveys (adapted from Guo et al., 2011).

identified using both personalized and aggregated features corresponding to searcher preferences and behaviors surrounding a switch (e.g., average click position, time to click). Predicting switches using the logs of a single engine is advantageous because measuring the occurrence of the event traditionally requires logs that contain queries on both engines, typically collected via client-side software such as browser-based logging or a browser toolbar.

10.2.6.2 Between-Session and Longer-Term Switches

Beyond within-session switches, there are other types of switch that transcend session boundaries. For example, searchers may switch on a task basis, especially if particular search systems are known to perform better for certain tasks. If this is the case, we may observe oscillations between search engines depending on the nature of the search task being attempted. More critical for search providers are long-term switches, or so-called defections where searchers may leave a search engine indefinitely. White et al. (2010) modeled long-term search engine switching and showed that there were three distinct searcher cohorts who either: (1) stuck with the same engine over time; (2) switched frequently between engines (perhaps reflecting task preferences and multiple searchers on the same machine); or (3) defected once to a different search engine and never returned. The cause for the third transition could be long-term dissatisfaction, or more innocuous reasons such as installing a new Web browser or operating system with a different default search engine, or software that changes the default engine as part of the installation process. The reluctance of people to change default settings has been well documented in terms of cognitive effort (Gigerenzer, 2008) and loss aversion (Tversky and Kahneman, 1991), and this is likely to impact multi-engine usage.

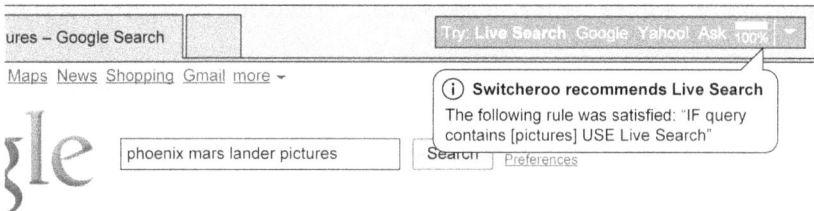

Figure 10.4. Screenshot of the *Switcheroo* system in action.

10.2.6.3 Promoting Engine Switching

Rather than simply studying search engine switching, researchers have also examined the promotion of engine switching when better search results can be predicted. Each commercial search engine has differences in the pages that it indexes and the ranking methods that it employs. We could always point the searcher to the best search engine if for each query we had a service that could poll the other engines and make predictions about whether the searcher was on the best engine for that query. White et al. (2008) devised a system called *Switcheroo* that could accurately predict the best engine to use based on features of the query, the results returned from both of the engines, and the intersection between those features (e.g., the overlap between the query terms and the titles of the returned documents). A model was learned from human-labeled relevance data to predict which of many engines had the most relevant results for the current query. Switcheroo was a Web browser plug-in that monitored queries/results on different commercial search engines, and alerted searchers if a better result set was available elsewhere for their current search query. Figure 10.4 shows a screenshot of the experience that searchers could be offered. In this case, the system is recommending a vertical search engine based on a manually-generated rule related to the quality of the engine for particular queries (in this case images).

Switcheroo and other similar support enable an engine-agnostic approach to search that is similar to that employed by meta-search engines, but does not require the searcher to adopt a new (meta-)search engine to benefit from the feature. In the model of the search process, searchers are always directed to the most performant search engine, and for the non-dominant search engines this could lead to an increase in query share for some search engines if searchers trusted Switcheroo to always identify the most performant search system on their behalf.

The amount of traffic that a search engine receives is dependent on factors beyond the relevance of its results, including brand loyalty and default settings. For the non-dominant search engines, it is likely that they perform better for more queries than is represented in their market share. If a minor search engine is struggling to make inroads on the search market, having searchers adopt a plug-in that directs them to the best search engine could significantly benefit the minor market player(s).The success of this approach depends on searchers trusting that a particular search engine is an unbiased broker of search engine traffic. The service may need to be released by an impartial third party to be fully trusted by searchers as a way to improve their search experience. Evidence shows that people can be persuaded to change their engrained search practices, if it is in their interests (Bateman et al., 2012; Agapie et al., 2013).

10.3 Application of Measures

Traditionally, experiments in search settings focus on outcome-oriented measures, such as relevance and task success. However, as the range of tasks for which search systems are used continues to grow, the search experience will become more involved. Many measures assume context independence when searcher choices are strongly dependent on their experiences and preferences, the search situation, and how the search engine responds to the information retrieved. Future measures need to consider what other information was shown to the searcher so as to understand their *preferences* in addition to their absolute implicit judgments (Joachims, 2002). A/B testing goes some way toward addressing this challenge, as does other research on personalized relevance (Dou et al., 2010), the consideration of skips and clicks in interest modeling (Shokouhi et al., 2013), and eye-gaze/cursor movements (Huang et al., 2011).

The measures vary in terms of ease of application, ranging from "easy to apply" (e.g., relevance, success, engagement, and satisfaction) to "requires specialist equipment/expertise to instantiate/interpret" (e.g., assessment of cognitive load using EEG, measurement of frustration using eye-gaze tracking). Some of the measures are also more open-ended and subjective than others. For example, learning and creativity are highly specific to an individual and challenging to measure objectively, but may reveal aspects of system performance that are not measurable using more traditional measures such as satisfaction or search success, from which inter-searcher inferences can be made based on consistent expected behaviors, such as dwelling for longer on satisfactory content (Fox et al., 2005; Liu et al., 2010; Kim et al., 2014). The specific measures also vary on both a system-by-system basis and a task-by-task basis. Designers should consider which of the measures (or combinations thereof) best meet their needs for answering their specific questions and determining system effectiveness. Although the primary system objective may simply be to make people more successful in their searching, this should not be at the expense of other factors, such as making the search process significantly less enjoyable or more frustrating. When designing search system evaluations, designers should consider utilizing both process-oriented measures (e.g., engagement and/or efficiency, because they may be easier to implement and do not require more than rudimentary system logging), and outcome-oriented measures (e.g., success and/or satisfaction).

Because there are some measures, such as cognitive load, which can be more or impossible to accurately measure retrospectively from historic records of search activity, a variety of methods are needed to fully understand search system performance. Thus far, criteria have been presented in isolation, but in actuality researchers and search providers would want to utilize appropriate subsets of these metrics and others to develop a complete picture of the search process and outcomes. For example, there are other criteria, such as whimsy or recreational searching (Wilson and Elsweiler, 2010), that are important parts of the search process, but it is unclear how to measure their success. Other researchers have suggested that metrics better reflecting actual searcher behavior can be produced by measuring search systems in the context of searchers performing tasks. For example, Reid (2000) proposed evaluating search systems based on result *utility* to a task rather than relevance; and Borlund (2000) proposed a framework for evaluating search systems by placing evaluators into task scenarios.

In operational settings, assessing search behaviors likely involves the computation of statistics across millions of searchers. In computing statistical significance in these cases, the sample sizes can be extremely large, meaning that small differences in mean averages can result in statistical significance. In interpreting these results, it is also important to consider measures such as effect size (see Kelley and Preacher, 2012; Cohen 1988), which attempt to capture the strength of a phenomenon and better represent the extent to which observed differences are meaningful versus significance testing alone.

On a final note, the emphasis in this chapter has been on the evaluation of search *systems*. However, it is also important to consider the performance of the searchers to understand the impact of variables such as search skill or search experience on the search process. Searcher performance could be measured independently as is traditionally done in laboratory studies or field experiments such as *Google-A-Day* (agoogleaday.com). However, there are other interesting ways in which this comparison could be performed. For example, in a competitive environment similar to Math Olympiads, individuals (or teams in the case of collaborative searching) could compete to complete search tasks of different types under a variety of constraints. The key learnings would be a better understanding of the tactics and strategies of those who were most performant, which could guide the design of tools and tutorials to help direct other searchers toward improving their search skills.

10.4 Summary

A number of evaluation measures were presented in this chapter, focused on the search process and search outcomes. There are some measures that are important that were not discussed. For example, the usability of search systems is an important issue (Nielsen, 1993) on which search engines place a lot of emphasis via user testing (including focus groups and laboratory studies) and flighting. Although the metrics were discussed independently, in practice *combinations* of metrics are needed to gain robust insights about system performance. In the next chapter, I discuss the evaluation methodologies that have been developed to evaluate search systems, as well as their strengths and weaknesses.

CHAPTER 11
Evaluation Methodologies

A range of methodologies can be used to evaluate search systems both in the laboratory and in the real world. Each has advantages and disadvantages. Methodologies range from offline test collections and simulations of people's search behavior, to living laboratories, instrumented panels, ethnography, and large-scale log analysis. Specific objectives determine the metrics and methodologies that are employed.

There are at least three important dimensions of the available methods: (1) *stage*: the point in the design process that the method is used (i.e., formative, as the experimental system is being designed – with outcomes being able to inform design decisions, and summative, once design is complete and the system has been developed); (2) *scale*: the scale at which the method is employed (small, medium, or large); and (3) *participants*: the people involved, e.g., searcher simulations, user study subjects, internal users (company employees test their own products; a process known as *dogfooding* [Harrison, 2006]), or external customers (either via parallel flighting or interleaving of the output of alternative algorithms). Dumais et al. [2014] divided a subset of experimental methodologies into two variants: (1) *observational* (where people may be observed searching naturally) and (2) *experimental* (where the search experience may be intentionally manipulated per an experimental design) (see Table 11.1).

The various methods provide different perspectives on search system performance. Although the methods are listed separately in Table 11.1 and discussed separately in this chapter, combinations of different methods are valuable to help search providers develop a more complete understanding of system effectiveness.

The focus in search system evaluation has been on designing experiments that are: insightful and able to assess successfully the attributes on which they focus; affordable with respect to the cost of creating and running the experiments; repeatable so that others can build on results; and explainable so that they can guide subsequent improvements (Liu and Oard, 2006). The primary focus has been component evaluation, involving the isolation and control of experimental variables that can interfere with the reliability of conclusions drawn.

Table 11.1. *Examples of experimental methodologies and variants of these methods focused on observing natural search practices versus controlled experimentation, where the experience may be manipulated*

Experimental Methodology	Typical Number of Participants	Variant	
		Observational	Experimental
Laboratory studies (rich data)	10–100s	In-laboratory behavior	In-laboratory controlled
Instrumented panels	100–1,000s	Ethnography	Clinical trials and field tests
Retrospective log analysis	1,000s–millions	Logs from one searcher	A/B testing of alternatives

Current methods are insufficient for evaluating complex systems for a number of reasons (Kelly, 2009), including the inadequacy of user models and task models for capturing all types of information-seeking tasks, activities, and situations. Web and search engine indices are constantly changing. Many search tasks are complex and evolve without having stable, definable end points. Longitudinal studies are needed to understand the performance of search systems over time.

There are excellent summaries of the various methodologies for evaluating search systems interactively (Kelly, 2009), using test collections (Sanderson, 2010; Harman, 2011) or via behavioral data (Dumais et al., 2014). As highlighted in Table 11.1, system evaluation can be performed at different scales, including large-scale deployment, medium-scale deployments to panels using instrumented software, and small-scale deployments in laboratory settings, where special software/hardware enables the capture of many attributes, ranging from interaction behaviors to physiological signals and affective cues.

11.1 Research Questions

Research questions motivate the study and help focus what needs to be done. The specification of the research questions is one of the first steps that an experimenter must take when undertaking scientific research that is quantitative or qualitative in nature. There are usually a small number of research questions in user studies of search systems. The questions can be focused on a particular component (e.g., what is the value of widget X for search?), or more broadly associated with a particular approach or technology (e.g., to what extent does searcher-perceived caption relevance match the relevance of the underlying document?).

Researchers may choose to express their experimental objectives as hypotheses. These are usually formulated as statements asserting that there is some relationship between the treatment and the dependent variables studied in the experiment. Traditionally, these alternative hypotheses are then compared against the null hypotheses using statistical hypothesis testing (Fisher, 1925) to assess the probability that any observed affect occurred by chance. Because many experiments that collect quantitative data use it to perform statistical hypothesis testing, it is important to define hypotheses early, both to shape experimental design decisions, as well as decisions about the specific data to be collected and the analysis mechanisms employed.

Because the experiment is guided by the research questions, they are a key determinant of experimental aspects such as the choice of metrics (e.g., those covered in the previous chapter) and the choice of experimental methods, covered in the next section. In some cases, if the questions are complex or a richer analysis of behavior is sought, then the researcher may elect to utilize a mixed methods approach to provide different perspectives on the variables of interest.

11.2 Methods

Different methodologies are now described, ordered from small scale to large scale.

11.2.1 Interviews and Focus Groups

Interviews involve one-to-one dialog between the experimental participant and the experimenter (or a third party). Interviews can be structured (often with set questions asked in a standardized order) or unstructured (which are informal discussions). Structured interviews are more commonly used in search evaluation given their replicability and the speed with which they can be conducted. Interviews are often performed following an experiment, giving the participant an opportunity to reflect on their experience in using the experimental system. Experimenters can probe deeply about particular aspects of the study, such as which aspects of the system the participants did and did not like. The advantage of this approach is the depth of the questioning, the opportunity for follow-up questions, and the richness of the data that results from the dialog. The disadvantages include the costs involved in performing the interview and transcribing the data, especially since each interview only contains the opinions of a single participant, albeit in great detail.

Focus groups can be used to address some of the shortcomings of interviews. These involve selected panels who participate in a structured interview process aimed at eliciting their perceptions, opinions, beliefs, and attitudes toward a new concept, design, or product; often a new system or new feature in our case. Focus-group methodologies have been discussed extensively (Kreuger, 2009; Kitzinger, 1995; Morgan, 1997), and has been employed to a limited extent in search evaluation (Eysenbach and Köhler, 2002). In focus groups, questions are asked in an interactive setting where participants are free to discuss their views with other group members. The groups usually comprise small groups of six to ten participants, unknown to each other, who are consulted in detail about their opinions during the formative stages of design. Sessions may last 1.5–2 hours and are conducted a setting that is conducive to discussion, such as a conference room. Typically, a new idea is presented to the focus group, with some example implementations and usage scenarios. The process is guided by a moderator, who asks questions (which are usually open-ended), and ensures that all participants have an opportunity to contribute to the discussion. Participants are then asked to provide their opinions on the idea presented to them.

Focus groups can be a cost-effective way to solicit the opinions of multiple people simultaneously (Marshall and Rossman, 1999) and effective way to get feedback on an idea before incurring the cost of running a full-blown user study or distributing a survey. They are also meant to be used early enough in the design cycle that the results from the focus group can be fed directly into the design of the system rather than waiting until it is in a more advanced state, at which point a user study might be a more effective method. On the downside, focus groups suffer from many of the same drawbacks as other forms of qualitative research, including: (1) where the findings of the study are subject to interpretation or bias by the experimenter (Rosenthal, 1966; Sackett, 1979); (2) participants may attempt to anticipate the desired responses of the experimenters (Rushkoff, 2005); or (3) only the opinions of the vocal participants are considered since others are less likely to express their opinions (Harding, 2013).

11.2.2 Field Studies

Understand how search systems are used in naturalistic settings requires ethnographic studies of current search practices and how systems are used. Freund et al. (2005) modeled how software engineers' work context was associated with their information behavior. Fieldwork allows for the capture of detailed information about the context surrounding the search task that can be difficult to interpret from studying search behaviors alone. Experimenters immerse themselves in the environment in which the systems are being used, and observing users of these systems in situ. Conducting fieldwork in participants' natural environment supports some aspects of the experimental process, such as selecting user-generated tasks, which may be spurred by the environment. While this approach can provide a detailed understanding of searchers' real information needs and search practices, it is less common in the information-seeking literature, although they are appropriate for some settings in which deeper insight in people's search practices is sought. For example, recent research on personal information management has applied ethnographic techniques to study how people interact with their own digital content (e.g., Kwasnik, 1989; Jones et al., 2005), task switching and interruptions (Czerwinski et al., 2004), and explorations of the role of affect in the search process (Nahl, 1998). These methodologies address some of the issues with experimental biases, such as demand characteristics (Brewer, 2000), discussed in more detail later in this chapter. In field studies, data can only be collected from a small number of searchers about a small number of tasks, which limits their generalizability.

11.2.3 Instrumented Panels

Instrumented panels utilize richer logging of interactions of hundreds or thousands of individuals, and usually incorporate some periodic probes associated with an activity of interest (e.g., soliciting judgments about searcher satisfaction at the end of a search session [Fox et al., 2005; Hassan et al., 2011]). The machines of those participating in these panels can be instrumented quite heavily (including keystroke logging and application tracking), with a view to collecting rich data about their search activities and the application context within which those activities occur. Panel participants consent to have their data recorded via specialized software that records data about their Web usage and other aspects of their computing environment, such as other active applications. In addition to capturing data, these plug-ins can administer surveys to capture demographic and other information, and elicit people's feedback about the search experience at salient points in the interaction process (e.g., when searchers abandon the search results (Diriye et al., 2012) or when they switch between search engines [Guo et al., 2011]). Detailed instrumentation of a user panel can provide rich data about the search process and the corresponding search context to enable deeper explorations of the information-seeking process that extend well beyond what is possible with search engine log data that may be several orders of magnitude larger, but are more limited in terms of what data they record.

These panels are flexible and can be performed over the short or long term, and with small or large user populations. Short-term panels are usually more task focused, whereas long-term panels are more focused on naturalistic behaviors. Even though studying behavior over long periods of time means that some (potentially large) fraction of data will be missed as participants will be lost from the study as they change machines, use different machines, and so on, such longitudinal analysis does provide additional insights into changes in search patterns over time, which may not be seen in shorter-term studies (Grimes et al., 2007). Panels can range in size; for example, Internet analytics company comScore maintains a panel of millions of panelists (incentivized by free software, entries into prize drawings, and other such rewards). The panel was validated to be representative of the online population and projectable to the United States population (Fulgoni, 2005). They track panelists' online behavior longitudinally to measure trends in Internet usage, such as the relative market share of Web search engines; an important statistic used by the engines for competitive analysis, and to inform and measure the impact of strategic decisions. That said, this is an example of an extremely large panel; most panels range from a few hundred to a few thousand participants.

11.2.4 Laboratory Studies

Laboratory studies are the primary means of evaluating interactive search systems and they have been used extensively for this purpose (Belkin et al., 1993; Koenemann and Belkin, 1996; Kelly et al., 2005; White et al., 2007). Laboratory studies afford more detailed insights and also more control than is possible with field studies. In a typical laboratory study, participants use one of more experimental search systems to find information described in a small number of prescribed topics, sometimes derived from common topic sets, such as a set of topics from one or more TREC tracks. Their interactions with the system(s) are recorded for later analysis, and they may provide feedback at various points about the efficacy of the system via surveys and other self-reporting techniques such as interviews and think-alouds. Usability measures can be computed based on questionnaire responses or system interactions; performance can be estimated using measures such as the number of relevant documents found and the time taken to do so. There are some excellent summaries of laboratory studies in the evaluation of interactive search systems (see, e.g., Kelly, 2009).

User studies of search systems can assume many forms, but the typical approach that is adopted in studies of search interaction have a few common elements:

- They usually include one or more experimental systems, including a baseline system without any of the additional functionality under test in the experiment. The experimental systems are typically created to answer the set of research questions devised by the experimenter in advance of the experiment.
- Experimental stimuli, usually in the form of task descriptions (e.g., simulated work task situations [Borlund, 2003]), are often created and assigned the experiments to motivate participants' information-seeking activity. Tasks should be understandable to participants, believable in the context of the task description, and sufficiently engaging to elicit realistic search behavior (Hsieh-Yee, 1993). These tasks can also be varied along a number of dimensions to evaluate the performance of the system in different ways (e.g., the experimenters may wish to vary the complexity of the task to understand how searcher performance on each of the systems changes as the task becomes more challenging). Having participants perform the same set of tasks removes the effect of the search task from the experimental process, which has been shown to impact behaviors and outcomes (Liu et al., 2010; White and Kelly, 2006). Some have argued that having participants bring their own search tasks (e.g., Russell and Grimes, 2007) improves the realism of the experiment, especially when full-session behavior is studied. Doing this makes comparisons between searchers difficult; while searchers may be attempting similar *types* of search tasks, there are also likely to be differences in the nature of the task.
- Instrumentation of the systems is used to record searcher activity, including interactions with the system and other measures such as participant attention, via eye-gaze tracking (e.g., Granka et al., 2004) and mouse cursor tracking (Rodden et al., 2008). Other forms of data collection – such as video/audio recording and application tracking – are often performed. The data produced by many of these additional methods need to be hand coded, which can be labor intensive, time consuming, and potentially unreliable, depending on the subjectivity of the criteria employed by the human judges. In-situ labeling by the experimental participants can be quite obtrusive.
- Experimental materials – including questionnaires, participant instructions, interview questions, consent forms, and so on are designed – to guide participants in conducting experiments and also to select reliable data to answer the research questions. The materials are often pilot tested with a small number of participants before the full study to ensure that the questions are worded clearly.
- Participants are recruited from some participant pool that is available to the experimenters – which can introduce some participant bias. For example, participant pools of search-related experiments run within academic settings are often skewed toward college students. Dedicated pools of user study participants, which attempt to balance demographics and can help make results more reliable, are available but can be expensive to use given costs associated with recruitment, compensation, and laboratory space for the experiment.
- The study usually lasts one to two hours and the participants are compensated in some way for their time, usually including a combination of financial reward and class credit. During the experiment the researcher will guide the participant through steps in the experimental protocol, explaining the systems and answering any questions that the participant may have. The experimental protocol describes

exactly how the experiment should be conducted so that it is consistent across all participants. The protocol is created in advance of the experiments and will be followed carefully by the experimenter as they walk the participant through the process. The experimenter may also perform other functions such as recording the amount of time that the participant takes to complete a search task. Some aspects of this guidance can also be provided by cues on the system (participants can provide answers in an interface created by experimenters, and they can indicate task start and stop events on the interface, reducing the load on the experimenter). As the participant attempts their assigned tasks, they may be asked to "think aloud," providing experimenters with more insight into their decision processes. Retrospectively, stimulated recall methods may be used to encourage participants to consider and reflect upon particular aspects of their searching (e.g., Kelly [2004] asked participants to discuss and label their last week of searching for use in experiments on the efficacy of implicit relevance feedback).

- An experimental design is created that governs how many tasks and systems each participant will attempt, whether a within-subjects or between-subjects design will be adopted, the order in which participants will attempt search tasks (e.g., will tasks be rotated to reduce learning effects associated with using tasks/systems in a particular order), and so on. The experimental design is also influenced greatly by the research questions and the *a posteriori* statistical analysis that will be performed. Data are collected to support that analysis.
- Once the results are collected, the experimenter collates the results and analyzes them using a variety of methods. Data such as interview responses and responses to open questions in questionnaires are hand coded by the experimenter(s) or (preferably) by third parties, and any trends in the responses are identified. Logs need to be parsed to extract the information about interaction behavior that is of interest in the study. Once the data are in a consistent format, appropriate statistical tests can be applied to determine the significance of any of the observed differences between the systems under test.

Laboratory studies are typically focused on the utility of a system component or system in a task-based setting. More general studies of system usability are also possible (Kuniavsky, 2003) and can yield useful insights about ease of use. Laboratory studies are often conducted onsite given logistical challenges associated with remote access, and because many aspects of the experimental process can be controlled at that location. If some control can be sacrificed, with careful design, remote variants of these studies can be developed using screen-sharing or crowdsourcing platforms.

11.2.5 Crowdsourced Studies

The recent emergence of crowdsourcing platforms such as *Mechanical Turk* and *Crowd-Flower* has enabled low-cost, carefully controlled studies of human behavior (Kittur et al., 2008, Paolacci et al., 2010). This approach is being used for a variety of experiments, including those associated with satisfaction modeling (Ageev et al., 2011), estimating attention (Lagun and Agichtein, 2011), and evaluating relevance (Alonso et al., 2008). These platforms provide access to crowdworkers who are paid a small amount of money to complete a simple human intelligence task such as assigning a category label to a query, comparing two result sets, or assigning a relevance label to a document given an assigned search query. With some careful experimental design, these platforms can be used to conduct more sophisticated, at-scale user studies that move beyond rudimentary labeling tasks to afford deeper understanding of issues such as belief dynamics during search (White, 2014). The search behaviors of remote participants can be captured by instrumenting the interface extensively using mouse cursor tracking and other mechanisms to record clicks, page views, and so on. In addition to evaluating different interface treatments, crowdsourcing can be useful as a means for cheaply gathering training data for machine learning purposes. However, there are concerns about the quality of data captured using a crowdsourced methodology (Alonso et al., 2008; Kazai, 2011).

11.2.6 Surveys

Surveys comprises a mixture of open and closed questions and can be useful in capturing participant opinions both after an experiment has concluded (in a laboratory setting) or more broadly, to canvas opinion from many members of a particular cohort. They can be a useful tool to capture subjective impressions from a large number of people, but they need to be carefully designed, both structurally and with easily understandable questions, to extract maximum value out of the replies received. Participant responses to open questions also need to be manually coded, which can be a time-consuming process, and it can be affected by some of the experimental biases described earlier. Surveys are also frequently retrospective, relying on participants' recall of past events, which can be skewed by the nature of the event (e.g., the effects of valence on the nature of memorability of an event [Taylor, 1991]).

11.2.7 Retrospective Log Analysis

The retrospective analysis of (usually aggregated) query log data containing records of user behavior captured in naturalistic settings can also be useful in understanding system performance, although typically not comparisons between systems. This is standard practice in the building better search engines and allows search providers to understand characteristics of the queries issued to the engine and to study people's search behavior. There have been a number of studies of search log behavior in the both large and the small scales (Silverstein et al., 1999; Jansen and Spink, 2005; Jansen, 2006b). Analyzing these logs offers a number of benefits, including being able to study the needs and intentions of searchers at scale, allowing for the development of taxonomies of Web search engines that can help inform system design (Broder, 2002; Rose and Levinson, 2004), and the fact that log data can be analyzed immediately (unlike other methods for which there is a need to manually label data, which can be time consuming). However, search logs provide a lot of evidence about what actions occurred, but little in the way of explanation for that activity. Pharo and Järvelin (2004) indicated that query log analysis is limited in its ability to provide the necessary data for studying the different factors and their relationships, and they proposed extensive data collection and analysis methods. Search log data can also be noisy, and log analysis provides little insight into the rationale behind the behavior. Complementary methods such as interviews, field studies, or laboratory studies need to be employed to more fully understand the observed search behavior (Grimes et al., 2007). Some progress has been made in automatically identifying searchers' goals based on search-result selection activity and hyperlink distributions (Lee et al., 2005).

11.2.8 Online Evaluation

Online evaluation involves real users searching for actual and current information needs. The method makes assumptions about the meaning behind observed behavior. For example, studies of examination of search results assume that observable aspects of people's online search behavior reflect aspects of relevance (Joachims, 2002). Specifically, searchers have a goal, they always acting in pursuit if their task goal during search, and they are not trying to provide spurious data to the system. As such, their behavior regarding the documents retrieved by the engine can be used to evaluate system performance. Marchionini and Shneiderman (1988) suggested that an examination of paths taken and decisions made during a search can support inferences about cognitive activity. Online evaluation methods have benefits over other methods in that (implicit) judgments are provided in situ, allowing the intentions of searchers to be accurately modeled, along with their intentions and state of knowledge at the time of the query. The cost of collecting judgments of this nature are also lower than they would be via dedicated, expert judges, as is the case in other circumstances such as TREC, as discussed in Section 10.2.9.

When employing online evaluation methods, there are two important decisions: (1) the unit of evaluation, whether the judgments are occurring at a document level (obtain a score for each document) or holistically at the full-ranking level (obtain an overall score for the ranking itself, to be able to evaluate retrieval functions); and (2) the nature of the judgment is either absolute (a value for the document independent of others) or relative (where the focus is on a comparison of one document, or result set, with another set).

Given that the focus is on obtaining metrics from online evaluation, such as time to click and the rank position of clicks in the result list (Kelly and Teevan, 2003; Wang et al., 2009; Huang et al., 2011), there are two main ways in which the experiment can be setup: (1) as a comparative experiment (i.e., baseline versus some number of comparative systems); or (2) as an combination experiment (i.e., combining the results retrieved by different retrieval algorithms in a single list, usually termed interleaved evaluation). Both of these methods involve controlling the presentation of the results and studying searcher interaction with the presented results.

11.2.8.1 Comparative Testing
Randomized controlled experiments are the standard means of comparing different variants of systems in online settings (Kohavi et al., 2009). Flighting (also known as "A-B testing") involves trialing different variants of the system by deploying them at scale to a small fraction of the user population and comparing and contrasting their behavior with that of other searchers in the non-experimental (control) group. This is the same as a between-subjects experimental design, which is commonly

used in various forms of experimental design to avoid carryover effects. Before the flight is initiated, success criteria are defined and the experimenters can determine whether the experimental system has been a success by whether or not the criteria have been met. The groups are typically small (1–5% of overall search engine traffic), and there is always at least one treatment group and a control group that does not have the new experience. Kohavi et al. (2009; 2010; 2011) offered insights into online experimentation, including the need for a single organizational metric that is not affected by issues such as experiment-wise error rates, the need for statistical power estimates to determine the sample size, and the need to consider primacy and newness effects. Similar insights were reported in some of their earlier work (Kohavi and Longbotham, 2007).

11.2.8.2 Combination Testing

Combination testing involves merging the results from different ranking algorithms and observing searchers' click preferences. The idea of combining search results from multiple rankings was first described by Kantor (1988), and the first interleaving algorithm was detailed and implemented by Joachims (2002a; 2002b), with the following four objectives:

- Be blind to the searcher with respect to the underlying retrieval function.
- Be robust to biases in the searcher's decision-making processes that does not relate to retrieval quality.
- Do not substantially alter the search experience.
- Lead to result clicks that reflect the searcher's preference.

It is important to note that the work on biases has primarily sought to control for positional bias, but there are a number of different biases that can affect result selection decisions that have not been considered by this model, including the effect of captions on click-through decisions (Clarke et al., 2007; Yue et al., 2010). As highlighted in Chapter 3, White and Horvitz (2013b) demonstrated that there may be more subtle effects, such as that the presence of potentially-alarming content in captions can significantly increase click-through rates on those captions.

A number of methods for performing interleaving have been proposed, including balanced interleaving, team draft interleaving, and probabilistic interleaving. Because searchers see results from both rankings (e.g., five from method A and five from method B, interwoven), this has the advantage of being able to establish within-subject preferences rather than the between-subject preferences that are attainable using parallel flighting. The same searchers with the same information need at the same time is shown the best results from each of the retrieval systems and directly chooses between them. This leads to greater sensitivity with interleaving than other approaches such as including abandonment and query reformulation (Radlinski et al., 2008; Joachims, 2002a; Chapelle et al., 2012).

Some of these methods address shortcomings in previous methods (e.g., probabilistic interleaving allows for the construction of a richer set of rankings than is possible with the less sophisticated team-draft interleaving method), but it remains a difficult decision to choose between them given a number of alternatives. The evaluation of these algorithms can be problematic because they require deployment at scale to many searchers, and they can make assumptions that are difficult to verify. Methods have also been proposed to decide on the optimal interleaving method formulated as an optimization problem and obtain better interleaving performance (Radlinski and Craswell, 2013). Radlinski and Craswell also showed how historic log-based methods can be adapted from other settings and used to evaluate different interleaving methods offline rather than requiring them to be deployed online (Li et al., 2011).

11.2.8.3 Limitations of Online Evaluation

While online evaluation has a number of advantages, there are still many limitations associated with the methodology:

- There is a high start-up cost associated with conducting online experimentation. They are typically only a viable evaluation option for investigators who have access to a popular system with a sufficiently large user base on which to experiment with manipulations of the search experience. Research in counterfactual estimation could be useful in understanding the potential impact of a change has shown to be useful in settings such as search result ranking (Li et al., 2014), online advertising (Lambert et al., 2007; Chan et al., 2010; Bottou et al., 2013), and content recommendation (Li et al., 2011).
- There is a lack of control over the types of queries that people submit. Even if evaluating using historic logs, the experimenter is still limited to the set of previously-issued queries and their associated interactions.
- The search log data that are collected during the online evaluation, especially the non-control-group data, is not easily reusable for later experiments.
- The focus on search behavior without truly understanding the rationale behind the decisions that searchers are observed to make. That rationale can be estimated from other complementary methods, such as user studies or focus groups, both described in more detail elsewhere in this chapter.
- Not all clicks are created equal. Clicks are more than just binary events. Clicks can be weighted based on a number of factors such as order, time spent, position in the result list, and so on. There are also potential biases associated with the visual presentation of results that can affect the performance of online evaluation methods. For example, varying the bolding of the title terms has been shown to skew paired click-through in interleaving experiments (Yue et al., 2010).
- Searchers may not be examining ranked lists of search results, as in many modern search engines, especially with the advent of touch devices where results are presented in different forms (e.g., two-dimensional grids). Even in cases in which a list of results is shown to searchers, the Web search results are often interspersed with multimedia content and answers (News answers, Image answers, etc.). Advertisements are also shown surrounding the search results, consuming searcher attention. In all of these cases, these additional elements impact examination behavior in a variety of ways. For example, Metrikov et al. (2014) showed that the inclusion of an image answer on the SERP can negatively impact advertising click-through because attention is directed away from advertisements and toward the more visually appealing content. Search providers need to be able to reliably

model how searchers interact with these aggregated SERPs and combine signals from multiple sources, including eye-gaze and cursor tracking as well as the more traditional signals such as queries and click-through, to more fully model the search examination process and better evaluate the impact of click-through decisions. Taking steps in this direction, Diaz et al. (2013) developed a method to predict the impact on examination behavior (proxied by cursor movement data using to train a machine-learned model) of adding new elements to the SERP.

The lack of the control and the reliance on large-scale user participation in online evaluations mean that *offline* evaluation methods, although much critiqued in the literature as being unrealistic, may still yield significant benefit for evaluation purposes. Offline methods can also improve their realism by settings parameters based on values from user studies or log analyses. Offline evaluation methods are now discussed in more detail.

11.2.9 Offline Evaluation

Although all methods described in this chapter can be controlled in some way, offline experiments refer to experimental methods most capable of rigorously answering experimental questions through carefully controlled experimental protocols. Although the simplistic role of the searcher in these experiments reduces their realism, they are necessary to run highly controlled experiments (Voorhees, 2009). Beyond realism, these models are also missing richer models of searchers, richer models of content, characterizations of queries/tasks, and metrics focused on the searcher. Offline experimentation with retrieval systems generally involves calculating an estimate of mean searcher utility or effectiveness over a representative set of tasks/information needs. This abstracts the human element and focuses primarily on the topical relevance of documents to queries. It is often argued that too much abstraction creates an artificial experimental setting from which the findings are less meaningful operationally. One of the main attributes of a controlled experiment is test collections comprising queries, a corpus of documents, and relevance judgments assessing the value of the documents with respect to the queries. These can be shared between researchers along with common guidelines, and in doing so it is possible to compare search systems both within-site and across experimental sites (something that is challenging, although not impossible with interactive experiments [Lagergren and Over, 1998]).

11.2.9.1 System-Oriented

There are a number of methods that have focused on evaluating the system-oriented effectiveness of search systems, the most famous are the Cranfield method (Cleverdon et al., 1966) and the Text Retrieval Conference (TREC), and other initiatives such as the Cross-Language Evaluation Forum (CLEF) and NII Testbeds and Community for Information access Research (NTCIR), which have continued this tradition. The principles under which information retrieval experimentation was conducted have been central in driving innovation in information retrieval. The core principles are to sample a set of queries that are representative of the searcher needs (e.g., queries sampled from search logs for use in evaluating Web search systems), run each of these queries against a number of different retrieval systems, pool and judge the top-ranked results from these systems, and evaluate how well the different retrieval methods retrieve and rank the results judged as relevant.

11.2.9.1.1 Cranfield

The Cranfield indexing experiments in the 1960s are often cited as the beginning of the modern era of computer-based retrieval system evaluation (Cleverdon et al., 1966). In the Cranfield studies, retrieval experiments were conducted on a variety of test databases in a controlled, laboratory-like setting. In the second series of experiments, known as Cranfield II, alternative indexing languages constituted the performance variable under investigation. The aim of the research was to find ways to improve the relative retrieval effectiveness of search systems through better indexing languages and methods (Cleverdon, 1970). The components of the Cranfield experiments were a small test collection of documents, a set of test queries, and a set of relevance judgments (that is, a set of documents judged to be relevant to each query). Human searchers, their interaction with the system, their interpretation of the query, and their process-formed relevance judgments were not factors included in these experiments. For purposes of performance comparisons, it was necessary to select quantitative measures of relevant documents output by the system under various controlled conditions. The measures used in the Cranfield II experiments are recall and precision, derivatives of the concept of relevance – described in Chapter 10.

11.2.9.1.2 Text Retrieval Conference (TREC)

Building on the Cranfield paradigm, the TREC (Text REtrieval Conference) began in 1992 and has run annually ever since. TREC is an ongoing series of workshops focusing on a list of different research areas within information retrieval, or tracks. Its purpose is to support and encourage research in information retrieval by providing the infrastructure necessary for large-scale evaluation of text retrieval methodologies and to increase the speed of laboratory-to-product transfer of technology.

Because TREC provides a forum within which research groups can compete on a common dataset and furnishes data and relevance judgments (performed by human assessors) as part of the process, it can catalyze significant advances in research and development on information retrieval. For example, the U.S. National Institutes of Standards and Technology (NIST) claims that within the first six years of the workshops, the effectiveness of retrieval systems approximately doubled. The conference was also the first to hold large-scale evaluations of non-English documents, speech, video, and retrieval across languages. Additionally, TREC has inspired many publications, as well as significant time and financial savings.[1]

The test collections developed at TREC are useful not only in helping researchers advance the state of the art, but also for allowing developers of new (commercial) retrieval products to evaluate their effectiveness on standard tests. In the past decade, TREC has created new tests for enterprise e-mail search, genomics search, spam filtering, e-discovery, and several other retrieval domains. TREC has been less effective at supporting interactive experimentation, in part because of issues with performing reliable comparisons between experimental sites. TREC has primarily provided a medium for the evaluation of algorithms underlying the analytic aspects of search systems, yet struggled because the experimental methods of batch retrieval are not suited to studies of interactive searching. Since TREC-3, the conference has extended its mandate to recognize the importance of the user in information seeking. The TREC Interactive Track (Dumais and Belkin, 2005; Harman, 1997) provided methods for comparing interactive search systems between experimental sites (Lagergren and Over, 1998).

The Interactive Track, and later the High Accuracy Retrieval from Documents (HARD) track (Allan, 2003), place searchers at the heart of the retrieval process. However, these tracks struggled to establish comparability between experimental sites in terms of the experimental systems devised and the measures used. They were also adversely affected by the reliance on relevance judgments and interactions between searchers, tasks, and systems. Nonetheless, the Interactive Track and the HARD Track were successful in highlighting and underscoring the importance of searchers in information seeking and developing protocols and best practices for the evaluation of interactive search systems. More recently, alternative tracks such as the Session Track (Kanoulas et al., 2010) and the Contextual Suggestion Track (Dean-Hall et al., 2013) (among others) emerged as ways in which interactivity and query-less search experiences can be represented within the TREC framework. It has also been suggested that repositories of data and tasks (similar to TREC) could be used to evaluate interactive search systems based on information visualization (Plaisant, 2004).

11.2.9.1.3 Limitations of the System-Oriented Approach

Several authors have noted the limitations of the offline evaluation approach (Belkin, 2008; Turpin and Hersh, 2001). One of the primary criticisms of the system-oriented approach has been the lack of realism. Search is an inherently noisy and unconstrained process and it is not clear that improvements noted in controlled experimental settings will translate to realistic search settings once the search system is deployed. Specifically, would searchers using the systems in practice agree with the relative ranking generated by the offline evaluation. As discussed in Chapter 10, there has been significant research on comparing the rankings of search system rankings obtained from offline experimentation against those from user studies (Turpin and Hersh, 2001; 2002). The system-oriented approach also largely ignores how people formulate needs and examine search results and the criteria that are important to them in making decisions about which results to view and when to stop searching. It also does not consider multiple queries in a search session and the evolution of information needs over the course of a session, all of which are important factors in determining search outcomes (although there are signs with recent research that the emphasis on single queries may be changing [Smucker and Clarke, 2012]). While simplifying many of these aspects is important for comparability, many of them should be modeled in some way as part of offline experiments, just as they are evident in online studies. Because information needs are rarely satisfied with the results from a single query, it is important to consider tasks, sessions, and search within a broader context when evaluating search systems in offline settings (as has been attempted in the TREC Session Track [Kanoulas et al., 2010]). For example, White et al. (2005) developed simulations of search behavior that included random *wandering* behavior that was purposely designed to model some of the noise that is inherent in search system usage. Some of the methods in the remainder of this chapter more completely model search system use.

11.2.9.2 Modeling Searcher Utility

The Cranfield methodology formed the foundation of controlled research in search experimentation. In these models, a keyword query is presented to the system as input, and the system in turn ranks the documents in decreasing order by a score assigned to the match between the query and the document. This ranked list of results is then evaluated per metrics designed to model the utility of these ranked results, both individually and the accumulation of this utility as people examine the result list.

Frameworks have been developed that model how people engage with lists of search results and how their utility is accumulated (Moffat and Zobel, 2005; Chapelle et al., 2009; Yilmaz et al., 2010). Each framework models a searcher examining a ranked list of search results generated by a system until the searcher decides to abandon the examination process. The frameworks differ in complexity, especially in terms of how they model the decision to stop examining a list of search results and whether they model the decision to examine a particular result.

Moffat and Zobel (2005) proposed rank-biased precision (RBP) with one parameter, theta, which represents the searcher's patience as they continue to browse down the ranked list of results. RBP models the linear traversal of result ranking, at each point making a decision whether to terminate the search or continue examining the search results. Expected reciprocal rank (ERR; see Chapelle et al. [2009]) considers the relevance of examined documents as part of the termination determination decision; and expected browsing utility (EBU; see Yilmaz et al. [2010]) integrates the relevance of the caption into the result click-through decision, and then decides to terminate their examination of results. Another model by Chapelle and Zhang (2009) modeled searcher patience, but leveraged a number of different parameters and considers the relevance of the results that searchers have observed thus far in the query impression (based on the assumption that searchers are more likely to terminate searching after discovering a highly-relevant document, and more likely to continue browsing after encountering a non-relevant document). A simpler version of the model considers whether searchers visit the landing page based on reading the result caption, then deciding whether to continue browsing.

Given these models for how people examine search results and make termination decisions, the utility that the searcher accumulates over the course of the session could also be represented if relevance (utility) judgments were available for the results examined. Judgments can be captured in a number of ways, including through human judges and also using implicit personalized judgments collected from behavioral data. By combining the relevance judgments with interaction models such as those described in this section, we can obtain a richer model of search interaction that more fully represents the search process during evaluation.

11.2.9.2.1 Role of Parameters

In many of these models, there are a number of free parameters that need to be set *a posteriori* by the experimenter. The parameters allow experimenters to model different types of searchers (e.g., impatient versus patient, searchers who stop searching after they encounter a single relevant document, or those who find all of the information that they need from result captions and do not need to click through to the landing page), as well as different tasks and experimental settings. Being able to understand the particular parameter settings (e.g., the specific population of searchers) for whom a system performs well is not only useful from a characterization perspective, it supports the selective application of different systems for these settings when the system is deployed in practice. Selectively applying rankers to different groups of searchers is different from personalization, because it does not presume to know anything about the individual, but rather makes assumptions based on what has worked well for searchers with similar information needs.

The particular parameter settings in these models may be determined based on the intuition of the experimenter or be determined by the experimental setting (e.g., one might expect searchers in a mobile setting to be more impatient than those in a desktop setting). However, they could also be determined from behavioral data collected from search engines as well as in user studies. Models of searcher utility will need to become more sophisticated as the ways in which people engage with search results changes and the range of signals that can be mined from their interactions expands.

11.2.9.3 Richer Searcher Simulations

Current models of evaluation assume a simple interaction model in which the searcher is assumed to consider a result list in descending order and select some subset of the documents shown. This is a crude, yet powerful, approximation of search behavior that has been employed to great effect in many evaluation paradigms, as described in this chapter. Although all user models represent a simulation of search acitivity, when "simulations" are mentioned in this book, they refer to attempts to model behavior in terms of more than just query and document selections. Simulations address many of the drawbacks associated with a lack of realism in (overly) controlled experiments. Simulations of search interaction behavior have been proposed to test the usability of websites (Chi et al., 2003), simulate the navigation of the World Wide Web (Fu and Pirolli, 2007), and in a search context, to evaluate the effectiveness of search systems without human participants (White et al., 2005c; Lin and Smucker, 2008; Keskustalo et al., 2008). Because they run automatically, simulations can test all possible ways in which searchers may interact with a system. Some of the methods (e.g., the *Bloodhound* system [Chi et al., 2003]) require a model of the search task in advance of their application, limiting their generalizability to the broad range of search tasks that people attempt. One way that simulations can mirror human searching is by adding a degree of randomness associated with searcher decisions into the simulated search processes (White et al., 2005c).

Evaluation of novel approaches that rely on behavioral data can be challenging for academic researchers who may not have the same access to data as those in industry. Logs analyzed by researchers in industry are typically gathered under strict terms of use. While these researchers may still pursue logs from other sources (e.g., purchase log data from comScore or other analytics companies, this may be prohibitively expensive, and the general lack of availability of large-scale log data hinders general research advancement. Although the search log data may not be shareable for privacy reasons, *models* of simulated searchers learned from search logs may be useful in evaluating search systems offline. Simulations of search behavior have value in approximating real searcher behavior via simplistic models of search activity that consider factors such as the amount of information gained per rank position or unit time in evaluation metrics

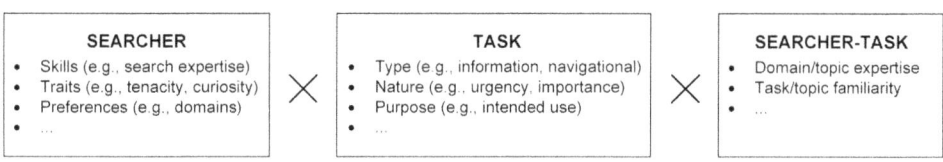

Figure 11.1. Aspects of searcher simulations. The cross is used to symbolize the cross product.

such as discounted cumulative gain and time-based gain (Järvelin and Kekäläinen, 2002; Smucker and Clarke, 2012).

Simulations have also been proposed as a way to evaluate implicit feedback models to represent search behavior according to pre-defined models of how searchers are likely to behave (White et al., 2005c). Parameters in these models can be tuned using behavioral data from user studies or search logs. Data from user studies, where the search goals are known, can be used to build simulations that more accurately represent search behavior (Azzopardi et al., 2011).

11.2.9.3.1 User Models[2]

User models could represent core components of the search process, such as query complexity and time taken to examine result pages for users of different types (e.g., search expert, domain novice, etc.). Previous work on stereotypes in the user modeling community (Rich, 1979) and on clustering searchers based on similarities in their behavioral patterns during search (White and Drucker, 2007; White and Morris, 2007; Castillo et al., 2010; Buscher et al., 2012) are also relevant. For example, in studying search abandonment, Castillo et al. (2010) identified tenacious searchers who are likely to expend significant effort in searching for information. For these searchers, evidence of abandonment is likely to be a negative signal. Tenacity, among many other searcher attributes, could be modeled in simulations. The simulations become significantly more compelling if they can be derived from behavioral data. This also allows the studies that use these models to consider the relative frequency of occurrence of each of the user types. Figure 11.1 provides an example of some of the aspects that could be modeled in simulations, all of which can be represented in some way in variables affecting search behavior and resource preferences.

Once a suite of simulated searchers has been created using both the aspects highlighted here and other aspects, the experimenter must select the appropriate user model or set of models to apply in their particular experimental context. Given models of search behavior, researchers could evaluate the performance of behavioral prediction methods, ranking algorithms and implicit feedback algorithms that learn from search behavior. To apply the suite of simulations, experimenters choose the appropriate searcher class from the suite (e.g., a cohort of domain novices, with general similarities in their behavior, but also specific searcher traits), plug the parameters into the model, and execute the simulation. The simulated searchers would then mimic the interactions of searchers in the selected cohort, performing actions from a finite set of possible behaviors (result clicks, search queries, etc.). Because the simulation includes some stochastic processes to improve realism (e.g., wandering behaviors [White et al., 2005c]), reproducibility is a concern. While simulations run, they should produce a recorded trace of parameter values and simulated interactions that allow the model to be re-run as tested for replicability by the experimenter or others.

11.2.9.3.2 Searcher Traits

More sophisticated simulations could be developed that consider factors such as searcher traits (e.g., the degree of curiosity, distractibility, and tenacity) that could impact search behavior and searcher preferences about how the search engine responds to their search requests. Given these various traits, a suite of searcher profiles can represent different searcher types. One way in which these profiles could be derived is based on psychological research on personality types, which is used to classify different types of individuals (Jung, 1923; Totton and Jacobs, 2001; Bernstein et al., 2008), and personality traits (Eysenck, 1991; McCrae and Costa, 1987), with the latter embodying a smaller grouping of behavioral tendencies (e.g., conscientiousness, novelty seeking, curiosity). Types are sometimes said to involve qualitative differences between people, whereas traits might be construed as quantitative differences. According to type theories, for example, introverts and extraverts are fundamentally different categories of people. According to trait theories, introversion and extraversion are part of a continuous dimension, with many people in the middle. While the relationship between these traits and traditional search behavior may be unclear, simulations of social interactions (González-Ibáñez et al., 2012) could benefit from richer models of how people interact (e.g., different pairings of introvert and extravert individuals exhibit different patterns of interpersonal interaction [Thorne, 1987]). Psychological models may not be directly transferrable to information seeking contexts, but they do provide examples of the types of searcher profiles that could be generated in simulations. For example, we may expect a conscientious searcher to explore many results before settling on the final answer.

Simulation parameters should be determined from laboratory studies (or instrumented panels) with searchers self-identified as conforming to various personality types, plus adapting the type schema as appropriate based on observations made in the search logs and the desired outcome of the simulation. The schema should be based on the needs of the evaluation (e.g., focusing on tenacious searchers when the goal is to study search abandonment [Castillo et al., 2010]). Rather than proposing the schema in advance and seeking participants from searchers conforming to a desired profile, an alternative is to generate profiles direct from search data. Clustering methods could be employed to identify groups of searchers who exhibit coherent search behaviors (e.g., navigators or explorers [White and Drucker, 2007]). Clustering methods have been used previously in the analysis of behavioral data (e.g., in grouping searchers based on their SERP examination patterns using mouse cursor data [Buscher et al., 2012]). Using the data as the starting point, we would not be limited by the criteria imposed by the various profile types (although it can be valuable to ground the research in related disciplines such as psychology, where people have explored profiling for decades).

Once sufficient samples of search behavior within each profile type have been observed, and differentiated from other types, signals from these profiles can be used to find similar searchers in query logs. Harel and Yom-Tov (2015) used clustering methods to find searchers who appeared to share a common medical condition. This can help further refine the behavioral profiles across a broader range of information needs.

Once these profiles have been developed, profile *attributes* (not the raw data) could be shared with the research community to promote experimentation. For example, a TREC track could require that participants evaluate the performance of ranking algorithms using a variety of different searcher profiles and measure robustness across the searcher cohorts.

The general approach of deriving user models from log data could offer a way in which some of the insights from large-scale search logs could be shared more broadly with the research community without privacy concerns associated with releasing individual searchers' data. The models could capture many of the behaviors present in the logs, tune parameters accurately based on the search behavior of millions of searchers, and develop a suite of profiles that researchers could use in the evaluation of their systems in a way that is grounded in naturalistic search behavior (rather than experimenter intuition), is comparable between experimental sites, and respects the privacy of searchers whose behavioral data is collected by search engines. I will discuss privacy in more detail in Chapter 12.

11.3 Comparing Methods

Search systems can perform well along a number of dimensions. Understanding their performance often requires combining different experimental methods so that weaknesses of some methods can be offset by the strengths of others. For example, ethnographic methods can be combined with laboratory studies and search log analyses to develop a more complete picture of system support for the search process (Grimes et al., 2007). Each of the methods outlined in this chapter has advantages and disadvantages that can be summarized in Table 11.2. In addition to listing the strengths and weaknesses of each the table also describes some of their key aspects, such as the scale at which they are deployed and the depth of the analysis that is possible using them methods. There are obvious tradeoffs between the methods in terms of factors such as scale versus the level of detail and the level of automation with the timeliness/longitudinality of the collection. Many of the methods (interviews, focus groups, surveys, etc.) rely on participants' natural information needs as stimuli, but they are leveraged as a way to understand system performance and searcher behavior in controlled experimental settings. In selecting methods, statistical testing needs to be considered, including the application of power analysis to determine the size of the data sample that is required (Cohen, 1988). Sakai (2014) provided suggestions on how to report effect sizes and confidence intervals within the context of information retrieval evaluation, with a view to making comparisons between systems more meaningful.

11.3.1 Experimental Biases

There are a number of biases that can affect experimental outcomes, including those associated with the design of the experiment itself, the experimental instruments used, and the selection of a participant sample. All of the methods involving self-report data, in particular those methods where participants come in direct contact with investigators – interviews, user studies, focus groups, and field studies – are also affected by

Table 11.2. *Strengths and weaknesses of the various evaluation methods (adapted from Grimes et al., 2007). Naturalistic methodologies are denoted using (N), and controlled methodologies are denoted (C)*

Method	Scale	Strengths/Weaknesses	Depth	Naturalness	Flexibility	Turnaround
Field studies (N)	O(50) users	+ Rich data − Small samples − Reliance on coding	Very detailed	Observed, may be artificial tasks	Altered midstream	~1 month
Instrumented Panels (N)	O(1,000) users	+ Rich data + In situ probes − Annoyance/interruption − Drop out over time	Observes computer environment, multitasking	Natural, may be edited by user	Difficult to change data collection	~2–4 weeks
Log analysis (N)	Millions	+ Large-scale + Naturalistic setting − No rationale	Limited; no contextual information	Completely natural	Easy to make changes on the server side	Real time to ~1 week
Interviews and Focus groups (C)	O(10) users	+ Opportunity for dialog + Cost effective (vs. individual interviews) − Experimental biases − Small-scale data − Interaction effects between participants	Very detailed	Recall or perception based	Highly flexible, based on the direction of the conversation	~1 month (time to encode)
Laboratory studies (C)	O(50) users	+ Direct comparisons + Statistical validity − Experimental biases − Realism of setting	Detailed	Unnatural, assigned tasks (could be natural in some settings [e.g., when people bring their own tasks])	Fairly inflexible once experimental protocol set	~1 month

Crowdsourcing (C)	O(100) users	+ Low cost + Rapid turnaround − Low quality data	Limited, although behavioral and qualitative data can be collected	Unnatural, assigned tasks	Fairly inflexible once experimental protocol set	~2–4 weeks
Surveys (C)	O(500) users	+ Rich data + Low cost − Recall-based − Respondent bias	Somewhat detailed, depending on questions	Recall or perception based	Inflexible once survey has been distributed	~2–4 weeks
Online (Flighting, interleaving) (C)	Millions	+ Realism + Broad coverage of information needs + Statistical validity + Reproducibility − High startup costs − Limited degree of experimental control	Limited to click behavior, and missing rationales	Controlled, but users have natural tasks	Fairly flexible, flights can be changed on server time	Real time to ~1 week
Offline (Cranfield, other simulations) (C)	Infinite	+ Reproducibility + High degree of experimental control + Statistical validity − Lack of realism/validation	Limited to behaviors and metrics studied	Unnatural	Flexible, all data and methods	Real time

biases. One of the main issues is demand characteristics, which describes an experimental artifact (regarded as an extraneous variable for experimental purposes) for which participants form an interpretation of the experiment's purpose and unconsciously change their behavior to fit that interpretation (Orne, 1962; 1969). Demand characteristics have been studied in detail in psychology, but to a lesser extent in information retrieval and related subdisciplines. There are a variety of different types of demand characteristics, related to rumors about the study, the experimental setting, or communication between the experimenter and the participant. Given the presence of these effects, participants may assume different roles in the experiment that can impact outcomes (Weber and Cook, 1972). Good participants attempt to detect the experimental hypothesis and attempt to confirm it. Bad participants attempt to discern the experimental purpose so as to destroy the credibility of the study. Faithful participants follow experimenter instructions exactly, whereas apprehensive participants are overly concerned about how their responses could be evaluated, meaning that they may choose to behave in a socially desirable manner. With a better understanding of the impact of factors related to the experimental context, user study outcomes can be generalized (Orne, 1962).

Many of the user studies conducted in the information retrieval community are susceptible to demand characteristics and related effects, primarily because it is often clear which system is the baseline (i.e., the system lacking the additional search support that resembles the current state-of-the-art in search technology), and which system is the experimental system (with some new functionality that may be directly visible to the participant); and the hypothesis that the experimental system outperforms the control, usually in completing some search task, is fairly easy to discern.

There are a number of ways in which demand characteristics can be handled during user studies. These include using deception to mislead participants about experimental goals, hide manipulations and measures so that the research hypothesis is unclear, take care with experimenters (e.g., hide hypothesis from those working directly with participants), focus on communication (e.g., provide specific and clear instructions, minimize interpersonal contact between experimenter and participant), and think carefully about experimental design (e.g., using a between-subjects design rather than a within-subjects design, so that participants are unaware of the different experimental variants under test; see Rubin and Badea [2010]). Birnbaum (2000) discusses the potential benefits of conducting Web-based (remote) experimentation to reduce demand and experimenter effects similar to those described in this section. They can be effective for this purpose because participants can be more fully shielded from undue influence from the experimenter and the experimental setup. In an investigation of delivery methods for user studies, Kelly and Gyllstrom (2011) reported the presence of potential demand characteristics associated with protocol by which participants elected to complete the experiment (e.g., those in the remote group may have felt that they should report higher search expertise because they were participating in the experiment more independently). In addition, there are other affects related to how experimenters choose to interpret collected data, if they are performing the coding themselves (Sackett, 1979).

11.3.2 Experimental Costs

The process of running experiments can be prohibitively expensive, especially at scale and especially for those who need to consider the costs of participant/usage recruitment, as well as data analysis. Finding searchers for a research system can be challenging. To help with this task and support the advancement of science, search engines could siphon off a small subset of their traffic for experimental purposes, share a carefully anonymized subset of their usage data, or sponsor the purchase and release of non-proprietary data from other sources to academic institutions for research purposes (e.g., in collaboration with analytics companies such as comScore). These methods are discussed in more detail in Chapter 12.

Another way in which experimental costs can be reduced is through the development of living laboratories. A living laboratory is a research concept that represents a participant-centric research methodology for sensing, prototyping, validating, and refining complex solutions in multiple and evolving real life contexts. Rather than individual research groups independently developing experimental search infrastructures and gathering their own groups of test searchers for evaluation purposes, a central and shared experimental environment could be developed to facilitate the sharing of resources, and the running of experiments, the data behind which would be available to the community, perhaps after some delay to accommodate publication timelines. The development of living laboratories would offer huge benefits to the research community, such as the availability of potentially larger cohorts of real searchers and their activity (e.g., querying behaviors), for experimentation purposes; cross-comparability across research centers; and greater knowledge transfer between industry and academia, when industry partners are involved (Kelly et al., 2009). The need for this methodology is further amplified by the increased reliance of experimentation on proprietary data (discussed in more detail in Chapter 12). Living laboratories offer a way to bridge the data divide between academia and industry. They could serve to bring together researchers from academia and industry, and provide them with the tools and participants needed to perform studies and foster collaborations for future investigations.

11.4 Summary

In this chapter, I have discussed ways in which investigators can perform evaluation of interactive search systems. It is clear from the range of methods covered that there are many options, each appropriate for different circumstances and stages in the development cycle. It is important to note that the focus was on cases for which there is a direct emphasis on comparing different search systems (versus more general analysis of current information-seeking behaviors on a single system), although the Section 11.2.7 covers this in some detail. Other methods – such as critical incident analysis (Flanagan, 1954) based on participant recollections of salient events – could also be employed to better understand the search process on a particular system.

One aspect that may permeate all of the evaluation methodologies described in this chapter is the amount of time over which any study is conducted. Many evaluation methods focus on the performance of the system at a particular point in time. However, many search tasks extend beyond session boundaries (over 50% of tasks per recent estimates [Agichtein et al., 2012]), and require being able to evaluate system performance longitudinally. This creates challenges in terms of identifying the various stages of the search process, including the conclusion (when searchers decide that their search task is complete). Longitudinal studies require sustained engagement with searchers, even if passive monitoring methods such as long-term log analysis can be employed. Recruiting participants for such long-term studies of search behavior can be challenging and requires significant compensation for active participation over a sustained period (e.g., Kelly [2004] gifted a laptop to each participant in her longitudinal study of implicit relevance feedback).

Although large-scale log analysis can be used to track search activity over time, the source logs contain only partial information about the searcher. They comprise their interactions with an online service and no information about other search behaviors. Client-side logging addresses some of these concerns, but there is still the related issue of identifying search-related behaviors amid many other interactions, and richer logging that captures additional contexts (similar to those described in Chapter 9) are needed, although valid concerns about privacy may still hinder progress.

Next-generation search systems will be more ubiquitous. It is therefore important to evaluate their performance within their device and application contexts, whereby we consider how the systems interact with other applications as well as evaluate their own support for serving search results and experiences from within those systems. In addition, evaluation mechanisms need to factor the search *situation* into the evaluation process (e.g., how would searchers and/or systems perform when searching under time pressure? [Crescenzi et al., 2013; Crescenzi, 2015]). Simulated work task situations (Borlund, 2001) facilitate the introduction of such contextual information in user studies, but in other settings (such as offline experiments in TREC and elsewhere), simulating search *situations* and their impact on searchers (in addition to searcher characteristics) is an important future research direction.

CHAPTER 12
Data, Tools, and Privacy

An important aspect of many of the methods covered in this book is the availability of data on how people interact with search systems. It is therefore important to discuss how searcher data are collected, and what data are available for research purposes. An important aspect in mining, analyzing, and applying these data is searcher privacy, which permeates all aspects of collection and use – from the consent of searchers to collect the data at the outset, to the de-identification, aggregation, and restrictions of sharing and applying data (Horvitz and Mulligan, 2015). The collection of such interaction data is standard practice for large commercial entities, such as Web search engines, who use the data to understand how people are interacting with their services and improve the user experience. Because of privacy concerns, once the data are collected, they are usually not shareable with external parties. Efforts to release data (e.g., by America Online in 2006) have led to serious privacy breaches associated with a failure to completely anonymize the dataset. Serious events such as this make future broad data releases unlikely. Limited releases under license to researchers and the extreme anonymization of datasets have been used as strategies to address privacy challenges and promote research into behavioral analysis and user modeling.

In this chapter, I discuss the need for the shared resources (e.g., datasets), tools (e.g., logging support), and infrastructure that are necessary to build and evaluate competitive search systems. These pillars are important when comparing or coordinating the performance of interactive search systems across multiple experimental sites. Lagergren and Over (1998) described an experimental design for cross-site comparisons of experimental results (i.e., a matrix design to which participating sites must strictly adhere) to address issues such as two-way interactions and effects specific to how the experiment was conducted at a particular site, in the context of the TREC Interactive Track (in which a single search system was used as a baseline at all sites). This involved significant coordination effort and was still focused on comparing *systems*. Important alternative goals include advancing our understanding of search behavior, improving the design of systems to support searching, and facilitating comparability between laboratory studies performed at different sites.

A repository of datasets – collected with appropriate consent from and privacy guarantees for searchers – would provide a point of collaboration for researchers and support the examination and analysis of data using a wide array of methods and techniques (Kelly, 2009). The benefits associated with the adoption of such data sharing practices are significant, including enabling multiple perspectives on the data, assisting with the identification of errors in the data, discouraging the publication of fraudulent results, and reducing the duplication of effort.

12.1 Logging

Search interaction behavior can be recorded in a number of ways, ranging from rich client-side logging of, among other things, keystrokes, cursor movements, and application usage, to more traditional server-side logging which may be less intrusive but also collects less complete data about search behavior and the search environment more generally. Lightweight toolbars and instrumented Web browsers offer a way for search engines to retrieve significant information about search interaction and the search situation, without the need to deploy heavyweight client-side logging software. The data collected from these applications are useful for tasks such as learning to rank (Agichtein et al., 2006; Bilenko and White, 2008) and content recommendation (White et al., 2009a).

12.1.1 Query and Click Logs

Search logs are captured directly by commercial search engines as people interact with the systems. Log entries typically form Hypertext Transfer Protocol (HTTP) requests that contain information about the event encoded as a single request. The request often contains a significant amount of information about, among other things, the search query, the specific resource(s) being accessed, the time at which the event occurred, a unique identifier for the searcher (or at least the machine or signed-in user profile) accessing the resource, the device used, and the physical location (primarily at the town/city level). Logs can also include other information such as the content present on the SERP at query time (e.g., result captions).

Search logs can be mined for a number of purposes, including directly improving result relevance by promoting search results that appear to interest many searchers for specific queries (e.g., those that align with the dominant *search intent* for a query; see Joachims [2002] and Agichtein et al. [2006]). Search engines retain the association between searchers and their online activity directly in search logs for time periods spanning many months. The timeframe varies depending on the service provider and the terms of use under which the data are collected. After that time, some services retain anonymized records for aggregate analysis (e.g., in applications such as Google *Trends*), but at that point, the connection between searcher identifiers and the recorded data are likely to have been removed. This disassociation between people and activity means that longitudinal *within-searcher* analysis (over, say, many years) is not feasible using search engine log data. There may be sources of large-scale behavioral data, such as those available for purchase from Internet analytics companies, that have fewer restrictions.

12.1.2 Browsing Logs

Search engines and other companies offer toolbars and Web browser add-ins that record search behavior beyond SERPs, given user consent. This consent is usually captured through explicit agreement with the terms of use / end user license agreement (EULA) during the installation of the application. If consent is obtained, data are collected in accordance with the terms outlined (e.g., some activity, such as sites accessed through secure connections or within organizational intranets, may not be logged per the terms of use). Each entry in these logs might not be as rich as those collected from the search engine directly, but they do have a broad coverage of most sites accessed, enabling an analysis of interaction behavior within and between different Web properties. This also facilitates the extraction of search and browsing trails (White and Drucker, 2007), as well as the detection and analysis of key competitive activities that transcend search engine boundaries, such as search engine switching (White and Dumais, 2009).

Browser toolbars can be offered to searchers via distribution deals with software and hardware partners. Data on browsing trails allows online service providers to make more relevant recommendations about resources of interest given the resource(s) that are currently being examined (e.g., for the *Suggested Sites* feature in the IE Web browser or the Web service *StumbleUpon*). People may be motivated to share their browsing histories to receive such functionality. Alternative incentivization schemes may also be effective, including those where people can claim rewards for agreeing to provide their data with a minimal privacy risk (Singla et al., 2014a).

12.1.3 Searchers and Locations

Logging physical location is important, especially given the correlation between search activity and physical location (Lymberopoulos et al., 2011). The availability of location data enables the development of models to better personalize (Bennett et al., 2012) and contextualize the search experience based on where people are (Bennett et al., 2011) and where they have been (White and Buscher, 2012).

12.1.3.1 Tracking Searchers

A unique identifier is needed to associate observed behaviors with a single searcher over time, either within the same session or longitudinally. This is important for applications such as personalization (Teevan et al., 2011b; Bennett et al., 2012), but also longitudinal analyses where searchers are first aligned based on landmark events (Richardson, 2008; White et al., 2014a). Identifiers are often one-way hexadecimal hashes, which cannot be linked directly to user-identifying information. User identifiers can be found in different forms:

- **HTTP Cookies:** A cookie, also known as a HTTP cookie, Web cookie, or browser cookie, is a small piece of data sent from a website and stored in a user's web browser while the user is browsing that website. Cookies are installed on the searcher's machine by a website, allowing the site to track future visits to the site, and other sites for applications such as display advertising. Every time a website user visits a page on the site, the browser sends the cookie to the server to notify the site of their prior activity. Cookies were designed to be reliable for websites to remember stateful information (such as shopping cart items) or to record browsing activity (including selecting particular buttons, logging in, or recording visited pages extending back over time). Cookies can be reset and are therefore susceptible to cookie churn (the effects of which can be mitigated by connecting [Dasgupta et al., 2012]).

- **Application Identifier:** This is an identifier assigned to an application such as a browser instance or a plug-in (e.g., a toolbar). Application identifiers are largely permanent until a new version of the application is installed, in which case a new identifier will be assigned to the searcher.
- **Searcher Credentials:** Searchers are increasingly being required to log in to devices and services using their credentials, typically in the form of a username and password. This information can be used (in encrypted form) to identify users from their remote requests (e.g., a hashed version of the username can be included in the request received by the service). Importantly, because this is a persistent identifier associated with the searcher and not with their device or applications, it can be used to support searchers as they move *between* devices or applications, and across domains. Persistent identifiers are important given the growth in ownership and use of multiple devices; being able to offer these searchers personalized experiences across applications, services, and devices is increasingly important.
- **IP Address:** An Internet Protocol (IP) address is a numerical label assigned to each device (e.g., computer, printer) participating in a computer network that uses the Internet Protocol for communication. This has been used historically as an identifier, but its popularity has decreased as other methods became more feasible. Using the IP address for user identification can be problematic if people access the Web through a proxy server, giving them all the same address. Mei and Church (2009) explored the use of the IP address for personalization. The IP address may be regarded as personally identifiable information (PII) primarily because it is associated with a particular machine (rather than an application that can be uninstalled or user credentials that they may elect not to use), meaning that IP addresses may not be logged by service providers.

12.1.3.2 Tracking Locations

In addition to serving as searcher identifier, the IP address can also be used to estimate the location of the searcher at the city, postal code, or region level. Although IP addresses do not correspond exactly to geographic locations, it is still possible in many cases to determine the physical location of IP addresses via geolocation. Determining the nation of an Internet searcher based on his or her IP address is relatively simple and accurate (95%–99%) because a country name is required information when an IP range is allocated and IP registrars already supply that information. Determining the physical location at a more granular level (city or postal code), is more challenging and less accurate because there is no official source for the information, searchers sometimes share IP addresses, and Internet service providers often base IP addresses in a city where the company is headquartered. Accuracy rates on deriving a city from an IP address can fluctuate between 50% and 80%. Even when not accurate, however, geolocation can place searchers in a bordering or nearby city, which may be sufficient for personalization purposes, depending on the application domain. For example, if a searcher seeks local restaurants in Bellevue, WA, it is not an egregious error for the search system to favor restaurants in neighboring Redmond, WA. However, if the searcher specifies the location directly in their query (e.g., [italian restaurants kirkland]), this should override any system inferences regarding the current location. Errors in accuracy can occur because a common geolocation method involves referencing an IP address against similar IP addresses with already-known locations.

There are a number of sources of mappings from IP addresses to physical locations, including the WHOIS databases, which tracks the owner of an IP address range (subnet or block) and the owner's postal address. This may be inaccurate for a number of reasons, including differences in the location of the person who registered the IP addresses and the physical location of those who use it to access the Web. Beyond IP addresses, wireless access points and cellphone tower signals (via trilateration or triangulation) can also be used to serve a similar locating purpose, often with better accuracy than methods based on reverse IP. GPS-enabled mobile devices such as smartphones and tablets, can accurately determine the searcher's location at search time (to within a few meters of the true location). There are important privacy concerns associated with the collection of such granular location data.

12.1.4 Client-Side Logging

Much of the focus of this chapter (and much of this book) is on mining and applying search interaction data at scale. Per the current state of the art, this involves server-side logging and means that the events that are recorded are limited to certain events such as queries and result clicks. Transferring data remotely for use in applications such as personalization can be a significant privacy concern for searchers (Volokh, 2000), and it can also limit the sophistication of user models and impact their performance (Jeh and Widom, 2003). Rather than performing logging server-side, it is also possible to log on the client. This is attractive for a number of reasons, primarily for perceived and actual privacy, because no information is shared outside of the machine. However, if the machine is stolen, thieves can have access to detailed personal information about the searcher by accessing the local data. Drive encryption mechanisms can protect data by encrypting all content on a device.

12.1.5 Important Tradeoffs

There are important tradeoffs that need to be made in the collection of data, associated with the application domain in which the logging occurs and constraints that may exist on bandwidth and battery usage, especially on mobile devices. Higher fidelity logging means that more information must be transmitted over networks and stored to remote servers. In contrast, lower fidelity logs may not capture as much searcher behavior, but have lower overhead in their collection, transport, and storage. Because network bandwidth, computational resources, and storage are finite, cost-benefit analysis is needed regarding which specific events to record, the granularity of those actions, and whether there is a sensible sampling rate for recording dynamic events such as eye-gaze position or cursor movement data (e.g., sampling movements every 250ms rather than every move) given the intended use for the data.

12.1.5.1 Alternatives to Large-Scale Logging

Search engines have access to large amounts of data about the search and browsing behavior of Web searchers. Given privacy constraints, these data are rarely released externally unless they have been anonymized and/or are accompanied by strict license agreements controlling who can access the data and its applications. Unfortunately, this leaves the academic community bereft of the type of data that they may need to perform research into searcher behavior and the application of behavioral signals for enhancing search relevance. To help address this shortcoming, researchers have distributed browser toolbars to collect data from volunteers within the research community. Unfortunately, uptake of this software has been low, in large part because of privacy concerns. Given the small number of people from a well-connected research community who are likely to install the toolbar, the chances of one individual being identified retrospectively via log analysis increases significantly. This creates a paradoxical situation whereby there is a reluctance from individuals to install applications with activity logging until there are many other users.

12.2 Cloud Storage

Storing people's content in the cloud provides them with access to that information from anywhere. It also provides search systems with the ability to leverage the content of those documents, and also interactions with them (e.g., time spent, edits made) and their social context (e.g., collaborators) to build profiles that can be useful for searching both cloud content and other purposes (e.g., Web search). Previous research on personalization has considered content that is stored client-side (Teevan et al., 2005; Matthijs and Radlinski, 2011), but as usage of multiple devices has grown in popularity, it is no longer prudent (or necessary) to couple content and behavior so strongly with a particular device and enforce artificial device boundaries on the information available for user profile construction. Through the use of persistent and secure user/machine identifiers, user generated content stored in the cloud can be accessed from anywhere and linked between multiple applications. With clear user consent, these cloud-based profiles can provide a rich source of additional signal from which to model searchers' persistent interests and active tasks. This could help set priorities or devise background models on which to base refined user models. This enables search systems to generate richer models of interests and intentions than is possible by only considering the recent, single-device search histories that are commonly employed in today's search systems.

In addition to employing the information stored in the cloud to generate user profiles, this content can also be searched from any machine. This is similar in some respects to searching local content or other retrieval settings, but there are some interesting challenges associated with handling different document types, multiple versions of the same document, connecting multiple accounts and locations, and keeping track of changes in user-generated content over time. Early research on searching distributed collections of content (Callan et al., 1995), and more recent research on federated search (Shokouhi and Si, 2011) are also highly relevant in the context of searching cloud-based content. As an alternative to using a single retrieval algorithm to search all available content (which is limited in terms of the content indexed and the ranking algorithm employed), systems may also select or recommend the most performant algorithm for the query (White et al., 2008).[1]

12.3 Release of Data

Large-scale behavioral data can be valuable for research purposes. Privacy concerns have prevented anything more than rudimentary data releases. There are some ways that usage data could be released for research purposes under contractual agreements clearly stipulating how the data could be used and shared.

12.3.1 General Release

The privacy risk of releasing usage data generally with no restrictions on its access or use is simply too great. An example of the risks involved can be found back in 2006, when America Online (AOL) released three months of query and click-through logs for approximately 650,000 users of AOL search engine. Although users of the search engine were not identified in the search logs explicitly, a numeric identifier for each user that allowed them to be tracked over time and multiple queries could be connected to the same user (Arrington, 2006; Adar, 2007). News organizations such as *The New York Times* and others were able to use the anonymized logs to identify individuals by cross referencing the logs with other sources, such as phonebook listings (Barbaro et al., 2006). The event was known as one of the year's "101 Dumbest Moments in Business" (Horowitz et al., 2007). Despite the retraction of the dataset, the AOL logs remain mirrored worldwide, and continue to be used for research in the search and data mining communities. Because it was retracted, the use of the AOL dataset for research purposes has been called unethical, and some outlets will not accept submissions for publication that use the dataset.

12.3.2 Data Challenges

Search engines can support research is via data challenges in which a select group of recipients receive access to the data under non-disclosure agreements (NDAs), or who receive the data in a highly anonymized format. Sensitive information redacted or replaced with numeric identifiers to mask its meaning, but still allow multiple instances of the same query to be found, that could have utility for some purposes (e.g., for studies of re-finding [Teevan et al., 2007] or engine switching [Savenkov et al., 2013]). It may still be possible to de-anonymize the data for some subset of the searchers by joining with other datasets for which personally identifiable information is available (e.g., social media postings). Two recent examples of data challenges are the Netflix Prize and the Yandex data challenge.

12.3.2.1 Netflix Prize

Netflix, a U.S.-based provider of on-demand Internet streaming media, offered one million U.S. dollars in return for a significant (10%) improvement in its recommendation algorithm for suggesting movies to viewers. The winning algorithm used machine-learning techniques to find that, for example, the rating system people use for older movies is different from that used for a movie they just saw. The mood of the day was important; that is, Friday afternoon ratings differed from Monday morning ratings (Bell and Koren, 2007).

As part of the challenge, Netflix has also released a training dataset for the competing developers to train their systems. While releasing this dataset they had provided a disclaimer: *To protect customer privacy, all personal information identifying individual customers has been removed and all customer IDs have been replaced by randomly assigned IDs*. However, researchers were able to connect the Netflix data with data from another database (in this case the Internet Movie Database (IMDB), using the date on which a rating was provided by a user, and partially de-anonymize the Netflix training database (Narayanan and Shmatikov, 2008). This process is known as a *linkage attack*, because it involves the connection of two or more separately innocuous databases using information present in both datasets. This highlights the significant difficulty in releasing data is truly anonymous, especially when others may treat the *identification* of people in the data as its own separate challenge.

12.3.2.2 Yandex Challenges

Although search logs cannot be joined with other sources as easily, it is still important to respect the privacy of searchers if their logs are going to be released publically. For example, the Russian search engine *Yandex* has released log data for a series of data challenges, including those on search engine switching and personalization, much of which was inspired by research referenced in this book. These logs have been carefully anonymized such that they do not contain any queries, results, or clicks directly, but instead use unique identifiers for the queries, the result URLs, and result clicks. This still enables studies of revisitation and various types of query and session analysis that are not dependent on characteristics of the query. Some query characteristics, such as the frequency with which the query appears in the logs and the click entropy, capturing the diversity of clicks when that query is observed, can still be estimated without access to query content. These query statistics can be useful in segmenting the query into different categories, such as informational intentions and navigational intentions (Broder, 2002), which also exhibit differences in how people interact with the results (e.g., higher click entropy for informational queries [Dou et al., 2007]).

Beyond releasing the log data, there are other ways in which behavioral data can be shared. For example, simulations comprising user models developed based on search logs (as described in the previous chapter) are one way in which search engines can support research and promote reproducibility without having to share sensitive usage data externally.

12.3.3 Games with a Purpose

Data can be collected in research environments is via "games with a purpose" (Von Ahn, 2006). These are meant to be fun and engaging applications during which people provide data that can be useful for a range of other research problems or application domains. The idea of games with a purpose was introduced by Luis Von Ahn and colleagues in their work on human computation (Von Ahn et al., 2003). Examples of this include cases in which people are asked to assign labels to images to guess what the other user also playing the game is thinking (Von Ahn and Dabbish, 2004). This has the useful byproduct of generating labeled data for image searching. Another application of human computation is to digitize books using Web security images known as "captchas" where users interpret images and type the text they see, so as to verify that they are indeed human (Von Ahn et al., 2008). This addresses the problem of automated traffic trawling websites (machines are not able to read the images as well as humans can, especially if the images are distorted). Captchas have a useful side benefit: the output of the human labeling can be used to digitize words in books that may be difficult for optical character recognition (OCR) algorithms to recognize with high confidence. Given the widespread use of captchas in websites across the globe, this could help digitize large numbers of books.

Within information retrieval, crowdworkers or participants sourced from elsewhere can be set search tasks and their activities could be recorded (Ageev et al., 2011). This crowdsourced methodology allows for controlled, yet realistic, scalable, and reproducible studies of search behavior; in the case of the study by Ageev and colleagues, the research focus was on measures of search success. A set of navigation paths through Wikipedia were collected as part of the human computation game *Wikispeedia* (West et al., 2009). Participants in the game were asked to navigate between two Wikipedia pages using only links in the documents. The dataset consists of more than 50,000 (source, destination) paths and is publically available.[2] The terms of participating in these studies can be crafted in such a way as to make it permissible to share the usage data (although concerns about user privacy still remain and participant privacy must be preserved in any such data). Data collected through such experiments can then be shared with others researchers, to either recreate the results of the original experiment (e.g., as a baseline in another study), to perform additional analysis, or to facilitate further research in this or related areas.

12.3.4 User Study Data

Moving beyond the data available from search engines, many research groups perform studies with human participants to evaluate new interfaces, prototypes, and other tools. The sharing of user study data has generally not been adopted as standard practice. One of the main reasons for this has been that there are so many differences between the experimental setups and methodologies at different sites, including differences in the research questions being addressed, the systems, and the experimental designs. It is therefore unclear whether the benefits of broad data sharing outweigh the costs associated with doing so. In terms of comparability, even a small difference in the experimental setup can make the comparison of results between experimental sites problematic or invalid – even if the same system(s) and tasks were used in both places.

In recent years, there has been a trend towards data sharing within the information retrieval research community. Some researchers are making their study data available publically. For example, Feild et al. (2010) made data from their study on searcher frustration available for other researchers. That dataset was unique in that it captured eye-gaze tracking and mouse movement data. It was used in a follow-on study to estimate document relevance from searcher engagement (Guo and Agichtein, 2012). This is an example of how the efforts of collecting data in laboratory settings (a notoriously expensive and time consuming process) can benefit the research community at large. This becomes mutually beneficial if there is reciprocity in data sharing between research groups.

As mentioned earlier, there have been concerted efforts to run user studies at multiple sites and to share the outcomes of the experiments (e.g., via TREC tracks, discussed in Section 12.3.4.1). Although TREC tracks shared tasks, baselines, and questions across different sites, the lack of the rigorous experimental controls meant that it was difficult to both compare experimental findings across sites and ask scientifically valuable questions. This was especially challenging to do within the TREC framework, given that a primary objective of initiative is to facilitate comparability between different methods for tackling the same set of search tasks. That said, there are some examples of successful cross-site experiments, albeit as part of the same research study. For example, White and Marchionini (2007) conducted a user study in which half of the participants were studied at one institution (University of Maryland) and half at another institution (University of North Carolina), both using the same baseline and experimental systems, and experimental methodology, including search tasks. The findings and participant demographics at the two sites were similar, and the researchers were able to pool the findings to create a larger study than was possible at either location alone.

12.3.4.1 TREC Tracks

The Interactive Track and the High Accuracy Retrieval from Documents (HARD) Track at TREC attempted to coordinate a consistent set of user experiments at different experimental sites. The tracks encountered difficulties connected with obtaining experimental consistency and in comparing the results between experimental sites.

12.3.4.1.1 Interactive Track

The primary goal of the TREC Interactive Track was to experiment with different interactive experiences, while controlling for variables such as the collections and the tasks. All participants used the same search system and results were returned in XML format. Task topics included "Looking for personal health information" and "Making travel plans," formulated in pre-determined ways (e.g., "Find any N short answers"). Participants were assigned an allotted time in which to complete the task (and participating groups had to report participant performance at the end of a ten-minute period, irrespective of how long they allowed for task completion). There were also requirements on the sample size and the number of tasks per participant. In some years, the track spanned a multi-year cycle. In the first year, participants performed an observational study of search behavior. In the second year of the study, experiments focused on controlled laboratory experiments on question answering using Web data.

12.3.4.1.2 High Accuracy Retrieval from Documents (HARD) Track
The goal of the HARD track was to achieve high accuracy retrieval by leveraging additional information about the searcher and/or the search context captured using targeted interaction with the searcher (Allan et al., 2005). The track involved the development of methods to attain highly detailed information on a searcher's information needs that could then be applied to the retrieval of specific target documents. This raised a number of interesting questions about methods to elicit these descriptions of information needs from searchers. Kelly et al. (2005) investigated the effectiveness of a document-independent technique for eliciting feedback from users about their information problems. They proposed that such a technique could be used to elicit terms from users for use in query expansion and as a follow-up when ambiguous queries are initially posed by searchers. The researchers designed a feedback form to obtain additional information, administered the form to searchers after initial querying, and created a series of experimental runs based on the information that we obtained from the form. Their results demonstrated that this approach was successful at eliciting more information from searchers and that this additional information improved retrieval performance. Their results also demonstrated a strong positive correlation between query length and performance. The value of these methods in commercial search engines is more unclear given that they perform worse for longer queries (Bailey et al., 2010). This may need to change; research suggests that than natural language queries are increasingly in popularity (Pang and Kumar, 2011; White et al., 2014).

12.3.5 Tools

There are a number of tools available to perform data analysis, including information visualization and data processing tools. Statistical packages help researchers to determine the levels of significance (if any) of the observed differences between systems, groups of searchers, or tasks.

12.3.5.1 Scalable Visualization Tools
Visual data exploration techniques enable researchers and data scientists can gain insight and formulate hypotheses about data (Keim, 2001). As discussed earlier in the book, there is a range of different visualization techniques, many of which offer key functions: overview, zoom and filter, and details-on-demand (Shneiderman, 1996). Toolkits and development environments such as *Lyra* (Satyanarayan and Heer, 2014) and *Processing* (Reas and Fry, 2010) can help develop custom data visualizations. However, many of the current visualization tools are designed to handle only moderately sized datasets. The enormity of the data generated by online services means that visualization tools need to scale to massive data. Challenges range from how data is processed prior to visualization, through the user experience, to if and how to display billions of data points in an intuitive and easily manipulated visualization.

Methods exists to support rapid full-data processing (where the data is stored main memory on a single machine or distributed across machines; see Melnik et al. [2010]), or progressive processing (where the system produces early results based on partial data and progressively refines the results as more data are processed; see Jermaine et al. [2007], Condie et al. [2010], and Hellerstein et al. [1999]). The latter approach is efficient and provides the analysts with the ability to terminate execution of the query once the required level of accuracy (or query incorrectness) is attained. Recent visualization techniques have successfully applied such incremental visualizations to increase analyst efficiency (Fisher et al., 2012; Barnett et al., 2013).

Given the large volumes and that they are typically stored on the server, there is no need to download these data to client machines (i.e., data can be visualized on the server and streamed to the client as needed). A range of companies offer cloud-based behavioral intelligence services, including the *Power BI* suite from Microsoft, which includes a number of tools for analyzing and visualizing data in the cloud, and stream their output. Online services such as Google *Trends* and Google *Correlate* help people to create rudimentary time series visualizations of data without requiring that they have access to the raw data.

12.3.5.2 Gathering and Processing Large Data Volumes

Depending on the context of use, the tools need to be scalable and able to either handle large volumes of data or sample the data in intelligent ways so that they provide representative outcomes. If the goal is to process large quantities of search log data, appropriate storage and processing methods are needed for handling large data volumes. Online service providers can help by providing a platform by which approved researchers could securely query data and receive summaries and overviews in response (in a similar way to Google *Trends* or Google *Correlate*), but do not provide access to the raw data directly.

Another important issue is the availability of searchers. There is little value in methods to store and analyze large volumes of data if there is no user base to generate the log records to be analyzed. Obtaining sizable numbers of users requires a significant marketing effort extending beyond a single academic institution. A commercial enterprise, however, could pursue this as part of academic outreach (e.g., by directing a small fraction of their search traffic to this service and/or by advertising the availability of research initiatives to a subset of its user population). Search engines could also provide a small test flight to academic researchers to help them run experiments and collect data that they could use in further analysis. This is a way for industry to assist academia in exploring aspects of information behavior at scale, while being extremely clear with consenting searchers that records of their search behavior might be used for research purposes.

12.3.5.3 Interactive Machine Learning

Earlier in the book, the importance of machine learning (ML) in helping to construct models of search behavior was discussed. Many applications of ML involve interactions with humans, and research has shown that many human factors researchers already apply ML methods (Moustakis, 1997). Humans may provide input to a learning algorithm (in the form of labels, demonstrations, corrections, rankings, or evaluations) while observing its outputs (in the form of feedback, predictions, or executions). Although humans are an integral part of the learning process, traditional ML algorithms used in these applications are agnostic to the fact that inputs/outputs are from/for humans. Researchers also face challenges associated with understanding ML models and in evaluating their performance (Patel et al., 2008). However, a growing community of researchers at the intersection of machine learning and human-computer interaction have considered human intervention to be a central part of developing systems that leverage machine learning methods (Fails and Olsen, 2003; Talbot et al., 2009; Kapoor et al., 2010).

12.3.5.4 Search Components

Components that can be easily plugged into experimental systems could be re-used by different researchers to monitor aspects of information behavior on their systems. One such component could be a behavioral logging tool that would record all interactions with a search system in a consistent format over the course of an experiment and also solicit searcher feedback where required (e.g., in popups when particular events are triggered) to supplement the search logs with additional context: others include: (1) analysis tools to support log data examination; (2) search tools that provide the top results from a search engine given a query; (3) search interface tools that enable new interface components to be easily added to an experimental search interface; and (4) toolkits to perform operations such as natural language processing (Quirk et al., 2012), machine learning (e.g., Microsoft Azure Machine Learning[3]), and machine intelligence (e.g., Microsoft Project Oxford[4]). These components should be pluggable and connectable, meaning that they can perform core functions without the need for multiple research groups to develop their own tools independently. This may be particularly attractive to researchers who may lack the expertise to develop their own services.

12.3.5.5 Interface Prototypes

An important part of the toolset of an experimenter is the ability to develop prototype systems to place in front of searchers to test their ideas. Prototypes must be functional and allow researchers to answer the question. They can be server-side (running on a remote server and utilizing application frameworks such as ASP.NET) or client-side applications (running as an executable on the local machine). The choice depends on at least the intended application domain and the experimental protocol (e.g., whether participation is going to be local or remote). If the goal is to develop a Web-based application, then it makes sense to develop prototypes that can be executed inside a Web browser. One challenge of deploying interactive applications is the logging of searcher events because mechanisms must also be included to return these logs to the experimenter. Complete logging can be difficult remotely, given the data volumes involved in the need to share these data over the wire to a central repository.

12.3.6 Obtaining Data

Access to large-scale behavioral data is useful for researchers in a range of communities for advancing science. Although this section has focused so far on the difficulties in obtaining access to large scale data resources, there are three ways in which researchers can obtain access to the samples of log data for use in research or product development: (1) public sector releases of data; (2) purchasing logs from Internet analytics companies; and (3) requests for proposals from online service providers.

12.3.6.1 Public Sector Releases

Recently there has been a push from within governmental agencies to release data for public consumption and use in research. Governmental initiatives such as Data.gov (United States) and Data.gov.uk (UK) are making a broad range of datasets, tools, and applications freely available for download in topics such as agriculture, health, and education. The New York City OpenData initiative[5] provides researchers with access to public data gathered from a variety of sources, ranging from the position of elements such as subway entrances or points of interest, to the results of surveys and inspections. The latter data source is an example of data connected to the original data stream that could be particularly useful as a form of ground truth. Shared data such as this can be used to complement observational data that is available from other sources, such as people's online activity in search engines and/or their postings to social media such as *Twitter*.[6] For example, a recent study has shown that activity on the social media platform *Twitter* can be used to predict in real time the restaurants that may be affected by food borne illnesses. The predictions can be validated using restaurant inspection results made publically available by health departments (see Sadilek et al. [2013]).

Given increased interest in transparency and accountability in government, more cities and governmental agencies are likely to release data for public use. Getting industry to follow suit is more challenging. Companies invest billions of dollars in methods to gather, store, and analyze these data to improve their services, and take the privacy of their users incredibly seriously. It is unlikely that companies will release log data in the foreseeable future except as part of targeted initiatives and trusted (contractual, non-disclosure) relationships with academic partners.

12.3.6.2 Purchasing Log Data

Log data can be purchased from Internet analytics companies such as comScore, who collect search log data from panelists across the world. Millions of panelists provide explicit permission to passively measure some of their online activities using monitoring software installed on their computers. Participants are selected such that they are representative of the general Web usage population in the United States (Fuglio, 2005). In exchange for joining the panel, participants are offered a variety of benefits, including computer security software, Internet data storage, virus scanning, and chances to win cash or prizes. Because these logs are available for purchase, they could be acquired and used by members of the academic community *in a replicable manner*. Although these logs can be expensive to purchase, they do provide access to large-scale usage data for analysis of search behavior that could be reproduced by others.

12.3.6.3 Search Engine Donations

In some circumstances, search engines may donate log data externally given appropriate confidentiality and licensing agreements. Some search engines have licensed limited subsets of carefully-anonymized search logs to academics for research purposes via a request for proposals (RFP). Interested parties respond outlining how they will use the data, and if their proposal is accepted, they are provided with the data under a licensing agreement that requires them to abide by the strict policies and procedures using to safeguard the query logs. These contracts may contain provisions that hold third parties responsible for privacy violations as an incentive to comply.

12.3.6.4 Academics as Contractors

Because proprietary datasets cannot be shared publically for privacy reasons, a potential solution to the data access challenge could be to bring people to the data (rather than releasing the data to them). Industry could hire academics as contractors, so that they could work with proprietary data from inside the organization.

12.3.7 Issues on Data Release by Providers and Researchers

Although the sharing of any data with the research community may be popular and admirable, the costs of collecting data are significant, including within academia – including the development of the systems, recruiting participants, and cleaning and distributing the logs. Given this large investment, researchers may wish to withhold the data collected and use it for their own research purposes. Studies in the medical community have shown that while the public sharing of research datasets is not yet common practice, publication of a study in prestigious venue or investigator seniority tended to increase the likelihood that the data would be shared (Piwowar and Chapman, 2010). Calls to researchers to make their datasets widely available to other researchers should consider the initial costs and provide sufficient time for those who collected the data to publish to their satisfaction.

In the biomedical community, some journals require that authors provide detailed datasets as a condition of publication (McCain, 1995). Many funding agencies, such as the U.S. National Institutes of Health, require a plan for how data generated as part of funded projects are going to be shared externally. Citing concerns about the reproducibility of research conducted on proprietary datasets, conferences in search and data mining (e.g., SIGIR, SIGKDD) are now emphasizing reproducibility in their acceptance criteria. Means of addressing these concerns range from carefully describing the procedures followed so that others could replicate the methods, to running simulation studies or sharing the data directly to accompany publication.

12.3.8 Overcoming Challenges in Data Release

As discussed thus far in this chapter (and covered in more detail in the next section), there are significant privacy considerations and ethical considerations associated with the release of behavioral data to the research community. As the Netflix case has highlighted, even anonymized data can pose significant privacy challenges if joined with other data sources. The opportunity to release data is not just limited to commercial enterprises collecting data as part of the provision and improvement of online services. Many organizations, including academic institutions, collect the behavioral log data through their proxy servers.

Although terms of use could be updated to include research purposes as one of the goals of collecting data from online services, general data releases are unlikely. A number of methods have been proposed to overcome challenges associated with data release:

- **Generating data:** Rather than releasing data directly, it is also possible to construct simulated query logs based on other sources. Dang and Croft (2010) constructed a simulated query log, or anchor log, from the anchor text of a TREC Web test collection, comprising 25 million documents from the .gov Web domain. They evaluated query reformulation techniques using both the anchor text log and a Web search engine query log, and show that the performance of the anchor log is at least as strong as the search log. Other researchers have demonstrated a similarity between anchor text and query logs, also demonstrating the potential in this direction. Nallapati et al. (2003) used anchor text as queries to train a retrieval model. Kraft and Zien (2004) showed that using anchor text is a better source of data for query refinement than sourcing refinements from the document collection. Studies have also shown that anchor text resembles real search queries in terms of term distribution and length (Eiron and McCurley, 2003). Other sources such as Web page titles or even the query suggestions provided by search engines (Bar-Yossef and Gurevich, 2008; Fourney et al., 2011) might be useful data sources for estimating signals found in query logs. Bar-Yossef and Gurevich demonstrated how statistics of search engine logs can be approximated using an importance sampling technique. Their methods estimated the popularity of certain keywords using parameterized models derived from the AOL logs, and by sampling auto-completions from search engines. Similarly, Fourney et al. (2011) mined query auto-completions to characterize usability issues with interactive applications.

- **Anonymizing data:** Search logs are the queries and resource identifiers have a high level of privacy risk. Jones et al. (2007) carefully applied a set of classifiers for the age, gender, and location of searchers, and revealed that they could be identified with much more likelihood than random chance. By anonymizing the information in these data sources, PII can be removed. Adar (2007) discussed schemes that have been employed for the anonymization of query logs, including removing unique queries, hashing rare queries, breaking sessions into shorter sessions, and fragmenting searchers into topical profiles. Kumar et al. (2007) showed that tokenizing a query, hashing the tokens and publishing the hashes does not preserve privacy because an adversary who has access to another log can reverse engineer the tokens by utilizing the frequency with which the query appears in the log. In addition, methods of k-anonymity (where searchers can be identified as one of k alternatives) have been employed (Navarro-Arribas et al., 2012), and perturbed query frequencies and query-click graphs have been generated (Korolova et al., 2009). The critical issue in the anonymization process is whether utility of the search log data is retained following the application of the particular anonymization method; many of the studies in this area include assessments of utility post anonymization.

- **Providing tools:** One approach that those without access to data can use is to leverage aggregated search data, such as that available for applications such as Google *Trends*. This can be used for a range of purposes in which the research focus is on aggregated patterns rather than specific query- or session-based interactions. For example, it could be used to estimate changes in the fraction of query volume that has question-answering intent (Pang and Kumar, 2011), to study trends in search behavior following a news event, or to track public health issues such as influenza (Ginsberg et al., 2009; Choi and Varian, 2012), although not without drawbacks related to the influence of the media (Butler, 2013).

- **Providing models:** Rather than making the data searchable in any form, aggregate or otherwise, we can instead make available models derived from that data that could be applied to evaluation support methods such as algorithms to learn from searcher behavior. Previous work has studied the application of stereotypes to cases for which models need to be developed for users (Rich, 1979) and applied for providing task support. A set of models depicting stereotypical search behavior could be created that could be applied to evaluate a number of different aspects of the systems. There is precedent in other domains, where models of human motion, fluid dynamics, physics, and so on have been created and then used as means to evaluate other proposed mechanisms. Models of search interaction behavior could be generated from large-scale behavioral data and/or our knowledge and intuitions about human cognition, which have been represented computationally in frameworks such as ACT-R (Anderson et al., 2004). Research on developing computational cognitive models of Web navigation behavior based on information foraging theory (SNIF-ACT; see Fu and Pirolli [2007]) and simulations of search interactions (White et al., 2005c) has blazed a trail for further advances in this area. There is still significant opportunity to develop such user models to form a central part of evaluating search systems from a user, or more accurately a "pseudo-user," perspective, but in a controlled and repeatable manner.
- **Providing sandboxes and flighting infrastructure:** As a way to help the community more directly than sharing user models, search engines could also provide a search sandbox or flighting platform that directs a small fraction of their traffic could to experimental search systems developed by academic researchers and hosted on commercial servers to ameliorate concerns in handling large data volumes. Alternatively, Web search engines could seek informed consent from a small fraction of volunteers to use a modified terms or use, allowing their search behavior to be shared with academic researchers or stored for a longer duration to facilitate the longitudinal analyses of search behavior that is needed to understand episodic searching (Paul et al., 2014).

All of these options have their own strengths and weaknesses. For example, anonymized data may help study query repetition, but linguistic analysis of query text is not possible. Sandboxes and flighting infrastructure have broad reach, but are only feasible for systems that scale, largely eliminating the use of heavyweight applications (e.g., those with sophisticated search interfaces or those that rely on access to client-side data).

12.4 Privacy and Ethics

The retention of long-term usage data by online service providers and the association of that data with user identifiers such as IP addresses and browser cookies can make people susceptible to privacy risks. Malicious attacks and surprising events such as the AOL data release (Arrington, 2006; Adar, 2007) and the de-anonymization of released Netflix logs (Narayanan and Shmatikov, 2008), both discussed earlier in this chapter, can result in privacy breaches. Cooper (2008) suggested that the risks are not limited to accidental or malicious disclosure of data, but also include: (1) the compelled disclosure to third parties (e.g., search logs subject to subpoena as part of civil litigation); (2) the disclosure to the government in the context of law enforcement or intelligence investigations; and (3) the misuse of user profiles of interests, preferences, and behaviors for unintended purposes, ranging from advertising to applications for insurance or financial credit.

PII such as social security numbers or physical addresses can be used to identify an individual if queries containing that data appear in the search logs. People feel ownership of their data and are concerned about who has access to that data and exactly what records are shared (e.g., they may be comfortable with sharing some subset of the data, but not everything). The choice of which data to share is also related to the sensitivity of the data (e.g., medical histories are likely more sensitive than other information). Privacy invasions can occur on a large scale, such as that in the AOL logs or on the level of a single user/household (intentionally or accidentally) when using shared computers. An example of an accidental release associated with shared machine usage is as follows: search results and/or advertisements are presented to the current searcher on a machine are affected by the previous queries of another searcher in the same household, or the search engine explicitly reveals the search history of the other searcher on the SERP or on related search engine pages. Search activity attribution methods (White et al., 2014) described earlier could help preserve privacy on shared machines by shielding histories from all users but the current searcher.

There are a number of ways to reduce privacy risk. These can be grouped into three classes: (1) *searcher controlled*; (2) *provider controlled*; and (3) *externally controlled*.

12.4.1 Searcher Controlled

Searcher controlled measures are steps that people can take to protect their own privacy.

12.4.1.1 Consent

When using online services users can provide their level of consent ranging from no consent to explicit opt-in consent (Cooper, 2008). Online services typically rely on implied consent, meaning that – given that the service provider discloses it privacy policies and people use the service – users are consenting for the service provider system to use their data as stipulated in the policy. The only means that people have to opt-out of this type of data collection is to terminate their usage of the service. Implied consent is practical at scale, but for some purposes, such as recording all of the websites that a person visits, opt-in consent is likely required and is frequently sought. In the opt-in approach, people are presented with an explicit choice about whether log data can be recorded and they must agree explicitly before any recording can start. Even though opt-in consent is common in medical research and may be required by law, opt-in consent can be optional and people may still use the service even if they do not agree to the logging. A significant challenge in obtaining opt-in consent is to design choices for people that are clear and understandable, preserving them over time so that they can be applied on each use of the system, and also providing the individual with mechanisms to revise their selection at any time.

12.4.1.2 Software

Searchers desire control over the information that they share with the search system and other applications. It is worth noting that the collection of query log data is not limited to the search providers themselves. Internet service providers (ISPs) have access to their subscribers' search traffic and could also disclose or sell these logs to third parties (Reimer, 2007). Privacy-enhancing tools can help those concerned about their privacy, independent of what action is being taken by service providers. For example, the use of proxy servers may shield identifying information from remote observers. Features of Web browsers and separate browser add-ins (e.g., *TrackMeNot* [Howe and Nissenbaum, 2008]) are emerging to put control of data collection and sharing back in the hands of searchers. For example, the *InPrivate* browsing feature of the IE Web browser deletes cookies and temporary Internet files, and does not store data about history, passwords, and other information, so as to not share a user's visitation history with other users of the same machine. The Google Chrome Web browser has an *Incognito* mode that has similar functionality. As discussed above, these capabilities are important in shared-machine settings. However, these methods do not protect the searcher against the use of tracking while using online services, nor do they protect against administrators or hackers on the network viewing an individual's Web traffic.

12.4.2 Provider Controlled

Provider controlled measures can be used by search systems to protect user privacy.

12.4.2.1 Methods

Cooper (2008) discussed some methods search providers employ to enhance user privacy. These include log deletion and various forms of obfuscation and refactoring, such as hashing queries or identifiers, deleting infrequent queries (Adar, 2007) or shortening search sessions to reduce the length of time that identifiers are associated with activity (Xiong and Agichtein, 2007). All of these approaches have tradeoffs in terms of information lost versus privacy gained. For example, shortening sessions may undermine methods to learn from within-session transitions (e.g., Jones et al., 2006). The outright deletion of logs as an extreme policy is the most effective way of protecting privacy, but also removes the value from the logs. Some online services provide a way for privacy-conscious individuals to remove personal information on request (e.g., *AskEraser* from search engine Ask.com [Dye, 2011]). This respects the wishes of these searchers while leaving the logs intact and preserving the benefits for others of logging search data.[7]

12.4.2.2 Privacy Policies

Online services such as Web search or e-commerce applications utilize the collection of logs as a way in which service providers can improve the quality of the services that they offer to their users given their consent. Although details about what is recorded can be provided to individuals, there is still some uncertainty over whether searchers understand the terms of use presented to them (Cranor, 2007). Such notices are often difficult to understand and recent estimates suggest that they are ignored by 40% of individuals (TechNet, 2012), and people are less likely to read them if they contain more legal terminology (Milne and Culnan, 2004). It is therefore questionable whether the consent to utilize behavioral logs can actually be relied upon as informed consent.

Although there are limitations on the duration of search history for which companies can store data about an individual (often twelve to eighteen months), this is still a sufficient duration for malicious parties to identify people given that each of the log entries is associated with a persistent identifier. Searchers' long-term behavioral traces are unique (ideal for personalization) but can contain clues about individual identities (e.g., through vanity searches, where people query for their own name). Organizations have restrictions on who can view log data internally and on how they may be analyzed and applied to enhance the search experience. For example, one policy may be that certain types of log data cannot be used as the basis for tailored advertising.

12.4.3 Externally Controlled

Externally controlled measures are used by outside agencies to protect searcher privacy.

12.4.3.1 Legislation

The presence of sensitive information about searchers in query logs, and the ability to identify individuals from their query statements, has raised concerns about privacy. The charges by the Federal Trade Commission against Facebook (FTC, 2011) and Google (FTC, 2012) highlight increasing concerns by privacy advocates and government institutions about the large-scale recording of personal data. Query logs have been subject to discovery by governmental agencies and others parties. Privacy legislation in the United States and the European Union covers a range of data types (e.g., census, health, financial, communications). These are handled using different protection schemes in the United States, including communications privacy laws designed for telephone communications, although how people's queries fit within this framework is still up for debate (Foley, 2007). Privacy is more comprehensively managed in the European Union (EU) through its Data Protection Directive (European Parliament, 1995), and the EU Article 29 which lays out the connection to search log data.[8] The EU directive states that personal data should not be processed unless there is a specific legal basis or people provide consent. This legislation assumes that privacy is best preserved by either requiring that the collected data be destroyed or anonymized, so that it cannot be directly connected back to the individual searcher.

Even though, as the AOL data release demonstrated, anonymization may be ineffective, interested parties were still able to identify searchers from queries alone. The need for these strategies have been called into question given the potential utility of search data for a range of purposes to benefit searchers (including personalization and improving general purpose ranking algorithms), or benefiting society in general (Dolin, 2010; Horvitz and Mulligan, 2015), many of which are highlighted in this book. There are also exceptions in the legislation for purposes including scientific, national and public security, defense, criminal prosecutions, and even ethics violations for regulated professions.[9] The need for anonymization or deletion of data could be lessened if appropriate practices were adopted that minimize unauthorized disclosure of personal data, similar to the mechanisms followed in health data, which is certainly more personal than search queries, but is retained indefinitely.

12.4.3.2 Institutional Review Boards

Institutional review boards (IRBs) comprise panels of experts that have been formally designated to approve, monitor, and review biomedical and behavioral research involving humans. They often conduct some form of risk-benefit analysis in an attempt to determine whether or not research should be done based on issues such as the risk to participants, the benefits of the study, and if and how informed consent has been obtained. Bar-Ilan (2007) suggested that IRBs may be useful in developing ways in which log data can be shared with the research community. IRBs can significantly shape experimental designs and protect people from unethical experimentation. Ethics covers both how the data that are collected are handled and the experimental protocol under which the data collection occurred during the experiment. In many retrospective log analyses, where search behavior is aggregated across many searchers, full IRB review may not be necessary because participants are not placed in any direct risk of harm during the experiment and accompanying analysis.

12.4.4 Utility

Ideally, methods to handling privacy in online services would enable searchers to benefit from the use of their behavioral data, yet also respect their preferences regarding what information, if any, to share with the search provider. There is a tradeoff between privacy and utility: protecting people's privacy to the extent that search systems record nothing of real personal significance may also render the logged data useless for its target application. People with privacy concerns may be unwilling to provide their data to the system, which may change if the service provider could communicate to searchers the likelihood of their data being logged and tailor incentives accordingly. Prior research in this area has focused on designing privacy-preserving methodologies that can provide control of a privacy-utility tradeoff (Adar, 2007; Krause and Horvitz, 2008). Research has also explored the feasibility of incorporating user preferences over what type of data can be logged (Xu et al., 2007; Cooper 2008; Olson et al., 2005; Ghosh et al., 2012). Krause and Horvitz (2008) addressed this issue specifically in the context of search personalization, where decisions need to be made about how much information to share with search systems versus the value of personalization for the searcher in tailoring the search experience.

There are a number of strategies to mitigate privacy risks. These include *stochastic privacy* (Singla et al., 2014a), which provides guarantees that could be offered by the service provider of the maximum likelihood that a searcher's logs will be selected from the pool of available searchers. This is referred to as the assessed or communicated privacy risk. The chances of an individual being selected are low, but if an individual is chosen, the service provider may want to compensate them appropriately through incentives such as increases in the quality of services, financial rewards, and so on. Another privacy-preserving approach is *differential privacy* (Dwork 2006), which formalizes the notion that for every possible output of the system, the probability of this output is almost unchanged by the addition or removal of any individual, where the probabilities are taken over coin flips of the mechanism (and not the dataset). Other methods have been proposed to preserve privacy, including generating perturbed query frequencies and query-click graphs for the purposes of releasing queries and result click-throughs publically (Korolova et al., 2009).

Much of the discussion in this chapter has assumed that searchers are providing either explicit or implicit consent to have their activity tracked. Increasingly, such consent may not always be sought. Retail location marketers such as *Turnstyle* are collecting signals from people's smartphones as they search for open wireless networks as they transition around the world. These data can then be sold back to companies as way to inform them about where their clientele are coming from or heading to after they depart. Although there have been attempts to create benchmarks for consumer privacy in such settings, Crawford and Schultz (2014) argued that all data are personal, that explicit opt-out functionality provides even more data to marketers, and questions whether industry self-regulation will be sufficient – that is, there may simply be too much financial benefit for businesses to not want to leverage the vast quantities of usage that they have been collecting.

Privacy preservation is clearly important. It is also a personal preference. Some people may be less concerned about their privacy and be willing to sell their data to the highest bidder. They could trade their information for the best price in a market in which people are assumed to be cognizant of the privacy risks. Users of online services (or users of store loyalty cards) are trading their personal data with every query they issue or item they purchase. This is captured to some extent in stochastic privacy, where the incentives to participate can be set higher for individuals with a high value of information (e.g., people from less well represented locations, searchers with less common topical interests, and so on). However, rather than having this be part of a privacy-preserving framework, personal data markets are emerging where people can sell their data to the highest bidder, and earn profits from the provision of their own information (see Lanier, 2013).

12.5 Obtaining Ground Truth

Although search data is large in scale, it offers a limited lens into the rationales behind the observed activity. That is, it captures the "how" and "what" of search behavior, but not the important "why" representing the motivation and the broader search task. To truly understand search behavior and make more than rudimentary inferences about the searcher interests and intentions (e.g., that actions are solely driven by information needs), we need to obtain ground truth data that helps us explain behaviors seen in the search logs. There are three main mechanisms that can be used to perform that function: (1) retrospective surveys; (2) client-side applications that display requests for labels/explanations when a particular event such as engine switching or abandonment occurs; and (3) survey-log linking, where a consenting survey respondent is represented by a unique identifier that is used to link their survey response with the same searcher in search engine log data. Table 12.1 summarizes the various advantages and disadvantages of the different methods.

The choice of approach varies based on the nature of the data that the experimenter wishes to collect. The survey is easy to deploy and, if the researcher is only interested in aggregate statistics across many searchers, this might be a reasonable method.

Table 12.1. *Advantages and disadvantages of various ground truth collection methods*

Method	Advantages	Disadvantages
Retrospective surveys and interviews	• Rich qualitative data	• No direct connection between the survey and the recorded behavior • Dataset could be small if interviews are employed
In situ probes	• Request made at query time • Explanations for recent activity • Tracks long-term search behavior	• Requires download/installation • High interruption cost • Limited qualitative data given the cost of interrupting users
Survey-log linking methodology	• Linking survey and activity • Simple mechanism (no need to explicitly install additional software) • Enables long-term tracking of search behavior	• Based on cookie or unique browser identifier (could expire or be reset when new Web browser instance is installed) • No in-situ explanations

Interviews can also be used as a way to understand information-searching behavior captured in logs of user search behavior of small participant groups (Kelly, 2004). Dedicated instrumentation also provides in situ data at each occurrence of a particular event of interest and can help explain the rationale for the observed behavior surrounding that event (e.g., the motivation behavior an observed switch in search engine [Guo et al., 2011]). The survey-log linking methodology is a simple approach enabling a direct connection between long-term search behavior and survey responses. This is useful for better understanding, say, life-changing events that could affect behavior over a prolonged period of time (e.g., receipt of a devastating diagnosis [Paul et al., 2014]).

A large part of what experiments are trying to establish with a determination of ground truth is a causal link between events in the lives of searchers or in the world, and search behaviors observed in search logs. Alternative methods to estimate this ground truth exist, including connecting variations in the search behavior over time with timelines of other events (e.g., using Granger causality that considers the relationship between surprising events appearing in two time series; see Granger [1969]), or temporal associations with data from different sources (e.g., emergency department admissions [West et al., 2013b]). This has applications in different aspects of search interaction modeling, including behavioral dynamics over time (Radinsky et al., 2013), the connection between search satisfaction and long-term search engine re-use (Hu et al., 2011; Song et al., 2013), and the connection between actions and outcomes (Kiciman and Richardson, 2015).

12.6 Summary

In this chapter, I discussed the means by which data are logged and data availability. I also discussed tools for data processing and examination, which are important for realizing value from the logs collected. Finally, I discussed important issues around data privacy and the trade-off between privacy and utility. When the experience is purposely manipulated, there are also significant ethical considerations in large-scale studies that should not be ignored. For example, Kramer et al. (2014) faced public backlash for studying emotional contagion (i.e., the transfer of emotional state) among hundreds of thousands of unwitting Facebook users by purposely manipulating the amount of positive and negative content presented in their newsfeed. While the academic research questions may have some value, there was widespread concern about the ethical implications of such direct manipulation of the emotional state of populations without their knowledge (Fiske and Hauser, 2014; Harriman and Patel, 2014; Tufecki, 2014). Kramer and colleagues argued that seeking explicit consent would have invalidated their findings because participants would be aware that their newsfeed was being manipulated. However, such consent should be acquired and institutional review boards should be more cognizant of the risks involved in population-scale studies of this kind.

As I described in many ways throughout this book, online search is an essential tool and the search log data collected from its usage has utility for many applications, including fundamental research on human behavior. This utility comes at a price: the outstanding opportunity to study the information-seeking activities of millions of searchers and leverage that behavior to improve a swathe of services is accompanied by the responsibility to fully respect searchers' privacy preferences so that they can continue to use online services without fear of privacy risks. Privacy frameworks are needed to balance the interests of all stakeholders, but searchers' preferences, understanding of what is being recorded, and control over the data collection process must be paramount. I concluded the chapter by comparing and contrasting various ways in which ground truth data can be collected from searchers, and how that could be used to inform log analysis and provide dependable data for tasks such as predictive modeling. It is important to note that the focus of this chapter has been on data and associated privacy costs, but there are other issues such as the financial and environmental costs in serving queries at scale that have recently received attention (Kayaaslan et al., 2011; Sazoglu et al., 2013; Friere et al., 2014).

PART IV
Opportunities and Challenges

As technology continues to evolve, many opportunities for advances in the development of search systems are emerging. Over the next decade and beyond, people will interact with search systems in new ways. There will be new, more natural and richer, interaction capabilities, as well access to knowledge mined from both data and human resources to help answer searchers' questions. With the move beyond the current reactive model, there are significant and exciting challenges in how to make search systems assume the role of a companion or intelligent assistant, in terms both of understanding query semantics as a human intermediary would, and – given that understanding – search the world's knowledge to get people to answers and information quickly. This support will help searchers explore and learn about new topics and domains, and facilitate effective decision making and action.

CHAPTER 13

New Directions and Domains

A large number of advances in the design of interactive search systems are attainable given recent technological developments, coupled with an expansion in the range of ways in which people employ search technology as it becomes more pervasive. In light of these developments, search technology will play an increasingly important role in how people tackle problems and challenges in the world. Beyond utilitarian goals, such as addressing information needs or solving problems, search is expanding into new important domains such as casual-leisure search (e.g., searching for fun; see Ross [1999], Fulton [2009], and Elsweiler et al. [2011]), diagnostic search (e.g., self-diagnosing a medical condition or debugging a problem with computer code; see Cartright et al. [2011]), and social searching (e.g., searching for people or information about people; see Evans and Chi [2008] and Horowitz and Kamvar [2010]). There are a number of new directions in the area of search interaction that will receive significant attention over the next decade and beyond. These advances can be framed in terms of technologies and opportunities. I touched on some of these earlier in the book, but in this chapter I provide more detail on each of these areas.

13.1 Mobile and Cloud Computing

The growth in mobile computing, in particular the ownership and use of smartphones and other mobile devices such as tablets and slates, has led to an increase in the volume of search traffic on new devices, especially in relevant search segments such as local search.[1] Beyond query volume, however, the *range* of tasks that people are attempting on their devices will also grow to accompany an evolution in user expectations. There are challenges associated with the transition from desktop to mobile searching that need to be addressed. For example, given the limited real screen estate on mobile devices and the difficulties associated with typed query input, the best search experience is yet to be determined (and we currently fall back to trusted presentation methods). Given different interaction paradigms, richer models of interaction with mobile devices (e.g., Guo et al., 2013), as well the development of dedicated search applications for these devices, are both important in next-generation search systems.

Despite the rise in mobile searching, the desktop computer will still be an important search entry point and will still be vital for tasks involving knowledge generation, synthesis of multiple resources, and document generation, and more research is also needed to effectively support *transitions* between devices (helping people be effective in cross-device, as well as cross-application, scenarios), in addition to focusing on single-device usage (Wang et al., 2013; Montañez et al., 2014). Given expected increases in the processing power and memory capacity of all devices, it seems reasonable for the longer-term that smartphones and/or tablets will become people's primary device. Docking stations appropriate for their location allow the functionality of existing systems to be replicated (e.g., keyboards and large displays for home and office use, or dashboard mounting with spoken dialog input, visible displays for turn-by-turn directions, and heads-up displays or audio output for the presentation of search results when operating automobiles or while exercising).

Cloud computing infrastructures enable profile information and any user-generated content to be available at any time and from anywhere. It also removes the need for retention locally on any device, which may have limited storage capabilities. Access to user-generated content from anywhere can facilitate improved productivity via better remote and mobile work capabilities. This information can be applied, with searcher consent, to improve the search experience by using constituent data to build richer user profiles to better model their long-term interests and intentions for applications such as personalization and recommendation. Simultaneously, when editing documents in the cloud independently or in collaboration with others, information about the document content, as well as social information obtained through collaborators and their respective interest profiles, can also be used by search providers for personalization and recommendation purposes.

13.2 Natural User Interaction

Driven largely by technological advances in other areas, such as speech and gesture recognition, search systems are becoming more capable of monitoring and utilizing natural search interactions. Hearst (2011) discussed the development of more natural search user interfaces, including the integration of voice and touch technology into mobile devices. There have been many other advances in the creation of immersive experiences, gesture recognition, and attention monitoring (primarily through the recent commoditization of eye-gaze tracking or proxies such as mouse-cursor tracking) that will revolutionize how people interact with search systems. Interactions with these systems are increasingly based on natural interaction methods, and systems will be able to monitor a range of aspects of search, from searcher attention to searcher affect based on a richer sensing of how people are engage with the system. Some limited progress has already been made in these areas, primarily around supporting speech-based query input and modeling the current affective state of the searcher (Arapakis et al., 2008; Feild et al., 2010).

13.3 Richer Sensing

There is a growing trend on the human-computer interaction community toward more aggressive sensing and tracking of signals over time. Devices such as eye-gaze trackers are able to detect in greater detail where people look on displays, but wearable computing devices also provide input on a range of different aspects, including health and well-being (e.g., *Fit Bit*, Microsoft *Band*, *Withings*), bionic contact lenses, and human motion in the physical world, be it based on geographic coordinates or indoor location sensing as enabled by recent advances in smartphone sensing technology (e.g., Google *Tango* devices). Armed with these additional signals, search systems can better model their users and their interests over time. I also expect to see an expansion of the ways in which people can communicate with systems by decoupling input from electronic displays, allowing the size of devices to be reduced. *SixthSense* (Mistry and Maes, 2009) utilizes computer vision to recognize hand gestures that can be used to control system input. *Skinput* (Harrison et al., 2010) provides a way in which the human body can be appropriated as an input surface using bio-acoustic sensing to localize finger taps on the skin. When augmented with a small projector, the device can also support direct manipulation of a graphical user interface, which could mean search interactions directly on the human body. Recent research on whole-body sensing (Junker et al., 2004; Cohn et al., 2012) has shown that it is possible to monitor whole body interactions with no environmental instrumentation, and only limited instrumentation of the user (to measure and digitize voltages detected by the human body [Cohn et al., 2011; 2012]) or inertial sensing of arm movements (Junker et al., 2004), among other things.

Thinking more broadly about how people will interact with systems, recent research on brain-computer interactions has focused on interfaces that allow humans to interact directly with the search system through mechanisms such as EEG (Wolpaw et al., 1991; Leuthardt et al., 2004; Nijholt and Tan, 2008). Brain sensing can be used for applications such as hands-free cursor control, but also for more sophisticated tasks by reconstructing a person's visual experience from measurements of brain activity alone (e.g., Kay et al., 2008) or to understand cognitive states (Mitchell et al., 2004), potentially useful for some applications, such as image search. The motivation behind research in this area lies in developing systems to probe searchers' thoughts in the absence of a specific stimulus. Research on decoding brain signals to infer cognitive states has made progress (e.g., Norman et al., 2006), and there has been recent work on the link between relevance and brain activity (Moshfeghi et al., 2013), but significant work needs to be done before these signals can in any way realize the vision of decoding aspects of information needs from brain activity alone. In reality, at least in the short term, "mind-reading" search systems are more likely to emerge from studying patterns of long-term search activity (e.g., re-finding [Teevan et al., 2007] and revisitation [Adar et al., 2008]) than by monitoring brain activity directly.

13.4 Augmented Reality

As search becomes more pervasive, there will be a growth in range of different ways in which search results are presented to searchers. Augmented reality (AR; Azuma et al., 2001; Feiner, 2002) can be used to present auditory and overlay information on a view of the physical world. Systems providing AR assume a number of forms, including hand-held devices (Rekimoto and Ayatsuka, 2000) and heads-up displays (Hoellerer et al., 1999). There is potential to augment people's view of the world using projective overlays with results, notifications, and other information projected onto any surface. It is also possible to use projections to augment the area surrounding large displays (e.g., Jones et al., 2013), with a view to utilizing the additional space surrounding the device to provide additional contextual information to support navigation and situate the searcher in the result space (e.g., displaying results for similar queries, showing popular follow-on pages). Moving beyond projection, Google *Glass* and Microsoft *HoloLens* provide results and additional information in a head-mounted display, and applications for smartphones make use of the device camera to provide a range of support from applying machine translation to street signs to using mapping technology and positional information about the phone to identify in-world landmarks. Such applications have the potential to both enrich our environment with salient information, and when coupled with voice input, also provide a means for seamless engagement with search systems. Despite the potential of AR to provide contextually-aware search experiences, the additional equipment can be cumbersome, expensive, and may intrude on social interactions or raise privacy concerns (as discussed in Chapter 12).

13.5 Machine Understanding and Intelligence

Equipping machines with capabilities to understand language and make intelligent decisions has long been an aspirational goal of the machine learning and artificial intelligence communities. Two areas of emerging focus in the search interaction space are enabling machines to comprehend queries and documents, and applying machine learning to support aspects of search interaction beyond result ranking.

13.5.1 Query and Document Understanding

Building machines that can understand search intent as expressed through search queries and estimate the meaning of documents could yield better result matching. Recent research on natural language understanding has the potential to contribute to these advances (Allen, 1987; Bates, 1995). Natural language understanding is a subtopic of natural language processing in artificial intelligence that deals with machine reading comprehension. The process of disassembling and parsing input is more complex than the reverse process of assembling output in natural language generation because of the occurrence of unknown and unexpected features in the input and the need to determine the appropriate syntactic and semantic schemes to apply to it, factors which are pre-determined when outputting language. A particular instantiation of natural language understanding is machine reading (Etzioni et al., 2006), whereby machines can understand the semantics of text, beyond the traditional syntactic matches relied on in current information retrieval systems. Progress is being made in the area of semantic search, but largely outside the core search community, which is focusing on the semantic

Web instead (Guha et al., 2003; Lei et al., 2006); more work is needed in this area for the vast majority of documents that lack semantic markup. Better understanding documents would advance search algorithms from syntactic matching of query terms to terms in documents to matching at higher levels of abstraction (and some progress has been made using topical information rather than query terms alone [Bennett et al., 2010] and deep learning [Song et al., 2014]). To complement machine-based comprehension of text, efforts in combining machine- and crowdsourced-understanding can leverage the collective intelligence of human workers and model meaning more accurately (Richardson et al., 2013).

13.5.2 Machine Learning and Artificial Intelligence

The explosive growth in research and development in machine learning in recent years has created a lot of opportunity for the integration of machine learning in search systems. Learning is already used extensively to rank search results based on many relevance features, but similar methods could also be applied to assist searchers dynamically in real time. Intelligent agents capable of sensing its environment (including richer modeling of the user, and even using wearable devices to obtain readings of pulse rate, blood pressure, galvanic skin response, and other characteristics to better model their current psychological state) can take actions that maximize the searcher's chances of success. Intelligent agents can help people complete a range of tasks, from complex to mundane (e.g., providing location sensitive reminders). Really complex tasks that these agents do not (presently) have the capability to handle can be redirected to humans via services such as FancyHands[2] and TaskRabbit.[3]

Efforts to develop intelligent agents capable of assisting users in their daily tasks (e.g., Maes, 1994) has met with some resistance from the user interface community, who believed that empowering people with more sophisticated user interfaces that place more control in their hands was the most effective way to assure success (Shneiderman, 1990). While support from intelligent agents may still be desirable in some forms, and as more such agents are emerging, care needs to be taken about how these agents present themselves and their recommendations to users. Ultimately, people need control over system operation. Mixed initiative user interfaces (Horvitz, 1999) blend together principals from both artificial intelligence and direct manipulation to develop automated services with aspects of searcher control. Although the mode of interaction with these agents will be spoken dialog, the medium need not be restricted to smartphones. For example, the Amazon *Echo* is a dedicated voice command device that provides answers and other functionality on demand.

13.6 Knowledge Assistants and Proactive Search

Search in its current form is reactive and recent advancements have added contextual signals to the ranking of search engines. Search systems can anticipate information needs and support task completion rather than relying on searchers to enter them explicitly. Systems are emerging that offer this type of support, e.g., Google *Now*, Microsoft *Cortana*, or Apple *Knowledge Navigator* (proposed in 1987, and replaced by the *Siri* voice activated personal assistant in 2011). These systems have access to a wealth of knowledge about the world through search engines and their partners. Moving beyond search assistance, such applications can pool information about schedules, skills, and general interests of people and their friends/family members to simplify common tasks that the individual performs often (e.g., making calendar appointments, setting reminders, performing long-running search tasks), filter noisy information and prioritize pending tasks, provide recommendations about activities worth pursuing (e.g., sightseeing for a group of conference attendees), or recommend corrective actions based on observed histories (search and otherwise; e.g., recommend exercise after a week of excess), or predict future events (e.g., forewarn of the danger of oversleeping given participation in late night social activities), although in such systems it is well understood that care needs to be taken over which actions are automated (Tambe et al., 2002). Providing such support also requires knowledge of searchers' high-level goals (e.g., weight loss, cholesterol reduction, exam preparation) and would need to be both carefully modeled and represented internally by the system and expressed explicitly by searchers as part of a periodic goal-setting activity.

These systems can develop awareness activities across a range of applications (e.g., mining events from calendars or email, monitoring interactions with productivity applications), allowing the systems to more fully model needs and intentions, and make recommendations to the searcher at the appropriate time. Many of these services access sensitive data on the searcher's device, and as such they will probably need to perform analysis of these data client-side; only sending selected information to the cloud (e.g., requests for flight status inferred from received emails) once approved by the user. Previous research on the development of intelligent agents (Horvitz et al., 1999), as well as research on attention and interruptions (Horvitz et al., 1999; Horvitz and Apacible, 2003; Czerwinski et al., 2004) is also relevant in terms of making decisions about when to engage people with recommendations. The ability to control settings such as quiet time (time periods during which the user does not want to be disturbed) or inner circles (preferred social contacts) could also be offered by the system to facilitate control and prioritization of interruptions.

13.7 New Search Scenarios

Beyond technological advancements, search is expanding to handle additional search scenarios that are not being adequately addressed with current search support. There are a few key directions in this area that I highlight in this section.

13.7.1 Diagnostic Search

People frequently use search engines to perform diagnosis of a range of problems, including health issues, fixing computer problems, and home and auto repair. I mentioned some of these topics earlier in the book when I covered problem solving. One area of diagnostic search that has received particular attention is the area of medical search (White and Horvitz, 2009; Cartright et al., 2011).

Table 13.1. *Probability of mention of cause given symptom (White and Horvitz, 2009)*

Symptom	Cause	Web Crawl	Web Search	Domain Search
headache	caffeine withdrawal	0.29	0.26	0.25
	tension	0.68	0.48	0.75
	brain tumor	0.03	0.26	0.00
muscle twitches	benign fasciculation	0.53	0.12	0.34
	muscle strain	0.40	0.38	0.66
	amyotrophic lateral sclerosis	0.07	0.50	0.00
chest pain	indigestion	0.28	0.35	0.38
	heartburn	0.57	0.28	0.52
	heart attack	0.15	0.37	0.10

Health information is one of the most widely searched topics on the Web. A recent survey by the Pew Internet and American Life Project found that 59% of U.S. adults have looked online for health information in the past year, with 35% of respondents seeking to diagnose a medical condition online; more than half of these searchers then proceed to engage directly with medical professionals (Fox and Duggan, 2013). Health information search is conducted using both search systems such as Internet search engines and via social media (e.g., advice from friends and others). However, studies have found that that cyberspace can be a costly and challenging place for those with no medical training.

The common task of performing self-diagnosis can lead to unwarranted anxiety and healthcare utilization associated with interactions between biases of indexing and retrieval in search engines and biases of human judgment and decision making (Tversky and Kahneman, 1974). Under these circumstances, common symptoms such as headaches or chest pains might transition to serious conditions such as brain tumors or heart attacks based on exposure to information online, even though the likelihood of experiencing any of these two conditions given that a searcher is experiencing either of the symptoms is extremely low.

Table 13.1 lists symptoms, some common non-serious explanations, and some more serious concerns, along with their associated probabilities, from random crawls of the Web, with the top-100 results from a Web search engine and a specialized domain search (White and Horvitz, 2009). As can be seen in Table 13.1, the estimates for Web search differ dramatically from those of Web crawl or for domain search, with more weight being given to serious conditions. For example, the co-occurrence statistics for the Web crawl may be interpreted naively by a searcher as indicating that there is a probability of 0.03 that "headache" is associated with "brain tumor," 0.29 for "caffeine withdrawal," and 0.68 for "tension." In reality, the probability of a brain tumor, given the chief complaint of headache, is much smaller than 0.03. Headaches are exceedingly common and the background chance per year of a brain tumor, based on the U.S. annual incidence rate, is 0.000116 (around 1:10,000). A naïve probability estimate of "brain tumor" given "headache" based on co-occurrence statistics in the top-ten Web search results was 0.26, more than eight times the Web estimate, and significantly higher than the general incidence rate. In comparison, co-occurrence statistics from domain search were roughly aligned with the Web estimate. Similar findings have been observed in more recent studies of bias in results, focusing on the accuracy of results given consensus answers from physicians (White, 2013) and authoritative resources such as Cochrane Reviews[4] (White and Hassan, 2014).

Concerning content on Web pages may lead to escalations in health concerns following review of the content on those pages (White and Horvitz, 2010). Search engines need to provide support for diagnostic activities, either directly in the search engine if it is equipped with such diagnostic support (Heckerman et al., 1989; Henrion et al., 1991), or it can direct searchers to dedicated diagnosis sites such as *WebMD*. Because results for symptom queries are often skewed toward concerning outcomes (e.g., [*brain tumor*] occurs frequently in the search results for the query [*headache*], and more than expected given base rates [White and Horvitz, 2009]), search engines may attempt to correct for biases in search results by using veracity-oriented features so that result distributions better match normative base rates.

Details of the pursuit of professional medical care may not be available from searchers directly owing to privacy concerns. However, it is possible to make inferences about the pursuit of this treatment from professional medical care from their online behavior. Healthcare utilization intentions (HUIs; see White and Horvitz [2010]) can be expressed in a number of ways, such as issuing a query indicating the pursuit of professional medical treatment at a particular location (e.g., querying for [*physician 98034*]) or seeking directions to a local medical facility. These Web-to-world transitions may be caused by the information that searchers are exposed to online, or may be facilitated by the Web. Either way, as part of supporting the diagnostic process, there is a need to support these transitions (e.g., by reminding users of salient historic symptom search episodes for discussion with their physician), especially if we can be confident that searchers will visit the medical facility based on their prior health-seeking activity or other information.

13.7.2 Slow Search

Following on from a number of slow movements, including "slow food," slow search refers to a class of information-seeking activities where the traditional focus on speed in generating search results is replaced by an emphasis on quality (Teevan et al., 2013). Recent research has shown that search tasks can span time and devices (Kotov et al., 2011; Wang et al., 2013), generating opportunities for search systems to use this downtime to generate better quality search results (e.g., via engagement with subject matter experts).

The implementation of slow search can take a number of forms, including synchronous social question answering (White et al., 2011), the human composition of direct answers for less frequent queries (Bernstein et al., 2012), and the integration of search systems into social networks (Hecht et al., 2012). The main premise in doing so is that for many tasks there may not be the need for an instant response and that by employing alternative finding and synthesizing resources from the Web, we can support searchers for these complex tasks. Recent research in this area has suggested that there are situations in which people may be willing to wait for an answer from the system if the search results were of sufficient quality (Teevan et al., 2013). In such cases, the search engine can involve humans in both phases of the search process – to clarify needs (query understanding) and to generate the set of search results that the user should see – perhaps by filtering or ordering the results that are returned by the search engine to select the results that are of most potential interest to searchers (Kim et al., 2014).

13.7.3 Social Search

Social search involves both the search for people and search that involves people (e.g., search or subject matter experts who may guide searchers through the stages of their search). The potential benefit from leveraging the crowd has received attention in recent years, and services such as *Aardvark* (Horowitz and Kamvar, 2010) and *IM-an-Expert* (White et al., 2011) provide askers with direct access to answerers synchronously, supporting real-time dialog to resolve uncertainty. Social search systems may leverage social network graphs in addition to textual and behavioral features to rank search results such that they the algorithm favors results visited (or preferred) by those proximal to the current searcher. Other forms of social search range from bookmark sharing or tagging (Chi, 2009) to more sophisticated models that combine human intelligence with ranking algorithms (e.g., social bookmarking or direct interaction with the search results such as promoting or demoting results perceived to be more or less relevant to the query). Human search engines such as ChaCha.com pair searchers with search experts who can help users clarify their request and find resources to help answer their questions; other systems such as Google *Helpouts* paired askers with expert answerers for higher fidelity answering experiences through video chat.

There will be a growth in many types of explicit support for social searching, especially with the advent of technologies to support real-time language translation (e.g., the Skype Translator) – facilitating communication between individuals anywhere in the world, irrespective of the language that they speak. In addition to explicit support, studies have shown that people are also repurposing social media for question answering purposes. Research on the best way to present questions to these networks to have the maximum possible likelihood of achieving an answer (Morris et al., 2010). Because this practice is expected to continue, there is a need to provide support to people to help them formulate more effective questions. Algorithms have been developed to help askers create better questions (that are less likely to result in clarification dialogs) in the context of synchronous social question-answering (Kato et al., 2013), but not in more commonly-used asynchronous social media such as Facebook or Twitter.

13.7.4 Task Continuation and Cross-Device Search

Many tasks extend over time. Recent estimates suggest that more than half of online search behavior relates to long-term tasks (Agichtein et al., 2012), which are often associated with complex, multi-stage events such as planning a wedding, making travel plans, or purchasing a home. There has been some work in this area on personal computers (Donato et al., 2010; Kotov et al., 2011), as well as research specifically focused on search tasks that transcend device boundaries (Wang et al., 2013; Montañez et al., 2014). As multi-device usage increases, there will be an increased need to support search across devices. A core component in supporting users as they move between devices is the identification of task continuation. If a system could identify that a searcher may resume their task, it can rehydrate previous search state, both cognitively by summarizing past activity and in terms of a set of historic task-related actions that the system can use for applications such as personalization (Tan et al., 2006). In its current form, search is largely stateless. Cross-session tasks could be supported by providing searchers with abilities to restore state as it pertains to a task of interest. This could take a number of forms, including (1) restoring state reactively (e.g., task-based views on people's search histories); (2) restoring state proactively (e.g., task-based personalization using historic actions pertaining only to the search task); or (3) task-based recommendations of future actions (based on modeling the searcher's current knowledge state and suggesting new information). While there is the opportunity to perform additional actions such as proactively retrieving content pertaining to tasks in the downtime between sessions (as advocated in literature on slow search, described earlier in this chapter), these three goals are both more pressing and more attainable in the short-to-medium term, especially given the existing work in this area. Recent research on "self-sourcing" (Teevan et al., 2014a) offers a way for people to manage long-term personal tasks by dividing tasks into easily attemptable pieces that searchers can complete when they have only a small amount of free time.

13.8 Applying Big Data

In addition to supporting search activity, there is value in the data collected during search interaction to support learning about the world. Big data provides incredible opportunities for understanding human interactions at a societal scale (e.g., computational social science has emerged as an important field of study [Lazer et al., 2009]), with rich spatial and temporal dynamics, and to detect complex interactions and nonlinearities among variables. Previous research in other domains has shown that valuable insights may be obtained from mining large quantities of data (e.g., Swanson [1988] discovered hidden connections between migraines and magnesium was made via a citation analysis and a manual review of terms in both literatures). Similar principles can be applied to the analysis of search logs, which may reveal rich signals about factors affecting people. These data can be used for a variety of purposes, including discovering adverse drug reactions (White et al., 2013b) and determining associations between queries, e.g., those related to the outcomes of actions (Kiciman and Richardson, 2015). The boundaries between the online and offline worlds continue to blur, and some of the most promising uses of the Internet rely on considering it an adjunct to the physical world, not a separate space. Data gleaned from search interactions can be used to inform action and decision processes in the real world.

Research on the use of long-term logs to understand changes in user interest over time is also worth pursuing. For example, Richardson (2008) showed that there are clear temporal relationships between real-world events that are evident in long-term query logs. Figure 13.1 visually represents the relationship between searches for [*interview*] and searches for both [*resume*] and [*moving*]. The figure shows quite clearly that

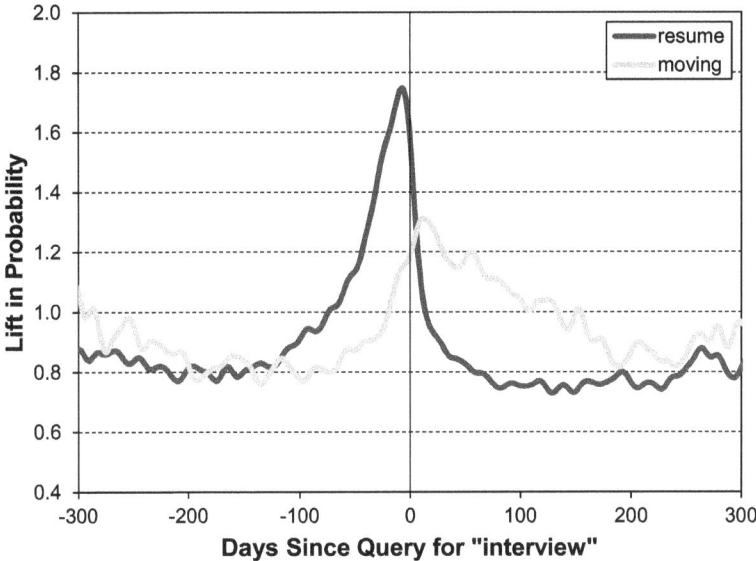

Figure 13.1. Lift in probability for the queries "resume" and "moving" given the reference query "interview." People begin looking for information on resumes up to 100 days before the interview query; most look immediately before. Users are more interested in moving after the interview query (adapted from Richardson, 2008).

searching for résumé-related information increases dramatically before interview searching and searches for moving-related information is more prevalent afterward.

The presence of such signals in search log data represents an incredible opportunity to obtain a lens into searchers' lives via log data that may not be attainable using other means. Such long-term analysis can be used for a range of purposes, from predictive advertising to discovering associations between concepts (e.g., links between magnesium and headaches [Swanson, 1988]) that can have profound implications for people's health and wellbeing.

13.8.1 Case Studies in Public Health

Big data can yield important insights for a number of domains. One domain of particular importance is public health, which can be costly and slow to study at scale. Researchers have explored the use of social media such as Twitter as a source of public health data (e.g., to track influenza [Paul and Dredze, 2011], detect health concerns associated with eating at particular restaurants [Sadilek et al., 2013], or monitor the spread of disease [Sadilek et al., 2012]). This demonstrates the potential from mining online behavior to track possible health risks in a timely and scalable manner.

Focusing specifically on aggregated records of *search interaction* (the focus of this book), models have been developed that leverage large volumes of search log data to make predictions about disease (e.g., influenza patterns [Johnson et al., 2004; Eysenbach, 2006; Polgreen et al., 2008; Ginsberg et al., 2009]), and track nutritional intake globally (West et al., 2013a). Figure 13.2 shows the predictions of these models

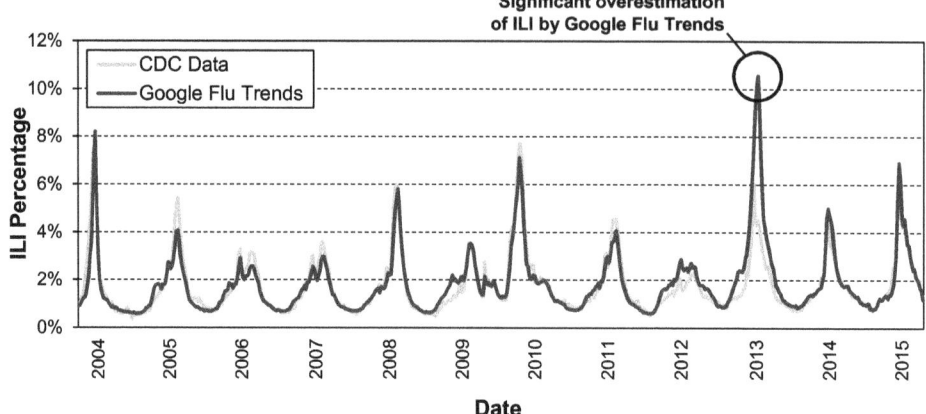

Figure 13.2. A comparison of model estimates for the United States (red) against CDC-reported ILI percentages (blue). *Data Source:* Google Flu Trends (www.google.org/flutrends). A point of significant overestimation of ILI by Google *Flu Trends* is marked in the figure.

regarding the incidence rates for influenza-like illness (ILI) for the United States for data from the Centers for Disease Control (CDC) and that from a predictive model based on search log data.

Additional discoveries can be made from log data such as potential interactions between medications that can be visible in the query stream. Searchers who are observed querying for a drug or pair of drugs may also be observed querying for side effects of those drugs which may not be known. The enormous potential of search logs as a tool for pharmacovigilance is yet to be unlocked, but offers an incredible potential for societal benefit from mining data in this way. White et al. (2013c) showed that they could identify evidence of an interaction between pravastatin and paroxetine using signals in search engine log data before that interaction effect became public knowledge (creating a serious confound for any behavioral analysis). They verified the utility of search logs for this purpose using a further set of sixty-four drug pairs, half of which were associated with hyperglycemia and half of which were not.

White et al. (2014a) studied the use of search behavior before and after a search for particular drugs as a way to automatically detect adverse events from search logs. The authors demonstrated the effectiveness of their methods using ground truth data from the observational medical outcomes partnership (OMOP), which contains a list of approximately 400 medications and labels indicating whether they are likely to cause one of four events. The research described showed that is possible to automatically detect adverse events associated with the drugs using search log data with an accuracy that is comparable to the industry mainstay, the adverse event reporting system provided by the U.S. Food and Drug Administration (FDA). Others have explored similar issues (e.g., Yom-Tov and Gabrilovich [2013]), but have also encountered challenges with obtaining ground truth data against which to verify their conclusions – a common difficulty in this and similar applications of big data. There are exciting opportunities to apply similar methods for *prospective* analysis, whereby can predict adverse drug events before they are found in other sources such as the FDA's Adverse Events Reporting System (FAERS). The Behavioral Log-based AERS (BLAERS) from Microsoft

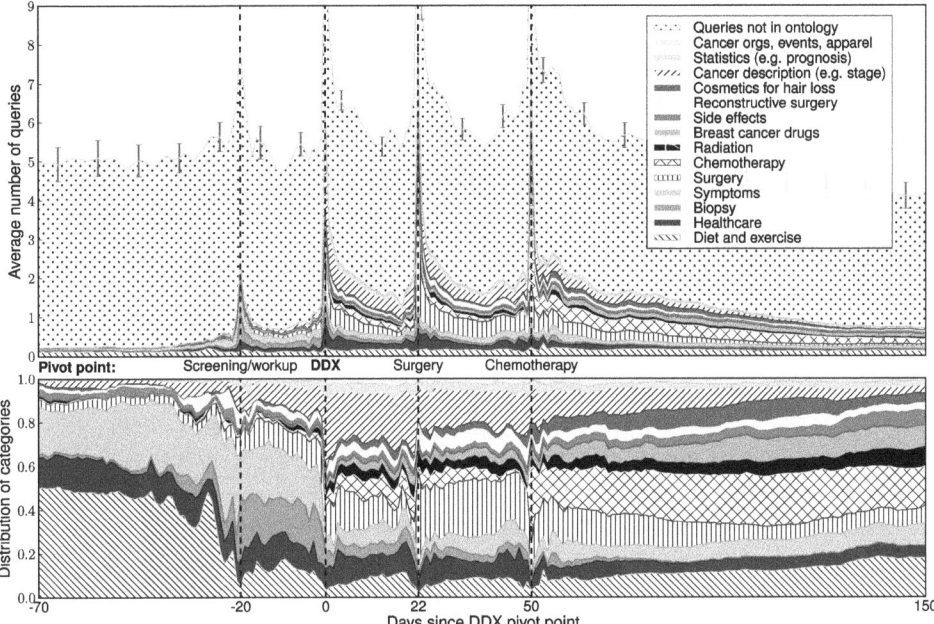

Figure 13.3. The raw (top) and normalized (bottom) average number of queries per day for different search categories. The day on the *x*-axis is with respect to the pivot point, whereas the *y*-axis value is averaged between the values of the two surrounding pivot points. Standard error of the unsmoothed values is shown for the topmost curve (Paul et al., 2014). (See color plate 13.3.)

Research leverages behavioral data for prospective adverse drug reaction (ADR) analysis and *n*-way drug interaction analysis.

The challenge in such investigations is in not only obtaining truth through known adverse events, but also finding the set of those that are not public knowledge at the time the prediction is made; general awareness through label changes and alerts could bias the signals gleaned from online user behavior. Harpaz et al. (2014) developed a time-indexed reference standard of ADRs based on FDA label change dates that can be used to evaluate predictive performance using only data available before the ADR was publically known. There may still be indications of ADRs before the label change date (e.g., discussions in Web fora) that may influence online searching, and tools such as the Internet Archive's Wayback machine[5] may be useful in identifying when information appears online and correcting label change dates accordingly.

More recent studies have shown that there is potential utility in search logs for applications such as tracking nutrition in populations using recipes accessed online (West et al., 2013a), characterizing and predicting mental health issues using search activity (Yom-Tov et al., 2014), and tracking episodes of information seeking associated with chronic conditions such as breast cancer and pregnancy over prolonged time periods (Paul et al., 2014; Fourney et al., 2015). Figure 13.3 presents timelines visualizing the temporal dynamics of searchers' health search intentions for those predicted to have been diagnosed with breast cancer. The day of diagnosis (DDX), estimated from the query stream based on human labeling, is marked on the figure, with other pivot points such as when surgery or chemotherapy are likely to begin.

13.8.1.1 A Cautionary Note

Although here are significant opportunities for scientific advances through big data (Lazer et al., 2009; Vespignani, 2009; King, 2011), care needs to be taken regarding issues such as validity, reliability, and dependencies among data (Boyd and Crawford, 2012). Care is also needed in making inferences that are usually reserved for sophisticated scientific mechanisms from data alone (especially repurposed data). A canonical example is the Google *Flu Trends* (GFT) service, which faced documented problems of overestimating instances of influenza from search queries (Butler, 2013; Lazer et al., 2014), as is visible in the highlighted part of Figure 13.2. Explanations for this overestimation include the effect of the media on online search behavior (e.g., more press coverage of influenza is likely to result in more searching about it; see Butler [2013] and Copeland et al. [2013]) and changes in the Google search services over time, including the ranking algorithm and query suggestions. Other challenges include the malicious use of the search engine to promote particular resources (e.g., Google Bombing, which involves manipulation of anchor text to promote pages for unrelated queries). Lazer et al. (2014) showed that combining the GFT signals with other sources such as near real-time health data from the Centers for Disease control, its performance could be significantly improved. The efficacy of combining offline and online data sources has been demonstrated in other studies (e.g., combining signals from query logs with those from the FAERS yields large gains in accuracy over using either of the sources alone [White et al., 2014a]). Besides verifying that we can obtain good or slightly better performance on tasks addressable successfully with current methods, big data should be used to tackle richer problems (e.g., predicting influenza rates at local levels), combined with qualitative and quantitative data from a variety of sources, and analyzed in innovative ways to learn about the world (Lazer et al., 2014).

Given the mixture of signals from different sources, visualization mechanisms need to be able summarize the main findings efficiently and present them in a clear and understandable manner, so that appropriate action can be taken. The primary focus is not on identifying issues directly, but rather narrowing the space of possibilities and providing guidance for follow-up studies, including those with human participants once a small set of research questions has been identified.

13.8.2 Biases and Behavior

With the use of large-scale behavioral data, there are obvious drawbacks related to the nature of the user cohort who provide these data. It may be unrepresentative of particular user groups (e.g., low income users who lack Internet access would likely be missing from the sample). Additionally, for the behaviors that are observed, there are a variety of biases that affect that behavior, including examination bias (Joachims et al., 2007), caption biases (Yue et al., 2010; White and Horvitz, 2013), and cognitive biases, which have only recently started to be explored in terms of search interaction (White, 2013; White and Horvitz, 2015). There has been significant research from those in the psychology community on understanding the impact of cognitive bias on a variety of settings. Biases permeate many aspects of how people make decisions and interact with the world around them, including their interactions with search engines. For example, it has been suggested that anchoring biases (whereby people remain attached to initial estimates [Tversky and Kahneman, 1974]), may impact query formulation decisions (Blair, 1980).

Cognitive biases have a marked effect on search behavior, yet there has been little research on the role of these biases on search activity, and the effect that this can ultimately have on search engines that learn from that behavior. The biases may also be counterproductive and lead searchers to incorrect answers, especially if they have strongly held beliefs that may not align with the correct answers (if one is known). Biases in search have typically focused on preference for search results presented high in the ranking, or a preference for particular resources (e.g., favoring one Web domain over another). The impact of biases in beliefs on behaviors and outcomes is an important emerging area that needs to be better understood. A recent study examined search-related bias in the context of yes-no questions (White, 2013). I showed that search engine results and result selections (even when they controlled for rank position) were skewed toward positive (*yes*) answers, irrespective of the truth, which was controlled experimentally to be evenly split between the two outcomes. A follow-on crowdsourced study that asked people about their beliefs directly before examining results confirmed the findings of the log-based investigation (White, 2013). Such cognitive biases, coupled with other biases, such as those associated with the examination of results in a particular order (discussed in more detail in Chapter 3), and the content of search results, which has shown to be skewed for certain types of query (White and Hassan, 2014), can bias people's perceptions about event likelihood (Tversky and Kahneman, 1973) and in-world decision making (Epstein and Robertson, 2015).

These biases can skew the data available for learning purposes, but could also affect the performance of the search engine, e.g., search engines are tailored to handle the types of requests that people ask, but if people are phrasing questions positively then engines may learn to prefer positively leaning content, irrespective of the search query that is posed. This highlights the nature of the challenges of learning from behavioral data, which is affected by a number of biases. It is not only search logs that could be affected by such biases. Data collected from online sources such as social media is affected by a number of biases, including different populations at a coarse level, including different demographics. Figure 13.4 illustrates relationships between content, results, and searchers.

Biases affect both beliefs/preferences and interaction behavior. Content generation is based on authors' estimation of readers'/searchers' future interests, which can be biased toward particular perspectives (e.g., alarming content in the case of online searching [White and Horvitz, 2009]) because that can attract more readers. The results that are served to searchers influence their beliefs, and if personalization is used, could be affected by their beliefs. Search engines also learn from aggregate and individual searcher behavior, which creates feedback loops whereby particular documents or those expressing a particular viewpoint are promoted over time given preferential attachment and the utilization of implicit feedback.

The decisions about what data to share publically in these outlets affect the nature and generalizability of conclusions drawn from the data. Studies are needed into the nature of biases and the extent of its impact on social media analysis. Kiciman (2012) targeted perceptions on social media about the weather. He found that extreme weather

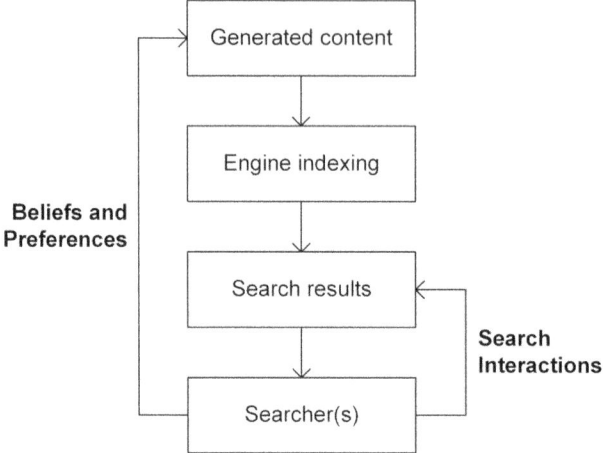

Figure 13.4. Interactions between content, results, and searchers.

conditions were likely to be overrepresented in Twitter data, leading to a biased dataset. Others studied biases in rumor propagation in social network data (Friggeri et al., 2014), which has implications for the beliefs and actions of those exposed to these rumors, especially if they are incorrect. Hecht and Stephens (2014) explored biases in the self-reporting of volunteered geographic information in Twitter, Flickr, and Foursquare, such that urban perspectives are more represented in the data than rural areas, even when normalizing for population.

Mechanisms are needed detect and mitigate these biases, such as smart sampling of actions or searchers from the population, or more balanced training of search systems irrespective of any biases toward positive outcomes observed in the data. There has been research on the removal of biases from data in the medical community (when seeking to fairly compare treatment and control groups in light of possible selection biases; see Rosenbaum and Rubin [1983]) and more recently in the context of learning from online data (Agrawal et al., 2011). Beyond bias mitigation, search systems may also want to simply indicate the *potential* for bias via a warning on the SERP (e.g., "Distribution of results does not agree with the published literature on this topic") or summarize the different viewpoints on a topic in a direct answer.

13.9 Evaluation

Because information seeking is a personal process, we would expect to see this mirrored in the types of metrics that are used to evaluate search system performance, both in small- and large-scale testing (e.g., personalized relevance or satisfaction judgments mined from click data). As the range of search tasks expands beyond the lookup scenarios that have traditionally been the focus in search evaluation, a range of different metrics (e.g., learning, enjoyment, cognitive load), and their combinations, may need to be adopted. Richer simulations of search behavior may help facilitate progress in this area. For example, more advanced models that are capable of learning during the search process (e.g., SNIF-ACT [Fu and Pirolli, 2007]) may provide accurate simulations of how searchers could adapt and learn during the search process. However, these methods are inherently limited by their automated nature (log data is human generated) and that will never provide the rich qualitative feedback and insight that is attainable from direct engagement with human subjects (both search logs and searcher simulations lack accompanying qualitative data). More open sharing of data and resources (including systems and materials) between researchers at different experimental sites is needed, accompanied by mechanisms for coordinating experiments at these sites, so as to attain required reproducibility in system evaluation. Without such a means, it is difficult to see how interactive experimentation can extend beyond a collection of isolated, one-off experiments, influenced by situational and environmental factors, and limiting the potential for studies to progressively build on the findings of previous research.

13.10 Summary

I have highlighted a number of potential new directions and domains in the area of search interaction. Technological advances are enabling many opportunities for richer, smarter, and more natural search experiences. Looking forward, intelligent agents will help searchers both reactively and proactively. Next-generation search systems will be equipped with capabilities to develop richer models of context to enhance retrieval, but also to push relevant content to searchers. Attention is turning to new, richer search scenarios such as diagnostic, slow, and social search, and the methods that are needed to support these types of search scenarios. Despite the promising future for search interaction, search providers face challenges in addressing biases inherent in log data that need to be counteracted if reliable behavioral signals are to be mined and applied effectively to these settings and others. Methods to more fully evaluate interactive search systems and compare results between experimental sites are also a necessity.

CHAPTER 14
Call to Action

14.1 Opportunities and Challenges

The future is bright for search interaction. This chapter outlines some of the grand challenges for search interaction and present a call to action for the researchers and practitioners of search systems to work collaboratively to meet these challenges. The confluence of a number of important technological advances means that there is significant opportunity for the search community to advance the process of information seeking well beyond its current state. New interaction techniques, cloud-based storage, and mobile devices are some of the most important recent advances that need to be investigated more thoroughly by the research community when designing next-generation search systems. Some of the other notable recent advances, such as big data and machine learning, have led to significant advances in the development of support for the search process (Liu, 2009). The goals of search, both in terms of the core capabilities of search systems and searcher expectations for what these systems can do, need to be expanded beyond information finding (a facility that all search systems must possess) to promote the development of search technology to help people explore, learn, gain insights, and apply their knowledge. The remainder of this chapter outlines key opportunities presently available to the search community to shape the future of search interaction. These can be grouped into four categories: (1) experiences; (2) data; (3) evaluation; and (4) external engagement.

1. Development of search experiences
   - *Capitalize on new technologies and interaction paradigms.* The pace of technological innovation is increasing rapidly. New devices are emerging that understand natural interactions such as touch, gesture, and voice, and can be used in many different settings. Although there has been some recent progress toward supporting the application of these new technologies in search interaction (see Hearst [2011] for a summary of some recent advances), research in the area

of natural user information retrieval (NUIR) is still in its infancy. Despite the importance and growing prevalence of devices and applications with new capabilities, the research community is largely still fixated on supporting desktop-based Web searching, with the keyboard and the mouse as the only input mechanisms, and textual query statements and a ranked list of search results as the primary means of engaging with search systems. Although interest in search across different types of devices is growing (Montañez et al., 2014), little attention has been paid to new modalities. These present opportunities for more advanced search systems that leverage spoken dialog and artificial intelligence, and richer and more rewarding search experiences (e.g., some of the interaction strategies for interpersonal communication [a dialog model] could help make the search process more natural, especially for complex tasks).
- *Develop proactive, engaging, and situational search experiences.* There has been insufficient research on the development of compelling new search experiences, including a lack of research on revising search interfaces beyond the traditional ranked list of results. More research on search interfaces is needed. As part of the support that they offer, search systems should be both proactive (promoting useful content that might be of interest to searchers), and reactive as they have been developed traditionally. They should also respond to the nature of the current situation based on modeling contextual factors that are likely to influence intentions, interests, interactions, and task outcomes.

2. Data collection and applications
   - *Collect and represent rich interaction data in a responsible and privacy preserving manner.* New interfaces and interaction methods mean that next-generation searcher activity logs may need to capture a broad array of different interaction streams, potentially much fuller than the current focus on query and click events in current logging. The collection of richer interaction data is in tension with the collection of massive volumes of search data at Web scale. Current logging schemes usually only record basic interaction events, given the desire to minimize the impact on system operation associated with logging and minimize data volumes for the recorded behaviors given storage costs. Research is needed into ways to generate condensed logging schemes that do not utilize too much storage space, and can allow search behavior to be collected with a minimal impact on the performance of search applications.
   - *Balance privacy and utility*: It is clear that searcher data, including data describing their online search and browsing activity, is useful for a number of applications, including modeling interests and intentions. With growth in the richness of the data collected from searchers, there is also a danger that data collection and modeling will become too invasive, leading to unacceptable levels of privacy risk. Privacy preserving methods such as stochastic privacy (Singla et al., 2014a) and differential privacy (Dwork, 2006) present the initial steps in preserving people's privacy while still being able to glean useful information from behavioral signals. More research is needed in the development of methods to balance important privacy concerns against the utility of using their data for improving the search experience and better understanding the world. Research has already shown that data preserving strict privacy guarantees can be useful

for important tasks such as studying human nature (specifically fears expressed in search queries) or keyword generation (Korolova et al., 2009).

- *Correct biases in searcher data and searcher sampling.* As suggested in the previous chapter, biases in searchers' examination behaviors can impact the behavioral signals used as implicit feedback by search engines to improve result ranking (Joachims, 2002). These biases may skew the behavioral signals and impact the accuracy and the overall relevance of the search results. They may be associated with known cognitive biases such as confirmation bias (Tversky and Kahneman, 1974), but they may also extend beyond search behavior and be associated with the selection of particular searcher samples for a study (e.g., people who use a particular Web service may not be representative of the general population). More research is needed in the development of methods to de-bias the data and create a cleaner behavioral signal for applications such as result ranking or query suggestion (White and Hassan, 2014). People can be persuaded to change their beliefs by the sequencing of the results returned by search systems (White, 2014; Epstein and Robertson, 2015). Methods from psychology may also be useful for handling and correcting misinformation in ways that convinces people with false beliefs to alter them (Lewandowsky et al., 2012), assuming that falsehood is determinable for the current topic.
- *Reflect carefully about data generation and sharing.* To foster collaboration and competition, search engines should explore ways to provide data to academic researchers, in the form of their own proprietary data (anonymized as needed) or some subset of third-party datasets (such as those from analytics companies such as Experian and comScore), licensed to institutions under non-disclosure agreements. The release of datasets is already standard practice in other communities such as biomedicine, even though there may well be publication and privacy sensitivities associated with that data. Some venues in the data-mining community require tests to be performed on simulated datasets in the case of proprietary data as a precondition for publication. A similar strategy could be employed within information retrieval. Alternatively, search engines could provide researchers with a means to generate their own interaction data (e.g., by providing a platform from which researchers can perform parallel flights [A-B testing] and gain access to large numbers of volunteer searchers as part of academic outreach). Although proprietary data can yield extremely valuable insights about online information-seeking processes, its scientific value is limited given the lack of replicability, verifiability, and extension in follow-on studies. Limited release of some subset of usage data is necessary from published studies to drive research on search interaction. The AOL data (described in Chapter 12) is fulfilling that function, albeit with ethical concerns since it was retracted. Logs from analytics companies such as comScore may meet this requirement since the logs are available to purchase by any researcher. Requiring that researchers report findings on a dataset such as that in addition to any proprietary data analysis would help promote reproducibility of any proposed methods and ultimately, the more rapid advancement of research on search interaction. Searcher simulations, with parameter settings directly derived from search log data and/or user study data may also help facilitate rapid reproducible experimentation.

3. Evaluation of search systems
   - *Develop and apply appropriate and novel evaluation methods.* The current methods of evaluation do not adequately capture the complexity of the interactions with search systems, or measure some of the aspects that are important objectives in the design of next-generation search systems, such as learning and searcher engagement. Richer simulations of search behavior would facilitate comparability in systems between experimental sites for some tasks, but will be insufficient on their own accord to determine search performance. Not only are more user studies needed in Information Retrieval research in general, but also more attention needs to be paid to evaluation methods that extend beyond the laboratory setting to consider longitudinal studies of experimental systems in situ. It is only through observing the how searchers utilize new search systems in practice that we can truly understand their utility.
   - *Consider a broader range of evaluation metrics individually and in combination.* Search systems can support searchers in multiple ways. It is important to understand how system usage affects, among other things, learning, cognitive load, and enjoyment, as well as more standard metrics such as success and satisfaction. Each metric offers different insight on the search experience, and salient combinations of metrics are needed for each system, task, and search situation. Considering the degree to which search systems help and hinder search processes and search outcomes is important in measuring holistic system value.
4. Learn from and engage with other communities
   - *Learn from other communities.* More interdisciplinary interaction is needed beyond the boundaries of the search community. As search becomes more pervasive, there is a need to consider the broader impact of search technology, and expand the range of search tasks being considered. Much can be learned from practices around design and evaluation in other communities such as psychology, cognitive science, sociology, and human computer interaction.
   - *Engage with other communities.* Beyond simply learning from the lessons of the other communities (which could be performed by reading the relevant literature), more can be achieved through direct engagement. Interdisciplinary events, journals, organizations, and working groups are needed to foster interactions between the communities and directly leverage strengths and insights from each community to design and evaluate next-generation search experiences.

14.2 Summary

Overall, it is clear from the opportunities summarized in the previous section and throughout this book that the study of interactive search systems is an important and evolving research area. Only by capitalizing and keeping pace with the important developments in technology can search systems offer the most compelling experiences to searchers. Although the core technologies will be hidden from the searchers, advances in areas such as deep learning, speech recognition, and computer vision, will enable the more natural expression of information needs as spoken queries and images, leading to an increase in queries of this nature. Although it may not always be clear how new technological advances can be applied in retrieval settings (e.g., the application of gestural input on large displays for search is not clearly understood but may be useful for some applications, such as those where exploration, immersion, or co-located collaboration are important; or cases in which an intelligent personal assistant can interpret both body language and gesture), research is needed on the development of applications that leverage such signals.

Ways in which research in these areas could be encouraged include the provision of funding from commercial or governmental sources, and establishing meetings and working groups specifically targeting search interaction and interactions between relevant research communities, focused first on the challenges that people face in searching and then on designing new methods to support information seeking. These activities, especially the former, could both further energize research on the development of interactive search systems, and facilitate significant advances in supporting searchers seeking to find, explore, and use information across a range of search situations. Armed with both small and big data, describing the individual in detail and the masses in general respectively, search systems are closing in on the aspirational goal of query-less, mind-reading search systems. Because such systems would still make mistakes and raise quite significant privacy concerns, the future of search systems lies in *synergies* between humans and machines, where intelligent and personalized search systems are capable of taking action on behalf of searchers for some scenarios, but mostly make recommendations and operate in a semi-supervised manner. These next-generation search experiences will empower searchers to realize and even exceed their potential, through interactions with search systems.

Notes

Foreword

1. Although logs provide little information on the rationale behind observed behavior, that can be captured through complementary methods such as in situ surveys asking about search intent (Broder, 2002), satisfaction (Fox et al., 2005, and others (e.g., search abandonment [Diriye et al., 2012] or search engine switching [Guo et al., 2011]) and stimulated recall, where people reflect on prior searches prompted by logs (Kelly, 2004).

Chapter 1. Introduction

1. A recent report from the International Data Corporation (IDC) forecasts that 87% of connected device sales by 2017 will be tablets and smartphones; www.idc.com/getdoc.jsp?containerId=prUS24314413.

Chapter 2. Collecting and Representing Search Interaction

1. Simulations of user behavior may be useful for assessing the utility and usability of search interface variants without human participants (Chi et al., 2003; White, 2006). Recent progress in counterfactual estimation (Bottou et al., 2013; Li et al., 2014) suggests that this could be possible in understanding the potential impact of a change.
2. Exceptions to this are parallel flighting (AB testing; see Kohavi et al. [2009]) and interleaving (Chapelle et al., 2012), which is discussed in Chapter 11.
3. In some cases the query itself is a navigation event, whereby the searcher is trying to reach a particular, known resource using the query as the means by which the navigation occurs. The searcher could equally type the Web address of the site they are trying to reach into the address bar of the browser, but querying is perceived by the searcher as being easier.
4. I use the phrases "selection," "result selection," and "click" synonymously throughout the book.
5. Other ways of selecting items include touch, gesture, and spoken dialog. In systems employing these modalities, there is often an action that assumes the role of a selector: tap in touch, hover or grab in gesture, and pause or specific voice command in spoken dialog.
6. The need for cognition is a personality trait that measures the extent to which people enjoy cognitively effortful activity (Cacioppo and Petty, 1982).
7. http://www.comscore.com.

8. http://www.nielsen.com.
9. http://www.experian.com/hitwise.
10. Different authors have used alternate terminology: Chierchetti et al. (2010) call this "control-click" because this action can be performed by holding the CTRL key and clicking; the word "branching" in Meiss et al. (2010) also includes Back button usage (which can be distinguished as *backtracking* to a previous page); Huang and White (2012) use the same terminology.
11. Even small increases in page load time can have a noticeable impact on searcher engagement (Shurman and Brutlag, 2009; Teevan et al., 2013; Arapakis et al., 2014).
12. http://www.w3.org/TR/touch-events.
13. http://google.com/dashboard.

Chapter 3. Modeling Interests and Intentions

1. This has also been referred to as "user behavior modeling." I prefer the term "searcher" here and throughout the book because it more accurately represents the role of the individual as an information seeker.
2. Research has explored the tradeoffs between data volumes and algorithm effectiveness, see – for example – the seminal paper by Banko and Brill (2001) from the natural language processing community, which demonstrated the benefits of increasing the size of the training data by orders of magnitude. Learning curves have been reported in studies on the impact of search behavior (e.g., Bilenko and White, 2008).
3. http://microsoft.com/band.
4. http://www.cs.waikato.ac.nz/ml/weka/.
5. It is important to note that because the learning-to-rank models can be computationally expensive, these simpler retrieval models may still be used in the generation of a filter set (or so-called "top-k retrieval") on which the learning-to-rank methods can be applied to generate a *ranking* of potentially relevant documents. Many good heuristics were proposed in the literature to accelerate the ranking, such as using document's static quality score and tiered indexes.

Chapter 4. Models and Frameworks for Information Seeking

1. Examining search processes beyond information workers interacting with information systems – a common focus in many studies of information behavior, especially before large-scale log analysis afforded (albeit limited) insight on the information behaviors of the general public.
2. In addition, research has shown that people rarely use the find-in-page functionality (Ctrl-F) and instead use potential inefficient strategies such as skimming and scanning to locate content within documents (Feild et al., 2013).
3. Exploitation is in contrast to exploration, whereby people seek to broaden their searching by accessing a material in a diverse set of areas and/or on a range of different regions across the information space.

Chapter 5. Helping People Search

1. Credit to Kevyn Collins-Thompson, who coined this phrase during discussions at Microsoft.
2. Uncertainty has been investigated in studies of information seeking (Bates, 1989; Dervin, 1983; Kuhlthau, 1991; Kuhlthau, 1993; Wilson et al., 2002), the uncertainty studied typically surrounds a user's state of knowledge, which may be high at the outset but reduces over time, as they review information (although not always [Wilson et al., 2002]).

3. "Jamming" (Eisenberg 1990) has a similar meaning to "flow," whereby people are deeply immersed and engaged, and through such activity they transcend the boundaries of their typical experience.
4. https://addons.mozilla.org/en-US/firefox/addon/rsccmanfasterfox/.
5. http://pewinternet.org/reports/2010/Mobile-Access-2010.aspx.
6. Derived from Greek mythology, where King Midas possessed the ability to turn everything that he touched to gold.
7. Although as we will discuss later in the section, there are a consumer devices designed to monitor gesture that require that people hold a sensor of some sort so that their gestures can be tracked.
8. http://googleblog.blogspot.com/2014/10/omg-mobile-voice-survey-reveals-teens.html.
9. There are other cases in which attentional resources may be constrained, such as during multi-tasking.
10. http://www.consumerphysics.com.
11. http://oculusvr.com/rift.

Chapter 6. Exploration, Complexity, and Discovery

1. http://www.google.com/notebook.
2. http://del.icio.us.
3. http://www.windowsphone.com/en-us/how-to/wp8/cortana/meet-cortana.
4. http://www.google.com/landing/now/.
5. http://www.apple.com/ios/siri/.

Chapter 7. Learning and Use

1. Although it has been considered in some models of the information search process (e.g., Marchionini, 1995).

Chapter 8. Interaction beyond the Individual

1. Note that an alternative is for the searcher to perform their own targeting: they select the people to ask based on personal connections or candidate answerers identified using expert-finding methods.

Chapter 9. Personalization and Contextualization

1. http://www.surfcanyon.com.
2. http://desktop.google.com/.
3. http://developer.apple.com/macosx/tiger/spotlight.html.
4. http://www.gnome.org/projects/beagle/.
5. http://dmoz.org.
6. http://wikipedia.org.
7. http://freebase.com.
8. The percentage of machine identifiers that comprise multiple users changes from 56% to around 20% if we only consider four weeks' of logs rather than the longer time frame of two years.
9. http://www.comscore.com/Press_Events/Press_Releases/2007/04/comScore_Cookie_Deletion_Report.
10. *PageRank* assigns a score proportional to the number of time that a "random surfer" would visit that page, if it surfed indefinitely from page to page, following all outlinks from a page with equal probability, and will eventually stop clicking according to some damping factor. Enhanced versions of PageRank have been proposed that guide the surfing based on estimates

of the relevance of the visited documents with respect to the query (the so-called "intelligent surfer model"; see Richardson and Domingos [2001]) or based on the information about people's browsing habits (the so-called "intentional surfer model" (Josang, 2007). Some of these same principles underlie computational models of information foraging (discussed in Chapter 4).

Chapter 10. Evaluation Measures

1. Such pooling will result in incomplete judgments since not every document in the collection will be judged. This is okay for assessing the precision of systems but not for assessing their recall, as for that task we need to reliably identify all relevant documents in the collection. In settings such as Web search, precision is more important (Lesk, 1997).
2. http://research.microsoft.com/en-us/um/people/nickcr/wscd2014.

Chapter 11. Evaluation Methodologies

1. http://www.nist.gov/director/planning/upload/report10-1.pdf.
2. The phrase "user model" is used even though "searcher" is preferred to "user" in this book. User model is the more commonly used phrase in the research literature.

Chapter 12. Data, Tools, and Privacy

1. Note that this is different from meta-search engines (e.g., *MetaCrawler* [Selberg and Etzioni, 1995]), which collate the results from multiple search engines, but in the process lose information about the algorithm-specific relevance scores used to generate the ranked list, as well as potentially useful interface support that may be available on those engines.
2. http://snap.stanford.edu/data/wikispeedia.html.
3. https://azure.microsoft.com/en-us/services/machine-learning.
4. http://www.projectoxford.ai.
5. https://nycopendata.socrata.com.
6. http://twitter.com.
7. Moving beyond logs to online content, the "Right to be forgotten" law in the European Union provides people with a privacy right that requires search engines to remove pages about a person at their request (Rosen, 2012).
8. http://ec.europa.eu/justice/data-protection/article-29/index_en.htm.
9. Council Directive 95/46, art. 13(1), 1995 O.J. (L 281) 31, 42.

Chapter 13. New Directions and Domains

1. http://www.biakelsey.com/Company/Press-Releases/120418-Mobile-Local-Search-Volume-Will-Surpass-Desktop-Local-Search-in-2015.asp. This 2012 study by BIA/Kelsey projects predicted that mobile local search volume will surpass desktop local search in 2015.
2. http://fancyhands.com.
3. http://taskrabbit.com.
4. http://community.cochrane.org/cochrane-reviews.
5. http://archive.org/web.

References

Aalbersberg, I.J. (1992). Incremental relevance feedback. In *Proceedings of the ACM SIGIR conference on research and development in information retrieval* (pp. 11–22). ACM Press.

Abowd, G.D., Atkeson, C.G., Hong, J., Long, S., Kooper, R., and Pinkerton, M. (1997). Cyberguide: A mobile context-aware tour guide. *ACM Wireless Networks*, 3, 421–433.

Abowd, G.D. and Mynatt, E.D. (2000). Charting past, present, and future research in ubiquitous computing. *ACM Transactions on Computer-Human Interaction*, 7(1), 29–58.

Abrams, D., Baecker, R., and Chignell, M. (1998). Information archiving with bookmarks: Personal Web space construction and organization. In *Proceedings of the ACM SIGCHI conference on human factors in computing systems* (pp. 41–48). ACM Press/Addison-Wesley Publishing Co.

Ackerman, M.A. and McDonald, D.W. (1998). Just talk to me: A field study of expertise location. In *Proceedings of conference on computer supported cooperative work* (pp. 315–324). ACM Press.

Ackerman, M.S. and McDonald, D.W. (1996). Answer Garden 2: Merging organizational memory with collaborative help. In *Proceedings of conference on computer supported cooperative work* (pp. 97–105). ACM Press.

Adamczyk, P.D. and Bailey, B.P. (2004). If not now, when? The effects of interruption at different moments within task execution. In *Proceedings of the ACM SIGCHI conference on human factors in computing systems* (pp. 271–278). ACM Press/Addison-Wesley Publishing Co.

Adamic, L.A., Zhang, J., Bakshy, E., and Ackerman, M.S. (2008). Knowledge sharing and yahoo answers: Everyone knows something. In *Proceedings of the international conference on the World Wide Web* (pp. 665–674). ACM Press.

Adar, E. (2007). User 4xxxxx9: anonymizing query logs. In *Proceedings of the query log analysis workshop at the international conference on the World Wide Web*.

Adar, E., Teevan, J., and Dumais, S.T. (2008). Large scale analysis of web revisitation patterns. In *Proceedings of the ACM SIGCHI conference on human factors in computing systems* (pp. 1197–1206). ACM Press/Addison-Wesley Publishing Co.

Adar, E., Teevan, J., and Dumais, S.T. (2009). Resonance on the web: Web dynamics and revisitation patterns. In *Proceedings of the SIGCHI conference on human factors in computing systems* (pp. 1381–1390). ACM Press/Addison-Wesley Publishing Co.

Agapie, E., Golovchinsky, G., and Qvarfordt, P. (2013). Leading people to longer queries. In *Proceedings of the ACM SIGCHI conference on human factors in computing systems* (pp. 3019–3022). ACM Press/Addison-Wesley Publishing Co.

Agarawala, A. and Balakrishnan, R. (2006). Keepin'it real: Pushing the desktop metaphor with physics, piles and the pen. In *Proceedings of the ACM SIGCHI conference on human factors in computing systems* (pp. 1283–1292). ACM Press/Addison-Wesley Publishing Co.

Agarwal, A., Chakrabarti, S., and Aggarwal, S. (2006). Learning to rank networked entities. In *Proceedings of the ACM SIGKDD conference on knowledge discovery and data mining* (pp. 14–23). ACM Press.

Agarwal, D., Li, L., and Smola, A.J. (2011). Linear-time estimators for propensity scores. In *Proceedings of the international conference on artificial intelligence and statistics* (pp. 93–100).

Ageev, M., Guo, Q., Lagun, D., and Agichtein, E. (2011). Find it if you can: A game for modeling different types of web search success using interaction data. In *Proceedings of the ACM SIGIR conference on research and development in information retrieval* (pp. 345–354). ACM Press.

Agichtein, E., Brill, E., Dumais, S., and Ragno, R. (2006). Learning user interaction models for predicting web search result preferences. In *Proceedings of the ACM SIGIR conference on research and development in information retrieval* (pp. 3–10). ACM Press.

Agichtein, E., White, R.W., Dumais, S.T., and Bennett, P.N. (2012). Search, interrupted: understanding and predicting search task continuation. In *Proceedings of the ACM SIGIR conference on research and development in information retrieval* (pp. 315–324). ACM Press.

Agichtein, E. and Zheng, Z. (2006). Identifying best bet web search results by mining past user behavior. In *Proceedings of the ACM SIGKDD conference on knowledge discovery and data mining* (pp. 902–908). ACM Press.

Agosti, M., Fuhr, N., Toms, E., and Vakkari, P. (2014). Evaluation methodologies in information retrieval (Dagstuhl seminar 13441), *Dagstuhl Reports*, 3(10), 92–126.

Agrawal, R., Gollapudi, S., Halverson, A., and Ieong, S. (2009). Diversifying search results. In *Proceedings of the ACM WSDM conference on web search and data mining* (pp. 5–14). ACM Press.

Ahlberg, C. and Shneiderman, B. (1994). Visual information seeking: Tight coupling of dynamic query filters with starfield displays. In *Proceedings of the ACM SIGCHI conference on human factors in computing systems* (pp. 313–317). ACM Press/Addison-Wesley Publishing Co.

Ahlberg, C., Williamson, C., and Shneiderman, B. (1992). Dynamic queries for information exploration: An implementation and evaluation. In *Proceedings of the ACM SIGCHI conference on human factors in computing systems* (pp. 619–626). ACM Press/Addison-Wesley Publishing Co.

Ahmad, F. and Kondrak, G. (2005). Learning a spelling error model from search query logs. In *Proceedings of the conference on human language technology and empirical methods in natural language processing* (pp. 955–962). Association for Computational Linguistics.

Ahn, J.W. and Brusilovsky, P. (2013). Adaptive visualization for exploratory information retrieval. *Information Processing and Management*, 49(5), 1139–1164.

Ahn, J.W., Brusilovsky, P., Grady, J., He, D., and Syn, S.Y. (2007). Open user profiles for adaptive news systems: Help or harm?. In *Proceedings of the international conference on the World Wide Web* (pp. 11–20). ACM Press.

Ali, K. and Chang, C. (2006). On the relationship between click-rate and relevance for search engines. In *Proceedings of data-mining and information engineering conference* (pp. 213–222). ACM Press.

Allan, J. (1995). Relevance feedback with too much data. In *Proceedings of the ACM SIGIR conference on research and development in information retrieval* (pp. 337–343). ACM Press.

Allan, J. (1996). Incremental relevance feedback for information filtering. In *Proceedings of the ACM SIGIR conference on research and development in information retrieval* (pp. 270–278). ACM Press.

REFERENCES

Allan, J. (2005). HARD track overview in TREC 2004: High accuracy retrieval from documents. In *Proceedings of TREC 2004* (pp. 25–35). NIST special publication 500-261.

Allan, J., Carterette, B., and Lewis, J. (2005). When will information retrieval be "good enough"? In *Proceedings of the ACM SIGIR conference on research and development in information retrieval* (pp. 433–440). ACM Press.

Allan, J., Croft, B., Moffat, A., and Sanderson, M. (2012). Frontiers, challenges, and opportunities for information retrieval: report from SWIRL 2012 the second strategic workshop on information retrieval in Lorne. *SIGIR Forum*, 46(1), 2–32.

Allen, J. (1987). *Natural language understanding*. New York: Benjamin/Cummings Publishing Company.

Allen, J.F., Byron, D.K., Dzikovska, M., Ferguson, G., Galescu, L., and Stent, A. (2001). Toward conversational human-computer interaction. *AI Magazine*, 22(4), 27.

Al-Maskari, A., Sanderson, M., Clough, P., and Airio, E. (2008). The good and the bad system: Does the test collection predict users' effectiveness? In *Proceedings of the ACM SIGIR conference on research and development in information retrieval* (pp. 59–66). ACM Press.

Almeida, R.B. and Almeida, V.A. (2004). A community-aware search engine. In *Proceedings of the international conference on the World Wide Web* (pp. 413–421). ACM Press.

Alonso, O., Rose, D.E., and Stewart, B. (2008). Crowdsourcing for relevance evaluation. *SIGIR Forum*, 42(2), 9–15. ACM Press.

Amar, R., Eagan, J., and Stasko, J. (2005). Low-level components of analytic activity in information visualization. In *Proceedings of the IEEE symposium on information visualization* (pp. 111–117). IEEE.

Amari, S.I., Cichocki, A., and Yang, H.H. (1996). A new learning algorithm for blind signal separation. In *Proceedings of the conference on neural information processing systems* (pp. 757–763). ACM Press.

Amento, B., Terveen, L., and Hill, W. (2000). Does "authority" mean quality? Predicting expert quality ratings of Web documents. In *Proceedings of the ACM SIGIR conference on research and development in information retrieval* (pp. 296–303). ACM Press.

Amershi, S. and Morris, M.R. (2008). CoSearch: A system for co-located collaborative web search. In *Proceedings of the ACM SIGCHI conference on human factors in computing systems* (pp. 1647–1656). ACM Press/Addison-Wesley Publishing Co.

Amitay, E., Har'El, N., Sivan, R., and Soffer, A. (2004). Web-a-where: geotagging web content. In *Proceedings of the ACM SIGIR conference on research and development in information retrieval* (pp. 273–280). ACM Press.

Anand, K., Mathew, G., and Reddy, V. (1995). Blind separation of multiple co-channel BPSK signals arriving at an antenna array. *IEEE Signal Processing Letters*, 2, 176–178.

Anderson, A., Huttenlocher, D., Kleinberg, J., and Leskovec, J. (2013). Steering user behavior with badges. In *Proceedings of the nternational conference on the World Wide Web* (pp. 95–106). International World Wide Web Conferences Steering Committee.

Anderson, A., Huttenlocher, D., Kleinberg, J., and Leskovec, J. (2014). Engaging with massive online courses. In *Proceedings of the international conference on World Wide Web* (pp. 687–698). International World Wide Web Conferences Steering Committee.

Anderson, J.R. (1976). *Language, Memory, and Thought*. Mahwah, NJ: Earlbaum.

Anderson, J.R. (1983). A spreading activation theory of memory. *Journal of Verbal Learning and Verbal Behavior*, 22(3), 261–295.

Anderson, J.R. (1990). *The Adaptive Character of Thought*. New York: Psychology Press.

Anderson, J.R. and Lebiere, C. (1998). *The Atomic Components of Thought*. Mahwah, NJ: Lawrence Erlbaum Associates.

REFERENCES

Anderson, J.R., Bothell, D., Byrne, M.D., Douglass, S., Lebiere, C., and Qin, Y. (2004). An integrated theory of the mind. *Psychological Review*, 1036–1060.

Anderson, L., Krathwohl, D., Airasian, P., Cruikshank, K., Mayer, R., Pintrich, P., and Wittrock, M. (2000). *A Taxonomy for Learning, Teaching, and Assessing: A Revision of Bloom's Taxonomy of Educational Objectives*, Abridged Version. Boston: Allyn and Bacon.

Anderson, L.W., Krathwohl, D.R., and Bloom, B.S. (2001). *A Taxonomy for Learning, Teaching, and Assessing: A Revision of Bloom's Taxonomy of Educational Objectives*. Boston: Allyn & Bacon.

Anderson, M.L. (2003). Embodied cognition: A field guide. *Artificial Intelligence*, 149(1), 91–130.

Andrade, L. and Silva, M. (2006). Relevance ranking for geographic IR. In *Proceedings of the ACM SIGIR workshop on geographic information retrieval*.

André, P., Teevan, J. and Dumais, S. (2009a). From x-rays to silly putty via Uranus: Serendipity and its role in Web search. In *Proceedings of the ACM SIGCHI conference on human factors in computing systems* (pp. 2033–2036). ACM Press/Addison-Wesley Publishing Co.

André, P., Teevan, J., and Dumais, S.T. (2009b). Discovery is never by chance: Designing for (un)serendipity. In *Proceedings of the ACM conference on creativity and cognition* (pp. 305–314). ACM Press.

Anick, P. (2003). Using terminological feedback for web search refinement: A log based study. In *Proceedings of the ACM SIGIR conference on research and development in information retrieval* (pp. 88–95). ACM Press.

Anick, P. and Tipirneni, S. (1999). The paraphrase search assistant: Terminological feedback for iterative information seeking. In *Proceedings of the ACM SIGIR conference on research and development in information retrieval* (pp. 153–159). ACM Press.

Anick, P.G., Brennan, J.D., Flynn, R.A., Hanssen, D.R., Alvey, B., and Robbins, J.M. (1989). A direct manipulation interface for boolean information retrieval via natural language query. In *Proceedings of the ACM SIGIR conference on research and development in information retrieval* (pp. 135–150). ACM Press.

Antin, J. and Churchill, E.F. (2011). Badges in social media: A social psychological perspective. In *Proceedings of the gamification workshop at the ACM SIGCHI conference* (pp. 1–4). ACM Press.

Antin, J., de Sa, M., and Churchill, E.F. (2012). Local experts and online review sites. In *Proceedings of the ACM CSCW conference on computer supported cooperative work companion* (pp. 55–58). ACM Press.

Arapakis, I., Bai, X., and Cambazoglu, B.B. (2014). Impact of response latency on user behavior in web search. In *Proceedings of the ACM SIGIR conference on research and development in information retrieval* (pp. 103–112). ACM Press.

Arapakis, I., Jose, J.M., and Gray, P.D. (2008). Affective feedback. In *Proceedings of the ACM SIGIR conference on research and development in information retrieval* (pp. 20–24). ACM Press.

Arapakis, I., Konstas, I., and Jose, J.M. (2009). Using facial expressions and peripheral physiological signals as implicit indicators of topical relevance. In *Proceedings of the ACM international conference on multimedia* (pp. 461–470). ACM Press.

Arlitt, M. (2000). Characterizing Web user sessions. *ACM SIGMETRICS Performance Evaluation Review*, 28(2), 50–63.

Armstrong, R., Freitag, D., Joachims, T., and Mitchell, T. (1995). WebWatcher: A learning apprentice for the world wide web. In *Proceedings of the AAAI spring symposium on information gathering from heterogeneous, distributed environments* (pp. 6–12). AAAI.

Arrington, M. (2006). AOL proudly releases massive amounts of private data. http://techcrunch.com/2006/08/06/aol-proudly-releases-massive-amounts-of-user-search-data/.

Article 29 Data Protection Working Party. (2008). Opinion on data protection issues related to search engines. http://ec.europa.eu/justice/data-protection/article-29/documentation/opinion-recommendation/files/2008/wp148_en.pdf. Accessed on October 12, 2015.

Attfield, S., Blandford, A., and Dowell, J. (2003). Information seeking in the context of writing: A design psychology interpretation of the "problematic situation." *Journal of Documentation*, 59(4), 430–453.

Auer, P. (2003). Using confidence bounds for exploitation-exploration trade-offs. *The Journal of Machine Learning Research*, 3, 397–422.

Aula, A. and Nordhausen, K. (2006). Modeling successful performance in web searching. *Journal of the Asosication for Information Science and Technology,* 57(12), 1678–1693.

Aula, A., Jhaveri, N., and Käki, M. (2005a). Information search and re-access strategies of experienced web users. In *Proceedings of the international conference on the World Wide Web* (pp. 583–592). International World Wide Web Conferences Steering Committee.

Aula, A., Khan, R.M., and Guan, Z. (2010a). How does search behavior change as search becomes more difficult? In *Proceedings of the ACM SIGCHI conference on human factors in computing systems* (pp. 35–44). ACM Press/Addison-Wesley Publishing Co.

Aula, A., Khan, R.M., Guan, Z., Fontes, P., and Hong, P. (2010b). A comparison of visual and textual page previews in judging the helpfulness of web pages. In *Proceedings of the international conference on the World Wide Web* (pp. 51–60). ACM Press.

Aula, A., Majaranta, P., and Räihä, K.J. (2005b). Eye-tracking reveals the personal styles for search result evaluation. In *Proceedings of human-computer interaction-INTERACT 2005* (pp. 1058–1061). Springer Berlin Heidelberg.

Aula, A. and Siirtola, H. (2005). Hundreds of folders or one ugly pile–strategies for information search and re-access. In *Proceedings of Human-Computer Interaction-INTERACT 2005* (pp. 954–957). Springer Berlin Heidelberg.

Avrahami, A., Fussel, S., and Hudson, S. (2008). IM waiting: Timing and responsiveness in semi-synchronous communication. In *Proceedings of the ACM conference on computer supported cooperative work* (pp. 285–294). ACM Press.

Ayers, E. and Stasko, J. (1995). Using graphic history in browsing the World Wide Web. In *Proceedings of the international conference on the World Wide Web*. International World Wide Web Conferences Steering Committee.

Azcarraga, J. and Suarez, M.T. (2012). Predicting academic emotions based on brainwaves, mouse behaviour and personality profile. In *Proceedings of PRICAI: Trends in artificial intelligence* (pp. 728–733). Springer Berlin Heidelberg.

Azizyan, M., Constandache, I., and Choudhury, R.R. (2009). Surroundsense: Mobile phone localization via ambience fingerprinting. In *Proceedings of the annual internation conference on mobile computing and networking* (pp. 261–272). ACM Press.

Azuma, R., Baillot, Y., Behringer, R., Feiner, S., Julier, S., and MacIntyre, B. (2001). Recent advances in augmented reality. *IEEE Computer Graphics and Applications*, 21(6), 34–47.

Azzopardi, L. (2011). The economics in interactive information retrieval. In *Proceedings of the ACM SIGIR conference on research and development in Information Retrieval* (pp. 15–24). ACM Press.

Azzopardi, L. (2014). Modelling interaction with economic models of search. In *Proceedings of the ACM SIGIR conference on research and development in information retrieval* (pp. 3–12). ACM Press.

Azzopardi, L., Järvelin, K., Kamps, J., and Smucker, M.D. (2011). Report on the SIGIR 2010 workshop on the simulation of interaction. *ACM SIGIR Forum*, 44(2), 35–47. ACM Press.

Azzopardi, L., Kelly, D., and Brennan, K. (2013). How query cost affects search behavior. In *Proceedings of the ACM SIGIR conference on research and development in information retrieval* (pp. 23–32). ACM Press.

Back, J. and Oppenheim, C. (2001). A model of cognitive load for IR: Implications for user relevance feedback interaction. *Information Research*, 6(2).

Baeza-Yates, R. and Ribeiro-Neto, B. (1999). *Modern Information Retrieval*. Boston, MA: Addison-Wesley Longman Publishing Company.

Bharat, K. (2000). SearchPad: Explicit capture of search context to support Web search. In *Proceedings of the international World Wide Web conference on computer networks* (pp. 493–501).

Bai, X., Cambazoglu, B.B., and Junqueira, F.P. (2011). Discovering URLs through user feedback. In *Proceedings of the ACM CIKM conference on information and knowledge management* (pp. 77–86). ACM Press.

Bailey, J.E. and Pearson, S.W. (1983). Development of a tool for measuring and analyzing computer user satisfaction. *Management Science*, 29(5), 530–545.

Bailey, P., White, R.W., Liu, H., and Kumaran, G. (2010). Mining historic query trails to label long and rare search engine queries. *ACM Transactions on the Web*, 4(4), 15.

Balabanovic, M. and Shoham, Y. (1995). Learning information retrieval agents: Experiments with automated web browsing. In *Proceedings of the AAAI spring symposium on information gathering from heterogeneous, distributed environments* (pp. 13–18).

Balabanović, M. and Shoham, Y. (1997). Fab: Content-based, collaborative recommendation. *Communications of the ACM*, 40(3), 66–72.

Balog, K., Azzopardi, L., and De Rijke, M. (2006). Formal models for expert finding in enterprise corpora. In *Proceedings of the ACM SIGIR conference on research and development in information retrieval* (pp. 43–50). ACM Press.

Balog, K. and de Rijke, M. (2007). Determining expert profiles (with an application to expert finding). In *Proceedings of the international joint conference on artificial intelligence* (pp. 2657–2662). Morgan Kaufmann Publishers.

Bandura, A. (1971). *Psychological Modelling*. New York: Lieber-Antherton.

Bandura, A. (1986). *Social Foundations of Thought and Action: A Social Cognitive Theory*. Englewood Cliffs, NJ: Prentice-Hall.

Banko, M. and Brill, E. (2001). Scaling to very very large corpora for natural language disambiguation. In *Proceedings of the annual meeting of the association for computational linguistics* (pp. 26–33). Association for Computational Linguistics.

Banko, M., Brill, E., Dumais, S., and Lin, J. (2002). AskMSR: Question answering using the worldwide Web. In *Proceedings of 2002 AAAI spring symposium on mining answers from texts and knowledge bases* (pp. 7–9). AAAI Press.

Barbaro, M., Zeller, T., and Hansell, S. (2006). A face is exposed for AOL searcher no. 4417749. *New York Times*, 9(2008), F8.

Barber, R.K. and Merton, E. (2006). *The travels and adventures of serendipity: A study in sociological semantics and the sociology of science (paperback ed.)*. Princeton, NJ: Princeton University Press.

Bar-Ilan, J. (2007). Position paper: Access to query logs – an academic researcher's point of view. In *Proceedings of the query log analysis workshop at the international conference on the World Wide Web*.

Barnett, M., Chandramouli, B., DeLine, R., Drucker, S., Fisher, D., Goldstein, J., Morrison, P., and Platt, J. (2013). Stat! An interactive analytics environment for big data. In *Proceedings of the ACM SIGMOD international conference on management of data* (pp. 1013–1016). ACM Press.

Baron-Cohen, S., Cox, A., Baird, G., Swettenham, J., Nightingale, N., Morgan, K., and Charman, T. (1996). Psychological markers in the detection of autism in infancy in a large population. *The British Journal of Psychiatry*, 168(2), 158–163.

Barroso, L.A., Dean, J., and Holzle, U. (2003). Web search for a planet: The Google cluster architecture. *Micro*, 23(2), 22–28. IEEE.

Barry, C.L. (1994). User-defined relevance criteria: An exploratory study. *Journal of the American Society for Information Science*, 45(3), 149–159.

Barry, C.L. (1998). Document representations and clues to document relevance. *Journal of the American Society for Information Science*, 49(14), 1293–1303.

Bar-Yossef, Z. and Gurevich, M. (2008). Mining search engine query logs via suggestion sampling. In *Proceedings of the VLDB Endowment* (pp. 54–65).

Bar-Yossef, Z. and Kraus, N. (2011). Context-sensitive query auto-completion. In *Proceedings of the international conference on the World Wide Web* (pp. 107–116). ACM Press.

Baskaya, F. Keskustalo, H., and Järvelin, K. (2013). Modeling behavioral factors in interactive information retrieval. In *Proceedings of the ACM CIKM conference on information and knowledge management* (pp. 2297–2302). ACM Press.

Baskaya, F., Keskustalo, H., and Järvelin, K. (2012). Time drives interaction: simulating sessions in diverse searching environments. In *Proceedings of the ACM SIGIR conference on research and development in information retrieval* (pp. 105–114). ACM Press.

Basu, C., Hirsh, H., and Cohen, W. (1998). Recommendation as classification: Using social and content-based information in recommendation. In *Proceedings of the AAAI conference on artificial intelligence* (pp. 714–720). AAAI Press.

Bateman, S., Teevan, J., and White, R.W. (2012). The search dashboard: how reflection and comparison impact search behavior. In *Proceedings of the ACM SIGCHI conference on human factors in computing systems* (pp. 1785–1794). ACM Press/Addison-Wesley Publishing Co.

Bates, M. (1989). The design of browsing and berry-picking techniques for the online search interface. *Online Review*, 13(5), 407–424.

Bates, M. (1995). Models of natural language understanding. In *Proceedings of the National Academy of Sciences*, 92(22), 9977–9982.

Bates, M.J. (1979a). Information search tactics. *Journal of the American Society for information Science*, 30(4), 205–214.

Bates, M.J. (1979b). Idea tactics. *Journal of the American Society for Information Science*, 30(5), 280–289.

Bates, M.J. (1990). Where should the person stop and the information search interface start? *Information Processing and Management*, 26(5), 575–591.

Bates, M.J. (1998). Indexing and access for digital libraries and the Internet: Human, database, and domain factors. *Journal of the American Society for Information Science*, 49(13), 1185–1205.

Bates, M.J. (2002). The cascade of interactions in the digital library interface. *Information Processing and Management*, 38(3), 381–400.

Bates, M.J. (2005). Are there optimal ways to do exploratory searching? Slides available online at: http://research.microsoft.com/en-us/um/people/ryenw/xsi/slides/bates.pdf. Accessed on August 17, 2015.

Bates, M.J. (2007). What is browsing – really? A model drawing from behavioural science research. *Information Research*, 12(4), paper 330.

Battelle, J. (2005). *The Search: How Google and Its Rivals Rewrote the Rules of Business and Transformed Our Culture*. New York: Penguin.

Bawden, D. (1986). Information systems and the stimulation of creativity. *Journal of Information Science*, 12(5), 203–216.

REFERENCES

Baudisch, P. and Brueckner, L. (2002). TV Scout: Lowering the entry barrier to personalized TV program recommendation. In *Proceedings of the international conference on adaptive hypermedia and adaptive web-based systems* (pp. 58–68).

Baudisch, P., Tan, D., Collomb, M., Robbins, D., Hinckley, K., Agrawala, M., and Ramos, G. (2006). Phosphor: Explaining transitions in the user interface using afterglow effects. In *Proceedings of the ACM UIST symposium on user interface software and technology* (pp. 169–178). ACM Press.

Bawden, D. (1986). Information systems and the stimulation of creativity. *Journal of Information Science*, 12, 203–216.

Beale, R. (2007). Supporting serendipity: using ambient intelligence to augment user exploration for data mining and web browsing. *International Journal of Human-Computer Studies*, 65(5), 421–433.

Beaulieu, M. (1997). Experiments on interfaces to support query expansion. *Journal of Documentation*, 53(1), 8–19.

Beaulieu, M. and Jones, S. (1998). Interactive searching and interface issues in the Okapi best match retrieval system. *Interacting with Computers*, 10(3), 237–248.

Bederson, B. and Hollan, J. (1994). Pad++: A zooming graphical interface for exploring alternative interface physics. In *Proceedings of the ACM UIST symposium on user interface software and technology* (pp. 17–26). ACM Press.

Beeferman, D. and Berger, A.L. (2000). Agglomerative clustering of a search engine query log. In *Proceedings of the ACM SIGKDD conference on knowledge discovery and data mining* (pp. 407–416).

Belkin, N. (1996). Intelligent information retrieval: Whose intelligence? In J. Krause, M. Herfurth, J. Marx (eds.). *ISI '96: Hearausfordurungen an die Informationswirtschaft Informationsverdichtung, Informationsbewertung and Datenvisualisierung. Konstanz*, Germany, University of Konstanz. 25–31.

Belkin, N.J. (1978). Information concepts for information science. *Journal of Documentation*, 34(1), 55–85.

Belkin, N.J. (1980). Anomalous state of knowledge for information retrieval. *Canadian Journal of Information Science*, 5, 133–143.

Belkin, N.J. (1990). The cognitive viewpoint in information science. *Journal of Information Science*, 16(1), 11–15.

Belkin, N.J. (1993). Interaction with texts: Information retrieval as information-seeking behavior. In *Proceedings of Information Retrieval* (pp. 55–66).

Belkin, N.J. (2000). Helping people find what they don't know. *Communications of the ACM*, 43(8), 59–61.

Belkin, N.J. (2008). Some(what) grand challenges for information retrieval. *ACM SIGIR Forum*, 42(1), 47–54. ACM Press.

Belkin, N.J. and Cool, C.A. (2002). Classification of interactions with information. In Emerging frameworks and methods. In *Proceedings of the COLIS conference on conceptions of library and information science* (pp. 1–15). Libraries Unlimited.

Belkin, N.J., Cool, C., Croft, W.B., and Callan, J.P. (1993). The effect multiple query representations on information retrieval system performance. In *Proceedings of the ACM SIGIR conference on research and development in information retrieval* (pp. 339–346). ACM Press.

Belkin, N.J., Cool, C., Kelly, D., Lee, H.-J., Muresan, G., Tang, M.C., and Yuan, X.J. (2003). Query length in interactive information retrieval. In *Proceedings of the ACM SIGIR conference on research and development in information retrieval* (pp. 205–212). ACM Press.

Belkin, N.J., Cool, C., Kelly, D., Lin, S.-J., Park, S.-Y., Perez-Carballo, J., and Sikora, C. (2001). Iterative exploration, design and evaluation for query reformulation in interactive information retrieval. *Information Processing and Management*, 37(3), 403–434.

Belkin, N.J., Cool, C., and Koenemann, J. (1996). On the potential utility of negative relevance feedback for interactive information retrieval. In *Proceedings of the ACM SIGIR conference on research and development in information retrieval* (p. 341). ACM Press.

Belkin, N.J., Cool, C., Stein, A., and Theil, U. (1995). Cases, scripts and information seeking strategies: On the design of interactive information retrieval systems. *Expert Systems with Applications*, 29(3), 325–344.

Belkin, N.J. and Croft, W.B. (1992). Information filtering and retrieval: Two sides of the same coin? *Communications of the ACM*, 35(12), 29–38.

Belkin, N.J., Oddy, R.N., and Brooks, H.M. (1982). ASK for information retrieval: Part I -background and theory. *Journal of Documentation*, 38(2), 61–71.

Belkin, N.J., Perez Carballo, J., Cool, C., Lin, S., Park, S.Y., Rieh, S.Y., Savage, P., Sikora, C., Xie, H., Cool, C., and Allan, J. (1998). Rutgers TREC-6 interactive track experience. In *Proceedings of the text retrieval conference* (pp. 597–610).

Bell, R.M. and Koren, Y. (2007). Lessons from the Netflix prize challenge. *ACM SIGKDD Explorations Newsletter*, 9(2), 75–79.

Bell, W.J. (1991). *Searching Behaviour: The Behavioural Ecology of Finding Resources*. London: Chapman and Hall.

Bendersky, M. and Croft, W.B. (2009). Analysis of long queries in a large scale search log. In *Proceedings of the 2009 workshop on web search click data* (pp. 8–14). ACM Press.

Benko, H., Wilson, A.D., and Baudisch, P. (2006). Precise selection techniques for multi-touch screens. In *Proceedings of the ACM SIGCHI conference on human factors in computing systems* (pp. 1263–1272). ACM Press.

Benford, S., Snowdon, D., Greenhalgh, C., Ingram, R., Knox, I., and Brown, C. (1995). VR-VIBE: A virtual environment for co-operative information retrieval. *Computer Graphics Forum*, 14(3), 349–360. Blackwell Science Ltd.

Bennett, P.N., Svore, K., and Dumais, S.T. (2010). Classification-enhanced ranking. In *Proceedings of the international conference on the World Wide Web* (pp. 111–120). ACM Press.

Bennett, P.N., Radlinski, F., White, R.W., and Yilmaz, E. (2011). Inferring and using location metadata to personalize web search. In *Proceedings of the ACM SIGIR conference on research and development in information retrieval* (pp. 135–144). ACM Press.

Bennett, P.N., White, R.W., Chu, W., Dumais, S.T., Bailey, P., Borisyuk, F., and Cui, X. (2012). Modeling the impact of short-and long-term behavior on search personalization. In *Proceedings of the ACM SIGIR conference on research and development in information retrieval* (pp. 185–194). ACM Press.

Berlyne, D.E. (1960). *Conflict, arousal and curiosity*, New York: McGraw Hill.

Bernstein, M.S., Tan, D., Smith, G., Czerwinski, M., and Horvitz, E. (2010). Personalization via friendsourcing. *ACM Transactions on Computer-Human Interaction*, 17(2), 6.

Bernstein, M.S., Teevan, J., Dumais, S., Liebling, D., and Horvitz, E. (2012). Direct answers for search queries in the long tail. In *Proceedings of the ACM SIGCHI conference on human factors in computing systems* (pp. 237–246). ACM Press.

Bernstein, M., Van Kleek, M., Karger, D., and schraefel, m.c. (2008). Information scraps: How and why information eludes our personal information management tools. *ACM Transactions on Information Systems*, 26(4), 24.

Bernstein, P. and Clarke-Stewart, R. (2008). *Psychology, 8th edition*. Boston, MA: Houghton Mifflin Company.

Bharat, K. (2000). SearchPad: Explicit capture of search context to support Web search. *Computer Networks*, 33(1), 493–501.

Bhavnani, S.K. (2002). Domain-specific search strategies for the effective retrieval of healthcare and shopping information. In *Proceedings of the ACM SIGCHI Conference on human factors in computing systems* (pp. 610–611). ACM Press.

Bhavnani, S.K., Christopher, B.K., Johnson, T.M., Little, R.J., Peck, F.A., Schwartz, J.L., and Strecher, V.J. (2003). Strategy hubs: Next-generation domain portals with search procedures. In *Proceedings of the ACM SIGCHI conference on human factors in computing systems* (pp. 393–400). ACM Press.

Biczok, G., Martinez, D., Jelle, T., and Krogstie, J. (2014). Navigating MazeMap: Indoor human mobility, spatio-logical ties and future potential. In *Proceedings of the IEEE International Conference on Pervasive Computing and Communications Workshops* (pp. 266–271). IEEE.

Biedert, R., Buscher, G., and Dengel, A. (2010). The eyeBook – using eye tracking to enhance the reading experience. *Informatik Spektrum*, 33, 3 (June), 272–281.

Biedert, R., Dengel, A., Buscher, G., and Vartan, A. (2012). Reading and estimating gaze on smart phones. In *Proceedings of the symposium on eye tracking research and applications* (pp. 385–388). ACM Press.

Bier, E.A., Stone, M.A., Pier, K., Buxton, W., and DeRose, T.D. (1993). Toolglass and magic lenses: The see through interface. In *Proceedings of the ACM SIGGRAPH conference on computer graphics and interactive techniques* (pp. 73–80). ACM Press.

Bilal, D. (2000). Children's use of the Yahooligans! Web search engine: I. Cognitive, physical, and affective behaviors on fact-based search tasks. *Journal of the American Society for information Science*, 51(7), 646–665.

Bilenko, M. and Richardson, M. (2011). Predictive client-side profiles for personalized advertising. In *Proceedings of the ACM SIGKDD conference on knowledge discovery and data mining* (pp. 413–421). ACM Press.

Bilenko, M. and White, R.W. (2008). Mining the search trails of surfing crowds: Identifying relevant websites from user activity. In *Proceedings of the international conference on the World Wide Web* (pp. 51–60). ACM Press.

Billerbeck, B. and Zobel J. (2004). Techniques for efficient query expansion. In *Proceedings of string processing and information retrieval* (pp. 30–42). Springer Berlin Heidelberg.

Billsus, D. and Pazzani, M.J. (1999). A personal news agent that talks, learns and explains. In *Proceedings of the conference on autonomous agents* (pp. 268–275). ACM Press.

Bingham, D. and Hailey, D.J. (1989). The time-urgency component of the type a behavior pattern: time pressure and performance. *Journal of Applied Social Psychology*, 19, 425–432.

Birchler, V. and Bütler, M. (2007). *Information economics*. Routledge, 1st edition.

Birnbaum, M.H. (2000). *Psychological experiments on the internet*. London: Academic Press.

Bishop, C.M. (2006). *Pattern recognition and machine learning*. New York: Springer.

Bishop, J. (1989). Incentives for learning: Why American high school students compare so poorly to their counterparts overseas (CAHRS Working Paper #89-09). Ithaca, NY: Cornell University, School of Industrial and Labor Relations, Center for Advanced Human Resource Studies. http://digitalcommons.ilr.cornell.edu/cahrswp/400.

Blair, D.C. (1980). Searching biases in large interactive document retrieval systems. *Journal of the American Society for Information Science*, 31(4), 271–277.

Blair, D.C. and Maron, M.E. (1985). An evaluation of retrieval effectiveness for a full-text document-retrieval system. *Communications of the ACM*, 28(3), 289–299.

Blattner, M., Sumikawa, D., and Greenberg, R. (1989). Earcons and icons: Their structure and common design principles. *Human Computer Interaction*, 4(1), 11–44.

Bloom, B.S., Englehard, E., Furst, W., and Krathwohl, D.R. (1956). *Taxonomy of Educational Objectives: The Classification of Educational Goals*. New York: McKay.

Boden, M.A. (1996). Agents and creativity. In Gorayska, G. and Mey, J.L. (Eds.). *Cognitive technology: In search of a humane interface*. Elsevier Science B.V. (pp. 119–127).

Boden, M.A. (2004). *The creative mind: myths and mechanisms*. Psychology Press.

Boldi, P., Bonchi, F., Castillo, C., Donato, D., Gionis, A., and Vigna, V. (2008). The query flow graph: Model and applications. In *Proceedings of the ACM CIKM conference on information and knowledge management* (pp. 609–618). ACM Press.

Bolger, F. and Wright, G. (1992). Reliability and validity in expert judgment. In Wright, G. and Bolger, F. (Eds.), *Expertise and decision support*. New York: Plenum (pp. 47–76).

Bolt, R.A. (1980). "Put-that-there": Voice and gesture at the graphics interface. *ACM Computer Graphics*, 14(3), 262–270. ACM Press.

Bonwell, C.C. and Eison, J.A. (1991). *Active Learning: Creating Excitement in the Classroom*. Washington, DC: George Washington University, ERIC Clearinghouse on Higher Education.

Borgman, C. (1984). Psychological research in human-computer interaction. *Annual Review of Information Science and Technology*, 19, 33–64.

Borgman, C.L. (1985). The user's mental model of an information retrieval system. In *Proceedings of the ACM SIGIR conference on research and development in informational retrieval* (pp. 268–273). ACM Press.

Borgman, C.L. (1986). The user's mental model of an information retrieval system: An experiment on a prototype online catalog. *International Journal of Man-Machine Studies*, 24(1), 47–64.

Borgman, C.L. (1996). Why are online catalogs hard to use? Lessons learned from information-retrieval studies. *Journal of the American Society for Information Science*, 37(6), 387–400.

Borlund, P. (2000). Experimental components for the evaluation of interactive information retrieval systems. *Journal of documentation*, 56(1), 71–90.

Borlund, P. (2003). The IIR evaluation model: A framework for evaluation of interactive information retrieval systems. *Information Research*, 8(3).

Borlund, P. and Ingwersen, P. (1998). Measures of relative relevance and ranked half-life: Performance indicators for interactive IR. In Proceedings of the *ACM SIGIR conference on research and development in informational retrieval* (pp. 324–331). ACM Press.

Bos, N., Olson, J., Gergle, D., Olson, G., and Wright, Z. (2002). Effects of four computer-mediated communications channels on trust development. In *Proceedings of the ACM SIGCHI conference on human factors in computing systems* (pp. 135–140). ACM Press.

Bottou, L. (1998). *Online Algorithms and Stochastic Approximations, Online Learning and Neural Networks*, edited by David Saad,Cambridge: Cambridge University Press.

Bottou, L., Peters, J., Quiñonero-Candela, J., Charles, D.X., Chickering, D.M., Portugaly, E., Snelson, E. (2013). Counterfactual reasoning and learning systems: The example of computational advertising. *The Journal of Machine Learning Research*, 14(1), 3207–3260.

Boud, D., Keogh, R., and Walker, D. (1985). *Reflection: Turning Experience into Learning*. London: Kogan Page.

Boyce, A. (1982). Beyond topicality: A two-stage view of relevance and the retrieval process. *Information Processing and Management*, 18(3), 105–109.

Boyd, D. and Crawford, K. (2012). Critical questions for big data: Provocations for a cultural, technological, and scholarly phenomenon. *Information, Communication and Society*, 15(5), 662–679.

Bradner, E., Kellogg, W., and Erickson, T. (1999). The adoption and use of babble: A field study of chat in the workplace. In *Proceedings of the ACM CSCW conference on computer supported cooperative work* (pp. 139–158). ACM Press.

Brajnik, G., Guida, G., and Tasso, C. (1987). User modeling in intelligent information retrieval. *Information Processing and Management*, 23(4), 305–320.

Brajnik, G., Mizzaro, S., and Tasso, C. (1996). Evaluating user interfaces to information retrieval systems: A case study of user support. In *Proceedings of the ACM SIGIR conference on research and development in information retrieval* (pp. 128–136). ACM Press.

Brajnik, G., Mizzaro, S., and Tasso, C. (2002). Strategic help in user interfaces for information retrieval. *Journal of the American Society for Information Science and Technology*, 53(5), 343–358.

Brand-Gruwel, S., Wopereis, I., and Vermetten, Y. (2005). Information problem solving by experts and novices: Analysis of a complex cognitive skill. *Computers in Human Behavior*, 21, 487–508.

Brandt, J., Guo, P.J., Lewenstein, J., Dontcheva, M., and Klemmer, S.R. (2009). Two studies of opportunistic programming: interleaving web foraging, learning, and writing code. In *Proceedings of the ACM SIGCHI conference on human factors in computing systems* (pp. 1589–1598). ACM Press.

Breese, J.S., Heckerman, D., and Kadie, C. (1998). Empirical analysis of predictive algorithms for collaborative filtering. In *Proceedings of the conference on uncertainty in artificial intelligence* (pp. 43–52). Morgan Kaufmann Publishers Inc.

Brewer, J.D. (2000). *Ethnography*. Philadelphia: Open University Press, p.10.

Brewster, S.A., Wright, P.C., and Edwards, A.D.N. (1993). An evaluation of earcons for use in auditory human-computer interfaces. In *Proceedings of InterCHI Conference* (pp. 222–227). ACM Press

Brewster, S.A., Wright, P.C. and Edwards, A.D.N. (1994). The design and evaluation of an auditory-enhanced scrollbar. In *Proceedings of the ACM SIGCHI conference on human factors in computing systems* (pp. 173–179). ACM Press, Addison-Wesley.

Brin, S. and Page, L. (1998). The anatomy of a large-scale hypertextual Web search engine. In *Proceedings of the international conference on the World Wide Web* (pp. 107–117).

Broder, A. (2002). A taxonomy of web search. *SIGIR Forum*, 36(2), 3–10. ACM Press.

Broder, A., Churchill, E., Hearst, M., Pell, B., Raghavan, P., and Tomkins, A. (2010). Search is dead!: Long live search (panel). In *Proceedings of the international conference on the World Wide Web*, (pp. 1337–1338).

Broder, A., Garcia-Pueyo, L., Josifovski, V., Vassilvitskii, S., and Venkatesan, S. (2014). Scalable K-Means by ranked retrieval. In *Proceedings of the ACM WSDM conference on Web search and data mining* (pp. 233–242). ACM Press.

Bron, M., Van Gorp, J., Nack, F., de Rijke, M., Vishneuski, A., and de Leeuw, S. (2012). A subjunctive exploratory search interface to support media studies researchers. In *Proceedings of the ACM SIGIR conference on research and development in information retrieval* (pp. 425–434). ACM Press.

Bronkhorst, A.W. (2000). The cocktail party phenomenon: A review on speech intelligibility in multiple-talker conditions. *Acta Acustica united with Acustica*, 86, 117–128.

Brooks, P. Phang, K.Y., Oard, D.W., White, R.W., Bradley, R., and Gumbretière, F. (2006). Measuring the utility of gaze detection for task modeling: A study design. In *Proceedings of the workshop on intelligent user interfaces for intelligence analysis*.

Brown, I. (1999). Developing a virtual reality user interface (VRUI) for geographic information retrieval on the Internet. *Transactions in GIS*, 3(3), 207–220.

Grigore C. Burdea, Philippe Coiffet. (2003). *Virtual reality technology*. Wiley-IEEE Press.

Bruffee, K. (1999). *Collaborative learning: Higher education, interdependence, and the authority of knowledge*. Baltimore: The Johns Hopkins University Press.

Bruner, J.S. (1961). The act of discovery. *Harvard Educational Review*, 31, 21–32.

Brünken, R., Steinbacher, S., Plass, J.L., and Leutner, D. (2002). Assessment of cognitive load in multimedia learning using dual-task methodology. *Experimental Psychology*, 49(2), 109–119.

Brusilovsky, P., Cassel, L., Delcambre, L., Fox, E., Furuta, R., Garcia, D.D., and Yudelson, M. (2010). Enhancing digital libraries with social navigation: The case of ensemble. In *Research and Advanced Technology for Digital Libraries* Springer Berlin Heidelberg (pp. 116–123).

Brusilovsky, P., Chavan, G., and Farzan, R. (2004). Social adaptive navigation support for open corpus electronic textbooks. In *Proceedings of international conference on adaptive hypermedia and adaptive Web-based systems* (pp. 24–33).

Buchanan, G. and Loizides, F. (2007). Investigating document triage on paper and electronic media. In *Proceedings of the European conference on digital libraries*, 416–427.

Buckley, C., Salton, G., and Allan, J. (1992). Automatic Retrieval with Locality Information Using Smart. In *The first Text REtrieval Conference (TREC-1), National Institute of Standards and Technology*, Gaithersburg, MD (pp. 59–72).

Buckley, C. and Voorhees, E.M. (2004). Retrieval evaluation with incomplete information. In *Proceedings of the ACM SIGIR conference on research and development in information retrieval* (pp. 25–32). ACM Press.

Budhu, M. and Coleman, A. (2002). The design and evaluation of interactivities in a digital library. *D-Lib Magazine*, 8(11).

Budzik, J. and Hammond, K.J. (2000). User interactions with everyday applications as context for justin-in-time information access. In *Proceedings of the annual conference on intelligent user interfaces* (pp. 44–51).

Bull, S. (2004). Supporting learning with open learner models. In *Proceedings of Hellenic conference on information and communication technologies in education* (pp. 47–61).

Burdea, G. and Coiffet, P. (2003). Virtual reality technology. *Presence: Teleoperators and Virtual Environments*, 12(6), 663–664.

Burges, C., Shaked, T., Renshaw, E., Lazier, A., Deeds, M., Hamilton, N., and Hullender, G. (2005). Learning to rank using gradient descent. In *Proceedings of the international conference on machine learning* (pp. 89–96). ACM Press.

Burke, M., Marlow, C., and Lento, T. (2009). Feed me: Motivating newcomer contribution in social network sites. In *Proceedings of the ACM SIGCHI conference on human factors in computing systems* (pp. 945–954). ACM Press.

Burke, M., and Settles, B. (2011). Plugged in to the community: social motivators in online goal-setting groups. In *Proceedings of the international conference on communities and technologies* (pp. 1–10). ACM Press.

Burke, R. (2002). Hybrid recommender systems: Survey and experiments. *User Modeling and User-Adapted Interaction*, 12(4), 331–370.

Burt, R.S. (2005). *Brokerage and closure: An introduction to social capital*. Oxford University Press: Oxford.

Buscher, G., Dengel, A. and Van Elst, L. (2008). Query expansion using gaze-based feedback on the subdocument level. In *Proceedings of the ACM SIGIR conference on research and development in information retrieval* (pp. 387–394). ACM Press.

Buscher, G., Dumais, S.T., and Cutrell, E. (2010). The good, the bad, and the random: an eye-tracking study of ad quality in web search. In *Proceedings of the ACM SIGIR conference on research and development in information retrieval* (pp. 42–49). ACM Press.

Buscher, G., van Elst, L., and Dengel, A. (2009). Segment-level display time as implicit feedback: A comparison to eye tracking. In *Proceedings of the ACM SIGIR conference on research and development in information retrieval* (pp. 67–74). ACM Press.

Buscher, G., White, R.W., Dumais, S., and Huang, J. (2012). Large-scale analysis of individual and task differences in search result page examination strategies. In *Proceedings of the ACM WSDM conference on web search and data mining* (pp. 373–382). ACM Press.

Bush, V. (1945). As we may think. *Atlantic Monthly*, 3(2), 37–46.

Butler, A., Izadi, S., and Hodges, S. (2008). SideSight: Multi-touch interaction around small devices. In *Proceedings of the ACM UIST symposium on user interface software and technology* (pp. 201–204). ACM Press.

Butler, D. (February 14, 2013). When Google got flu wrong. *Nature*, 494(7436), 155–156.

Butler, E.S., Aasheim, C., and Williams, S. (2007). Does telecommuting improve productivity? *Communications of the ACM*, 50(4), 101–103.

Buxton, B. (2007). Multi-touch systems that I have known and loved. *Microsoft Research*, 56, 1–11.

Byström, K. and Järvelin, K. (1995). Task complexity affects information seeking and use. *Information Processing and Management*, 31(2), 191–213.

Cacioppo, J.T., and Petty, R.E. (1982). The need for cognition. *Journal of Personality and Social Psychology*, 42(1), 116.

Cadez, I., Heckerman, D., Meek, C., Smyth, P., and White, S. (2003). Visualization of navigation patterns on a web site using model based clustering. *Data Mining and Knowledge Discovery*, 7, 399–424.

Cadoz, C. (1994). *Les réalités virtuelles*. Dominos, Flammarion.

Callan, J. P. (1994). Passage-level evidence in document retrieval. In *Proceedings of the ACM SIGIR conference on research and development in information retrieval* (pp. 302–310). Springer-Verlag New York, Inc.

Callan, J.P., Lu, Z., and Croft, W.B. (1995). Searching distributed collections with inference networks. In *Proceedings of the ACM SIGIR conference on research and development in information retrieval* (pp. 21–28). ACM Press.

Calvo, R.A. and Sidney D'Mello (2010). Affect detection: An interdisciplinary review of models, methods, and their applications. *IEEE Transactions on Affective Computing*, 1(1), 18–37.

Camerer, C.F. and Johnson, E.J. (1991). The process-performance paradox in expert judgment: How can the experts know so much and predict so badly? In K. A. Ericsson and J. Smith, eds., *Towards a General Theory of Expertise: Prospects and Limits* (pp. 195–217). Cambridge: Cambridge University Press.

Campbell, I. (2000). Interactive evaluation of the ostensive model using a new test collection of images with multiple relevance assessments. *Information Retrieval*, 2(1), 89–114.

Campbell, I. and van Rijsbergen, C.J. (1996). The ostensive model of developing information needs. In *Proceedings of the COLIS conference on conceptions of library and information science* (pp. 251–268).

Capra, R. and Pérez-Quiñones, M.A. (2005). Using Web search engines to find and refind information. *IEEE Computer*, 38(10), 36–42.

Capra, R., Arguello, J., Crescenzi, A., and Vardell, E. (2015). Differences in the use of search assistance for tasks of varying complexity. In *Proceedings of the ACM SIGIR conference on research and development in information retrieval* (pp. 23–32). ACM Press.

Caracciolo, C. and de Rijke, M. (2006). Generating and retrieving text segments for focused access to scientific documents. In *Proceedings of the European conference on advances in information retrieval* (pp. 350–361).

Carbonell, J. and Goldstein, J. (1998). The use of MMR, diversity-based reranking for reordering documents and producing summaries. In *Proceedings of the ACM SIGIR conference on research and development in information retrieval* (pp. 335–336). ACM Press.

Card, S.K., Mackinlay, J. D., and Shneiderman, B. (eds.). (1999). *Readings in information visualization: Using vision to think*. Morgan Kaufmann.

Card, S.K., Moran, T.P., and Newell, A. (1983). *The Psychology of Human-Computer Interaction*. Hillsdale, NJ: Lawrence Erlbaum Associates.

Card, S.K., Pirolli, P., Van Der Wege, M., Morrison, J.B., Reeder, R.W., Schraedley, P.K., and Boshart, J. (2001). Information scent as a driver of Web behavior graphs: Results of a protocol analysis method for Web usability. In *Proceedings of the ACM SIGCHI conference on human factors in computing systems* (pp. 498–505). ACM Press.

Card, S.K., Robertson, G.C., and Mackinlay, J.D. (1991). The information visualizer, an information workspace. In *Proceedings of the ACM SIGCHI conference on human factors in computing systems* (pp. 181–188). ACM Press

Card, S. K., Robertson, G.G., and York, W. (1996). The WebBook and the Web forager: An information workspace for the World-Wide Web. In *Proceedings of the ACM SIGCHI conference on human factors in computing systems* (pp. 111-ff). ACM Press.

Cardoso, J.F.C. (1998). Blind signal separation: Statistical principles. In *Proceedings of the IEEE*, 86(10), 2009–2025.

Carmagnola, F. and Cena, F. (2009). User identification for cross-system personalisation. *Information Sciences*, 179(1), 16–32.

Carmel, E., Crawford, S., and Chen, H. (1992). In browsing in hypertext: A cognitive study. In *Proceedings of the IEEE transactions on systems, man and cybernetics* (pp. 865–884).

Carrington, P.J., Scott, J., and Wasserman, S. (Eds.). (2005). *Models and Methods in Social Network Analysis*. Cambridge, MA: Cambridge University Press.

Carroll, J.M. and Anderson, N.S. (1987). Mental models in human-computer interaction: Research issues about what the user of software knows (No. 12). Olson, J. R. (Ed.). National Academies.

Carroll, J.M. and Rosson, M.B. (1992). Getting around the task-artifact cycle: how to make claims and design by scenario. *ACM Transactions on Information Systems*, 10(2), 181–212. ACM Press.

Carroll, J.M. and Thomas, J.C. (1988). Fun. *SIGCHI Bulletin*, 19(3), 21–24. ACM Press.

Carta, T., Paternò, F., and Santana, V. (2011). Support for remote usability evaluation of web mobile applications. In *Proceedings of the ACM international conference on design of communication* (pp. 129–136). ACM Press.

Carterette, B. and Jones, R. (2007). Evaluating search engines by modeling the relationship between relevance and clicks. In *Proceedings of the conference on advances in neural information processing systems* (pp. 217–224).

Cartright, M.A., White, R.W., and Horvitz, E. (2011). Intentions and attention in exploratory health search. In *Proceedings of the ACM SIGIR conference on research and development in information retrieval* (pp. 65–74). ACM Press.

Case, D.O. (2002). *Looking for Information: A Survey of Research on Information Seeking, Needs, and Behavior*. London: Academic Press.

Castillo, C., Gionis, A., Lempel, R., and Maarek, Y. (2010). When no clicks are good news. Presentation at the SIGIR 2010 industry day. http://www.eurospider.com/fileadmin/pdf/SIGIR_Industry_Track_2010/11_SIGIR-2010-CASTILLO.pdf. Accessed on August 16, 2015.

Catledge, L.D. and Pitkow, J.E. (1995). Characterizing browsing strategies in the World-Wide Web. *Computer Networks and ISDN systems*, 27(6), 1065–1073.

Ceaparu, I., Lazar, J., Bessiere, K., Robinson, J., and Shneiderman, B. (2004). Determining causes and severity of end-user frustration. *International Journal of Human-Computer Interaction*, 17(3), 333–356.

Cegarra, J. and Chevalier, A. (2008). The use of tholos software for combining measures of mental workload: Toward theoretical and methodological improvements. *Behavior Research Methods*, 40(4), 988–1000.

Chakrabarti, S., Frieze, A., and Vera, J. (2005). The influence of search engines on preferential attachment. In *Proceedings of the ACM-SIAM symposium on discrete algorithms* (pp. 293–300). Society for Industrial and Applied Mathematics.

Chaiken, R., Jenkins, B., Larson, P.Å., Ramsey, B., Shakib, D., Weaver, S., and Zhou, J. (2008). SCOPE: Easy and efficient parallel processing of massive data sets. In *Proceedings of the VLDB Endowment*, 1(2), 1265–1276.

Chalmers, M., Rodden, K., and Brodbeck, D. (1998). The order of things: Activity-centred information access. *Computer Networks and ISDN Systems*, 30(1), 359–367.

Chan, D., Ge, R., Gershony, O., Hesterberg, T., and Lambert, D. (2010). Evaluating online ad campaigns in a pipeline: Causal models at scale. In *Proceedings of the ACM SIGKDD conference on knowledge discovery and data mining* (pp. 7–16). ACM Press.

Chan, R.C.K., Shum, D., Toulopoulou, T., Chen, E.Y.H., R., Shum, D., Toulopoulou, T., and Chen, E. (2008). Assessment of executive functions: Review of instruments and identification of critical issues. *Archives of Clinical Neuropsychology*, 23(2), 201–216.

Chang, S. and Rice, R. (1993). Browsing: A multidimensional framework. *Annual review of information science and technology (ARIST)*, 28, 231–276.

Chapelle, O., Joachims, T., Radlinski, F., and Yue, Y. (2012). Large scale validation and analysis of interleaved search evaluation. *ACM Transactions on Information Systems*, 30(1), 6.

Chapelle, O., Metlzer, D., Zhang, Y., and Grinspan, P. (2009). Expected reciprocal rank for graded relevance. In *Proceedings of the ACM CIKM conference on information and knowledge management* (pp. 621–630). ACM Press.

Chapelle, O. and Zhang, Y. (2009). A dynamic bayesian network click model for web search ranking. In *Proceedings of the international conference on World Wide Web* (pp. 1–10). ACM Press.

Charnov, E.L. (1976). Optimal foraging, the marginal value theorem. *Theoretical Population Biology*, 9, 129–136.

Chase, W.G. and Simon, H.A. (1973). The mind's eye in chess. In Chase, W.G. (Ed.), *Visual Information Processing*. New York: Academic Press, pp. 215–281.

Chau, M. and Betke, M. (2005). *Real Time Eye Tracking and Blink Detection with USB Cameras*. Boston, MA: Boston University Computer Science Department.

Chaudhuri, S. and Kaushik, R. (2009). Extending autocompletion to tolerate errors. In *Proceedings of the ACM SIGMOD conference on management of data* (pp. 707–718). ACM Press.

Chawla, S., Hartline, J.D., and Sivan, B. (2012). Optimal crowdsourcing contests. In *Proceedings of the ACM SIAM symposium on discrete algorithms* (pp. 856–868). SIAM.

Chen, G., and Chiu, M.M. (2008). Online discussion processes. *Computers and Education*, 50, 678–692.

Chen, H. and Karger, D.R. (2006). Less is more: Probabilistic models for retrieving fewer relevant documents. In *Proceedings of the ACM SIGIR conference on research and development in information retrieval* (pp. 429–436). ACM Press.

Chen, J. and Ji, Q. (2015). A probabilistic approach to online eye gaze tracking without explicit personal calibration. *IEEE Transactions on Image Processing*, 24(3), 1076–1086.

Cheng, Z., Caverlee, J., Barthwal, H., and Bachani, V. (2014). Who is the barbecue king of Texas?: A geo-spatial approach to finding local experts on Twitter. In *Proceedings of the ACM SIGIR conference on research and development in information retrieval* (pp. 335–344). ACM Press.

Cheverst, K., Davies, N., Mitchell, K., Friday, A., Efstratiou, C. (2000). Developing a context-aware electronic tourist guide: Some issues and experiences. In *Proceedings of the ACM SIGCHI conference on human factors in computing systems* (pp. 17–24). ACM Press.

Chi, E.H. (2009). Information seeking can be social. *IEEE Computer*, 42(3), 42–46.

Chi, E.H. (2012). Who knows?: Searching for expertise on the social web. *Communications of the ACM*, 55(4), 110–110.

Chi, E.H., Hong, L., Gumbrecht, M., and Card, S.K. (2005). ScentHighlights: Highlighting conceptually-related sentences during reading. In *Proceedings of the ACM IUI conference on intelligent user interfaces* (pp. 272–274). ACM Press.

Chi, E. H., Pirolli, P., Chen, K., and Pitkow, J. (2001). Using information scent to model user information needs and actions and the Web. In *Proceedings of the ACM SIGCHI conference on human factors in computing systems* (pp. 490–497). ACM Press.

Chi, E.H., Pirolli, P., and Lam, S.K. (2007). Aspects of augmented social cognition: Social information foraging and social search. In *Proceedings of Online Communities and Social Computing* (pp. 60–69). Springer Berlin Heidelberg.

Chi, E.H., Pirolli, P., and Pitkow, J. (2000). The scent of a site: A system for analyzing and predicting information scent, usage, and usability of a web site. In *Proceedings of the ACM SIGCHI conference on human factors in computing systems* (pp. 161–168). ACM Press.

Chi, E.H., Rosien, A., Supattanasiri, G., Williams, A., Royer, C., Chow, C., and Cousins, S. (2003). The bloodhound project: Automating discovery of web usability issues using the InfoScent simulator. In *Proceedings of the ACM SIGCHI conference on human factors in computing systems* (pp. 505–512). ACM Press.

Chi, M.T., Glaser, R., and Farr, M.J. (Eds.). (2014). *The Nature of Expertise*. Psychology Press.

Chi, M.T.H., Glaser, R., and Rees, E. (1982). Expertise in problem solving. In Sternberg, R.S. (Ed.), *Advances in the Psychology of Human Intelligence*. Hillsdale, NJ Erlbaum, Vol. 1 (pp. 1–75).

Chierichetti, F., Kumar, R., and Raghavan, P. (2011). Optimizing two-dimensional search results presentation. In *Proceedings of the ACM WSDM conference on web search and data mining* (pp. 257–266). ACM Press.

Chierichetti, F., Kumar, R., and Tomkins, A. (2010). Stochastic models for tabbed browsing. In *Proceedings of the international conference on World Wide Web* (pp. 241–250). ACM Press.

Chirita, P.A., Nejdl, W., Paiu, R., and Kohlschütter, C. (2005). Using ODP metadata to personalize search. In *Proceedings of the ACM SIGIR conference on research and development in information retrieval* (pp. 178–185). ACM Press.

Cho, J. and Roy, S. (2004). Impact of search engines on page popularity. In *Proceedings of the international conference on the World Wide Web* (pp. 20–29). ACM Press.

Choi, H., and Varian, H. (2012). Predicting the present with google trends. *Economic Record*, 88(s1), 2–9.

Chon, Y., Lane, N.D., Li, F., Cha, H., and Zhao, F. (2012). Automatically characterizing places with opportunistic crowdsensing using smartphones. In *Proceedings of the ACM conference on ubiquitous computing* (pp. 481–490). ACM Press.

Choo, C.W., Detlor, B., and Turnbull, D. (2000). Information seeking on the Web: An integrated model of browsing and searching. *First Monday*, 5(2).

Chu, W. and Keerthi, S.S. (2005). New approaches to support vector ordinal regression. In *Proceedings of the international conference on machine learning* (pp. 145–152). ACM Press.

Chun, M.M. and Potter, M.C. (1995). A two-stage model for multiple target detection in rapid serial visual presentation. *Journal of Experimental Psychology: Human Perception and Performance*, 21(1), 109.

Churchill, E.F. and Munro, A.J. (2001). Work/place: Mobile technologies and arenas of activity. *ACM SigGroup Bulletin*, 22(3), 3–9.

Clark, H.H. and Brennan, S.E. (1991). Grounding in communication. In Resnick, L.B., Levine, J.M., and Teasley, S.D. (eds.). *Perspectives on Socially Shared Cognition* (pp. 127–149). American Psychological Association.

Clarke, C.L.A., Agichtein, E., Dumais, S.T., and White, R.W. (2007). The influence of caption features on clickthrough patterns in web search. In *Proceedings of the ACM SIGIR conference on research and development in information retrieval* (pp. 135–142). ACM Press.

Clarke, C.L., Kolla, M., Cormack, G.V., Vechtomova, O., Ashkan, A., Büttcher, S., and MacKinnon, I. (2008). Novelty and diversity in information retrieval evaluation. In *Proceedings of the ACM SIGIR conference on research and development in information retrieval* (pp. 659–666). ACM Press.

Claypool, M., Le, P., Waseda, M., and Brown, D. (2001). Implicit interest indicators. In *Proceedings of the ACM IUI on intelligent user interfaces* (pp. 33–40). ACM Press.

Cleverdon, C.W. (1970). *The effect of variations in relevance assessments in comparative experimental tests of index languages*. Cranfield: Cranfield Institute of Technology. (Cranfield Library Report No. 3)

Cleverdon, C.W., Mills, J., and Keen, E.M. (1966). *Factors determining the performance of indexing systems*. Cranfield: Aslib Cranfield Research Project, College of Aeronautics. (Vol. 1: Design; Vol. 2: Results)

Clough, P., Ford, N., and Stevenson, M. (2011). Personalizing access to cultural heritage collections using pathways. In *Proceedings of workshop on personalized access to cultural heritage*.

Cockburn, A. and B. McKenzie. (2001). What do Web users do? An empirical analysis of Web use. *International Journal of Human-Computer Studies*, 54(6), 903–922.

Cohen, J. (1988). *Statistical Power Analysis for the Behavioral Sciences (2nd ed.)*. Lawrence Erlbaum Associates.

Cohen, N. (2010). "Suicide" query prompts Google to offer hotline. In *New York Times*, April 2010.

Cohen, W.W., Shapire, R.E., and Singer, Y. (1999). Learning to order things. *Journal of Artificial Intelligence Research*, 10, 243–270.

Cohn, G., Morris, D., Patel, S., and Tan, D. (2012). Humantenna: Using the body as an antenna for real-time whole-body interaction. In *Proceedings of the ACM SIGCHI conference on human factors in computing systems* (pp. 1901–1910). ACM Press.

Cohn, G., Morris, D., Patel, S.N., and Tan, D.S. (2011). Your noise is my command: Sensing gestures using the body as an antenna. In *Proceedings of the ACM SIGCHI conference on human factors in computing systems* (pp. 791–800). ACM Press.

Cole, M.J., Gwizdka, J., Liu, C., Belkin, N.J., and Zhang, X. (2013). Inferring user knowledge level from eye movement patterns. *Information Processing and Management*, 49(5), 1075–1091.

Cole, M.J., Gwizdka, J., Liu, C., Bierig, R., Belkin, N.J., and Zhang, X. (2011). Task and user effects on reading patterns in information search. *Interacting with Computers*, 23(4), 346–362.

Cole, M.J., Hendahewa, C., Belkin, N.J., and Shah, C. (2014). Discrimination between tasks with user activity patterns during information search. In *Proceedings of the ACM SIGIR conference on research and development in information retrieval* (pp. 567–576). ACM Press.

Collins, A., Brown, J.S., and Newman, S.E. (1989). Cognitive apprenticeship: teaching the crafts of reading, writing, and mathematics. *Knowing, learning, and instruction: Essays in honor of Robert Glaser*, 18, 32–42.

Collins-Thompson, K. (2009a). Accounting for stability of retrieval algorithms using risk-reward curves. In *Proceedings of the SIGIR workshop on the future of IR evaluation* (pp. 27–28).

Collins-Thompson, K. (2009b). Reducing the risk of query expansion via robust constrained optimization. In *Proceedings of the ACM CIKM conference on information and knowledge management* (pp. 837–846). ACM Press.

Collins-Thompson, K., Bennett, P.N., White, R.W., de la Chica, S., and Sontag, D. (2011). Personalizing web search results by reading level. In *Proceedings of the ACM CIKM conference on information and knowledge management* (pp. 403–412). ACM Press.

Comon, P. (1994). Independent component analysis: A new concept? *Signal Processing*, 36(3): 287–314.

Condie, T., Conway, N., Alvaro, P., Hellerstein, J.M., Elmeleegy, K., and Sears, R. (2010). MapReduce online. In *Proceedings of Symposium on Networked Systems Design and Implementation*, 10(4), 20.

Cong, G., Wang, L., Lin, C.Y., Song, Y.I., and Sun, Y. (2008). Finding question-answer pairs from online forums. In *Proceedings of the ACM SIGIR conference on research and development in information retrieval* (pp. 467–474). ACM Press.

Consolvo, S., McDonald, D., and Landay, J. (2009). Theory-driven design strategies for technologies that support behavior change in everyday life. In *Proceedings of the ACM SIGCHI conference on human factors in computing systems* (pp. 405–414). ACM Press.

Convertino, G., Mentis, H.M., Rosson, M.B., Slavkovic, A., and Carroll, J.M. (2009). Supporting content and process common ground in computer-supported teamwork. In *Proceedings of the SIGCHI conference on human factors in computing systems* (pp. 2339–2348). ACM Press.

Cool, C. (2001). The concept of situation in information science. *Annual review of information science and technology*, 35, 5–42.

Cool, C. and Belkin, N.J. (2002) A classification of interactions with information. In *Proceedings of the COLIS conference on conceptions of library and information science* (pp. 1–15).

Cool, C., Park, S., Belkin, N.J., Koenemann, J., and Ng, K.B. (1996). Information seeking behavior in new searching environment In *Proceedings of the COLIS conference on conceptions of library and information science* (pp. 403–416).

Cool, C. and Spink, A. (2002). Issues of context in information retrieval (IR): An introduction to the special issue. *Information Processing and Management*, 38(5), 605–611.

Cooper, A. (2008). A survey of query log privacy-enhancing techniques from a policy perspective. *ACM Transactions on the Web*, 2(4), 19.

Cooper, D.G., Arroyo, I., Woolf, B.P., Muldner, K., Burleson, W., and Christopherson, R. (2009). Sensor model student self-concept in the classroom. In *Proceedings of the conference on user modeling and personalization* (pp. 30–41).

Cooper, M.D. (1972). A cost model for evaluating information retrieval systems. *Journal of the American Society for Information Science*, 23(5), 306–312.

Cooper, W. (1968). Expected search length: A single measure of retrieval effectiveness based on the weak ordering action of retrieval systems. *American Documentation*, 19(1), 30–41.

Cooper, W.S., Gey, F.C., and Dabney, D.P. (1992). Probabilistic retrieval based on staged logistic regression. In *Proceedings of the ACM SIGIR conference on research and development in information retrieval* (pp. 198–210). ACM Press.

Corbett, A.T., Koedinger, K.R., and Anderson, J.R. (1997). Intelligent tutoring systems. *Handbook of Human–Computer Interaction* (pp. 849–874).

Corston-Oliver, S., Ringger, E., Gamon, M., and Campbell, R. (2004). Task-focused summarization of email. In *Proceedings of the ACL workshop: text summarization branches out* (pp. 43–50).

Cosijn, E. and Ingwersen, P. (2000). Dimensions of relevance. *Information Processing and Management*, 36(4), 533–550.

Cranor, L. (2007). Making privacy disclosures to consumers more usable. *Bureau of Consumer Protection*.

Craswell, N. and Szummer, M. (2007). Random walks on the click graph. In *Proceedings of the ACM SIGIR conference on research and development in information retrieval* (pp. 239–246). ACM Press.

Craswell, N., Zoeter, O., Taylor, M., and Ramsey, B. (2008). An experimental comparison of click position-bias models. In *Proceedings of the ACM WSDM conference on web search and data mining* (pp. 87–94). ACM Press.

Crawford, K. and Schultz, J. (2014). Big data and due process: Toward a framework to redress predictive privacy harms. *Boston College Law Review*, 55, 93.

Crescenzi, A., Capra, R., and Arguello, J. (2013). Time pressure, user satisfaction and task difficulty. *American Society for Information Science and Technology*, 50(1), 1–4.

Crescenzi, A. (2015). Time pressure in information search. In *Proceedings of the ACM SIGIR Conference on Research and Development in Information Retrieval* (pp. 1050–1055). ACM Press.

Croft, W.B., Metzler, D., and Strohman, T. (2010). *Search engines: Information retrieval in practice*. Reading: Addison-Wesley.

Croft, W.B. and Thompson, R.H. (1987). I^{3}R: A new approach to the design of document retrieval systems. *Journal of the American Society for Information Science*, 38(6), 389–404.

Cronen-Townsend, S., Zhou, Y., and Croft, W.B. (2002). Predicting query performance. In *Proceedings of the ACM SIGIR conference on research and development in information retrieval* (pp. 299–306). ACM Press.

Cropley, A.J. (2000). Defining and measuring creativity: Are creativity tests worth using? *Roeper Review*, 23(2), 72–79.

Csikszentmihalyi, M. (1991). *Flow: The Psychology of Optimal Experience*. New York: Harper-Perennial.

Csikszentmihalyi, M. (1997). *Flow and the Psychology of Discovery and Invention*. New York: Harper-Perennial.

Cucerzan, S. and Brill, E. (2004). Spelling correction as an iterative process that exploits the collective knowledge of Web users. In *Proceedings of the conference on empirical methods in natural language processing* (pp. 293–300).

Cui, H., J.R. Wen, J.Y. Nie, and W. Ma (2002). Probabilistic query expansion using query logs. In *Proceedings of the international conference on the World Wide Web* (pp. 325–332).

Culliss, G. (1999). User popularity ranked search engines. http://web.archive.org/web/20000302121422/http://www.infonortics.com/searchengines/boston1999/culliss/index.htm.

Cutrell, E., Dumais, S.T., and Teevan, J. (2006). Searching to eliminate personal information management. *Communications of the ACM*, 49(1), 58–64.

Cutrell, E. and Guan, Z. (2007). What are you looking for?: An eye-tracking study of information usage in web search. In *Proceedings of the ACM SIGCHI conference on human factors in computing systems* (pp. 407–416). ACM Press.

Cutting, D.R., Karger, D.R., Pedersen, J.O., and Tukey, J.W. (1992). Scatter/gather: A cluster-based approach to browsing large document collections. In *Proceedings of the ACM SIGIR conference on research and development in information retrieval* (pp. 318–329). ACM Press.

Czerwinski, M., Horvitz, E., and Cutrell, E. (2001). Subjective duration assessment: An implicit probe for software usability. In *Proceedings of IHM-HCI conference* (pp. 167–170).

Czerwinski, M., Cutrell, E., and Horvitz, E. (2000). Instant messaging and interruptions: Influence of task type on performance. In *Proceedings of OZCHI* (pp. 356–361).

Czerwinski, M., Gage, D., Gemmell, J., Marshall, C., Perez-Quinonesis, M., Skeels, M., and Catarci, T. (2006). Digital memories in an era of ubiquitous computing and abundant storage. *Communications of the ACM*, 49(1), 44–50.

Czerwinski, M. and Horvitz, E. (2002). An investigation of memory for daily computing events. In *Proceedings of People and Computers XVI-Memorable Yet Invisible* (pp. 229–245). Springer London.

Czerwinski, M., Horvitz, E., and Cutrell, E. (2001). Subjective duration assessment: An implicit probe for software usability. In *Proceedings of IHM-HCI 2001 conference* (pp. 167–170).

Czerwinski, M., Horvitz, E., and Wilhite, S. (2004). A diary study of task switching and interruptions. In *Proceedings of the ACM SIGCHI conference on human factors in computing systems* (pp. 175–182). ACM Press.

Dan, O., Dmitriev, P., and White, R.W. (2012). Mining for insights in the search engine query stream. In *Proceedings of the international conference companion on the World Wide Web* (pp. 489–490). ACM Press.

Dang, V. and Croft, W.B. (2010). Query reformulation using anchor text. In *Proceedings of the ACM WSDM conference on Web search and data mining* (pp. 41–50). ACM Press.

Daoud, L. Tamine-Lechani, L., Boughanem, M., and Chebaro, B. (2009). A session based personalized search using an ontological user profile. In *Proceedings of the ACM symposium on applied computing* (pp. 1732–1736). ACM Press.

Das Sarma, A., Gollapudi, S., and Ieong, S. (2008). Bypass rates: Reducing query abandonment using negative inferences. In *Proceedings of the ACM SIGKDD conference on knowledge discovery and data mining* (pp. 177–185). ACM Press.

Dasgupta, A., Gurevich, M., Zhang, L., Tseng, B., and Thomas, A.O. (2012). Overcoming browser cookie churn with clustering. In *Proceedings of the ACM WSDM conference on web search and data mining* (pp. 83–92). ACM Press.

Daumé, H. and Brill, E. (2004). Web search intent induction via automatic query reformulation. In *Proceedings of the conference of the north american chapter of the association for computational linguistics – human language technologies: short papers* (pp. 49–52). Association for Computational Linguistics.

Davenport, T.H. and Beck, J.C. (2013). *The Attention Economy: Understanding the New Currency of Business*. Cambridge, MA: Harvard Business Press.

Davies, G. and Thomson, D., eds. (1988). *Memory in Context: Context in Memory*. Wiley: England.

Davis, S.F. and Palladino, J.J. (1995). *Psychology*. Englewood Cliffs, NJ: Prentice Hall.

Dean, J. and Barroso, L.A. (2013). The tail at scale. *Communications of the ACM*, 56(2), 74–80.

Dean, J. and Ghemawat, S. (2008). MapReduce: Simplified data processing on large clusters. *Communications of the ACM*, 51(1), 107–113.

Dean-Hall, A., Clarke, C.L.A., Kamps, J., Thomas, P., Simone, N., and Voorhees, E. (2013). Overview of the trec 2013 contextual suggestion track. University of Waterloo (Ontario).

De Brouwer, S., Missal, M., Barnes, G., and Lefèvre, P. (2002). Quantitative analysis of catch-up saccades during sustained pursuit. *Journal of Neurophysiology*, 87(4), 1772–1780.

De Choudhury, M., Morris, M.R., and White, R.W. (2014). Seeking and sharing health information online: Comparing search engines and social media. In *Proceedings of the ACM SIGCHI conference on human factors in computing systems* (pp. 1365–1376). ACM Press.

de Jong, F.P. and Simons, R.J. (1988). Self-regulation in text processing. *European Journal of Psychology of Education*, 3(2), 177–190.

De Vries, A. P., Kazai, G., and Lalmas, M. (2004). Tolerance to irrelevance: A user-effort oriented evaluation of retrieval systems without predefined retrieval unit. In *Proceedings of the conference on computer-assisted information retrieval (RIAO)* (pp. 463–473).

Deci, E.L., Koestner, R., and Ryan, R.M. (1999). A meta-analytic review of experiments examining the effects of extrinsic rewards on intrinsic motivation. *Psychological Bulletin*, 125(6), 627–668.

Dennis, S., McArthur, R., and Bruza, P.D. (1998). Searching the World Wide Web made easy? The cognitive load imposed by query refinement mechanisms. In *Proceedings of the Australian document computing symposium* (pp. 65–71).

Dennis, S., Bruza, P., and McArthur, R. (2002). Web searching: A process-oriented experimental study of three interactive search paradigms. *Journal of the American Society for Information Science and Technology*, 53(2), 120–133.

Dervin, B. (1983). An overview of sense-making research: Concepts, methods, and results to date. In *Proceedings of the annual meeting of the international communication association*, Dallas, TX.

Dervin, B. (1992). From the mind's eye of the user: The sense-making qualitative-quantitative methodology. *Qualitative research in information management*, 61, 84.

Dervin, B. (1998). Sense-making theory and practice: An overview of user interests in knowledge seeking and use. *Journal of knowledge management*, 2(2), 36–46.

Dervin, B. and Nilan, M. (1986). Information needs and uses. *Annual review of information science and technology*, 21, 3–33.

Deville, P., Linard, C., Martin, S., Gilbert, M., Stevens, F.R., Gaughan, A.E., and Tatem, A.J. (2014). Dynamic population mapping using mobile phone data. In *Proceedings of the National Academy of Sciences*, 111(45), 15888–15893.

De Vries, A.P., Kazai, G., and Lalmas, M. (2004). Tolerance to irrelevance: A user-effort oriented evaluation of retrieval systems without predefined retrieval unit. In *Proceedings of RIAO* (pp. 463–473).

Dewey, J. (1933). *How We Think*. Boston: D.C. Heath.

Diaz, F. (2007). Performance prediction using spatial autocorrelation. In *Proceedings of the ACM SIGIR conference on research and development in information retrieval* (pp. 583–590). ACM Press.

Diaz, F., White, R., Buscher, G., and Liebling, D. (2013). Robust models of mouse movement on dynamic web search results pages. In *Proceedings of the ACM CIKM conference on information and knowledge management* (pp. 1451–1460). ACM Press.

Dieberger, A. (1997). Supporting social navigation on the World Wide Web. *International Journal of Human-Computer Studies*, 46(6), 805–825.

Dieberger, A., Dourish, P., Höök, K., Resnick, P., and Wexelblat, A. (2000). Social navigation: Techniques for building more usable systems. *Interactions*, 7(6), 36–45.

DiGioia, P. and Dourish, P. (2005). Social navigation as a model for usable security. In *Proceedings of the symposium on usable privacy and security* (pp. 101–108). ACM Press.

Dillon, A. and Watson, C. (1996). User analysis in HCI: The historical lessons from individual differences research. *International Journal of Human-Computer Studies*, 45(6), 619–637.

Dincer, B.T., Macdonald, C., and Ounis, I. (2014). Hypothesis testing for the risk-sensitive evaluation of retrieval systems. In *Proceedings of the ACM SIGIR conference on research and development in information retrieval* (pp. 23–32). ACM Press.

Dix, A.J. and Beale, R. (1996). *Remote Cooperation: CSCW Issues for Mobile and Teleworkers*. New York: Springer-Verlag.

Diriye, A., White, R., Buscher, G., and Dumais, S. (2012). Leaving so soon? Understanding and predicting web search abandonment rationales. In *Proceedings of the ACM CIKM conference on information and knowledge management* (pp. 1025–1034). ACM Press.

Dolin, R.A. (2010). Search query privacy: The problem of anonymization. *Hastings Science and Technology Law Journal*, 2, 137.

Domingos, P. (2012). A few useful things to know about machine learning. *Communications of the ACM*, 55(10), 78–87.

Donath, J. and Robertson, N. (1994). The sociable web. In *Proceedings of the annual international World Wide Web conference*.

Donato, D., Bonchi, F., Chi, T., and Maarek, Y. (2010). Do you want to take notes?: Identifying research missions in Yahoo! search pad. In *Proceedings of the international conference on the World Wide Web* (pp. 321–330). ACM Press.

Dong, A., Zhang, R., Kolari, P., Bai, J., Diaz, F., Chang, Y., Zheng, Z., and Zha, H. (2010). Time is of the essence: Improving recency ranking using twitter data. In *Proceedings of the international conference on the World Wide Web* (pp. 331–340). ACM Press.

Dontcheva, M., Drucker, S., Wade, G., Salesin, D., and Cohen, M. (2006). Summarizing personal web ubrowsing sessions. In *Proceedings of the ACM UIST symposium on user interface software and technology* (pp. 115–124). ACM Press.

Dontcheva, M., Drucker, S.M., Salesin, D., and Cohen, M.F. (2007). Relations, cards, and search templates: User-guided web data integration and layout. In *Proceedings of the ACM UIST symposium on user interface software and technology* (pp. 61–70). ACM Press.

Dörk, M., Carpendale, S., and Williamson, C. (2011). The information flaneur: A fresh look at information seeking. In *Proceedings of the ACM SIGCHI conference on human factors in computing systems* (pp. 1215–1224). ACM Press.

Dou, Z., Song, R., and Wen, J.R. (2007). A large-scale evaluation and analysis of personalized search strategies. In *Proceedings of the international conference on the World Wide Web* (pp. 581–590). ACM Press.

Dourish, P. and Chalmers, M. (1994). Running out of space: Models of information navigation. In *Proceedings of the human-computer interaction conference* (pp. 23–26).

Dourish, P. and Bellotti, V. (1992). Awareness and coordination in shared workspaces. In *Proceedings of the ACM CSCW conference on computer-supported cooperative work* (pp. 107–114). ACM Press.

Downey, D., Dumais, S., Liebling, D., and Horvitz, E. (2008). Understanding the relationship between searchers' queries and information goals. In *Proceedings of the ACM CIKM conference on information and knowledge management* (pp. 449–458). ACM Press.

Downey, D., Dumais, S.T., and Horvitz, E. (2007). Models of searching and browsing: Languages, studies, and application. In *Proceedings of the international joint conference on artificial intelligence* (pp. 2740–2747).

Dreyfus, S.E. and Dreyfus, H.L. (1980). A five-stage model of the mental activities involved in directed skill acquisition (No. ORC-80-2). California Univ Berkeley Operations Research Center.

Drewes, H. and Schmidt, A. (2007). Interacting with the computer using gaze gestures. In *Proceedings of Human-Computer Interaction–INTERACT 2007* (pp. 475–488). Springer Berlin Heidelberg.

Duggan, G.B. and Payne, S.J. (2008). Knowledge in the head and on the web: Using topic expertise to aid search. In *Proceedings of the ACM SIGCHI conference on human factors in computing systems* (pp. 39–48). ACM Press.

Dumais, S., Banko, M., Brill, E., Lin, J., and Ng, A. (2002). Web question answering: Is more always better? In *Proceedings of the ACM SIGIR conference on research and development in information retrieval* (pp. 291–298). ACM Press.

Dumais, S.T. and Belkin, N.J. (2005). The TREC interactive tracks: Putting the user into search. In Voorhees, E.M. and Harman, D. (Eds.). *TREC: Experiment and evaluation in information retrieval* (pp. 123–152). Cambridge: MIT Press.

Dumais, S.T., Buscher, G., and Cutrell, E. (2010). Individual differences in gaze patterns for web search. In *Proceedings of the IIiX symposium on information interaction in context* (pp. 185–194). ACM Press.

Dumais, S.T., Cutrell, E., Cadiz, J.J., Jancke, G., Sarin, R., and Robbins, D.C. (2003). Stuff I've seen: A system for personal information retrieval and re-use. In *Proceedings of the ACM SIGIR conference on research and development in information retrieval* (pp. 72–79). ACM Press.

Dumais, S., Cutrell, E., and Chen, H. (2001). Optimizing search by showing results in context. In *Proceedings of the ACM SIGCHI conference on human factors in computing systems* (pp. 277–284). ACM Press.

Dumais, S., Cutrell, E., Sarin, R., and Horvitz, E. (2004). Implicit queries (IQ) for contextualized search. In *Proceedings of the ACM SIGIR conference on research and development in information retrieval* (pp. 594–594). ACM Press.

Dumais, S., Jeffries, R., Russell, D. M., Tang, D., and Teevan, J. (2014). Understanding user behavior through log data and analysis. In Olson, J.S. and Kellogg, W.A. (Eds.). Ways of Knowing in HCI (pp. 349–372), New York, NY: Springer.

Dumas, J.S. and Redish, J.C. (1999). *A Practical Guide to Usability Testing*. Bristol: Intellect Books.

Duncker, K. and Lees, L.S. (1945). On problem solving. *Psychological Monographs*, 58(5), i.

Dunlop, M. (1997). Time, relevance and interaction modelling for information retrieval. In *Proceedings of the ACM SIGIR conference on research and development in information retrieval* (pp. 206–213). ACM Press.

Dupret, G.E. and Piwowarski, B. (2008). A user browsing model to predict search engine click data from past observations. In *Proceedings of the ACM SIGIR conference on research and development in information retrieval* (pp. 331–338). ACM Press.

Dwork, C. (2006). Differential privacy. In *Proceedings of the international colloqium on automata, languages, and programming* (pp. 1–12). Springer Verlag Heidelberg.

Dye, J. (2009). Consumer privacy advocates seek search engine solution. *EContent*. March 2009. http://www.econtentmag.com/Articles/News/News-Feature/Consumer-Privacy-Advocates–Seek-Search-Engine-Solution-52679.htm. Accessed on August 15, 2015.

Eckles, D., Karrer, D., and Ugander, J. (2015). *Design and analysis of experiments in networks: Reducing bias from interference.* (forthcoming)

Edelman, B. (2004). *Earnings and Ratings at Google Answers*. Unpublished Manuscript.

Edmonds, A., White, R.W., Morris, D., and Drucker, S.M. (2007). Instrumenting the dynamic Web. *Journal of Web Engineering*, 6(3), 243–260.

Efthimiadis, E.N. (1993). A user-centered evaluation of ranking algorithms for interactive query expansion. In *Proceedings of the ACM SIGIR conference on research and development in information retrieval* (pp. 146–159). ACM Press.

Efthimiadis, E.N. (1996). Query expansion. *Annual Review of Information Systems and Technology*, 31, 121–187.

Efthimiadis, E.N. and Hendry, D.G. (2005). Search engines and how students think they work. In *Proceedings of the ACM SIGIR conference on research and development in information retrieval* (pp. 595–596). ACM Press.

Egan, D.E., Remde, J.R., Gomez, L.M., Landauer, T.K., Eberhardt, J., and Lochbaum, C.C. (1989). Formative design evaluation of superbook. *ACM Transactions on Information Systems*, 7(1), 30–57

Ehmke, C., and Wilson, S. (2007). Identifying web usability problems from eye-tracking data. In *Proceedings of the British HCI group annual conference on people and computers* (pp. 119–128). British Computer Society.

Eickhoff, C., Collins-Thompson, K., Bennett, P., and Dumais, S. (2013). Designing human-readable user profiles for search evaluation. In *Proceedings of the European conference on information retrieval* (pp. 701–705). Springer-Verlag.

Eickhoff, C., Dungs, S., and Tran, V. (2015). An eye-tracking study of query reformulation. In *Proceedings of the ACM SIGIR conference on research and development in information retrieval* (pp. 13–22). ACM Press.

Eickhoff, C., Teevan, J., White, R., and Dumais, S. (2014). Lessons from the journey: A query log analysis of within-session learning. In *Proceedings of the ACM WSDM conference on Web search and data mining* (pp. 223–232). ACM Press.

Eiron, N. and McCurley, K.S. (2003). Analysis of anchor text for web search. In *Proceedings of the ACM SIGIR conference on research and development in information retrieval* (pp. 459–460). ACM Press.

Eisenberg, E.M. (1990). Jamming: Transcendence through organizing. *Communication Research* 17(2), 139–164.

Eisenberg, M.B. and Berkowitz, R.E. (1990). *Information Problem Solving: The Big Six Skills Approach to Library and Information Skills Instruction*. Norwood, NJ: Ablex Publishing Corporation.

Eisenberg, M.B. and Berkowitz, R.E. (1992). Information problem-solving: The big six skills approach. *School Library Media Activities Monthly*, 8(5), 27.

Ekman, P. and Friesen, W.V. (1976). Measuring facial movement. *Environmental Psychology and Nonverbal Behavior*, 1(1), 56–75.

Elliott, R. (2003). Executive functions and their disorders. *British Medical Bulletin*, 65, 49–59.

Ellis, D. (1989). A behavioural approach to information retrieval system design. *Journal of Documentation*, 45(3), 171–212.

Ellis, D. (1993). Modeling the information-seeking patterns of academic researchers: A grounded theory approach. *The Library Quarterly*, 469–486.

Ellis, D. and Haugan, M. (1997). Modelling the information seeking patterns of engineers and research scientists in an industrial environment. *Journal of Documentation*, 53(4), 384–403.

Ellis, H.C. (1965). *The Transfer of Learning*. New York: The Macmillan Company.

Elkahky, A.M., Song, Y., and He, X. (2015). A multi-view deep learning approach for cross domain user modeling in recommendation systems. In *Proceedings of the international conference on the World Wide Web* (pp. 278–288). International World Wide Web Conferences Steering Committee.

Elsas, J.L. and Dumais, S.T. (2010). Leveraging temporal dynamics of document content in relevance ranking. In *Proceedings of the ACM WSDM conference on web search and data mining* (pp. 1–10). ACM Press.

Elsweiler, D., Wilson, M.L., and Lunn, B.K. (2011). Understanding casual-leisure information behaviour. *Library and Information Science*, 1, 211–241.

Engelbart, D. (1962). Augmenting human intellect: A conceptual framework. *Summary Report AFOSR-3233*. Menlo Park, CA: Stanford Research Institute.

Epstein, R. and Robertson, R.E. (2015). The search engine manipulation effect (SEME) and its possible impact on the outcomes of elections. *Proceedings of the National Academy of Sciences*, 112(33), 512–521.

Eraut, M. (1994). *Developing Professional Knowledge and Competence*. London: Falmer Press.

Erdelez, S. (1999). Information encountering: It's more than just bumping into information. *Bulletin of the American Society for Information Science*, 25(3), 25–29.

Erdelez, S. (2004). Investigation of information encountering in the controlled research environment. *Information Processing and Management*, 40(6), 1013–1025.

Ericsson, K.A. (2006). The influence of experience and deliberate practice on the development of superior expert performance. In Ericsson, K.A., Charness, N., Feltovich, P.J., and Hoffman, R.R. (Eds.). *The Cambridge Handbook of Expertise and Expert Performance* (pp. 683–703). Cambridge University Press.

Ericsson, K.A., Krampe, R.T., and Tesch-Römer, C. (1993). The role of deliberate practice in the acquisition of expert performance. *Psychological Review*, 100(3), 363.

Ericsson, K.A. and Smith, J. (Eds.). (1991). *Toward a General Theory of Expertise: Prospects and Limits*. Cambridge: Cambridge University Press.

Etzioni, O., Banko, M., and Cafarella, M.J. (2006). Machine reading. In *Proceedings of the AAAI conference on artificial intelligence* (pp. 1517–1519). AAAI Press.

Eugster, M.J., Ruotsalo, T., Spapé, M.M., Kosunen, I., Barral, O., Ravaja, N., and Kaski, S. (2014). Predicting term-relevance from brain signals. In *Proceedings of the ACM SIGIR conference on research and development in information retrieval* (pp. 425–434). ACM Press.

European Parliament. (1995). Directive 95/46/EC of the European Parliament and of the Council of 24 October 1995 on the protection of individuals with regard to the processing of personal data and on the free movement of such data.

Evans, B.M. and Chi, E.H. (2008). Towards a model of understanding social search. In *Proceedings of the ACM CSCW conference on computer supported cooperative work* (pp. 485–494). ACM Press.

Eysenbach, G. (2006). Infodemiology: Tracking flu-related searches on the web for syndromic surveillance. In *Proceedings of the annual symposium of the American medical informatics association* (pp. 244–248).

Eysenbach, G. and Köhler, C. (2002). How do consumers search for and appraise health information on the world wide web? Qualitative study using focus groups, usability tests, and in-depth interviews. *British Medical Journal*, 324(7337), 573.

Eysenck, H. (1991). Dimensions of personality: 16: 5 or 3? Criteria for a taxonomic paradigm. *Personality and Individual Differences*, 12, 773–790.

Faber, D. (2006). Google's Marissa Mayer: Speed wins. *ZDNet*. November 9, 2006.

Fails, J.A. and Olsen, D.R.J. (2003). Interactive machine learning. In *Proceedings of the international conference on intelligent user interfaces* (pp. 39–45). ACM Press.

Fanelli, G., Weise, T., Gall, J., and Van Gool, L. (2011). Real time head pose estimation from consumer depth cameras. *Pattern Recognition* (pp. 101–110). Springer Berlin Heidelberg.

Farago, J.H., Williams, H.E., Walsh, J.E., Whyte, N.A., Goel, K.J., Fung, P., and Ray, E.N. (2010). Object search UI and dragging object results. U.S. Patent No. 7,664,739. Washington, DC: U.S. Patent and Trademark Office.

Fawcett, T. and Provost, F. (1997). Adaptive fraud detection. *Data Mining and Knowledge Discovery*, 1(3), 291–316.

Fayyad, U.M., Wierse, A., and Grinstein, G.G. (Eds.). (2002). *Information Visualization in Data Mining and Knowledge Discovery*. San Francisco, CA: Morgan Kaufmann.

Federal Trade Commission. (2011). Facebook settles FTC charges that it deceived consumers by failing to keep privacy promises. *Federal Trade Commission*. Np, 11, 29.

Federal Trade Commission. (2012). Google Will Pay $22.5 million to settle FTC charges it misrepresented privacy assurances to users of apple's safari internet browser. *Federal Trade Commission*. Np, 8, 9.

Feild, H., White, R.W., and Fu, X. (2013). Supporting orientation during search result examination. In *Proceedings of the ACM SIGCHI conference on human factors in computing systems* (pp. 2999–3008). ACM Press.

Feiner, S., Macintyre, B., and Seligmann, D. (1993). Knowledge-based augmented reality. *Communications of the ACM*, 36(7), 53–62.

Feiner, S.K. (April 2002). Augmented reality: A new way of seeing. *Scientific American*, 48–55.

Fels, S.S. and Hinton, G.E. (1993). Glove-talk: A neural network interface between a data-glove and a speech synthesizer. *IEEE Transactions on Neural Networks*, 4(1), 2–8.

Ferrucci, D., Brown, E., Chu-Carroll, J., Fan, J., Gondek, D., Kalyanpur, A. A., and Welty, C. (2010). Building Watson: An overview of the DeepQA project. *AI magazine*, 31(3), 59–79.

Fertig, S., Freeman, E., and Gelernter, D. (1996). Lifestreams: An alternative to the desktop metaphor. In *Proceedings of the ACM SIGCHI conference on human factors in computing systems* (pp. 410–411).

Fidel, R., Bruce, H., Pejtersen, A.M., Dumais, S.T., Grudin, J., and Poltrock, S. (2000). Collaborative information retrieval (CIR). *The New Review of Information Behaviour Research*, 1 (January), 235–247.

Fidel, R., Pejtersen, A.M., Cleal, B., and Bruce, H. (2004). A multidimensional approach to the study of human-information interaction: A case study of collaborative information retrieval. *Journal of the American Society for Information Science and Technology*, 55(11), 939–953.

File, T. and Ryan, C. (2013). Computer and Internet Use in the United States. https://www.census.gov/history/pdf/acs-internet2013.pdf. Accessed on August 17, 2015.

Fisher, D., Popov, I., and Drucker, S. (2012). Trust me, I'm partially right: Incremental visualization lets analysts explore large datasets faster. In *Proceedings of the ACM SIGCHI conference on human factors in computing systems* (pp. 1673–1682). ACM Press.

Fisher, R. (1925). *Statistical Methods for Research Workers*, Edinburgh: Oliver and Boyd, p. 43.

Fishkin, K. and Stone, M.C. (1995). Enhanced dynamic queries via movable filters. In *Proceedings of ACM SIGCHI conference on human factors in computing systems* (pp. 415–420). ACM Press.

Fiske, S.T., and Hauser, R.M. (2014). Protecting human research participants in the age of big data. *Proceedings of the National Academy of Sciences*, 111(38), 13675–13676.

Fitts, P.M. (1954). The information capacity of the human motor system in controlling the amplitude of movement. *Journal of Experimental Psychology*, 47(6), 381.

Flanagan, J.C. (1954). The critical incident technique. *Psychological Bulletin*, 51(4), 327.

Florance, V. and Marchionini, G. (1995). Information processing in the context of medical care. In *Proceedings of the ACM SIGIR conference on research and development in information retrieval* (pp. 158–163). ACM Press.

Fogarty, J., Tan, D., Kapoor, A., and Winder, S. (2008). CueFlik: Interactive concept learning in image search. In *Proceedings of the ACM SIGCHI conference on human factors in computing systems* (pp. 29–38). ACM Press.

Fogg, B.J. (2002). Motivating, influencing, and persuading users. In Jacko, J. and Sears, A. (Eds.) *The Human-Computer Interaction Handbook* (pp. 358–370). Hillsdale, NJ: Lawrence Erlbaum Associates Inc.

Foley, J. (2007). Are google searches private: an originalist interpretation of the fourth amendment in online communication cases. *Berkeley Technology Law Journal*, 22, 447.

Foltz, P. and Landauer, T. (2007). Helping people find and learn from documents: Exploiting synergies between human and computer retrieval with SuperManual. In Landauer, T.K., McNamara, D.S., Dennis, S., and Kintsch, W. (Eds.), *The Handbook of Latent Semantic Analysis*, pp. 323–345. Mahwah, NJ: Erlbaum.

Ford, N. (1980). Levels of understanding and the personal acceptance of information in higher education. *Studies in higher education*, 5(1), 63–70.

Ford, N. (1999). Information retrieval and creativity: Towards support for the original thinker. *Journal of Documentation*, 55(5), 528–542.

Ford, N., Miller, D., and Moss, N. (2005). Web search strategies and human individual differences. *Journal of the American Society for Information Science and Technology*, 56(7), 741–756.

Foster, A. (2004). A nonlinear model of information-seeking behavior. *Journal of the American Society for Information Science and Technology*, 55(3), 228–237.

Foster, A. and Ford, N. (2003). Serendipity and information seeking: An empirical study. *Journal of Documentation*, 59(3), 321–340.

Fourney, A., Mann, R., and Terry, M. (2011). Characterizing the usability of interactive applications through query log analysis. In *Proceedings of the ACM SIGCHI conference on human factors in computing systems* (pp. 1817–1826). ACM Press.

Fourney, A. and Morris, M.R. (2013). Enhancing technical Q&A forums with CiteHistory. In *Proceedings of the international conference n weblogs and social media*. AAAI Press.

Fourney, A., Lafreniere, B., Chilana, P., and Terry, M. (2014). InterTwine: Creating interapplication information scent to support coordinated use of software. In *Proceedings of the ACM UIST symposium on user interface software and technology* (pp. 429–438). ACM Press.

Fourney, A., White, R.W., and Horvitz, E. (2015). Exploring time-dependent concerns about pregnancy and childbirth from search logs. In *Proceedings of the ACM SIGCHI conference on human factors in computing systems* (pp. 737–746). ACM Press.

Fox, S. and Duggan, M. (2013). Online Health 2013. Pew Internet and American Life Project. http://www.pewinternet.org/2013/01/15/health-online-2013. Accessed August 16, 2015.

Fox, S., Karnawat, K., Mydland, M., Dumais, S., and White, T. (2005). Evaluating implicit measures to improve web search. *ACM Transactions on Information Systems*, 23(2), 147–168.

Franzen, K. and Karlgren, J. (2000). Verbosity and interface design. SICS Research Report.

Freire, A., Macdonald, C., Tonellotto, N., Ounis, I., and Cacheda, F. (2014). A self-adapting latency/power tradeoff model for replicated search engines. In *Proceedings of the ACM WSDM conference on web search and data mining* (pp. 13–22). ACM Press.

Freund, L., Toms, E.G., and Clarke, C.L. (2005). Modeling task-genre relationships for IR in the workplace. In *Proceedings of the ACM SIGIR conference on research and development in information retrieval* (pp. 441–448). ACM Press.

Freyne, J., Farzan, R., Brusilovsky, P., Smyth, B., and Coyle, M. (2007). Collecting community wisdom: Integrating social search and social navigation. In *Proceedings of the international conference on intelligent user interfaces* (pp. 52–61). ACM Press.

Friedman, J.H. (1999). *Stochastic Gradient Boosting*. Technical report, Stanford University.

Friggeri, A., Adamic, L.A., Eckles, D., and Cheng, J. (2014). Rumor cascades. In *Proceedings of the international AAAI conference on weblogs and social media*.

Froehlich, J., Findlater, L., and Landay, J. (2010). The design of eco-feedback technology. In *Proceedings of the ACM SIGCHI Conference on human factors in computing systems* (pp. 1999–2008). ACM Press.

Fu, X. (2010). Towards a model of implicit feedback for Web search. *Journal of the American Society for Information Science and Technology*, 61(1), 30–49.

Fu, W.-T. and Pirolli, P. (2007). SNIF-ACT: A cognitive model of user navigation on the world wide web. *Human-Computer Interaction*, 22(4), 355–412.

Fu, X., Budzik, J., and Hammond, K.J. (2000). Mining navigation history for recommendation. In *Proceedings of the international conference on intelligent user interfaces* (pp. 106–112). ACM Press.

Fuhr, N. (1989). Optimum polynomial retrieval functions based on the probability ranking principle. *ACM Transactions on Information Systems*, 7(3), 183–204.

Fulgoni, G.M. (2005). The "Professional Respondent" Problem in Online Survey Panels Today. Slides online at: http://www.sigmavalidation.com/tips/05_06_02_Online_Survey_Panels.ppt. Accessed on August 17, 2015.

Fulton, C. (2009). The pleasure principle: The power of positive affect in information seeking. *Aslib Proceedings: New Information Perspectives*, 61(3), 245–261.

Funes Mora, K.A., and Odobez, J. (2012). Gaze estimation from multimodal Kinect data. In *Computer vision and pattern recognition workshops* (pp. 25–30). IEEE.

Furnas, G.W. (1986). Generalized fisheye views. In *Proceedings of the ACM SIGCHI conference on human factors in computing systems* (pp. 16–23). ACM Press.

Furnas, G. (2002). On recommending. *Journal of the American Society of Information Science and Technology*, 53 (9), 747–763.

Furnas, G.W. (1985). Experience with an adaptive indexing scheme. *ACM SIGCHI Bulletin*, 16(4), 131–135. ACM Press.

Furnas, G.W., Landauer, T.K., Gomez, L.M., and Dumais, S.T. (1987). The vocabulary problem in human-system communication. *Communications of the ACM*, 30(11), 964–971.

Gao, J., Yuan, W., Li, X., Deng, K., and Nie, J.Y. (2009). Smoothing clickthrough data for web search ranking. In *Proceedings of the ACM SIGIR conference on research and development in information retrieval* (pp. 355–362). ACM Press.

Gao, R., Zhao, M., Ye, T., Ye, F., Wang, Y., Bian, K., and Li, X. (2014). Jigsaw: Indoor floor plan reconstruction via mobile crowdsensing. In *Proceedings of the international conference on mobile computing and networking* (pp. 249–260). ACM Press.

Gara, T. (2014). *My Life, and Past, as Seen Through Google's Dashboard*. http://www.wsj.com/articles/SB10001424127887324170004578638402779534498. Accessed on August 15, 2015.

Garfield, E. (1970). When is a negative search result positive? *Essays of an Information Scientist*, 1, 117–118.

Gauch, S., Chaffee, J., and Pretschner, A. (2003). Ontology-based personalized search and browsing. *Web Intelligence and Agent Systems*, 1(3), 219–234.

Ge, Y., Xiong, H., Tuzhilin, A., Xiao, K., Gruteser, M., and Pazzani, M. (2010). An energy-efficient mobile recommender system. In *Proceedings of the ACM SIGKDD conference on knowledge discovery and data mining* (pp. 899–908). ACM Press.

Gemmell, J., Bell, G., and Lueder, R. (2006). MyLifeBits: A personal database for everything. *Communications of the ACM*, 49(1), 88–95.

Gemmell, J., Bell, G., Lueder, R., Drucker, S., and Wong, C. (2002). MyLifeBits: Fulfilling the Memex vision. In *Proceedings of the ACM conference on multimedia* (pp. 235–238). ACM Press.

Ghani, J.A. and Deshpande, S.P. (1994). Task characteristics and the experience of optimal flow in human-computer interaction. *The Journal of Psychology*, 128(4), 381–391.

Ghosh, A., Roughgarden, T., and Sundararajan, M. (2012). Universally utility-maximizing privacy mechanisms. *SIAM Journal on Computing*, 41(6), 1673–1693.

Giannopoulos, G., Brefeld, U., Dalamagas, T., and Sellis, T. (2011). Learning to rank user intent. In *Proceedings of the ACM CIKM conference on information and knowledge management* (pp. 195–200). ACM Press.

Gigerenzer, G. (2008). Why heuristics work. *Perspectives on Psychological Science*, 3, 20–281.

Ginsberg, J., Mohebbi, M.H., Patel, R.S., Brammer, L., Smolinski, M.S., and Brilliant, L. (2009). Detecting influenza epidemics using search engine query data. *Nature*, 457(7232), 1012–1014.

Gladwell, M. (2008). *Outliers: The Story of Success*. Hachette UK.

Glowacka, D., Ruotsalo, T., Konuyshkova, K., Kaski, S., and Jacucci, G. (2013). Directing exploratory search: Reinforcement learning from user interactions with keywords. In *Proceedings of the international conference on intelligent user interfaces* (pp. 117–128). ACM Press.

Goffman, W.A. (1964). Searching procedure for information retrieval. *Information Storage and Retrieval*, 2, 73–78.

Golbeck, J.A. (2005). Computing and applying trust in web-based social networks. *Unpublished doctoral dissertation*. Baltimore: University of Maryland at College Park.

Goldberg, J.H., Stimson, M.J., Lewenstein, M., Scott, N., and Wichansky, A.M. (2002). Eye tracking in web search tasks: Design implications. In *Proceedings of the symposium on eye tracking research and applications* (pp. 51–58). ACM Press.

Goldman, E. (2008). Search engine bias and the demise of search engine utopianism. *Web Search*, 14(III), 121–133.

Goldstein F.C. and Levin H.S. (1987). Disorders of reasoning and problem-solving ability. In M. Meier, A. Benton, and L. Diller (Eds.), *Neuropsychological Rehabilitation* (pp. 327–344). London: Taylor and Francis Group.

Golovchinsky, G. (1997a). What the query told the link: The integration of hypertext and information retrieval. In *Proceedings of the ACM conference on hypertext* (pp. 67–74).

Golovchinsky, G. (1997b). Queries? Links? Is there a difference?. In *Proceedings of the ACM SIGCHI conference on human factors in computing systems* (pp. 407–414). ACM Press.

Golovchinsky, G., Adcock, J., Pickens, J., Qvarfordt, P., and Back, M. (2008). Cerchiamo: A collaborative exploratory search tool. In *Proceedings of the ACM CSCW conference on computer supported cooperative work* (pp. 8–12). ACM Press.

Golovchinsky, G., Dunnigan, A., and Diriye, A. (2012). Designing a tool for exploratory information seeking. In *Proceedings of the ACM SIGCHI extended abstracts on human factors in computing systems* (pp. 1799–1804). ACM Press.

Gomez, L.M., Lochbaum, C.C., and Landauer, T.K. (1990). All the right words: Finding what you want as a function of richness of indexing vocabulary. *Journal of the American Society for Information Science*, 41(8), 547–559.

González-Ibáñez, R., Shah, C., and White, R.W. (2012). Pseudo-collaboration as a method to perform selective algorithmic mediation in collaborative IR systems. In *Proceedings of the American Society for Information Science and Technology*, 49(1), 1–4.

González-Ibáñez, R., Shah, C., and White, R.W. (2015). Capturing collabportunities: A method to evaluate collaboration opportunities in information search using pseudocollaboration. *Journal of the Association for Information Science and Technology*, 66(9), 1897–1912.

Google Webmaster Central Blog. (April 9, 2010). Using site speed in web search ranking. http://bit.ly/acUf3Q.

Gould, J.D. and Lewis, C. (1985). Designing for usability: Key principles and what designers think. *Communications of the ACM*, 28(3), 300–311.

Granger, C.W.J. (1969). Investigating causal relations by econometric models and cross-spectral methods. *Econometrica*, 37(3), 424–438.

Granka, L.A., Joachims, T., and Gay, G. (2004). Eye-tracking analysis of user behavior in WWW search. In *Proceedings of the ACM SIGIR conference on research and development in information retrieval* (pp. 478–479). ACM Press.

Granovetter, M. (1973). Strength of weak ties. *American Journal of Sociology*, 78, 1360–1380.

Gray, B. (1989). *Collaborating: Finding Common Ground for Multiparty Problems.* San Francisco, CA: Jossey-Bass.

Green, T.R. (1991). Describing information artifacts with cognitive dimensions and structure maps. *In Human Computer Interaction*, 91(748), 297–315.

Greenberg, S. and Cockburn, A. (1999). Getting back to back: Alternate behaviors for a Web browser's back button. In *Proceedings of the annual human factors and the Web conference.*

Greer, J.E., McCalla, G.I., Cooke, J.E., Collins, J., Kumar, V.S., Bishop, A., and Vassileva, J.I. (1998). The intelligent helpdesk: Supporting peer-help in a university course. In *Proceedings of the intelligent tutoring systems conference* (pp. 494–505).

Grimes, C., Tang, D., and Russell, D.M. (2007). Query logs alone are not enough. In *Proceedings of the query log analysis workshop at the international conference on the World Wide Web.*

Grudin, J. (1994). Groupware and social dynamics: Eight challenges for developers. *Communications of the ACM*, 37(1), 92–105.

Guha, R., McCool, R., and Miller, E. (2003). Semantic search. In *Proceedings of the international conference on the World Wide Web* (pp. 700–709). ACM Press.

Guilford, J.P. (1967). *The nature of human intelligence.* New York: McGraw-Hill.

Guimbretière, F. and Nguyen, C. (2012). Bimanual marking menu for near surface interactions. In *Proceedings of the ACM SIGCHI annual conference on human factors in computing systems* (pp. 825–828). ACM Press.

Guinan, C. and Smeaton, A.F. (1992). Information retrieval from hypertext using dynamically planned guided tours. In *Proceedings of the ACM conference on hypertext* (pp. 122–130). ACM Press.

Gunduz, S.U. and Özsu, M.T., (2003). Recommendation models for user accesses to web pages. In *Proceedings of the conference on artificial neural networks* (pp. 1003–1010).

Guo, Q. and Agichtein, E. (2008). Exploring mouse movements for inferring query intent. In *Proceedings of the ACM SIGIR conference on research and development in information retrieval* (pp. 707–708). ACM Press.

Guo, Q., Agichtein, E., Clarke, C.L., and Ashkan, A. (2009). In the mood to click? Towards inferring receptiveness to search advertising. In *Proceedings of the international joint conference on Web intelligence and intelligent agent technology* (pp. 319–324). IEEE Computer Society.

Guo, Q. and Agichtein, E. (2010). Ready to buy or just browsing? Detecting web searcher goals from interaction data. In *Proceedings of the ACM SIGIR conference on research and development in information retrieval* (pp. 130–137). ACM Press.

Guo, Q., White, R.W., Dumais, S.T., Wang, J., and Anderson, B. (2010). Predicting query performance using query, result, and user interaction features. In *Proceedings of adaptivity, personalization and fusion of heterogeneous information* (pp. 198–201).

Guo, Q. and Agichtein, E. (2012). Beyond dwell time: estimating document relevance from cursor movements and other post-click searcher behavior. In *Proceedings of the international conference on the World Wide Web* (pp. 569–578). ACM Press.

Guo, Q., Diaz, F., and Yom-Tov, E. (2013). *Updating users about time critical events. In* Proceedings of the European conference on information retrieval (pp. 483–494). Springer-Verlag.

Guo, Q., Yuan, S., and Agichtein, E. (2011). Detecting success in mobile search from interaction. *In* Proceedings of the ACM SIGIR conference on research and development in information retrieval (pp. 1229–1230). ACM Press.

Guo, Q., Jin, H., Lagun, D., Yuan, S., and Agichtein, E. (2013). Mining touch interaction data on mobile devices to predict web search result relevance. In *Proceedings of the ACM SIGIR conference on research and development in information retrieval* (pp. 153–162). ACM Press.

Guyon, I. and Elisseeff, A. (2003). An introduction to variable and feature selection. *The Journal of Machine Learning Research*, 3, 1157–1182.

Gwizdka, J. (2008). Revisiting search task difficulty: Behavioral and individual difference measures. *Proceedings of the American Society for Information Science and Technology*, 45(1), 1–12.

Gwizdka, J. (2010). Distribution of cognitive load in web search. *Journal of the American Society for Information Science and Technology*, 61(11), 2167–2187.

Gwizdka, J. and Spence, I. (2006). What can searching behavior tell us about the difficulty of information tasks? A study of web navigation. In *Proceedings of the American society for information science and technology*, 43(1), 1–22.

Gwizdka, J. and Spence, I. (2007). Implicit measures of lostness and success in web navigation. *Interacting with Computers*, 19(3), 357–369.

Gwizdka, J. and Zhang, Y. (2015). Differences in eye-tracking measures between visits and revisits to relevant and irrelevant web pages. In *Proceedings of the ACM SIGIR conference on research and development in information retrieval* (pp. 811–814). ACM Press.

Hammond, N. and Allison, L. (1988). Travels around a learning support environment: Rambling, orienteering, or touring? In *Proceedings of the ACM SIGCHI conference on human factors in computing systems* (pp. 269–273). ACM Press.

Han, J., Kamber, M., and Pei, J. (2006). *Data Mining: Concepts and Techniques*. San Francisco, CA: Morgan Kaufmann.

Han, S., Yue, Z., and He, D. (2013). Automatic detection of search tactic in individual information seeking: A hidden markov model approach. In *Proceedings of the iConference* (pp. 712–716).

Hancock-Beaulieu, M. and Walker, S. (1992). An evaluation of automatic query expansion in an online library catalog. *Journal of Documentation*, 48, 406–421.

Hansen, P. and Järvelin, K. (2000). The information seeking and retrieval process at the Swedish patent and registration office. In *Proceedings of the ACM SIGIR Workshop on Patent Retrieval*.

Harding, J. (2013). *Qualitative Data Analysis from Start to Finish*. London, SAGE Publishers.

Harel, M.G.O. and Yom-Tov, E. (2015). Modularity-based query clustering for identifying users sharing a common condition. In *Proceedings the ACM SIGIR conference on research and development in information retrieval* (pp. 819–822). ACM Press.

Harman, D. (1988). Towards interactive query expansion. In *Proceedings of the ACM SIGIR conference on research and development in information retrieval* (pp. 321–331).

Harman, D. (1993). Overview of the first TREC conference. In *Proceedings of the ACM SIGIR conference of research and development in information retrieval* (pp. 36–47).

Harman, D.K. (1997). The TREC conferences. In Jones, K.S. (Ed.), *Readings in Information Retrieval* (pp. 247–256). San Francisco, CA: Morgan Kaufmann Publishers Inc.

Harman, D. (2011). Information retrieval evaluation. *Synthesis Lectures on Information Concepts, Retrieval, and Services*, 3(2), 1–119.

Hart, W., Albarracín, D., Eagly, A.H., Brechan, I., Lindberg, M.J., and Merrill, L. (2009). Feeling validated versus being correct: A meta-analysis of selective exposure to information. *Psychological bulletin*, 135(4), 555.

Haro, A., Essa, I., and Flickner, M. (2000). A non-invasive computer vision system for reliable eye tracking. In *Proceedings of the ACM SIGCHI extended abstracts on human factors in computing systems* (pp. 167–168). ACM Press.

Harpaz, R., Odgers, D., Gaskin, G., DuMouchel, W., Winnenburg, R., Bodenreider, O., Ripple, A., Szarfman, A., Sorbello, A., Horvitz, E., White, R.W., and Shah, N. (2014). A time-indexed reference standard of adverse drug reactions. *Nature Scientific Data*, 1.

Harper, D.J., Coulthard, S., and Yixing, S. (2002). A language modelling approach to relevance profiling for document browsing. In *Proceedings of the joint conference on digital libraries* (pp. 76–83). ACM Press.

Harper, D.J., Koychev, I., Sun, Y. and Pirie, I. (2004). Within-document retrieval: A user-centred evaluation of relevance profiling. *Information Retrieval*, 7(3–4), 265–290.

Harper, F.M., Raban, D., Rafaeli, S., and Konstan, J.A. 2008. Predictors of answer quality in online QandA sites. In *Proceedings of the ACM SIGCHI conference on human factors in computing systems* (pp. 865–874). ACM Press.

Harriman, S. and Patel, J. (2014). The ethics and editorial challenges of internet-based research. *BMC Medicine*, 12(1), 124.

Harrison, C., Tan, D., and Morris, D. (2010). Skinput: Appropriating the body as an input surface. *Proceedings of the ACM SIGCHI conference on human factors in computing systems* (pp. 453–462). ACM Press.

Harrison, W. (2006). Eating your own dog food. *IEEE Software*, 23(3), 5–7.

Hart, S.G. and Staveland, L.E. (1988). Development of NASA-TLX (Task Load Index): Results of empirical and theoretical research. *Advances in psychology*, 52, 139–183.

Harter, S.P. (1992). Psychological relevance and information science. *Journal of the American Society for Information Science*, 43(9), 602.

Hassan, A. (2012). A semi-supervised approach to modeling web search satisfaction. In *Proceedings of the ACM SIGIR conference on research and development in information retrieval* (pp. 275–284). ACM Press.

Hassan, A. and White, R.W. (2012). Task tours: Helping users tackle complex search tasks. In *Proceedings of the ACM CIKM conference on information and knowledge management* (pp. 1885–1889). ACM Press.

Hassan, A., Jones, R., and Klinkner, K.L. (2010). Beyond DCG: User behavior as a predictor of a successful search. In *Proceedings of the ACM WSDM conference on web search and data mining* (pp. 221–230). ACM Press.

Hassan, A., Song, Y., and He, L.W. (2011). A task level metric for measuring web search satisfaction and its application on improving relevance estimation. In *Proceedings of the ACM conference on information and knowledge management* (pp. 125–134). ACM Press.

Hassan, A. and White, R.W. (2013). Personalized models of search satisfaction. In *Proceedings of the ACM CIKM conference on information and knowledge management* (pp. 2009–2018). ACM Press.

Hassan, A., White, R.W., and Wang, Y.M. (2013). Toward self-correcting search engines: Using underperforming queries to improve search. In *Proceedings of the ACM SIGIR conference on research and development in information retrieval* (pp. 263–272). ACM Press.

Hassan, A., White, R.W., Dumais, S.T., and Wang, Y.M. (2014). Struggling or exploring?: Disambiguating long search sessions. In *Proceedings of the ACM WSDM conference on web search and data mining* (pp. 53–62). ACM Press.

Hassan Awadallah, A., White, R.W., Pantel, P., Dumais, S.T., and Wang, Y.M. (2014). Supporting complex search tasks. In *Proceedings of the ACM CIKM conference on information and knowledge management* (pp. 829–838). ACM Press.

Hassan Awadallah, A., Kulkarni, R.G., Ozertem, U. and Jones, R. (2015). Characterizing and predicting voice query reformulation. In *Proceedings of the ACM CIKM conference on information and knowledge management* (in press). ACM Press.

Hauff, C., Kelly, D., and Azzopardi, L. (2010). A comparison of user and system query performance predictions. In *Proceedings of the ACM CIKM conference on information and knowledge management* (pp. 979–988). ACM Press.

Hauff, C., Hiemstra, D., and de Jong, F. (2008). A survey of pre-retrieval query performance predictors. In *Proceedings of the ACM CIKM conference on information and knowledge management* (pp. 1419–1420). ACM Press.

He, B. and Ounis, I. (2004). Inferring query performance using pre-retrieval predictors. In *String Processing and Information Retrieval* (pp. 43–54). Springer Berlin Heidelberg.

REFERENCES

He, D., Göker, A., and Harper, D.J. (2002). Combining evidence for automatic web session identification. *Information Processing and Management*, 38(5), 727–742.

He, J., Larson, M., and De Rijke, M. (2008). Using coherence-based measures to predict query difficulty. In *Advances in Information Retrieval* (pp. 689–694). Springer Berlin Heidelberg.

He, Q., Kifer, D., Pei, J., Mitra, P., and Giles, C.L. (2011). Citation recommendation without author supervision. In *Proceedings of the ACM WSDM conference on web search and data mining* (pp. 755–764). ACM Press.

Healey, J. and Picard, R.W. (1998). Startlecam: a cybernetic wearable camera. In Proceedings of the international symposium on *wearable computers* (pp. 42–49). IEEE.

Hearst, M. (2009). *Search User Interfaces*. Cambridge: Cambridge University Press.

Hearst, M., Elliott, A., English, J., Sinha, R., Swearingen, K., and Yee, K.P. (2002). Finding the flow in web site search. *Communications of the ACM*, 45(9), 42–49.

Hearst, M. A. (1995). TileBars: Visualization of term distribution information in full text information access. In *Proceedings of the ACM SIGCHI conference on human factors in computing systems* (pp. 59–66). ACM Press/Addison-Wesley Publishing Co.

Hearst, M.A. (1997). TextTiling: Segmenting text into multi-paragraph subtopic passages. *Computational linguistics*, 23(1), 33–64.

Hearst, M.A. (1999). User interfaces and visualization. In R. Baeza-Yates and B. Ribeiro-Neto (eds.), *Modern Information Retrieval* (pp. 257–323). Reading, MA: Addison Wesley Longman.

Hearst, M.A. (2000). Next generation web search: Setting our sites. *IEEE Data Engineering Bulletin*, 23(3), 38–48.

Hearst, M.A. (2006). Clustering versus faceted categories for information exploration. *Communications of the ACM*, 49(4), pp. 59–61.

Hearst, M.A. (2011). "Natural" search user interfaces. *Communications of the ACM*, 54(11), 60–67.

Hearst, M.A. (2014a). What's missing from collaborative search? *IEEE Computer*, 3, 58–61.

Hearst, M. A. (2014b). Seeking simplicity in search user interfaces. In *Proceedings of the ACM SIGIR conference on research and development in information retrieval* (pp. 333–334). ACM Press.

Hearst, M.A. and Karadi, C. (1997). Cat-a-Cone: An interactive interface for specifying searches and viewing retrieval results using a large category hierarchy. *ACM SIGIR Forum*, 31(SI), 246–255. ACM Press.

Hearst, M.A. and Plaunt, C. (1993). Subtopic structuring for full-length document access. In *Proceedings of the ACM SIGIR conference on research and development in information retrieval* (pp. 59–68). ACM Press.

Heath, A.P. and White, R.W. (2008). Defection detection: Predicting search engine switching. In *Proceedings of the international conference on the World Wide Web* (pp. 1173–1174). ACM Press.

Hecht, B. and Stephens, M. (2014). A tale of cities: Urban biases in volunteered geographic information. In *Proceedings of the international conference on weblogs and social media*. AAAI Press.

Hecht, B., Teevan, J., Morris, M.R., and Liebling, D.J. (2012). SearchBuddies: Bringing search engines into the conversation. In *Proceedings of the international conference on weblogs and social media* (pp. 138–145). AAAI Press.

Heckerman, D.E., Horvitz, E.J., and Nathwani, B.N. (1989). The Pathfinder system. In *Proceedings of the annual symposium on computer application [sic] in medical care* (pp. 203–207). American Medical Informatics Association.

Heer, J. and Chi, E.H. (2001). Identification of web user traffic composition using multi-modal clustering and information scent. In *Proceedings of the workshop on web mining, siam conference on data mining* (pp. 51–58).

Heitz, G. and Koller, D. (2008). Learning spatial context: Using stuff to find things. *In Computer Vision–ECCV 2008* (pp. 30–43). Springer Berlin Heidelberg.

Hellerstein, J.M., Avnur, R., Chou, A., Hidber, C., Olston, C., Raman, V., and Haas, P.J. (1999). Interactive data analysis: The control project. *Computer*, 32(8), 51–59.

Hendahewa, C. and Shah, C. (2015). Implicit search feature based approach to assist users in exploratory search tasks. *Information Processing and Management*, 51(5), 643–661.

Hendry, D.G. and Harper, D.J. (1997). An informal information-seeking environment. *Journal of the American Society for Information Science*, 48(11), 1036–1048.

Henrion, M., Breese, J.S., and Horvitz, E.J. (1991). Decision analysis and expert systems. *Artificial Intelligence Magazine*, 12(4), 64.

Henze, N., Rukzio, E., and Boll, S. (2012). Observational and experimental investigation of typing behaviour using virtual keyboards for mobile devices. In *Proceedings of the ACM SIGCHI conference on human factors in computing systems* (pp. 2659–2668). ACM Press.

Henzinger, M.R. (2001). Hyperlink analysis for the Web. *Internet Computing*, 5(1), 45–50.

Herder, E. (2005). Characterizations of user Web revisit behavior. In *Proceedings of workshop on adaptivity and user modeling in interactive systems*.

Herlocker, J.L., Konstan, J.A., and Riedl, J. (2000). Explaining collaborative filtering recommendations. In *Proceedings of the ACM CSCW conference on computer supported cooperative work* (pp. 241–250). ACM Press.

Hersh, W., Turpin, A., Price, S., Chan, B., Kramer, D., Sacherek, L., and Olson, D. (2000). Do batch and user evaluations give the same results? In *Proceedings of the ACM SIGIR conference on research and development in information retrieval* (pp. 17–24). ACM Press.

Hess, E.H., and Polt, J.M. (1960). Pupil size as related to interest value of stimuli. *Science*, 132(3423), 349–350.

Hilbert, M. and López, P. (2011). The world's technological capacity to store, communicate, and compute information. *Science*, 332(6025), 60–65.

Hill, J.R. and Hannafin, M.J. (1997). Cognitive strategies and learning from the World Wide Web. *Educational Technology Research and Development*, 45(4), 37–64.

Hill, J.R. (1999). A conceptual framework for understanding information seeking in open-ended information systems. *Educational Technology Research and Development*, 47(1), 5–27.

Hill, W.C., Hollan, J.D., Wroblewski, D., and McCandless, T. (1992). Edit wear and read wear. In *Proceedings of the ACM SIGCHI conference on human factors in computing systems* (pp. 3–9). ACM Press.

Hill, W.C. and Hollan, J.D. (1994). History-enriched digital objects: Prototypes and policy issues. *The Information Society*, 10(2), 139–145.

Hill, W.C., Hollan, J.D., Wroblewski, D., and McCandless, T. (1992). Edit wear and read wear. In *Proceedings of the ACM SIGCHI conference on human factors in computing systems* (pp. 3–9). ACM Press.

Himmelstein, M. (2005). Local search: The internet is the yellow pages. *IEEE Computer*, 38(2), 26–34.

Hinkelmann, K., and Kempthorne, O. (1994). *Design and Analysis of Experiments: Volume 1: Introduction to Experimental Design*. Hoboken, NJ: John Wiley and Sons.

Hinckley, K., Zhao, S., Sarin, R., Baudisch, P., Cutrell, E., Shilman, M., and Tan, D. (2007). InkSeine: In situ search for active note taking. In *Proceedings of the ACM SIGCHI conference on human factors in computing systems* (pp. 251–260). ACM Press.

Hinton, G.E. and Salakhutdinov, R.R. (2006). Reducing the dimensionality of data with neural networks. *Science*, 313(5786), 504–507.

Hirshfield, L.M., Chauncey, K., Gulotta, R., Girouard, A., Solovey, E.T., Jacob, R.J.K., Sassaroli, A., and Fantini, S. (2009). Combining electroencephalograph and functional near infrared spectroscopy to explore users' mental workload. In *Foundations of Augmented Cognition. Neuroergonomics and Operational Neuroscience* (pp. 239–47). Springer Berlin / Heidelberg.

Hirsh-Pasek, K., Golinkoff, R.M., Berk, L.E., and Singer, D. (2008). *A Mandate for Playful Learning in Preschool: Applying the Scientific Evidence*. Oxford: Oxford University Press.

Hoellerer, T., Feiner, S., Terauchi, T., Rashid, G.,and Hallaway, D. (1999). Exploring mars: Developing indoor and outdoor user interfaces to a mobile augmented reality system. *Computers and Graphics*, 23(6), 779–785.

Höller, J., Tsiatsis, V., Mulligan, C., Karnouskos, S., Avesand, S., and Boyle, D. (2014). *From Machine-to-Machine to the Internet of Things: Introduction to a New Age of Intelligence*. Elsevier.

Hölscher, C. and Strube, G. (2000). Web search behavior of Inter-net experts and newbies. *Computer Networks*, 33, 337–346.

Holz, C. and Wilson, A. (2011). Data miming: inferring spatial object descriptions from human gesture. In *Proceedings of the ACM SIGCHI conference on human factors in computing systems* (pp. 811–820). ACM Press.

Hong, J. (2013). Considering privacy issues in the context of Google glass. *Communications of the ACM*, 56(11), 10–11.

Horowitz, A., Jacobson, D., McNichol, T., and Thomas, O. (2007). 101 dumbest moments in business, the year's biggest boors, buffoons, and blunderers. *CNN Money*. http://money.cnn.com/galleries/2007/biz2/0701/gallery.101dumbest_2007/index.html.

Horowitz, D., and Kamvar, S.D. (2010). The anatomy of a large-scale social search engine. In *Proceedings of the international conference on World Wide Web* (pp. 431–440). ACM.

Horvitz, E. (1997). Models of continual computation. In *Proceedings of the AAAI conference on artificial intelligence* (pp. 286–293). AAAI Press.

Horvitz, E. (1998). Continual computation policies for utility-directed prefetching. In *Proceedings of the ACM CIKM conference on information and knowledge management* (pp. 175–184). ACM Press.

Horvitz, E. (1999). Principles of mixed-initiative user interfaces. In *Proceedings of the ACM SIGCHI conference on human factors in computing systems* (pp. 159–166). ACM Press.

Horvitz, E. (2001). Principles and applications of continual computation. *Artificial Intelligence*, 126(1), 159–196.

Horvitz, E. and Apacible, J. (2003). Learning and reasoning about interruption. In *Proceedings of the international conference on multimodal interfaces* (pp. 20–27). ACM Press.

Horvitz, E. and Barry, M. (1995). Display of information for time-critical decision making. In *Proceedings of the conference on uncertainty in artificial intelligence* (pp. 296–305). Morgan Kaufmann Publishers Inc.

Horvitz, E., Dumais, S., and Koch, P. (2004). Learning predictive models of memory landmarks. In *Proceedings of the annual meeting of the cognitive science society* (pp. 583–588). Lawrence Erlbaum Associates.

Horvitz, E., Jacobs, A., and Hovel, D. (1999). Attention-sensitive alerting. In *Proceedings of the conference on uncertainty in artificial intelligence* (pp. 305–313). Morgan Kaufmann Publishers Inc.

Horvitz, E. and Mulligan, D. (2015). Data, privacy, and the greater good. *Science*, 349(6245), 253–255.

Horvitz, E. and Rutledge, G. (1991). Time-dependent utility and action under uncertainty. In *Proceedings of the conference on uncertainty in artificial intelligence* (pp. 151–158). Morgan Kaufmann Publishers Inc.

Horvitz, E. and Seiver, A. (1997). Time-critical action: Representations and application. In *Proceedings of the conference on uncertainty in artificial intelligence* (pp. 250–257). Morgan Kaufmann Publishers Inc.

Horvitz, E. and Shwe, M. (1995). In pursuit of effective handsfree decision support: Coupling bayesian inference. In *Proceedings of the anuual symposium on computer applications in medical care. toward cost-effective clinical computing.*

Howe, D. and Nissenbaum, H. (2008). TrackMeNot: Resisting surveillance in web search. In *On the Identity Trail: Privacy, Anonymity and Identity in a Networked Society.* Oxford: Oxford University Press.

Hoyle, R., Templeman, R., Armes, S., Anthony, D., Crandall, D., and Kapadia, A. (2014). Privacy behaviors of lifeloggers using wearable cameras. In *Proceedings of the ACM international joint conference on pervasive and ubiquitous computing* (pp. 571–582). ACM Press.

Hsieh, G. and Counts, S. (2009). Mimir: A market-based real-time question and answer service. In *Proceedings of the ACM SIGCHI on human factors in computing systems* (pp. 769–778). ACM Press.

Hsieh-Yee, I. (1993). Effects of search experience and subject knowledge on the search tactics of novice and experience users. *Journal of the American Society for Information Science*, 44(3), 161–174.

Hu, V., Stone, M., Pedersen, J., and White, R.W. (2011). Effects of search success on search engine re-use. In *Proceedings of the ACM CIKM conference on information and knowledge management* (pp. 1841–1846). ACM Press.

Huang, J. and Diriye, A. (2012). Web user interaction mining from touch-enabled mobile devices. In *Proceedings of the symposium on human-computer interaction and retrieval.*

Huang, J. and Efthimiadis, E.N. (2009). Analyzing and evaluating query reformulation strategies in web search logs. In *Proceedings of the ACM CIKM conference on information and knowledge management* (pp. 77–86). ACM Press.

Huang, J. and White, R.W. (2010). Parallel browsing behavior on the web. In *Proceedings of the ACM conference on hypertext and hypermedia* (pp. 13–18). ACM Press.

Huang, J., White, R.W., and Buscher, G. (2012). User see, user point: Gaze and cursor alignment in web search. In *Proceedings of the ACM SIGCHI conference on human factors in computing systems* (pp. 1341–1350). ACM Press.

Huang, J., White, R.W., and Dumais, S.T. (2011). No clicks, no problem: Using cursor movements to understand and improve search. In *Proceedings of the ACM SIGCHI conference on human factors in computing systems* (pp. 1225–1234). ACM Press.

Huang, P.S., He, X., Gao, J., Deng, L., Acero, A., and Heck, L. (2013). Learning deep structured semantic models for web search using clickthrough data. In *Proceedings of the ACM CIKM conference on information and knowledge management* (pp. 2333–2338). ACM Press.

Huberman, B.A., Pirolli, P.L., Pitkow, J.E., and Lukose, R.M. (1998). Strong regularities in world wide web surfing. *Science*, 280(5360), 95–97.

Huffman, S.B. and Hochster, M. (2007). How well does result relevance predict session satisfaction?. In *Proceedings of the ACM SIGIR conference on research and development in information retrieval* (pp. 567–574). ACM Press.

Hughes, R.N. (1997). Intrinsic exploration in animals: Motives and measurement. *Behavioural Processes*, 41(3), 213–226.

Huvila, I. and Widén-Wulff, G. (2006). Perspectives to the classification of information interactions: the Cool and Belkin faceted classification scheme under scrutiny. In *Proceedings of the IIiX conference on information interaction in context* (pp. 144–152). ACM Press.

Hunt, R.R. (1995). The subtlety of distinctiveness: What von Restorff really did. *Psychonomic Bulletin and Review*, 2, 105–112.

Hutchinson, T.E., White Jr, K.P., Martin, W.N., Reichert, K.C., and Frey, L.A. (1989). Human-computer interaction using eye-gaze input. *IEEE Transactions on Systems, Man and Cybernetics*, 19(6), 1527–1534.

Hyldegård, J. (2006). Collaborative information behaviour: Exploring Kuhlthau's Information Search Process model in a group-based educational setting. *Information Processing and Management*, 42(1), 276–298.

Hyldegård, J. (2009). Beyond the search process: Exploring group members' information behavior in context. *Information Processing and Management*, 45(1), 142–158.

IBM (2013). What is big data? – Bringing big data to the enterprise. http://www-01.ibm.com/software/in/data/bigdata. Accessed on August 26, 2013.

Inagaki, Y., Sadagopan, N., Dupret, G., Dong, A., Liao, C., Chang, Y., and Zheng, Z. (2010). Session based click features for recency ranking. In *Proceedings of the AAAI conference on artificial intelligence* (pp. 1334–1339). AAAI Press.

Ieong, S., Mishra, N., Sadikov, E., and Zhang, L. (2012). Domain bias in Web search. In *Proceedings of the ACM WSDM conference on web search and data mining* (pp. 413–422). ACM Press.

Ingwersen, P. (1982). Search procedures in the library analysed from the cognitive point of view. *Journal of Documentation*, 38, 165–191.

Ingwersen, P. (1984). A cognitive view of three selected online search facilities. *Online Information Review*, 8(5), 465–492.

Ingwersen, P. and Pejtersen, A.M. (1986). User requirements – empirical research and information systems design. In *Information technology and information use: Towards a unified view of information and information technology* (pp. 111–124). Taylor Graham Publishing.

Ingwersen, P. (1992). *Information Retrieval Interaction*. London: Taylor Graham.

Ingwersen, P. (1994). Polyrepresentation of information needs and semantic entities elements of a cognitive theory for information retrieval interaction. In *Proceedings of the ACM SIGIR conference on research and development in information retrieval* (pp. 101–110). Springer London.

Ingwersen, P. (1996). Cognitive perspectives of information retrieval interaction: Elements of a cognitive IR theory. *Journal of Documentation*, 52(1), 3–50.

Ingwersen, P. (2002). Cognitive perspectives of document representation. In *Proceedings of the COLIS conference on conceptions of library and information science* (pp. 285–300).

Ingwersen, P. and Järvelin, K. (2005). *The Turn: Integration of Information Seeking and Retrieval in Context*. New York: Springer-Verlag.

Intons-Peterson, M.J. and Fournier, J. (1986). External and internal memory aids: When and how often do we use them?. *Journal of Experimental Psychology: General*, 115(3), 267.

Iqbal, S.T. and Horvitz, E. (2007). Disruption and recovery of computing tasks: field study, analysis, and directions. In *Proceedings of the ACM SIGCHI conference on human factors in computing systems* (pp. 677–686). ACM Press.

Iqbal, S.T., Zheng, X.S., and Bailey, B.P. (2004). Task-evoked pupillary response to mental workload in human-computer interaction. In *Proceedings of the ACM SIGCHI extended abstracts on human factors in computing systems* (pp. 1477–1480). ACM Press.

Isaacs, E., Walendowski, A., Whittaker, S., Schiano, D.J., and Kamm, C. (2002). The character, functions, and styles of instant messaging in the workplace. In *Proceedings of the ACM CSCW computer supported cooperative work* (pp. 11–20). ACM Press.

Issacs, E.A. and Clark, H. (1987). References in conversations between experts and novices. *Journal of Experimental Psychology*, 116(1), 26–37.

Ives, B., Olson, M.H., and Baroudi, J.J. (1983). The measurement of user information satisfaction. *Communications of the ACM*, 26(10), 785–793.

Iwayama, M. (2000). Relevance feedback with a small number of relevance judgements: Incremental relevance feedback vs. document clustering. In *Proceedings of the ACM SIGIR conference on research and development in information retrieval* (pp. 10–16). ACM Press.

Jacob, R.J. (1990). What you look at is what you get: Eye movement-based interaction techniques. In *Proceedings of the ACM SIGCHI conference on human factors in computing systems* (pp. 11–18). ACM Press.

Jacques, R.D. (1996). The nature of engagement and its role in hypermedia evaluation and design. Unpublished doctoral dissertation, South Bank University, London.

Jaggi, M. and Sulovsk, M. (2010). A simple algorithm for nuclear norm regularized problems. In *Proceedings of the international conference on machine learning* (pp. 471–478).

Janes, J.W. (1991). Relevance judgements and the incremental presentation of document representations. *Information Processing and Management*, 27(6), 629–646.

Jansen, B.J. (2006a). Search log analysis: What it is, what's been done, how to do it. *Library and Information Science Research*, 28(3), 407–432.

Jansen, B.J. (2006b). The Wrapper: An open source application for logging user-system interactions during search studies. In *Proceedings of the workshop on logging traces of web activity at the World Wide Web conference*.

Jansen, B.J., Booth, D., and Smith, B. (2009). Using the taxonomy of cognitive learning to model online searching. *Information Processing and Management*, 45(6), 643–663.

Jansen, B.J. and Spink, A. (2005). How are we searching the World Wide Web? A comparison of nine search engine transaction logs. *Information Processing and Management*, 42(1), 248–263.

Jansen, B.J., Spink, A., Blakely, C., and Koshman, S. (2007). Defining a session on Web search engines. *Journal of the American Society for Information Science and Technology*, 58(6), 862–871.

Jansen, B.J., Spink, A., and Saracevic, T. (2000). Real life, real users, and real needs: A study and analysis of user queries on the web. *Information Processing and Management*, 36 (2), 207–227.

Jardine, N. and Van Rijsbergen, C.J. (1971). The use of hierarchic clustering in information retrieval. *Information storage and retrieval*, 7(5), 217–240.

Järvelin, K. and Kekäläinen, J. (2002). Cumulated gain-based evaluation of IR techniques. *ACM Transactions on Information Systems* 20(4), 422–446.

Järvelin, K., Price, S.L., Delcambre, L.M., and Nielsen, M.L. (2008). Discounted cumulated gain based evaluation of multiple-query IR sessions. In *Proceedings of the European conference on information retrieval* (pp. 4–15). Springer Berlin Heidelberg.

Jarvis, P., Holford, J., and Griffin, C. (Eds.). (2003). *The Theory and Practice of Learning*. London: Routledge.

Jeh, G. and Widom, J. (2003). Scaling personalized web search. In *Proceedings of the international conference on the World Wide Web* (pp. 271–279). ACM Press.

Jennings, R.B., Nahum, E.M., Olshefski, D.P., Saha, D., Shae, Z.Y., and Waters, C. (2006). A study of internet instant messaging and chat protocols. *IEEE, Network*, 20(4), 16–21. IEEE.

Jensen, C., Farnham, S.D., Drucker, S.M., and Kollock, P. (2000). The effect of communication modality on cooperation in online environments. In *Proceedings of the ACM SIGCHI conference on human factors in computing systems* (pp. 470–477). ACM Press.

Jermaine, C., Aramugam, S., Pol, A., and Dobra, A. (2007). Scalable approximate query processing with the DBO engine. In *Proceedings of the ACM SIGMOD conference on the management of data* (pp. 725–736). ACM Press.

Jiang, J., Hassan, A., Jones, R., Ozertem, U., Zitouni, I., Kulkarni, R.G., and Khan, O.Z. (2015). Automatic online evaluation of intelligent assistants. In *Proceedings of the international conference on the World Wide Web* (pp. 506–516). International World Wide Web Conferences Steering Committee.

Jiang, J., Hassan, A., Shi, X., and White, R.W. (2015). Understanding and predicting graded search satisfaction. In *Proceedings of the ACM WSDM conference on Web search and data mining*. (pp. 57–66). ACM Press.

Jiang, J., He, D., Han, S., Yue, Z., and Ni, C. (2012). Contextual evaluation of query reformulations in a search session by user simulation. In *Proceedings of the ACM CIKM international conference on information and knowledge management* (pp. 2635–2638). ACM Press.

Joachims, T. (2002a). Evaluating retrieval performance using click through data. In *Proceedings of the workshop on mathematical/formal methods in IR* (pp. 12–15).

Joachims, T. (2002b). Optimizing search engines using clickthrough data. In *Proceedings of the ACM SIGKDD conference on knowledge discovery and data mining* (pp. 133–142). ACM Press.

Joachims, T., Freitag, D., and Mitchell, T. (1997). WebWatcher: A tour guide for the world wide web. In *Proceedings of the joint international conference on artificial intelligence* (pp. 770–775).

Joachims, T., Granka, L., Pan, B., Hembrooke, H., and Gay, G. (2005). Accurately interpreting clickthrough data as implicit feedback. In *Proceedings of the ACM SIGIR conference on research and development in information retrieval* (pp. 154–161). ACM Press.

Joachims, T., Granka, L., Pan, B., Hembrooke, H., Radlinski, F., and Gay, G. (2007). Evaluating the accuracy of implicit feedback from clicks and query reformulations in web search. *ACM Transactions on Information Systems*, 25(2), 7.

Johnson, E.A. (1965). Touch display: A novel input/output device for computers. *Electronics Letters* 1(8), 219–220

Johnson, E.A. (1967). Touch displays: A programmed man-machine interface. *Ergonomics*, 10(2), 271–277.

Johnson, H.A., Wagner, M.M., Hogan, W.R., Chapman, W., Olszewski, R.T., Dowling, J., and Barnas, G. (2004). Analysis of Web access logs for surveillance of influenza. *Studies in Health Technology and Informatics*, 107(Pt 2), 1202–1206.

Johnson-Laird, P.N. (1983). *Mental Models: Towards a Cognitive Science of Language, Inference, and Consciousness (No. 6)*. Cambridge, MA: Harvard University Press.

Jones, B.R., Benko, H., Ofek, E., and Wilson, A.D. (2013). IllumiRoom: Peripheral projected illusions for interactive experiences. In *Proceedings of the ACM SIGCHI conference on human factors in computing systems* (pp. 869–878). ACM Press.

Jones, B., Sodhi, R., Murdock, M., Mehra, R., Benko, H., Wilson, A., and Shapira, L. (2014). RoomAlive: Magical experiences enabled by scalable, adaptive projector-camera units. In *Proceedings of the ACM UIST symposium on user interface software and technology* (pp. 637–644). ACM Press.

Jones, R., Hassan, A., and Diaz, F. (2008). Geographic features in web search retrieval. In *Proceedings of the international workshop on geographic information retrieval* (pp. 57–58). ACM Press.

Jones, R. and Klinkner, K.L. (2008). Beyond the session timeout: Automatic hierarchical segmentation of search topics in Query logs. In *Proceedings of the ACM CIKM conference on information and knowledge management* (pp. 699–708). ACM Press.

Jones, R., Kumar, R., Pang, B., and Tomkins, A. (2007). I know what you did last summer: Query logs and user privacy. In *Proceedings of the ACM CIKM conference on information and knowledge management* (pp. 909–914). ACM Press.

Jones, R., Rey, B., Madani, O., and Greiner, W. (2006). Generating query substitutions. In *Proceedings of the international conference on the World Wide Web* (pp. 387–396). ACM Press.

Jones, W. (2007). Personal information management. *Annual Review of Information Science and Technology*, 41(1), 453–504.

Jones, W., Phuwanartnurak, A. J., Gill, R., and Bruce, H. (2005). Don't take my folders away!: Organizing personal information to get things done. In *Proceedings of the ACM SIGCHI extended abstracts on human factors in computing systems* (pp. 1505–1508). ACM Press.

Jøsang, A. (2007). Trust and reputation systems. In Aldini, A. (Ed.), *Foundations of Security Analysis and Design IV* (pp. 209–245). Springer-Verlag.

Jose, J.M., Furner, J., and Harper, D.J. (1998). Spatial querying for image retrieval: a user-oriented evaluation. In *Proceedings of the ACM SIGIR conference on research and development in information retrieval* (pp. 232–240). ACM Press.

Juan, Y.F. and Chang, C.C. (2005). An analysis of search engine switching behavior using click streams. In *Proceedings of the international conference on the World Wide Web* (pp. 1050–1051). ACM Press.

Jung, C.G. (1923). *Psychological Types*. Routledge: London.

Jung, C.G. (1953). *Two Essays on Analytical Psychology*. Routledge: London.

Junker, H., Lukowitz, P., and Troester, G. (2004). Continuous recognition of arm activities with body-worn inertial sensors. In *Proceedings of the International Semantic Web Conference* (pp. 188–189). IEEE.

Jurczyk, P. and Agichtein, E. (2007). Discovering authorities in question answer communities by using link analysis. In *Proceedings of the ACM CIKM conference on nformation and knowledge management* (pp. 919–922). ACM Press.

Kaasten, S. and Greenberg, S. (2000). Designing an integrated bookmark/history system for Web browsing. In *Proceedings of the western computer graphics symposium*.

Kaki, M. (2005). Findex: Search result categories help users when document ranking fails. In *Proceedings of the ACM SIGCHI conference on human factors in computing systems* (pp. 131–140). ACM Press.

Kammerer, Y., Nairn, R., Pirolli, P., and Chi, E.H. (2009). Signpost from the masses: learning effects in an exploratory social tag search browser. In *Proceedings of the ACM SIGCHI conference on human factors in computing systems* (pp. 625–634). ACM Press.

Kanoulas, E., Carterette, B., Clough, P., and Sanderson, M. (2010). Session track overview. In *Proceedings of the text retrieval conference* (p. 11).

Kanoulas, E., Carterette, B., Clough, P.D., and Sanderson, M. (2011). Evaluating multi-query sessions. In *Proceedings of the ACM SIGIR conference on research and development in information retrieval* (pp. 1053–1062). ACM Press.

Kantor, P. (1988). National, language-specific evaluation sites for retrieval systems and interfaces. In *Proceedings of the RIAO conference on computer-assisted information retrieval* (pp. 139–147).

Kantor, P., Bores, E., Melamed, B., Neu, D., Menkov, V., and Kim, M.H. (1999). Ant World. In *Proceedings of the ACM SIGIR conference on research and development in information retrieval* (p. 323). ACM Press.

Kantor, P.B., Boros, E., Melamed, B., Meñkov, V., Shapira, B., and Neu, D.J. (2000). Capturing human intelligence in the net. *Communications of the ACM*, 43(8), 112–115.

Kaplan, K. (2014). Telecommuting: No place like home. *Nature*, 506(7486), 121–123.

Kapoor, A., Burleson, W., and Picard, R.W. (2007). Automatic prediction of frustration. *International Journal of Human-Computer Studies*, 65(8), 724–736.

Kapoor, A., Lee, B., Tan, D., and Horvitz, E. (2010). Interactive optimization for steering machine classification. In *Proceedings of the ACM SIGCHI conference on human factors in computing systems* (pp. 1343–1352). ACM Press.

Kapoor, A., Mota, S., and Picard, R.W. (2001). Towards a learning companion that recognizes affect. In *Proceedings of the AAAI fall symposium* (pp. 2–4).

Kapoor, A. and Picard, R.W. (2005). Multimodal affect recognition in learning environments. In *Proceedings of the ACM international conference on multimedia* (pp. 677–682). ACM Press.

Kaptelinin, V. and Nardi, B. (2006). *Acting with Technology: Activity Theory and Interaction Design*. Cambridge: MIT Press.

Kari, J. and Hartel, J. (2007). Information and higher things in life: Addressing the pleasurable and the profound in information science. *Journal of the American Society for Information Science and Technology*, 58(8), 1131–1147.

REFERENCES

Karimzadehgan, M., White, R.W., and Richardson, M. (2009). Enhancing expert finding using organizational hierarchies. In *Proceedings of the European conference on information retrieval* (pp. 177–188). Springer Berlin Heidelberg.

Karlson, A.K., Iqbal, S.T, Meyers, B., Ramos, G., Lee, K., and Tang, J.C. (2010). Mobile taskflow in context: A screenshot study of smartphone usage. In *Proceedings of the ACM SIGCHI conference on human factors in computing systems* (pp. 2009–2018). ACM Press.

Kashdan, T., Rose, P., and Fincham, F. (2004). Curiosity and exploration: Facilitating positive subjective experiences and personal growth opportunities. *Journal of Personality Assessment*, 82(3), 291–305.

Kato, M.P., White, R.W., Teevan, J., and Dumais, S.T. (2013). Clarifications and question specificity in synchronous social Q&A. In *Proceedings of the ACM SIGCHI extended abstracts on human factors in computing systems* (pp. 913–918). ACM Press.

Kato, M.P., Yamamoto, T., Ohshima, H., and Tanaka, K. (2014). Cognitive search intents hidden behind queries: a user study on query formulations. In *Proceedings of the companion publication of the international conference on the World Wide Web* (pp. 313–314). International World Wide Web Conferences Steering Committee.

Kautz, H., Selman, B., and Milewski, A. (1996). Agent amplified communication. In *Proceedings of the AAAI conference on artificial intelligence* (pp. 3–9). AAAI Press.

Kautz, H., Selman, B., and Shah, M. (1997). Referral-Web: Combining social networks and collaborative filtering. *Communications of the ACM*, 40(3), 63–65.

Kay, J. (2006). Scrutable adaptation: Because we can and must. In *Proceedings of the international conference on adaptive hypermedia and adaptive Web-based systems* (pp. 11–19). Springer Verlag.

Kay, K.N., Naselaris, T., Prenger, R.J., and Gallant, J.L. (2008). Identifying natural images from human brain activity. *Nature*, 452(7185), 352–355.

Kayaaslan, E., Cambazoglu, B.B., Blanco, R., Junqueira, F.P., and Aykanat, C. (2011). Energy-price-driven query processing in multi-center web search engines. In *Proceedings of the ACM SIGIR conference on research and development in information retrieval* (pp. 983–992). ACM Press.

Kazai, G. (2011). In search of quality in crowdsourcing for search engine evaluation. In *Proceedings of the European conference on information retrieval* (pp. 165–176). Springer Berlin Heidelberg.

Keim, D. (2001). Visual exploration of large data sets. *Communications of the ACM*, 44(8), 39–44.

Kekäläinen, J. (2005). Binary and graded relevance in IR evaluations: Comparison of the effects on ranking of IR systems. *Information Processing and Management*, 41(5), 1019–1033.

Kellar, M., Watters, C., and Shepherd, M. (2007). A field study characterizing Web-based information-seeking tasks. *Journal of the American Society for Information Science and Technology*, 58(7), 999–1018.

Kellar, M., Watters, C., and Shepherd, M. (2006). A goal-based classification of web information tasks. In *Proceedings of the American Society for Information Science and Technology*, 43(1), 1–22.

Keller, M., Mühlschlegel, P., and Hartenstein, H. (2013). Search result presentation: supporting post-search navigation by integration of taxonomy data. In *Proceedings of the companion publication of the international conference on the World Wide Web* (pp. 1269–1274). ACM Press.

Keller, R., Wolf, S., Chen, J., Rabinowitz, J., and Mathe, N.A. (1997). Bookmarking service for organizing and sharing URLs. *Computer Networks and ISDN Systems*, 29(8–13), 1103–1114.

Kelley, K. and Preacher, K.J. (2012). On effect size. *Psychological methods*, 17(2), 137.

Kelly, D. (2004). *Understanding implicit feedback and document preference: A naturalistic user study*. Ph.D. Dissertation, Rutgers University.

Kelly, D. (2009). Methods for evaluating interactive information retrieval systems with users. *Foundations and Trends in Information Retrieval*, 3(1–2), 1–224.

Kelly, D. and Belkin, N.J. (2001). Reading time, scrolling and interaction: Exploring sources of user preferences for relevance feedback during interactive information retrieval. In *Proceedings of the ACM SIGIR conference on research and development in information retrieval* (pp. 408–409). ACM Press.

Kelly, D. and Belkin, N.J. (2004). Display time as implicit feedback: Understanding task effects. In *Proceedings of the ACM SIGIR conference on research and development in information retrieval* (pp. 377–384). ACM Press.

Kelly, D. and Cool, C. (2002). The effects of topic familiarity on information search behavior. In *Proceedings of the joint conference on digital libraries* (pp. 74–75).

Kelly, D., Cushing, A., Dostert, M., Niu, X., and Gyllstrom, K. (2010). Effects of popularity and quality on the usage of query suggestions during information search. In *Proceedings of the ACM SIGCHI conference on human factors in computing systems* (pp. 45–54). ACM Press.

Kelly, D., Dollu, V.D., and Fu, X. (2005). The loquacious user: A document-independent source of terms for query expansion. In *Proceedings of the ACM SIGIR conference on research and development in information retrieval* (pp. 457–464). ACM Press.

Kelly, D. and Gyllstrom, K. (2011). An examination of two delivery modes for interactive search system experiments: Remote and laboratory. In *Proceedings of the ACM SIGCHI conference on human factors in computing systems* (pp. 1531–1540). ACM Press.

Kelly, D. and Teevan, J. (2003). Implicit feedback for inferring user preference. *SIGIR Forum*, 37 (2), 18–28.

Kelly, G.A. (1963). *Theory of Personality: The Psychology of Personal Constructs*. New York: W.W. Norton.

Kemp, C. and Ramamohanarao, K. (2002). Long-term learning for web search engines. In *Proceedings of the European conference on principles and practice of knowledge discovery in databases* (pp. 263–274).

Kerne, A., Koh, E., Smith, S., Webb, A., and Dworaczyk, B. (2008). combinFormation: Mixed-initiative composition of image and text surrogates promotes information discovery. *ACM Transactions on Information Systems*, 27(1), 5. ACM Press.

Kerne, A., Webb, AM., Smith, S.M., Linder, R., Lupfer, N., Qu, Y., Moeller, J., and Damaraju, S. (2014). Using metrics of curation to evaluate information-based ideation. *ACM Transactions on Computer-Human Interaction*, 21(3), 14. ACM Press.

Keskustalo, H., Järvelin, K., and Pirkola, A. (2008). Evaluating the effectiveness of relevance feedback based on a user simulation model: Effects of a user scenario on cumulated gain value. *Information Retrieval*, 11(3), 209–228.

Khan, K. and Locatis, C. (1998). Searching through the cyber-space: The effects of link display and link density on information retrieval from hypertext on the World Wide Web. *Journal of the American Society for Information Science and Technlogy*, 49(2), 176–182.

Kiciman, E. (2012). OMG, I have to tweet that! A study of factors that influence tweet rates. In *Proceedings of the international AAAI conference on weblogs and social media*.

Kiciman, E. and Richardson, M. (2015). Towards decision support and goal achievement: Identifying action-outcome relationships from social media. In *Proceedings of the ACM SIGKDD conference on knowledge discovery and data mining* (pp. 547–556). ACM Press.

Kim, J. (2006). *Task as a predictable indicator of information seeking behavior on the Web*. Ph.D. Disseration, Rutgers University.

Kim, J., Oard, D.W., and Romanik, K. (2000). *Using Implicit Feedback for User Modelling in Internet and Intranet Searching*. College Park: College of Library and Information Services, University of Maryland.

Kim, Y.M. and Rieh, S.Y. (2005). Dual-task performance as a measure for mental effort in library searching and web searching. In *Proceedings of the annual meeting of the American society for information science and technology*, 42(1).

Kim, J.Y., Collins-Thompson, K., Bennett, P.N., and Dumais, S.T. (2012). Characterizing web content, user interests, and search behavior by reading level and topic. In *Proceedings of the ACM WSDM international conference on Web search and data mining* (pp. 213–222). ACM Press.

Kim, S. and Soergel, D. (2005). Selecting and measuring task characteristics as independent variables. In *Proceedings of the American society for information science and technology*, 42(1).

Kim, Y., Hassan, A., White, R.W., and Wang, Y.M. (2013). Playing by the rules: Mining query associations to predict search performance. In *Proceedings of the ACM WSDM conference on web search and data mining* (pp. 133–142). ACM Press.

Kim, Y., Hassan, A., White, R.W., and Zitouni, I. (2014). Modeling dwell time to predict click-level satisfaction. In *Proceedings of the ACM WSDM conference on web search and data mining* (pp. 193–202). ACM Press.

Kim, K., Turner, S.A., and Pérez-Quiñones, M.A. (2009). Requirements for electronic note taking systems: A field study of note taking in university classrooms. *Education and Information Technologies*, 14(3), 255–283.

King, G. (2011). Ensuring the data-rich future of the social sciences. *Science*, 331(6018), 719–721.

Kintsch, W. (1998). *Comprehension: A Paradigm for Cognition*. New York: Cambridge University Press.

Kirk, T. (1974). Problems in library instruction in four-year colleges. In Lubans, J., Jr. (Ed.), *Educating the Library User*, New York: R. R. Bowker (pp. 83–103).

Kiseleva, J., Crestan, E., Brigo, R., and Ditte, R. (2014). Modelling and detecting changes in user satisfaction. In *Proceedings of the ACM CIKM conference on information and knowledge management* (pp. 1449–1458). ACM Press.

Kittur, A., Chi, E.H., and Suh, B. (2008). Crowdsourcing user studies with Mechanical Turk. In *Proceedings of the ACM SIGCHI conference on human factors in computing systems* (pp. 453–456). ACM Press.

Kitzinger, J. (1995). Qualitative research. Introducing focus groups. *British medical journal*, 311(7000), 299.

Klein, G., Moon, B. and Hoffman, R.F. (2006). Making sense of sensemaking I: Alternative perspectives. *IEEE Intelligent Systems*, 21(4), 70–73. IEEE.

Klein, G., Orasanu, J., Calderwood, R., and Zsambok, C.E. (1993). *Decision Making in Action: Models and Methods*: Norwood, NJ: Ablex Publishing Co.

Kleinberg, J. (2000). The small-world phenomenon: An algorithmic perspective. In *Proceedings of the ACM symposium on theory of computing* (pp. 163–170). ACM Press.

Kleinberg, J.M. (1999). Authoritative sources in a hyperlinked environment. *Journal of the ACM*, 46(5), 604–632. ACM Press.

Klepeis, N.E., William, C.N., Wayne, R.O., John, P.R., Andy M.T., Paul, S., Joseph V.B., Stephen C.H., and William H.E. (2001). The national human activity pattern survey. *Journal of Exposure Analysis and Environmental Epidemiology*, 11(3), 231–252.

Knight, F.H. (1924). Some fallacies in the interpretation of social cost. *The Quarterly Journal of Economics*, 38(4), 582–606.

Kobsa, A. (2007). Privacy-enhanced personalization. *Communications of the ACM*, 50(8), 24–33.

Kodagoda, N. and Wong, B.L.W. (2008). Effects of low and high literacy on user performance in information search and retrieval. In *Proceedings of the British HCI group annual conference on people and computers* (pp. 173–181). British Computer Society.

Koenemann, J. and Belkin, N.J. (1996). A case for interaction: A study of interactive information retrieval behavior and effectiveness. In *Proceedings of the ACM SIGCHI conference on human factors in computing systems* (pp. 205–212). ACM Press.

Kohavi, R., Henne, R.M., and Sommerfield, D. (2007). Practical guide to controlled experiments on the web: Listen to your customers not to the hippo. In *Proceedings of the ACM SIGKDD conference on knowledge discovery and data mining* (pp. 959–967). ACM Press.

Kohavi, R. and Longbotham, R. (2007). Online experiments: Lessons learned. *Computer*, 40(9), 103–105.

Kohavi, R., Longbotham, R., Sommerfield, D., and Henne, R.M. (2009). Controlled experiments on the web: Survey and practical guide. *Data Mining and Knowledge Discovery*, 18(1), 140–181.

Kohavi, R., Longbotham, R., and Walker, T. (2010). Online experiments: Practical lessons. *Computer*, 43(9), 82–85.

Kohavi, R. and Longbotham, R. (2011). Unexpected results in online controlled experiments. *ACM SIGKDD Explorations Newsletter*, 12(2), 31–35.

Kohn, A. (1989). *Fortune or Failure: Missed Opportunities and Chance Discoveries*. Cambridge, MA: Blackwell.

Kolb, D. (1985). *Learning Style Inventory: Self Scoring Inventory and Interpretation Booklet*. Boston, MA: McBer and Company.

Komlodi, A. (2002). *Search History for User Support in Information-Seeking Interfaces*. Unpublished doctoral dissertation, University of Maryland, College Park.

Komlodi, A. (2002). The role of interaction histories in mental model building and knowledge sharing in the legal domain. *Journal of Universal Computer Science*, 8(5), 557–566.

Komlodi, A., Soergel, D., and Marchionini, G. (2006). Search histories for user support in user interfaces. *Journal of the American Society for Information Science and Technology*, 57(6), 803–807.

Komogortsev, O.V., Ryu, Y.S., Koh, D.H., and Gowda, S.M. (2009). Instantaneous saccade driven eye gaze interaction. In *Proceedings of the international conference on advances in computer entertainment technology* (pp. 140–147). ACM Press.

Kong, W., Aktolga, E., and Allan, J. (2013). Improving passage ranking with user behavior information. In *Proceedings of the ACM CIKM conference on information and knowledge management* (pp. 1999–2008). ACM Press.

Konstan, J.A. and Riedl, J. (2012). Recommender systems: From algorithms to user experience. In *Proceedings of the conference on user modeling and user-adapted interaction* (pp. 1–23). Springer Verlag.

Kopalle, P.K. and Neslin, S. (2001). The economic viability of frequency reward programs in a strategic competitive environment. Tuck School of Business at Dartmouth Working Paper (01–02).

Korfhage, R.R. (1991). To see or not to see – is that the query? In *Proceedings of the ACM SIGIR conference on research and development in information retrieval* (pp. 134–141), ACM Press.

Korolova, A., Kenthapadi, K., Mishra, N., and Ntoulas, A. (2009). Releasing search queries and clicks privately. In *Proceedings of the international conference on World Wide Web* (pp. 171–180). ACM Press.

Kotov, A., Bennett, P. N., White, R. W., Dumais, S.T., and Teevan, J. (2011). Modeling and analysis of cross-session search tasks. In *Proceedings of the ACM SIGIR conference on research and development in information retrieval* (pp. 5–14). ACM Press.

Kozierok, R. and Maes, P. (1993). A learning interface agent for scheduling meetings. In *Proceedings of the ACM IUI conference on intelligent user interfaces* (pp. 81–88). ACM Press.

REFERENCES

Kraft, R. and Zien, J. (2004). Mining anchor text for query refinement. In *Proceedings of the international conference on the World Wide Web* (pp. 666–674).

Kramer, A.D., Guillory, J.E., and Hancock, J.T. (2014). Experimental evidence of massive-scale emotional contagion through social networks. In *Proceedings of the National Academy of Sciences*, 111(24), 8788–8790.

Krathwohl, D.R. (2002). A revision of Bloom's taxonomy: An overview. *Theory into practice*, 41(4), 212–218.

Krause, A. and Horvitz, E. (2008). A utility-theoretic approach to privacy and personalization. In *Proceedings of the AAAI conference on artificial intelligence* (pp. 1181–1188). AAAI Press.

Krebs, J.R. and Davies, N.B. (1989). *An Introduction to Behavioral Ecology*. Oxford: Blackwell Scientific Publications.

Krueger, R.A. (2009). *Focus Groups: A Practical Guide for Applied Research*. Thousand Oaks, CA: Sage.

Krumm, J. and Horvitz, E. (2006). Predestination: Inferring destinations from partial trajectories. In *Proceedings of the conference on ubiquitous computing* (pp. 243–260). Springer Berlin Heidelberg.

Krumm, J. and Rouhana, D. (2013). Placer: Semantic place labels from diary data. In *Proceedings of the ACM international joint conference on pervasive and ubiquitous computing* (pp. 163–172). ACM.

Kuhlthau, C. (1988). Developing a model of the library search process: Cognitive and affective aspects. *Retrieval Quarterly*, 28(2), 232–242.

Kuhlthau, C. (1991). Inside the search process: Information seeking from the user's perspective. *Journal of the American Society for Information Science*, 42(5), 361–371.

Kuhlthau, C.C. (1993). A principle of uncertainty for information seeking. *Journal of documentation*, 49(4), 339–355.

Kuhn, T.S. (1970). *The Structure of Scientific Revolutions*. Chicago: Chicago University Press.

Kules, B. (2005). Supporting creativity with search tools. In *Proceedings of NSF Workshop on Creativity Support Tools* (pp. 53–64).

Kules, B., and Shneiderman, B. (2008). Users can change their web search tactics: Design guidelines for categorized overviews. *Information Processing and Management*, 44(2), 463–484.

Kulkarni, A., Teevan, J., Svore, K.M., and Dumais, S.T. (2011). Understanding temporal query dynamics. In *Proceedings of the ACM WSDM conference on web search and data mining* (pp. 167–176). ACM Press.

Kumar, M., Garfinkel, T., Boneh, D., and Winograd, T. (2007). Reducing shoulder-surfing by using gaze-based password entry. In *Proceedings of the symposium on usable privacy and security* (pp. 13–19). ACM Press.

Kumar, R., Novak, J., Pang, B., and Tomkins, A. (2007). On anonymizing query logs via token-based hashing. In *Proceedings of the international conference on the World Wide Web* (pp. 629–638).

Kumar, V., Furuta, R., and Allen, R. (1998). Metadata visualization for digital libraries: Interactive timeline editing and review. In *Proceedings of the ACM conference on digital libraries* (pp. 126–133).

Kumaran, G. and Carvalho, V.R. (2009). Reducing long queries using query quality predictors. In *Proceedings of the ACM SIGIR conference on research and development in information retrieval* (pp. 564–571). ACM Press.

Kumaran, G., Jones, R., and Madani, O. (2005). Biasing web search results for topic familiarity. In *Proceedings of the ACM conference on information and knowledge management* (pp. 271–272). ACM Press.

Kumpulainen, S. and Järvelin, K. (2010). Information interaction in molecular medicine: Integrated use of multiple channels. In *Proceedings of the IIiX symposium on information interaction in context* (pp. 95–104). ACM Press.

Kuniavsky, M. (2003). *Observing the User Experience: A Practioner's Guide for User Research*. San Francisco, CA: Morgan Kaufman.

Kurtenbach, G. and Hulteen, E.A. (1990). Gestures in human-computer communication. In Laurel, B. (ed.) *The art of human-computer interface design* (pp. 309–317). Boston, MA: Addison-Wesley Longman Publishing Co.

Kwasnik, B. (1989). How a personal document's intended use or purpose affects its classification in an office. *ACM SIGIR Forum*, 23(SI), 207–210. ACM Press.

Kwasnik, B.H. (1999). The role of classification in knowledge representation and discovery. *Library Trends*, 48(1), 22–47.

Lagergren, E. and Over, P. (1998). Comparing interactive information retrieval systems across sites: the TREC-6 interactive track matrix experiment. In *Proceedings of the ACM SIGIR conference on research and development in information retrieval* (pp. 164–172). ACM Press.

Lagun, D. and Agichtein, E. (2011). Viewser: Enabling large-scale remote user studies of web search examination and interaction. In *Proceedings of the ACM SIGIR conference on research and development in information retrieval* (pp. 365–374). ACM Press.

Lagun, D., Ageev, M., Guo, Q., and Agichtein, E. (2014a). Discovering common motifs in cursor movement data for improving web search. In *Proceedings of the ACM WSDM conference on Web search and data mining* (pp. 183–192). ACM Press.

Lagun, D., Hsieh, C. H., Webster, D., and Navalpakkam, V. (2014b). Towards better measurement of attention and satisfaction in mobile search. In *Proceedings of the ACM SIGIR conference on research and development in information retrieval* (pp. 113–122). ACM Press.

Lalmas, M., O'Brien, H., and Yom-Tov, E. (2014). Measuring user engagement. *Synthesis Lectures on Information Concepts, Retrieval, and Services*, 6(4), 1–132.

Lalmas, M. and Ruthven, I. (1998). Representing and retrieving structured documents using the dempster-shafer theory of evidence: modelling and evaluation. *Journal of Documentation*, 54(5), 529–565.

Lam, H., Russell, D., Tang, D., and Munzner, T. (2007). Session viewer: Visual exploratory analysis of web session logs. In *Proceedings of the IEEE symposium on visual analytics science and technology* (pp. 147–154). IEEE.

Lam-Adesina, A.M. and Jones, G.J.F. (2001). Applying summarization techniques for term selection in relevance feedback. In *Proceedings of the ACM SIGIR conference on research and development in information retrieval* (pp. 1–9). ACM Press.

Lambert, D. and Pregibon, D. (2007). More bang for their bucks: Assessing new features for online advertisers. In *Proceedings of the international workshop on data mining and audience intelligence for advertising* (pp. 7–15). ACM Press.

Landauer, T.K. (1996). *The Trouble with Computers*. Cambridge, MA: The MIT Press.

Landauer, T.K. (2002). On the computational basis of learning and cognition: Arguments from LSA. *The Psychology of Learning and Motivation*, 41, 43–84.

Landauer, T., Egan, D., Remde, J., Lesk, M., Lochbaum, C., and Ketchum, D. (1993). Enhancing the usability of text through computer delivery and formative evaluation: the SuperBook project. In McKnight, C., Dillon, A., and Richardson, J. (Eds.) *Hypertext: A Psychological Perspective* (pp. 71–136). New York: Ellis Horwood.

Landgren, J. (2006). Making action visible in time-critical work. In *Proceedings of the ACM SIGCHI conference on human factors in computing systems* (pp. 201–210). ACM.

Landy, F.J., Rastegary, H., Thayer, J., and Colvin, C. (1991). Time urgency: The construct and its measurement. *Journal of Applied Psychology*, 76(5), 644.

Lanier, J. (2013). *Who owns the future?* New York: Simon and Schuster.

Larsen, J.T., Norris, C.J., and Cacioppo, J.T. (2003). Effects of positive and negative affect on electromyographic activity over zygomaticus major and corrugator supercilii. *Psychophysiology*, 40(5), 776–785.

Lashkari, T., Metral, M., and Maes, P. (1994). Collaborative interface agents. In *Proceedings of the AAAI conference on artificial intelligence* (pp. 444–449). AAAI Press.

Lauckner, C. and Hsieh, G. (2013). The presentation of health-related search results and its impact on negative emotional outcomes. In *Proceedings of the ACM SIGCHI conference on human factors in computing systems* (pp. 333–342). ACM Press.

Laxman, S., Tankasali, V., and White, R.W. (2008). Stream prediction using a generative model based on frequent episodes in event sequences. In *Proceedings of the ACM SIGKDD conference on knowledge discovery and data mining* (pp. 453–461). ACM Press.

Lazer, D., Kennedy, R., King, G., and Vespigiani, A. (2014). The parable of google flu: Traps in big data analysis. *Science*, 343(6176), 1203–1205.

Lazer, D., Pentland, A.S., Adamic, L., Aral, S., Barabasi, A.L., Brewer, D., and Van Alstyne, M. (2009). Life in the network: The coming age of computational social science. *Science*, 323(5915), 721.

Lazonder, A.W., Biemans, H.J.A., and Worpeis, I.G.J.H. (2000). Differences between novice and experienced users in searching information on the World Wide Web. *Journal of the American Society for Information Science and Technology*, 51(6), 576–581.

Lebanon, G. (2014). Challenges and new directions in recommendation systems. Practice and experience talk at the conference on web search and data mining.

Lee, U., Liu, Z., and Cho, J. (2005). Automatic identification of user goals in web search. In *Proceedings of the international conference on the World Wide Web* (pp. 391–400). ACM.

Lehmann, S., Schwanecke, U., and Dörner, R. (2010). Interactive visualization for opportunistic exploration of large document collections. *Information Systems*, 35(2), 260–269.

Lehmann, J., Lalmas, M., Yom-Tov, E., and Dupret, G. (2012). Models of user engagement. In *Proceedings of the conference on user modeling, adaptation, and personalization* (pp. 164–175). Springer Berlin Heidelberg.

Lei, Y., Uren, V., and Motta, E. (2006). Semsearch: A search engine for the semantic web. In *Proceedings of the international conference on knowledge engineering and knowledge management* (pp. 238–245). Springer Berlin Heidelberg.

Leigh, R.J. and Zee, D.S. (1999). *The Neurology of Eye Movements (Vol. 90).* New York: Oxford University Press.

Leiva, L. (2011). Restyling website design via touch-based interactions. *In Proceedings of Mobile HCI* (pp. 599–604).

Leiva, L.A. and Huang, J. (2015). Building a better mousetrap: Compressing mouse cursor activity for web analytics. *Information Processing and Management*, 51(2), 114–129.

Lesk, M., Cutting, D., Pedersen, J., Noreault, T., and Koll, M. (1997). Real life information retrieval (panel): commercial search engines. *ACM SIGIR Forum*, 31(SI), 333. ACM Press.

Leskovec, J., Dumais, S., and Horvitz, E. (2007). Web projections: Learning from contextual subgraphs of the web. In *Proceedings of the international conference on the World Wide Web* (pp. 471–480). ACM Press.

Lettner, F. and Holzmann, C. (2012). Heat maps as a usability tool for multi-touch interaction in mobile applications. In *Proceedings of the international conference on mobile and ubiquitous multimedia* (p. 49). ACM Press.

Leuthardt, E.C., Schalk, G., Wolpaw, J.R., Ojemann, J.G., and Moran, D.W. (2004). A brain–computer interface using electrocorticographic signals in humans. *Journal of Neural Engineering*, 1(2), 63.

Leiva, L.A. (2011). Restyling website design via touch-based interactions. In *Proceedings of the international conference on human computer interaction with mobile devices and services* (pp. 599–604). ACM Press.

Lewandowsky, S., Ecker, U., Seifert, C.M., Schwarz, N., and Cook, J. (2012). Misinformation and its correction continued influence and successful debiasing. *Psychological Science in the Public Interest*, 13(3), 106–131.

Lewis, M. (2004). The influence of loyalty programs and short-term promotions on customer retention. *Journal of Marketing Research*, 41(3), 281–292.

Li, D., Babcock, J., and Parkhurst, D. (2006). openEyes: A low-cost head-mounted eye-tracking solution. In *Proceedings of the symposium on eye tracking research and applications* (pp. 95–100). ACM Press.

Li, I., Forlizzi, J., and Dey, A. (2010). Know thyself: Monitoring and reflecting on facets of one's life. In *Proceedings of the ACM SIGCHI extended abstracts on human factors in computing systems* (pp. 4489–4492). ACM Press.

Li, I., Nichols, J., Lau, T., Drews, C., and Cypher, A. (2010). Here's what i did: Sharing and reusing web activity with ActionShot. In *Proceedings of the ACM SIGCHI conference on human factors in computing systems* (pp. 723–732). ACM Press.

Li, J., Huffman, S., and Tokuda, A. (2009). Good abandonment in mobile and PC internet search. In *Proceedings of the ACM SIGIR conference on research and development in information retrieval* (pp. 43–50). ACM Press.

Li, L., Chen, S., Kleban, J., and Gupta, A. (2015). Counterfactual estimation and optimization of click metrics in search engines: a case study. In *Proceedings of the international conference on the World Wide Web companion* (pp. 929–934). International World Wide Web Conferences Steering Committee.

Li, L., Chu, W., Langford, J., and Wang, X. (2011). Unbiased offline evaluation of contextual-bandit-based news article recommendation algorithms. In *Proceedings of the ACM WSDM conference on Web search and data mining* (pp. 297–306). ACM Press.

Li, Y. (2010). Gesture search: A tool for fast mobile data access. In *Proceedings of the ACM UIST symposium on user interface software and technology* (pp. 87–96). ACM Press.

Liang, R.H. and Ouhyoung, M. (1998). A real-time continuous gesture recognition system for sign language. In *Proceedings of IEEE international conference on automatic face and gesture recognition* (pp. 558–567). IEEE.

Liao, Z., Song, Y., He, L.W., and Huang, Y. (2012). Evaluating the effectiveness of search task trails. In *Proceedings of the international conference on the World Wide Web* (pp. 489–498). ACM Press.

Licklider, J.C.R. (1960). Man–computer symbiosis. *IRE Transactions on Human Factors in Electronics*, v. HFE-1, pp. 4–11.

Lieberman, H. (1995). Letizia: An agent that assists web browsing. In *Proceedings of the international joint conference on artificial intelligence* (pp. 475–480).

Lieberman, H., Fry, C., and Weitzman, L. (2001). Exploring the web with reconnaissance agents. *Communications of the ACM*, 44(7), 69–75.

Liebling, D.J., Bennett, P.N., and White, R.W. (2012). Anticipatory search: Using context to initiate search. In *Proceedings of the ACM SIGIR conference on research and development in information retrieval* (pp. 1035–1036). ACM Press.

Lin, J. and Smucker, M.D. (2008). How do users find things with PubMed? Towards automatic utility evaluation with user simulations. In *Proceedings of the ACM SIGIR conference on research and development in information retrieval* (pp. 19–26). ACM Press.

Ling, K., Beenen, G., Ludford, P., Wang, X., Chang, K., Li, X, Cosley, D., Frankowski, D., Terveen, L., Rashid, A.M., Resnick, P., and Kraut, R. (2005). Using social psychology to motivate contributions to online communities. *Journal of Computer-Mediated Communication*, 10(4), 10.

Liu, B. and Oard, D.W. (2006). One-sided measures for evaluating ranked retrieval effectiveness with spontaneous conversational speech. In *Proceedings of the ACM SIGIR conference on research and development in information retrieval* (pp. 673–674). ACM Press.

Liu C., White, R.W., and Dumais, S. (2010). Understanding web browsing behaviors through Weibull analysis of dwell time. In *Proceedings of the ACM SIGIR conference on research and development in information retrieval* (pp. 379–386).

Liu, F., Yu, C., and Meng, W. (2002). Personalized web search by mapping user queries to categories. In *Proceedings of the ACM CIKM conference on information and knowledge management* (pp. 558–565). ACM Press.

Liu, F., Yu, C., and Meng, W. (2004). Personalized web search for improving retrieval effectiveness. *IEEE Transactions on Knowledge and Data Engineering*, 16(1), 28–40.

Liu, J., Belkin, N.J., Zhang, X., and Yuan, X. (2013). Examining users' knowledge change in the task completion process. *Information Processing and Management*, 49(5), 1058–1074.

Liu, J., Cole, M.J., Liu, C., Bierig, R., Gwizdka, J., Belkin, N.J., Zhang, J., and Zhang, X. (2010a). Search behaviors in different task types. In *Proceedings of the Joint Conference on Digital Libraries* (pp. 69–78).

Liu, J., Gwizdka, J., Liu, C., and Belkin, N.J. (2010b). Predicting task difficulty for different task types. In *Proceedings of the American Society for Information Science and Technology*, 47(1), 1–10.

Liu, Q., Agichtein, E., Dror, G., Maarek, Y., and Szpektor, I. (2012). When web search fails, searchers become askers: Understanding the transition. In *Proceedings of the ACM SIGIR conference on research and development in information retrieval* (pp. 801–810). ACM Press.

Liu, T.Y. (2009). Learning to rank for information retrieval. *Foundations and Trends in Information Retrieval*, 3(3), 225–331.

Liu, X., Croft, W.B., and Koll, M. (2005). Finding experts in community-based question-answering services. In *Proceedings of the ACM CIKM conference on information and knowledge management* (pp. 315–316). ACM Press.

Liu, Y., Bian, J., and Agichtein, E. (2008). Predicting information seeker satisfaction in community question answering. In *Proceedings of the ACM SIGIR conference on research and development in information retrieval* (pp. 483–490). ACM Press.

Livne, A., Gokuldas, V., Teevan, J., Dumais, S.T., and Adar, E. (2014). CiteSight: Supporting contextual citation recommendation using differential search. In *Proceedings of the ACM SIGIR conference on research and development in information retrieval* (pp. 807–816). ACM Press.

Loewenstein, G. (1994). The psychology of curiosity: A review and reinterpretation. *Psychological Bulletin*, 116(1), 75–98.

Loizides, F. and Buchanan, G.R. (2008). The myth of find: User behaviour and attitudes towards the basic search feature. In *Proceedings of the Joint Conference on Digital Libraries* (pp. 48–51).

London, S. (1995). *Collaboration and Community*. Retrieved from http://scottlondon.com/reports/ppcc.html

Lopatovska, I. and Arapakis, I. (2011). Theories, methods and current research on emotions in library and information science, information retrieval and human–computer interaction. *Information Processing and Management*, 47(4), 575–592.

Lopez, S.J. and Snyder, C.R. (2011). *The Oxford Handbook of Positive Psychology*. Oxford: Oxford University Press.

Lorigo, L., Haridasan, M., Brynjarsdóttir, H., Xia, L., Joachims, T., Gay, G., Granka, L. A., Pellacini, F., and Pan, B. (2008). Eye tracking and online search: Lessons learned and challenges ahead. *Journal of the American Society for Information Science and Technology*, 59(7), 1041–1052.

Low, Y., Agarwal, D., and Smola, A.J. (2011). Multiple domain user personalization. In *Proceedings of the ACM SIGKDD conference on knowledge discovery and data mining* (pp. 123–131). ACM Press.

Lowe, D.G. (1999). Object recognition from local scale-invariant features. In *Proceedings of the IEEE conference on computer vision* (pp. 1150–1157). IEEE.

Lucchese, C., Orlando, S., Perego, R., Silvestri, F., and Tolomei, G. (2013a). Modeling and predicting the task-by-task behavior of search engine users. In *Proceedings of the conference on open research areas in information retrieval* (pp. 77–84).

Lucchese, C., Orlando, S., Perego, R., Silvestri, F., and Tolomei, G. (2013b). Discovering tasks from search engine query logs. *ACM Transactions on Information Systems*, 31(3), 14.

Ludford, P.J., Cosley, D., Frankowski, D., and Terveen, L. (2004). Think different: Increasing online community participation using uniqueness and group dissimilarity. In *Proceedings of ACM SIGCHI conference on human factors in computing systems* (pp. 631–638). ACM Press.

Ludford, P. J., Priedhorsky, R., Reily, K., and Terveen, L. (2007). Capturing, sharing, and using local place information. In *Proceedings of ACM SIGCHI conference on human factors in computing systems* (pp. 1235–1244). ACM Press.

Lymberopoulos, D., Zhao, P., Konig, C., Berberich, K., and Liu, J. (2011). Location-aware click prediction in mobile local search. In *Proceedings of the ACM CIKM conference on information and knowledge management* (pp. 413–422). ACM Press.

Lynch, K. (1960). *The Image of the City*. Cambridge MA: MIT Press.

Lv, Y., Lymberopoulos, D., and Wu, Q. (2012). An exploration of ranking heuristics in mobile local search. In *Proceedings of the ACM SIGIR conference on research and development in information retrieval* (pp. 295–304). ACM Press.

MacArthur, R.H. and Pianka, E.R. (1966). Optimal use of a patchy environment. *The American Naturalist*, 100, 603–609.

Macdonald, C. and White, R.W. (2009). Usefulness of click-through data in expert search. In *Proceedings of the ACM SIGIR conference on research and development in information retrieval* (pp. 816–817). ACM Press.

MacKay, D. (1960). What makes a question? *The Listener*, May 5, 789–790.

MacKay, D.M. (1969). *Information Mechanism and Meaning*. Boston, MA: MIT Press.

MacKenzie, I.S. (1992). Fitts' law as a research and design tool in human-computer interaction. *Human-Computer Interaction*, 7(1), 91–139.

MacKenzie, I.S. and Zhang, X. (2008). Eye typing using word and letter prediction and a fixation algorithm. In *Proceedings of the symposium on eye tracking research and applications* (pp. 55–58). ACM Press.

Mackinlay, J.D., Rao, R., and Card, S.K. (1995). An organic user interface for searching citation links. In *Proceedings of the ACM SIGCHI conference on, human factors in computing systems* (pp. 67–73). ACM Press.

MacQueen, J.B. (1967). Some methods for classification and analysis of multivariate observations. In *Proceedings of the symposium on math, statistics, and probability* (pp. 281–297).

Madsen, M., El Kaliouby, R., Goodwin, M., and Picard, R. (2008). Technology for just-in-time in-situ learning of facial affect for persons diagnosed with an autism spectrum disorder. In *Proceedings of the ACM SIGACCESS conference on computers and accessibility* (pp. 19–26). ACM Press.

Maekawa, T., Hara, T., and Nishio, S.A. (2006). Collaborative Web browsing system for multiple mobile users. In *Proceedings of the IEEE conference on pervasive computing and communications* (pp. 22–35). IEEE.

Maes, P. (1994). Agents that reduce work and information overload. *Communications of the ACM*, 37(7), 30–40.

Maglio, P.P., Barrett, R., Campbell, C.S., and Selker, T. (2000). SUITOR: An attentive information system. In *Proceedings of the ACM IUI conference on intelligent user interfaces* (pp. 169–176). ACM Press.

Maior, H., Pike, M., Wilson, M., and Sharples, S. (2013). Directly evaluating the cognitive impact of search user interfaces: a two-pronged approach with fNIRS. In *Proceedings of EuroHCIR* (pp. 43–46). ACM Press.

Majaranta, P. and Räihä, K.J. (2002). Twenty years of eye typing: Systems and design issues. In *Proceedings of the symposium on eye tracking research and applications* (pp. 15–22). ACM Press.

Malacria, S., Scarr, J., Cockburn, A., Gutwin, C., and Grossman, T. (2013). Skillometers: Reflective widgets that motivate and help users to improve performance. In *Proceedings of the ACM UIST symposium on user interface software and technology* (pp. 321–330). ACM Press.

Malone, T. (1982). What makes computer games fun? *ACM SIGSOC Bulletin*, 13(2–3), 143. ACM Press.

Malone, T.W. (1981). Toward a theory of intrinsically motivating instruction. *Cognitive Science*, 5(4), 333–369.

Malone, T.W. (1983). How do people organize their desks?: Implications for the design of office information systems. *ACM Transactions on Information Systems*, 1(1), 99–112.

Mander, R., Salomon, G., and Wong, Y.Y. (1992). A 'pile' metaphor for supporting casual organization of information. In *Proceedings of ACM SIGCHI conference on human factors in computing systems* (pp. 627–634). ACM Press.

Manglano, V., Beaulieu, M., and Robertson, S. (1998). Evaluation of interfaces for IRS: Modelling end-user searching behavior. *In Proceedings of the colloquium on information retrieval* (pp. 137–146).

Mankiw, G. (2010). *Principles of Macroeconomics*. SouthWestern Cengage Learning.

Mann, S. (1997). Wearable computing: A first step toward personal imaging. *Computer*, 30(2), 25–32.

Manning, C., Raghavan, P., and Schütze, H. (2008). *Introduction to Information Retrieval*. Cambridge: Cambridge University Press.

Manski, C.F. (2000). Economic analysis of social interactions. *The Journal of Economic Perspectives*, 14, 115–136.

Marchionini, G. (1989a). Making the transition from print to electronic encyclopaedias: Adaptation of mental models. *International journal of man-machine studies*, 30(6), 591–618.

Marchionini, G. (1989b). Information-seeking strategies of novices using a full-text electronic encyclopedia. *Journal of the American Society for Information Science*, 40(1), 54–66.

Marchionini, G. (1995). *Information Seeking in Electronic Environments*. Cambridge: Cambridge University Press.

Marchionini, G. (2004). From information retrieval to information interaction. In *Proceedings of the European conference on information retrieval*, 1–11.

Marchionini, G. (2006a). Exploratory search: From finding to understanding. *Communications of the ACM*, 49(4), 41–46.

Marchionini, G. (2006b). Toward human-computer information retrieval. *Bulletin of the American Society for Information Science and Technology*, June/July.

Marchionini, G. (2011). HCIR: Now the tricky part. *Keynote presentation at the symposium on human-computer interaction and information retrieval*.

Marchionini, G. and Komlodi, A. (1998). Design of interfaces for information seeking. *Annual Review of Information Science and Technology*, 33, 89–130.

Marchionini, G. and Shneiderman, B. (1988). Finding facts vs. browsing knowledge in hypertext systems. *IEEE Computer*, 21(1), 70–80.

Marchionini, G., and White, R. (2007). Find what you need, understand what you find. *International Journal of Human-Computer Interaction*, 23(3), 205–237.

Marchionini, G. and White, R.W. (2009). Information-seeking support systems. *Computer*, 42(3), 30–32.

Marchionini, G., Song, Y., and Farrell, R. (2009). Multimedia surrogates for video gisting: Toward combining spoken words and imagery. *Information Processing and Management*, 45(6), 615–630.

Marcotte, E. (2011). *Responsive Web Design*. Editions Eyrolles.

Maron, ME. (1988). Probabilistic design principles for conventional and full-text retrieval systems. *Information Processing and Management*, 24(3), 249–256.

Marshall, A. (2009). *Principles of Economics: Abridged Edition*. Cosimo Classics.

Marshall, C. and Rossman, G.B. (1999). Designing qualitative research (3rd Ed.). Thousand Oaks: Sage Publications.

Marshall, C.C., Shipman III, F.M., and Coombs, J.H. (1994). VIKI: Spatial hypertext supporting emergent structure. In *Proceedings of the ACM European conference on hypermedia technology* (pp. 13–23). ACM Press.

Martin, F.G. (2012). Will massive open online courses change how we teach?. *Communications of the ACM*, 55(8), 26–28.

Martins, B., Anastácio, I., and Calado, P. (2010). A machine learning approach for resolving place references in text. In *Proceedings of the AGILE conference on geographical information science* (pp. 221–236). Springer Berlin Heidelberg.

Matthijs, N. and Radlinski, F. (2011). Personalizing web search using long term browsing history. In *Proceedings of ACM WSDM conference on web search and data mining* (pp. 25–34). ACM Press.

Maxwell, D. and Azzopardi, L. (2014). Stuck in traffic: How temporal delays affect search behaviour. In *Proceedings of the IIiX symposium on information interaction in context* (pp. 155–164). ACM Press.

Mayer, R.E. (1999). Fifty years of creativity research. In Sternberg, R.J. (Ed.). *Handbook of Creativity*. Cambridge: Cambridge University Press.

McCain, K.W. (1995). Mandating sharing journal policies in the natural sciences. *Science Communication*, 16(4), 403–431.

McCarthy, J.C., Miles, V.C., and Monk, A.F. (1991). An experimental study of common ground in text-based communication. In *Proceedings of the ACM SIGCHI conference on human factors in computing systems* (pp. 209–215). ACM Press.

McCay-Peet, L. and Toms, E.G. (2010). The process of serendipity in knowledge work. In *Proceedings of the IIiX symposium on information interaction in context* (pp. 377–382). ACM Press.

McCrae, R.R. and Costa, P.C., Jr. (1987). Validation of the five-factor model across instruments and observers. *Journal of Personality and Social Psychology*, 52, 81–90.

McDonald, D.W. and Ackerman, M.S. (2000). Expertise recommender: A flexible recommendation architecture. In *Proceedings of the ACM CSCW conference on computer supported cooperative work* (pp. 231–240). ACM Press.

McKenzie, P. (2003). A model of information practices in accounts of everyday-life information seeking. *Journal of Documentation*, 59(1), 19–40.

McKenzie, P.J. and Davies, E. (2002). Time is of the essence: Social theory of time and its implications for LIS research. In *Proceedings of the annual conference of CAIS/ASCI* (pp. 1–13).

McKinney, V., Yoon, K., and Zahedi, F.M. (2002). The measurement of web-customer satisfaction: an expectation and disconfirmation approach. *Information systems research*, 13(3), 296–315.

Meadow, C.T. (1979). Computer as a search intermediary. *Online*, 3(3), 54–59.

Mei, Q. and Church, K. (2008). Entropy of search logs: How hard is search? with personalization? with backoff?. In *Proceedings of the ACM WSDM conference on web search and data mining* (pp. 45–54). ACM Press.

Mei, Q., Liu, C., Su, H., and Zhai, C. (2006). A probabilistic approach to spatiotemporal theme pattern mining on weblogs. In *Proceedings of the international conference on the World Wide Web* (pp. 533–542). ACM.

Meiss, M.R., Gonçalves, B., Ramasco, J.J., Flammini, A., and Menczer, F. (2010). Agents, bookmarks and clicks: a topical model of web navigation. In *Proceedings of the ACM conference on hypertext and hypermedia* (pp. 229–234). ACM.

Mellon, C.A. (1986). Library anxiety: A grounded theory and its development. *College and Research Libraries*, 47(2), 160–165.

Melnik, S., Gubarev, A., Long, J.J., Romer, G., Shivakumar, S., Tolton, M., and Vassilakis, T. (2010). Dremel: Interactive analysis of web-scale datasets. In *Proceedings of the VLDB Endowment*, 3(1–2), 330–339.

Melville, P., Mooney, R.J., and Nagarajan, R. (2002). Content-boosted collaborative filtering for improved recommendations. In *Proceedings of the AAAI conference on artificial intelligence* (pp. 187–192). AAAI Press.

Merrill, D. and Maes, P. (2007). Augmenting looking, pointing and reaching gestures to enhance the searching and browsing of physical objects. In *Proceedings of conference on pervasive computing* (pp. 1–18). Springer Berlin Heidelberg.

Metcalfe, J.E. and Shimamura, A.P. (1994). *Metacognition: Knowing About Knowing*. The MIT Press.

Metrikov, P., Diaz, F., Lahaie, S., and Rao, J. (2014). Whole page optimization: How page elements interact with the position auction. In *Proceedings of the ACM EC conference on economics and computation* (pp. 583–600). ACM Press.

Milic-Frayling, N., Jones, R., Rodden, K., Smyth, G., Blackwell, A., and Sommerer, R. (2004). Smartback: Supporting users in back navigation. In *Proceedings of the international conference on the World Wide Web* (pp. 63–71). ACM Press.

Millen, D.R. and Feinberg, J. (2006). Using social tagging to improve social navigation. In *Proceedings of workshop on the social navigation and community based adaptation technologies*.

Miller, G.A. (1956). The magical number seven, plus or minus two: Some limits on our capacity for processing information. *Psychological Review*, 63(2), 81–97.

Miller, G. (1983). Informavores. In F. Machlup and U. Mansfield (eds.), *The study of information: Interdisciplinary messages* (pp. 111–113). Wiley-Interscience.

Milne, G.R. and Culnan, M.J. (2004). Strategies for reducing online privacy risks: Why consumers read (or don't read) online privacy notices. *Journal of Interactive Marketing*, 18, 24–25.

Mishra, N., White, R.W., Ieong, S., and Horvitz, E. (2014). Time-critical search. In *Proceedings of the ACM SIGIR conference on research and development in information retrieval* (pp. 747–756). ACM Press.

Mistry, P. and Maes, P. (2009). SixthSense: a wearable gestural interface. In *Proceedings of ACM SIGGRAPH ASIA Sketches* (p. 11). ACM Press.

Mistry, P. and Wang, H. (2011). Precursor. http://www.pranavmistry.com/projects/precursor/.

Mitchell, T. (1997). *Machine Learning*, Burr Ridge, IL: McGraw Hill.

Mitchell, T.M., Caruana, R., Freitag, D., McDermott, J., and Zabowski, D. (1994). Experience with a learning personal assistant. *Communications of the ACM*, 37(7), 80–91.

Mitchell, T.M., Hutchinson, R., Niculescu, R.S., Pereira, F., Wang, X., Just, M., and Newman, S. (2004). Learning to decode cognitive states from brain images. *Machine Learning*, 57(1–2), 145–175.

Mitra, M., Singhal, A., and Buckley, C. (1998). Improving automatic query expansion. In *Proceedings of the ACM SIGIR conference on research and development in information retrieval* (pp. 206–214). ACM Press.

Mizarro, S. and Tasso, C. (2002). Ephemeral and persistent personalization in adaptive information access to scholarly publications on the Web. In *Proceedings of the international conference* on adaptive hypermedia and adaptive Web based systems (pp. 306–316). Springer Berlin Heidelberg.

Mizzaro, S. (1997). Relevance: The whole history. *Journal of the American Society for Information Science*, 48(9), 810–832.

Moffat, A. and Zobel, J. (2008). Rank-biased precision for measurement of retrieval effectiveness. *ACM Transactions on Information Systems*, 27(1), 2.

Monroe, M., Lan, R., Lee, H., Plaisant, C., and Shneiderman, B. (2013). Temporal event sequence simplification. IEEE Transactions *on Visualization and Computer Graphics*, 19(2), 2227–2236.

Monsell, S. (2003). Task switching. *TRENDS in Cognitive Sciences*, 7(3), 134–140.

Montaner, M., Lopez, B., and de la Rosa, J.L. (2002). Developing trust in recommender agents. In *Proceedings of the international joint conference on autonomous agents and multiagent* (pp. 304–305).

Montañez, G.D., White, R.W., and Huang, X. (2014). Cross-device search. In *Proceedings of the ACM CIKM conference on information and knowledge management* (pp. 1669–1678). ACM Press.

Moore, P. (1995). Information problem solving: A wider view of library skills. *Contemporary educational psychology*, 20(1), 1–31.

Moore, D S. (1997). New pedagogy and new content: The case of statistics. *International Statistical Review/Revue Internationale de Statistique*, 123–137.

Moraveji, N., Morris, M.R., Morris, D., Czerwinski, M., and Riche, N. (2011a). ClassSearch: Facilitating the development of web search skills through social learning. In *Proceedings of the ACM SIGCHI conference on human factors in computing systems* (pp. 1797–1806). ACM Press.

Moraveji, N., Russell, D., Bien, J., and Mease, D. (2011b). Measuring improvement in user search performance resulting from optimal search tips. In *Proceedings of the ACM SIGIR conference on research and development in information retrieval* (pp. 355–363). ACM Press.

Morgan, D.L. (1997). *Focus Groups as Qualitative Research (Vol. 16)*. London: Sage.

Morita, M. and Shinoda, Y. (1994). Information filtering based on user behavior analysis and best match text retrieval. *In Proceedings of the ACM SIGIR conference on research and development in information retrieval* (pp. 272–281). ACM Press.

Morris, D., Morris, M.R., and Venolia, G. (2008). SearchBar: A search-centric web history for task resumption and information re-finding. In *Proceedings of the ACM SIGCHI conference on human factors in computing systems* (pp. 1207–1216). ACM Press.

Morris, D., Collett, P., Marsh, P., and O'Shaughnessy, M. (1980). *Gestures*. New York, NY: Stein and Day.

Morris, M.R. (2008). A survey of collaborative web search practices. In *Proceedings of the ACM SIGCHI conference on human factors in computing systems* (pp. 1657–1660). ACM Press.

Morris, M.R. (2012). Web on the wall: Insights from a multimodal interaction elicitation study. In *Proceedings of the ACM ITS conference on interactive tabletops and surfaces* (pp. 95–104). ACM Press.

Morris, M.R. (2013). Collaborative search revisited. In *Proceedings of the ACM CSCW conference on computer supported cooperative work* (pp. 1181–1192). ACM Press.

Morris, M.R. and Horvitz, E. (2007). SearchTogether: An interface for collaborative Web search. In *Proceedings of the ACM UIST conference on user interface software and technology* (pp. 3–12). ACM Press.

Morris, M.R. and Horvitz, E. (2007). S3: Storable, shareable search. In *Proceedings of the conference on Human-Computer Interaction–INTERACT* (pp. 120–123). Springer Berlin Heidelberg.

Morris, M.R., Paepcke, A., and Winograd, T. (2006). TeamSearch: Comparing techniques for co-present collaborative search of digital media. In *Proceedings of the IEEE international workshop on horizontal interactive human-computer systems* (pp. 97–104). IEEE.

REFERENCES

Morris, M.R., Teevan, J., and Panovich, K. (2010). What do people ask their social networks, and why?: A survey study of status message Q&A behavior. In *Proceedings of the ACM SIGCHI conference on human factors in computing systems* (pp. 1739–1748). ACM Press.

Morrison, J.B., Pirolli, P., and Card, S.K. (2001). A taxonomic analysis of what World Wide Web activities significantly impact people's decisions and actions. In *Proceedings of the ACM SIGCHI conference on human factors in computing systems* (pp. 163–164). ACM Press.

Moshfeghi, Y. and Jose, J.M. (2013a). On cognition, emotion, and interaction aspects of search tasks with different search intentions. In *Proceedings of the international conference on the World Wide Web* (pp. 931–942). International World Wide Web Conferences Steering Committee.

Moshfeghi, Y. and Jose, J.M. (2013b). An effective implicit relevance feedback technique using affective, physiological and behavioural features. In *Proceedings of the ACM SIGIR conference on research and development in information retrieval* (pp. 133–142). ACM Press.

Moshfeghi, Y., Pinto, LR., Pollick, F.E., and Jose, J.M. (2013). Understanding relevance: An fMRI study. In *Proceedings of the European conference on information retrieval* (pp. 14–25). Springer Berlin Heidelberg.

Moustakis, V. (1997). Do people in HCI use machine learning? In *Advances in human factors/ergonomics*, 95–98.

Mueller, F., and Lockerd, A. (2001). Cheese: Tracking mouse movement activity on websites, a tool for user modeling. In *Proceedings of the ACM SIGCHI extended abstracts on human factors in computing systems* (pp. 279–280). ACM Press.

Mulder, A. (1996). Hand gestures for HCI. hand centered studies of human movement project, Technical Report, 96-1. Simon Fraser University.

Mumford, M.D. (2003). Where have we been, where are we going? Taking stock in creativity research. *Creativity Research Journal*, 15, 107–120.

Munro, A.J., Höök, K., and Benyon, D. (Eds.). (1999). *Social Navigation of Information Space*. London, New York: Springer.

Muralidharan, A., Gyongyi, Z., and Chi, E. (2012). Social annotations in web search. In *Proceedings of the ACM SIGCHI conference on human factors in computing systems* (pp. 1085–1094). ACM Press.

Muramatsu, J. and Pratt, W. (2001). Transparent queries: Investigating users' mental models of search engines. In *Proceedings of the ACM SIGIR conference on research and development in information retrieval* (pp. 217–224). ACM Press.

Murphy, K. (2012). *Machine Learning: A Probabilistic Perspective*. Boston, MA: MIT Press.

Murray, G.C., Lin, J., and Chowdhury, A. (2006). Identification of user sessions with hierarchical agglomerative clustering. In *Proceedings of the American association for information science and technology*, 43(1), 1–5.

Murugiah, K., Vallakati, A., Rajput, K., Sood, A., and Challa, N. (2011). Youtube as a source of information on cardiopulmonary resuscitation. *Resuscitation*, 82(3), 332–334.

Mynatt, B. and Tullio, J. (2001). Inferring calendar event attendance. In *Proceedings of the ACM IUI conference on intelligent user interfaces* (pp. 121–128). ACM Press.

Nahl, D. (1998). Ethnography of novices' first use of Web search engines: Affective control in cognitive processing. *Internet Reference Services Quarterly*, 3(2), 51–72.

Nahl, D. and Bilal, D. (Eds.). (2007). *Information and Emotion: The Emergent Affective Paradigm in Information Behavior Research and Theory*. Medford, NJ: Information Today for ASIST.

Nakazato, M. and Huang, T.S. (2001). 3d Mars: Immersive virtual reality for content-based image retrieval. In *Proceedings of the International Conference on Multimedia and Expo* (pp. 12). IEEE.

Nallapati, R., Croft, W.B., and Allan, J. (2003). Relevant query feedback in statistical language modeling. In *Proceedings on ACM CIKM conference on information and knowledge management* (pp. 560–563). ACM Press.

Narayanan, A. and Shmatikov, V. (2008). Robust deanonymization of large sparse datasets. In *Proceedings of the IEEE symposium on security and privacy* (pp. 111–125). IEEE.

Nardi, B., Whittaker, S., and Bradner, E. (2000). Interaction and outeraction: Instant messaging in action. In *Proceedings of the ACM CSCW conference on computer supported cooperative work* (pp. 79–88). ACM Press.

Navalpakkam, V. and Churchill, E. (2012). Mouse tracking: Measuring and predicting users' experience of web-based content. In *Proceedings of the ACM SIGCHI conference on human factors in computing systems* (pp. 2963–2972). ACM Press.

Navarro-Arribas, G., Torra, V., Erola, A., and Castellà-Roca, J. (2012). User k-anonymity for privacy preserving data mining of query logs. *Information Processing and Management*, 48(3), 476–487.

Navarro-Prieto, R., Scaife, M., and Rogers, Y. (1999). Cognitive strategies in web searching. In *Proceedings of the conference on human factors and the Web* (pp. 43–56).

Newell, A., and Simon, H.A. (1972). *Human Problem Solving (Vol. 104, No. 9)*. Englewood Cliffs, NJ: Prentice-Hall.

Nichols, D.M. (1997). Implicit ratings and filtering. In *Proceedings of the DELOS workshop on filtering and collaborative filtering* (pp. 31–36).

Nielsen, J. (1993). *Usability Engineering*. San Francisco, CA: Morgan Kaufmann.

Nielsen, J. (April 11, 2011). Incompetent research skills curb users' problem solving. Alertbox. (available at: http://www.useit.com/alertbox/search-skills.html). Accessed on August 15, 2015.

Nielsen, J. and Levy, J. (1994). Measuring usability – preference vs. performance. *Communications of the ACM*, 37(4), 66–75.

Nielsen, J. and Loranger, H. (2006). *Prioritizing Web Usability*. Thousand Oaks, CA: New Riders Publishing.

Nielsen, J. and Norman, D.A. (2000). Web-site usability: usability on the web isn't a luxury. *InformationWeek*, January 14.

Nielsen, J. and Pernice, K. (2010). *Eyetracking Web Usability*. Thousand Oaks, CA: New Riders Publishing.

Nijholt, A. and Tan, D. (2008). Brain-computer interfacing for intelligent systems. *Intelligent Systems, IEEE*, 23(3), 72–79.

Ninio, A. and Bruner, J. (1978). The achievement and antecedents of labelling. *Journal of Child Language*, 5, 1–15.

Nippert-Eng, C.E. (2008). *Home and Work: Negotiating Boundaries through Everyday life*. Chicago, IL: University of Chicago Press.

Niu, X. and Kelly, D. (2014). The use of query suggestions as idea tactics during information search. *Information Processing and Management*, 50(1), 218–234.

Norman, D.A. (1983). Some observations on mental models. *Mental models*, 1.

Norman, K.A., Polyn, S.M., Detre, G.J., and Haxby, J.V. (2006). Beyond mind-reading: Multi-voxel pattern analysis of fMRI data. *Trends in cognitive sciences*, 10(9), 424–430.

Oard, D. and Kim, J. (2001). Modeling information content using observable behaviors. In *Proceedings of the annual meeting of the American society for information science and technology* (pp. 38–45).

O'Brien, H.L. and Toms, E.G. (2013). Examining the generalizability of the user engagement scale (UES) in exploratory search. *Information Processing and Management*, 49(5), 1092–1107.

Obendorf, H., Weinreich, H., Herder, E., and Mayer, M. (2007). Web page revisitation revisited: Implications of a long-term click-stream study of browser usage. In *Proceedings of the ACM SIGCHI conference on human factors in computing systems* (pp. 597–606). ACM Press.

O'Brien, H.L., and Toms, E.G. (2008). What is user engagement? A conceptual framework for defining user engagement with technology. *Journal of the American Society for Information Science and Technology*, 59(6), 938–955.

O'Brien, H.L. and Toms, E.G. (2010). The development and evaluation of a survey to measure user engagement. *Journal of the American Society for Information Science and Technology*, 61(1), 50–69.

O'Connor, B (1988). Fostering creativity: Enhancing the browsing environment. *International Journal of Information Management*, 8(3), 203–210.

O'Day, V. and Jeffries, R. (1993). Orienteering in an information landscape: How information seekers get from here to there. In *Proceedings of the INTERACT and CHI conference on human factors in computing systems* (pp. 438–445). ACM Press.

Oddy, R.N. (1977). Information retrieval through man-machine dialogue. *Journal of Documentation*, 33(1), 1–14.

Ofek, E., Iqbal, S.T., and Strauss, K. (2013). Reducing disruption from subtle information delivery during a conversation: Mode and bandwidth investigation. In *Proceedings of the ACM SIGCHI conference on human factors in computing systems* (pp. 3111–3120). ACM Press.

Oliveira, F.T., Aula, A., and Russell, D.M. (2009). Discriminating the relevance of web search results with measures of pupil size. In *Proceedings of the ACM SIGCHI conference on human factors in computing systems* (pp. 2209–2212). ACM Press.

Oliver, P.E. and Marwell, G. (1988). The paradox of group size in collective action: A theory of the critical mass. II. *American Sociological Review*, 1–8.

Oliver, R.L. (1980). A cognitive model of the antecedents and consequences of satisfaction decisions. *Journal of Marketing Research*. 17(4), 460–470.

Oliver, R.L. (2010). *Satisfaction: A behavioral perspective on the consumer*. New York: ME Sharpe.

Olson, J.S., Grudin, J., and Horvitz, E. (2005). A study of preferences for sharing and privacy. In *Proceedings of ACM SIGCHI extended abstracts on human factors in computing systems* (pp. 1985–1988). ACM Press.

Olson, M.A., Bostic, K., and Seltzer, M.I. (1999). Berkeley DB. In *Proceedings of USENIX annual technical conference, FREENIX Track* (pp. 183–191).

Olson, M.H. (1983). Remote office work: Changing work patterns in space and time. *Communications of the ACM*, 26(3), 182–187.

Olston, C. and Chi, E.H. (2003). ScentTrails: Integrating browsing and searching on the Web. *ACM Transactions on Computer-Human Interaction*, 10(3).

Orne, M.T. (1962). On the social psychology of the psychological experiment: With particular reference to demand characteristics and their implications. *American Psychologist*, 17, 776–783.

Orne, M.T. (1969). Demand characteristics and the concept of quasi-controls. In R. Rosenthal and R. Rosnow (Eds.), *Artifact in Behavioral Research*. New York: Academic Press, 143–179.

Ortiz, J.R., Zhou, H., Shay, D.K., Neuzil, K.M., Fowlkes, A.L., and Goss, C.H. (2011). Monitoring influenza activity in the United States: A comparison of traditional surveillance systems with Google Flu Trends. *PloS One*, 6(4), e18687.

Öquist, G. and Goldstein, M. (2003). Towards an improved readability on mobile devices: Evaluating adaptive rapid serial visual presentation. *Interacting with Computers*, 15(4), 539–558.

Ozmutlu, S. (2006). Automatic new topic identification using multiple linear regression. *Information Processing and Management*, 42(4), 934–950.

Pace, S. (2004). A grounded theory of the flow experiences of web users. *International Journal of Human–Computer Studies*, 60(3), 327–363.

Paek, T., Dumais, S., and Logan, R. (2004). WaveLens: A new view onto internet search results. In *Proceedings of the SIGCHI conference on human factors in computing systems* (pp. 727–734). ACM Press.

Palen, L. (2008). Online social media in crisis events. *Educause Quarterly*, 31(3), 12.

Palen, L., Vieweg, S., Sutton, J., Liu, S.B., and Hughes, A.L. (2007). Crisis informatics: Studying crisis in a networked world. In *Proceedings of the international conference on e-social science*.

Pandit, S. and Olston, C. (2007). Navigation-aided retrieval. In *Proceedings of the international conference on the World Wide Web* (pp. 391–400).

Pang, B. and Kumar, R. (2011). Search in the lost sense of query: Question formulation in web search queries and its temporal changes. In *Proceedings of the annual meeting of the association for computational linguistics: human language technologies (short papers)* (Vol. 2, pp. 135–140). Association for Computational Linguistics.

Pao, M.L. (1993). Term and citation retrieval: A field study. *Information Processing and Management*, 29(1), 95–112.

Paolacci, G., Chandler, J., and Ipeirotis, P.G. (2010). Running experiments on amazon mechanical turk. *Judgment and Decision making*, 5(5), 411–419.

Pariser, E. (2011). *The Filter Bubble: How the New Personalized Web is Changing What We Read and How We Think*. New York, NY: Penguin.

Patel, K., Fogarty, J., Landay, J.A., and Harrison, B.L. (2008). Examining difficulties software developers encounter in the adoption of statistical machine learning. In *Proceedings of the AAAI conference on artificial intelligence* (pp. 1563–1566). AAAI Press.

Patterson, E.S., Roth, E.M., and Woods, D.D. (2001). Predicting vulnerabilities in computer-supported inferential analysis under data overload. *Cognition Technology and Work*, 3(4), 224–237.

Paul, M.J. and Dredze, M. (2011). You are what you Tweet: Analyzing Twitter for public health. In *Proceedings of the international conference on weblogs and social media* (pp. 265–272).

Paul, M.J., White, R.W., and Horvitz, E. (2014). Search and breast cancer: On disruptive shifts of attention over life histories of an illness. Microsoft Research Technical Report: MSR-TR-2014-144.

Pavlovic, V.I., Sharma, R., and Huang, T.S. (1997). Visual interpretation of hand gestures for human-computer interaction: a review. *IEEE Transactions on Pattern Analysis and Machine Intelligence*, 19(7), 677–695.

Pease, A. (2004). *The Definitive Guide to Body Language*. London: Orion.

Pedersen, J. (2008). *The Machine Learned Ranking Story*. http://docslide.us/documents/jan-pedersen the-machine-learned-ranking-story.html.

Petajan, E., Bischoff, B., Bodoff, D., and Brooke, N.M. (1988). An improved automatic lipreading system to enhance speech recognition. In *Proceedings of the ACM SIGCHI conference on human factors in computing systems* (pp. 19–25). ACM Press.

Petter, M., Fragoso, V., Turk, M., and Baur, C. (2011). Automatic text detection for mobile augmented reality translation. In *Proceedings of the IEEE computer vision workshops* (pp. 48–55). IEEE.

Pfeuffer, K., Vidal, M., Turner, J., Bulling, A., and Gellersen, H. (2013). Pursuit calibration: Making gaze calibration less tedious and more flexible. In *Proceedings of the ACM UIST symposium on user interface software and technology* (pp. 261–270). ACM Press.

Pharo, N. (1999). Web information search strategies: A model for classifying Web interaction? In *Proceedings of the COLIS conference on conceptions of library and information science* (pp. 207–218). Libraries Unlimited.

Pharo, N. and Järvelin, K. (2004). The SST method: A tool for analysing Web information search processes. *Information Processing and Management*, 40(4), 633–654.

Piaget, J. (1952). *The Origins of Intelligence in Children*. New York: International Universities Press.

Piaget, J. (1978). La equilibración de las estructuras cognitivas: problema central del desarrollo.

Picard, R.W. (1995). *Affective Computing*. MIT Tech Report.

Picard, R. (1997). *Affective Computing*. Cambridge, MA: MIT Press.

Picard, R.W. (2000). Toward computers that recognize and respond to user emotion. *IBM Systems Journal*, 39(3–4), 705–719.

Pickens, J., Golovchinsky, G., Shah, C., Qvarfordt, P., and Back, M. (2008). Algorithmic mediation for collaborative exploratory search. In *Proceedings of the ACM SIGIR conference on research and development in information retrieval* (pp. 315–322). ACM Press.

Pirhonen, A., Brewster, S., and Holguin, C. (2002). Gestural and audio metaphors as a means of control for mobile devices. In *Proceedings of the SIGCHI conference on human factors in computing systems* (pp. 291–298). ACM Press.

Pirolli, P. (1997). Computational models of information scent-following in a very large browsable text collection. In *Proceedings of the ACM SIGCHI conference on human factors in computing systems* (pp. 3–10). ACM Press.

Pirolli, P. (2007). *Information Foraging Theory: Adaptive Interaction with Information*. Oxford: Oxford University Press.

Pirolli, P. (2007). Exploratory Search Systems. http://web.mac.com/peter.pirolli/Professional/Blog/Entries/2007/5/18_Exploratory_Search_Systems.html. Accessed December 15, 2008.

Pirolli, P. (2009). An elementary social information foraging model. In *Proceedings of the ACM SIGCHI conference on human factors in computing systems* (pp. 605–614). ACM Press.

Pirolli, P. and Card, S. (2005). The sensemaking process and leverage points for analyst technology as identified through cognitive task analysis. In *Proceedings of International Conference on Intelligence Analysis* (Vol. 5, pp. 2–4).

Pirolli, P. and Card, S. (1995). Information foraging in information access environments. In *Proceedings of the ACM SIGCHI conference on human factors in computing systems* (pp. 51–58). ACM Press/Addison-Wesley Publishing Co.

Pirolli, P. and Card, S.K. (1999). Information foraging. *Psychological Review*, 106, 643–675.

Pirolli, P., Card, S.K., and Van Der Wege, M.M. (2003). The effects of information scent on visual search in the Hyperbolic Tree Browser. *ACM Transactions on Computer-Human Interaction*, 10(1), 20–53.

Pirolli, P. and Fu, W.T. (2003). SNIF-ACT: A model of information foraging on the World Wide Web. In *Proceedings of the user modeling conference* (pp. 45–54). Springer Berlin Heidelberg.

Pirolli, P., Pitkow, J., and Rao, R. (1996a). Silk from a sow's ear: Extracting usable structures from the Web. In *Proceedings of the ACM SIGCHI conference on human factors in computing systems* (pp. 118–125). ACM Press.

Pirolli, P. and Rao, R. (1996). Table lens as a tool for making sense of data. In *Proceedings of the working conference on advanced visual interfaces* (pp. 67–80).

Pirolli, P. and Russell, D.M. (2011). Introduction to special issue on sensemaking. *In Human Computer Interaction*, 26(1), 1–8.

Pirolli, P., Schank, P., Hearst, M., and Diehl, C. (1996b). Scatter/gather browsing communicates the topic structure of a very large text collection. In *Proceedings of the ACM SIGCHI conference on human factors in computing systems* (pp. 213–220). ACM Press.

Pitkow, J., Schutze, H., Cass, T., Cooley, R., Turnbull, D., Edmonds, A., Adar, E., and Breuel, T. (2002). Personalized seach. *Communications of the ACM*, 45(9), 50–55.

Piwowar, H.A. and Chapman, W.W. (2010). Public sharing of research datasets: A pilot study of associations. *Journal of Infometrics*, 4(2), 148–156.

Piwowarski, B., Dupret, G., and Jones, R. (2009). Mining user web search activity with layered bayesian networks or how to capture a click in its context. In *Proceedings of the ACM WSDM conference on web search and data mining* (pp. 162–171). ACM Press.

Plaisant, C. (2004). The challenge of information visualization evaluation. In *Proceedings of the working conference on advanced visual interfaces* (pp. 109–116).

Plaisant, C., Milash, B., Rose, A., Widoff, S., and Shneiderman, B. (1996). LifeLines: Visualizing personal histories. In *Proceedings of the ACM SIGCHI conference on human factors in computing systems* (pp. 221–227). ACM Press.

Plan, Y. (2011). *Compressed Sensing, Sparse Approximation, and Low-rank Matrix Estimation*. Unpublished Doctoral Dissertation, California Institute of Technology.

Platt, J. (2000). AutoAlbum: Clustering digital photographs using probabilistic model merging. *IEEE workshop on content-based access of image and video libraries*, 96–100.

Poddar, A. and Ruthven, I. (2010). The emotional impact of search tasks. In *Proceedings of the IIiX conference on information interaction in context* (pp. 35–44). ACM Press.

Poh, M.Z., Loddenkemper, T., Reinsberger, C., Swenson, N.C., Goyal, S., Madsen, J.R., and Picard, R.W. (2012). Autonomic changes with seizures correlate with postictal EEG suppression. *Neurology*, 78(23), 1868–1876.

Polgreen, P.M., Chen, Y., Pennock, D.M., and Forrest, N.D. (2008). Using internet searches for influenza surveillance. *Clinical Infectious Diseases*, 47(11), 1443–1448.

Pollack, M.E. (1985). Information sought and information provided: An empirical study of user/expert dialogues. *ACM SIGCHI Bulletin*, 16(4), 155–159. ACM Press.

Potter, M.C. (1976). Short-term conceptual memory for pictures. *Journal of Experimental Psychology: Human Learning and Memory*, 2(5), 509.

Pousman, Z., Stasko, J. and Mateas, M. (2007). Casual information visualization: depictions of data in everyday life. *IEEE Transactions on Visualization and Computer Graphics*, 13(6), 1145–1152.

Pratt, W., Hearst, M.A., and Fagan, L.M. (1999). A knowledge-based approach to organizing retrieved documents. In *Proceedings of the AAAI conference on artificial intelligence* (pp. 80–85). AAAI Press.

Pratt, W., and Yetisgen-Yildiz, M. (2003). LitLinker: Capturing connections across the biomedical literature. In *Proceedings of the international conference on knowledge capture* (pp. 105–112).

Pretschner, A. and Gauch, S. (1999). Ontology based personalized search. In *Proceedings of the IEEE international conference on tools with artificial intelligence* (pp. 391–398). IEEE.

Psotka, J., Massey, L.D., and Mutter, S.A. (Eds.). (1988). *Intelligent Tutoring Systems: Lessons Learned*. Hillsdale, NJ: Psychology Press.

Qu, Y. and Furnas, G.W. (2008). Model-driven formative evaluation of exploratory search: A study under a sensemaking framework. *Information Processing and Management*, 44(2), 534–555.

Qiu, F. and Cho, J. (2006). Automatic identification of user interest for personalized search. In *Proceedings of the international conference on the World Wide Web* (pp. 727–736). ACM Press.

Quine, W.V. (1953). Identity, ostension, and hypostasis. In Quine, W.V. (Ed.), *From a Logical Point of View* (pp. 65–79). Cambridge, MA: Harvard University Press.

Quine, W.V. (1969). Natural kinds. In Quine, W.V. (Ed.), *Ontological relativity and other essays* (pp. 114–138). New York: Columbia University Press.

Quine, W.V. and Quine, W.V.O. (1969). *Ontological Relativity and Other Essays (No. 1)*. New York: Columbia University Press.

Quine, W.V.O. (1980). *From a Logical Point of View: 9 Logico-Philosophical Essays (Vol. 9)*. Cambridge, MA: Harvard University Press.

Quirk, C., Choudhury, P., Gao, J., Suzuki, H., Toutanova, K., Gamon, M., and Cherry, C. (2012). MSR SPLAT, a language analysis toolkit. In *Proceedings of the conference of the North American chapter of the association for computational linguistics: human language technologies: Demonstration session* (pp. 21–24). Association for Computational Linguistics.

Radinsky, K. and Horvitz, E. (2013). Mining the web to predict future events. In *Proceedings of the ACM WSDM conference on web search and data mining* (pp. 255–264). ACM Press.

Radinsky, K., Svore, K.M., Dumais, S.T., Shokouhi, M., Teevan, J., Bocharov, A., and Horvitz, E. (2013). Behavioral dynamics on the web: Learning, modeling, and prediction. *ACM Transactions on Information Systems*, 31(3), 16.

Radlinski, F. and Craswell N. (2013). Optimized interleaving for online retrieval evaluation. In *Proceedings of the ACM WSDM conference on web search and data mining* (pp. 245–254). ACM Press.

Radlinski, F., and Dumais, S. (2006). Improving personalized web search using result diversification. In *Proceedings of the ACM SIGIR conference on research and development in information retrieval* (pp. 691–692). ACM Press.

Radlinski, F. and Joachims, T. (2005). Query chains: Learning to rank from implicit feedback. In *Proceedings of the ACM SIGKDD conference on knowledge discovery in data mining* (pp. 239–248). ACM Press.

Radlinski, F., Kurup, M., and Joachims, T. (2008). How does clickthrough data reflect retrieval quality? In *Proceedings of the ACM CIKM conference on information and knowledge management* (pp. 43–52). ACM Press.

Rafaeli, S., Raban, D., and Ravid, G. (2007). How social motivation enhances economic activity and incentives in the google answers knowledge sharing market. *International Journal of Knowledge and Learning*, 3(1), 1–11.

Raman, K., Bennett, P.N., and Collins-Thompson, K. (2013). Toward whole session relevance: Exploring intrinsic diversity in web search. In *Proceedings of the ACM SIGIR conference on research and development in information retrieval* (pp. 463–472). ACM Press.

Rao, R. and Card, S.K. (1994). The table lens: Merging graphical and symbolic representations in an interactive focus + context visualization for tabular information. In *Proceedings of the ACM SIGCHI conference on human factors in computing systems* (pp. 318–322). ACM Press.

Rayner, K. (1998). Eye movements in reading and information processing: 20 years of research. *Psychological Bulletin*, 124(3), 372.

Reas, C. and Fry, B. (2010). *Getting Started with Processing*. Sebastopol, CA: O'Reilly Media.

Reich, S., Carr, L., De Roure, D., and Hall, W. (1999). Where have you been from here? Trials in hypertext systems. *ACM Computing Surveys*, 31(4es), 11.

Reid, J. (2000). A task-oriented non-interactive evaluation methodology for information retrieval systems. *Information Retrieval*, 2(1), 115–129.

Rieh, S.Y. and Xie, H.I. (2006). Analysis of multiple query reformulations on the web: The interactive information retrieval context. *Information Processing and Management*, 42(3), 751–768.

Reimer, J. (2007). Your ISP may be selling your web clicks. *Ars Technica*. http://arstechnica.com/news.ars/post/20070315-your-isp-may-be-selling-your-web-clicks.html. Accessed on August 15, 2015.

Reis, S., and Church, K. (2013). Insights into co-located shared mobile search. In *Proceedings of the ACM SIGCHI extended abstracts on human factors in computing systems* (pp. 1401–1406). ACM Press.

Reisner. P. (1963). Construction of a growing thesaurus by conversational interaction in a man-machine system. In *Proceedings of the annual meeting of the american documentation institute*.

Reisner. P. (1966). Evaluation of a 'growing thesaurus'. Research Paper RC-1662. IBM Watson Research Center. Yorktown Heights, N.Y.

Rekimoto, J. and Ayatsuka, Y. (2000). Cybercode:designing augmented reality environments with visual tags. In *Proceedings of designing augmented reality environments* (pp. 1–10).

Ren, Y., Tomko, M., Ong, K., Bai, Y.B., and Sanderson, M. (2014). The influence of indoor spatial context on user information behaviours. In *Proceedings of the i-ASC 2014 Workshop* (p. 13).

Resnick, P. and Varian, H.R. (1997). Recommender systems. *Communications of the ACM*, 40(3), 56–58.

Resnick, P. and Virzi, R.A. (1995). Relief from the audio interface blues: Expanding the spectrum of menu, list, and form styles. *ACM Transactions on Computer-Human Interaction*, 2(2), 145–176.

Rheingold, H. (1991). *Virtual Reality: Exploring the Brave New Technologies*. Simon and Schuster Adult Publishing Group.

Rheingold, H. (2000). *The Virtual Community: Home-steading on the Electronic Frontier*. Boston, MA: MIT Press.

Rhodes, B.J. and Starner, T. (1996). Remembrance agent: A continuously running automated information retrieval system. In *Proceedings of the international conference on the practical application of intelligent agents and multi agent technology* (pp. 487–495).

Ribak, A., Jacovi, M., and Soroka, V. (2002). Ask before you search: peer support and community building with ReachOut. In *Proceedings of the ACM CSCW conference on computer supported cooperative work* (pp. 126–135). ACM Press.

Ricci, F., Rokach, L., Shapira, B., and Kantor, P.B. (2011). Introduction to recommender systems handbook. *Recommender Systems Handbook* (pp. 1–35). Springer.

Rich, E. (1979). User modeling via stereotypes. *Cognitive Science*, 3(4), 329–354.

Rich, E. (1983). Users are individuals: Individualizing user models. *International Journal of Man-machine Studies*, 18(3), 199–214.

Richardson, M. (2008). Learning about the world through long-term query logs. *ACM Transactions on the Web*, 2(4), 21.

Richardson, M., Burges, C.J., and Renshaw, E. (2013). McTest: A challenge dataset for the open-domain machine comprehension of text. In *Proceedings of the conference on empirical methods in natural language processing* (Vol. 1, p. 2).

Richardson, M. and Domingos, P. (2002). The intelligent surfer: Probabilistic combination of link and content information in pagerank. In *Proceedings of advances in neural information processing systems* (pp. 1441–1448).

Richardson, M., Dominowska, E., and Ragno, R. (2007). Predicting clicks: Estimating the click-through rate for new ads. In *Proceedings of the international conference on the World Wide Web* (pp. 521–530). ACM Press.

Richardson, M., Prakash, A., and Brill, E. (2006). Beyond PageRank: Machine learning for static ranking. In *Proceedings of the international conference on the World Wide Web* (pp. 707–715). ACM Press.

Richardson, M. and White, R.W. (2011). Supporting synchronous social Q&A throughout the question lifecycle. In *Proceedings of the international conference on the World Wide Web* (pp. 755–764). ACM Press.

Rimé, B. (1982). The elimination of visible behaviour from social interactions: Effects on verbal, nonverbal and interpersonal variables. *European Journal of Social Psychology*, 12(2), 113–129.

Rimé, B., & Schiaratura, L. (1991). Gesture and speech, In Feldman R.S. and Rimé B. (Eds.), Fundamentals of nonverbal behavior (pp. 239–281), Cambridge: Cambridge University Press.

Ringel, M., Cutrell, E., Dumais, S., and Horvitz, E. (2003). Milestones in time: The value of landmarks in retrieving information from personal stores. In *Proceedings of Human-Computer Interaction–INTERACT 2003* (pp. 184–191).

Roberts, R.M. (1989). *Serendipity: Accidental Discoveries in Science*. New York: Wiley VCH.

Robertson, G., Czerwinski, M., Larson, K., Robbins, D.C., Thiel, D., and Van Dantzich, M. (1998). Data mountain: Using spatial memory for document management. In *Proceedings of the ACM UIST symposium on user interface software and technology* (pp. 153–162). ACM Press.

Robertson, S.E. (1977). The probability ranking principle in IR. *Journal of Documentation*, 33(4), 294–304.

Robins, D. (2000). Shifts of focus on various aspects of user information problems during interactive information retrieval. *Journal of the American Society for Information Science*, 51(10), 913–928.

Rocchio, J.J. (1971). Relevance feedback in information retrieval. In Salton, G. (Ed.), *The SMART retrieval system – experiments in automatic document processing* (pp. 313–323). Upper Saddle River, NJ: Prentice-Hall, Inc.

Rodden, K. (1998). About 23 million documents match your query. In *Proceedings of the ACM SIGCHI conference on human factors in computing systems* (Doctoral Consortium). (pp. 64–65). ACM Press.

Rodden, K., Basalaj, W., Sinclair, D., and Wood, K. (2001). Does organisation by similarity assist image browsing?. In *Proceedings of the ACM SIGCHI conference on human factors in computing systems* (pp. 190–197). ACM Press.

Rodden, K., Fu, X., Aula, A., and Spiro, I. (2008). Eye-mouse coordination patterns on web search results pages. In *Proceedings of the ACM SIGCHI extended abstracts on human factors in computing systems* (pp. 2997–3002). ACM Press.

Rotter, J.B. (1954). *Social learning and clinical psychology*. Englewood Cliffs, NJ, US: Prentice-Hall, Inc

Rose, D.E. and Levinson, D. (2004). Understanding user goals in web search. In *Proceedings of the international conference on the World Wide Web* (pp. 13–19). ACM Press.

Rosen, J. (2012). The right to be forgotten. *Stanford Law Review Online*, 64, 88.

Rosenbaum, P. and Rubin, D. (1983). The central role of propensity score in observational studies for causal effects. *Biometrica*, 70, 41–55.

Rosenholtz, R., Li, Y., and Nakano, L. (2007). Measuring visual clutter. *Journal of Vision*, 7(2), 1–22.

Rosenthal R. (1966). *Experimenter Effects in Behavioral Research*. New York: Appleton-Century-Crofts 464.

Ross, C. (1999). Finding without seeking: the information encounter in the context of reading for pleasure. *Information Processing and Management*, 35(6), 783–799.

Rubin, M., and Badea, C. (2010). The central tendency of a social group can affect ratings of its intragroup variability in the absence of social identity concerns. *Journal of Experimental Social Psychology*, 46, 410–415.

Rubin, V.L., Burkell, J., and Quan-Haase, A. (2011). Facets of serendipity in everyday chance encounters: A grounded theory approach to blog analysis. *Information Research*, 16(3).

Ruotsalo, T., Jacucci, G., Myllymäki, P., and Kaski, S. (2015). Interactive intent modeling: Information discovery beyond search. *Communications of the ACM*, 58(1), 86–92.

Rushinek, A. and Rushinek, S.F. (1986). What makes users happy? *Communications of the ACM*, 29(1), 594–598.

Rushkoff, D. (2005). *Get Back in the Box: Innovation from the Inside Out*, New York: Harper Collins.

Russell, D.M. (2010). Why is search easy and hard? Understanding serendipity and expertise in search. Keynote presentation of the workshop on human-computer interaction and informational retrieval.

Russell, D.M. and Grimes, C. (2007). Assigned tasks are not the same as self-chosen Web search tasks. In *Proceedings of the annual Hawaii international conference on system sciences* (pp. 83–83). IEEE.

Russell, D.M. Stefik, M.J., Pirolli, P., and Card, S.K. (1993). The cost structure of sensemaking. In *Proceedings of the INTERACT and SIGCHI conference on human factors in computing systems* (pp. 269–276). ACM Press.

Russell-Rose, T., and Tate, T. (2012). *Designing the Search Experience: The Information Architecture of Discovery*. San Francisco, CA: Morgan Kaufman.

Ruthven, I. (2001). *Abduction, Explanation and Relevance Feedback*. Unpublished doctoral dissertation, Glasgow: University of Glasgow.

Ruthven, I. (2002). On the use of explanations as mediating device for relevance feedback. In *Proceedings of the European conference on digital libraries* (pp. 338–345).

Ruthven, I. (2003). Re-examining the potential effectiveness of interactive query expansion. In *Proceedings of the ACM SIGIR conference on research and development in information retrieval* (pp. 213–220). ACM Press.

Ruthven, I. (2008). Interactive information retrieval. *Annual review of information science and technology*, 42(1), 43–91.

Ruthven, I. and Kelly, D. (2012). *Interactive Information-Seeking Behaviour and Retrieval*. London: Facet Publishing.

Ruthven, I., Lalmas, M., and Van Rijsbergen, C.J. (2002). Ranking expansion terms using partial and ostensive relevance. In *Proceedings of the COLIS conference on conceptions of library and information science* (pp. 199–219).

Rzeszotarski, J.M. and Morris, M.R. (2014). Estimating the social costs of friendsourcing. In *Proceedings of the ACM SIGCHI conference on human factors in computing systems* (pp. 2735–2744). ACM Press.

Sackett, D.L. (1979). Bias in analytic research. *Journal of Chronic Diseases*, 32(1–2), 5–63.

Sadilek, A., Brennan, S., Kautz, H., and Silenzio, V. (2013). nEmesis: Which restaurants should you avoid today?. In *Proceedings of the AAAI conference on human computation and crowd sourcing*.

Sadilek, A. and Krumm, J. (2012). Far out: Predicting long-term human mobility. In *Proceedings of the AAAI conference on artificial intelligence* (pp. 814–820). AAAI Press.

Sadilek, A., Kautz, H.A., and Silenzio, V. (2012). Predicting disease transmission from geo-tagged micro-blog data. In *Proceedings of the AAAI conference on artificial intelligence* (pp. 136–142). AAAI Press.

Sahib, N.G., Tombros, A., and Ruthven, I. (2010). Enabling interactive query expansion through eliciting the potential effect of expansion terms. In *Proceedings of the European conference on information retrieval* (pp. 532–543). Springer Berlin Heidelberg.

Saito, H. and Miwa, K. (2001). A cognitive study of information seeking processes in the WWW: Effects of searcher's knowledge and experience. In *Proceedings of the conference Web information systems engineering* (pp. 321–327). IEEE.

Sakai, T. (2014). Statistical reform in information retrieval? *SIGIR Forum*, 48(1), 3–12.

Säljö, R. (1979). Learning in the learner's perspective. *I. Some common-sense conceptions*, Reports from the Institute of Education, University of Gothenburg, 76.

Salojärvi, J., Puolamäki, K., and Kaski, S. (2005). Implicit relevance feedback from eye movements. In *Proceedings of artificial neural networks: biological inspirations* (pp. 513–518). Springer Berlin Heidelberg.

Salton, G. (1971). *The SMART Retrieval System: Experiments in Automatic Document Processing*. Englewood Cliffs, NJ: Prentice-Hall.

Salton, G., Allan, J., and Buckley, C. (1993). Approaches to passage retrieval in full text retrieval systems. In *Proceedings of the ACM SIGIR conference on research and development in information retrieval* (pp. 49–58). ACM Press.

Salton, G. and Buckley, C. (1990). Improving retrieval performance by relevance feedback. *Journal of the American Society for Information Science*, 41(4), 288–297.

Salton, G., Wong, A., and Yang, C.S. (1975). A vector space model for automatic indexing. *Communications of the ACM*, 18(11), 613–620.

REFERENCES

San Agustin, J., Skovsgaard, H., Mollenbach, E., Barret, M., Tall, M., Hansen, D.W., and Hansen, J.P. (2010). Evaluation of a low-cost open-source gaze tracker. In *Proceedings of the symposium on eye-tracking research and applications* (pp. 77–80). ACM Press.

Sanderson, M. (2010). *Test Collection Based Evaluation of Information Retrieval Systems*. Foundations and Trends in Information Retrieval. Now Publishers Inc.

Sanderson, M. and Dumais, S. (2007). Examining repetition in user search behavior. In *Proceedings of the European conference on information retrieval* (pp. 597–604). Springer Berlin Heidelberg.

Sanderson, M., Paramita, M.L., Clough, P., and Kanoulas, E. (2010). Do user preferences and evaluation measures line up?. In *Proceedings of the ACM SIGIR conference on research and development in information retrieval* (pp. 555–562). ACM Press.

Sandstrom, P.E. (1994). An optimal foraging approach to information seeking and use. *Library Quarterly*, 64, 414–449.

Sankar, A. and Seitz, S. (2012). Capturing indoor scenes with smartphones. In *Proceedings of the ACM UIST symposium on user interface software and technology* (pp. 403–412). ACM Press.

Santos, R.L., Macdonald, C., and Ounis, I. (2010). Exploiting query reformulations for web search result diversification. In *Proceedings of the international conference on the World Wide Web* (pp. 881–890). ACM Press.

Santos, R. L., Macdonald, C., and Ounis, I. (2011). Intent-aware search result diversification. In *Proceedings of the ACM SIGIR conference on research and development in information retrieval* (pp. 595–604). ACM Press.

Saracevic, T. (1975). Relevance: A review of and framework for the thinking on the notion in information science. *Journal of the American Society for Information Science*, 26(6), 321–343.

Saracevic, T. (1991). Individual differences in organizing, searching and retrieving information. In *Proceedings of the annual meeting of the American society for information science* (Vol. 28, pp. 82–86).

Saracevic, T. (1996). Relevance reconsidered. In *Proceedings of the COLIS conference on conceptions of library and information science* (pp. 201–218). ACM Press.

Saracevic, T. (1997). The stratified model of information retrieval interaction: Extension and applications. In *Proceedings of the annual meeting for the American society for information science* (Vol. 34, pp. 313–327).

Saracevic, T. (2007). Relevance: A review of the literature and a framework for thinking on the notion in information science. Part III: Behavior and effects of relevance. *Journal of the American Society for Information Science and Technology*, 58(13), 2126–2144.

Saracevic, T., and Kantor, P. (1988). A study of information seeking and retrieving. III. Searchers, searches, and overlap. *Journal of the American Society for Information Science*, 39(3), 197–216.

Satyanarayanan, M. (2001). Pervasive computing: Vision and challenges. *IEEE Personal Communications*, 8(4), 10–17.

Sauro, J. and Dumas, J.S. (2009). Comparison of three one-question, post-task usability questionnaires. In *Proceedings of the ACM SIGCHI conference on human factors in computing systems* (pp. 1599–1608). ACM Press.

Savenkov, D., Lagun, D., and Liu, Q. (2013). Search engine switching detection based on user personal preferences and behavior patterns. In *Proceedings of the ACM SIGIR conference on research and development in information retrieval* (pp. 33–42). ACM Press.

Savenkov, D. and Agichtein, E. (2014). To hint or not: Exploring the effectiveness of search hints for complex informational tasks. In *Proceedings of the ACM SIGIR conference on research and development in information retrieval* (pp. 1115–1118). ACM Press.

Savolainen, R. (1995). Everyday life information seeking: approaching information seeking in the context of "way of life". *Library and Information Science Research*, 17(3), 259–294.

Savolainen, R. (2006). Time as a context of information seeking. *Library and Information Science Research*, 28(1), 110–127.

Sazoglu, F.B., Cambazoglu, B.B., Ozcan, R., Altingovde, I.S., and Ulusoy, Ö. (2013). A financial cost metric for result caching. In *Proceedings of the ACM SIGIR conference on research and development in information retrieval* (pp. 873–876). ACM Press.

Scaria, A. T., Philip, R. M., West, R., and Leskovec, J. (2014). The last click: Why users give up information network navigation. In *Proceedings of the ACM WSDM conference on web search and data mining* (pp. 213–222). ACM Press.

Schamber, L. (1994). Relevance and information behavior. *Annual Review of Information Science and Technology*, 29(1), 3–48.

Schamber, L., Eisenberg, M.B., and Nilan, M.S. (1990). A re-examination of relevance: toward a dynamic, situational definition. *Information Processing and Management*, 26(6), 755–776.

Schein, A.I., Popescul, A., Ungar, L.H., and Pennock, D.M. (2002). Methods and metrics for cold-start recommendations. In *Proceedings of the ACM SIGIR conference on research and development in information retrieval* (pp. 253–260). ACM Press.

Scheirer, J., Fernandez, R., Klein, J., and Picard, R.W. (2002). Frustrating the user on purpose: a step toward building an affective computer. *Interacting with Computers*, 14(2), 93–118.

Schmeck, R.R. (1988). *Learning Strategies and lLearning Styles (Perspectives on Individual Differences)*. New York: Plenum Press

Schmeck, R.R. and Geisler-Brenstein, E. (1989). Individual differences that affect the way students approach learning. *Learning and Individual Differences*, 1, 85–124.

Scholer, F., Kelly, D., Wu, W.-C., Lee, H.S. and Webber, W. (2013). The effect of threshold priming and need for cognition on relevance calibration and assessment. In *Proceedings of the ACM SIGIR conference on research and development in information retrieval* (pp. 623–632). ACM Press.

Scholer, F., Williams, H., and Turpin, A. (2004). Query association surrogates for web search. *Journal of the American Society on Informatin Science and Technology*, 55(7), 637–650.

schraefel, m.c. (2009). Building knowledge: what's beyond keyword search? *IEEE Computer*, 42(3), 52–59.

schraefel, m.c., Smith, D.A., Owens, A., Russell, A., Harris, C., and Wilson, M.L. (2005). The evolving mSpace platform: Leveraging the semantic web on the trail of the Memex. In *Proceedings of the ACM conference on hypertext and hypermedia* (pp. 174–183). ACM Press.

Schulz, L.E., and Bonawitz, E.B. (2007). Serious fun: Preschoolers engage in more exploratory play when evidence is confounded. *Developmental Psychology*, 43(4), 1045.

Schunk, D. (2004). *Learning Theories: An Educational Perspective* (4th ed.). Upper Saddle River, NJ: Pearson.

Schwarz, J. and Morris, M. (2011). Augmenting web pages and search results to support credibility assessment. In Proceedings of the ACM SIGCHI conference on human factors in computing systems (pp. 1245–1254). ACM Press.

Schwartz, K.L., Roe, T., Northrup, J., Meza, J., Seifeldin, R., and Neale, A.V. (2006). Family medicine patients' use of the internet for health information: A metronet study. *The Journal of the American Board of Family Medicine*, 19(1), 39–45.

Scientific American. (2008). How It Works: Multitouch Surfaces Explained. http://www.scientificamerican.com/article/how-it-works-touch-surfaces-explained/ Retrieved January 9, 2010.

Sears, A., Plaisant, C., Shneiderman, B. (1992). A new era for high-precision touchscreens. In Hartson, R., and Hix, D. (Eds.), Advances in Human-Computer Interaction, Vol. 3, Ablex (pp. 1–33).

Seligman, M.E. and Csikszentmihalyi, M. (2000). Positive psychology: An introduction. *American Psychologist*, 55(1), 5. American Psychological Association.

Sellen, A.J., Murphy, R., and Shaw, K.L. (2002). How knowledge workers use the web. In *Proceedings of the ACM SIGCHI conference on human factors in computing systems* (pp. 227–234). ACM Press.

Sellen, A.J. and Whittaker, S. (2010). Beyond total capture: A constructive critique of lifelogging. *Communications of the ACM*, 53(5), 70–77.

Serdyukov, P., Taylor, M., Vinay, V., Richardson, M., and White, R.W. (2011). Automatic people tagging for expertise profiling in the enterprise. In *Proceedings of the European conference on information retrieval* (pp. 399–410). Springer Berlin Heidelberg.

Sewell, W. and Komogortsev, O. (2010). Real-time eye gaze tracking with an unmodified commodity webcam employing a neural network. In *Proceedings of the ACM SIGCHI extended abstracts on human factors in computing systems* (pp. 3739–3744). ACM Press.

Shafer, G. (1976). *A Mathematical Theory of Evidence* (Vol. 1). Princeton: Princeton university press.

Shah, C. (2010a). Collaborative information seeking: A literature review. *Advances in librarianship*, 32, 3–33.

Shah, C. (2010b). Coagmento: A collaborative information seeking, synthesis and sense-making framework. In *Proceedings of the ACM CSCW conference on computer supported cooperative work: demonstrations* (pp. 6–11).

Shah, C. (2014). Collaborative information seeking. *Journal of the Association for Information Science and Technology*, 65(2), 215–236.

Shah, C. and González-Ibáñez, R. (2011). Evaluating the synergic effect of collaboration in information seeking. In *Proceedings of the ACM SIGIR conference on research and development in information retrieval* (pp. 913–922). ACM Press.

Shah, C., and Pomerantz, J. (2010). Evaluating and predicting answer quality in community QA. In *Proceedings of the ACM SIGIR conference on research and development in information retrieval* (pp. 411–418). ACM Press.

Shah, C. and Marchionini, G. (2010). Awareness in collaborative information seeking. *Journal of the American Society for Information Science and Technology*, 61(10), 1970–1986.

Shah, C. (2013). Effects of Awareness on Coordination in Collaborative Information Seeking. *Journal of the American Society for Information Science and Technology*, 64(6), 1122–1143.

Shahaf, D., Guestrin, C., and Horvitz, E. (2012). Trains of thought: Generating information maps. In *Proceedings of the international conference on the World Wide Web* (pp. 899–908). ACM Press.

Shami, N.S., Ehrlich, K., and Millen, D.R. (2008). Pick me!: Link selection in expertise search results. In *Proceedings of the ACM SIGCHI conference on human factors in computing systems* (pp. 1089–1092). ACM Press.

Shapira, B., Kantor, P.B., and Melamed, B. (2001). The effect of extrinsic motivation on user behavior in a collaborative information finding system. *Journal of the American Society for Information Science and Technology*, 52(11), 879–887.

Shardanand, U. and Maes, P. (1995). Social information filtering: Algorithms for automating "word of mouth". In *Proceedings of the ACM SIGCHI conference on human factors in computing systems* (pp. 210–217). ACM Press/Addison-Wesley Publishing Co.

Sharma, A. and Cosley, D. (2013). Do social explanations work?: Studying and modeling the effects of social explanations in recommender systems. In *Proceedings of the international conference on the World Wide Web* (pp. 1133–1144). ACM Press.

Sheldon, D., Shokouhi, M., Szummer, M., and Craswell, N. (2011). LambdaMerge: Merging the results of query reformulations. In *Proceedings of the ACM WSDM conference on web search and data mining* (pp. 795–804). ACM Press.

Shen, X., Tan, B., and Zhai, C. (2005a). Context-sensitive information retrieval using implicit feedback. In *Proceedings of the ACM SIGIR conference on research and development in information retrieval* (pp. 43–50).

Shen, X., Tan, B., and Zhai, C. (2005b). Implicit user modeling for personalized search. In *Proceedings of the ACM CIKM conference on information and knowledge management* (pp. 824–831). ACM Press.

Sherman, C. (2005). A new F-word for Google search results. *Search Engine Watch*. Retrieved March 8, 2005 from http://searchenginewatch.com/showPage.html?"3488076.

Sheth, B. and Maes, P. (1993). Evolving agents for personalized information filtering. In *Proceedings of the IEEE conference on artificial intelligence for applications* (pp. 345–352). IEEE.

Shipman, F.M., Furuta, R., Brenner, D., Chung, C.C., and Hsieh, H.W. (2000). Guided paths through Web-based collections: Design, experiences, and adaptations. *Journal of the American Society for Information Science*, 51(3), 260–272.

Shneiderman, B. (1984). Response time and display rate in human performance with computers. *Computing Surveys*, 16(3), 265–285.

Shneiderman, B. (1990). Human values and the future of technology: A declaration of empowerment. *ACM SIGCAS Computers and Society*, 20(3), 1–6.

Shneiderman, B. (1991). Touch screens now offer compelling uses. *IEEE Software*, 8(2), 93–94.

Shneiderman, B. (1992). Tree visualization with tree-maps: 2-d space-filling approach. *ACM Transactions on Graphics*, 11(1), 92–99.

Shneiderman, B. (1994). Dynamic queries for visual information seeking. *IEEE Software*, 11(6), 70–77.

Shneiderman, B. (1996). The eyes have it: a task by data type taxonomy for information visualizations, In *Proceedings of the IEEE symposium on visual languages* (pp. 336–343). IEEE.

Shneiderman, B. (1998). *Designing the User Interface: Strategies for Effective Human-Computer Interaction* (3rd ed.). Reading, MA: Addison-Wesley.

Shneiderman, B. (2000). Creating creativity: user interfaces for supporting innovation. *ACM Transactions on Computer-Human Interaction*, 7(1), 114–138.

Shneiderman, B. (2002). Creativity support tools. *Communications of the ACM*, 45(10), 116–120.

Shneiderman, B. (2007). Creativity support tools: Accelerating discovery and innovation. *Communications of the ACM*, 50(12), 20–32.

Shneiderman, B. and Maes, P. (1997). Direct manipulation vs. interface agents. *Interactions*, 4(6), 42–61.

Shneiderman, B., Byrd, D. and Croft, W.B. (1998). Sorting out searching: A user-interface framework for text searches. *Communications of the ACM*, 41(4), 95–98.

Shneiderman, B., Plaisant, C., and Hesse, B. (2013). Improving health and healthcare with interactive visualization tools. *IEEE Computer*, 46(5), 26–34.

Shokouhi, M. (2013). Learning to personalize query auto-completion. In *Proceedings of the ACM SIGIR conference on research and development in information retrieval* (pp. 103–112). ACM Press.

Shokouhi, M. and Guo, Q. (2015). From queries to cards: re-ranking proactive card recommendations based on reactive search history. In *Proceedings of the ACM SIGIR conference on research and development in information retrieval* (pp. 695–704). ACM Press.

Shokouhi, M. and Radinsky, K. (2012). Time-sensitive query auto-completion. In *Proceedings of the ACM SIGIR conference on research and development in information retrieval* (pp. 601–610). ACM Press.

Shokouhi, M. and Si, L. (2011). Federated search. *Foundations and Trends in Information Retrieval*, 5(1), 1–102.

Shokouhi, M., White, R.W., Bennett, P., and Radlinski, F. (2013). Fighting search engine amnesia: Re-ranking repeated results. In *Proceedings of the ACM SIGIR conference on research and development in information retrieval* (pp. 273–282). ACM Press.

REFERENCES

Shokouhi, M., White, R.W., and Yilmaz, E. (2015). Anchoring and adjustment in relevance estimation. In *Proceedings of the ACM SIGIR conference on research and development in information retrieval* (pp. 963–966). ACM Press.

Shtok, A., Kurland, O., and Carmel, D. (2009). Predicting query performance by query-drift estimation. In *Proceedings of the international conference on the theory of information retrieval* (pp. 305–312). Springer Berlin Heidelberg.

Shurman, E. and Brutlag, J. (2009). Performance related changes and their user impact. *Velocity*. http://oreil.ly/fTmYwz. Accessed on August 15, 2015.

Shute, S.J. and Smith, P.J. (1993). Knowledge-based search tactics. *Information Processing and Management*, 29(1), 29–45.

Sibert, L.E. and Jacob, R.J. (2000). Evaluation of eye gaze interaction. In *Proceedings of the ACM SIGCHI conference on human factors in computing systems* (pp. 281–288). ACM Press.

Sidney, K.D., Craig, S.D., Gholson, B., Franklin, S., Picard, R., and Graesser, A.C. (2005). Integrating affect sensors in an intelligent tutoring system. In *Proceedings of affective interactions: the computer in the affective loop workshop* (pp. 7–13).

Sieg, A., Mobasher, B., and Burke, R. (2007). Web search personalization with ontological user profiles. In *Proceedings of the ACM CIKM conference on information and knowledge management* (pp. 525–534). ACM Press.

Silverstein, C., Marais, H., Henzinger, M., and Moricz, M. (1999). Analysis of a very large web search engine query log. *SIGIR Forum*, 33(1), 6–12.

Simon, H.A. (1971). Designing organizations for an information-rich world. *Computers, Communication, and the Public Interest*, 37, 40–41

Sinervo, B. (1997). *Optimal Foraging Theory: Constraints and Cognitive Processes. Behavioral Ecology*. Santa Cruz, CA: University of California.

Singer, N. (2012). *You've won a badge (and now we know all about you)*. New York Times, 4 February 2012.

Singla, A., Horvitz, E., Kamar, E., and White, R. (2014a). Stochastic privacy. In *Proceedings of the AAAI conference on artificial intelligence* (pp. 152–158). AAAI Press.

Singla, A., White, R.W., Hassan, A., and Horvitz, E. (2014b). Enhancing personalization via search activity attribution. In *Proceedings of the ACM SIGIR conference on research and development in information retrieval* (pp. 1063–1066). ACM Press.

Singla, A., White, R.W., and Huang, J. (2010). Studying trailfinding algorithms for enhanced web search. In *Proceedings of the ACM SIGIR conference on research and development in information retrieval* (pp. 443–450). ACM Press.

Singley, K., Lai, J., Kuang, L., and Tang, J.-M. (2008). BlueReach: Harnessing synchronous chat to support expertise sharing in a large organization. In *Proceedings of the ACM SIGCHI conference on human factors in computing systems* (pp. 2001–2008). ACM Press.

Skinner, B.F. (1974). *About Behaviorism*. New York: Knopf (distributed by Random House).

Slater, M. (1999). Measuring presence: A response to the witmer and singer presence questionnaire. *Presence*, 8(5), 560–565.

Smirnova, E. and Balog, K. (2011). A user-oriented model for expert finding. In *Proceedings of the European conference on information retrieval* (pp. 580–592). Springer-Verlag.

Smith, C.L. and Kantor, P.B. (2008). User adaptation: good results from poor systems. In *Proceedings of the ACM SIGIR conference on research and development in information retrieval* (pp. 147–154). ACM Press.

Smith, S., Glenberg, A., and Bjork, R. (1978). Environmental context and human memory. *Memory and Cognition*, 6(4), 342–353.

Smucker, M.D. and Jethani, C.P. (2010). Human performance and retrieval precision revisited. In *Proceedings of the ACM SIGIR conference on research and development in information retrieval* (pp. 595–602). ACM Press.

Smucker, M.D. and Clarke, C.L. (2012a). Time-based calibration of effectiveness measures. In *Proceedings of the ACM SIGIR conference on research and development in information retrieval* (pp. 95–104). ACM Press.

Smucker, M.D., and Clarke, C.L. (2012b). Modeling user variance in time-biased gain. In *Proceedings of the symposium on human-computer interaction and information retrieval* (p. 3). ACM Press.

Soergel, D. (1999). The rise of ontologies or the reinvention of classification, *Journal of the American Society for Information Science and Technology*, 50(12), 1119–1120.

Solovey, E., Schermerhorn, P., Scheutz, M., Sassaroli, A., Fantini, S., and Jacob, R. (2012). Brainput: Enhancing interactive systems with streaming fnirs brain input. In *Proceedings of the ACM SIGCHI conference on human factors in computing systems* (pp. 2193–2202). ACM Press.

Song, Y., Shi, X., and Fu, X. (2013). Evaluating and predicting user engagement change with degraded search relevance. In *Proceedings of international conference on the World Wide Web* (pp. 1213–1224).

Song, Y., Wang, H., and He, X. (2014). Adapting deep ranknet for personalized search. In *Proceedings of the ACM WSDM conference on web search and data mining* (pp. 83–92). ACM Press.

Song, Y., Zhuang, Z., Li, H., Zhao, Q., Li, J., Lee, W.C., and Giles, C.L. (2008). Real-time automatic tag recommendation. *Proceedings of the ACM SIGIR conference on research and development in information retrieval* (pp. 515–522). ACM Press.

Sontag, D., Collins-Thompson, K., Bennett, P.N., White, R.W., Dumais, S., and Billerbeck, B. (2012). Probabilistic models for personalizing web search. In *Proceedings of the ACM WSDM conference on web search and data mining* (pp. 433–442). ACM Press.

Spärck-Jones, K. (1972). A statistical interpretation of term specificity and its application in retrieval. *Journal of Documentation*, 28(1), 11–21.

Spärck-Jones, K., Robertson, S.E., and Sanderson, M. (2007). Ambiguous requests: Implications for retrieval tests, systems, and theories. *SIGIR Forum*, 41(2), 8–17.

Spärck-Jones, K. and van Rijsbergen, C.J. (1976). Information retrieval test collections. *Journal of Documentation*, 32(1), 59–75.

Spärck-Jones, K., Walker, S., and Robertson, S.E. (2000). A probabilistic model of information retrieval: Development and comparative experiments: Part 1. *Information Processing and Management*, 36(6), 779–808.

Speicher, M. (2012). *W3touch: Crowdsourced Evaluation and Adaptation of Web Interfaces for Touch*. Master's thesis, ETH Zurich.

Spence, R. (2002). Rapid, serial and visual: A presentation technique with potential. *Information Visualization*, 1(1), 13–19.

Sperber, D., and Wilson, D. (1995). *Relevance: Communication and cognition* (2nd ed.). Oxford: Blackwell.

Speretta, M. and Gauch, S. (2005). Personalized search based on user search histories. In *Proceedings of IEEE/WIC/ACM conference on Web intelligence* (pp. 622–628). IEEE.

Spink, A., Goodrum, A., Robins, D., and Wu, M.M. (1996). Search intermediaries elicitations during mediated online searching. In *Proceedings of the ACM SIGIR conference on research and development in information retrieval* (pp. 120–127). ACM Press.

Spink, A., Griesdorf, H., and Bateman, J. (1998). From highly relevant to not relevant: Examining different regions of relevance. *Information Processing and Management*, 34(5), 599–621.

Spink, A. and Losee, R.M. (1996). Feedback in information retrieval. *Annual Review of Information Science and Technology*, 31(1), 33–78.

Spink, A., Park, M., Jansen, B.J., and Pedersen, J. (2006). Multitasking during Web search sessions. *Information Processing and Management*, 42(1), 264–275.

Spink, A. and Saracevic, T. (1997). Interactive information retrieval: Sources and effectiveness of search terms during mediated online searching. *Journal of the American Society for Information Science*, 48(8), 741–761.

Spivey, M.J., Grosjean, M., and Knoblich, G. (2005). Continuous attraction toward phonological competitors. *Proceedings of the National Academy of Sciences of the United States of America*, 102(29), 10393–10398.

Spoerri, A. (1993). InfoCrystal: A visual tool for information retrieval and management. In *Proceedings of the ACM CIKM conference on information and knowledge management* (pp. 11–20). ACM Press.

Sriram, S., Shen, X. and Zhai, C. (2004). A session-based search engine. In *Proceedings of the ACM SIGIR conference on research and development in information retrieval* (pp. 492–493). ACM Press.

Stanton, I., Ieong, S., and Mishra, N. (2014). Circumlocution in diagnostic medical queries. In *Proceedings of the ACM SIGIR conference on Research and development in information retrieval* (pp. 133–142). ACM Press.

Stephens, D.W. and Krebs, J. R. (1986). *Foraging Theory*. Princeton, NJ: Princeton University Press.

Sternberg, R.J. (1999). *Handbook of Creativity*. Cambridge: Cambridge University Press.

Sternberg, R.J. and Lubart, T.I. (1999). The concept of creativity: Prospects and paradigms. In Sternberg, R.J. (Ed.), *Handbook of Creativity* (pp. 3–15). Cambridge: Cambridge University Press.

Sternberg, R.J., Kaufman, J.C., and Pretz, J.E. (2002). *The Creativity Conundrum: A Propulsion Model of Kinds of Creative Contributions*. New York: Psychology Press.

Stigler, G.J. (1961). The economics of information. *The Journal of Political Economy*, 69(3), 213–225.

Stoica, E. and Hearst, M. (2004). Nearly automated metadata hierarchy creation. In *Proceedings of the annual conference of the North American chapter of the association for computational linguistics (Companion Volume)* (pp. 117–120).

Stone, M.C., Fishkin, K., and Bier, E.A. (1994). The movable filter as a user interface tool. In *Proceedings of the ACM SIGCHI conference on human factors in computing systems* (pp. 306–312). ACM Press.

Su, L.T. (1992). Evaluation measures for interactive information retrieval. *Information Processing and Management*, 28(4), 503–516.

Su, L.T. (2003). A comprehensive and systematic model of user evaluation of Web search engines. *Journal of the American Society for Information Science and Technology*, 54(13), 1175–1192.

Suchman, L.A. (1987). *Plans and Situated Actions*. New York: Cambridge University Press.

Sugiyama, K., Hatano, K., and Yoshikawa, M. (2004). Adaptive web search based on user profile constructed without any effort from users. In *Proceedings of the international conference on the World Wide Web* (pp. 675–684). ACM Press.

Sun, J.-T., Zeng, H.-J., Liu, H., Lu, Y., and Chen, Z. (2005). CubeSVD: A novel approach to personalized Web search. In *Proceedings of the international conference on the World Wide Web* (pp. 382–390).

Svennevig, J. (2000). *Getting Acquainted in Conversation: A Study of Initial Interactions* (Vol. 64). John Benjamins Publishing.

Swanson, D.R. (1988). Migraine and magnesium: Eleven neglected connections. *Perspectives in biology and medicine*, 31(4), 526–557.

Sweller, J., van Merrienboer, J., and Paas, F. (1998). Cognitive architecture and instructional design. *Educational Psychology Review*, 10(3), 251–296.

Tagliacozzo, R. (1977). Estimating the satisfaction of information users. *Bulletin of the Medical Library Association*, 65(2), 243–249.

Tague-Sutcliffe, J. (1992). The pragmatics of information retrieval experimentation revisited. *Information Processing and Management*, 28(4), 467–490.

Takano, H. and T. Winograd. (1998). Dynamic bookmarks for the WWW. In *Proceedings of ACM conference on hypertext and hypermedia* (pp. 297–298). ACM Press.

Talbot, J., Lee, B., Kapoor, A., and Tan, D. (2009). Ensemble matrix: Interactive visualization to support machine learning with multiple classifiers. In *Proceedings of the ACM SIGCHI conference on human factors in computing systems* (pp. 1283–1292). ACM Press.

Talja, S. and Hansen, P. (2006). Information sharing. In Spink, A. and Cole, C. (Eds.), *New Directions in Human Information Behavior*. Springer Netherlands (pp. 113–134).

Tambe, M., Scerri, P., and Pynadath, D.V. (2002). Adjustable autonomy for the real world. *Journal of Artificial Intelligence Research*, 17(1), 171–228.

Tan, B., Shen, X., and Zhai, C. (2006). Mining long-term search history to improve search accuracy. In *Proceedings of the ACM SIGKDD on knowledge discovery and data mining* (pp. 718–723). ACM Press.

Tan, C., Gabrilovich, E., and Pang, B. (2012). To each his own: Personalized content selection based on text comprehensibility. In *Proceedings of the ACM WSDM international conference on web search and data mining* (pp. 233–242). ACM Press.

Tang, J.C. (2011). Reflecting on the DARPA Red Balloon Challenge. *Communications of the ACM*, 54(4), 78–85.

Tang, R. and Solomon, P. (1998). Toward an understanding of the dynamics of relevance judgment: An analysis of one person's search behavior. *Information Processing and Management*, 34(2), 237–256.

Tao, J. and Tan, T. (2005). Affective computing: A review. In *Proceedings of the conference on affective computing and intelligent interaction* (pp. 981–995).

Tauscher, L. and Greenberg, S. (1997). How people revisit Web pages: Empirical findings and implications for the design of history systems. *International Journal of Human-Computer Studies*, 47(1), 97–137.

Taylor, N.J., Dennis, A.R., and Cummings, J.W. (2013). Situation normality and the shape of search: The effects of time delays and information presentation on search behavior. *Journal of the American Society for Information Science and Technology*, 64(5), 909–928.

Taylor, R.S. (1968). Question-negotiation and information seeking in libraries. *College and Research Libraries*, 29, 178–194.

Taylor, S.E. (1991). Asymmetrical effects of positive and negative events: The mobilization-minimization hypothesis. *Psychological Bulletin*, 110(1), 67.

Technet. (2012). Privacy and technology in balance. http://blogs.microsoft.com/on-the-issues/2012/10/26/privacy-and-technology-in-balance/. Accessed on August 15, 2015.

Teevan, J. (2006). How people recall search result lists. In *Proceedings of the ACM SIGCHI extended abstracts on human factors in computing systems* (pp. 1415–1420). ACM Press.

Teevan, J. (2007). The re: Search engine: Simultaneous support for finding and re-finding. In *Proceedings of the ACM UIST symposium on user interface software and technology* (pp. 23–32). ACM Press.

Teevan, J., Adar, E., Jones, R., and Potts, M.A. (2007). Information re-retrieval: Repeat queries in Yahoo's logs. In *Proceedings of the ACM SIGIR conference on research and development in information retrieval* (pp. 151–158). ACM Press.

Teevan, J., Alvarado, C., Ackerman, M.S., and Karger, D.R. (2004). The perfect search engine is not enough: a study of orienteering behavior in directed search. In *Proceedings of the ACM SIGCHI conference on human factors in computing systems* (pp. 415–422). ACM Press.

Teevan, J., Collins-Thompson, K., White, R.W., Dumais, S.T., and Kim, Y. (2013). Slow search: Information retrieval without time constraints. In *Proceedings of the symposium on human-computer interaction and information retrieval* (p. 1). ACM Press.

REFERENCES

Teevan, J., Cutrell, E., Fisher, D., Drucker, S.M., Ramos, G., André, P., and Hu, C. (2009a). Visual snippets: Summarizing web pages for search and revisitation. In *Proceedings of the ACM SIGCHI conference on human factors in computing systems* (pp. 2023–2032). ACM Press.

Teevan, J., Dumais, S.T. and Liebling, D.J. (2008). To personalize or not to personalize: modeling queries with variation in user intent. In *Proceedings of the ACM SIGIR conference on research and development in information retrieval* (pp. 163–170). ACM Press.

Teevan, J., Dumais, S., and Horvitz, E. (2010). Potential for personalization. *ACM Transactions on Computer-Human Interaction*, 17(1), 31.

Teevan, J., Dumais, S.T., and Horvitz, E. (2005). Beyond the commons: Investigating the value of personalizing web search. In *Proceedings of the Workshop on New Tech. for Personalized Information Access* (pp. 84–92).

Teevan, J., Karlson, A., Amini, S., Brush, A.J., and Krumm, J. (2011a). Understanding the importance of location, time, and people in mobile local search behavior. In *Proceedings of the international conference on human computer interaction with mobile devices and services* (pp. 77–80). ACM Press.

Teevan, J., Liebling, D.J., and Ravichandran G.G. (2011b). Understanding and predicting personal navigation. In *Proceedings of the ACM WSDM conference on web search and data mining* (pp. 85–94). ACM Press.

Teevan, J., Liebling, D.J., and Lasecki, W.S. (2014a). Selfsourcing personal tasks. In *Proceedings of the ACM SIGCHI extended abstracts on human factors in computing systems* (pp. 2527–2532). ACM Press.

Teevan, J., Morris, M.R., and Bush, S. (2009b). Discovering and using groups to improve personalized search. In *Proceedings of the ACM WSDM conference on web search and data mining* (pp. 15–24). ACM Press.

Teevan, J., Ringel Morris, M., and Azenkot, S. (2014b). Supporting interpersonal interaction during collaborative mobile search. *IEEE Computer*, 47(3), 54–57.

Telang, R., Mukhopadhyay, T., and Wilcox, R. (1999). An empirical analysis of the antecedents of internet search engine choice. In *Proceedings of the Workshop on Information Systems and Economics*.

Thaler, R.H. and Sunstein, C.R. (2008). *Nudge: Improving Decisions about Health, Wealth, and Happiness*. New Have, CT: Yale.

Thatcher, A. (2008). Web search strategies: The influence of Web experience and task type. *Information Processing and Management*, 44(3), 1308–1329.

Thibaut, J.W. and Kelley, H.H. (1959). *The Social Psychology of Groups*. New York: John Wiley and Sons, Inc.

Thomas, P. and Hawking, D. (2006). Evaluation by comparing result sets in context. In *Proceedings of the ACM CIKM conference on information and knowledge management* (pp. 94–101). ACM Press.

Thorisson, K.R. (1996). Communicative humanoids: A computational model of psychosocial dialogue skills (Doctoral dissertation, Massachusetts Institute of Technology).

Thorndike, E.L. and Woodworth, R.S. (1901). The influence of improvement in one mental function upon the efficiency of other functions. *Psychological Review*, 8.

Thorne, A. (1987). The press of personality: A study of conversations between introverts and extraverts. *Journal of Personality and Social Psychology*, 53(4), 718.

Tianmiyu, M.A. and Ajiferuke, I.Y. (1988). A total relevance a document interaction effects model for the evaluation of information retrieval processes. *Information Processing and Management*, 24(4), 391–404.

Tintarev, N. and Masthoff, J. (2007). Effective explanations of recommendations: User-centered design. In *Proceedings of the ACM RECSYS conference on recommender systems* (pp. 153–156). ACM Press.

Tombros, A. and Sanderson, M. (1998). Advantages of query biased summaries in information retrieval. In *Proceedings of the ACM SIGIR conference on research and development in information retrieval* (pp. 2–10). ACM Press.

Toms, E. (2000a). Understanding and facilitating the browsing of electronic text. *International Journal of Human-Computer Studies*, 52(3), 423–452.

Toms, E.G. (2000b). Serendipitous information retrieval. In *Proceedings of the DELOS workshop: information seeking, searching and querying in digital libraries*.

Totton, N. and Jacobs, M. (2001). *Character and Personality Types*. Philadelphia, PA: Open University Press.

Trattner, C., Helic, D., Singer, P., and Strohmaier, M. (2012). Exploring the differences and similarities between hierarchical decentralized search and human navigation in information networks. In *Proceedings of the conference on knowledge management and knowledge technologies* (p. 14). ACM Press.

Trigg, R.H. (1988). Guided tours and tabletops: tools for communicating in a hypertext environment. *ACM Transactions on Information Systems*, 6(4), 398–414.

Tsai, M.-J. and Tsai, C.-C. (2003). Information searching strategies in web-based science learning: The role of internet self-efficacy. *Innovations in Education and Teaching International*, 40(1), 43–50.

Tufekci, Z. (2014). Engineering the public: Big data, surveillance and computational politics. *First Monday*, 19(7).

Tukey, J.W. (1977). *Exploratory Data Analysis*. Reading, PA: Addison-Wesley.

Tulving, E. and Thomson, D. (1973). Encoding specificity and retrieval processes in episodic memory. *Psychological Review*, 80, 352–373.

Tungare, M. and Pérez-Quiñones, M.A. (2009). Mental workload in multi-device personal information management. In *Proceedings of the ACM SIGCHI extended abstracts on human factors in computing systems* (pp. 3431–3436). ACM Press.

Tunkelang, D. (2009). *Faceted Search*. San Rafael, CA: Morgan and Claypool.

Turkle, S. (1984). *The Second Self: Computers and the Human Spirit*. New York: Simon and Shuster.

Turpin, A.H. and Hersh, W. (2001). Why batch and user evaluations do not give the same results. In *Proceedings of the ACM SIGIR conference on research and development in information retrieval* (pp. 225–231). ACM Press.

Turpin, A. and Hersh, W. (2002). User interface effects in past batch versus user experiments. In *Proceedings of the ACM SIGIR conference on research and development in information retrieval* (pp. 431–432). ACM Press.

Turpin, A. and Scholer, F. (2006). User performance versus precision measures for simple search tasks. In *Proceedings of the ACM SIGIR conference on research and development in information retrieval* (pp. 11–18).

Turpin, A., Scholer, F., Järvelin, K., Wu, M., and Culpepper, J.S. (2009). Including summaries in system evaluation. In *Proceedings of the ACM SIGIR conference on research and development in information retrieval* (pp. 508–515).

Tversky, A. and Kahneman, D. (1974). Judgment under uncertainty: Heuristics and biases. *Science*, 185(4157), 1124–1131.

Tversky, A. and Kahneman, D. (1991). Loss aversion in riskless choice: A reference-dependent model. *The Quarterly Journal of Economics*, 106(4), 1039.

Twidale, M., and Nichols, D. (1996). Interfaces to support collaboration in information retrieval. *Information Retrieval and Human Computer Interaction*, 25–28.

Twidale, M.B., Nichols, D.M., and Paice, C.D. (1997). Browsing is a collaborative process. *Information Processing and Management*, 33(6), 761–783.

Tyler, J.R. and Tang, J.C. (2003). When can I expect an email response? A study of rhythms in email usage. In *Proceedings of the European conference on computer supported cooperative work* (pp. 239–258). Netherlands: Springer.

Tyler, S.K. and Teevan, J. (2010). Large scale query log analysis of re-finding. In *Proceedings of the ACM WSDM conference on web search and data mining* (pp. 191–200). ACM Press.

Tyler, S.K., Teevan, J., Bailey, P., de la Chica, S. and Dandekar, N. (2015). *Large scale log analysis of individuals' domain preferences in web search*. Microsoft Research Technical Report (MSR-TR-2015-48).

Twidale, M.B., Nichols, D.M., and Paice, C.D. (1997). Browsing is a collaborative process. *Information Processing and Management*, 33(6), 761–783.

Udsen, L. and Jørgensen, A. (2005). The aesthetic turn: Unravelling recent aesthetic approaches to human-computer interaction. *Digital Creativity*, 16(4), 205–216.

Urban, J., Jose, J.M., and van Rijsbergen, C.J. (2006) An adaptive technique for content-based image retrieval. *Multimedia Tools and Applications*, 31(1), 1–28.

Ustinovskiy, Y., Gusev, G., and Serdyukov, P. (2015). An optimization framework for weighting implicit relevance labels for personalized web search. In *Proceedings of the international conference on the World Wide Web* (pp. 1144–1154). ACM Press.

Ustinovskiy, Y. and Serdyukov, P. (2013). Personalization of web-search using short-term browsing context. In *Proceedings of the ACM CIKM conference on information and knowledge management* (pp. 1979–1988). ACM Press.

Vakkari, P. (1999). Task complexity, problem structure and information actions: Integrating studies on information seeking and retrieval. *Information Processing and Management*, 35(6), 819–837.

Vallet, D. and Castells, P. (2012). Personalized diversification of search results. In *Proceedings of the ACM SIGIR conference on research and development in information retrieval* (pp. 841–850). ACM Press.

Van Andel, P. (1994). Anatomy of the unsought finding. Serendipity: origin, history, domains, traditions, appearances, patterns and programmability. *The British Journal for the Philosophy of Science*, 45(2), 631–648.

Van Bergen, A. (1968). *Task Interruption*. Amsterdam: North Holland Publishing Co.

Van Kleek, M., Moore, B., Xu, C., and Karger, D.R. (2010). Eyebrowse: real-time web activity sharing and visualization. In *Proceedings of the ACM SIGCHI extended abstracts on human factors in computing systems* (pp. 3643–3648). ACM Press.

Vardi, M.Y. (2012). Will MOOCs destroy academia?. *Communications of the ACM*, 55(11), 5.

Varian, H.R. (1999). Economics and search. *SIGIR Forum*, 33(1), 1–5.

Vespignani, A. (2009). Predicting the behavior of techno-social systems. *Science*, 325(5939), 425.

Vickery, A. and Brooks, H.M. (1987). PLEXUS: The expert system for referral. *Information Processing and Management*, 23(2), 99–117.

Viégas, F.B., Wattenberg, M., van Ham, F., Kriss, J., and McKeon, M. (2007). Many eyes: A site for visualization at internet scale. *IEEE Transactions on Visualization and Computer Graphics*, 13(6), 1121–1128.

Villa, R., Cantador, I., Joho, H., and Jose, J.M. (2009). An aspectual interface for supporting complex search tasks. In *Proceedings of the ACM SIGIR conference on research and development in information retrieval* (pp. 379–386). ACM Press.

Vlachos, M., Meek, C., Vagena, Z., and Gunopulos, D. (2004). Identification of similarities, periodicities and bursts for online search queries. In *Proceedings of the ACM SIGMOD conference on the management of data* (pp. 131–142). ACM Press.

Volokh, E. (2000). Personalization and privacy. *Communications of the ACM*, 43(8), 84–88.

Von Ahn, L. (2006). Games with a purpose. *IEEE Computer*, 39(6), 92–94. IEEE.

Von Ahn, L., Blum, M., Hopper, N.J., and Langford, J. (2003). CAPTCHA: Using hard AI problems for security. In *Proceedings of the EUROCRYPT conference on advances in cryptology* (pp. 294–311). Springer Berlin Heidelberg.

Von Ahn, L. and Dabbish, L. (2004). Labeling images with a computer game. In *Proceedings of the ACM SIGCHI conference on human factors in computing systems* (pp. 319–326). ACM Press.

Von Ahn, L., Maurer, B., McMillen, C., Abraham, D., and Blum, M. (2008). Recaptcha: Human-based character recognition via web security measures. *Science*, 321(5895), 1465–1468.

Voorhees, E. and Harman, D. (Eds.). (2005). *TREC Experiment and Evaluation in Information Retrieval*. Boston, MA: MIT Press.

Voorhees, E.M. (1999). TREC-8 question answering track report. In *Proceedings of the text retrieval conference* (pp. 77–82).

Voorhees, E.M. (2009). I come not to bury Cranfield, but to praise it. In *Proceedings of the workshop on human-computer interaction and retrieval* (pp. 13–16).

Voorhees, E.M. and Harman, D.K. (Eds.). (2000). *TREC-9. The ninth text retrieval conference*. Washington, DC: GPO.

Vosniadou, S. and Brewer, W.F. (1987). Theories of knowledge restructuring in development. Review of educational research, 57(1), 51–67.

Vygotsky, L. (1962). *Thought and Language*: Cambridge, MA: MIT Press.

Vygotsky, L.S. (1978). Mind in society: The development of higher psychological processes. Cambridge, MA: Harvard University Press.

Wærn, A. (2004). User involvement in automatic filtering: An experimental study. *User Modeling and User-Adapted Interaction*, 14(2–3), 201–237.

Wang, C., Xie, X., Wang, L., Lu, Y., and Ma, W.Y. (2005). Web resource geographic location classification and detection. In *conference companion of the international conference on the World Wide Web* (pp. 1138–1139). ACM Press.

Wang, H., He, X., Chang, M.W., Song, Y., White, R.W., and Chu, W. (2013). Personalized ranking model adaptation for web search. In *Proceedings of the ACM SIGIR conference on research and development in information retrieval* (pp. 323–332). ACM Press.

Wang, H., Lymberopoulos, D., and Liu, J. (2014a). Local business ambience characterization through mobile audio sensing. In *Proceedings of the international conference on the World Wide Web* (pp. 293–304).

Wang, H., Zhai, C., Liang, F., Dong, A., and Chang, Y. (2014b). User modeling in search logs via a nonparametric bayesian approach, In *Proceedings on the ACM WSDM conference on web search and data mining* (pp. 203–212). ACM Press.

Wang, J. and Zhu, J. (2009). Portfolio theory of information retrieval. In *Proceedings of the ACM SIGIR conference on research and development in information retrieval* (pp. 115–122). ACM Press.

Wang, K., Walker, T., and Zheng, Z. (2009). PSkip: Estimating relevance ranking quality from web search clickthrough data. In *Proceedings of the ACM SIGKDD international conference on knowledge discovery and data mining* (pp. 1355–1364). ACM Press.

Wang, L., Wang, C., Xie, X., Forman, J., Lu, Y., Ma, W.Y., and Li, Y. (2005). Detecting dominant locations from search queries. In *Proceedings of the ACM SIGIR conference on research and development in information retrieval* (pp. 424–431). ACM Press.

Wang, T., Plaisant, C., Quinn, A.J., Stanchak, R., Murphy, S., and Shneiderman, B. (2008). Aligning temporal data by sentinel events: Discovering patterns in electronic health records. In *Proceedings of the ACM SIGCHI conference on human factors in computing systems* (pp. 457–466). ACM Press.

Wang, X. and Zhai, C. (2009). Beyond hyperlinks: Organizing information footprints in search logs to support effective browsing. In *Proceedings of the ACM CIKM conference on information and knowledge management* (pp. 1237–1246). ACM Press.

REFERENCES

Wang, J. and Zhu, J. (2009). Portfolio theory of information retrieval. In *Proceedings of the ACM SIGIR conference on research and development in information retrieval* (pp. 115–122). ACM Press.

Wang, Y., Huang, X., and White, R.W. (2013). Characterizing and supporting cross-device search tasks. In *Proceedings of the ACM WSDM conference on Web search and data mining* (pp. 707–716). ACM Press.

Want, R., Hopper, A., Falcao, V., and Gibbons, J. (1992). The active badge location system. *ACM Transactions on Information Systems*, 10(1), 91–102.

Wasserman, S. and Faust, K. (1994). Social network analysis in the social and behavioral sciences. In Wasserman, S. and Faust, K. (eds.), *Social Network Analysis: Methods and Applications*. Cambridge: Cambridge University Press (pp. 1–27).

Watanabe, Y., Okada, Y., Kim, Y.-B., and Takeda, T. (1998). Translation camera. In *Proceedings of the international conference on pattern recognition* (pp. 613–617).

Watts, D.J. and Strogatz, S.H. (1998). Collective dynamics of 'small-world' networks. *Nature*, 393(6684), 440–442.

Weber, I. and Castillo, C. (2010). The demographics of web search. In *Proceedings of the ACM SIGIR conference on Research and development in information retrieval* (pp. 523–530). ACM Press.

Weber, S.J. and Cook, T.D. (1972). Subject effects in laboratory research: An examination of subject roles, demand characteristics, and valid inference. *Psychological Bulletin*, 77(4), 273.

Weber, I., Garimella, V.R.K., and Borra, E. (2012). Mining web query logs to analyze political issues. In *Proceedings of the Annual ACM Web Science Conference* (pp. 330–334). ACM Press.

Webster, J., and Ho, H. (1997). Audience engagement in multimedia presentations. *The DATA BASE for Advances in Information Systems*, 28(2), 63–77.

Wedig S. and Madani, O. (2006). A large-scale analysis of query logs for assessing personalization opportunities. In *Proceedings of the ACM SIGKDD conference on knowledge discovery and data mining* (pp. 742–747). ACM Press.

Weinreich, H., Obendorf, H., Herder, E., and Mayer, M. (2006). Off the beaten tracks: Exploring three aspects of web navigation. In *Proceedings of the international conference on the World Wide Web* (pp. 133–142). ACM Press.

Weinreich, H., Obendorf, H., Herder, E., and Mayer, M. (2008). Not quite the average: An empirical study of Web use. *ACM Transactions on the Web*, 2(1), 5.

Weiser, M. (1993). Some computer science issues in ubiquitous computing. Communications of the ACM, 36(7), 75–84.

Weisz, J.D., Erickson, T., and Kellogg, W.A. (2006). Synchronous broadcast messaging: The use of ICT. In *Proceedings of the ACM SIGCHI conference on human factors in computing systems* (pp. 1293–1302). ACM Press.

West, R. and Leskovec, J. (2012a). Automatic versus human navigation in information networks. In *Proceedings of the international conference on weblogs and social media*. AAAI Press.

West, R. and Leskovec, J. (2012b). Human wayfinding in information networks. In *Proceedings of the international conference on the World Wide Web* (pp. 619–628). ACM Press.

West, R., Pineau, J., and Precup, D. (2009). Wikispeedia: An online game for inferring semantic distances between concepts. In *Proceedings of the international joint conference on artifical intelligence* (pp. 1598–1603).

West, R., White, R.W., and Horvitz, E. (2013a). From cookies to cooks: Insights on dietary patterns via analysis of web usage logs. In *Proceedings of the international conference on the World Wide Web* (pp. 1399–1410). International World Wide Web Conferences Steering Committee.

West, R., White, R.W., and Horvitz, E. (2013b). Here and there: Goals, activities, and predictions about location from geotagged queries. In *Proceedings of the ACM SIGIR conference on research and development in information retrieval* (pp. 817–820). ACM Press.

Wexelblat, A. and Maes, P. (1999). Footprints: History-rich tools for information foraging. In *Proceedings of the ACM SIGCHI conference on human factors in computing systems* (pp. 270–277). ACM Press.

Weybrew, B.B. (1984). The Zeigarnik phenomenon revisited: Implications for enhancement of morale. *Perceptual and Motor Skills*, 58(1), 223–226.

Wheeldon, R. and Levene, M. (2003). The best trail algorithm for assisted navigation of web sites. In *Proceedings of the latin American web congress* (pp. 166–178). IEEE.

White, R., Ruthven, I., and Jose, J.M. (2002a). Finding relevant documents using top ranking sentences: An evaluation of two alternative schemes. In *Proceedings of ACM SIGIR conference on research and development in information retrieval* (pp. 57–64). ACM Press.

White, R., Ruthven, I., and Jose, J.M. (2002b). The use of implicit evidence for relevance feedback in web retrieval. In *Advances in Information Retrieval* (pp. 93–109). Springer Berlin Heidelberg.

White, R.W. (2004). A visualisation technique to communicate implicit feedback decisions. In *Proceedings of the European conference on information retrieval* (Vol. 2, pp. 23–24).

White, R.W. (2006). Using searcher simulations to redesign a polyrepresentative implicit feedback interface. *Information Processing and Management*, 42(5), 1185–1202.

White, R.W. (2011). Interactive techniques. In Ruthven, I. and Kelly, D. (Eds.), *Interactive Information Seeking, Behaviour and Retrieval* (pp. 171–188). London: Facet Publishing.

White, R.W. (2013). Beliefs and biases in Web search. In *Proceedings of the ACM SIGIR conference on research and development in information retrieval* (pp. 3–10). ACM Press.

White, R.W. (2014). Belief dynamics in Web search. *Journal of the Association for Information Science and Technology*, 65(11), 2165–2178.

White, R.W., Bailey, P., and Chen, L. (2009a). Predicting user interests from contextual information. In *Proceedings of the ACM SIGIR conference on research and development in information retrieval* (pp. 363–370). ACM Press.

White, R.W., Bilenko, M., and Cucerzan, S. (2007). Studying the use of popular destinations to enhance web search inter-action. In *Proceedings of the ACM SIGIR conference on research and development in information retrieval* (pp. 159–166). ACM Press.

White, R.W. and Buscher, G. (2012a). Text selections as implicit relevance feedback. In *Proceedings of the ACM SIGIR conference on research and development in information retrieval* (pp. 1151–1152). ACM Press.

White, R.W. and Buscher, G. (2012b). Characterizing local interests and local knowledge. In *Proceedings of the SIGCHI conference on human factors in computing systems* (pp. 1607–1610). ACM.

White, R.W., Chu, W., Hassan, A., He, X., Song, Y., and Wang, H. (2013a). Enhancing personalized search by mining and modeling task behavior. In *Proceedings of the international conference on the World Wide Web* (pp. 1411–1420). International World Wide Web Conferences Steering Committee.

White, R.W. and Drucker, S.M. (2007). Investigating behavioral variability in web search. In *Proceedings of the international conference on the World Wide Web* (pp. 21–30). International World Wide Web Conferences Steering Committee.

White, R.W. and Dumais, S.T. (2009). Characterizing and predicting search engine switching behavior. In *Proceedings of the ACM CIKM conference on information and knowledge management* (pp. 87–96). ACM Press.

White, R.W., Dumais, S.T., and Teevan, J. (2009b). Characterizing the influence of domain expertise on web search behavior. In *Proceedings of the ACM WSDM conference on web search and data mining* (pp. 132–141). ACM Press.

White, R.W., Harpaz, R., Shah, N., DuMouchel, W., and Horvitz, E. (2014a). Toward enhanced pharmacovigilance using patient-generated data on the internet. *Nature Clinical Pharmacology and Therapeutics*, 96(2), 239–246.

White, R.W. and Hassan, A. (2014). Content bias in online health search. *ACM Transactions on the Web*, 8(4), 25.

White, R.W. and Hassan Awadallah, A. (2015). Personalizing search on shared devices. In *Proceedings of the ACM SIGIR conference on research and development in information retrieval* (pp. 523–532). ACM Press.

White, R.W., Hassan, A., Singla, A. and Horvitz, E. (2014b). From devices to people: Attribution of search activity in multi-user settings. In *Proceedings of the international conference on the World wide web* (pp. 431–442). ACM Press.

White, R.W. and Horvitz, E. (2009). Cyberchondria: Studies of the escalation of medical concerns in web search. *ACM Transactions on Information Systems*, 27(4), 23.

White, R.W. and Horvitz, E. (2010). Web to World: Predicting transitions from self-diagnosis to the pursuit of local medical assistance in web search. In *Proceedings of the annual symposium of the American medical informatics association* (p. 882). American Medical Informatics Association.

White, R.W. and Horvitz, E. (2013a). Captions and biases in diagnostic search. *ACM Transactions on the Web*, 7(4): 23.

White, R.W. and Horvitz, E. (2013b). From web search to healthcare utilization: privacy-sensitive studies from mobile data. *Journal of the American Medical Informatics Association*, 20(1), 61–68.

White, R.W. and Horvitz, E. (2015). Belief dynamics and biases in web search. *ACM Transactions on Information Systems*, 33(4), 18.

White, R.W. and Huang, J. (2010). Assessing the scenic route: Measuring the value of search trails in web logs. In *Proceedings of the ACM SIGIR conference on research and development in information retrieval* (pp. 587–594). ACM Press.

White, R.W., Jose, J.M., and Ruthven, I. (2003). A task-oriented study on the influencing effects of query-biased summarisation in web searching. *Information Processing and Management*, 39(5), 707–733.

White, R.W., Jose, J.M., and Ruthven, I. (2005a). Using top-ranking sentences to facilitate effective information access. *Journal of the American Society for Information Science and Technology*, 56(10), 1113–1125.

White, R.W., Kapoor, A., and Dumais, S.T. (2010). Modeling long-term search engine usage. In *Proceedings of the conference on user modeling, adaptation, and personalization* (pp. 28–39). Springer Berlin Heidelberg.

White, R.W. and Kelly, D. (2006). A study on the effects of personalization and task information on implicit feedback performance. In *Proceedings of the ACM international conference on information and knowledge management* (pp. 297–306). ACM Press.

White, R.W., Kules, B., Drucker, S.M., and schraefel, m.c. (2006a). Supporting exploratory search, *Communications of the ACM*, 49(4), 36–39.

White, R.W. and Marchionini, G. (2007). Examining the effectiveness of real-time query expansion. *Information Processing and Management*, 43(3), 685–704.

White, R. W. and Morris, D. (2007). Investigating the querying and browsing behavior of advanced search engine users. In *Proceedings of the ACM SIGIR conference on research and development in information retrieval* (pp. 255–262). ACM Press.

White, R.W., Muresan, G., and Marchionini, G. (2006b). Report on the ACM SIGIR 2006 workshop on evaluating exploratory search systems. *SIGIR Forum*, 40(2), 52–60. ACM Press.

White, R.W. and Richardson, M. (2012). Effects of expertise differences in synchronous social Q&A. In *Proceedings of the ACM SIGIR conference on research and development in information retrieval* (pp. 1055–1056). ACM Press.

White, R.W., Richardson, M., Bilenko, M., and Heath, A.P. (2008). Enhancing web search by promoting multiple search engine use. In *Proceedings of the ACM SIGIR conference on research and development in information retrieval* (pp. 43–50). ACM Press.

White, R.W., Richardson, M., and Liu, Y. (2011). Effects of community size and contact rate in synchronous social Q&A. In *Proceedings of ACM SIGCHI conference on human factors in computing systems* (pp. 2837–2846). ACM Press.

White, R.W. and Roth, R.A. (2009). *Exploratory Search: Beyond the Query-Response Paradigm*. San Rafael, CA: Morgan and Claypool.

White, R.W. and Ruthven, I. (2007). A study of interface support mechanisms for interactive information retrieval. *Journal of the American Society for Information Science and Technology*, 57(7), 933–948.

White, R.W., Ruthven, I., and Jose, J.M. (2002b). The use of implicit evidence for relevance feedback in web retrieval. In *Proceedings of European colloquium on information retrieval research* (pp. 93–109). Springer.

White, R.W., Ruthven, I., and Jose, J.M. (2005b). A study of factors affecting the utility of implicit relevance feedback. In *Proceedings of the ACM SIGIR conference on research and development in information retrieval* (pp. 35–42). ACM Press.

White, R.W., Ruthven, I., Jose, J.M., and Van Rijsbergen, C.J. (2005c). Evaluating implicit feedback models using searcher simulations. *ACM Transactions on Information Systems*, 23(3), 325–361.

White, R.W. and Singla, A. (2011). Finding our way on the web: Exploring the role of waypoints in search interaction. In *Proceedings of the nternational conference companion on the World Wide Web* (pp. 147–148). International World Wide Web Conferences Steering Committee.

White, R.W., Tatonetti, N.P., Shah, N.H., Altman, R.B., and Horvitz, E. (2013b). Web-scale pharmacovigilance: Listening to signals from the crowd. *Journal of the American Medical Informatics Association*, 20(3), 404–408.

Whittaker, S. (1996). Talking to strangers: An evaluation of the factors affecting electronic collaboration. In *Proceedings of the ACM CSCW conference on computer supported cooperative work* (pp. 409–418). ACM Press.

Whittaker, S. and Sidner, C. (1996). Email overload: Exploring personal information management of email. In *Proceedings of the ACM SIGCHI conference on human factors in computing systems* (pp. 276–283). ACM Press.

Wickens, C.D. (2002). Multiple resources and performance prediction. *Theoretical Issues in Ergonomics Science*, 3(2), 159–177.

Wigdor, D., Forlines, C., Baudisch, P., Barnwell, J., and Shen, C. (2007). Lucid touch: A see-through mobile device. In *Proceedings of the ACM UIST symposium on user interface software and technology* (pp. 269–278). ACM Press.

Wildemuth, B.M. (2004). The effects of domain knowledge on search tactic formulation. *Journal of the American Society for Information Science and Technology*, 55(3), 246–258.

Williams, J.G., Sochats, K.M., and Morse, E. (1995). Visualization. In Williams, M.E. (Ed.), *Annual Review of Information Science and Technology*, 30 (pp. 161–207). Medford, NJ: ASIS/Information Today Inc.

Williams, K.D. and Karau, S.J. (1991). Social loafing and social compensation: The effects of expectation of co-worker performance. *Journal of Personality and Social Psychology*, 61(4), 570–581.

Williamson, C., and Shneiderman, B. (1992). The Dynamic HomeFinder: Evaluating dynamic queries in a real-estate information exploration system. In *Proceedings of the ACM SIGIR conference on research and development in information retrieval* (pp. 338–346). ACM Press.

Williamson, K. (1998). Discovered by chance: The role of incidental information acquisition in an ecological model of information use. *Library Information Science Research*, 20(1), 23–40.

Wilson, M. (2002). Six views of embodied cognition. *Psychonomic Bulletin and Review*, 9(4), 625–636.

Wilson, M.J. and Wilson, M.L. (2013). A comparison of techniques for measuring sensemaking and learning within participant-generated summaries. *Journal of the American Society for Information Science and Technology*, 64(2), 291–306.

Wilson, M.L. and Elsweiler, D. (2010). Casual-leisure searching: The exploratory search scenarios that break our current models. In *Proceedings of the workshop on human-computer interaction and information retrieval*.

Wilson, M.L., Kules, B., and Shneiderman, B. (2010). From keyword search to exploration: Designing future search interfaces for the web. *Foundations and Trends in Web Science*, 2(1), 1–97.

Wilson, T.D. (1997). Information behaviour: An interdisciplinary perspective. *Information Processing and Management*, 33(4), 551–572.

Wilson, T.D. (1999). Models in information behaviour research. *Journal of Documentation*, 55(3), 249–270.

Witten, I.H. and Frank, E. (2005). *Data Mining: Practical Machine Learning Tools and Techniques*. San Francisco, CA: Morgan Kaufmann.

Wittenburg, K., Das, D., Hill, W., and Stead, L. (1995). Group asynchronous browsing on the World Wide Web. In *Proceedings of the international conference on the World Wide Web* (pp. 51–62). International World Wide Web Conferences Steering Committee.

Wittrock, M. (1974). Learning as a generative activity. *Educational Psychologist*, 11, 87–95.

Wobbrock, J.O., Forlizzi, J., Hudson, S.E., and Myers, B.A. (2002). WebThumb: Interaction techniques for small-screen browsers. In *Proceedings of the ACM UIST symposium on user interface software and technology* (pp. 205–208). ACM Press.

Wobbrock, J.O., Morris, M.R., and Wilson, A.D. (2009). User-defined gestures for surface computing. In *Proceedings of the ACM SIGCHI Conference on human factors in computing systems* (pp. 1083–1092). ACM Press.

Wobbrock, J.O., Rubinstein, J., Sawyer, M.W., and Duchowski, A.T. (2008). Longitudinal evaluation of discrete consecutive gaze gestures for text entry. In *Proceedings of the symposium on eye tracking research and applications* (pp. 11–18). ACM Press.

Wolf, G. (2010). The data-driven life. *The New York Times*, 28.

Wolfe, J.M. (1994). Guided search 2.0: A revised model of visual search. *Psychonomic Bulletin and Review*, 1(2), 202–238.

Wolpaw, J.R., McFarland, D.J., Neat, G.W., and Forneris, C.A. (1991). An EEG-based brain-computer interface for cursor control. *Electroencephalography and Clinical Neurophysiology*, 78(3), 252–259.

Wongsuphasawat, K., Guerra Gómez, J.A., Plaisant, C., Wang, T.D., Taieb-Maimon, M., and Shneiderman, B. (2011). LifeFlow: Visualizing an overview of event sequences. In *Proceedings of the ACM SIGCHI conference on human factors in computing systems* (pp. 1747–1756). ACM Press.

Woodruff, A., Faulring, A., Rosenholtz, R., Morrsion, J., and Pirolli, P. (2001). Using thumbnails to search the Web. In *Proceedings of the ACM SIGCHI conference on human factors in computing systems* (pp. 198–205). ACM Press.

Wu, H.Y., Rubinstein, M., Shih, E., Guttag, J., Durand, F., and Freeman, W. (2012). Eulerian video magnification for revealing subtle changes in the world. *ACM Transactions on Graphics*, 31(4), 65.

Wu, S., Liu, S., Cosley, D., and Macy, M. (2011). Mining collective local knowledge from Google MyMaps. In *Proceedings of the international conference companion on the World Wide Web* (pp. 151–152). ACM Press.

Wu, W.C., Kelly, D., and Sud, A. (2014). Using information scent and need for cognition to understand online search behavior. In *Proceedings of the ACM SIGIR conference on research and development in information retrieval* (pp. 557–566). ACM Press.

Xiang, B., Jiang, D., Pei, J., Sun, X., Chen, E., and Li, H. (2010). Context-aware ranking in Web search. In *Proceedings of the ACM SIGIR conference of research and development in information retrieval* (pp. 451–458). ACM Press.

Xie, I. and Cool, C. (2009). Understanding help seeking within the context of searching digital libraries. *Journal of American Society for Information Science and Technology*, 60(3), 477–494.

Xiong, L. and Agichtein, E. (2007). Towards privacy-preserving query log publishing. In *Proceedings of the workshop on query log analysis: social and technological challenges*.

Xu, D., Liu, Y., Zhang, M., Ma, S., and Ru, L. (2012). Incorporating revisiting behaviors into click models. In *Proceedings of the ACM WSDM international conference on web search and data mining* (pp. 303–312). ACM Press.

Xu, S., Jiang, H., and Lau, F.C.M. (2011). Mining user dwell time for personalized web search re-ranking. In *Proceedings of the international joint conference on artificial intelligence* (pp. 2367–2372).

Xu, Y. and Mease, D. (2009). Evaluating web search using task completion time. In *Proceedings of the ACM SIGIR conference on research and development in information retrieval* (pp. 676–677). ACM Press.

Xu, Y., Wang, K., Zhang, B., and Chen, Z. (2007). Privacy-enhancing personalized web search. In *Proceedings of the international conference on the World Wide Web* (pp. 591–600). ACM Press.

Xu, Y. and Yin, H. (2008). Novelty and topicality in interactive information retrieval. *Journal of the American Society for Information Science and Technology*, 59(2), 201–215.

Yamauchi, T. (2013). Mouse trajectories and state anxiety: Feature selection with random forest. In *Proceedings of the humaine association conference on* affective computing and intelligent interaction (pp. 399–404). IEEE.

Yamauchi, T., Kohn, N., and Yu, N.Y. (2007). Tracking mouse movement in feature inference: Category labels are different from feature labels. *Memory and Cognition*, 35(5), 852–863.

Yan, J., Chu, W., and White, R.W. (2014). Cohort modeling for enhanced personalized search. In *Proceedings of the ACM SIGIR conference on research and development in information retrieval* (pp. 505–514). ACM Press.

Yang, J., Yang, W., Denecke, M., and Waibel, A. (1999). Smart sight: A tourist assistant system. In *Proceedings of the international symposium on wearable computers* (pp. 73–78). IEEE.

Yankelovich, N., Levow, G.A., and Marx, M. (1995). Designing SpeechActs: Issues in speech user interfaces. In *Proceedings of the ACM SIGCHI conference on human factors in computing systems* (pp. 369–376). ACM Press/Addison-Wesley Publishing Co.

Yankelovich, N., Meyrowitz, N., and van Dam, A. (1985). Reading and writing the electronic book. *IEEE Computer*, 18(10), 15–30.

Yarbus, A.L. (1967). *Eye Movements and Vision*. New York: Plenum Press.

Yap, K.K., Srinivasan, V., and Motani, M. (2005). MAX: Human-centric search of the physical world. In *Proceedings of the international conference on embedded networked sensor systems* (pp. 166–179). ACM Press.

Yee, K.P., Swearingen, K., Li, K., and Hearst, M. (2003). Faceted metadata for image search and browsing. In *Proceedings of the ACM SIGCHI conference on human factors in computing systems* (pp. 401–408). ACM Press.

Yilmaz, E., Shokouhi, M., Craswell, N., and Robertson, S. (2010). Expected browsing utility for web search evaluation. In *Proceedings of the ACM CIKM international conference on information and knowledge management* (pp. 1561–1564). ACM Press.

Yilmaz, E., Verma, M., Craswell, N., Radlinski, F., and Bailey, P. (2014). Relevance and effort: An analysis of document utility. In *Proceedings of the ACM CIKM conference on conference on information and knowledge management* (pp. 91–100). ACM Press.

Yin, P., Luo, P., Lee, W.-C., and Wang, M. (2013). Silence is also evidence: Interpreting dwell time for recommendation from psychological perspective. In *Proceedings of the ACM SIGKDD conference on knowledge discovery and data mining* (pp. 989–997). ACM Press.

Yom-Tov, E., Fine, S., Carmel, D., and Darlow, A. (2005). Learning to estimate query difficulty: Including applications to missing content detection and distributed information retrieval. In *Proceedings of the ACM SIGIR conference on research and development in information retrieval* (pp. 512–519). ACM Press.

Yom-Tov, E., Dumais, S., and Guo, Q. (2013). Promoting civil discourse through search engine diversity. *Social Science Computer Review*, 32(3), 145–154.

Yom-Tov, E., and Gabrilovich, E. (2013). Postmarket drug surveillance without trial costs: Discovery of adverse drug reactions through large-scale analysis of web search queries. *Journal of Medical Internet Research*, 15(6).

Yom-Tov, E., Lalmas, M., Dupret, G., Baeza-Yates, R., Donmez, P., and Lehmann, J. (2012). The effect of links on networked user engagement. In *Proceedings of the international conference companion on the World Wide Web* (pp. 641–642). ACM Press.

Yu, S., Yu, K., and Tresp, V. (2005). Collaborative ordinal regression. In *Proceedings of the NIPS workshop on learning to rank*.

Yuan, X. and White, R.W. (2012). Building the trail best traveled: Effects of domain knowledge on web search trailblazing. In *Proceedings of the ACM SIGCHI conference on human factors in computing systems* (pp. 1795–1804). ACM Press.

Yue, Y., Patel, R., and Roehrig, H. (2010). Beyond position bias: Examining result attractiveness as a source of presentation bias in clickthrough data. In *Proceedings of the international conference on the World Wide Web* (pp. 1011–1018). ACM Press.

Zaiane, O.R. and Strilets, A. (2002). Finding similar queries to satisfy searches based on query traces. In *Advances in Object-Oriented Information Systems* (pp. 207–216). Springer Berlin Heidelberg.

Zamir, O., and Etzioni, O. (1999). Grouper: A dynamic clustering interface to Web search results. *Computer Networks*, 31(11), 1361–1374.

Zelazo, P.D., Carter, A., Reznick, J., and Frye, D. (1997). Early development of executive function: A problem-solving framework. *Review of General Psychology*, 1(2), 198–226.

Zellweger, P.T. (1989). Scripted documents: A hypermedia path mechanism. In Proceedings of the ACM conference on hypertext and hypermedia (pp. 1–14). ACM Press.

Zellweger, P.T., Regli, S.H., Mackinlay, J.D., and Chang, B.W. (2000). The impact of fluid documents on reading and browsing: An observational study. In *Proceedings of the ACM SIGCHI conference on human factors in computing systems* (pp. 249–256). ACM Press.

Zhai, S., Morimoto, C., and Ihde, S. (1999). Manual and gaze input cascaded (MAGIC) pointing. In *Proceedings of the ACM SIGCHI conference on human factors in computing systems* (pp. 246–253). ACM Press.

Zhang, M., Ackerman, M.S., and Adamic, L. (2007). Expertise networks in online communities: Structure and algorithms. In *Proceedings of the international conference on the World Wide Web* (pp. 221–230). ACM Press.

Zhang, M., Jansen, B.J., and Spink, A. (2006). Information searching tactics of web searchers. In *Proceedings of the annual meeting of the American society for information science and technology*, 43(1), 1–14.

Zhang, X., Cole, M., and Belkin, N. (2011). Predicting users' domain knowledge from search behaviors. In *Proceedings of the ACM SIGIR conference on research and development in information retrieval* (pp. 1225–1226). ACM Press.

Zhang, Y., Wang, D., Wang, G., Chen, W., Zhang, Z., Hu, B., and Zhang, L. (2010). Learning click models via probit bayesian inference. In *Proceedings of the ACM CIKM conference on information and knowledge management* (pp. 439–448). ACM Press.

Zhao, L. and Callan, J. (2010). Term necessity prediction. In *Proceedings of the ACM CIKM conference on information and knowledge management* (pp. 259–268). ACM Press.

Zhao, Y., Scholer, F., and Tsegay, Y. (2008). Effective pre-retrieval query performance prediction using similarity and variability evidence. In *Proceedings of the European conference on information retrieval* (pp. 52–64). Springer Berlin Heidelberg.

Zhou, K., Cummins, R., Lalmas, M., and Jose, J.M. (2012). Evaluating reward and risk for vertical selection. In *Proceedings of the ACM CIKM conference on information and knowledge management* (pp. 2631–2634). ACM Press.

Zhou, Y. and Croft, W.B. (2006). Ranking robustness: A novel framework to predict query performance. In *Proceedings of the ACM CIKM conference on information and knowledge management* (pp. 567–574). ACM Press.

Zhuang, Z., Brunk, C., and Giles, C.L. (2008). Modeling and visualizing geo-sensitive queries based on user clicks. In *Proceedings of the international workshop on location and the Web* (pp. 73–76).

Ziegarnik, B. (1927). Uber das Behalten von erledigten und unerledigten handlungen. *Psychologische Forschung*, 9, 1–85.

Ziegler, C., McNee, S.M., Konstan, J.A., and Lausen, G. (2005). Improving recommendation lists through topic diversification. In *Proceedings of the international conference on the World Wide Web* (pp. 22–32). ACM Press.

Ziemkiewicz, C., Crouser, R.J., Yauilla, A.R., Su, S.L., Ribarsky, W., and Chang, R. (2011). How locus of control influences compatibility with visualization style. In *Proceedings of the IEEE conference on visual analytics science and technology* (pp. 81–90). IEEE.

Zimmermann, P., Guttormsen, S., Danuser, B., and Gomez, P. (2003). Affective computing: A rationale for measuring mood with mouse and keyboard. *International Journal of Occupational Safety and Ergonomics*, 9(4), 539–551.

Zimmerman, T.G., Lanier, J., Blanchard, C., Bryson, S., and Harvill, Y. (1987). A hand gesture interface device. *ACM SIGCHI Bulletin*, 18(4), 189–192. ACM Press.

Zuccon, G., Koopman, B., and Palotti, J. (2015). Diagnose this if you can. In *Proceedings of the European conference on information retrieval* (pp. 562–567). Springer International Publishing.

Zukerman, I. and Albrecht, D.W. (2001). Predictive statistical models for user modeling. *User Modeling and User-Adapted Interaction*, 11(1–2), 5–18.

Index

A-B testing, 345, 407
abandonment, 16, 28, 43, 44, 70, 71, 254, 265, 329, 346, 353, 354, 382, 411
actionable insights, 16, 86, 113, 225
active learning, 233
active search, 99
activity attribution, 274, 275, 276, 302, 378
adaptive indexing, 75
adaptive thesaurus, 75
advanced operators, 79, 164, 165, 240
affective computing, 176, 184
affective feedback, 10, 71, 177, 185, 191, 317
affective models, 71, 189
affective state, 19, 56, 107, 185, 186, 189, 282, 388
afterglow effects, 170
agile views, 142
algorithmically mediated collaboration, 252
anchor text, 153, 283, 376, 400
anomalous state of knowledge, 22, 103, 235
anonymization, 244, 361, 376, 377, 380
Apple Siri, xiv, 61, 222
Apple Watch, 181
application context, 54, 75, 87, 181, 184, 271, 281, 294, 340, 360
applying knowledge, 246
appropriateness, 9, 117, 227, 308
apps, 168
archiving answers, 264
areas of interest, 44
artificial intelligence, 2, 60, 85, 182, 390, 391, 406
asynchronous collaboration, 253, 254

asynchronous communication, 249, 253, 256
atomic interaction events, 17
attentional resources, 39, 98, 117, 413
attentive systems, 158, 210, 211
attractiveness bias, 66
attribution-based personalization, 274
audio interfaces, 191
augmented reality, xv, 11, 181, 389
automatic query expansion, 148

backtracking, 30, 31, 36, 105, 118, 120, 122, 313, 412
bad abandonment, 43, 71, 265
badges, 263, 265
balanced interleaving, 346
base rates, 394
behavior-based interface agents, 210
berrypicking, 32, 102, 114, 120, 121, 122, 123, 130, 157, 236
big data, xiii, 17, 60, 63, 83, 227, 396, 397, 398, 400, 405, 409
binary preference, 320
blind zones maps, 46
branching, 36, 130, 136
behavioral biases, xiii, 325
behavioral dynamics, 295, 383
behavioral ecology, 116
behavioral learning, 233
behavioral tendencies, 354
biases, xiii, 8, 17, 23, 25, 63, 65, 66, 67, 74, 84, 87, 91, 128, 129, 144, 277, 329, 340, 344, 346, 347, 355, 356, 393, 394, 400, 401, 402, 403, 407

Bloom's taxonomy of learning, 233
bookmarking, 124, 216
brain sensing, 315, 389
brain-computer interactions, 389
bright pupil gaze tracking, 41
broadcasting questions, 257
brokerage, 129
browse trails, 29, 77
browser toolbars, 28, 29, 33, 35, 69, 73, 87, 220, 332, 366
browsing context, 270, 287
browsing logs, 217, 218

captchas, 369
caption bias, 66, 400
captions, 24, 25, 27, 43, 47, 52, 64, 65, 66, 71, 117, 144, 160, 170, 247, 271, 346, 351
cascade model, 64
casual-leisure search, 387
categorical overviews, 159
characterizations of search behavior, 142, 143
childhood development, 231
chunking, 19
clarity score, 81
click entropy, 74, 316, 368
click perplexity, 65
click prediction, 19, 59, 64, 65, 97, 288
clickable snippets, 146
click-through inversions, 25, 26, 86, 144
click-through rate, 25, 77, 88, 288, 319, 325, 329
client-side applications, 33, 73, 161, 373, 382
client-side instrumentation, 28, 36
client-side personalization, 194
cloud computing, xiii, 60, 388
cloud-based content, 367
cocktail party effect, 183
cognitive actor, 281
cognitive analysis, 318
cognitive bias, xiii, 17, 66, 241, 400, 401, 407
cognitive dimensions framework, 133
cognitive effort, 40, 98, 237, 313, 332
cognitive engineering, 161
cognitive flow, 162, 316
cognitive gap, 22, 126
cognitive learning, 246, 311
cognitive load, 9, 151, 157, 166, 299, 305, 307, 313, 314, 315, 319, 334, 402, 408
cognitive model, 102, 103, 104, 119, 133, 377
cognitive model of information transfer, 103, 104

cognitive overlap, 105
cognitive prosthetic, 2, 98, 212, 228
cognitive resources, 126, 151, 166, 314
cognitive search intents, 105
cognitive workload, 315
cohorts, 16, 54, 71, 74, 96, 188, 227, 262, 268, 279, 282, 332, 355, 359
cold start problem, 212
collaborative filtering, 119, 212, 213, 222, 252, 293
collaborative search, 56, 63, 125, 191, 197, 250, 251, 252, 253, 265, 282, 335
collabportunities, 252
collection overviews, 102, 107
collective knowledge, 215, 216
co-located collaborative search, 253
combination testing, 346
combinations of metrics, 335, 408
commercial search engine, xii, 9, 21, 74, 131, 164, 268, 277, 285, 323, 333, 362, 371
common ground, 250, 256
comparability, 11, 311, 350, 359, 361, 369, 370, 408
comparative testing, 345
comparison with other searchers, 247
complex search tasks, 6, 20, 78, 79, 111, 128, 133, 141, 147, 155, 185, 201, 202, 206, 207, 218, 248, 391, 394, 406
compression techniques, 199
compromised need, 22
computational resources, 80, 212, 331, 365
computational social science, 396
computer vision, 182, 389, 408
computer-supported collaborative work, 125
concept drift, 296
confirmation bias, 407
conscious need, 2, 22
constraint assumption, 116
constructivist learning theories, 231
content examination, 99
content recommendation, xiv, 94, 105, 347, 362
content-based filtering, 212, 213
content-based image retrieval, 197
content-based personalization, 270, 271
content-based recommender systems, 213
context bias, 66
context-sensitive recommendations, 207
contextual data, 281
contextual information, 54, 82, 122, 158, 211, 300, 356, 360, 390
contextual understanding, 180

contextualization, 10, 21, 77, 108, 267, 268, 269, 270, 280, 296, 301, 303, 320, 326, 363
contextually aware search experiences, 390
continual computation, 163
control group, 77, 310, 346
controlled experimental settings, 350, 355
controlled laboratory setting, 237
conversational systems, 180
cookie churn, 276, 364
cookies, 199, 274, 276, 363, 383
cost of interaction, 326
cost structure analysis, 121, 311
cost-benefit analysis, 121, 199, 365
counterfactual analysis, 67, 347, 411
coverage, 32, 252
Cranfield studies, 323, 325, 348, 349, 351, 357
creative process, 135, 136, 137, 330
creativity, 97, 135, 136, 137, 162, 201, 239, 316, 330, 334
creativity support tools, 137, 330
crisis informatics, 297
critical incident analysis, 359
cross-application search, 9, 55, 168, 192, 194, 388
cross-device, xv, 59, 70, 194, 199, 208
cross-device search, 9, 17, 195, 290, 388
cross-domain search, 9
cross-session, 396
cross-site experiments, 370
crowdsourcing, 9, 79, 92, 196, 265, 343
curiosity, 2, 101, 102, 129, 130, 325, 331, 354
currency assumption, 115
cursor movements, 5, 16, 34, 36, 38, 42, 44, 71, 163, 174, 187, 281, 318, 334, 348, 362, 366
cursor tracking, 16, 38, 42, 43, 44, 48, 49, 53, 82, 83, 143, 237, 342, 344, 348, 388

dark pupil gaze tracking, 41
data challenges, 367, 368
data compression, 82
data release, 375, 377, 380
data revolution, xii, 13
data sources, 73, 80, 81, 87, 143, 171, 199, 222, 269, 295, 375, 376, 400
data visualization, 225, 226, 228
data volume, 8, 84, 86, 87, 168, 198, 371, 372, 373, 377, 406, 412
day-of-week effects, 87
decision assumption, 115

decision making, 1, 3, 4, 6, 55, 60, 98, 108, 128, 158, 185, 187, 200, 201, 205, 228, 232, 233, 247, 316, 401
declarative knowledge, 242
deep learning, 90, 391, 408
defection, 331
demand characteristics, 8, 318, 340, 358
demographics, 109, 138, 213, 342, 370, 401
development of cognitive skills, 129
device boundaries, 9, 194, 366, 395
device-appropriate information, 195
diagnostic search, 387, 392
dialog model, 406
diet width, 115
differential privacy, 381, 406
diminishing returns, 115, 121
direct manipulation, 8, 177, 179, 194, 212, 384, 389, 391
directed browsing, 100, 315
discounted cumulative gain, 321, 322, 353
discovering new insights, 201
discovery learning, 233
dissatisfaction, 27, 29, 34, 68, 70, 285, 318, 331, 332
distributed collections, 367
diversification of search results, 327
diversity, 32, 54, 74, 81, 115, 122, 158, 217, 251, 268, 273, 282, 327, 328, 331, 368
document context, 282, 283
document retention, 4, 124, 152, 237
domain expertise, 80, 162, 165, 237, 238, 239, 240, 273, 280
domain experts, xiv, 215, 238, 250, 259, 261, 331
domain knowledge, 6, 22, 54, 80, 133, 138, 239, 245, 249, 261, 282
domain novices, 34, 214, 215, 256, 312, 353
domain preferences, 17, 26
dominant search intent, xiii, 8, 27, 73, 74, 77, 184, 279, 284, 362
dwell time, 34, 35, 36, 37, 49, 68, 69, 71, 80, 81, 91, 152, 153, 155, 185, 237, 309, 315, 327, 329
dynamic queries, 142, 206, 212, 224, 228, 239
dynamic rank, 283

earcons, 184
economic incentives, 263
economic models, 103
economic theory, 103, 113
edit and read wear, xiii, 168, 219, 244

editable user models, 303
effect size, 88, 335, 355
efficiency, 87, 134, 215, 233, 307, 311, 312, 334, 372
e-learning, 185, 215, 231
electro-encephalography, 314
electronic mail, xiii, 108, 170, 208, 229, 256, 271, 284
empowering searchers, 165
en vitro, 54
en vivo, 54
end user license agreement, 363
engagement, 1, 17, 25, 38, 44, 49, 55, 64, 77, 86, 128, 149, 173, 187, 199, 213, 223, 226, 237, 249, 287, 308, 311, 312, 318, 319, 334, 360, 370, 390, 394, 403, 405, 408, 412
enjoyment, 1, 162, 313, 317, 402, 408
episodic model, 111, 113
epistemic gestures, 177
ergotic gestures, 177
ethics, 259, 367, 375, 380, 381, 384, 407
ethnography, 337, 340, 355
evaluation metrics, 90, 248, 295, 307, 352, 408
event sequences, 17, 224
examination behavior, 39, 43, 47, 48, 49, 143, 153, 347, 348, 407
examination bias, 400
examining results, 201
executive functions, 135
expected browsing utility, 351
expected reciprocal rank, 351
expected search length, 326
experimental design, 325, 337, 339, 343, 344, 345, 358, 361, 369, 381
experimental materials, 342
experimental protocol, 100, 342, 356, 357, 373, 381
experimental stimuli, 342
experimental systems, 16, 148, 342, 350, 370, 373, 408
expert recruitment, 262
expert searchers, 62, 215, 217, 250
expertise location, 258, 262
explanations, 16, 72, 123, 205, 223, 269, 301, 302, 303, 382, 383, 393, 400
explicit feedback, 151, 155, 315
exploration and exploitation, 101
exploration suggestions, 220, 221
exploratory behavior, 100, 101, 102, 114, 202, 203, 204
exploratory browsing, 101, 102, 206
exploratory data analysis, 5, 129, 226
exploratory search, 97, 101, 102, 107, 109, 128, 129, 130, 131, 132, 148, 157, 200, 205, 206, 241, 302, 308, 310, 317
exploratory search systems, 129, 132, 205
exploratory search tasks, 147, 159
explorers, 30, 143, 285, 354
exploring session, 203, 204
extrinsic incentives, 263
eye gaze, 5, 38, 40, 41, 48, 51, 143, 172, 173, 237
eye-gaze interaction, 172

faceted navigation, 159, 160
faceted search interfaces, 142
facial affect detection, 188
facial recognition, 56, 174, 186, 188, 291
feature engineering, 68, 89, 93
feature generation, 85, 89
feature selection, 89, 90
federated search, 367
feedback loops, 24, 401
field studies, 340, 341, 345, 355, 356
fieldwork, 340
filter bubble, xiii, 222, 277
fixed vocabulary gestures, 176
flighting, 9, 54, 335, 337, 345, 346, 357, 377, 411
fluid documents, 147
F-measure, 321
focus groups, 339, 340, 347, 355, 356
focused attention, 318
formalized need, 22
formulating and testing hypotheses, 202
freshness, 295
frustration, 71, 72, 79, 86, 88, 105, 106, 107, 173, 183, 185, 187, 188, 209, 308, 317, 318, 334, 370
functional fixedness, 241, 246
functional near infrared spectroscopy, 314
functional visibility, 150, 157, 166

galvanic skin response, 71, 72, 187, 391
games with a purpose, 369
gaze patterns, 38, 46, 47, 237
gaze trackers, 38, 40, 41, 42, 51, 172, 173, 389
gaze tracking, 10, 15, 36, 38, 39, 40, 41, 43, 44, 46, 48, 49, 51, 55, 67, 83, 151, 153, 172, 183, 198, 237, 314, 318, 319, 334, 342, 370, 388
geographic retrieval, 197
geolocation, 82, 195, 291, 364

gestural feedback, 56
gestural interaction, xv, 57, 179, 287
gestural vocabularies, 178
gesture based search systems, 180
gisting, 144
glimpses, 102
goal-directed tasks, 102, 135
good abandonment, 43, 71, 265, 329
Google Glass, xv, 181, 182, 191, 390
Google Now, xiv, 7, 10, 210, 222, 271, 391
Granger causality, 383
groupization, 279
groupware systems, 254
guided tours, 34, 63, 73, 167, 205, 214, 217, 218, 232

hand gestures, 181, 389
HCIR. *See* human-computer information retrieval
healthcare utilization intentions, 290, 394
heart rate, 71, 72, 180, 186, 187, 188
heatmaps, 39, 45, 46, 49
hierarchical category representations, 272
hints and tips, 165, 242, 312
histories, 7, 9, 21, 23, 57, 73, 77, 79, 119, 123, 137, 157, 158, 168, 169, 183, 192, 194, 196, 205, 207, 219, 221, 228, 251, 268, 271, 274, 286, 299, 363, 366, 378, 392, 396
hover, 43, 48, 53, 174, 176, 178, 189, 198, 411
human intelligence, 2, 98, 344, 395
human memory, 181, 214, 299
human navigation behavior, 100
human-computer information retrieval, 4, 141
human-in-the-loop, 293
hybrid recommender systems, 213
hyperlink analysis, 249
hyperlink clicks, 24, 65, 170, 283, 287

I'm feeling lucky, 122, 156
idea tactics, 110, 220
ideation, 136, 330
immersive search experiences, 8, 197
implicit feedback, 4, 5, 8, 15, 16, 21, 24, 35, 36, 38, 39, 49, 55, 56, 67, 76, 91, 102, 124, 150, 152, 153, 154, 155, 161, 185, 271, 315, 353, 401, 407
implied consent, 378
in situ surveys, 331, 411
incremental feedback, 152
individual differences, 41, 71, 81, 143, 161, 173, 189, 310

infinite scrolling, xiv, 5
information behavior, xvi, 5, 8, 20, 55, 97, 99, 100, 104, 108, 110, 116, 117, 132, 138, 201, 281, 340, 372, 373, 412
information coverage, 131
information filtering, 7, 208, 209, 210, 212, 303
information finding, 4, 6, 132, 138, 141, 160, 405
information foraging, 30, 97, 100, 102, 114, 116, 117, 118, 119, 120, 121, 123, 127, 130, 132, 138, 377, 414
information foraging theory, 113, 116, 117, 120
information fragments, 124, 192, 193
information gain, 89, 114, 115, 130, 206, 218
information gathering, 114, 122, 123, 135, 143
information patch, 113, 117, 118
information retrieval evaluation, 309, 355
information scent, 25, 29, 33, 98, 100, 116, 117, 118, 119, 120, 158, 192, 220, 283
information search process, 97, 105, 107, 310, 413
information use, 3, 4, 8, 10, 108, 118, 124, 132, 133, 135, 158, 165, 229, 233, 246, 247, 271, 316
information visualization, 1, 4, 8, 101, 142, 172, 202, 205, 206, 224, 225, 226, 227, 228, 229, 311, 350, 371, 372
informational nuggets, 327
information-seeking activity, 98, 100, 185, 342
information-seeking behavior, 8, 17, 37, 102, 103, 104, 107, 108, 111, 120, 133, 280
information-seeking context, 28, 53, 315
information-seeking process, 2, 102, 107, 108, 129, 185, 231, 233, 295, 341
information-seeking strategy, 111, 122, 132
information-seeking support systems, 99
informavores, 117
innovation, 24, 108, 137, 330, 405
in-situ data collection, 16, 44, 211, 329
instant answers, xiv, 44, 130, 265, 299, 394
instant messaging, 134, 251, 253, 254, 255, 257
instant search, 149
institutional review boards, 381, 384
instructional scaffolding, 245
instrumented Web browsers, 123, 362
intellect augmentation, 98
intelligence amplification, 98, 232
intelligent agents, xiv, 11, 61, 184, 194, 211, 222, 234, 391, 392, 403
intelligent assistants, 7, 223

intelligent personal assistants, 6, 17, 20, 59, 70, 133, 134, 210, 229, 271, 290, 409
intelligent tutoring, 188, 231, 246, 317
intelligent tutoring system, 188, 246
interacting with strangers, 249, 260, 261, 263, 265
interaction monitoring, 318
interactive experimentation, 349, 403
interactive information retrieval, 4
interactive machine learning, 91
interactive query expansion, 148
interactive visualization systems, 224
interface mediated collaboration, 252
interleaved evaluation, 345
interleaving, 54, 67, 125, 144, 276, 325, 337, 346, 347, 357
internet of things, xii
interpersonal interactions, 249
interruption cost, 383
interruption management, 209
interruptions, 173, 209, 255, 259, 262, 326, 340, 356, 392
interviews, 55, 143, 227, 237, 310, 313, 316, 318, 339, 341, 345, 355, 356, 383
intrinsic exploration, 101, 102
intrinsic incentives, 263
IP addresses, 274, 280, 289, 291, 364, 365, 377
item-to-item collaborative filtering, 212
iterative search behavior, 131

judgment and decision making, 393
just-in-time information access, 192, 210, 229

knowledge acquisition, 108, 127, 128, 129, 130, 232, 238, 242
knowledge building, 232
knowledge discovery, 97, 160, 193, 212
knowledge gap, 126, 235

laboratory setting, 36, 54, 55, 83, 237, 310, 325, 330, 338, 344, 370, 408
laboratory studies, 237, 246, 335, 338, 341, 343, 345, 354, 355, 356, 361
landing pages, 24, 34, 35, 69, 71, 144, 145, 146, 175, 283
large displays, xv, 172, 178, 191, 388, 390, 409
lazy loading, 44, 199
learning, 9, 60, 62, 63, 64, 97, 126, 129, 130, 138, 160, 162, 202, 233, 243, 247, 310, 334
learning loop complex, 235

learning process, 91, 101, 132, 233, 235, 236, 238, 242, 245, 308, 372
learning theory, 236
learning to rank, 49, 76, 89, 92, 93, 217, 362
life-long learning, 232
living laboratories, 337, 359
local knowledge, 292, 293, 294
location context, 289
locus of control, 227
log analysis, 16, 17, 20, 30, 49, 147, 158, 237, 276, 331, 337, 338, 344, 360, 366, 384, 412
log duration, 87
longitudinal analysis, 77, 88, 341
longitudinal studies, 105, 360, 408
long-lived interests, 208
long-term learning, 138, 238
long-term tasks, 7, 20, 62, 395
lookup model, 2, 3, 5, 79, 121
lookup searches, 130, 236

machine learning, xi, xv, 2, 13, 51, 59, 60, 67, 76, 85, 89, 90, 91, 92, 93, 94, 96, 188, 225, 344, 372, 373, 390, 391, 405
machine learning algorithms, 61, 76, 89, 93, 94, 372
machine reading, 390
machine translation, 182, 262, 390
machine-learned ranking, 92, 93, 94, 153, 327
Map Reduce, 84, 85
marginal value theorem, 115, 116, 118
massive open online courses, 232, 238
mean average precision, 320
mean reciprocal rank, 320, 321, 322
measuring creativity, 137, 330
measuring engagement, 319
measuring learning, 310, 311, 312
measuring serendipity, 316
memex, 214
memory landmarks, 299, 300
metacognitive knowledge and skills, 132
metric agreement, 324
metro maps, 218
Microsoft Band, 71, 72, 181, 184, 187, 188, 389
Microsoft Cortana, xiv, 7, 10, 61, 210, 222, 271, 391
Microsoft HoloLens, xvi, 172, 390
Microsoft Kinect, 51, 186, 188
Midas touch, 172
misses, 48, 51, 314
missions, 7, 19, 110, 169
mixed control, 157, 303

mixed initiative interfaces, 193, 391
mobile applications, xv, 138, 168
mobile computing, xi, xv, 59, 61, 81, 96, 99, 161, 387
mobile devices, xv, 10, 15, 36, 38, 50, 52, 60, 70, 163, 168, 182, 190, 191, 222, 253, 288, 290, 365, 387, 388, 405
mobile search, 71, 81, 253, 289, 387, 388
modeling expertise level, 239
motifs, 38, 135, 284, 329
multi-device usage, 195, 396
multi-level judgments, 327
multimodal systems, 180
multi-query sessions, 49
multitasking, 37, 254, 255, 315, 356
multi-touch, 52, 174

natural language queries, 164, 182
natural language understanding, 390
natural search interactions, 81, 388
natural settings, 16, 55, 56, 83
natural user information retrieval, 142, 406
natural user interaction, 8, 52, 59, 61, 99, 142, 161, 171, 172, 186, 388, 405
natural user interfaces, 60
naturally occurring gestures, 176
navigation by information scent, 117
navigators, 30, 143, 285, 354
near-surface interactions, 174
need for cognition, 25, 411
negative relevance feedback, 155
negative search, 166
nested model of context, 281
next-generation search experiences, 59, 408
next-generation search interaction, 9, 10, 59, 61, 63, 90, 161
next-generation search systems, xi, 2, 6, 8, 9, 10, 57, 60, 64, 82, 96, 97, 108, 188, 191, 194, 197, 198, 206, 217, 248, 253, 267, 300, 302, 303, 307, 309, 388, 405, 408
non-hyperlink clicks, 16, 24, 28
normalized discounted cumulative gain, 114, 269, 320, 323
novelty, 32, 101, 115, 116, 122, 131, 136, 222, 251, 252, 316, 327, 328, 331, 354
novice searchers, 215, 246

offline experiments, 138, 324, 325, 327, 348, 350, 360
one from many, 251
ongoing search, 59, 99

online advertising, 8, 65, 347
online experiments, 63, 67, 95, 324, 345, 346, 347, 348
on-task behavior, 252, 279, 280, 284
ontologies, 272
open user models, 303
open-ended questions, 318
open-mindedness, 136
optical character recognition, 291, 369
optimal foraging theory, 114, 115, 116
optimality modeling, 115
opt-in consent, 378
orientation, 122, 145, 173, 177, 186
orienteering, 32, 33, 102, 114, 120, 122, 123, 124, 129
ostension, 154, 169
outcome-oriented measures, 334

page load time, 16, 35, 44, 95, 163, 199, 287, 412
page prediction models, 209
page-zero experiences, 207
pagination, 5, 18, 24, 25, 27, 88, 209, 285
panels, 4, 28, 337, 338, 339, 340, 341, 354, 356, 381
parameter settings, 352, 407
participant recruitment, 342
passive attention, 99
passive search, 99
patch enrichment, 118
patience, 176, 203, 351
perceptual measures, 319
personal assistants, 61, 62, 222, 223
personal data markets, 382
personal informatics, 243
personal information management, 60, 193, 294, 299, 340
personal location preferences, 291
personal navigation, 27, 74, 92, 143, 271, 272, 279
personal preferences, 223, 331
personalized ranking models, 91
personalized relevance judgments, 320
personalized search, xiv, 7, 94, 274, 276, 303, 409
personally identifiable information, 143, 199, 364, 368, 378
personas, 275, 276
persuasion, 245, 277
persuasive systems, 243
persuasive technologies, 243

physical context, 56
physical environment, 7, 197, 289
physical location, 54, 60, 63, 138, 194, 275, 287, 289, 362, 363, 364, 365
physiological measures, 313, 314, 319
physiological signals, 6, 56, 72, 180, 185, 191, 314, 319, 338
pile metaphor, 125
pleasure, 1, 222, 316, 317
polyrepresentation, 104
pooling, 92, 323, 414
popular destinations, 32, 131, 148, 158, 168
portfolio theory, 113
position bias, 65
positive affect, 317, 318
positive psychology, 316
post-search browsing activity, 3, 18, 29, 33, 76, 123, 144, 168, 219, 287
potential for personalization, 269, 276
potentially alarming content, 144, 346
poverty of attention, 117
precision and recall, 91, 307, 321, 322, 323
preference judgment, 325
preferential attachment, 24, 155, 401
pre-fetching, 73, 79, 163, 195, 209, 220
preparedness, 136, 227
pre-search browsing activity, 208, 285, 287
pre-search search activity, 285
pre-searchbrowsing activity, 287
presentation bias. *See* position bias
privacy, xiii, 8, 11, 16, 54, 55, 199, 213, 223, 274, 276, 303, 352, 360, 361, 366, 368, 369, 374, 375, 377, 378, 379, 380, 381, 382, 383, 384, 394, 407
privacy concerns, xvi, 57, 143, 168, 189, 191, 212, 301, 355, 361, 365, 366, 367, 381, 390, 394, 406, 409
privacy expectations, 194
privacy frameworks, 384
privacy guarantees, 362, 406
privacy legislation, 380
privacy preservation, 382, 406
privacy risks, 168, 295, 302, 363, 367, 376, 377, 381, 382, 384, 406
proactive search, 1, 10, 11, 61, 62, 94, 192, 209
probabilistic interleaving, 346
problem identification, 86, 138
problem solving, 105, 117, 132, 133, 134, 135, 222, 225, 231, 233, 239, 246, 392
problematic situation, 2, 103, 133

procedural knowledge, 242, 310
process model, 102, 105
process-oriented measures, 309, 318, 334
production theory, 113
productivity, xiv, 95, 138, 192, 193, 252, 266, 294, 388, 392
productivity applications, xiv, 192, 193, 392
progress updates, 205, 207
progressive revealment, 24, 175
projected displays, 176, 191
pseudo-relevance feedback, 149, 155
psychological state, 391
public health, 8, 17, 376, 397

quality-in, quality-out principle, 22
query alterations, 97
query auto-completion, 15, 21, 22, 23, 97, 118, 149, 207, 295, 296, 376
query chains, 18, 74, 75, 77, 92, 285
query expansion, 22, 23, 35, 105, 142, 144, 147, 148, 149, 153, 155, 166, 271, 278, 302, 371
query formulation, 4, 18, 21, 23, 30, 35, 99, 103, 107, 138, 147, 149, 152, 156, 157, 160, 166, 168, 246, 273, 310, 315, 324, 329, 346, 376, 401
query operators, 164, 241
query performance prediction, 70, 80, 81
query statements, 5, 21, 23, 38, 120, 131, 135, 137, 163, 164, 165, 200, 209, 238, 283, 285, 287, 312, 380, 406
query substitutions, 147
query suggestion, 1, 4, 8, 21, 23, 24, 27, 48, 70, 75, 97, 131, 141, 147, 148, 150, 156, 220, 268, 284, 285, 287, 376, 400, 407
query trails, 29
query understanding, 395
question answering, 3, 60, 130, 164, 250, 251, 253, 254, 255, 256, 257, 260, 261, 263, 264, 265, 293, 322, 370, 376, 394, 395
quick-backs, 91, 285

rank-biased precision, 320, 351
rational analysis, 117, 119
reading level, 238, 273, 277, 278
real-time query expansion, 23, 149, 207, 302
recommendation system, 281
recommender systems, 152, 207, 212, 213, 214, 250, 268, 282, 301
reconnaissance agents, 163, 196, 208, 211
reference librarians, 4, 55, 97, 134, 141, 164

re-finding, 20, 27, 122, 143, 169, 170, 171, 183, 244, 271, 272, 310, 367, 389
reflection, 60, 62, 160, 172, 181, 202, 243, 244, 245, 247
reinforcement learning, 90, 101
related searches. *See* query suggestion
relative expertise, 246, 250, 258
relevance, 32, 52, 53, 155, 183
relevance assessments, 67, 93, 151, 152, 269, 276, 278, 279, 320, 322, 324, 326, 327, 348, 349, 350, 351
relevance feedback, xii, 4, 24, 53, 76, 107, 141, 144, 148, 150, 151, 152, 154, 155, 166, 185, 206, 301, 302, 314, 317, 343, 360
relevance judgment. *See* relevance assessments
relevance metrics, 92, 321, 325
relevance models, 73, 74
remote locations, 55, 291
remote work, 276
repeat queries, 27, 77, 207, 272
research questions, 17, 206, 338, 339, 342, 343, 369, 384, 400
resource bias, 66
result clicks, 16, 25, 35, 37, 68, 73, 75, 76, 86, 91, 92, 144, 169, 271, 285, 317, 329, 353, 365, 368, 382
result examination, 108, 401
result ranking, 5, 17, 19, 24, 32, 64, 74, 76, 83, 89, 91, 152, 166, 220, 285, 295, 347, 351, 390, 407
result re-ranking, 35, 50, 71, 153, 157, 270, 271, 273, 277, 278, 287, 302
retrospective surveys, 331, 332, 382, 383
review browsing, 100
revisitation, 65, 78, 99, 143, 169, 170, 193, 197, 206, 368, 389
richer sensing, xii, 7, 10, 56, 71, 107, 388
risk and reward, 277, 278

saccade paths, 46
sampling, 87, 88
sampling bias, 17, 83
sandboxes, 377
satisfaction, 9, 19, 34, 35, 53, 59, 67, 68, 69, 70, 71, 73, 81, 89, 106, 155, 162, 163, 267, 296, 312, 325, 329, 330, 340, 383
satisfaction models, 50, 69, 70, 71, 78, 97, 204, 296, 329, 343
scalable visualization tools, 371
scan browsing, 100
scientific discovery, 129, 330

search as learning, 233
search context, 94, 108, 156, 160, 174, 183, 205, 207, 284, 285, 292, 303, 341, 352, 371
search engine switching, 72, 81, 86, 317, 319, 331, 332, 333, 363, 367, 368, 382, 411
search expertise, 164, 165, 221, 238, 240, 246, 273, 312, 358
search experts, 134, 240, 241, 243, 249, 280, 312, 395
search goals, 1, 15, 19, 32, 110, 129, 353
search outcomes, 67, 70, 80, 204, 249, 309, 320, 324, 335, 350, 408
search sessions, 7, 18, 20, 31, 37, 68, 70, 76, 78, 79, 110, 111, 114, 123, 130, 135, 143, 205, 206, 237, 242, 285, 299, 329, 331, 379
search situations, 7, 71, 77, 82, 92, 176, 267, 360, 409
search skills, 165, 240, 242, 243, 244, 245, 335
search state, 170, 196, 205, 271, 396
search strategies, 3, 4, 7, 110, 130, 131, 151, 156, 170, 217, 238, 244, 249, 285, 325
search success, 69, 147, 204, 220, 243, 245, 282, 328, 331, 334, 369
search tactics, 110, 240
search trails, 29, 30, 33, 37, 63, 73, 76, 77, 136, 143
searcher attention, 25, 36, 37, 38, 39, 43, 44, 48, 50, 51, 52, 65, 144, 147, 170, 172, 173, 174, 219, 347, 388
searcher control, 148, 151, 155, 156, 302, 378, 391
searching to learn, 232, 236
search-oriented browsing, 100
search-result click-through, 38, 50, 68, 73, 138, 351
self-reports, xv, 237, 318
selfsourcing, 78, 396
semi-directed browsing, 100, 236
semiotic gestures, 177
semi-supervised learning, 90
sensemaking, 22, 97, 102, 121, 126, 127, 128, 144, 162, 232, 233, 235, 311
serendipity, 60, 136, 201, 206, 212, 222, 315, 316
session trails, 29
simulations, 9, 29, 83, 114, 119, 120, 125, 161, 337, 350, 352, 353, 354, 357, 368, 377, 402, 403, 407, 408
situated navigation, 123
situational relevance, 109, 131

skill level, 63, 132, 162, 223, 240, 241, 242, 245, 273
skin temperature, 72
skips, 48, 49, 51, 309, 334
slow search, xv, 7, 62, 96, 196, 208, 250, 394, 396
small data, xii, 60, 62
SNIF-ACT, 119, 377, 402
social bookmarking, 120, 216, 395
social capital, 129, 261
social computing, 60
social context, 7, 249, 281, 282, 366
social explanations, 301
social learning, 165, 312
social media, 6, 9, 20, 35, 60, 63, 128, 129, 262, 293, 295, 297, 368, 374, 393, 395, 397, 401
social navigation, xiii, 34, 125, 215, 216
social networks, xiii, xiv, 30, 60, 63, 83, 84, 128, 222, 232, 254, 260, 261, 312, 394
social search, 189, 216, 232, 258, 387, 395, 403
social sensemaking, 128
spatial context, xiv, 292
spatial hypertext, 125
spatial mobility, 292
specialized search services, 138
speech recognition, xv, 13, 60, 134, 182, 183, 190, 262, 408
spelling correction, 23
spoken dialog, xv, 1, 15, 52, 57, 60, 94, 134, 161, 178, 182, 183, 189, 202, 253, 287, 388, 391, 406, 411
spreading activation, 119
standing queries, 7, 11, 208, 223
static rank, 76, 94, 283
statistical testing, 88, 225, 227, 335, 338, 355
stereotypes, 157, 353, 377
stimulated recall, 16, 143, 309, 318, 343, 411
stochastic privacy, 381, 382, 406
strategic models, 103, 110
strategic search support, xiii, 21, 215
stratified models, 97, 103, 109, 110
struggling session, 203
sub-goals, 215
subject matter expertise, 66, 75, 132, 236, 238, 239, 280, 312
subject matter experts, 134, 136, 236, 245, 249, 260, 261, 394, 395
subjective experiences, 318
subjective measures, 313
subjective perception of time, 319

subject-matter expertise, 4, 34, 63, 132, 328
subtopic structuring, 144
summary generation, 247
supervised learning, 90
supporting exploration, 23, 212, 222, 308
supporting learning, 231, 233, 241, 248
supporting website navigation, 219
surprise, 66, 186, 308, 325
survey-log linking methodology, 383
surveys, 4, 143, 227, 237, 341, 344, 355, 357, 374
synchronous collaboration, 252, 254
synchronous communications, 254
synthesis, 63, 97, 100, 124, 126, 129, 132, 138, 157, 192, 232, 234, 239, 388
system mediated collaboration, 252

tabbed browsing, 36
tacit knowledge, 255
tag clouds, 228
tail answers, 265
tangible search artifacts, 196
targeted distribution of questions, 259
task completion, 1, 2, 5, 32, 59, 61, 78, 99, 158, 192, 194, 197, 223, 247, 309, 311, 312, 314, 370, 391
task context, 4, 78, 157, 281
task continuation, 20, 396
task difficulty, 79, 80, 162, 185
task expertise, 238, 241, 284
task models, 74, 79, 153, 284, 338
task resumption, xv, 7, 9, 62, 99, 169
task scenarios, 245, 335
task switching, 340
task taxonomy, 143, 226
task tours, 168, 218, 220
taxonomies of learning, 233, 310
team draft interleaving, 346
teleportation, 122, 216
temporal dynamics, 296, 396, 399
temporal query patterns, 147
ten blue links, 2
terms of use, 54, 88, 352, 362, 363, 375, 379
Text Retrieval Conference, 3, 207, 348, 349
text selections, 28, 43
text tiling, 144
theory of learning, 236
think-alouds, 55, 237, 309, 313, 318, 319, 341
time estimation, 329
time-aware information access, 295
time-biased gain, 114, 115, 326, 353

time-critical search, 143, 297, 298
timeline visualization, 300
time-varying goals, 193
topic hierarchies, 272
touch devices, 174
touch gestures, 174, 176
touch interactions, 10, 15, 38, 51, 52, 53, 70, 82, 174, 176, 318
tours and trails, 32, 167, 217, 220
trailblazers, xiii, 28, 214
trailblazing, 29, 34, 158, 214, 217
trailfinding, 33, 219
traits, 227, 326, 353, 354
transfer of learning, 239, 241, 311
treatment group, 77, 84, 346
TREC. *See* Text Retrieval Conference
TREC Contextual Suggestion Track, 207, 350
TREC High Accuracy Retrieval from Documents Track, 350, 370, 371
TREC Interactive Track, 220, 350, 361, 370
TREC Session Track, 324, 350
triangulation of data, 212
triggers, 73, 123, 294
trust bias. *See* position bias

unconventional thinking, 136
undirected browsing, 20, 99, 100
unsupervised learning, 85, 90
urgency, 143, 183, 295, 297, 298, 299, 300
usability, 28, 50, 53, 79, 117, 120, 161, 231, 308, 329, 335, 341, 343, 352, 376, 411
user mediated collaboration, 252
user models, xiii, 2, 61, 157, 193, 210, 215, 320, 338, 352, 353, 355, 365, 377, 414

user profiles, 9, 51, 62, 96, 168, 196, 213, 237, 262, 267, 270, 272, 274, 282, 303, 362, 366, 378, 388
user studies, 5, 23, 72, 131, 147, 148, 149, 187, 217, 219, 260, 309, 311, 317, 324, 337, 338, 340, 342, 344, 347, 348, 350, 352, 353, 355, 358, 360, 369, 370, 408
user study data, 309, 353, 369
utility, 163, 166, 317, 320, 322, 323, 324, 327, 335, 348, 351, 352, 381, 383, 384, 398, 399

verbose queries, 134, 164
verification, 214, 331
viewport, 36, 49, 50, 51, 53, 70, 81, 174, 176, 178
virtual reality, 197
visceral need, 22
visual analytics, 202
visual search, 101
vocabulary problem, 75
voice query, 183
Von Restorff effect, 27

wandering behavior, 350, 352, 353
waypoints, 32
wearable, xv, xvi, 6, 7, 10, 71, 72, 181, 182, 187, 197, 389, 391
web behavior graphs, 30, 118, 135
web cameras, 51, 172, 174, 188
work tasks, 63, 78, 79, 104, 281, 299, 309, 312, 342, 360
workspaces, 124, 125, 205, 206, 207

zone of proximal development, 232, 245

For EU product safety concerns, contact us at Calle de José Abascal, 56–1°,
28003 Madrid, Spain or eugpsr@cambridge.org.

www.ingramcontent.com/pod-product-compliance
Ingram Content Group UK Ltd.
Pitfield, Milton Keynes, MK11 3LW, UK
UKHW051938220326
469255UK00009B/122